Diversity in Contact

Koloniale und Postkoloniale Linguistik
Colonial and Postcolonial Linguistics

Edited by Stefan Engelberg,
Peter Mühlhäusler, Doris Stolberg, Thomas Stolz
and Ingo H. Warnke

Volume 21

Diversity in Contact

Edited by
Nataliya Levkovych

DE GRUYTER

ISBN 978-3-11-221546-3
e-ISBN (PDF) 978-3-11-132375-6
e-ISBN (EPUB) 978-3-11-132412-8

Library of Congress Control Number: 2023945297

Bibliographic information published by the Deutsche Nationalbibliothek
The Deutsche Nationalbibliothek lists this publication in the Deutsche Nationalbibliografie; detailed bibliographic data are available on the internet at http://dnb.dnb.de.

© 2025 Walter de Gruyter GmbH, Berlin/Boston
Dieser Band ist text- und seitenidentisch mit der 2023 erschienenen gebundenen Ausgabe.
Printing and binding: CPI books GmbH, Leck

www.degruyter.com

Preface

Language contact is not a monolithic phenomenon but the cover term for an enormously rich and diverse catalogue of processes, settings, structures, triggers, and results connected with the interaction of several languages and speech communities. This edited volume reflects some of this diversity. The contributions included in this collection approach language contact from very different perspectives and address issues which are not usually raised in the mainstream of language-contact studies. In this way, new strands of research are presented in the hope that they induce other scholars to investigate further.

Already the preceding edited volume (Levkovych 2022) was intended to show that it makes sense for our discipline to broaden our horizons empirically and add new topics to the canon of research projects. Since diversity is important for the organization of this edited volume, the different contributions are not necessarily closely interrelated in terms of theory, methodology, phenomena, and languages. In point of fact the replica languages featured in the articles range from Latvian via Jordanian Chechen, Basque, Maltese, West African English, West African French to Pidgins and Creoles. On the side of the donor languages, the readers will find French, English, German, Polish, Arabic, Gascon, Italian/Sicilian, as well as autochthonous languages of Togo, Nigeria and Ghana. Language contact situations in Africa, the Americas, Asia (Middle East and Indian Ocean), Australia, and Europe are in the focus of the different papers.

Colonial and postcolonial settings are discussed in the contributions by Marcus Callies, Nicole Nau, Julia Nintemann and Nicole Hober, Andreas Jäger and Jascha de Bloom as well as Magnus Fischer, Andreas Jäger, Carolin Patzelt, and Ingo H. Warnke. There is thus a direct link to the leitmotif of the series KPL/CPL. The papers by Marcus Callies, Diana Forker and Ala Al Sheshani, Martin Haase, Nicole Nau, Maike Vorholt, and Andreas Jäger and Jascha de Bloom represent detailed case studies whereas Julia Nintemann and Nicole Hober as well as Magnus Fischer, Andreas Jäger, Carolin Patzelt, and Ingo H. Warnke discuss their findings in comparative perspective. Thomas Stolz and Nataliya Levkovych evaluate phonological systems according to the principles of areal typology. The same authors are responsible for a second paper which addresses parallel borrowing behavior of languages in a geographical macroarea. The contribution by Yaron Matras provides a new theoretical and methodological framework for language contact studies in situations of multilingualism.

For the orientation of the reader, I shortly summarize each paper individually in the order of their appearance in the volume. There is a general division in two parts. Part I comprises those studies which approach language contact from the point of view of established structural and functional categories. Part II is reserved for papers which investigate language contact from the perspective of metapragmatics.

Part I

The contribution of **Nicole Nau** deals with language contact in unusual colonial settings. Her case study addresses the impact of the colonial languages German and Polish on the grammatical structures of two written varieties of Latvian. The author suggests that the structural differences in these varieties are to a great extent explicable with reference to the different sociolinguistic situation in the colonial contexts.

Marcus Callies contributes to the current debates on the diversity in World Englishes from the perspective of the connection between language and culture. He investigates how indigenous proverbs and idioms in the languages of Nigeria and Ghana affect the proverbs and idioms in the corresponding English varieties of these African countries.

In their case study on the migrant variety of the Nakh-Daghestanian language Chechen, **Diana Forker and Ala Al Sheshani** survey the impact of Arabic as a donor language on the grammar of Jordanian Chechen. They compare their findings with Caucasian Chechen as an autochthonous (minority) language in the Russian Federation.

Martin Haase reviews different contact scenarios in the language isolate Basque. Special attention is paid to the hitherto understudied contact between Basque and Gascon. Beside lexical loans, the Romance language Gascon had noticeable effects on the phonology, morphology, and syntax of non-standard varieties of Basque making the dialectal map of this language more diverse.

Maike Vorholt's in-depth study focuses on the impact of the intensive language contact between the Semitic language Maltese and Italian/Sicilian on the system of Maltese adpositions. By means of quantitative methods the author discusses the connection between the token frequencies and the Semitic or Romance origin of the Maltese adpositions.

Julia Nintemann and Nicole Hober research the new languages which typically emerge directly in colonial contexts – pidgins and creoles. In their study the authors investigate some aspects of morphosyntax of place names, namely the coding of Ground phrases in Goal and Source constructions and compare their results to those of studies dedicated to languages outside the domain of language contact.

The typological study of **Thomas Stolz and Nataliya Levkovych** deals with the distribution of specific phonological properties – places and manners of articulation in 210 languages of Europe. It is shown that the geographic distribution of many of these phenomena is neither random nor correlated to the genetic affiliation of languages. In many cases language contact (linguistic areas) could be invoked to explain the facts.

Thomas Stolz and Nataliya Levkovych contribute a second study to this volume in which they take stock of the many cases of conjunction borrowing in languages of the Middle East and Southeast Asia which have been exposed to language contact with Arabic and/or Persian. It is shown that the processes observed in the replica languages constitute perfect parallels to other language contact situations in which either Arabic or Persian are involved as donor languages.

Part II

The topic of **Yaron Matras**'s paper are multilingual spaces in urban contexts (Manchester). He specifically looks at the use of linguistic repertoires in institutional contexts and their connection to language policy and transnational identities. The study is embedded in the general framework of decolonization.

Magnus Fischer, Andreas Jäger, Carolin Patzelt, and Ingo H. Warnke continue the strand of research of decolonized settings by way of applying metapragmatics to language contact situations in Mauritius and Australia. They aim at redefining the notion of colonial language on the backdrop of fluid registers as opposed to the traditional concepts of fixed languages.

In preparation of a future research project **Andreas Jäger and Jascha de Bloom** discuss the phenomenon of code-switching involving French, German, Ewe, and further autochthonous language of Togo. The facts are inspected with the help of metapragmatics in order to determine the social hierarchy of prestige of the languages under review.

I am grateful to the editors of the series KPL/CPL for accepting this collection of articles in the series. I also like to express my gratitude to Thomas Stolz for supporting me during the editing process of this volume. All remaining errors are mine.

Nataliya Levkovych
Bremen, August 2023

References

Levkovych, Nataliya (ed.). 2022. *Susceptibility vs. resistance. Case studies on different structural categories in language-contact situations*. Berlin & Boston: De Gruyter.

Contents

Nataliya Levkovych
Preface —— V

Part I

Nicole Nau
Differential impact of colonial languages on written languages —— 3

Marcus Callies
Contact in World Englishes at the nexus of language and culture —— 91

Diana Forker and Ala Al Sheshani
Far beyond the Caucasus —— 111

Martin Haase
Scenarios of Basque Language Contact —— 145

Maike Vorholt
The relevance of origin —— 165

Julia Nintemann and Nicole Hober
On the morphosyntax of place names vs. common nouns in pidgins and creoles —— 195

Thomas Stolz and Nataliya Levkovych
Places, manners, and the areal phonology of Europe —— 249

Thomas Stolz and Nataliya Levkovych
Travellers in time and space —— 327

Part II

Yaron Matras
The city as multilingual utopia —— 369

Magnus Fischer, Andreas Jäger, Carolin Patzelt and Ingo H. Warnke
Fluid registers and fixed language concepts in postcolonial spaces —— 439

Andreas Jäger and Jascha de Bloom
Prolegomena to a study of code-switching in Togo and its metapragmatic functions —— 477

Index of Authors —— 513

Index of Languages, Language Families, and Linguistic Areas —— 521

Index of Subjects —— 527

Part I

Nicole Nau
Differential impact of colonial languages on written languages

A case study from Latvia in the early 19th century

Abstract: Two written varieties of Latvian developed in a colonial setting under the influence of two different dominant languages, German and Polish. This case study shows their impact on grammatical constructions in two versions of a manual of beekeeping from the early 19th century, a pioneering example of this register in Latvian. The findings indicate the entanglement of two driving forces in the development of grammatical structures, language contact and register features of written texts, and point out differences in the sociolinguistic situation as explanations for different outcomes of language contact.

Keywords: Contact-induced language change; written language; word order; discontinuos noun phrase; passive; necessity; connectives; Latvian; Latgalian

1 Introduction

Until 1918, when the Republic of Latvia was founded, the territory where Latvian is spoken belonged to various foreign powers, and speakers of Latvian were politically, economically, and culturally dominated by others. While the political rulers changed, established elites remained powerful in many domains. This had a lasting effect on the development of the Latvian language, especially its written forms. For centuries, the most powerful language was German: it was the language of the "crusaders" that conquered the territory in the 13th century, the language of the Livonian Confederation that ruled the whole territory until the mid-16th century, the language of the nobility established during that time, the language of the landowners, the language of trade and of the guilds in towns, and, after the Reformation, the language of the Protestant Church, the language of education and of upward mobility. In the western and central part of Latvia, this situation changed only in the second half of the 19th century. In the eastern part

---

Nicole Nau, Adam Mickiewicz University in Poznan, Department of Scandinavian Studies, al. Niepodległości 4, PL 61-874 Poznań, Poland. E-Mail: Nicole.Nau@amu.edu.pl

of Latvia, on the territory called Latgalia (*Latgale* in Latvian), the power of German diminished considerably already in the 17th century, when Latgalia became part of the Polish-Lithuanian Commonwealth. Polish became the language of the nobility and the landowners, and it was the language of the Catholic Church which ruled religious life and education in this region. While not as powerful as German in western Latvia, Polish in Latgalia had many characteristics of a colonial language and lost its dominance only in the second half of the 19th century, when the region experienced a period of Russification.

The political and confessional border that separated Latgalia from the western parts of Latvia led to the development of two distinct written languages, both under the influence of the respective colonial language. These written varieties were created and maintained not by native speakers of Latvian, but by speakers of German and Polish, respectively, mostly members of the clergy. They were based on different dialects of Latvian, and I will refer to them as (Old Written) Low Latvian and (Old Written) High Latvian. In Latvian dialectology, "High Latvian" comprises dialects spoken in Latgalia and some neighboring territories, while "Low Latvian" is a cover term for Central and Coastal dialects. Old Written Low Latvian and modern Standard Latvian are based on Central dialects. I will keep the name *Latvian* without modifiers to cover all varieties of this language, written and spoken, old and current; the ISO code for this concept is LAV. For written and spoken varieties of modern (Low) Latvian (ISO code LVS, formerly LTV), I will use the term *Standard Latvian*, while *Latgalian* (LTG) comprises varieties of spoken and written High Latvian.

The existence of the two distinct historical written languages offers the opportunity to study the influence that different colonial languages exerted on one language, and the impact they had on the development of writing. It is well known in linguistics that writing creates a new code, a new kind of language, and gives rise to more register variation (cf. Chafe and Tannen 1987; Miller and Weinert 1998; Biber 2009). The absence of prosody, mimics and gestures, the distance between author and recipient in time and space, the extended time for planning the message and other factors require or facilitate new solutions for expressing and structuring one's thoughts. Furthermore, new registers develop that exist only in or through writing. In the history of many languages, the development of writing is influenced by other languages and cultures, at various stages: from graphization and codification to differentiation of registers and spread of literacy practices (cf. Smalley 1994).

In this chapter, I show the entanglement of language contact and general principles of written languages in detailed analyses of grammatical phenomena. I subscribe to the view that language contact as a driving force in language change is best studied in its interplay with other factors (e.g., Chamoreau and Léglise 2012). Furthermore, language production and the texts that result from it must be analysed in their historical and sociolinguistic context, which in this study is a special, European, situation of colonialism. Thereby, this study relates to the fields of *Colonial Linguistics* and *Missionary Linguistics*, which have seen growing interest and an increasing number of contributions during the past two decades (for some overviews see Migge and Léglise 2007: 3–10; Zwartjes 2012; Engelberg and Stolberg 2012; Zimmermann and Kellermeier-Rehbein 2015; Warnke et al. 2016). Research in these fields is almost always devoted to situations of European colonization and missionizing of parts of Meso- and South America, Africa, or Asia. However, as the above sketch of the historic sociolinguistic situation on Latvian territories should have shown, there are good reasons to include this inner-European setting of cultural hegemony and (meta)linguistic dominance into colonial linguistic studies; a similar claim was made by Saagpakk (2015). We find here the characteristics singled out by Warnke et al. (2016: 4–5), and the practices described by Migge and Léglise (2007: 5–10). The parallels as well as differences between the Baltic situation and intercontinental colonialism deserve further investigation and are beyond the scope of this paper. In any case, the results of this study are of relevance for broader questions about colonialism and its linguistic consequences. I will argue that the differential impact of the contact languages on the grammar of Old Written Low and High Latvian reflects differences in the colonial settings.

The main research questions of this investigation are: (i) In which areas of grammar do the written languages of the early 19th century show the impact of the colonial language? (ii) Which phenomena can be explained by principles of written language or the characteristics of special written registers? (iii) How do differences between Low and High Old Written Latvian reflect differences in the sociolinguistic situation in which they developed?

My case study is based on the Low Latvian and the High Latvian version of a book on beekeeping (Launitz 1803 and Akielewicz 1832). The focus of this study is on grammatical constructions that are typical for written registers, or which often show qualitative or quantitative differences in written and spoken varieties of a language, such as the structure and use of referring expressions, word order, passive constructions, or techniques of clause combining. The two books offer a snapshot of the Latvian written languages at the beginning of the 19th century, after several centuries of language planning by non-native speakers. Launitz (1803) is a typical example of Old Written Low Latvian, written in a code that was already normalized and codified at the time, with a clear German impact and rules that were partly independent of the spoken vernacular. Akielewicz (1832) in turn reflects the highly multilingual situation in Latgalia and is closer to spoken varieties.

The structure of this chapter is as follows. Section 2 gives an overview of the history of Old Written Low and High Latvian and summarizes the findings of prior work on the influence of German on Low Latvian. In Section 3 I provide information about the two investigated books and other material used in the case study and briefly explain its methods. Section 4 contains the results of my detailed analyses of selected structures and their discussion; a summary is provided in Section 4.8. In Section 5, I draw some general conclusions from my findings.

2 The development of two written varieties of Latvian

This section provides the necessary historical background of my study. Although the history of Latvian can hardly be understood without knowledge of the history of its speakers, the latter can only be touched upon here. For more information the reader is referred to Plakans (2011) and other books about the history of Latvia or the Baltic States.

2.1 History of Old Written Low Latvian and the role of German in its development

Written varieties of Latvian started to develop in the 16th century, in the aftermath of the Protestant Reformation and the Catholic Counter-Reformation. There was no earlier tradition of writing in Latvian, but Latvian names and a few individual words appear in Latin and German texts from the 13th century on (Ozols 1965: 40–54; Vanags 2019: 58–59). In the development of Old Written Low Latvian, an early, middle, and later period are distinguished (Ozols 1965: 11–14). I will follow here the periodization as described by Vanags (2013, 2019), who characterizes the three periods based on general principles of standardization. The first period, from the beginnings until the middle of the 17th century, is described as the period of graphization and code-selection; the second period, from the middle of the 17th to the middle of the 18th century, shows efforts of standardization and codification of a norm, while in the third period, from the mid-18th to the mid-19 century, we witness stabilization of the norm (Vanags 2019: 57). The most important documents of the first period comprise catechisms (the oldest surviving are the *Catechismus Catholicorum* 1585 and the Lutheran *Enchiridion* of

1586), hymnals (starting in 1587 with *Undeutsche Psalmen und geistliche Lieder* [Non-German psalms and spiritual Songs]) and selected texts of the Gospels and other parts of the New Testament (the oldest published as *Evangelien und Episteln* [Gospels and epistles] in 1587). The second period starts with the works of Georg Mancelius. His texts, which were written, edited and published several times in the 1630s to 1650s, show his endeavor to normalize Latvian spelling and grammar, to develop Latvian prose (especially in his book of sermons *Lettische Postill* [Latvian postil], 1654), and to expand its vocabulary and phraseology; he is also the author of two German-Latvian dictionaries. At the end of the 18th century, the Bible is translated into Latvian by Ernst Glück (New Testament published in 1685, the whole Bible in 1695). While this is an important milestone in the history of any European language, it was only the revised second edition of the Bible, published in 1739, which would serve as a model text for more than a century. It shows the result of conscious language planning by a group of influential clergymen, and it marks the end of the second period. The orthographic and grammatical standard that was achieved at that time was used with little variation throughout the third period of Old Written Low Latvian. The most important changes and achievements of this third period are an expansion of the registers and types of texts, especially non-religious literature, both translated and original. Gotthard Friedrich Stender wrote short moralizing and entertaining stories and poems for young and adult readers, partly inspired by fairytales and folksongs. He is also the author of the first Latvian book in the field of popular science (*Augstas Gudribas Grahmata no Pasaules un Dabbas* [A book of high wisdom on the world and nature], first edition 1774). His son Alexander Johann Stender was the first to translate plays into Latvian. The second half of the 18th century is also the beginning of technical literature, practical guides to questions of agriculture, health care, housekeeping, and others. Such texts are first published in periodicals and yearbooks (calendars), which are also an innovation of the period. Launitz' (1803) book on beekeeping is among the first book-length texts of this register.

During all this time, almost all authors of Latvian texts were native speakers of other languages[1], and in the overwhelming majority they were German clergymen. Some of them had acquired spoken Latvian in their childhood from caretakers and servants, others had learned the language only later in life and attained various degrees of competence. Their languages of education were German and Latin. Moreover, during the first and second period, not only writers, but also

---

[1] Plakans (1993: 208) reports of an estimate of 3% native Latvians among authors of original work in Latvian in 1844.

readers of Latvian texts were mainly Germans. Most of the books published in the 16th and 17th century were addressed to the clergy, and only indirectly to their parishioners. The title page of the first Lutheran catechism states this bluntly:

> Die fuenff Heuptstuecke des heiligen Catechismi: Neben Der Beicht / Frage und Antwort / die da sonderlich den einfeltigen Bawren vor und nach der Predigt sollen fein deutlich und langsam vorgelesen und gebetet werden. (Enchiridion 1586)[2]

Most of the Low Latvian books of the first period had their title pages and prefaces in German, or sometimes in Latin, but not in Latvian. For a rather long time, Latvians experienced literacy in a passive way – by being read to. Only at the end of the 17th century were reading skills among Latvians promoted; the first Latvian primers date from the 1680s (Vanags 2019: 64), a century after the first texts were printed in that language. The first edition of the Bible that appeared at that time was still meant for the clergy to read aloud during church service, not for farmers to read at home. This can be inferred from its bulky format, weight, and limited print run (Ozols 1965: 268–269). This situation had certainly effects on the development of Old Written Low Latvian during the first two periods. First, for native speakers of Latvian it probably was a code of its own, somehow understandable, but clearly different from their everyday language as well as the language of their own verbal art. This may have furthered the acceptance of imported constructions unknown in spoken Latvian. Second, native speakers had very little influence on the development of this variety of their language – they were not supposed to, and probably also did not dare (or care) to criticize it. All corpus planning was done by the same German clergymen who were the authors and readers of Old Low Latvian texts.

In the third period, the situation changes as more and more texts are written for a growing Latvian readership and authors slowly start to reflect about the needs and expectations of their readers. Literacy skills and practices among Latvians become more varied. The first primers that explicitly teach writing in addition to reading appear at the end of the 18th century. At the same time, more thorough research and description of the language is carried out, starting with Gotthard Friedrich Stender's grammar (*Neue vollständigere lettische Grammatik* [New and more complete grammar of Latvian], 1761; new edition as *Lettische Grammatik* [A grammar of Latvian] in 1783). Subsequently, researchers and activists of the Enlightenment publicly discuss the quality of Old Written Low Latvian

---

[2] 'The five main parts of the Holy Catechism: As well as Question and Answer / of the Confession / that shall be read aloud and said in prayer articulately and slowly to the simple farmers before and after the sermon.' All translations of titles and quotes are mine.

and criticize German influence on its syntax. Christoph Harder gives the first systematic account of German-like word order in written Latvian (Harder 1790: 64–72). He demonstrates the phenomenon and its effects, taking the perspective of the Latvian reader:

> in der Prosa aber findet man wohl ganze Bücher, wo durchaus von Wort zu Wort die reine teutsche Construction beybehalten ist. Man kan sich leicht vorstellen, daß ein solcher Styl dem Letten ungefehr so gefallen wird, als wenn man im Teutschen sagen wollte: *Ich ihm es wohl hab gesagt, aber nicht er hört, und es nicht er will thun.* u. s. w. Man kan diese Worte freylich wohl verstehen: man denke doch aber auch, was wird man wohl haben empfinden, wenn ein ganzes Buch in solchem Ton immer fort gehet. (Harder 1790: 65)[3]

Despite this early critique, it took another century to get rid of many German-based patterns in the written language that were in disaccord with the inner rules of Latvian, and this was the end of Old Written Low Latvian. In the second half of the 19th century, native speakers of Latvian took over both as authors of Latvian texts and as the main activists of language planning (cf. Vanags 2008) and started to create modern Standard Latvian.

There are several ways by which German has exerted an influence on Old Written Low Latvian. Their relative importance varies across time, texts, authors, as well as the part of language system that was affected. The following four ways or channels may be distinguished:
1) Imitation of a model when translating a text from German,
2) German influence manifest in spoken varieties of Latvian,
3) interference from the author's native language,
4) continuation of German models already established in Old Written Low Latvian.

For the first published texts, the first two channels were the most important. There was not yet any tradition of writing Latvian, and the spoken language on which the translations are based was that of Riga, a multicultural city where German had a strong influence on Latvian (Vanags 1993: 165). From the 17th century on, rural dialects of Latvian became more important as input for written registers, as many authors were parsons in the country. Translations continued to make up the greatest part of literature in Old Written Low Latvian, even towards the end

---

[3] 'But in prose one finds whole books where a purely German construction is followed word by word. It is easy to imagine that such a style may please a Latvian about as much as [it would please us] if one said in German: *Ich ihm es wohl hab gesagt, aber nicht er hört, und es nicht er will thun.* [I him it have said, but not he listens, and it not he wants do]. One may of course understand these words. However, think of what people might feel when a whole book goes on and on in such a way.'

of the third period, when practical literature and popular novels and plays were translated. However, with the growing body of texts in the target language, direct transfers from German into Latvian during the translation process decreased – the translations became freer, the translators used already established patterns. As concerns individual interference, one must remember that most authors and translators were learned men who spoke, read, and wrote not only in their mother tongue. They were fluent in Latin and had at least a reading knowledge of Greek and Hebrew, thus they were familiar with languages of different types.

The German influence on Old Written Low Latvian is most obvious and most stable in the writing system. As languages of cultures belonging to Western Christianity, both Low Latvian and High Latvian use the Latin alphabet, but other elements of the writing systems differ sharply and make the German and the Polish model, respectively, visible at first sight. Old Written Low Latvian is printed in blackletter, while High Latvian uses the roman and the italic type. For a long time, in several parts of Europe the use of blackletter was associated with Protestantism and/or a German cultural influence. The roman type was more neutral and widespread but could stand for Catholic culture and the Latin language when contrasted to blackletter. In the Baltic region, the contrast between a "Protestant" and a "Catholic script" was maintained still in the 19th century. The association with the "wrong" confession and the difficulty to read a script to which one is not used contributed to the independent development of the two traditions of writing. The use of blackletter in print may also be one of the causes why writing skills developed much later than reading skills among speakers of Low Latvian, as handwritten letters had a different shape and had to be learned separately.

Old Low Latvian spelling was from the very beginning based on spelling conventions for German, but it took two centuries, individual initiatives and active language planning by influential groups to arrive at the standard manifest in the second edition of the Latvian Bible from 1739. This standard was observed in most of the texts produced in the third period of Old Written Low Latvian, with very little variation. Its colonial nature was pointed out by Christoph Harder, who remarked:

> Bey Einrichtung der lettischen *orthographie* hat man mehr den Vortheil des Teutschen der lettisch lernen will, als des Letten selbst vor Augen gehabt: denn sonst hätte sie vor ein Kind, das lesen lernen soll, wohl noch etwas leichter seyn können. (Harder 1790: 3)[4]

---

[4] 'When creating the Latvian orthography, one was guided more by advantages for Germans who want to learn Latvian as for Latvians themselves. Otherwise, it surely could have been made easier for a child that is to learn how to read.'

The development of Old Written Low Latvian orthography is well documented in several individual studies of documents of all three periods, and in the overviews by Rūķe-Draviņa (1977) and Bergmane and Blinkena (1986).

In the vocabulary, German influence is manifest in numerous loanwords, loan translations, semantic loans, as well as tendencies in word formation. Material loanwords were supposedly frequent also in spoken varieties of Latvian and therefore a natural choice for writers. During the first four centuries of colonization, Low German was used along High German, first as the dominant language, then slowly losing ground to High German. Many of the loanwords that entered Latvian in the 13th–16th century have a Middle Low German model (see Jordan 1995; Low and High German loanwords in Latvian were studied by Sehwers 1934; a short overview is given by Karulis 2000). Loan translations, on the other hand, often arose through a literal translation of a (Low or High) German model in a text. They were also consciously created by writers lacking an appropriate term in Latvian. Semantic loans typically involve the addition of abstract meanings to a word with a basic concrete meaning. For example, in Latvian dialects, the Latvian preposition *caur* 'through' is used only in a concrete local sense, while in Old Written Low Latvian it is often found in the meaning 'by', marking an instrument, force, cause, or agent (Vanags 1993: 174, 2015: 59). Like loan translations, semantic loans may be the result of conscious coining or of unconscious transfer. A phenomenon connected to loan translations, but not limited to them, is a high number of nominal compounds in Old Written Low Latvian. Compounding as such is not an imported technique, but German influence has surely contributed to its increase. Compounds in the works of Georg Mancelius were studied by Skujiņa (2006).

German influence on the grammar, especially the syntax of Old Written Low Latvian is often mentioned in the literature on the history of Latvian, but rarely studied in detail. Most often authors just name some phenomena where they assume the imitation of a German pattern. The most systematic study that I found is Vanags' (1993) investigation of possible German influence on the grammar of the oldest written Latvian documents. He chose texts which in all likelihood had been translated and in use already in the first half of the 16th century, though the eldest preserved prints date from 1586–1587 (Vanags 1993: 164). The model texts were written in Low German. Vanags examines various grammatical phenomena where a German influence on Latvian is likely to occur and compares the Latvian sentences with the corresponding Low German model. Most of the identified instances of German-inspired patterns are also found in later texts and can count as examples of German influence on Old Written Low Latvian in general (see list below). Thus, there seems to be no specific Low German influence on the grammar, unlike what we find in vocabulary. I only found one phenomenon that reflects Low German grammar in contrast to High German, only observed in texts of the first period: the non-distinction of dative and accusative in first and second person pronouns (mentioned in Vanags 2013: 181). Phenomena showing German influence in the field of grammar are usually mentioned in studies of the language of individual writers or documents, for example, Jēgers (1975) on the sample translation made by Jānis Reiters in 1675; Vanags (2015) on the history book written by Friedrich Bernhard Blaufuß in 1753; Karulis (1988) on Friedrich Gotthard Stender's book *Augstas Gudribas Grahmata* [A book of high wisdom] (1774, second edition 1799). They can also be found in general accounts of the history of the language (Ozols 1965; Vanags 2013) or more specialized studies of the development of parts of the grammatical system (most important sources are Pokrotniece 2002, 2007). The following list of phenomena is based on these sources. It includes phenomena mentioned by at least two authors. Ozols (1965) is here cited for his comments on the language of Mancelius. Several of the listed phenomena are also found in Launitz (1803) and will be described in detail in Section 4.

List of salient phenomena showing a German influence on the grammar of Old Written Low Latvian (based on the literature)
Nominal constructions and categories
- Use of the demonstrative pronoun *tas* 'that' as a definite article; use of the numeral *viens* 'one' as an indefinite article – observed in all periods (Vanags 1993: 168; Ozols 1965: 190; Jēgers 1975: 49; Vanags 2015: 50, 52; Karulis 1988: 540; Barbare 2002: 340).
- Use of a preposition 'in' instead of the locative – typical for the first period, still frequent in the second period, occasionally observed in the third period (Vanags 1993: 166; Ozols 1965: 84–85; Jēgers 1975: 50; Vanags 2015: 59; Nītiņa 2007: 31).
- Use of the personal pronoun instead of the reflexive pronoun for first and second person – all periods (Vanags 1993: 167; Barbare 2002: 315, 327–328; Harder 1790: 28).
- Use of an agreeing possessive pronoun instead of the genitive of the personal pronoun in first and second person plural and third person (Latvian having agreeing possessive pronouns only for 1SG and 2SG and as possessive pronoun) – only first and second period (Jēgers 1975: 47; Barbare 2002: 331–332).

– Position of a modifying genitive after instead of before the head noun – all periods (Vanags 1993: 176–177; Ozols 1965: 189; Vanags 2015: 68; Harder 1790: 26).

Verbal constructions
– Pleonastic use of a reflexive or personal pronoun with reflexive verbs – first and second period (Vanags 1993: 169; Ozols 1965: 190–191; Jēgers 1975: 49; Veidemane 2002: 424–425).
– Passive construction with an auxiliary 'become' – all periods, especially frequent in the third period (Vanags 2015: 56; Veidemane 2002: 415–418).
– Necessive construction with 'be' + infinitive and a nominative subject (instead of a dative) – occasionally observed in all periods (Vanags 1993: 179; Jēgers 1975: 48, 50; Vanags 2015: 54).
– Causative or permissive construction with the auxiliary *likt* + infinitive and an accusative (instead of a dative) – occasional in different periods (Jēgers 1995: 48; Karulis 1988: 547).

Clause constructions
– Lack of negative concord in clauses with a negative pronoun – all periods (Vanags 1993: 177–178; Ozols 1965: 189–190; Jēgers 1975: 49; Vanags 2015: 68; Karulis 1988: 541, 547; Barbare 2002: 402).
– Order of clause constituents – all periods (Vanags 1993: 176; Vanags 2015: 68; Harder 1790).
– Formation of polar questions by fronting of the finite verb – all periods (Vanags 2013: 181).

Vanags (1993) also mentions explicitly four grammatical phenomena where a German impact on the Latvian construction was *not* observed in the early translations he investigated, despite differences between the two languages:
– no grammaticalization of a verb 'have', but consequent observation of the Latvian pattern with the verb 'be' and a dative possessor,
– no grammaticalization of a future auxiliary, but correct use of the synthetic future,
– no confusion of active and passive past participles,
– no violation of the rule that the negative marker immediately precedes the finite verb.

These Latvian constructions remain stable throughout the time of Old Written Low Latvian.

2.2 History of Old Written High Latvian

The oldest preserved book in Old Written High Latvian was published in 1753 and contains the texts from the Gospels to be read at Sunday services and a short appendix with the words of the confession, the Ten Commandments, explanations of religious rules, and prayers (*Evangelia Toto Anno* 1753). While the existence of earlier printed books is doubtful (Stafecka 2004: 320; Jansone and Stafecka 2013: 228–229), it is very likely that High Latvian had been written at least from the beginning of the 18th century on, for the *Evangelia Toto Anno* 1753 shows already the results of graphization and code selection. It is based on southern dialects of Latgalian and serves as an important model text for the coming century. The time from the beginning of High Latvian writing in the 18th century and the middle of the 19th century is regarded as one period in the history of Old Written High Latvian (Vanags 2019: 82), and in terms of standardization processes it corresponds partly to the second and partly to the third period distinguished in the history of Old Written Low Latvian (Section 2.1). Throughout this time, we observe in High Latvian writings a search for a unified spelling as well as variation in morphology (corresponding to the second period), but also a diversification of registers that partly corresponds to that of Low Latvian in its third period. Primers are among the earliest printings, and at least some of the early books were intended for a Latvian readership (Vanags 2019: 74). At the end of the period, the body of work written in High Latvian comprises religious books of various genres (texts from the Bible, catechisms, prayer books, hymnals, sermons, hagiographic texts), practical literature for farmers, and some short entertaining and/or educating texts published mainly in calendars (for details, see Stafecka 2004).

The authors of Old Written High Latvian texts were Catholic priests, missionaries, and monks. Their language of upbringing was mainly Polish, in some cases Lithuanian and Polish, and in some cases German. A very important role was played by the Jesuit order, who maintained missions and educational institutions on the territory of Latgalia and whose members were especially active in using, teaching and normalizing Old Written High Latvian. Important authors include[5] Jan Kariger (1664–1729), author of a High Latvian-Polish-Latin dictionary that was widely in use, though not published in print (see Kolbuszewski 1977); Jan Łukaszewicz (1699–1779), who may have been one of the translators of the *Evan-*

---

[5] Information on authors compiled from Bukšs (1952); Kolbuszewski (1966, 1973, 1977); Stafecka (2004); Jansone and Stafecka (2013), and the portal *Latgales dati* (http://latgalesdati.du.lv/, accessed 22.02.2022).

gelia toto anno 1753; Michael Roth (1721–1785), who wrote a catechism and primer, poems, religious lessons in questions and answers, and retellings of Bible stories; Józef Akielewicz (1768 or 1769–1842), author of the book on beekeeping studied in this chapter; he also published a short grammar of High Latvian in Polish that before circulated as a manuscript; Tomasz Kossowski (1798–1856), who published another version of this grammar[6] and wrote two volumes of sermons; Jan Kurmin (1795–1860), who also wrote sermons and published the first printed High Latvian-Polish-Latin dictionary; Józef Macilewicz (1805–1872), author of a practical book about agriculture translated from Lithuanian; Gustaw Manteuffel (1832–1916), the only laic among the authors mentioned here, who published the first High Latvian calendars as well as law texts, folk songs, religious books and some secular texts.

While Old Written High Latvian ends at about the same time as Old Written Low Latvian, the reasons are very different: publishing in High Latvian was disrupted by the ban of printing in the Latin alphabet, which was imposed in 1865 in those parts of the Russian Empire where Polish (and Catholic) cultural influence had been strong, affecting High Latvian as well as Lithuanian. The ban was lifted only in 1904. During this period, the first Latgalian intelligentsia had grown up and was ready to take charge of the development of a Latgalian standard language.

Like in the case of Low Latvian, the influence of the colonial language (here: Polish) on Old Written High Latvian is most apparent in the writing system and the visual appearance of printed books. Title pages and prefaces are written in Polish or Latin. As a "Catholic language", Old Written High Latvian uses the Latin alphabet and is printed in roman letters. The spelling is based on the Polish spelling system and in the course of time reflects Polish spelling reforms, for example, by replacing < y > by < j > in diphthongs; see Stafecka (2004). There is no unified system for indicating vowel length: some publications use accents, but inconsistently, in others, vowel length is simply ignored. Nevertheless, Old Written High Latvian is not difficult to read for those who know the spoken language – but, in contrast to Old Written Low Latvian, it is not convenient for learners of the language who only speak the colonial language. The spelling used in Akielewicz's book will be explained in Section 3.2.

In the vocabulary, Polish loanwords are most frequent in the religious domain, but also found elsewhere. Slavic loanwords are also common in spoken dialects of High Latvian, and it is often not clear which was the donor language.

---

6 On Akielewicz's and Kossowski's grammars and their common source see Strods (1937); Kristovska (1996).

In Old Written High Latvian, in addition to Standard Polish, regional varieties of Polish as used on the territory of Lithuania and Latgalia have to be taken into account as well as relicts of the Ruthenian chancery language, which may be the source of East Slavonic shapes of words, even if they entered Latgalian through Polish. I am not aware of studies dedicated to an inventory of Polish or Slavic loanwords in Old Written High Latvian. Likewise, Polish influence on the grammar of Old Written High Latvian has not been investigated yet. Interestingly, some phenomena that may be candidates of Polish influence in the grammar of *Evangelia toto anno* 1753 are attributed to a Latin model by Bukšs (1952: 65–66): the postposition of modifiers (adjectives, possessive pronouns, modifying genitives) and the use of *un* 'and' in the meaning 'also'.

Finally, it should be noted that also Old Written Low Latvian had an influence on Old Written High Latvian, evident in the vocabulary and more subtle in the grammar. A side effect is the introduction of German patterns into Old Written High Latvian which were part of the Low Latvian writing tradition.

3 Material and methods of the case study

To analyze the impact of German on Old Written Low Latvian and that of Polish and other languages on Old Written High Latvian, two books were chosen that offer the same content in the two codes: Christian Friedrich Launitz, *Bißchu=gramatiņa jeb ihßa un ßkaidra Pamahzißchana no bittehm un bißchu kohpßchanaß* ('The little book of bees, or a short and clear teaching about bees and beekeeping', 1803), in this paper also referred to by the abbreviation LL (Low Latvian), and Józef Akielewicz, *Eysa mociba ap audzieyszonu biszu* ('Short teaching about beekeeping', 1832), also referred to as AL (High Latvian). Akielewicz (1832) is a free translation of Launitz' book, which in turn is a free translation of a German book with the title *Das Wahre und Nützliche in der Bienenzucht* ('The true and the useful in beekeeping') by the Prussian precentor Daniel Gottlieb Settegast (1798). Three years earlier, Settegast had published a longer version of this book, which was subsequently translated into Lithuanian (by the author himself) and Polish. These translations seem to have played no role for the two Latvian versions, which represent the content and style of the shorter book of 1798. Most importantly, I found no cue in the High Latvian text that Akielewicz may have used the Polish or the Lithuanian version. His book is clearly a free translation of the Low Latvian book by Launitz, and text parts that have no correspondence there most likely were written by Akielewicz himself.

Akielewicz's *Eysa mociba...* (1832) is the first secular book in Old Written High Latvian (disregarding primers and grammatical sketches) and is among the first 20 printed High Latvian books of which copies have survived. The first title page is in Polish, a second one with the same content in Old Written High Latvian. The book is preceded by a dedication to Count Zyberk (Michał Plater-Zyberk), written in Polish, in which the author thanks him for the book in Low Latvian (*w języku Kurlandzkim* 'in the language of Courland') and the incitation to translate it into High Latvian (*na język Inflandzko-Łotewski* 'into the Latvian language of Polish Livonia'). Józef Akielewicz studied at the seminary in Krāslava and worked for long years as canon in the parish of Līksna. I could not find information about his origin and life before he entered the seminary. His year of birth (1768 or 1769) is inferred from the inscription on his gravestone, which says that he died in 1842 at the age of 73.[7] He is supposed to be of Polish origin, but his surname may also be Lithuanian. His version of the book on beekeeping shows a very good knowledge of spoken Latgalian, which he probably used daily in contact with his parishioners, as well as Old Written High and Low Latvian. Knowledge of Lithuanian cannot be proven but is possible. Polish and Latin were his languages of education and daily work. As he lived at a time when Latvia and most parts of Lithuania belonged to the Russian Empire, we may assume a knowledge of Russian. He also worked some years in Kiev, where he may have used Russian or Ukrainian. He was a truly multilingual person.

Christian Friedrich Schmidt von der Launitz (1773–1832) was a Baltic German Lutheran cleric, born in Grobiņa near Liepāja in Courland, where his father was pastor and later provost. After studying in Germany, he returned to his hometown, worked as a pastor at the side of his father and later became provost himself. The *Bißchu=gramatiņa* was his first book in Latvian, but he had already published Latvian texts in periodicals and would continue writing secular and religious texts, including hymns, primers, and an explanation of the terms of the abolition of serfdom in Courland in 1817 (Recke and Napiersky 1831: 24–27). Launitz' work and his endeavors to educate Latvian farmers makes him a representative of the Popular Enlightenment (see Daija 2017), and his translation of Settegast's book belongs to the first manuals on agricultural and household matters, which at that time started to become popular (Daija 2017: 51–52). Settegast's book on beekeeping contains both descriptive parts (describing the life of bees) and procedural parts (telling the reader how to do all kinds of tasks connected to beekeeping). For the language of the descriptive parts, Launitz could draw on

---

[7] Pictures of the gravestone are included in his entry in the database *Latgales dati* at http://latgalesdati.du.lv/persona/10977.

some already existing Low Latvian texts, including Stender's *Augstas gudribas grahamata* [Book of high wisdom], which had just appeared in its second, revised edition (published in 1799), but also some of the religious literature. Procedural texts, however, were still a novelty.[8]

At the beginning of the 19th century, Old Written Low Latvian was already well established as a book language (cf. Section 2.1). The norm achieved at that time is apparent in orthography, grammar and vocabulary of Launitz' book. Latvian sources do not count Launitz among the best writers of his time (for example, he is not mentioned by Vanags 2013: 187), probably because his writing is rather conservative and retains features of German influence which his more progressive contemporaries tried to avoid. This, however, qualifies his book for the present case study, whose aim is to find examples of the impact of German on the grammar of Old Written Low Latvian. The comparison with the High Latvian version by Akielewicz will further help in identifying these features. In a short comparison of parts of the two books, Leikuma (1992) found that the language of Akielewicz is closer than that of Launitz to Latvian as spoken in its respective region. In the present study I will show that this reflects the fact that Launitz wrote in an established code that had developed as a written register, while the sources on which Akielewicz drew were more varied.

For this study, the texts of the investigated books were compiled into two separate corpora, using the tools at the platform Sketch Engine (sketchengine.eu). This allows a quantitative comparison of selected expression means as well as a more convenient way of searching the texts. The corpus of LL (Launitz 1803) contains 16,152 words, that of AL (Akielewicz 1832) 12,392. Neither corpus is annotated; there are (yet) no tools for automatic annotation of these varieties of Latvian. As Launitz' book was printed in blackletter, the text had first to be transliterated; the principles are explained in Section 3.1 together with a general explanation of the spelling.

In addition to the corpora, I prepared tables for a sentence-by-sentence comparison, based on selected chapters or parts of chapters where each sentence in LL has a corresponding sentence in AL. In some instances, I also compared sentences from LL with the German model text (Settegast 1798). However, though Launitz' book clearly is a translation, it is a free translation that does not directly mirror the German constructions used in the model.

In Section 4, selected grammatical phenomena are investigated in detail in the two texts. For an evaluation of the spread of the phenomenon, I checked other

---

[8] For example, the first cookbook in Latvian, translated from German, was published by Christoph Harder in 1795.

Old Written Low and High Latvian texts. I used the corpus SENIE Unicode, which contains many Low Latvian texts of all three periods as well as the High Latvian *Evangelia toto anno* 1753. For the latter, I also used the edited print version with its index. I also looked into some other Old Written High Latvian texts, but the search options in full texts (partly available to me only as photographs) are limited. Another important source for Low Latvian were the grammars by Stender (1761), Hesselberg (1841), and Rosenberger (1852) and the comments and additions by Harder (1790). For Old Written High Latvian, there are no comparable grammars, only some sketches intended for teaching the language that were of little use for the current purpose.

3.1 Writing system in Launitz (1803) and principles of transliteration

Old Written Low Latvian is printed in blackletter. It uses the Latin alphabet and some diacritics to mark Latvian sounds. Figure 1 shows an extract of the printed book by Launitz and the way it was transliterated for the present study.

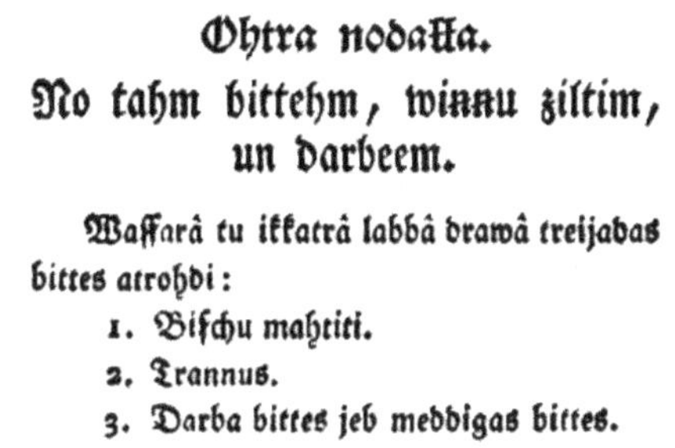
Ohtra nodalla.
No tahm bittehm, winnu ziltim, un darbeem.
Waſſarâ tu ikkatrâ labbâ drawâ treijadas bittes atrohdi:
1. Biſchu mahtiti.
2. Trannus.
3. Darba bittes jeb meddigas bittes.

Ohtra nodaļļa.

No tahm bittehm, wiņņu ziltim,
un darbeem.

Waßßarâ tu ikkatrâ labbâ drawâ treijadaß bitteß atrohdi:
1. Bißchu mahtiti.
2. Trannuß.
3. Darba bitteß jeb meddigaß bitteß.

'Second chapter. Of the bees, their colonies, and their work.
In summer, you find in any good apiary three kinds of bees:
1. The queen bee.
2. Drone bees.
3. Working bees or hunting bees.'

Figure 1: Extract from Launitz (1803) with transliteration and translation

The spelling system shows its German origin quite clearly. The letters <b, d, f, g, h, j, k, l, m, n, p, r, t> have the same value as in modern Latvian and modern

German, and their pronunciation is straightforward. The letter <w> is pronounced as in German, i.e. [v]. In modern Latvian, the letter <v> is used instead.

To indicate the palatal consonants of Latvian which have no equivalent in German, the letters <g, k, l, n, r> were crossed by a thin stroke (see the second and the sixth word in the example in Figure 1). In my transliteration, I use the modern Latvian letters <ģ, ķ, ļ, ņ, ŗ>. The corresponding sounds are [ɟ c ʎ ɲ rʲ].

The most complicated among consonants is the rendering of sibilants. First, the blackletter type has three letters which may correspond to a modern German <s>. Second, three sounds are rendered by a combination of letters. Table 1 shows the letters and combinations in question, the way they are transliterated here, the corresponding letter in modern Latvian, and their phonetic value.

Table 1: Writing convention for sibilants in Old Written Low Latvian

Text	Transliteration	Modern Latvian letter	Pronunciation (IPA)
ʃ	s	z	[z]
ʃch	sch	ž	[ʒ]
st **)	st	st	[st]
s *)	ß	s	[s]
f	ß	s	[s]
ʃch	ßch	š	[ʃ]
tʃch	tßch	č	[tʃ]
z	z	c	[ts]

*) appears at the end of a word or prefix; **) ligature

Although the system of consonant letters in the old "German style" writing looks more complicated than in modern Latvian, it is equally phonemic, and the letters and combinations could automatically be replaced by modern equivalents. With vowels, this is not the case. The greatest problem here is an inconsequent system of distinguishing long and short vowels, for which modern Latvian spelling has a simple and unambiguous rule: long vowels are distinguished by a macron. In Old Latvian writing, vowel length is sometimes indicated by the letter <h>, for example <mahte> (modern spelling *māte*) 'mother'. However, this is done mostly in roots, while derivational and inflectional suffixes may lack an indicator of vowel length, for example <maht-it-e> (*māt-īt-e*) 'mother-DIM-NOM.SG'. In a locative ending, vowel length is indicated by a circumflex, for example <draw-â> (*drav-ā*) 'apiary-LOC'. In some pronominal roots in turn, a long vowel is indicated by a grave accent: <kà> (*kā*) 'how'. On the other hand, a short vowel may be indicated by the doubling of the preceding consonant, as in <bitte> (*bite*) 'bee', <nodaḷḷa> (*nodaḷa*) 'chapter'. Thus, Old Written Low Latvian has copied from German spelling many inconsistencies and difficulties in distinguishing long and short vowels.

When it comes to vowel quality, both old and modern Latvian writing use the letter <e> for [ɛ] as well as [æ], which belong to different phonemes (both short and long). Another inconvenient heritage from the old spelling system is the use of the letter <o> for both the vowel [ɔ] and the diphthong [uɔ], the latter being much more frequent. The diphthong [iɛ], on the other hand, was unambiguously written as <ee> in Old Written Low Latvian, which was replaced by *ie* in modern spelling, for example <weenß> (*viens*) 'one'.

3.2 Spelling in Akielewicz (1832)

Old Written High Latvian did not reach the same level of normalization as Old Written Low Latvian. Although, as mentioned in Section 2.2, the *Evangelia toto anno* 1753 served as a model text, the beginning of the 19th century saw rather more than less variation in spelling.

High Latvian spelling was based on Polish orthography but also included some conventions of the Low Latvian tradition. One of these is the use of the letter <o> for both the single vowel and the diphthong. This is even more problematic in High Latvian, where both /o/ and /uo/ are frequent phonemes. The reader has to know the words and morphemes in order to read them correctly. For example, <jodor> 'must do' is pronounced [juɔdɔr]; modern spelling: *juodor*. Typical German conventions, such as the use of <h> for vowel length or doubling of consonants to indicate short vowels, are not found in High Latvian writing. In the *Evangelia toto anno* 1753, vowel length is often, but not consistently indicated by accents. Akielewicz does not use accents, and most often vowel length is not indicated at all – a knowledge of the language is necessary for correct reading. Occasionally, a long vowel is indicated by a doubling of the respective letter. This technique is found mostly with <i>, for example <ziima> (*zīma*) 'winter', <ciits> (*cīts*) 'hard', <tiisa> (*tīsa*) 'right', but also two times with <u>: <łuupu> (*lūpu*) 'cattle.GEN.PL', and <guudam> (*gūdam*) 'honor.DAT.SG'. Instead of <ii>, occasionally <ij> is found, for example <cijti> (*cīti*) 'closed', and <j> and <y> may indicate a long [iː] as well. More often than for [iː], the letter <y> stands for the sound [ɨ], as in Polish and in modern Latgalian spelling, for example <cyts> (*cyts*) 'other'. It is also used as the second part of a diphthong, where modern Polish uses <j> and modern Latgalian <i> or (at the end of a verbal stem) <j>, for example <tay> (*tai*) 'so',

<treys> (*treis*) 'three', <dzieywoy> (*dzeivoj*) 'live.PRS.3', <gaydey> (*gaidej*) 'wait.IMP.2SG'.

The spelling of consonants in Old Written High Latvian follows a Polish model. In contrast to Latvian, Latgalian has palatalized consonants; palatalization is partly phonemic, partly conditioned by the position of the consonant. The indication of palatalization is inconsistent in Old High Latvian writing and has not yet been fully solved in modern Latgalian orthography.

In Akielewicz's text, the accent <'> has partly the same function as in Polish: it indicates palatalization, for example <ń> for [nʲ] and <ć> for [tsʲ], and also <ź> for [zʲ]. However, <ź> also (and more often) stands for [ʒ], which is spelled by <ż> in Polish and <ž> in modern Latgalian. The letter <l> is used for palatalized [lʲ], while <ł> indicates a non-palatalized [l]. Two sounds are written by digraphs: <sz> stands for [ʃ] and <cz> for [tʃ]. Table 2 gives a summary of these conventions.

Table 2: Some conventions for the spelling of consonants in Akielewicz (1832)

Text	Modern Latgalian	Pronunciation (IPA)
w	v	[v]
z	z	[z]
ź	ž	[ʒ]
s	s	[s]
sz	š	[ʃ]
cz	č	[tʃ]
c	c	[ts]
ł	l	[l]
l	ļ	[lʲ]
ń	ņ	[nʲ]
ź	z *⁾	[zʲ]
ś	s *⁾	[sʲ]
ć	c *⁾	[tsʲ]

*⁾ Palatalization not indicated

Palatalization of a consonant (other than [lʲ]) may be indicated by the letter <i> between the consonant and a following <a, o, u>. Examples: <aćtiniom> (*actiņom*) [atsʲtʲinʲɔm] 'eye.DIM.DAT.PL', <ulenius> (*ūleņus*) [u:lʲenʲus] 'egg.DIM.ACC.PL', <pukiu> (*puķu*) [pukʲu] 'flower.GEN.PL'. This rule is also applied before <e>, but not consistently. Example: <niedelu> and <nedelu> (*nedeļu*) [nʲedʲelʲu] 'week (ACC.SG or GEN.PL)'. Furthermore, open [æ] after a palatalized consonant may be written by <e> or by

<a>, which gives rise to further variation. For example, the word *reizē* (in modern spelling) 'once; together', pronounced [rʲæjzʲæː] is found in four variants: <reyze>/ <reyzie> / <reyzia> / <rayzie>.

Notwithstanding such variation and inconsistencies, the High Latvian text is closer to modern writing than the Low Latvian text. However, it demands a higher command of the spoken language.

4 Case study: Grammatical constructions in Old Written Low and High Latvian

This section presents and discusses the findings of the investigation of selected grammatical constructions in the two versions of the little book on beekeeping, LL (Launtiz 1803, Low Latvian) and AL (Akielewicz 1832, High Latvian). Examples are cited from the corpora compiled from these texts, with an indication of the respective chapter. For example, "LL 2-08" refers to chapter 8 of the second part of Launitz (1803). The examples are cited as written in the sources, for LL using the transliteration explained in Section 3.1. Occasionally, obvious typographic errors were corrected; these occur mostly in AL. When a general citation form for words was needed, I used modern Standard Latvian. For example, *viņš* 'he' stands for the pronoun *wiṇßch* in LL and *winsz* in AL.

4.1 Referring expressions

Maybe the most conspicuous feature of Old Written Low Latvian is the use of a definite article, homonymous to the demonstrative pronoun *tas* 'that'. A less obvious feature is the overuse of the third person pronoun *viņš*. Both phenomena belong to the domain of discourse reference. A comparison of LL and AL shows clear differences in this domain, which mostly can be attributed to German influence on Low Latvian writing, while AL is closer to spoken language. Table 3 gives an overview of these differences, and Table 4 shows the frequency of individual pronouns in the texts. The high frequency, both absolute and relative, of *tas* 'that', 'the' in LL reflects its use as a definite article, while the much lower frequency of *weenß* 'one', 'a', which equals the frequency of High Latvian *wins*, is a hint that we do not find a grammaticalization of an indefinite article parallel to that of the definite article. The singular masculine nominative is used as the citation form; corpus searches included all inflected forms of the respective pronoun.

Table 3: Use of referring expressions in LL and AL compared

	LL	AL
Determiner and noun	very often	rarely
Bare noun	Rarely	very often
Demonstrative pronoun	more often than AL	less often than LL
Third person pronoun	very often	less often than LL
Zero	less often than AL	more often than LL

Table 4: Frequency of selected pronouns and determiners in LL and AL

	LL	AL	LL per 1000	AL per 1000
Third person pronoun	wiņßch (294)	winsz (44) jis (122) = 166	18.2	13.4
Demonstrative/definite determiner 'that', 'the'	taß (1252)	tys (305)	77.5	24.6
Demonstrative 'this'	ßchis (87)	szys (21)[9]	5.4	1.7
Numeral/indefinite determiner 'one', 'a'	weenß (125)	wins (95)	7.7	7.7

In High Latvian dialects and in modern Latgalian, the third person pronoun is *jis* (*jis* 'he', *jei* 'she', *jī* 'they.M', *juos* 'they.F'). In Old High Latvian writing, also *winsz* (*winsz, winia, wini, winias*) is used, most probably taken over from Low Latvian writing; for more details on forms of personal pronouns in Old Written High Latvian see Stafecka (1989).

Extracts (1) and (2) illustrate the use of referring expressions in a paragraph. The extracts are divided into clauses (a–i). Each clause contains a reference to the topic of the paragraph, the larvae. It is introduced in the first clause in both texts by a bare noun; the corresponding noun phrase in the German text has an indefinite article. For the first reference after this introduction, LL uses a noun phrase with the definite article, after that, pronouns (four times the third person pronoun *wiņßch*, once the emphatic pronoun *patß* 'itself'), or zero for a subject in coordinated clauses (conjunction reduction). Zero reference is marked in the

---

[9] The Latgalian word for 'this', *itys*, is not found in the corpus.

translations by "[_]". In AL we find a bare noun three times after the introduction, only two instances of the third person pronoun, and zero in conjunction reduction (clause 2i) as well as in situations where the previous mention was as an object (2d, 2h). Another difference between the two languages is that LL uses the singular for generic referents ('a/the larva'), while AL uses the plural ('larvae'). This difference rule can be observed throughout the books.

(1) Low Latvian[10] [LL 2-04]
    a. *No   ta   pauta,   ko   ta*
       from   DEM.GEN.SG.M egg.GEN.SG WH.ACC DEM.NOM.SG.F
       *mahte   dehj,   **zirmiņßch**   tohp* [...]
       mother.NOM.SG lay_eggs.PRS.3 **larva.NOM.SG** become.PRS.3
       'From the egg that the mother lays, **a larva** hatches [...].'
    b. *Irr   **taß**   **zirmiņßch**   jeb   kahpurß,*
       be.PRS.3 **DEM.NOM.SG.M** **larva.NOM.SG** or maggot.NOM.SG
       ißaudsiß
       grow_up.PST.PA.SG.M
       'When **the larva** or maggot has grown up,'
    c. *tad   tahß   bitteß   **winna**   kanniņu   ar*
       then DEM.NOM.PL.F bee.NOM.PL **3.GEN.SG.M** cell.ACC.SG with
       waßka   wahku   aißßlehds.
       wask.GEN.SG lid.ACC.SG lock_up.PRS.3
       'the bees lock up **its** cell with a wask lid.'
    d. *Tà   aißßlehgtß   **winßch**   gull   beß   barribaß*
       so lock_up.PST.PP.SG.M **3.NOM.SG.M** sleep.PRS.3 without food.GEN.SG
       'Locked up in such a way, **it** sleeps without food'
    e. *kamehr   **winßch**   par   kuhnu   tohp.*
       until **3.NOM.SG.M** for pupa.ACC.SG become.PRS.3
       'until **it** becomes a pupa.'
    f. *Tad   **winßch**   to   wahku   atkal   ußgruhßch*
       then **3.NOM.SG.M** DEM.ACC.SG lid.ACC.SG again push_off.PRS.3
       'Then **it** pushes off the lid'
    g. *un   no   tahm   bittehm   tohp   ehdinahtß,*
       and from DEM.DAT.PL.F bee.DAT.PL become.PRS.3 feed.PST.PP.SG.M
       'and [_] is fed by the bees'

---

10 The glossing of examples follows the Salos Glossing Rules (Nau and Arkadiev 2015), which are based on the Leipzig Glossing Rules (2015).

h.   *kamehr*   **patß**   *kà pilniga*
until   EMPH.NOM.SG.M   as complete.NOM.SG.F
bitte   *ißaug*
bee.NOM.SG   grow_up.PRS.3
'until [it] **itself** has grown into a fully-fledged bee,'

i.   *un*   *pee*   *darba*   *eet.*
and   to   work.GEN.SG   go.PRS.3
'and [_] goes to work.'

(2)   High Latvian; translation of (1)   [AL 07]

a.   *Nu*   *tu*   *uleniu,*   *kotrus*   *motieyte*
from   DEM.GEN.PL   egg.GEN.PL   REL.ACC.PL.M   mother.DIM.NOM.SG
pideja,   **cirmini**   *top [...]*
PVB.lay_eggs.PST.3   **larva.NOM.PL**   become.PRS.3
'From these eggs which the queen laid, **larvae** hatch [...].'

b.   *Kad*   *jau*   **cirmini**   *nu*   *syłtuma*   *drusieyti*
when   already   **larva.NOM.PL**   from   warmth.GEN.SG   a_bit
piaug,
PVB.grow.PRS.3
'When [the] **larvae** have grown a bit from the warmth,'

c.   *tułayk*   *bites*   **cirminius**   *kambareytem*[11]
then   bee.NOM.PL   **larva.ACC.PL**   cell.DAT.PL
ar   *wosku*   *ayzmyurey;*
with   wax.ACC.SG   wall_up.PRS.3
'the bees wall up [the] **larvae** in cells with wax;'

d.   *tay*   *ayzmyureti*   *otkon*   *par kaydu*   *łayku*
so   wall_up.PST.PP.PL.M   again   for   some.ACC.SG   time.ACC.SG
bez   *bareybas*   *gul,*
without   food.GEN.SG   sleep.PRS.3
'walled up in such a way, [_] [= the larvae] sleep again for some time without food,'

e.   *kolsz*   **wini**   *par*   *kapurim*   *way*   *pusbitem*
until   3.NOM.PL.M   for   pupa.DAT.PL   or   half_bee.DAT.PL
palik,
become.PRS.3
'until **they** become pupae or half-bees.'

---

[11] AL consequently uses a dative form in locative function in the plural of feminine nouns.

f. *tułayk* **cirmini** *poszy* *tos*
    then **larva.NOM.PL** EMPH.NOM.PL.M DEM.ACC.PL.F
    kambareytes *ayzsłagtas* *ar* *wosku* *porgrauź*,
    cell.ACC.PL lock_up.PST.PP.PL.M with wax.ACC.SG PVB.gnaw.PRS.3
    'Then [the] **larvae** themselves gnaw through those wax-locked cells,'
g. *un* *bites* *tyuleń* *izsoka* **winius** *barot*,
    and bee.NOM.PL at_once start.PRS.3 3.ACC.PL.M feed.INF
    'and the bees start at once to feed **them**,'
h. *kołeyt* *par* *pyłnom* *bitem* *napalik*,
    until for full.DAT.PL.F bee.DAT.PL NEG.become.PRS.3
    'until [_] [= the larvae] become full bees,'
i. *un* *tułayk* *jau* *isoka* *it* *dorba*.
    and then already start.PRS.3 go.INF work.LOC.SG
    'and [_] start going to work.'

For non-human discourse referents, reference tracking by nouns is more characteristic for modern Latvian than the frequent use of the third person pronoun, (see Nau 2016: 233). In this respect, AL conforms to modern High Latvian, and presumably also to the spoken language of the period, while LL deviates from spoken Low Latvian and modern Standard Latvian. The high frequency of the pronoun *viņš* in old Low Latvian writing was criticized by Endzelīns ([1920] 1979). His recommendation, which soon became a prescriptive norm, was to use the demonstrative pronoun *tas* 'that' when referring to non-human referents. However, a replacement of *wiņßch* by *tas* in (1c–f) and similar passages of LL does not result in a more natural language. Rather, the pronoun may be replaced by a noun, or dropped (zero reference). Interestingly, Barbare (2002: 319–320) found that the use of the third person pronoun *viņš* for inanimate referents increased in written Low Latvian in the second half of the 19th century, that is, in the period where native speakers of Latvian became the main authors and the influence of German lessened. There may be several reasons for this increase. First, it may reflect the greater number of texts whose topics are not human beings (in contrast to most stories as well as religious texts), especially descriptions and instructions, for example, in schoolbooks, from which Barbare (2002: 320) gives several examples. LL may here be just pioneering. Second, authors who started writing in Latvian (their native language) may have felt the need of more explicit reference in written texts and inserted the pronoun in situations where zero reference would be sufficient and more natural in a conversation.

The use of the demonstrative *tas* 'that' as a definite article in Old Written Low Latvian has often been singled out as an example for the German influence on

Old Latvian grammar (cf. Section 2.1 above). It can be observed from the earliest documents on until the end of the 19th century, but individual authors differ in their usage (Barbare 2002: 340–343). It is hard to judge in how far we can speak of an article system characteristic for Old Written Low Latvian, and more studies of individual texts would be necessary to describe such a system. The 17th century grammars explicitly call *tas* an article, while Stender (1761) and later grammars deny the existence of articles in Latvian. However, until the middle of the 19th century, all authors of Latvian grammars are themselves inconsistent in their use of determiners in their examples and in their other works. Latvian sources also report the use of the numeral *viens* 'one' as an indefinite article, especially in 16th and 17th century texts (cf. Mieze 2002: 251); however, it seems that this was less grammaticalized.

In LL, the numeral *weenß* (*viens* 'one') may be used when introducing a new discourse referent. A noun phrase with this determiner usually refers to a certain exemplar in a set of already established referents or concepts. It is unspecific, but its existence is presupposed for the sentence in which it occurs. A typical context is the protasis of a conditional sentence, as in (3).

(3) Low Latvian [LL 2-13]
Kad **weenß** *kohziß [..]* *no* *wezzeem* *un*
when **one.NOM.SG.M** hive.NOM.SG from old.DAT.PL.M and
melneem *kahŗeem* *pilnß* *irraid*
black.DAT.PL.M comb.DAT.PL full.NOM.SG.M be.PRS.3
'If **a hive** is full of old and black combs'

This use of 'one' as indefinite determiner is occasionally found in AL as well, cf. the first occurrence of *wins* in (4), while the second time *wins* is a numeral.

(4) High Latvian [AL 21]
War *un* *tys* *nutykt,* *kad* *pi*
can.PRS.3 ADD DEM.NOM.SG.M happen.INF that at
wina *Spita* *wayrok* *atsyrodas*
one.GEN.SG.M swarm.GEN.SG more be_located.PRS.3.RFL
motiniu *na* *kay* **wina**
mother.DIM.GEN.PL NEG as **one.NOM.SG.M**
'It may also happen that in **a** swarm there is more than **one** queen.'

Thus, there is no noticeable difference in the use of *viens* 'one' between the two investigated texts.

The use of *tas* as a definite article, on the other hand, is ubiquitous in LL, as many of the examples in this chapter show, but not found in AL. Compared to some of his contemporaries, Launitz is very consequent in its use. He also often uses a noun phrase with a definite article in situations where a pronoun could have been used. In (5), the noun phrases 'the queen' and 'the colony' may have been chosen for disambiguation of two referents which would have had the same form of the third person pronoun. In the German model sentence in (6), the referents can be distinguished by number ('she' vs 'they').

(5) Low Latvian [LL 1-02]
Tà   kà   ta   mahtite   wairß   ne   dehj,
so   as   DEM.NOM.SG.F   mother.DIM.NOM.SG   more   NEG lay.PRS.3
ta   ßaime   taißahß,   no   teem
DEM.NOM.SG.F   family.NOM.SG prepare.PRS.3.RFL from DEM.DAT.PL.M
pehdigeem   pauteem   jaunaß   mahteß   ißperreht.
last.DAT.PL.M   egg.DAT.PL   new.ACC.PL.F   mother.ACC.PL PVB.hatch.INF
'As soon as **the queen** stops laying eggs, **the colony** is ready to hatch new queens from the last eggs.'

(6) German, model sentence of (5) [Settegast 1798: 12]
sobald   sie   ihnen   aufhört   Eier   zu   legen; so   machen
as_soon_as she   3PL.DAT   stop.PRS.3 egg.PL to   lay.INF so   make.INF
sie   sogleich   Anstalt,   sich   aus   ihren   zuleßt   gelegten
they   at_once   institution   RFL   of   her   lastly   lay.PST.PTCP
Eiern   etliche   junge   Mütter   auszubrüten.
egg.PL.DAT   several.PL   young.PL   mother.PL   PVB.to.hatch.INF
'As soon as **she** stops to lay eggs for them, **they** go at once about to hatch a number of new queens from the eggs she had laid last.'

However, there are also some contexts where definite articles are *not* used, in contrast to German. First, natural forces such as wind, rain and sunshine usually appear without article: *lai* **wehjßch** *ne nopuhßch* 'so that (the) **wind** won't blow [it] down', *kad ßaule ßpihd* 'when (the) **sun** is shining'. Second, time expressions in the locative or with a preposition are used without article (as in English, but not German), for example *seemâ* 'in winter', *par seemu* 'during winter', *ap deenaß=widdu laiku* (around day.GEN.SG=middle.ACC.SG time.ACC) 'around noon', German *um die Mittagszeit*. Third, more generally articles are often lacking in the locative and with prepositions or relational adverbs; cf. (7).

(7) Low Latvian [LL 2-19]

Bet kad tee tranni jau preekſch
but when DEM.NOM.PL.M drone.NOM.PL already before
puſſdeenaſ **preekſch zauruma** *(gahteſ)*
midday.GEN.SG **in_front_of hole.GEN.SG** gate.GEN.SG
ſpehle, un kad dauds bitteſ **kohzî** *jeb*
play.PRS.3 and when much bee.NOM.PL **hive.LOC.SG** or
kohkâ appakſchâ *kņuhpu jeb tſchuppôſ ſagull*
tree.LOC.SG below huddled_up or pile.LOC.PL PVB.lie.PRS.3
'But when the drones already before noon are playing **in front of [the] [entrance] hole**, and when many bees are huddled up or lying in piles **in [the] hive** or **below [the] hive**.'

A German equivalent often contains a form where preposition and article are contracted (for example, *vorm* < *vor dem* 'in front of the.DAT.SG.M', *zur* < *zu der* 'towards the.DAT.SG.F'). German translation equivalents of the highlighted expressions in (7) would be *vorm Loch* 'in front of the hole', *im Stock* 'in the hive' and *unterm Stock* 'under the hive'.[12] A contraction of article and preposition is not possible when the noun is modified. Similarly, in LL we find the definite article within prepositional phrases if there is a modifier, as in (8).

(8) Low Latvian [LL 2-10]

leez weenu dehliti preekſch **ta**
put.IMP.2SG one.ACC.SG desk.DIM.ACC.SG in_front_of **DEM.GEN.SG.M**
iſſkreijama zauruma
PVB.fly.PRS.PP.GEN.SG.M hole.GEN.SG
'put a little desk in front of **the** entrance hole'

Summing up: the use of the definite article in LL is very similar to that of the definite article in German, but not identical. Considering further the absence of indefinite articles, we may state that LL shows its own system of article use, which is inspired by, but not copied from German. AL has no definite article. Both texts show an occasional use of the numeral *viens* 'one' as indefinite pronoun ('a certain'), but it does not develop into an indefinite article.

---

[12] These equivalents are constructed. The German model text differs slightly in the wording.

4.2 The structure of the noun phrase

In modern Standard Latvian and Latgalian, noun phrases are constructed identically (for details see Nau 1998: 47–50; Nau 2011: 63–65), while the texts studied here show considerable differences with respect to cohesion and complexity of noun phrases as well as the position of modifiers. These differences can be connected to differences between planned, more formal written language and spontaneous speech which have been observed in many languages. It is well known that noun phrases in spontaneous speech are usually shorter and less complex than in writing and may show more variation with respect to word order. Based on data from several European languages, Miller and Weinert (1998) assume that the complex noun phrases known from modern standard languages have arisen as part of the development of written registers. They put forward the following hypothesis:

> the combining of demonstratives, quantifiers, adjectives, and nouns into NPs happens as groups of language users develop written languages (Miller and Weinert 1998: 176).

This hypothesis will probably not hold in a strong version. Complex noun phrases with strict rules for the combination of elements may also be found in languages without written registers, and languages where writing is well developed may have noun phrases that are less cohesive and rule-governed – a striking example being Classical Latin (cf. Spevak 2010: 223–224, 280; 2014). However, when understood as a description of tendencies in language history, the texts under investigation agree well with Miller and Weinert's statement. In LL, which reflects an established tradition of writing in Low Latvian, we observe the same structures as in modern Standard Latvian, while noun phrases in AL show more variation and characteristics of spoken language: they are less complex, they may be discontinuous, and word order is freer. These differences are especially clear where AL otherwise is a true translation of LL, as in examples (9) vs (10).

(9) Low Latvian [LL 2-11]
Tahda   neaugliga   mahte   irr
such.NOM.SG.F infertile.NOM.SG.F mother.NOM.SG   be.PRS.3
leela   nelaime   preekſch   bittehm
big.NOM.SG.F   misfortune.NOM.SG for   bee.DAT.PL
'Such an infertile queen is a great misfortune for bees'

(10) High Latvian, translation of (9) [AL 13]
Motie   naaugliga   leła   ir
mother.NOM.SG infertilbe.NOM.SG.F great.NOM.SG.F   be.PRS.3

> *nałayme*   *del*   *Biszu;*
> misfortune.NOM.SG   for   bee.GEN.PL
> 'An infertile queen is a great misfortune for bees'

In LL, the noun phrases have the structure (DETERMINER) ADJECTIVE HEAD. In AL, the first NP has no determiner and the adjective follows the head noun, and in the second NP adjective and noun are separated by the copula, that is, *leła ... nelaime* 'great misfortune' is a discontinuos noun phrase. Discontinuos noun phrases are attested in many languages all over the world (Fanselow and Féry 2006: 6–12 give a good overview) and have been the subject of research especially from a formal point of view, as they pose problems for some theories of syntax. This research is not relevant for the current purpose, and I will restrict my presentation of the phenomenon to a short description of the data.

4.2.1 Discontinuous noun phrases in AL

Discontinuous noun phrases are well attested in Akielewicz's text. In all instances that I found, the interrupting element is the finite verb, or a complex of finite modal verb and infinitive (11). The extrapolated constituent may be an adjective, as in (10), a participle or participle phrase (11 and 13), or a quantifier (12; see also 4 above). Most often, it is only one word that is extrapolated (an adjective or a quantifier), but more complex constituents or even a combination of two constituents (13) also appear, leaving the noun alone after the verb. The most common communicative effect of this construction seems to be emphasis of the modifying or quantifying constituent; less often it marks a contrast, for example, in (11), where different types of available food are contrasted, or in (12), where a holder of many beehives is contrasted to one who holds few.

(11) High Latvian [AL 4]
     kur   **sieu**   **patykamu**   *war*   *dabut*   **bareybu**
     where   RFL.DAT   pleasant.ACC.SG   can.PRS.3   get.INF   food.ACC.SG
     'where they can get **food they like**'

(12) High Latvian [AL 19]
     kam   **daudz**   *ir*   **biszu**
     WH.DAT   a_lot   be.PRS.3   bee.GEN.PL
     '[a man] who has **a lot of bees**'

(13) High Latvian [AL 15]
*joże   tod   **kocz   winu   apputynotu   boltu***
if.PTC then   albeit   one.ACC.SG sprinkle.PST.PP.ACC.SG white.ACC.SG
pasorgosit   biti,
discover.FUT.2PL   bee.ACC.SG
'for when you discover **even a single bee sprinkled white**'

Also modifiers of an adjective phrase may be extrapolated, cf. (14)

(14) High Latvian [AL 17]
*Otkon   jo   ruden   **lut**   ir   **slapnis***
again   if   autumn   **very**   be.PRS.3   **wet**
'again, when autumn is **very wet**'

Discontinuous phrases similar to these are well attested in spoken varieties of Slavic languages, and they are also found in spoken Low Latvian (Nau 1998: 50) as well as Lithuanian (Ambrazas 1997: 701). There is no need to assume that the examples in AL follow a Polish or Russian model, though the existence of this construction in more than one of the author's languages (including Latin) may have strengthened his inclination to use it. In any case, it is a structure typical for spontaneous spoken language, and modern Baltic and Slavic languages, as well as German, seem to avoid it in standard written registers. A reason for this avoidance may be the lack of prosody in writing, for discontinuous phrases are often associated with certain intonational patterns (see Fanselow and Féry 2006 and other work by those authors; Schultze-Berndt and Simard 2012). In written texts, linear order and adjacency of phrase constituents play a greater role for the understanding of structures. Nevertheless, also in writing word order may have pragmatic functions. This has been well described for the noun phrase in Classical Latin, where discontinuity (in classical philology known as *hyperbaton*) is used for emphasis or marking a focus (Powell 2010; Spevak 2010: 274–279). The use of hyperbaton in Latin varies across authors as well as across registers of one author. Powell (2010) found that Cicero used it most frequently in letters to a friend and sometimes in philosophical treaties (which are presented in the form of dialogues) and in speeches, while there are no examples of hyperbaton in more objective, descriptive or instructive texts such as Cato's *De agricultura*. He concludes that "it has uses in both formally rhetorical and informally conversational genres of writing" and is prone to appear in texts "which approach most closely the character of a reasonably close imitation or evocation of oral discourse"

(Powel 2010: 184). This characterization does not fit the Latvian books on apiculture and the German model text. While Settegast's first book on beekeeping used the question-and-answer method for teaching, the author abolished this form in the shorter compendium (Settegast 1798) which was the model for Launitz' (1803). The style became more neutral and objective. Akielewicz's use of hyperbaton in AL is most probably a transfer from oral language use made possible by the lack of a stylistic standard for secular written texts. The fact that such constructions were used in classical Latin texts may have contributed to their acceptability.

4.2.2 Noun phrase complexity in AL and LL

Other "oral" characteristics of noun phrases in AL are (i) that they are often less complex than their equivalents in LL, and (ii) that more complex modifiers tend to follow the head noun. In the model sentence from LL in (15), the noun phrase contains two modifiers, while the translation in AL in (16) has only one, omitting the participle.

(15) Low Latvian [LL 2-11]
*Tahß   bitteß   ikdeenaß   **ißmirrußchuß***
DEM.NOM.PL.F bee.NOM.PL   every_day   PVB.**die**.PST.PA.ACC.PL.M
trannu   behrnuß   *ißmett.*
drone.GEN.PL child.ACC.PL PVB.throw.PRS.3
'Every day the bees throw out **dead drone children**.' (i.e. 'young male bees that have died')

(16) High Latvian [AL 13]
*Tułayk   bites   ikdinas   **Truniu**   **barnus***
then   bee.NOM.PL   each_day   **drone.GEN.PL**   **child.ACC.PL**
wałk   ora.
pull.PRS.3   out
'Then the bees every day pull out **drone children**.'

Long noun phrases in AL may result from the use of synonyms or semantically close words, which are either combined by *way* 'or' or simply juxtaposed. In (17), two alternative terms are used for 'cell' (*actinia* 'eye.DIM' and *kambareyte* 'chamber.DIM'), and two alternative modifiers describing them are juxtaposed.

(17) High Latvian [AL 11]
nu wiersa kora wajag byut **actiniom**
of top.GEN.SG comb.GEN.SG need.PRS.3 be.INF **cell.DAT.PL**
way kambareytem ayzsłagtom **ayzklejotom**
or cell.DAT.PL lock_up.PST.PP.DAT.PL.F seal.PST.PP.DAT.PL.F
'At the top of the comb there should be **locked, sealed cells**'

The model sentence for (17) in LL, given in (18), contains a shorter noun phrase with only one word for 'cell' (*kanniņa* 'pot.DIM') and only one participle for 'closed, locked up', but it has an additional modifier, thus it may be seen as more complex despite being shorter.

(18) Low Latvian [LL 2-08]
Itt augßcham waijaga buht
quite above need.PRS.3 be.INF
aißßlehgtahm behrnu kanniņahm
lock_up.PST.PP.DAT.PL.F child.GEN.SG cell.DAT.PL
'On the very top there should be **locked children's cells.**'

Extract (19) gives another example of a long noun phrase in AL with alternative terms and losely coordinated modifiers. It also contains a relative clause, which is the preferred means for giving additional information about a noun in both AL and LL. Finite relative clauses always contain a relative pronoun and always follow the head noun. In (19), and similar in (17), also adjectives and participles follow the head noun, which is not the most usual order (see below).

(19) High Latvian (this sentence has no model in LL) [AL-10]
Ir tieu **Awils** *way* **trauks** *ar* **bitem**
be.PRS.3 2SG.DAT hive.NOM.SG or hive.NOM.SG with bee.DAT.PL
wacs sapuwis, kura rodas
old.NOM.SG.M rotten.NOM.SG.M which.LOC.SG appear.PRS.3
kory malni way sapelejuszy
comb.NOM.PL black.NOM.PL.M or mold.PST.PA.NOM.PL.M
[*nu tayda trauka kończe wajag bites da jaunam traukam pordzieyt.*]
'If you have an **old or rotten beehive** in which there are **black or molded combs** [from such a hive, you definitely have to drive the bees into a new hive.]'

4.2.3 Position of agreeing modifiers in AL

In modern standard Latvian and Latgalian, modifiers with agreement markers (adjectives, participles, determiners and demonstratives, possessive pronouns and some quantifying pronouns) regularly precede the head noun (for details see Nau 1998: 47–50, 2011: 63–65). This rule is also strictly observed in LL. In AL, it is a strong tendency, but adjectives, participles and some pronouns may also appear after the head noun. Table 5 gives an overview of the findings concerning individual classes of modifiers.

Table 5: Position of agreeing noun modifiers in AL

Word class	Position
Demonstrative pronouns (*tys* 'this, that', *szys* 'this', *tayds* 'such a')	always before the head noun
Quantifying pronouns (*wyss* 'all', *kayds* 'some', *nekayds* 'not any')	usually before the head, sometimes following
Possessive pronouns (*sows* 'RPOSS', *tows* 'your (SG)')	mostly before the head (94% of counted instances)
Adjectives	mostly before the head (82% of counted instances; see Table 6 below)
Participles	without complements mostly before, with complements mostly after the head
Ordinal numbers	precede or follow the head; within clauses they more often precede, in chapter titles they more often follow

Posing one of these modifiers after the head may have pragmatic reasons and/or follow a Polish model. In the 19th century, the position of adjectives in the Polish noun phrase was freer than today and partly influenced by the meaning of the adjective; much more often than in modern Polish adjectives and some other modifiers followed the noun (Sankowska 1962: 41, with further references; Berneker 1900: 135–143).

The post-head position of ordinal numbers in AL is most certainly due to Polish influence. It appears in 21 of 28 chapter headings, for example, *ATDALA CZETURPACMITA* 'Chapter Fourteenth'; this is (still today) the usual order in chapter headings in Polish books. The inverse order is used seven times in a title, for example in *PICPACMITA ATDALA* 'Fifteenth Chapter', while it is the only possible order in chapter headings in LL as well as modern Latvian books. When a chapter is referred to in the text, the numeral more often precedes the word *atdala* 'chapter': twelve instances, nine with the ordinal number spelled as a word and three as a digit, against five instances where the number followed the noun 'chapter' (four times spelled out, one time as a digit). The form of the chapter headings in AL may be seen as a stylistic calque from written Polish, or even from Latin. Berneker (1900: 138) supposes Latin influence on this construction in Old Polish.

The reflexive possessive pronoun *sows* is used five times after and 62 times before the noun, and the second person possessive pronoun *tows* appears only once after and 26 times before the head. There is no apparent pragmatic or stylistic reason for the deviation from the normal order (modifier-head); a Polish model is possible, as in 19th century Polish possessive pronouns were used in both positions without pragmatic or stylistic motivation (Berneker 1900: 140, 143).

With adjectives and participles, the situation is different: in many (though not all) instances of post-head positioning, a pragmatic motivation can be found. This order appears most often in a context of contrast, as in (20) and (21). In (22) the adjective singles out a group of referents ('young bees') without explicitly mentioning the contrast, which is, however, clearly implied ('older bees').

(20) High Latvian [AL15]
Topec **bites** **stypras** *na top*
therefore bee.NOM.PL strong.NOM.PL.F NEG become.PRS.3
plestas, *bet tik* **wojas** *nu styproku*
tear.PST.PP.PL.F but only weak.NOM.PL.F from stronger.GEN.PL
palik *kryudeytas*
become.PRS.3 kill.PST.PP.PL.F
'Therefore **strong bees** are not slain, only **weak** [bees] are killed by stronger ones.'

(21) High Latvian [AL 19]
kad pec cik **dinu** *sołtu,* *słapniu,* *un*
when after some day.GEN.PL cold.GEN.PL wet.GEN.PL and
padebesigu, *reyzia cielas* **dina** *gaysza*
cloudy.GEN.PL at_once arise.PRS.3 day.NOM.SG clear.NOM.SG.F
un *syłta.*
and warm.NOM.SG.F
'when some **cold, wet and cloudy days** are followed immediately by a **clear and warm day**'

(22) High Latvian [Al 29]
 Baroy **bites jaunas,** un worgules
 feed.IMP.2SG **bee.ACC.PL young.ACC.PL.F** and weakling.ACC.PL
 'feed **young bees** and weaklings' (= 'feed those bees that are young or weak, not bees in general')

However, not in all contexts of explicit or implicit contrast adjectives are positioned after the head: this is only a stylistic possibility, not a syntactic rule. The position of the adjective before the head is the main rule, against which the post-head position is marked. It may be used to mark a contrast or more generally for emphasis. It seems that semantic or lexical factors also play a role. For example, the most frequent adjective, *jauns* 'new', 'young', appears only once after the head, against 47 instances of the regular pre-head position. Table 6 gives numbers for some frequent adjectives. Instances where adjective and noun form a discontinuous (split) noun phrase (as in 10 above) were counted separately.

Table 6: Position of selected adjectives with respect to the head noun

	Adj N	**N Adj**	**Split**	**sum**
jauns 'new', 'young'	47	1	0	48
wacs 'old'	32	4	0	36
lels 'big'	14	3	5	22
mozs 'small'	6	2	1	9
sauss 'dry'	7	3	0	10
wojsz 'weak'	4	3	0	7
styprs 'strong'	1	2	0	3
	111 = 82.2%	18 =13.3%	6 = 4.4 %	135 = 100%

The corpus is, however, too small and the number of occurrences of most adjectives not sufficient to draw conclusions about semantic factors or lexical preferences.

4.2.4 Position of genitive modifiers in LL and AL

The position of genitives as modifiers and complements in a noun phrase is subject to clear rules in modern Standard Latvian and Latgalian: they appear almost always before the head noun; the genitive follows when the noun expresses a measure or quantification, for example in Standard Latvian *kilograms ogu* 'a kilogram of berries', *glāze šampaniešа* 'a glass of champagne'. This situation was already described by Harder (1790), who states that, except for nouns of measure, the normal position of a genitive is before the head noun and that constructions where it follows the noun are a result of literal translation and not genuine Latvian (Harder 1790: 26).

In LL, the same rules are generally observed, for example *pußßteeßa bißchu* 'one half of the bees', but *bißchu mahtite* 'bees' mother' (= 'queen bee'), *bißchu kurwiß* 'bees' basket', 'skep', *bißchu dahrs* 'bees' garden' ('bee garden'). Deviations from these rules occur, but they are rare. First, with head nouns that express some quantification but not a measure in a narrow sense, the genitive may appear after or before the head noun; cf. (23) and (24).

(23) Low Latvian [LL 2-18]
Tahda jauna mahtite **leelu**
such.NOM.SG.F new.NOM.SG.F mother.DIM.NOM.SG **big.ACC.SG**
pulku bißchu *ßew apkahrt ßapulzina*
swarm.ACC.SG bee.GEN.PL RFL.DAT around gather.PRS.3
'Such a new queen gathers around herself **a big swarm of bees**.'

(24) Low Latvian [LL 2-25]
Ne ilgi pehz pee tahß mahteß [...]
NEG long after to DEM.GEN.SG.F mother.GEN.SG
leelß bißchu pulkß *ßanahkß*
big.NOM.SG.M bee.GEN.PL swarm.NOM.SG come_together.FUT.3
'Not long afterwards, **a big swarm of bees** will gather at this queen'

The head noun in examples (23) and (24) is *pulkß*, a noun designating a certain amount of living beings, translating according to context as 'swarm', 'flock', 'troop', 'cohort', and other. This noun is used more often in western dialects of Latvian, where it may bleach to the general meaning of 'a lot, many'. In LL *pulkß* appears seven times together with a genitive. In four instances the genitive precedes and in three instances it follows the head noun. Such variation, or a prehead position of a genitive, is also found with other nouns which may or may not be interpreted as measuring. In AL, a genitive always follows such a noun.

Second, there are a few instances in LL where a qualifying genitive follows the head noun. So far I have detected only four such instances. In all four instances, the genitive noun phrase contains a determiner, cf. (25) and (26).

(25) Low Latvian [LL 1-03]
 Ta *mahtite* [...] *irr*
 DEM.NOM.SG.F mother.DIM.NOM.SG be.PRS.3
 ta *waldineeze* *to* *bißchu.*
 DEM.NOM.SG.F governor(FEM).NOM.SG DEM.GEN.PL bee.GEN.PL
 'The queen [...] is the governer **of the bees**.'

(26) Low Latvian [LL 2-17]
 Tee *wahki* **tahdu** **kanniņu**
 DEM.NOM.PL.M lid.NOM.PL **such.GEN.PL** **cell.GEN.PL**
 ne *staw* *appali*
 NEG stand.PRS.3 round.NOM.PL.M
 'The lids **of such cells** are not convex'

All four instances were found in sentences that are not directly translated from German, two of them within one paragraph that Launitz added. Nevertheless, the construction is the same as in German, and a German model is likely. Such an imitation of a German noun phrase is, however, exceptional: there are many instances where the German model text has a genitive modifier following the noun while in Launitz' translation the genitive appears before the head noun, according to Latvian rules, or it is simply dropped. This is especially apparent with nominalizations (see below).

In AL, we find much more instances of a postposed genitive in a noun phrase, though the general rules are the same as in modern Latvian and non-quantified genitives more often precede the head noun (***biszu dorz*** '**bees**' garden', ***Diwa swetibas*** '**God's** blessing', ***boda łayka*** 'in times **of hunger**'). Like adjectives (cf. 4.2.3), genitive modifiers may be placed after the noun for contrastive emphasis, cf. (27).

(27) High Latvian [AL 2]
 Taypot *un* *mads* *nu* ***łobuma*** ***zidu***
 likewise also honey.NOM.SG from **quality.GEN.SG** **flower.GEN.PL**
 na *nu* *Biszu* *pait*
 NEG from bee.GEN.PL PVB.go.PRS.3
 'Likewise, the [quality of the] honey comes from **the quality of the flowers** and not from the bees.'

However, a pragmatic motivation for the deviant order of genitive and head is not always obvious (less often than with adjectives). Sometimes the position seems to be a matter of free choice, and we find variation as in (28) and (29) in the same chapter.

(28) High Latvian [AL 2]
 tus tyuleń wajag aizsmereyt ar
 DEM.ACC.PL.M at_once be_needed.PRS.3 smear_up.INF with
 biszu masti
 bee.GEN.PL tallow.ACC.SG
 'one has to smear up these [cracks] at once with **bee tallow**'

(29) High Latvian [AL 2]
 tus ayzsmierey ar **masti biszu**
 DEM.ACC.PL.M smear_up.IMP.2SG with **tallow.ACC.SG bee.GEN.PL**
 'smear these [cracks] up with **bee tallow**'

There is one construction where a post-head position of a genitive is the rule rather than the exception in AL: action nominals with the suffix *-szon-*. These nominalizations are found in all varieties of Latvian. The corresponding forms of the suffix are *-ßchan-* in LL and *-šan-* in modern Standard Latvian. These deverbal nouns are used in both texts in typical Latvian constructions, independently of the model. They are a bit more frequent in AL than in LL (7.4 vs 5.0 per thousand words). Another difference is that in AL, in half of the observations (45 = 49%), the noun is combined with a genitive expressing the direct object (39 instances) or the subject (six instances) of the underlying verb, while in LL, only 20 (25%) of the nominalizations with *-ßchan-* are accompanied by a genitive (17 corresponding to the object and one to the subject of the verb; two other). The position of the genitive after the nominalization is clearly preferred in AL (35 vs 10 instances), while it is rare in LL (2 vs 18 instances). Examples (30)–(34) illustrate the word order possibilities in both languages.

(30) Low Latvian, genitive preceding head [LL 2-19]
 Pee **medduß ißgreeßchanaß** sinnamß
 at **honey.GEN.SG PVB.cut.ACN.GEN.SG** know.PRS.PP.NOM.SG.NA
 duhmi waijaga.
 fume.NOM.PL be_needed.PRS.3
 'As is well known, one needs fumes when **cutting honey**.'

(31) Low Latvian, genitive-head combination marked as compound [LL 2-05]
   No   bißchu=ehdinaßchanaß.
   of   bee.GEN.PL=eat.CAUS.ACN.GEN.SG
   'About bee-feeding' (chapter heading)

(32) Low Latvian, genitive following the head noun [LL 1-01]
   Trihß   leetaß   peederr   pee   labbaß
   three   thing.NOM.PL   belong.PRS.3   at   good.GEN.SG.F
   ißdohßchanaß   **to**   **bißchu**:
   succeed.ACN.GEN.SG **DEM.GEN.PL** **bee.GEN.PL**
   'Three things are needed for **bees succeeding** well' ('for a good success of bees')

(33) High Latvian, genitive follows [AL 17]
   Tys   ir   wysym   zynoms,   kad   pi
   DEM.NOM.SG.M   be.PRS.3   all.DAT.PL.M   know.PRS.PP.NOM.SG.M   that   at
   raudzieszonas   **biszu**   wajag   dyumu;
   sort.ACN.GEN.SG **bee.GEN.PL** be_needed.PRS.3 fume.GEN.PL
   'It is known to everybody that fumes are needed at **the sorting of bees**.'

(34) High Latvian, genitive precedes [AL Introduction]
   Ap   **Biszu**   **audzieyszonu**   nawajag   ni
   for   **bee.GEN.PL**   **raise.ACN.ACC.SG**   NEG.be_needed.PRS.3 NEG
   gryutas   pracas,   ni   dorga   kosta
   hard.GEN.SG.F   labor.GEN.SG   NEG   expensive.GEN.SG   cost.GEN.SG
   'For **the raising of bees**, one needs neither hard labor nor high expenses.'

An influence of a Polish model for the order Action Noun – Genitive is quite likely. In addition, language internal reasons may play a role. Given the partly verbal nature of action nouns, this order corresponds to the general rule of VO, which is more pronounced in AL (and in modern Latvian) than in LL, where OV dominates (see Section 4.3 below). The two investigated texts also differ in the position of complements of adjectives such as *pilns* 'full': in LL they precede while in AL they follow the head, cf. (35) and (36).

(35) Low Latvian [LL 1-06]
   ne   wißßaß   pukkeß   irr   **barribaß**   **pilnaß**
   NEG   all.NOM.PL.F   flower.NOM.PL   be.PRS.3   **food.GEN.SG**   **full.NOM.PL.F**
   'not all flowers are **full of food**.'

(36) High Latvian [AL 14]
    kocz   *trauks*   *byutu*   **pyłns**   *dorba*
    even_if   hive.NOM.SG   be.IRR   **full.NOM.SG.M**   work.GEN.SG
    'even if the hive were **full of work**'

To sum up the observations on word order in the noun phrase, the Polish influence on AL seems to be stronger than the German influence on LL. A possible explanation for this is the fact that in LL the rules for the order of elements in the noun phrase are already settled, while AL shows more variation and more possibilities of using word order for pragmatic purposes (emphasis, contrast). This kind of variation is also found in 19th century Polish texts and in Classical Latin, which may have furthered the acceptance of non-canonical word order.

4.3 The order of clause constituents

The earliest printed documents of Low Latvian contain many examples of word-by-word translations from German, resulting in constructions that are alien to Latvian. In the period of consolidation (mid-18th to mid-19th century), on which this study focuses, we no longer find a simple imitation of German word order. Instead, there are some quite clear rules which result from an individual development based on both spoken Latvian (i.e. Latvian spoken by native speakers) and German-influenced written Latvian (i.e. Latvian written by non-native speakers). These rules are well documented in grammatical descriptions of the period, first by Harder (1790: 67–72), then by Hesselberg (1841: 146–151), and Rosenberger (1852: 121–124), who bases his description on Harder (1790). All authors, however, point out that violations of the rules are still frequent in writing. For Harder this was the main motivation to write down the rules which, according to him, characterize "real" Latvian. At the end of his treatise, he admits the difficulty of determining the correct way of constructing sentences, as Latvians themselves are often "very unsure" ("sehr unsicher") – partly because they often hear and read German-type constructions in Latvian (Harder 1790: 71–72).

    The most detailed description of word order in 19th century Latvian is given by Hesselberg (1841: 146–151). In a summary (1841: 150), he lists the order of six possible components of a clause, which may be translated into modern terminology as the following six slots, cf. (37), where > means "precedes" and < > "may precede or follow".

(37) Order of clause constituents according to Hesselberg (1841: 150)
connective > subject > arguments in the genitive, dative, or accusative < > oblique arguments and adverbials > finite verb > infinitive or participle

These word-order regularities are found throughout the studied text LL. Extract (38) illustrates the slots given in (37). Clause (38a) is a copula clause, for which another rule may be added: the copula 'be' is placed between the subject and the predicative, not at the end as other finite verbs (though it occasionally appears in clause-final position). Clause (38b) contains a finite modal verb and two infinitives, (38c), (38d), and (38e) contain intransitive verbs and show the order (subject) > adverbial > verb, and (38f) ends with a transitive verb preceded by a direct object. Clauses (38a), (38b), (38c) are independent or main clauses, (38e) is an adverbial clause with the subordinator *kad* 'when', and (38d and f) are two parts of a relative clause. The word order in (38d–f) corresponds to that of German, while the order in the independent clauses (38b–c) differs from German.

(38) Low Latvian [LL 2-02]
    a. ßchee   waßku=tarphi   **irr**   leela
        DEM.NOM.PL.M   wax.GEN.PL=worm.NOM.PL   **be.PRS.3**   big.NOM.SG.F
        nelaime   pee   bittehm,
        misfortune.NOM.SG   at   bee.DAT.PL
        'These wax-worms are a great misfortune for bees.'
    b. jo   winnuß   tik   lehti   **ne**   **warr**   **ißdsiht**
        for   3.ACC.PL.M   so   easily   **NEG**   **can.PRS.3**   **drive_off.INF**
        un   **ißdeldeht.**
        and   **exterminate.INF**
        'for one **cannot** easily **drive** them away or **exterminate** them.'
    c. Winni   no   weena   pelleka   taurina
        3.NOM.PL.M   from   one.GEN.SG.M   grey.GEN.SG.M   moth.GEN.SG
        zellahß
        arise.PRS.3.RFL
        'They **come** from a certain grey moth'
    d1. kaß   naktß=laikâ   un
        WH.NOM   night=time.LOC.SG   and
        'which during the night and'
    e. kad   tahß   bitteß   uß   lauku   **irr**,
        when   DEM.NOM.PL.F   bee.NOM.PL   on   field.ACC.SG   **be.PRS.3**
        'when the bees **are** outside'

d2.	*tannîß*	*kohkôß*	*un*	*kurwjôß*	**eeleen,**	
	DEM.LOC.PL.M	hive.LOC.PL	and	skep.LOC.PL	**PVB.creep.PRS.3**	

'**creep** into the hives and skeps'

f.	*un*	*tur*	*wißßur*	*ßawuß*	*pautuß*	**dehj.**
	and	there	everywhere	RPOSS.ACC.PL.M	egg.ACC.PL	**lay.PRS.3**

'and **lay** their eggs there everywhere.'

From the rules in (37) and the extract in (38) we may infer that the basic word order in Old Written Low Latvian is SOV. The 19th century grammars often state explicitly that the verb is placed at the end of the clause. In modern Latvian, on the other hand, the basic word order is SVO. MLLVG II (1962: 459) states that the most common place for the direct object is after the verb. Do we have to assume a change in basic word order in Latvian between the mid-19th and the mid-20th century? However, already in the middle of the 18th century Stender, who unfortunately does not go into details of word order, notes that a direct object (referred to as "the accusative") normally follows the verb (Stender 1761: 104). The answer to this puzzle lies in register differences. A clause-final position of the verb is characteristic for descriptions, especially those written in present tense and with third person subjects. In LL, it is observed in all parts that describe the life of bees. In narrative texts, on the other hand, we find SVO (or more generally, a position of the verb somewhere in the middle of the clause) already in the 18th century. This register difference is noted by Endzelin (1922: 830), whose grammar is based on a great variety of written and spoken Latvian of the late 19th and early 20th century. Endzelins quotes Berneker's finding that in Slavic languages a clause-final position is typical for "static presentations, depictions, judgements, and observations" ("bei stillstehender Darstellung, bei Schilderungen, Urteilen, Betrachtungen"; Berneker 1900: 58). The word-order change that took place in Latvian in the 19th and 20th century thus concerns only texts and text parts with these characteristics, or a generalization of SVO across registers.

In the High Latvian text AL, the verb is likewise found most often at the end of a clause in the descriptive parts. However, there are several instances where the verb is placed before arguments and adverbials. Extract (39) is the equivalent text part of extract (38). Compare (38e) with (39b), and (38d2) with (39a2).

(39) High Latvian [AL 16]

a1.	*Wini*	*tułayk*
	3.NOM.PL.M	then

'They at the time'

b. kad   bites   **izit**   ora   del   dorba,
    when   bee.NOM.PL   **PVB.go.PRS.3**   out   for   work.GEN.SG
    'when the bees **go out** for work'

c. way   nakti   kad   bites   **gul**,
    or   night.LOC.SG   when   bee.NOM.PL   **sleep.PRS.3**
    'or at night when the bees **are asleep**'

a2. **ilin**   traukus,
    PVB.creep.PRS.3   hive.LOC.PL
    '**creep** into the hives'

d. un   tur   pa   wysim   szkirbinim
    and   there   in   all.DAT.PL.M   crack.DIM.DAT.PL
    sowas   ułas   **dej**.
    RPOSS.ACC.PL.F   egg.ACC.PL   **lay.PRS.3**
    'and **lay** their eggs there into all little cracks.'

The tendency to place the verb at the end of the clause is thus more pronounced in LL than in AL. I see several possible reasons for this difference. First, word order in AL is freer because Akielewicz takes more inspiration from the spoken language around him than does Launitz (as we already have seen with the noun phrase). Second, word order in LL follows the model of other non-narrative texts written in Old Low Latvian, while AL did not have such models. Third, while an SOV order as such is most probably an inherited feature (a thesis supported by facts from the history of Slavic languages and Lithuanian, cf. Berneker 1900), its retention in descriptive and explanatory texts may also show some German influence. Typical for such texts is a high amount of non-main clauses (relative clauses, complement clauses, adverbial clauses), where the verb in German appears in final position. In all such clauses the word order in Old Latvian writing corresponds to that of German. Also, the order OV with infinitives and participles that is found in LL has a parallel in German. The constant contact with German may thus have had a conserving effect for the older word order SOV, and the decrease of German influence at the end of the 19th century gave way for the spread of the newer order SVO across registers.

In addition to these general rules of constituent order, where German may have supported already existing tendencies, we also find a direct influence on word order which creates structures not typical for Latvian. Several phenomena that were noted by Harder (1790), Hesselberg (1841), and Rosenberger (1852) can be found in LL.

First, according to the rule stated above in (37), if a predicate consists of a finite auxiliary and a participle, the auxiliary should precede the participle. This is also explicitly stated by Hesselberg (1841: 148). While LL mostly follows this rule, as in examples (40) with a present perfect and (41) with a passive, there are also several instances where the auxiliary follows the participle, cf. (42) and (43). The latter order undoubtedly is taken over from German; Hesselberg (1841: 149) notes that it is found in books, but never heard in the speech of Latvians.

(40) Low Latvian [LL Pee-1]
  Kad tu tawu medu **eßßi ißgreesiß**
  when 2SG.NOM POSS2SG.ACC.SG honey.ACC.SG **be.PRS.2SG PVB.cut.PST.PA.SG.M**
  'When you **have cut out** your honey'

(41) Low Latvian [LL 2-03]
  [*bet taß newa weena alga,*]
  kurrâß kanniņâß tee **tohp dehti**
  which.LOC.PL.F cell.LOC.PL DEM.NOM.PL.M **AUX.PRS.3 lay.PST.PP.PL.M**
  'but it is not all the same into which cells they **are laid**.'

(42) Low Latvian [LL 2-05]
  pehz to kad tu to ehdamaju
  after DEM.ACC.SG that 2SG.NOM DEM.ACC.SG food.ACC.SG
  eelizziß eßßi
  PVB.put.PST.PA.SG.M be.PRS.2SG
  'after you **have put in** the food'

(43) Low Latvian [LL 2-3]
  No teem pauteem, kaß tâß
  from DEM.DAT.PL.M egg.DAT.PL WH:NOM DEM.LOC.PL.F
  leelakâß kanniņâß **dehti tohp**
  bigger.LOC.PL.F cell.LOC.PL **lay.PST.PP.PL.M AUX.PRS.3**
  'From the eggs that **are laid** into the bigger cells'

Furthermore, when the past passive participle of a passive construction is (correctly) placed at the end of the clause, the auxiliary may be separated from the participle by several other constituents instead of immediately preceding it. The same is found in combinations of a modal verb and an infinitive. Both Harder (1790: 70) and Hesselberg (1841: 148) insist that auxiliaries and modal verbs should be adjacent to participles and infinitives. In modern Standard Latvian, the passive auxiliary *tikt* almost always immediately precedes the passive participle (Nau et al. 2020: 48), and a cursory look at corpus data (corpus LVK2018) suggests that the modal verb *varēt* 'can' immediately precedes an infinitive in the great majority of instances (82% of instances of the lemma *varēt* 'can' were immediately followed by an infinitive).

Another Germanism found in Old Latvian writing, to be avoided according to 19th century grammarians, is the inversion of subject and verb to form a question. This is not observed in LL, but inversion is sometimes used in the protasis of a conditional sentence (see Section 4.7 below).

4.4 Existential, possessive, and copula clauses

All varieties of Latvian use the verb 'be' as auxiliary, as copula, and as existential verb. These three functions can be associated with different clause types, even if they may not always be clearly distinguished (cf. Nau 2016: 124–134). Existential clauses and copula clauses have various subtypes, which accounts for a high frequency of forms of the verb 'be' in texts. The texts studied here are no exception.

Table 7: Forms of be.PRS.3 ('is', 'are', 'is not', 'are not')

	LL		AL	
be.PRS.3	irr	229	ir	147
be.PRS.3	irraid	32		
NEG.be.PRS.3	newaid	44		
NEG.be.PRS.3	newa	12	nawa	25
Sum		317		172
per 1000		19.6		13.9

The most frequent form of 'be' is the third person present tense, for which both the positive and the negated form are suppletive. The frequency of all forms is notably higher in LL than in AL. Table 7 shows the variants of these two forms found in the investigated texts. It is interesting that only in LL the old forms *irraid* and *newaid* are attested, while in contemporary Latvian they are found more often in Latgalian than in Standard Latvian

The difference in frequency reflects a higher number of constructions with 'be' in LL, especially copula constructions. The equivalent of these constructions in AL often is a simple verb, for example, for the meanings 'be silent', 'be called', 'be visible; appear' AL uses a verb, while LL uses an adjective and a copula; or a different construction is used, as in (45) vs (44). In general, AL is "more verby" than LL.

(44) Low Latvian [LL 1-07]
    Kad   tawi   kaimiņi   apkahrt   tewiß
    if   POSS2SG.NOM.PL.M neighbor.NOM.PL around   2SG.GEN
    jau   **bitteneeki**   **irraid**
    already **beekeeper.NOM.PL** **be.PRS.3**
    'If the neighbors around you already **are beekeepers**'

(45) High Latvian [AL 4]
    Jo   *towi*   *kaymini*   *apleyk*   *tiewi*
    if   POSS2SG.NOM.PL.M neighbor.NOM.PL around   2SG.ACC
    daudz   ***Biszu***   ***audziey***
    a_lot   **bee.GEN.PL** **rear.PRS.3**
    'If the neighbors around you **keep a lot of bees**'

The copula constructions in LL usually have an equivalent in German (though not always in the respective part of the model text), and it is likely that German influence is directly or indirectly responsible for the preference of copula constructions in Old Written Low Latvian. It may also be a register feature of descriptive and explanatory written texts and reflect the fact that this register is more developed in Low Latvian than in High Latvian. For example, Stender's *Augsta Gudribas Grahmata* [Book of high wisdom] is full of copula clauses.

In all functions, the third person present tense form of 'be' may be omitted. This happens more often in dependent than in independent clauses, as in examples (46) and (47).

(46) Low Latvian [LL 2-19]
    kad   *labß*   *ßiltß*   *un*   *agraiß*
    when good.NOM.SG.M warm.NOM.SG.M and early.NOM.SG.M.DEF
    pawaßßarß
    spring.NOM.SG
    'when [there is] a nice warm and early spring'

(47) Low Latvian [LL 2-19]
    kad   *wiņņahm*   *badß*
    when   3.DAT.PL.F   hunger.NOM.SG
    'when they [have] hunger', 'when they experience a period of famine'

I did not find a difference between LL and AL with respect to the frequency of omission of 'be'. Such a difference might be suspected, as a German model would hinder the omission and a Polish model may favor it. Quantitative data are hard to get in this case, as one cannot search a corpus for instances where a form is *not* used. I therefore went through my selection of parallel sentences and noted how clauses with *irr* or *irraid* in LL were rendered in AL. There was only one example where a copula was omitted, or rather, replaced by a demonstrative (see 52). Otherwise, where AL did not have a corresponding form of 'be', I found constructions with a lexical verb, as mentioned above, or a completely different way of expressing the content.

One of the functions of 'be' in Latvian is the expression of predicative possession, with the possessor in the dative. This construction distinguishes Latvian from Lithuanian, which possesses a verb 'have', *turėti*. In both spoken and written varieties of Latvian of earlier times, one sometimes finds the cognate verb *turēt* in the meaning 'have' (examples from dialects are given in the dictionary by Mühlenbach and Endzelin, ME). However, it never seems to become a regular expression of predicative possession. In both LL and AL there are some constructions where *turēt* may be translated as 'have', but the meaning is more specific and fits into the broad range of meanings that *turēt* has in historical varieties as well as in today's Standard Latvian: 'hold' (both in a physical sense and as cognitive verb), 'keep' (for example, in *keep bees*), 'have at one's disposal', and others. Some more idiomatic constructions may have come into the language as calques, but there is little evidence for a contact-induced lexicalization of a verb meaning 'have' in Old Written Low or High Latvian. The construction with 'be' and the dative is very robust and may block the grammaticalization of a 'have' verb with a nominative subject. Examples (48)–(51) show some of the uses of *turēt* in the texts which are a bit unusual from the point of view of the modern languages.

(48) High Latvian [AL 9]
    rods   *byusi*   **turedams**   *zoposu*   *mada*
    happy.NOM.SG.M   be.FUT.2SG   **hold.CVB.SG.M**   reserve.ACC.SG   honey.GEN.SG
    'you will be happy to **have at your disposal** a supply of honey'

(49) Low Latvian [LL 2-19]
    Tee   *wißßai*   *agraji*   *ßpeeti*   *newaid*
    DEM.NOM.PL.M   very   early.NOM.PL.M   swarm.NOM.PL   NEG.be.PRS.3
    labbi,   *jo*   *winni*   *mehds*   *knappu*
    good.NOM.PL.M   for   3.NOM.PL.M   use.PRS.3   poor.ACC.SG
    ßaimi   **turreht**
    family.ACC.SG   **hold.INF**

'The very early swarms are no good, for they usually **keep** a poor (= small) colony'

(50) Low Latvian [LL 2-13]
Ne **turri** *schelumu,*
NEG **hold.IMP.2SG** pity.ACC.SG
kad tew dauds irr ja=ißgreesch
if 2SG.DAT much be.PRS.3 DEB=PVB.cut
'Don't be sorry (literally: don't **have pity**) if you have to cut off a lot'

(51) High Latvian [AL 14]
Na **turgi** *żelestibas,*
NEG **hold.IMP.2SG.PTC** pity.GEN.SG
[*kocz tys trauks nu goła da gołam bytu płns ciita mada.*]
'Don't be sorry (literally: don't **have pity**), [even if the hive is full to the brim of hard honey]'

Copula clauses in AL occasionally contain a demonstrative pronoun or the particle *to*, which is reminiscent of copula constructions in Polish and Russian. However, I found only one clause where a demonstrative pronoun is used instead of a copula (52). In other instances, the demonstrative, taking up the subject, is placed before the copula (53), or the emphatic particle *to* follows the copula (54).

(52) High Latvian [AL 3]
Matieyte, **tiey** *waldinieyca un*
mother.DIM.NOM.SG **DEM.NOM.SG.F** governor(FEM).NOM.SG and
rendinieyca wysas draudzes biszu
ruler(FEM).NOM.SG all.GEN.SG.F community.GEN.SG bee.GEN.PL
'The queen **is** the governor and ruler of the whole bee community.'

(53) High Latvian [AL 3]
Dorba Bites **tos** *ir wysmozokas*
work.GEN.SG bee.NOM.PL **DEM.NOM.PL.F** be.PRS.3 smallest.NOM.PL.F
'The working bees **are** the smallest'

(54) High Latvian [AL 3]
Bites **ir** *to putnieni lut tieyri*
bee.NOM.PL **be.PRS.3** PTC bird.DIM.NOM.PL very clean.NOM.PL.M
'Bees **are** very clean little birds.'

Such copula constructions with a demonstrative or the particle *to* are also found in modern spoken and written varieties of Latgalian and I assume that their use in AL reflects the spoken language of the time. They are probably genuine Baltic but may have been supported by similarities with Slavic contact languages, as they are not used in the western varieties of Latvian.

4.5 Passive constructions

The Baltic languages have an inherited passive construction consisting of the past passive participle and the auxiliary 'be'. In modern Standard Latvian this construction is a stative passive, while in Lithuanian it may be stative or dynamic. In addition, Low Latvian and Lithuanian each developed a second construction for a dynamic passive. Here, Lithuanian uses the present passive participle and the auxiliary 'be', while the Latvian construction contains the past passive participle and an auxiliary with the basic meaning 'become'. For details on passive constructions in modern Latvian and Lithuanian see Nau et al. (2020).

It is most likely that the Latvian passive construction with an auxiliary 'become' arose (or was at least enforced) under the influence of German, where the construction with *werden* 'become' is the basic passive. An imitation of the German pattern is also found in Old Prussian, where a passive was first formed with the Prussian verb *postātwei* 'become' (Eckert et al. 1994: 402–403). In Latvian, different verbs with the basic meaning 'become' were used as passive auxiliaries in the course of time (see Veidemane 2002: 415–422). From the very beginning of Latvian writing, we find the verb *tapt*, which remains the main auxiliary for a dynamic passive until the second half of the 19th century and is still frequently used at the beginning of the 20th century. From the 17th to the 19th century, the verb *kļūt*, and from the late 18th century on the verb *tikt* were used as variants. The latter starts as a regional variant in writings from Vidzeme and later becomes the main passive auxiliary in Standard Latvian, ousting the other verbs during the 20th century.

(55) and (56) are examples for *tapt* and *kļūt* as passive auxiliaries in Old Low Latvian Writing of the first and second period, and (57) is an early attestation of the passive auxiliary *tikt*.

(55) Low Latvian [SENIE Unicode, EvEp1587]
vnde	**tope**	exkan	to	Helles	Vggunne
and	**AUX.PRS.3**	inside	DEM.ACC.SG	hell.GEN.SG	fire.ACC.SG

	e	*meeſtcz*			
	PVB	throw.PST.PP.SG.M			

'and **is thrown** into the fire of the hell'

(56) Low Latvian [SENIE Unicode, LGL1685]

Palaiſts		*kļuhſt*	*tas*	*Barrabas* /
release.PST.PP.SG.M		AUX.PRS.3	DEM.NOM.SG.M	Barrabas.NOM.SG
Kas	*bij*	*Dſelfis*	*eekalts*	
WH.NOM	be.PST.3	iron.LOC.PL	PVB.forge.PST.PP.SG.M	

'Barabbas **is released** / who had been enchained'

(57) Low Latvian [SENIE Unicode, CekFJ1790_KD]

Wifslabban,	*kad*	*tahs*	*tà*	*teek*	*ſtahditas:*
best	if	DEM.NOM.PL.F	so	AUX.PRS.3	plant.PST.PP.PL.F

literally: 'It is best if they (= the potatoes) **are planted** in the following way:'

A passive with *tapt* 'become' is also attested In Old High Latvian writing, but it is much rarer than in Low Latvian. This further supports the thesis of a German model for this construction in early Low Latvian writing. Its occurrence in High Latvian, in turn, is most probably due to the influence of Low Latvian religious texts, which were model texts for High Latvian in the 17th and 18th century. In *Evangelia toto anno* 1753, there are about a dozen instances of a construction with *tapt* and a past passive auxiliary. However, as noted by Nau and Holvoet (2015: 10), it is not so clear whether these are instances of a grammaticalized passive construction: some instances are formulaic, in others *tapt* has still its literal meaning 'become, get', highlighting a change of state, and the participle may be interpreted as a nominal predicate.[13] The same is observed in 19th century Old High Latvian writing, where the construction seems to be even rarer than in the *Evangelia*. An example is given in (58).

(58) High Latvian [Kurmin 1859: 8]

ku	*dareyt*	*kad*	***toptu***	*izpesteyts*
WH:ACC	do.INF	that	**become.IRR**	save.PST.PP.SG.M

'what [he had] to do in order to **be/get** saved'

---

13 Furthermore, there is ground to assume that the verb *tapt* 'become' as such has been borrowed from Low Latvian (Lidija Leikuma, personal communication). This would explain the form *top* instead of (expected for High Latvian) *tup* (modern spelling: *tūp*) for the third person present tense in Old Written High Latvian.

On the other hand, in High Latvian writing of the 19th century we find constructions with the verb *palikt* 'stay, remain; become', which probably are calqued from the Polish passive construction with the verb *zostać* with the same basic meanings; cf. (59). To the best of my knowledge, this verb does not appear as an auxiliary in Low Latvian writing.

(59) High Latvian [Kossowski 1852: 21]
 Misti, **paliks** **sajaukti** *un ar*
 town.NOM.PL **AUX.FUT.3** **raze.PST.PP.PL.M** and with
 ziemi **salejdzinoti.**
 earth.ACC **level.PST.PP.PL.M**
 'The towns **will be torn down** and **razed** to the ground.'

However, this construction seems not to be very frequent, as far as this can be judged from my cursory look at Old High Latvian texts. More detailed investigations, including the question how similar this construction is to the one with *zostać* in Polish, have to wait until suitable corpora will be available; for a history of the Polish construction, see Wiemer (2004: 298–304).

The frequency of the passive construction with an auxiliary 'become' in Old Low Latvian was investigated by Ruta Veidemane in a small corpus study (Veidemane 2002: 415–422). She took samples of 20,000 words from nine different Old Low Latvian texts published between 1654 and 1894 and counted the number of passive constructions with 'become', as well as the use of different auxiliaries (*tapt, kļūt, tikt*) in these constructions. Three of her sources represent the period studied here: the Bible of 1739, a legal text of 1818, and the first volume of the journal *Latviešu avīzes* from 1822. The number of passive constructions in these three samples of together 60,000 words is 413, thus 6.9 per thousand words. Veidemane shows that this number is considerably higher than in texts of the second half of the 19th century which were written by native speakers of Latvian. In her three samples from periodicals of that period (the *Pēterburgas Avīzes* from 1862, *Latviešu Avīzes* from 1872, and *Austrums* from 1894), she counted 126 passive constructions in 60,000 words, thus 2.1 per thousand (all figures based on those given by Veidemane 2002: 416). This shows that passive constructions with the then dominating auxiliary *tapt* were a typical feature of Old Low Latvian writing, while its (over)use was avoided by those later writers who were trying to get rid of German constructions and consciously developed a more genuine Latvian standard variety.

A critical evaluation of the construction starts in the middle of the 19th century. Stender (1761: 37) still describes the Latvian passive with 'become' in a neutral way, and Harder (1790) does not raise objections. Hesselberg (1841: 28, 34, 109) and Rosenberger (1852: 4), on the other hand, both start their sections on the passive by stating that these constructions are not characteristic of Latvian, and that Latvians usually use an active verb where Germans use the passive. Hesselberg explicitly characterizes the passive with a 'become' auxiliary as "very unusual" ("sehr ungebräuchlich", Hesselberg 1841: 28), "germanizing and imposed on Latvians" ("germanisirend und dem Letten aufgedrungen", 109), and "rather to be read in books than to be heard in speech" ("sind aber in Büchern mehr zu lesen als im Munde des Letten zu hören", 34). This last remark is very apt: passive constructions have always had a firm place in certain registers of written, published (non-fiction) texts, and while their use was reduced by the next generations of writers, they never abolished it completely (in contrast to, for example, the definite article).

In LL, a passive construction with *tapt* is found 67 times, which corresponds to 4.1 per thousand words. No other 'become' verb is used as auxiliary. The form of the auxiliary *tapt* is third person present (*tohp*) in 61 out of 67 occurrences, future (*tapß*) and conditional (*taptu*) are each attested once, and in four instances the auxiliary has the form of the past active participle and is part of a compound tense (*irr tappiß*, *ir tappußchaß*).

While the frequency of a passive with *tapt* in LL is lower than the average of the samples drawn by Veidemane (2002) from texts of the period (4.1 vs 6.9 per thousand), it is still more than twice as high than in Veidemane's sample of the later period (2.1 per thousand). Furthermore, its status as a characteristic feature of Written Old Low Latvian becomes apparent in comparison to the High Latvian book, where a passive with 'become' is found only seven times (0.6 per thousand). Table 8 summarizes the observations.

Table 8: Passive constructions with an auxiliary 'become'

	LL = 4.1 per 1000	AL = 0.6 per 1000
Auxiliary *tapt*	67	3
Auxiliary *palikt*	0	4

All occurrences of a 'become' passive in AL have a direct model in LL. Akielewicz uses both *tapt* and *palikt* to translate the auxiliary *tapt* of the model, see (60–61).

(60) Low Latvian [LL 2-15]

*Stippraß   bitteß   **ne tohp**   **aplaupihtaß**,*
strong.NOM.PL.F bee.NOM.PL   NEG AUX.PRS.3 PVB.**rob**.PST.PP.PL.F
jo   tahß   prettim   turrahß;   wahjaß
for DEM.NOM.PL.F against   hold.PRS.3.RFL weak.NOM.PL.F
*ween no   zittahm   **tohp**   **apmekletaß**.*
only   from other.DAT.PL.F AUX.PRS.3   **visit**.PST.PP.PL.F

'Strong bees **are not robbed**, for they defend themselves, only weak ones **are visited** by others.'

(61) = (20) High Latvian, translation of (60); [AL 15]

*Topec   bites   stypras   **na***
therefore   bee.NOM.PL strong.NOM.PL.F   NEG
***top   plestas**,   bet   tik   wojas*
become.PRS.3 **tear**.PST.PP.PL.F but only   weak.NOM.PL.F
*nu   styproku   **palik**   **kryudeytas***
from stronger.GEN.PL **become**.PRS.3   **kill**.PST.PP.PL.F

'For strong bees **are not slain**, only weak [bees] **are killed** by stronger ones.'

In other instances, Akielewicz translated a passive construction with *tapt* in LL by a passive construction with the auxiliary 'be' (62, 63) or with an active predicate (64, 65). Quite often sentences with a passive in LL do not have direct equivalents in AL: either the same content is rendered in a very different form, or the respective paragraph is missing in AL. For example, the sentence in (66) with a present perfect of a passive with *tapt* has no equivalent in AL.

(62) = (43) Low Latvian [LL 2-3]

No   teem   pauteem,   kaß   tâß
from   DEM.DAT.PL.F   egg.DAT.PL   WH:NOM   DEM.LOC.PL.F
*leelakâß   kanniņâß   **dehti**   **tohp**,*
bigger.LOC.PL.F cell.LOC.PL **lay**.PST.PP.PL.M   AUX.PRS.3
tranni   ißnahk
drone.NOM.PL PVB.come.PRS.3

'From the eggs that **are laid** into the bigger cells, drones come out.' (The order of passive auxiliary and passive participle follows the German model of subordinate clauses, see Section 4.3)

(63) High Latvian, translation of (62) [AL 7¹⁴]
Nu tu, kotry lełokom kambareytem
from DEM.GEN.PL REL.NOM.PL.M bigger.DAT.PL.F cell.DAT.PL
ir deti, Truni izit
be.PRS.3 lay.PST.PP.PL.M drone.NOM.PL PVB.go.PRS.3
'From those which **are laid** into the bigger cells, drones come out.'

(64) = (1g) Low Latvian [LL 2-3]
un no tahm bittehm **tohp ehdinahtß**
and from DEM.DAT.PL.F bee.DAT.PL **become.PRS.3 feed.PST.PP.SG.M**
'and **is fed** by the bees'

(65) = (2g) High Latvian [AL 7]
un bites tyuleń izsoka winius barot
and bee.NOM.PL at_once start.PRS.3 3.ACC.PL.M feed.INF
'and the bees start at once to feed them'

(66) Low Latvian [LL 2-06]
tad wiṇṇaß ne ka ne atraddußchaß, jeb no
then 3.NOM.PL.F NEG WH:GEN NEG find.PST.PA.PL.F or from
wehtra **irr** atpakkal **dsihtaß tappußchaß**
storm.GEN.SG **be.PRS.3** back **drive.PST.PP.PL.F AUX.PST.PA.PL.F**
'then they have found nothing, or **have been driven** back by the wind.'
(The order of elements in the verbal complex equals that of German *sind zurückgetrieben worden* 'have been driven back')

As can be seen in examples (60), (61), (64), and (66), a passive construction in both LL and AL may contain an agent expressed in a phrase with the preposition *no* 'of, from' (LL *no zittahm* 'by others', AL *nu styproku* 'by stronger ones'). There is also one example with the preposition *caur* 'through'. An agent phrase is another feature of Old Written Low Latvian that is most probably due to German influence. In spoken varieties of Latvian, and in modern Standard Latvian and modern Latgalian, passives do not contain an agent; cf. Nau et al. (2020: 34, 49). While the passive with 'become' as such has made it into the modern standard varieties, agent phrases were categorized as undesirable, and agent omission was identified as the prerequisite for using a passive (cf. Endzelin 1922: 763). In Lithuanian, agents may be expressed by a genitive phrase without preposition. Thus,

---

14 Another example for the dative plural instead of the locative, cf. footnote 10.

both the possibility of adding an agent in a predicative passive construction and the specific form it takes (with a preposition 'of, from') can be traced back to a German model. This construction was well established in Old Written Low Latvian; in LL, an agent phrase is found in 11% (6 of 67) of passive constructions with *tapt*. Interestingly, Akielewicz does not avoid agent phrases. There are even instances where only AL, but not LL, has an agent phrase, and they appear in both passive constructions: with 'become' and with 'be'. Extract (67) is one of two instances in LL with an impersonal passive with the auxiliary *tapt*. The same construction is used in the German model sentence (in Chapter 6 of Settegast 1798). In the High Latvian version in (68), the translator changed the auxiliary from 'become' to 'be' and added an agent phrase.

(67) Low Latvian [LL 1-9]
[*Bittehm jastahwßaußâ, ßkaidrâ, ruhmigâ un klußßâ meerigâ weetâ*],
kur	**ne**	**tohp**	dauds	**staigahtß**,	brauktß,
where	NEG	AUX.PRS.3	much	walk.PST.PP.NA	drive.PST.PP.NA

ahmerehtß,	bambahtß	jeb	klabbinahtß.
hammer.PST.PP.NA	knock.PST.PP.NA	or	rap.PST.PP.NA

'[Bees have to stand at a dry, clean, spacious and calm peaceful place,] where **people don't walk**, drive, hammer, knock or rap much.' (German original: [...] *wo **nicht** oft **gegangen**, gefahren, gehammert, gestoßen, geschlagen* [...] **wird**)

(68) High Latvian [AL 1]
[*Aysto Bitem wajag stowet sausa, skaydra, kłusa, un mireyga wita,*]
kur	nawa	staygots,	braukalets,
where	NEG.be.PRS.3	walk.PST.PP.NA	drive.ITER.PST.PP.NA

bambats,	un	kłabynots
knock.PST.PP.NA	and	rap.PST.PP.NA

tay	**nu**	**lauźu,**	**kay**	**nu**	**łuupu.**
as	from	people.GEN.PL	so	from	cattle.GEN.PL

'[Bees need to stand at a dry, clean, calm and peaceful place,] where neither people nor cattle walk, drive, knock and rattle about.' (literally "where it is not walked ... **either by people or by cattle**").

Impersonal passives with an overt agent are attested in Lithuanian, though they are very rare when the meaning is generic (Lindström et al. 2020: 147). Maybe knowledge of Lithuanian made this construction acceptable to Akielewicz.

The impersonal passive construction with 'become' in (67) may have been inspired by a German model. However, impersonal (subjectless) passives with the auxiliary 'be' are quite common in the Baltic languages, and Latvian and Lithuanian both have developed further, language-specific impersonal passive constructions (see Nau et al. 2020: 87–113; Lindström et al. 2020). German influence may have supported the formation of a subjectless passive with an auxiliary 'become' in Latvian, but the existence of subjectless passives with generic reference is probably genuine Baltic. From the point of view of today's Latvian, if we only exchange the auxiliary *tapt* by *tikt*, the sentence in (67) sounds more natural than those with a personal passive in (60), (62), (64), and (66), where a modern writer would rather use the active voice.

In LL, but not in AL, there are two more, mutually related, functions where a passive with 'become' is used. They appear only in certain passages which show a very high concentration of passive constructions. Interestingly, in these passages LL makes much more use of the passive than the German model text. The first function is to show "how other people do it" and appears in Chapters 2-28 and 2-29. In LL 2-28, a passage of 74 words contains 8 passive predicates with 6 occurrences of the auxiliary *tohp* 'become(s)' (two times the auxiliary has scope over two participles). The corresponding German text passage has only 2 passives in 87 words. In the other clauses that correspond to clauses with the passive in LL, German uses the active with the indefinite (general personal) pronoun *man* 'one'. In Chapter 2-29, where Launitz talks about different ways of getting honey out of the combs, two passages contain a similar concentration of passive predicates, without a corresponding German model. Both passages are introduced with a clause saying 'they do it this way:'. Thus, Launitz uses the dynamic passive for general descriptions of human behavior and activities. This use is not characteristic for modern Standard Latvian, where an active form without subject is preferred in this function (cf. Nau et al. 2020: 67; Nau 2021). The same can be said for the other function, that of describing a procedure in order to instruct ("how to do it"). In this function the passive is used only in one passage in Chapter 1-05. Again, the corresponding passage in German uses some passives and (more often) the impersonal with *man*. That this passage is an instruction rather than a description of an activity becomes evident when Launitz switches from the passive to the imperative. While each sentence of the German model has a content-wise equivalent sentence in the Low Latvian translation, the translator almost always used different constructions. The passages in Latvian and German are shown in (69) and (70). For reasons of space, I refrain from interlinear glossing, but imitate the constructions in the free translation.

(69) German   [Settegast 1798: 20–21]

[1] *Die Untersäzze* **dienen** *dazu, denen Bienen zum Zuarbeiten mehr Raum zu verschaffen.* [2] **Man hat** *Untersäzze von Holz, auch von Stroh.* [3] *Die von Stroh können 6 bis 8 Fuß hoch seyn und* **werden** *so rund und weit* **geflochten***, als der Korb unten ist, der darauf stehen soll.* [4] *Die hölzernen* **schägt man** *aus 4 Brettern zusammen und* **nagelt** *über die eine offene Seite dieses Kastens andere etwas überstehende Bretter zum Anfaßen.* [5] *Nachdem in sie ein rundes Loch* **ausgesäget ist, stellet man** *den Korb darüber.* [6] *In beiderlei Untersäzze* **wird** *vorher 3 Zoll von unten ein Loch zum Ausflug* **gemacht** *und ein Flugbrett dadurch* **hineingesteckt***, das mit seinem Ende oben am Rande des Korbes oder Kastens* **festgemacht ist.**

'[1] 'The socles **serve** to procure the bees with more space for their work. [2] There are (literally: **one has**) socles of wood and of straw. [3] The ones [made] of straw may be 6 to 8 feet high, and they **are woven** as round and broad as the bottom of the skep on which they are to stand. [4] **One hews** the wooden ones of 4 boards and **nails** other, slightly protruding boards onto one of the open sides of this box as handles. [5] After a round hole **has been sawn** into it, **one puts** the skep on top. [6] Before that, in both types of socles, a hole of 3 inches **is made** and a flying board **is** inserted through it, which **is fixed** with its end on the upper side of the skep or box.'

(70) Low Latvian, translation of (69)   [LL 1-05]

[1] *Tee pakurwji jeb tahß palahdeß* **tohp** *appakßch teem kurwjeem* **likti***, kad tahm bittehm ruhmeß peetruhkst.* [2] *Tee pakurwji (gredseni)* **tohp** *no ßalmeem* **pihti***, tahß palahdeß no kohka* **taißitaß***.* [3] *Tee pakurwji jeb gredseni warr 2 lihds 3 pehdaß augsti buht, un tik pat platti un appaḷi* **tohp pihti** *kà tee kurwji irr, jo teem uß wiṇṇeem jastahw wirßu.* [4] *Tahß palahdeß* **tohp** *kà zittaß lahditeß no tßschetrahm ihßahm dehlehm ar dibbeni* **ßanaglotaß***.* [5] *Taî dibbenî* **eegreesi** *appaḷu zaurumu, kur taß kurwiß warr wirßû stahweht.* [6] *Eekßch abbeem (tik labbi eekßch pakurwjeem, kà eekßch palahdehm)* **eegreesi** *ißeijamu zaurumu, eebahsi taî tahdu ßchkippelihti, kà taß zettortâ nodaḷḷâ mahzihtß irr, un* **peetaißi** *to itt zeeti.*

'[1] The mats or pedestals **are put** under the skeps when the bees lack space. [2] The mats (rings) **are woven** of straw, and the pedestals **made** of wood. [3] The mats or rings may have a height of 2 or 3 feet, and they **are woven** as broad and round as the skeps are, for they have to stand on them. [4] The pedestals **are nailed together** like other boxes of four short boards and a bottom. [5] **Cut** a round hole into the bottom above which the skep can stand. [6] **Cut** into both (into mats as well as pedestals) an exit hole, **put** into it such a small board in form of a spade as has been explained in Chapter 4, and **fasten** it tightly.'

This example shows that the passive construction with 'become' belongs to the Low Latvian repertoire of the translator and he uses it independently of the model. However, he uses it in the same functions as the corresponding construction is used in German. At the same time, he seems to lack the generic impersonal construction with the active voice, which is more characteristic for modern Latvian in this function, and which would be the best choice to translate German *man*. In extract (70), the translation is monotonous in its repetition of the passive construction, while the original is much more varied.

4.6 Expressions of necessity

The main communicative goal of the investigated texts is to instruct, to tell the reader what to do to be successful in beekeeping, and how to do it. Instructions are given in various forms: direct instructions using the imperative ('feed your bees with honey'), general statements of necessity ('bees have to be fed with honey'), recommendations ('it is advisable to feed bees with honey'), or, as we saw in Section 4.5 on the passive, by describing successful behavior in generic statements ('bees are fed with honey'). In those parts of the texts which are mostly procedural, the main means of giving instructions is the imperative mood. In addition, we find in these parts (as well as in some of the more descriptive passages) various constructions expressing necessity, which are the subject of this section.

Latvian and Lithuanian have each developed their own inventories of modal expressions, and the specific means of expressing necessity differ in the two languages (cf. Holvoet 2007: 33–56). In Old Written Low Latvian, four main constructions are used, which all are found in LL:

(i) the infinitive in combination with the third person future tense form of the verb 'be' (*būs darīt* 'must do');
(ii) the debitive, a form consisting of the prefix *jā-* and the third person present tense form of the verb, with the possible addition of a finite auxiliary 'be' ((AUX) *jādara*);
(iii) the impersonal verb *vajadzēt*, combined with an infinitive (present tense: *vajag darīt*);
(iv) the present passive participle with a finite form of the verb 'be' ((AUX) *darāms*).

All constructions have in common that the actor (the person obliged to do something), if it is expressed, takes the form of a dative argument. This pattern is thus very strong in Latvian, where we do not find verbs or constructions meaning 'must', 'need', or 'should' with a nominative subject.

The first two constructions are described under various names in the older grammars (cf. Veidemane 2002: 444–448). Stender (1761: 56–57) calls both (i) and (ii) *Modus necessitatis*. Harder (1790: 32) describes the notional differences between the two: the debitive as in (ii) denotes an internal necessity and may be used in recommendations, while the construction with *būs* in (i) belongs to commands given by an authority ("ist mehrentheils die entscheidende und gebietende Sprache, wo alles Widersprechen aufhört",[15] Harder (1790: 32)). Rosenberger (1852: 9–10) seems to be the first to list all four constructions, and he describes their different functions by a constructed example. According to him, using the construction (iv), the speaker expresses merely an opinion, with (iii) they state a necessity without a call for action, while (ii) includes the necessity of action and (i) expresses a command. A similar distinction is made by Endzelin (1922: 759), who describes construction (i) as a categorical command, (ii) as an expression of objective necessity, and (iii) of internal necessity, characterizing its meaning as "notwendig, sofern nützlich" ("necessary if beneficial"). He also states that (iv) is the weakest expression of necessity, though in folksongs it is used alongside the debitive without difference in meaning (Endzelin 1922: 759).

The construction with *būs* and the infinitive is the oldest one, having developed from constructions with 'be' and an infinitive with more general modal meanings found in Baltic and Slavic languages (Holvoet 2007: 195–216). It is attested in the very first Latvian books both in the positive ('you must', 'you have to') and with negation ('you must not' = 'are not allowed'), cf. (71) and (72). The meaning of this construction is mostly that of deontic necessity.

(71) Low Latvian   [SENIE unicode, Ench1586]
      Ta   **buhs**   *thöw*   *vs*   *tho*   *Baſnicekunge*   **ſatczyt.**
      then   **be.FUT.3**   2SG.DAT   to   DEM.ACC.SG   priest.ACC.SG   **say.INF**
      'Then you **shall say** to the priest.'

(72) Low Latvian   [SENIE Unicode, Ench1586]
      Thöw   **nhe**   **buhs**   *no*   *tho*   **ehſt**
      2SG.DAT   NEG   **be.FUT.3**   from   DEM.ACC.SG   **eat.INF**
      'You **shall not eat** from it.'

---

15 '[it] is mostly [a feature of] a ruling and commanding speech, where all objection ends'

The construction remains frequent in Old Written Low Latvian and is still used in Standard Latvian in the 20th century, but its frequency starts to decline in the 19th century, and in modern Latvian it is stylistically highly marked, evoking associations to the language of the Bible and especially the Ten Commandments. In Old High Latvian the construction is less frequent than in Old Low Latvian, and it is possible that it follows a Low Latvian model rather than being a construction in active use in spoken High Latvian of the time (but see Nau 2012: 283 for examples from orally transmitted fairytales). In the *Evangelia toto anno* 1753, *būs* + infinitive is used only in the Ten Commandments and the rules of the Catholic Church (on pages 104–105 of the book), but not in the text of the gospels, nor in other texts of the appendix.

The debitive is attested in Low Latvian writing as an expression of necessity from the early 17th century on (Vanags 2000; Veidemane 2002: 445). It has become the main grammatical means of expressing necessity in modern Standard Latvian. For the language of his time, Harder (1790: 32) remarks that the debitive is hardly ever used with negation, but this is not true for contemporary Standard Latvian, where a negated debitive is regularly used to indicate that something does not have to be done. In Old High Latvian writing, the debitive is not frequent and not used by all authors. However, some authors, including Akielewicz, do use it freely, and it is not clear whether it has arisen due to influence from Low Latvian (as stated for modern Latgalian by Cibuļs and Leikuma 2003: 83).

The most usual means of expressing necessity in High Latvian, both in historical variants and today's Latgalian, is by the impersonal verb *vajadzēt* (PRS.3 *vajag*) 'need, must'. This verb goes back to a particle borrowed from a Baltic Finnic language that became a verb in Latvian; cf. Nau (2012: 480–481). In Low Latvian texts of the 17th and 18th century, *vajag* is sometimes still used as an uninflected wordform that can combine with a finite form of 'be' (Vanags 2015: 66–67), while in High Latvian texts it seems always to be a verb. Another difference between the varieties is that in Low Latvian, *vajadzēt* often combines with a noun phrase ('need something'), while in High Latvian it combines with an infinitive in the majority of uses ('need to/must do something'). This tendency is also obvious in the investigated texts (see below). The conditional form *vajadzētu* is used to express recommendations ('should do').

The use of the present passive participle as expression of necessity is again more often found in Low Latvian than in High Latvian (for modal meanings of this participle in Lithuanian and Standard Latvian see Nau et al. 2020: 63–74). In LL, it is moderately frequent, but only with transitive verbs and without overt expression of an actor. It corresponds to the German construction with *zu* and infinitive (German *etwas ist zu tun* = Latvian *kaut kas ir darāms* 'something is/has to be done'). Although the forms are different, it is possible that the equivalence of the Latvian construction with the German one supports its use in Old Written Low Latvian.

Table 9 gives an overview of the frequency with which the four constructions are found in the investigated texts. It shows that the constructions with *būs* and, to a lesser degree, with the present passive participle, are clearly more frequent in LL than in AL, while AL makes much more use of the construction with *vajadzēt*. The frequency of the debitive is similar in both texts. Two further forms used only in AL are added. Constructions containing negation are counted separately in Table 10.

Table 9: Constructions expressing necessity in LL and AL

	LL tokens	LL per 1000	AL per 1000	AL tokens
būs + INF	42	2.6	0.2	2
DEBITIVE	45	2.8	2.1	26
vajadzēt + INF	14	0.9	4.8	60
PRS.PP	18	1.1	0.2	3
lai būs + PST.PP			0.6	8
piederēt			0.2	2

Table 10: Negated necessity in LL and AL

	LL	AL
nebūs + INF 'must not', 'shall not'	9	1 (quote from the Bible)
nevajadzēt + INF 'does not have to'; 'should not'	2	2
DEBITIVE negated 'does not have to'; 'must not'	3	0

In the investigated texts, the differentiation of meaning of the three main techniques (*būs* + infinitive, the debitive, and *vajadzēt* + infinitive) described in the above quoted grammars is not observed. All are used to express the kind of necessity that is most typical for the text: something has to be done in order to achieve a certain goal (the overall goal being success in beekeeping). In LL, also the fourth technique, the present passive participle, is used in this function, and in AL there is one curious instance of a combination of a present passive participle with the debitive prefix (78). The following examples (73)–(78) illustrate the constructions. I found no cue in the context for a regular difference in meaning.

(73) Low Latvian [LL 2-04]
Tam **buhß** *ßawaß* *bitteß* *pee*
DEM.DAT.SG.M **be.FUT.3** RPOSS.ACC.PL.F bee.ACC.PL at
laika **ehdinaht**
time.GEN.SG **feed.INF**
'He (= a good beekeeper) **must feed** his bees in time.'

(74) Low Latvian [LL 2-05]
Bitteß *daudsreis* **irr** **jaehdina.**
bee.NOM.PL often **be.PRS.3** **DEB.feed**
'Bees often **have to be fed**.' ('There are many occasions when one must feed the bees.')

(75) Low Latvian [LL 2-27]
ßliktâ *laikâ* *tahdi* *ßpeeti*
bad.LOC.SG weather.LOC.SG such.NOM.PL.M swarm.NOM.PL
irr **ehdinajami.**
be.PRS.3 **feed.PRS.PP.NOM.PL.M**
'In bad weather such swarms **must be fed**.'

(76) High Latvian [AL 09]
Jaunus *Spitus* *to* *że* **barot** *wajag;*
new.ACC.PL.M swarm.ACC.PL PTC PTC **feed.INF** need.PRS.3
'New swarms **have to be fed** as well.'

(77) High Latvian [AL 29]
Łopu *menesi* *wel* *bites* **jobaroy**
leaf.GEN.PL month.LOC.SG still be.ACC.PL **DEB.feed**
'In May you still **have to feed** the bees.'

(78) High Latvian (translation of 74) [AL 09]
Bites *daudzreyz* **jobarojamas** *ir*
bee.NOM.PL often **DEB.feed.PRS.PP.NOM.PL.F** be.PRS.3
'Bees often **have to be fed**.'

Furthermore, the expressions of necessity often alternate with an imperative, both within one language version and in translation equivalents. In (79), Akielewicz uses the debitive to translate clauses with the imperative (80).

(79) High Latvian, translation of (80) [AL 13]
[*Nu taydagi trauka, koleyt wel ir styproks, pyrma Jakaba dinas,*]
wysus	*korus*	***jogryź***	*ora*	*un*
all.ACC.PL.M	comb.ACC.PL	**DEB.cut**	out	and

nugyutu	*moti*	***jakaun***	*ziemie.*
catch.PST.PP.ACC.SG	mother.ACC.SG	**DEB.kill**	down

'[From such a hive, as long as it is still strong, before Saint Jacob,] you **must cut** out all combs and **must kill** the queen'

(80) Low Latvian [LL 2-11]
Tahdam	*kurwjam*	***ißgreesi***	*preekßch*	*Jehkabu,*
such.DAT.SG.M	skep.DAT.SG	**PVB.cut.IMP.2SG**	before	Jacob.GEN.PL

kamehr	*winßch*	*wehl*	*stiprß*	*irr,*	*wißßuß*
while	3.NOM.SG.M	still	strong.NOM.SG.M	be.PRS.3	all.ACC.PL.M

kahruß,	***noķeŗŗ***	*to*	*mahti*	*un*
comb.ACC.PL	**catch.IMP.2SG**	DEM.ACC.SG	mother.ACC.SG	and

kauj	*wiņņu*	*semmê.*
kill.IMP.2SG	3.ACC.SG	down

'Of such a hive, **cut out** all combs before Saint Jacob, while it is still strong, **catch** the queen and **kill** it.'

While the construction with *būs* + infinitive is rare in AL, Akielewicz uses another construction with this auxiliary in the meaning of a recommendation ('you should'): *būs* + past passive participle in combination with the modal particle *lai*; cf. (81).

(81) High Latvian [AL 2]
wina	*mola*	*nu*	*pryksza*
one.LOC.SG	edge.LOC.SG	from	front.GEN.SG

łay	***byus***	*łudzinsz*	***izgrysts***
PTC	**be.FUT.3**	window.DIM.NOM.SG	**PVB.cut.PST.PP.SG.M**

'At one edge at the front a small window (literally:) **should be cut out**' = 'you should cut out a small window'

The origin of this construction is unknown to me. It seems like a mixture of the Low Latvian necessity construction with *būs* + infinitive and the Low Latvian passive in its instructive function as described in Section 4.5. Various constructions with the particle *lai* in diverse varieties of Latvian may express a wish, a command, and other nuances of deontic modality (see Holvoet 2001: 63–81). In Low Latvian (or at least in modern Standard Latvian), however, the particle does not combine with the future tense of verbs.

The High Latvian construction with the verb *pīderēt*, whose base meaning is 'belong', is most likely a calque from Polish, where the verb *należeć* has the meanings 'belong', 'be suitable (behavior)', and 'to be done; must'. In Polish as well as in Latvian, this verb is constructed with a dative, and in AL the construction is used in the same meaning as the debitive (or *vajadzēt*), as can be seen in example (82).

(82) High Latvian [AL 05]

Łobam	**Bitinikam**	nu	pawasara	kay	tig
good.DAT.SG.M	beekeeper.DAT.SG	from	spring.GEN.SG	as	only
snigs	izsoka	kust,	apleyk	Awilim	
snow.NOM.SG	start.PRS.3	melt.INF	around	hive.DAT.PL	
snigu	**pidar**	**nurakt**,		un	
snow.ACC.SG	belong.PRS.3	PVB.shovel.INF		and	
wydus	trauku	tieyri	**jo**	**isłauciey**.	
inside.ACC.PL	hive.GEN.PL	clean.ADV	DEB	PVB.sweep	

'In early spring, as soon as the snow begins to melt, a good beekeeper **must shovel** away the snow around the hives and **must sweep** clean the insides of the hives.'

Several general observations and conclusions can be drawn from this study of necessity in the two old written languages. First, we observe a relatively large set of expression means which, at least in these texts, can be used interchangeably: they have the same meaning (external and internal necessity) and the same communicative functions (instruct, recommend). Second, all these expression means have in common that the actor, or "debitor", is expressed by a dative argument, or omitted. Taken together, these two observations show that new expression means for non-epistemic necessity arise again and again according to the same grammatical pattern – what Nau (2012) called a system-defining principle. The borrowed construction with 'belong' in High Latvian also fits this pattern.

The principle "Express the debitor in the dative" is very strong in Latvian (as well as Finnish, but less so in Lithuanian, Estonian, and Slavic languages; see

Nau 2012: 494–495). In the history of Old Written Low Latvian as well as in written and spoken varieties of High Latvian, there are a few examples of constructions that go against this principle, that is, where the debitor is expressed as a nominative subject. In Old Written Low Latvian, this is occasionally attested with the construction with *būs* + infinitive (Vanags 1993: 179; Jēgers 1975: 48, 50; Vanags 2015: 54). However, the dative is clearly the norm in all periods of Old Written Low Latvian.

In High Latvian varieties, the verb *turēt* 'hold; have at one's disposition' (cf. Section 4.4), which governs a nominative subject, is sometimes found in the meaning 'must'. This use has been noted and attributed to Polish influence in the earliest grammatical descriptions (see Strods 1937: 119–120). However, in this instance a Lithuanian influence seems more likely than a Polish influence, as the cognate Lithuanian verb *turėti* means both 'have' and 'have to, must'. Or the fact that the construction is used in both Lithuanian and Polish may have furthered its use in High Latvian. In modern varieties of Latgalian, the construction is sometimes, presumably consciously, used by writers who by their choice of forms and constructions emphasize parallels between Latgalian and Lithuanian and differences between Latgalian and Standard Latvian.[16] Otherwise it is uncommon. It is safe to conclude that in both Low Latvian and High Latvian there is a certain resistance against necessive constructions with a nominative subject. This corresponds to the stability of the dative construction for predicative possession (cf. Section 4.4).

Another interesting observation is the stability of the construction with *būs* + infinitive in Old Written Low Latvian. For the 19th century, we may assume that the debitive and the construction with *vajadzēt* were already more frequent in spoken varieties of Low Latvian, but in written varieties the dominance of the construction with *būs* seems to have slowed their spread. Authors such as Launitz continued the tradition of Old Written Low Latvian as codified with the second Bible edition and preferred to use familiar patterns. This tendency could also be seen in other phenomena discussed above, such as the passive construction, the use of definite articles, or some word order patterns.

---

[16] For example, *turēt* for 'must' is found in the Latgalian translation of the "Constitution of the Republic of Užupis" as part of the Lithuanian art project *Republic of Užupis* (see http://uzhupisembassy.eu/uzhupis-constitution/).

4.7 Clause linkage

Clauses as syntactic units can be identified in both spoken and written varieties of a language. The concept of *sentence*, on the other hand, is clearly connected to the written mode of language production (cf. Miller and Weinert 1998, Chapter 2; Givón 2001: 355). Rules for the formation of sentences evolve as part of the development of written registers. This involves rules for the graphic separation of sentences and their parts by punctuation marks as well as lexical and grammatical techniques for marking the relation between clauses. The latter may be based on techniques that already exist in oral uses of the language, but often new means are developed. In the history of many languages, we see how such techniques arise after the model of other languages which already have more elaborate written registers. In medieval Europe, Latin was such a model for many vernacular languages. In later times, various examples can be found in colonial settings (e.g. Bakker and Hekking 2012).

A full analysis of sentence formation in the investigated texts and how it reflects the impact of other languages is beyond the scope of the present study. I will therefore restrict myself to connectives as lexical means in clause combining and a few observations about word order and the use of participles and converbs.

Influence of a model language on clause combining may be manifest in various ways. In the history of Latvian, the following phenomena are attested:
– Material borrowing of connectives,
– structural borrowing (loan translation) of complex connectives,
– semantic borrowing, change of the functional range of a connective,
– change of the syntactic range of a word, for example when an adverb or preposition is used to combine finite clauses,
– imitation of word order patterns to mark subordination,
– use of finite clauses instead of participles and converbs.

Material borrowing is detected most easily as the result of language contact (see Stolz and Levkovych 2022 for a recent survey of borrowed connectives), while for the other phenomena listed, the model of another language may have played a major or minor role in combination with other factors.

An early material borrowing from German in Low Latvian is *un* 'and'. It is attested in the earliest written documents and probably was used in the spoken language already before the beginning of writing. In 16th and 17th century Old Written Low Latvian documents, this word appears in the forms *und, unde, unnde*, and *un*; the shortest variant soon becomes the most frequent and then the norm in later centuries (Blinkena 2007: 126–131). Besides *un*, there is also *in* for 'and', which is either borrowed from a Low German variant or arose as a mixture of borrowed *un* and inherited *ir* (compare Lithuanian *ir*; on *in* see Blinkena 2007: 118–122). The word *ir* is still found as a conjunction in 17th century Low Latvian texts (Blinkena 2007: 123), but more often, and for a longer time, *ir* is used in Latvian as an additive particle with the meanings 'also', 'even'. As the word is homophonous with the third person present form of 'be', an orthographic norm was established, distinguishing *irr* 'be.PRS.3' and *ir* 'also; even'. This norm is observed by Launitz.

It is likely that before Latvian borrowed the coordinator 'and' from German, (i) *ir* was used as both coordinator and additive particle, (ii) there were also other ways of marking coordination (for example by constructions with 'with' or by simple juxtaposition), and (iii) clause combining with 'and' was less frequent than it is in both historical and modern written texts. Thus, borrowed *un* did not simply replace an inherited coordinator, but the material borrowing was part of a set of lexical and syntactic changes which are difficult to reconstruct because of the scarcity and quality of data from the 16th and 17th century.

Low Latvian *un* has also a firm place in Old Written High Latvian, while in High Latvian dialects the form *i* (a shortened form of *ir*, cf. Blinkena 2007: 124–125) is more common. In the *Evangelia toto anno* 1753, the following forms for 'and' are attested: *und, un, in*, all of them also used as the additive 'also'. In Akielewicz (1832) we find *un* in both functions; examples for *un* as additive particle can be seen in (4) and in (27). Thus, in High Latvian, the use of the same element as both coordinating conjunction and additive (focus) particle is preserved, while in Low Latvian the two functions are differentiated – probably because they are expressed by different words in German (*und* 'and' vs *auch* 'also'). Akielewicz (1832) has also four instances of *i* as a particle (not as conjunction).

Another material borrowing in Low and High Latvian is disjunctive *vai* 'or' (LL *woi*, AL *way*). This word is of Fennic origin and has entered Latvian in prehistoric times; it is also used as question particle (see Stolz 1991: 65–68; Porīte 2007: 338). Launitz additionally uses the inherited *jeb* for 'or'. This word most often combines nouns or phrases and then often (but not always) has the function of metalinguistic disjunction ('in other words'), for example *zirmiņßch jeb kahpurß* 'larva or maggot' in example (1b). This is the function of *jeb* in Standard Latvian. However, Launitz uses *jeb* also as a synonym to *woi* in proper disjunction, for example, *ßlima jeb wezza* (LL 2-10) 'ill or old', and a few times for the disjunction of clauses. On the competition between *vai* and *jeb* in the history of Latvian see Blinkena (2007: 153–166); on the origin of *jeb* Ostrowski (2010). In Akielewicz's text, *jeb* is not used, but there are three instances of *aba* for 'or'. This word is attested in various functions in 17th and 18th century Old Written Low Latvian, and its origin is not clear (Blinkena 2007: 150). For Old Written High Latvian, its resemblance to Polish *albo* 'or' as well as to Lithuanian *arba* 'or' may, however, have played a role, independently of etymological relationships.

As adversative conjunction, both Low and High Latvian use the inherited *bet* 'but'. In spoken Latgalian, *a* is used instead of or in addition to *bet* (depending on the dialect). It is not clear whether *a* is borrowed from a Slavic language (Polish, Russian, and Belarusian *a* 'and; but') or inherited. In varieties where both *bet* and *a* are used, *a* is a marker of discontinuity, similar to *a* in the neighboring Slavic languages and Lithuanian *o* (cf. Mauri 2007: 194–195). In AL, there are thirteen attestations of *a*, and its use may reflect an influence from Polish as well as from spoken Latgalian, and maybe also from Lithuanian *o*.

Table 11 presents an overview of the discussed coordinators. The last column shows the main coordinator with the respective meaning in Lithuanian. The comparison with Lithuanian shows the separate development of coordinating connectives in the two main branches of East Baltic. This is in principle also the case when we consider (potentially) subordinating connectives, but here, High Latvian shares a bit more with Lithuanian than with Low Latvian, especially in the old written languages. Table 12 shows the main simple connectives used in the investigated texts for expressing adverbial relations and the complementizer 'that', and Table 13 lists connectives that consist of more than one word.

Table 11: Main coordinators in the investigated texts with absolute number of occurrences

	LL	AL	Lithuanian
Conjunction ('and')	*un* (695)	*un* (563)	*ir*
Disjunction ('or')	*woi* (108) [*] *jeb* (115)	*way* (191) [*] *aba* (3)	*arba*
Adversative ('bet')	*bet* (161)	*bet* (98) *a* (13)	*bet* *o*

[*] The numbers for *woi, way* include all uses of this word, as coordinator and as question particle.

Table 12: Complementizer and simple adverbial connectives

English	LL	AL	Lithuanian
'that' (complementizer)	*ka*	*kad*	*kad*
'so that' (final)	*lai*	*kad*	*kad*

English	LL	AL	Lithuanian
'when'	kad	kad kay	kada kai
'if'	kad ja (43)	(kad) jo [jɔ] (125)	(kad) jej, jeigu
'because; for'	jo [juɔ] (43)	aysto (46) bo (2)	nes (bo in Old Lithuanian)
'although; even if'	kaut (4)	kocz (16)	nors (koc in Old Lithuanian)
'while, as long as, until'	kamehr (24)	koleyt (11), kolsz (4)	kol, kolei
'before'	pirmß (2)	-	-

Table 13: Compound adverbial connectives

Meaning	LL	AL	Lithuanian
'because'	tapehz ka (1)	del to kad (1)	dėl tuo, kad
'as soon as'	tà kà (4)	kay tik (10)	kai tik
'even if'	lai arri (3)	kocz un (4), kocz i (1)	kad ir
'after'	pehz kad (1) pehz to kad/ka (2)	peć kay (1)	po to, kai
'before'	pirmß ka (6)	-	-

An influence of German on LL may be seen in the use of *kad* 'when' in conditional clauses, as in German, *wenn* means both 'when' and 'if'. While this polyfunctionality is also found in AL, it is much rarer there: much more often, the monofunctional connective *jo* [jɔ] 'if' is used in conditional clauses, while the cognate Low Latvian *ja* 'if' is used less often in LL. Furthermore, the word *kad* in AL has more functions than *kad* in LL: it is also the complementizer 'that' (LL *ka*) and used in final clauses ('so that', LL *lai*). Compared with Lithuanian, it combines the functions of Lithuanian *kad* and *kada*. This multifunctional use of *kad* is also found in the *Evangelia toto anno* 1753, where, however, also *ka* for 'that' is attested. Historically, *ka* is derived from *kad* by elision of the final stop. In modern varieties of Latgalian, *ka* is used for 'that' and 'if', less often also for 'when' and 'because', while *kad* or *kod* is only used in the temporal meaning (Nau 2018) – in other words, Latgalian *ka* corresponds to Lithuanian *kad*, while Latgalian *kad* corresponds to Lithuanian *kada*. In Old Written High Latvian, the model of Low Latvian may have been responsible for conserving the final stop in *kad* where it was dropped in the spoken language.

The main (simple) markers of a causal relation differ in all three East Baltic languages without evidence for language contact. In addition, in AL we find another instance of a borrowed connective: *bo* 'because, for'. The donor language may be Polish or Belarusian, and the word may be borrowed either directly or via Old Lithuanian, for in all three languages we find a word *bo* with this meaning. A similar case is High Latvian *kocz* 'although', which has a parallel in Old Written Lithuanian *koc*, borrowed from Polish *choć* 'although' (Lithuanian data from LKŽ). These two connectives reflect the influences in the development of written languages in the area of the Grand Duchy of Lithuania, where Slavic languages and Lithuanian were in close contact. A closer link between High Latvian and Lithuanian as opposed to Low Latvian can further be seen in the form of connectives meaning 'while, as long as, until'.

Two more parallels between High Latvian and Lithuanian are worth noting. First, there is no connective with the meaning 'before' for combining finite clauses. To express a relation of posteriority between states of affairs, the connective with the meaning 'until, as soon as' (AL *koleyt, kolsz*) may be used with negation ('as long as not yet p' = 'before p'; cf. Nau 2018: 82 for spoken Latgalian), or a more complex construction is used: 'not yet p when already q' (= 'q before p'), cf. (83) and (84). Low Latvian has additionally developed a clause connective 'before' out of a preposition with this meaning. In LL, this connective appears in the simple form *pirmß* 'before' (the same as the preposition) as well as in combination with *ka* 'that' or *kà* 'as', cf. (85).

(83) Low Latvian [LL 2-21]
Taß *pirmaiß* *ßpeetß* **wehl** *tik*
DEM.NOM.SG.M first.NOM.SG.M.DEF swarm.NOM.SG **still** PTC
***ne**waid* *nometteeß,* *ka* *jau* *ohtrß,*
NEG.be.PRS.3 settle.PST.PA.SG.M.RFL **when** **already** second.NOM.SG.M
treßch, *zettortaiß* *arri* *ißeet*
third.NOM.SG.M fourth.NOM.SG.M.DEF also exit.PRS.3
'The first swarm **has not yet** settled down **when already** the second, third, fourth [swarm] also comes out' = 'the second swarm comes out before the first has settled'

(84) High Latvian [AL 19]
wel	*pyrmays*	*Spits*	**na**baydzie	sadynotys,
still	first.NOM.SG.M.DEF	swarm.NOM.SG	**NEG**.finish.PST.3	settle.INF.RFL
jau	utrys,	tresz,	un	caturts
already	second.NOM.SG.M	third.NOM.SG.M	and	fourth.NOM.SG.M
otkon	izjt			
again	exit.PRS.3			

'The first swarm **still** did **not** finish settling, **already** the second, third and fourth [swarm] comes out'

(85) Low Latvian, no equivalent in AL [LL 2-18]
kad	tee	behrni	peemettahß	**pirmß kà**
if	DEM.NOM.PL.M	child.NOM.PL	sit_down.PRS.3.RFL	**before as**
ta	mahte	atgahjußi		
DEM.NOM.SG.F	mother.NOM.SG	arrive.PST.PA.SG.F		

'if the swarm already settles **before** the queen has arrived'

The connective *pirmß (kā)* 'before' is attested throughout the history of Old Written Latvian (Blinkena 2007: 233–236). I find it likely that the grammaticalization of an adverbial subordinator 'before' reflects a German model. More characteristic for Latvian is the combination with an action noun. This is found two times in LL (with the preposition *preekßch* 'for, before') and one time in AL (preposition *pyrma* 'before').

As shown in Table 13, lexicalized connectives consisting of more than one word are not frequent in either LL or AL. In modern Standard Latvian, *tāpēc ka* (< 'therefore that') 'because' is the most frequent causal connective, but its equivalent occurs only once in LL. It is, however, well attested in Old Written Low Latvian from the 17th century on, for example, in the Bible of 1685–1689. In High Latvian, compound causal connectives with *ka* 'that' or *kai* 'as' develop slower, there are more competing variants which still exist in modern Latgalian (cf. Nau 2018: 88). Of these, only *del to kad* (< 'for that that') 'because' is attested in AL. It also occurs only once in the *Evangelia toto anno* 1753. It has an exact parallel in Lithuanian. More frequent in AL is the temporal compound connective *kay tik* (< 'as only') 'as soon as', which also has a parallel in Lithuanian (*kai tik*). The Low Latvian connective with this meaning in LL is *tà kà* ('so as'), which in turn is parallel to, and probably a loan translation from German *sowie*. LL uses *tà kà* also in another meaning shared with German *sowie*: 'as well as'.

In sum, the comparison of connectives in LL and AL shows several instances of German influence on the creation and the functional range of adverbial connectives in Old Written Low Latvian, while Old Written High Latvian shows more similarities with Lithuanian, which are the mixed result of common heritage, common borrowings from Slavic languages, or direct influence of Lithuanian on Latgalian. In addition, the use of the coordinator *un* 'and' instead of a form of the inherited *ir* shows an impact of Old Written Low Latvian on Old Written High Latvian.

As stated in Section 4.3 above, in LL, the word order in complement and adverbial clauses does not differ from that of main clauses: a final position of the verb is the main trend in both. There is, however, one construction where word order is used as a technique in clause combining: in sentence-initial conditional clauses without connective the verb is placed at the beginning of the clause, usually followed by the subject; cf. (86). This technique is well known in German, where subject-verb inversion is used in conditional clauses as well as in questions (which are probably the source for this kind of conditional clauses). The inversion in (86) and other instances in LL is not due to a literal translation of the model sentence (87), which shows that the technique is part of the translator's repertoire.

(86) Low Latvian [LL 2-07]
Warri *tu to mahti atrast, tad*
can.PRS.2SG 2SG.NOM DEM.ACC.SG mother.ACC.SG find.INF then
noķeŗŗ to, un eeleez to papreekßch
catch.IMP.2SG DEM.ACC.SG and insert.IMP.2SG DEM.ACC.SG first
taî jaunâ kurwî, tad wißßaß bitteß
DEM.LOC.SG new.LOC.SG skep.LOC.SG then all.NOM.PL.F bee.NOM.PL
paßchaß no ßewiß pakkaļ eeß.
EMPH.NOM.PL.F of self.GEN after go.FUT.3
'**If you can** find the queen then catch her and put her first into the new skep, then all bees will follow her on their own.'

(87) German [Settegast 1798: 50]
Suchet die Mutter zu erhaschen und
try.IMP.2PL DEF.ACC.SG.F mother.SG to catch.INF and
sezzet sie zuerst in den neuen Korb hinein;
put.IMP.2PL she.ACC first in DEF.ACC.SG.M new.OBL skep into
[*so folgen ihr alle Bienen von selbst nach.*]

'Try to catch the queen and put her first into the new skep; [then all bees will follow her on their own.]'

Akielewicz never imitates this construction. His equivalent sentences usually contain the connective *jo* 'if', as in (88).

(88) High Latvian [AL 10]
Jo wareysi pi to dorba pasorgot
if can.FUT.2SG at DEM.GEN.SG work.GEN.SG discover.INF
motieyti un nugyut,
mother.DIM.ACC.SG and catch.INF
to ju nugywis iłayd da jaunam
PTC 3.ACC.SG catch.PST.PA.SG.M insert.IMP.2SG to new.DAT.SG.M
traukam, **tułayk** poszas bites ti sajs;
hive.DAT.SG **then** EMPH.NOM.PL.F bee.NOM.PL there gather.FUT.3
'**If** during this task **you can** find the queen and catch her, **then, having caught her**, put her into the new hive, **then** the bees themselves will gather there.'

The second half of extract (88) illustrates another phenomenon of clause combining: the use of a past active participle for an anterior action. This is also found in LL, but less frequently than in AL, and not in (86), in the model sentence for (88). Furthermore, AL uses these participles in structures that are reminiscent of clause chaining rather than subordination. For example, in (88), line three, the participle and the finite verb share the object (*ju nugywis iłayd* 'having caught **her** insert [her]'). The corresponding part in LL has two finite verbs, each with its object pronoun (*noķeŗŗ to, un eeleez to* 'catch **her**, and insert **her**'). Clause chaining with past active participles is characteristic for traditional oral varieties of Latgalian (see Nau 2018: 62–63).

Constructions with participles and converbs are typical clause-combining techniques in Baltic. Their occurrence in Old Written Low Latvian is noted by Latvian scholars as a token of the author's competence, of genuine Latvian expressions (for example, Vanags 2013: 186). Such constructions are found in both investigated texts, but in AL they are more frequent. The converb with the suffix -*dam*- (marking a simultaneous action with the same subject) occurs in LL 51 times (3.2 per 1000) and in AL 70 times (5.6 per 1000). This difference is similar to what we find in the modern languages, where Latgalian also uses this converb more often than Standard Latvian. The latter more often uses the other converb of simultaneity, with the suffix -*ot*. This converb is only rarely used in LL: there are five examples in my corpus (0.3 per 1000). The cognate form in High Latvian is found eleven times in AL (0.9 per 1000). Thus, we do not observe in these texts the difference in the choice of converb that distinguishes modern Standard Latvian and Latgalian, but a higher frequency of all converbs in AL (including the past active participle in converb use). This reflects a preference for finite clause combining in Old Written Low Latvian, which is an important part of the development of complex sentences.

4.8 Summary of findings

The detailed analyses in Sections 4.1–4.7 revealed several grammatical phenomena that distinguish Old Written Low and High Latvian, as well as differences between the Old Written languages and modern varieties of Latvian. The aim was to detect the specific impact of two driving forces in language change: language contact and the development of written registers. Accordingly, the findings may be grouped into the following categories:
(a) Phenomena that show the impact of German on Old Written Low Latvian, and phenomena that show the impact of Polish and other languages on Old Written High Latvian,
(b) phenomena that reflect differences between written and spoken varieties of a language, more specifically: the already established conventions of writing in Low Latvian found in LL and patterns that are more typical for spoken varieties in AL.

While the two driving forces often work together, in this summary I try to disentangle them and list the phenomena in four groups.

First group: Copying of a German model observed in LL
– Grammaticalization of a definite article from a demonstrative pronoun (4.1): systematic, ubiquitous.
– Genitive after head noun (4.2.4): rare.
– Auxiliary after participle or infinitive (4.3): occasional.
– Subject-verb inversion in conditional clauses (4.7): occasional as alternative to connective 'if'.
– Copula construction instead of lexical verb (4.4): conspicuous in comparison with AL.
– Passive with an auxiliary 'become' (4.5): systematic.
– Passive in instructions (4.5): occasional; conspicuous in comparison with AL.

- Material borrowing of coordinator 'and' (4.7): systematic, no alternative (old borrowing, also in AL).
- Distinction between coordinator 'and' and additive 'also' (4.7): systematic; conspicuous in comparison with AL.

Second group: Characteristics of planned written language in general or characteristics of the register (written instructive text with descriptive and procedural parts) in LL
- Overuse of third person pronouns for reference (instead of full noun phrases or zero) (4.1): conspicuous in comparison with AL.
- Complex noun phrases with strict rules for the order of modifiers (4.2). systematic, as in modern Standard Latvian; conspicuous in comparison with AL.
- SOV, or verb final order in general in main and subordinate clauses in descriptions (4.3): systematic; conspicuous in comparison to other registers.
- Frequent use of passive in descriptions (4.5).
- Conservation of passive auxiliary *tapt* against other variants (4.5).
- Conservation of the necessive construction with *būs* + infinitive (+ dative) against other variants (4.6).
- Development of sentences as units of written text, including complex sentences with finite subordinate clauses (4.7).

Third group: Copying of a Polish model in AL
- Order in chapter titles 'Chapter n-th' (4.2.3): very frequent; Latin model possible as well.
- Order N GEN and N POSS without pragmatic motivation (4.2.3 and 4.2.4): occasional.
- Passive auxiliary *palikt* 'stay; become' (model: Polish *zostać*) (4.5): rare; equally rare is the use of the passive auxiliary *tapt* 'become' after the model of Low Latvian.
- Modal auxiliary *pīderēt* 'belong; be necessary' (model: Polish *należeć*) (4.6): rare.
- Material borrowing of connectives *bo* 'because, for', *kocz* 'although' (4.7); material borrowing of *un* 'and' from Low Latvian (< German).

Fourth group: Structures more typical for spoken than written registers in AL (in addition, all listed phenomena have a parallel in 19th century Polish)
- Discontinuous noun phrases (4.2.1).
- Pragmatic use of position of noun modifiers (adjectives, genitives) (4.2.3 and 4.2.4).

- Copula clauses with demonstrative or particle *to* (4.4).
- Additive particle *i* and contrastive particle/connective *a* (4.7).

There are also a couple of phenomena where other driving forces seem to be more likely:
- Use of the numeral 'one' as indefinite determiner ('a certain') in both LL and AL (4.1) – may be an independent development.
- Genitive before measure noun in LL (4.2.4): probably a regional development in Western Latvian; a further step in fixing the pre-head position of genitives.
- Complements of action nouns and adjectives follow the head in AL (4.2.4): in line with the order VO that is stronger in AL than LL (nevertheless, a further parallel between High Latvian and Polish).
- Impersonal passives with 'become' (4.5): impersonal passives as such are typical for Baltic languages; their use with a new passive construction is not surprising (nevertheless it is a further parallel between Latvian and German).

In addition, it is worth noting where both LL and AL resisted a possible influence of their contact languages: for the expression of predicative possession and for non-epistemic necessity, only constructions with a dative argument are used. There are no constructions with a nominative subject and a verb 'have' or 'must', as have been occasionally found in other varieties of Latvian in contact with German, Polish, or Lithuanian.

5 Conclusions

Two written Latvian languages were in use from the 16th (Low Latvian) or 18th (High Latvian) century until the middle of the 19th century. These written languages are peculiar linguistic varieties that were developed in a colonial situation by speakers of the colonial language with only minimal direct contributions of the speech communities themselves. It was the colonial cultural elite who codified the writing system and determined how to write, what was written, and for which purposes native speakers of Latvian should use literacy.

During the 18th and the first half of the 19th century, German in western and central Latvia and Polish in Latgalia played similar roles in the respective societies: as the language of nobility and landowners, as the language of the dominant confession (Lutheran in the west and Catholic in the east), the language of education and upward mobility. However, there are some differences between the situations, and these partly explain differences in their impact on the respective variety of Latvian. First, German had been present in the region for a much longer time (since the 13th century), and the development of Old Written Low Latvian by speakers of German had started already in the 16th century. By the mid-18th century, it had become an established code with its own codified rules. At that time, writing in High Latvian was at an earlier stage of development and showed much more variation. Second, the society in Latgalia in all layers, but especially the "higher" layers, including the Catholic Church, was linguistically more diverse than was the case in western and central Latvia. The nobility spoke German and Polish, the Catholic Church used Latin besides Polish, and missionary institutions such as the powerful Jesuits recruited members with diverse linguistic backgrounds, including Lithuanian. Other languages (Belarusian, Russian, Yiddish) also were more present in the sociolinguistic landscape of Latgalia. This contrasts with the almost binary opposition between German and Low Latvian in western and central Latvia, where other languages played a minor role. Third, in several areas of morphosyntax, Latvian is more similar to Slavic languages than to German. For the German missionaries in the west of the region, Latvian was therefore more "exotic" than it was for the Polish missionaries in the east, especially if the latter were already familiar with Lithuanian. This had consequences not only for the ease of understanding and the willingness to use grammatical constructions, but also for attitudes towards the language and its speakers.

My case study showed reflexes of these differences in the language of the two investigated books: the impact of German on grammatical constructions in the Low Latvian book (LL) is much stronger and more obvious than the impact of Polish on the High Latvian version (AL). Furthermore, constructions that may have been copied from Polish in AL also have parallels in other contact languages. A summary of phenomena showing a German or Polish model was given in Section 4.8.

In Section 2.1, four different channels for the influence of the colonial language on the developing written language were named. Although the investigated books are translations (from German into Low Latvian, and from Low into High Latvian), they rarely show grammatical patterns caused by a literal translation of the original. Both authors have a repertoire of expression means which they use independently of their model to render the given content and meet the communicative goal at hand (information or instruction). Launitz, the author of the Low Latvian book, mainly draws on expression means that have already been established by previous writers and language planners of Old Written Low Latvian as a code. This includes several patterns that had arisen under a German model. Thus, the use of these patterns is not a token of unconscious interference from the author's native language, but rather reflects two characteristics of written languages: they perpetuate constructions independently of what goes on in spoken varieties, and they have a more regular (regulated) syntax. Clear examples in LL are the definite article, which Launitz uses very regularly, although it had already been criticized as being not genuine for Latvian for half a century (Section 4.1), as well as the strong tendency for a clause-final position of the verb in descriptions, which was described as the norm in grammars of the time (4.3). Also, the preference for the necessive construction with *būs* against other constructions (4.6) and of the passive auxiliary *tapt* against other auxiliaries (4.5) evidence the conserving character of Old Written Low Latvian.

Akielewicz, the author of the High Latvian version, seems to draw on a broader repertoire of expression means. Old Written High Latvian had not yet been normalized to such a degree as Old Written Low Latvian, but there were certain model texts. Their influence is evident in AL, for example, in the use of *un* for 'and', or the passive construction with 'become', both presumably imported from Low Latvian. However, while LL is a typical representative of its code (Old Written Low Latvian), AL shows more individual solutions, more constructions from spoken language, more freedom in word order, and in general more variation – also in spelling (see 3.2) and in vocabulary, which was not part of this study.

My case study of the Old Latvian books on beekeeping was mainly a synchronic one, though the existing documentation of Old Written Low Latvian sometimes allowed for diachronic considerations. While the two old written languages are commonly (and reasonably) treated as codes in their own right, an interesting question lying beyond the scope of this paper is that of the relation of these codes to the modern languages, especially in the case of Old Written Low Latvian and modern Standard Latvian. Some of the constructions that characterize the variety described here have been consciously and completely abolished (most significantly and somehow astonishingly: the definite article), others have remained in spite of open critique (the passive with 'become', with a new auxiliary), still others have faded away without acts of language planning (SOV order in descriptions, the necessive construction with *būs*). Thus, while the current study investigated language contact and the development of written languages in a colonial situation, future studies may turn to the effects of language contact in a postcolonial perspective.

Abbreviations

1/2/3	first, second, third person
ACC	accusative
ACN	action noun
ADD	additive particle
ADJ	adjective
ADV	adverb
AUX	auxiliary
CAUS	causative
CVB	converb
DAT	dative
DEB	debitive
DEF	definite
DEM	demonstrative
DIM	diminutive
EMPH	emphatic pronoun
F	feminine
FEM	female
FUT	future
GEN	genitive
IMP	imperative
INF	infinitive
IRR	irrealis
ITER	iterative
LOC	locative
M	masculine
N	noun
NA	non-agreement form
NEG	negation
NOM	nominative
OBL	oblique case (in German)
PA	active participle
PL	plural
POSS	possessive pronoun
PP	passive participle
PRS	present
PST	past
PTC	particle
PTCP	participle (in German)
PVB	preverb
REL	relative pronoun
RFL	reflexive
RPOSS	reflexive possessive pronoun
SG	singular
WH	interrogative, indefinite and relative pronoun 'what/who'

Sources

Books for the case study

AL = Akielewicz, Józef. 1832. *Eysa mociba ap audzieyszonu biszu. Wysim bitinikim un wysuwayrok łatweyszu* nu wina ju drauga Leyksnas baznieyc-kunga strupay un skaydri saraksteyta un da drukam paduta. Wilna pi Dworca 1832. [= High Latvian adaptation of Launitz 1803]

LL = Launitz, Christian Friedrich. 1803. *Bißchu=gramatiņa jeb ihßa un ßkaidra Pamahzißchana no bittehm un bißchu kohpßchanaß. Wißßeem bitteneekeem Kursemmê un Widsemmê* par labbu ßarakstita no Krißchana Wridriķķa Launitz, Grohbines draudseß jaunaka Mahzitaja. Jelgawâ 1803. Eeßpeesta pee J. W. Steffenhagen un dehla. [= Low Latvian adaptation of Settegast 1798]

Settegast, Daniel Gottlieb. 1798. *Das Wahre und Nützliche in der Bienenzucht*. Allen Bienen-Freunden auf dem Lande nach lauter eigenen Erfahrungen kurz und deutlich gelehrt von D. G. Settegast, Präz. in Prökuls. Königsberg: Hartung.

Other sources

Enchiridion 1586 = Enchiridion. Der kleine Catechismus: Oder Christliche zucht für die gemeinen Pfarherr und Prediger auch Hausueter etc. Durch D. Martin Luther. Nun aber aus dem Deudschen ins undeudsche gebracht und von wort zu wort wie es von D. M. Luthero gesetzet gesfasset worden. [Enchiridion. The small catechism. ...] Königsberg: Georg Osterberger. [Text available online as part of the corpus SENIE, http://senie.korpuss.lv/source.jsp?codificator=Ench1586]. [Accessed March 2022]

Evangelia toto anno 1753. Pirmā latgaliešu grāmata [Evangelia toto anno 1753. The first Latgalian book]. Riga: LU Latviešu valodas institūts. 2004. [Facsimile; text also available online as part of the corpus SENIE, http://senie.korpuss.lv/source.jsp?codificator=EvTA1753]. [Accessed March 2022]

Kossowski, Tomasz. 1852. *Conciones. Mocibas* [Teachings]. 2 volumes. Riga: Hartung.

Kurmin, Jan. 1859. *Jaunas mocibas uz abskaydrynoszonas laużu sprostu ab ticeybu swatu un irodumiem* [New teachings for the enlightening of simple folk about the holy religion and its practices]. Wilna: Drukarnie Jezupa Zawacku.

LVK2018. Balanced corpus of modern texts in Standard Latvian. Available at www.korpuss.lv. [Accessed March 2022]

LKŽ = *Lietuvių kalbos žodynas* (t. I–XX, 1941–2002): elektroninis variantas [Dictionary of Lithuanian (vol. I–XX, 1941–2002): electronic version]. Redaktorių kolegija: Gertrūda Naktinienė (vyr. redaktorė), Jonas Paulauskas, Ritutė Petrokienė, Vytautas Vitkauskas, Jolanta Zabarskaitė. Programuotojai: Evaldas Ožeraitis, Vytautas Zinkevičius. – Vilnius: Lietuvių kalbos institutas, 2005 (atnaujinta versija, 2017). Available at www.lkz.lt. [Accessed March 2022]

ME = *K. Mühlenbachs lettisch-deutsches Wörterbuch. Redigiert, ergänzt und fortgesetzt von J. Endzelin* [The Latvian-German dictionary by K. Mühlenbach. Edited, supplemented and continued by J. Endzelin]. 1923–1932. Riga: Lettisches Bildungsministerium.

SENIE Unicode. Corpus of Old Latvian texts. Available at www.korpuss.lv. [Accessed March 2022]

References

Ambrazas, Vytautas (ed.). 1997. *Lithuanian grammar*. Vilnius: Baltos lankos.
Bakker, Dik & Ewald Hekking. 2012. Clause combining in Otomi before and after contact with Spanish. *Linguistic Discovery* 10(1). 42–61.
Barbare, Dzidra. 2002. Vietniekvārds [The pronoun]. In Kornēlija Pokrotniece (ed.), *Latviešu literārās valodas morfoloģiskās sistēmas attīstība. Lokāmās vārdšķiras* [The development of the morphological system of Standard Latvian. Inflective parts of speech], 309–408. Riga: LU Latviešu valodas institūts.
Bergmane, Anna & Aina Blinkena. 1986. *Latviešu rakstības attīstība. Latviešu literārās valodas vēstures pētījumi* [The development of Latvian writing. Studies on the history of Standard Latvian]. Rīga: Zinātne.
Berneker, Erich. 1900. *Die Wortfolge in den slavischen Sprachen* [Word order in Slavic languages]. Berlin: E. Behr.
Biber, Douglas. 2009. Are there linguistic consequences of literacy? Comparing the potentials of language use in speech and writing. In David R. Olson & Nancy Torrance (eds.), *The Cambridge handbook of literacy*, 75–91. Cambridge: Cambridge University Press.
Blinkena, Anna. 2007. Konjunkcija (Saiklis) [The conjunction]. In Kornēlija Pokrotniece (ed.), *Latviešu literārās valodas morfoloģiskās sistēmas attīstība. Nelokāmās vārdšķiras* [The development of the morphological system of Standard Latvian. Non-inflective parts of speech], 100–309. Riga: LU Latviešu valodas institūts.
Bukšs, M. 1952. *Vacōkī rakstnīceibas pīminekli* [The oldest attestations of [Latgalian] writing]. [no place] Vl. Lōča izdevnīceiba.
Chafe, Wallace & Deborah Tannen. 1987. The relation between written and spoken language. *Annual Review of Anthropology* 16. 383–407.
Chamoreau, Claudine & Isabelle Léglise. 2012. A multi-model approach to contact-induced language change. In Claudine Chamoreau & Isabelle Léglise (eds.), *Dynamics of contact-induced language change*, 1–15. Berlin: De Gryuter Mouton.
Cibuļs, Juris & Lidija Leikuma. 2003. *Vasals! Latgaliešu valodas mācība* [Practical grammar of Latgalian]. Riga: n.i.m.s.
Daija, Pauls. 2017. *Literary history and popular enlightenment in Latvian culture*. Newcastle upon Thyne: Cambridge Scholars Publishing.
Eckert, Rainer, Elvira-Julia Bukevičiūtė & Friedhelm Hinze. 1994. *Die baltischen Sprachen. Eine Einführung* [The Baltic languages. An introduction]. Leipzig: Langenscheidt Verlag Enzyklopädie.
Endzelīns, Janis. [1920] 1979. kurš un viņš [On the pronouns *kurš* and *viņš*]. In H. Bendiks (ed.), *Janis Endzelins. Darbu izlase. Izbrannye trudy. Ausgewählte Werke* [Selected works of Jānis Endzelins]. Vol. 3, 72–73. Rīga: Zinātne.
Endzelin, J. 1922. *Lettische Grammatik* [Latvian grammar]. Riga: Kommissionsverlag A. Gulbis.
Engelberg, Stefan & Doris Stolberg. 2012. Einleitung: Die Koloniallinguistik und ihre Forschungsfelder [Introduction: Colonial Linguistics and its fields of research]. In Stefan Engelberg & Doris Stolberg (eds.), *Sprachwissenschaft und kolonialzeitlicher Sprachkontakt: Sprachliche Begegnungen und Auseinandersetzungen* [Linguistics and colonial language contact: Linguistic encounters and conflicts], 7–13. Berlin: Akademie Verlag.

Fanselow, Gisbert, & Caroline Féry. 2006. *Prosodic and morphosyntactic aspects of discontinuous noun phrases – a comparative perspective*. Unpublished Manuscript. Potsdam: University of Potsdam.
Givón, Talmy. 2001. *Syntax: An introduction*. Vol. II. Amsterdam: Benjamins.
Harder, Christoph. 1790. *Anmerkungen und Zusäzze zu der neuen lettischen Grammatik des Herrn Probst Stender* [Comments and additions to the new Latvian grammar of Provost Stender]. Papendorf: [Ch. Harder].
Hesselberg, Heinrich. 1841. *Lettische Sprachlehre* [Latvian grammar]. Mitau: Steffenhagen und Sohn.
Holvoet, Axel. 2001. *Studies in the Latvian verb*. Kraków: Wydawnictwo Uniwersytetu Jagiellońskiego.
Holvoet, Axel. 2007. *Mood and modality in Baltic*. Kraków: Wydawnictwo Uniwersytetu Jagiellońskiego.
Jansone, Ilga & Anna Stafecka. 2013. Latviešu rakstības attīstība: lejzemnieku un augšzemnieku tradīcija [The development of Latvian writing: the Low Latvian and the High Latvian traditions]. In Inga Jansone & Andrejs Vasks (eds.), *Latvieši un Latvija I. Latvieši* [Latvians and Latvia I. The Latvians], 204–244. Riga: Latvijas Zinātņu akadēmija.
Jēgers, B. 1975. Jānis Reiters un viņa Übersetzungsprobe [Jānis Reiters and his Übersetzungsprobe]. In Jānis Reiters, *Tulkojuma paraugs. 1675. gada Rīgā iznākušo latviešu bībeles tekstu faksimiliespiedums* [Translation sample. Reprint of the text of from the Latvian Bible published 1685 in Riga], 35–73. Stockholm: Daugava.
Jordan, Sabine. 1995. *Niederdeutsches im Lettischen: Untersuchungen zu den mittelniederdeutschen Lehnwörtern im Lettischen* [Low German elements in Latvian: Studies of the Middle Low German loanwords in Latvian]. Bielefeld: Verlag für Regionalgeschichte.
Karulis, Konstantīns. 1988. G. F. Stendera valoda un rakstība [The language and writing system of G. F. Stender]. In Gothards Frīdrihs Stenders, *Augstas gudrības grāmata no pasaules un dabas. 1796. gada izdevuma teksts ar komentāriem* [The book of high wisdom about the world and nature. Text of the 1796 edition with comments], 539–555. Riga: Liesma.
Karulis, Konstantīns. 2000. Baltisches Deutsch und Lettisch. Zur sprachlichen Interferenz [Baltic German and Latvian. On linguistic interference]. In Jochen D. Range (ed.), *Aspekte baltistischer Forschung* [Aspects of Baltistic research], 146–173. Essen: Die Blaue Eule.
Kolbuszewski, Stanisław Franciszek. 1966. Kariger, Jan. *Polski słownik biograficzny* [Polish biographical dictionary], tom 12, 44–45. Wrocław: Ossolineum.
Kolbuszewski, Stanisław Franciszek. 1973. Łukaszewicz, Jan. *Polski słownik biograficzny* [Polish biographical dictionary], tom 18, 540–541. Wrocław: Ossolineum.
Kolbuszewski, Stanisław F. 1977. *Jana Karigera słownik polsko-łotewski na tle leksykografii b. Inflant Polskich* [Jan Kariger's Polish-Latvian dictionary on the background of the lexicography of Polish Livonia]. Poznań: Uniwersytet im. Adama Mickiewicza w Poznaniu.
Kristovska, Ineta. 1996. *19. gadsimta latgaliešu gramatikas* [19th century grammars of Latgalian]. PhD thesis, University of Latvia.
Leikuma, Lidija. 1992. J. Akeleviča grōmotai par bišu audzēšonu – 160 [160 years since the publication of J. Akeliewicz's book on beekeeping]. *Tāvu zemes kalendars* 56, 164–167.
Lindström, Liina, Nicole Nau, Birutė Spraunienė & Asta Laugalienė. 2020. Impersonal constructions with personal reference: Reference of deleted actors in Baltic and Estonian. *Baltic Linguistics* 11. 129–213.

Mauri, Caterina. 2007. Conjunctive, disjunctive and adversative constructions in Europe: Some areal considerations. In Paolo Ramat & Elisa Roma (eds.), *Europe and the Mediterranean linguistic areas*, 182–214. Amsterdam: Benjamins.
Mieze, Silvija. 2002. Skaitļa vārds [The numeral]. In Kornēlija Pokrotniece (ed.), *Latviešu literārās valodas morfoloģiskās sistēmas attīstība. Lokāmās vārdšķiras* [The development of the morphological system of Standard Latvian. Inflective parts of speech], 243–308. Riga: LU Latviešu valodas institūts.
Migge, Bettina & Isabelle Léglise. 2007. Language and colonialism. Applied linguistics in the context of creole communities. In Marlis Hellinger & Anne Pauwels (eds.), *Handbook of language and communication: Diversity and change*, 297–338. Berlin: Mouton de Gruyter.
Miller, Jim & Regina Weinert. 1998. *Spontaneous spoken language: Syntax and discourse*. Oxford: Clarendon Press.
MLLVG II = E. Sokols (ed. in chief). 1962. *Mūsdienu latviešu literārās valodas gramatika. II Sintakse* [Grammar of modern Standard Latvian. Vol. II Syntax]. Riga: LPSR Zinātņu akadēmijas izdevniecība.
Nau, Nicole. 1998. *Latvian*. München: LINCOM.
Nau, Nicole. 2011. *A short grammar of Latgalian*. München: LINCOM.
Nau, Nicole. 2012. Modality in an areal context: The case of a Latgalian dialect. In Björn Wiemer, Bernhard Wälchli & Björn Hansen (eds.), *Grammatical replication and grammatical borrowing in language contact*, 471–514. Berlin: Mouton de Gruyter.
Nau, Nicole. 2016. *Wortarten und Pronomina. Studien zur lettischen Grammatik* [Word classes and pronouns. Studies on Latvian grammar]. E-Book. Poznań: Wydział Neofilologii UAM.
Nau, Nicole. 2018. Adverbial clause combining in Latgalian: Temporal, conditional, causal and concessive relations in spontaneous speech. *Baltic Linguistics* 9. 45–109.
Nau, Nicole. 2021. When one is singular: Notes on zero-person constructions in Latvian. In Peter Arkadiev, Jurgis Pakerys, Inesa Šeškauskienė & Vaiva Žeimantienė (eds.), *Studies in Baltic and other Languages. A Festschrift for Axel Holvoet on the occasion of his 65th birthday*, 248–267. Vilnius: Vilnius University Press.
Nau, Nicole & Peter Arkadiev. 2015. Towards a standard of glossing Baltic languages: The Salos Glossing Rules. *Baltic Linguistics* 6. 195–241.
Nau, Nicole & Axel Holvoet. 2015. Voice in Baltic – an overview. In Axel Holvoet and Nicole Nau (eds.), *Voice and argument structure in Baltic*, 1–36. Amsterdam: Benjamins.
Nau, Nicole, Birutė Spraunienė & Vaiva Žeimantienė. 2020. The Passive Familiy in Baltic. *Baltic Linguistics* 11. 27–128.
Nītiņa, Daina. 2007. Prepozicija (prievārds) [The preposition]. In Kornēlija Pokrotniece (ed.), *Latviešu literārās valodas morfoloģiskās sistēmas attīstība. Neokāmās vārdšķiras* [The development of the morphological system of Standard Latvian. Non-inflective parts of speech], 31–99. Riga: LU Latviešu valodas institūts.
Ostrowski, Norbert. 2010. Latvian *jeb* 'or' – from conditional to disjunctive conjunction. In Nicole Nau & Norbert Ostrowski (eds.), *Particles and connectives in Baltic*, 135–150. Vilnius: Vilniaus Universitetas and Associacija "Academia Salensis".
Ozols, Arturs. 1965. *Veclatviešu rakstu valoda* [Old Written Latvian]. Riga: Liesma.
Plakans, Andrejs. 1993. From a regional vernacular to the language of a state: The case of Latvian. *International Journal of the Sociology of Language* 100/101. 203–219.
Plakans, Andrejs. 2011. *A concise history of the Baltic States*. Cambrdige: Cambridge University Press.

Pokrotniece, Kornēlija (ed.). 2002. *Latviešu literārās valodas morfoloģiskās sistēmas attīstība. Lokāmās vārdšķiras* [The development of the morphological system of Standard Latvian. Inflective parts of speech]. Riga: LU Latviešu valodas institūts.
Pokrotniece, Kornēlija (ed.). 2007. *Latviešu literārās valodas morfoloģiskās sistēmas attīstība. Nelokāmās vārdšķiras* [The development of the morphological system of Standard Latvian. Non-inflective parts of speech]. Riga: LU Latviešu valodas institūts.
Porīte, Tamara. 2007. Partikula [The particle]. In Kornēlija Pokrotniece (ed.), *Latviešu literārās valodas morfoloģiskās sistēmas attīstība. Neokāmās vārdšķiras* [The development of the morphological system of Standard Latvian. Non-inflective parts of speech], 310–343. Riga: LU Latviešu valodas institūts.
Powell, Jonathan G. F. 2010. Hyperbaton and register in Cicero. In Eleanor Dickey & Anna Chahoud (eds), *Colloquial and literary Latin*, 163–185. Cambridge: Cambridge University Press.
Recke, Johann Friedrich von & Karl Eduard von Napiersky. 1831. *Allgemeines Schriftsteller- und Gelehrten-Lexicon der Provinzen Livland, Esthland und Kurland* [Encyclopedia of writers and academics of the provinces Livonia, Estonia, and Courland]. Volume 3. Mitau: Steffenhagen und Sohn.
Rosenberger, Otto Benj. Gottfr. 1852. *Der lettischen Grammatik zweiter Theil, Syntax* [Grammar of Latvian, part two: Syntax]. Mitau: Steffenhagen und Sohn.
Rūķe-Draviņa, Velta. 1977. *The standardization process in Latvian: 16th century to the present.* Stockholm: Stockholm University.
Saagpakk, Maris. 2015. Sprache steht zur Debatte – Diskussionen um die Zukunft der estnischen Sprache um die Mitte des 19. Jahrhunderts [Language is up for debate. Discussions about the future of the Estonian language at the middle of the 19th century]. In Anne Sommerlat-Michas (ed.), *Das Baltikum als Konstrukt: von einer Kolonialwahrnehmung zu einem nationalen Diskurs (18.-19. Jahrhundert)* [The Baltic as a construct: from a colonial perception to a national discours (18th-19th century)], 95–111. Würzburg: Königshausen und Neumann.
Sankowska, Julia. 1962. Szyk przymiotników we współczesnej polszczyźnie [The position of adjectives in modern Polish]. *Język Polski* 11(1). 41–85.
Schultze-Berndt, Eva & Candide Simard. 2012. Constraints on noun phrase discontinuity in an Australian language: The role of prosody and information structure. *Linguistics* 50(5). 1015–1058.
Sehwers, Johann. 1934. *Die deutschen Lehnwörter im Lettischen* [German loanwords in Latvian]. Inaugural-Dissertation. Universität Zürich.
Skujiņa, Valentīna. 2006. *Salikteņi G. Manceļa vārdnīcā "Lettus" un krājumā "Phraseologia Lettica"* [Compounds in G. Mancelius's dictionary "Lettus" and his collection "Phraseologia Lettica"]. Riga: LU Latviešu valodas institūts.
Smalley, William A. 1994. Codification by means of foreign systems. In Hartmut Günther & Otto Ludwig (eds.), *Schrift und Schriftlichkeit. Ein interdisziplinäres Handbuch internationaler Forschung* [Writing and its use. An interdisciplinary handbook of international research], Vol. 1, 697–708. Berlin: de Gruyter.
Spevak, Olga. 2010. *Constituent order in Classical Latin prose.* Amsterdam: Benjamins.
Spevak, Olga. 2014. *The noun phrase in Classical Latin prose.* Leiden: Brill.
Stafecka, Anna. 1989. Sistema mestoimenij v pamjatnikax latgal'skoj pis'mennosti (1753–1871) [The system of pronouns in old documents of Latgalian writing (1753–1871)). In

Verxnelatyšskij dialekt. Sbornik naučnyx trudov [The High Latvian dialect. Collection of academic work], 100–142. Riga: Latvijskij gosudarstvennyj universitet im. P. Stučki.

Stafecka, Anna. 2004. "Evangelia toto anno.." (1753) and the development of the written word in Latgale. In: *Evangelia toto anno 1753. Pirmā latgaliešu grāmata* [*Evangelia toto anno 1753*. The first Latgalian book], 316–345. Rīga: LU Latviešu valodas institūts.

Stender, Gotthard Friedrich. 1761. *Neue vollständigere Lettische Grammatik nebst einem hinlänglichen Lexico, wie auch einigen Gedichten* [A new and more complete grammar of Latvian, together with a sufficient dictionary, as well as some poems] Gedruckt im Fürstl. großen Waisenhause, Braunschweig.

Stolz, Thomas. 1991. *Sprachbund im Baltikum? Estnisch und Lettisch im Zentrum einer sprachlichen Konvergenzlandschaft* [Sprachbund in the Baltic. Estonian and Latvian in the center of a linguistic convergence landscape]. Bochum: Universitätsverlag Brockmeyer.

Stolz, Thomas & Nataliya Levkovych. 2022. On loan conjunctions: A comparative study with special focus on the languages of the former Soviet Union. In Nataliya Levkovych (ed.), *Susceptibility vs. resistance: Case studies on different structural categories in language-contact situations*, 259–392. Berlin: De Gruyter.

Strods, P. 1937. Bazneickungu J. Rimkeviča, J. Akileviča un T. Kosovska latvīšu volūdas (latgaļu dialekta) gramatika [The Latvian (Latgalian) grammar of the priests J. Rimkiewicz, J. Akielewicz and T. Kossowski]. *Zīdūnis* 7. 115–120.

Vanags, Pēteris. 1993. Die möglichen Formen deutschen Einflusses auf die grammatische und syntaktische Struktur der ältesten lettischen Texte [Possible forms of German influence on the grammatical and syntactic structure of the oldest Latvian texts]. *Linguistica Baltica* 2. 163–181.

Vanags, Pēteris. 2000. Debitīva formu lietojums visvecākajos latviešu rakstos. [The debitive form in the earliest Latvian texts]. *Baltu filoloģija* 11. 143–156.

Vanags Pēteris. 2008. Latviešu valodas standartizācijas problēma 19. gadsimtā: valodas kopēju maiņa. [Issues in standardization of Latvian in the 19th century: changes in planners]. *Latvijas Universitātes raksti* 731. 62–71.

Vanags, Pēteris. 2013. Latviešu literārās valodas attīstība. In Inga Jansone & Andrejs Vasks (eds.), *Latvieši un Latvija I. Latvieši* [Latvians and Latvia 1. The Latvians], 177–203. Riga: Latvijas Zinātņu akadēmija.

Vanags, Pēteris. 2015. Valoda "Stāstos" [The language of the "stāsti"]. In F. B. Blaufūss (ed.), *Vidzemes Stāsti. Stāsti no tas vecas un jaunas būšanas to Vidzemes ļaužu, uzrakstīti 1753* [Livonian history. Stories of old and new situation of Livonian folk, written down in 1753], 43–74. Riga: Vēstures izpētes un popularizēšanas biedrība.

Vanags, Pēteris. 2019. Latviešu valoda pirms Latvijas valsts [The Latvian language before the Latvian state]. In Andrejs Veisbergs (ed.), *Valoda un valsts*, 55–86. Riga: Zinatne.

Veidemane, Ruta. 2002. Darbības vārds [Verbs]. In Kornēlija Pokrotniece (ed.), *Latviešu literārās valodas morfoloģiskās sistēmas attīstība. Lokāmās vārdšķiras* [The development of the morphological system of Standard Latvian. Inflective parts of speech], 409–509. Riga: LU Latviešu valodas institūts.

Warnke, Ingo H., Thomas Stolz & Daniel Schmidt-Brücken. 2016. Perspektiven der Postcolonial Language Studies [Perspectives of postcolonial language studies]. In Thomas Stolz, Ingo H. Warnke & Daniel Schmidt-Brücken (eds.), *Sprache und Kolonialismus. Eine interdisziplinäre Einführung zu Sprache und Kommunikation in kolonialen Kontexten* [Language and colonialism. An interdisciplinary introduction to language and communication in colonial contexts], 1–25. Berlin & Boston: de Gruyter.

Wiemer, Björn. 2004. The evolution of passives as grammatical constructions in Northern Slavic and Baltic languages. In Walter Bisang, Nikolaus Himmelmann & Björn Wiemer (eds.), *What makes grammaticalization? A look from its fringes and its components*, 271–331. Berlin: Mouton de Gruyter.

Zimmermann, Klaus & Birte Kellermeier-Rehbein (eds). 2015. *Colonialism and Missionary Linguistics*. Berlin, München & Boston: De Gruyter.

Zwartjes, Otto. 2012. The historiography of Missionary Linguistics: present state and further research opportunities. *Historiographia Linguistica* 39. 185–242.

Marcus Callies
Contact in World Englishes at the nexus of language and culture
Proverbs and idioms

Abstract: This contribution proposes to broaden the scope of contact linguistics by discussing the nexus of language and culture in World Englishes with regard to the influence of Nigerian Pidgin English proverbs on the process of acculturation/nativisation in Nigerian English. Proverbs illustrate the linguistic impact of folk culture and traditional wisdom of the different indigenous cultures. Calquing from indigenous languages has been identified as a frequent process in West African Pidgin Englishes, especially with a view to proverbs and idioms which can thus be assumed to be a rich source of culture-specific lexis and conceptualisations in West African Englishes.

Keywords: World Englishes, West Africa, Ghanaian English, Nigerian English, Nigerian Pidgin English, proverbs, idioms, metaphor, language contact, culture

> The most fundamental values in a culture will be coherent with the metaphorical structure of the most fundamental concepts in the culture.
> (Lakoff and Johnson 1980: 22)

> Proverbs are the palm-oil with which words are eaten. (Achebe 1996: 5)

1 Introduction

The spread of the English language around the world and the evolution of postcolonial Englishes has brought about an enormous proliferation of research on the diversity, inclusivity, and equality of World Englishes. This research testifies to the fact that English has become increasingly "localised", a process frequently also referred to as indigenisation or nativisation. Questions of the role of the local

---

Marcus Callies, University of Bremen, FB 10: English-Speaking Cultures, Universitäts-Boulevard 13, 28359 Bremen, Germany. E-Mail: callies@uni-bremen.de

https://doi.org/10.1515/9783111323756-002

linguistic ecologies and how they interact with sociolinguistic and cultural factors in that process remain central to this day. In particular, the linguistic impact of the pragmatic, cognitive, and cultural features of English-speaking communities around the world in the "glocalisation" of Englishes have received much less attention to date (but see Wolf and Polzenhagen 2009; Anchimbe 2018; Callies and Onysko 2017; Sadeghpour and Sharifian 2021; Callies and Degani 2021; Peters and Burridge 2021 for recent publications in that direction). The cognitive and culture-specific grounding of figurative language as manifest, for example, in metaphors, proverbs and idioms, has largely been neglected to date. This seems to equally apply to other pluricentric languages such as French, Spanish, or Portuguese (see Soares da Silva 2021 for an exception but also the (lack of) relevant contributions to the volumes edited by Soares da Silva 2013 and Kristiansen et al. 2021).

The point of departure of this chapter is the nexus of language and culture / cultural models: a language (or a variety of that language) reflects the cultural context of its speech community (Kövecses 2005). In the localisation of Englishes, cultural conceptualisations encoded in other (indigenous) languages are progressively encoded in various features of the English language as used by local speech communities around the world to express their culturally constructed conceptualisations and world views (see Palmer 1996, chapter 2, for some history of this term as used in linguistic anthropology). The worldwide diversification of English provides rich potential for exploring if and how culturally diverse settings in which these Englishes have formed and are developing influence figurative language use. Such use is often grounded in cultural conceptualizations and reflects salient cultural practices, one example being the various linguistic surface forms used to express veiled bribes in West African Englishes (Callies 2021; Polzenhagen and Wolf 2021).

In Section 2 it will be argued that the specific role of culture and the conceptual system as a locus of language contact has been underrepresented in contact linguistics. I will discuss three more recent strands of research that examine the nexus of language and culture in contact situations, especially with a view to Englishes around the world. Section 3 zooms in on proverbs as a type of figurative language and their cultural significance in Nigerian Pidgin English as they illustrate the linguistic impact of folk culture and traditional wisdom of the different indigenous cultures. Section 4 elaborates on the cognitive motivation of idioms and proverbs, also discussing their role in language contact and the acculturation/nativisation of Nigerian English. A brief conclusion and outlook in Section 5 rounds off the chapter.

2 Contact linguistics and the nexus of language and culture

In research on the development of Englishes around the world, Schneider's (2007) Dynamic Model of the Evolution of Postcolonial Englishes (PCEs) has become one of the most influential frameworks. The model assumes that emerging varieties of English in postcolonial contexts typically follow an underlying, fundamentally uniform evolutionary process brought about by the social dynamics between two parties involved, i.e. a settler strand (STL) and an indigenous population (IDG). Similar historical, political, psychological and (socio-)linguistic factors are thought to be at work in all colonial contact situations, and some synchronically observable differences between PCEs may be regarded as consecutive stages in a diachronic process. Stronger social contact between STL and IDG leads to greater linguistic interaction, and language contact in general depends heavily on the social and political conditions, also with a view to the established four-part classification of colonization types into trade colonies, exploitation colonies, settlement colonies, and plantation (settlement) colonies (Schneider 2007: 24f.).

Language contact thus plays a major role in Schneider's model. On the one hand, it is essentially linked to social contact which triggers linguistic and cultural interaction and the re-writing and development of identity constructions. On the other, with a view to linguistic accommodation between the two strands, language contact is identified as one of three major clusters of sources and processes of the nativisation of PCEs on a structural level (Schneider 2007: 100), e.g. in phonology, vocabulary, lexico-grammar and syntax. Contact includes the selection and adoption of elements from different, competing systems (esp. indigenous languages), notably in the form of borrowing or calquing which often reflect and describe local phenomena such as flora and fauna, but also more complex concepts of local culture which in turn can also lead to the coinage of new (hybrid and complex) words. Another scenario is the addition of new meanings to established English words. For example, FAMILY has a much wider conceptual scope in e.g. Aboriginal Australian English (Sharifian 2015: 484) and West African Englishes (Wolf and Polzenhagen 2009: 73–74) when compared to British English in that people who form close personal bonds and those living in the same village can be referred to by kinship terms such as *brother* or *cousin*. Lexical items can thus carry distinct, culture-specific conceptualizations.

Moreover, nativisation does not only take place on a structural-linguistic but also on a broader cultural-cognitive level as a reflection of the local culture(s) and the functional-pragmatic norms of interaction of its speakers. Used in that sense, it is also referred to as "acculturation" (Sridar 2012), a process "by which a language takes on the cultural cloak of its speakers. In the case of varieties of English, acculturation is often accompanied by deculturation, where the new variety of English divests itself of cultural references to older varieties, such as British English" (Kirkpatrick 2015: 460). In a study of cultural keywords in South-Asian Englishes, Mukherjee and Bernaisch (2015: 412) use "linguistic acculturation" to refer to the process of cultural entrenchment of the English language in newly emerging Anglophone speech communities in postcolonial contexts.

It appears that the specific role of culture and the conceptual system as a locus of language contact has been underrepresented in contact linguistics. In two recently published handbooks of the field, culture does not feature prominently as a determinant of language contact. In Grant (2019) there is no dedicated chapter, and in the opening chapter (and throughout the rest of the volume) culture is merely mentioned with a view to "cultural borrowing", i.e. the borrowing of lexical items from the dominant culture. The same observation applies to the second edition of Hickey (2020). While there is a chapter on "Contact and African Englishes" (Mesthrie 2020), a topic most relevant to the present contribution, it largely focuses on the effects of language contact on linguistic features in phonology, morphosyntax and vocabulary, often in terms of code-switching and lexical borrowing. Bartens (2013: 81) notes in the context of creole languages that "[c]ultural aspects continue to be treated in other fields such as Anthropology, Folkloristics, Religious Studies, Musicology, and History" while "over the past few years, this situation has changed to some extent, particularly when the object of study is the language-culture interface, e.g. specific types of discourse". Bartens refers to studies of culture-specific politeness phenomena in the Caribbean region published in Mühleisen and Migge (2005). She concludes that "it would be (at least) as desirable for creolists to pay (even) more attention to issues of variation and language change, language use and policy, as well as the intricate relationships between language and (the rest of) culture in the future" (Bartens 2013: 137). More recently, we have seen the emergence of various strands of research that more explicitly examine the nexus of language and culture in contact situations, especially with a view to Englishes around the world. These will be briefly discussed below.

2.1 Research on cultural keywords

Cultural keywords are words and phrases that have a particular cultural significance in a speech community. According to Levisen and Waters (2017), cultural keywords are "culturally laden words around which whole discourses are organised". They "govern the shared cognitive outlook of speakers and encode certain culture-specific logics, and impose on their speakers a certain interpretative grid through which they make sense of the world" (Levisen and Waters 2017: 3). Research on cultural keywords has been carried out from various perspectives and in various disciplines (see, for example, Callies 2024, for an overview). Different methodologies, both qualitative and quantitative, have been used to identify cultural keywords in language use. Williams (1976) is one of the first studies on cultural keywords from a lexicographic perspective. The study of cultural keywords gained further visibility and prominence through the work of Wierzbicka and colleagues who have analysed these words by means of a distinct metalanguage, the Natural Semantic Metalanguage (Wierzbicka 1997). Wierzbicka (1997: 15–16) also acknowledges that keywords are words which are particularly important and revealing in a given culture, at the same time drawing attention to the conceptual-methodological challenge for research on cultural keywords to decide what counts as a keyword. While she generally highlights the importance of frequency as evidence for the "cultural salience" of a keyword (Wierzbicka 1997: 12, 15), she is critical of what the appropriate "discovery procedure" may be.

One widely-used discovery procedure ever since the availability of large electronic text corpora and the popularisation of corpus linguistics as a methodology has been the corpus-based approach to the identification and description of cultural keywords. Stubbs' (1996, 2002) work has been highly influential in showing how corpus methods can provide systematic evidence for the significance of keywords in English, emphasizing that words should be studied in the text types and collocations in which they typically occur. The culture-specificity of the (sometimes evaluative) meanings of cultural keywords thus often derive from the typical contexts in which they are habitually used. In corpus analyses of such keywords highly frequent lexical items and their collocations are examined in a large and representative corpus of a language or language variety in order to identify salient cultural keywords and describe the lexico-grammatical patterns in which they occur. Frequency is thus used as a proxy for salience or significance in a speech community, and in turn provides important insights into the socio-cultural setting of that community and, potentially, specific linguistic acculturation processes of English. By means of the corpus approach, the qualitative work on cultural keywords and its assumptions regarding their significance can thus be put to the empirical test, and additionally allows insights into collocational patterns and the textual patterns of such items, motivated in turn by underlying conceptualizations.

More recently, cultural keywords have been studied within cognitive-linguistic and cultural-linguistic approaches to World Englishes (see also 2.3. below). The importance of cultural keywords has been foregrounded in the seminal work of Wolf and Polzenhagen (see, for example, Wolf and Polzenhagen 2009) who emphasize that it is the cultural background knowledge and cultural conceptualizations that are essential for the interpretation of lexis, phraseology and figurative language use in varieties of English around the world that have developed in culturally diverse settings. Wolf's and Polzenhagen's work on cultural conceptualisations and cultural keywords has focused on the Englishes in Asian and West Africa (e.g. Polzenhagen and Wolf 2021; Wolf and Chan 2016) and also uses quantitative measures to determine cultural keywords. The frequency of a respective word in a target corpus of the variety under study in comparison to the frequency of the same word in a reference corpus is used as a measure to determine the salience, and hence the keyness of a cultural keyword (Wolf and Polzenhagen 2009: 38). The culture-specific lexis of World Englishes has recently also gained interest in lexicography (see, for example, Lambert 2020 and Salazar 2021).

2.2 Cognitive contact linguistics

Cognitive contact linguistics is a very recent field that has emerged as a research paradigm at the interface of contact linguistics and Cognitive Linguistics (Zenner et al. 2019). It seeks to reframe traditional questions in contact linguistics and reconceptualise existing contact phenomena through the lens of Cognitive Linguistics (CL). One major aim is to examine how the core principles of CL, in particular the usage-based hypothesis (i.e. that the mental representation of language structure is derived from the cognitive processing of language use), "apply to the bi- or multilingual mind in its dynamic bi- and multilingual environment, how this feeds back to our general understanding of these guiding principles, and how we can as a result better grasp how the interaction between cognition and context results in contact-induced variation and change" (Zenner et al. 2019: 4). An exemplary study is Finzel and Wolf (2019) that applies cognitive contact linguistics to conceptual metaphors in World Englishes and argues that these constitute contact phenomena, albeit more covert ones when compared to the more visible outcomes of language contact such as code-switching or lexical borrowing. Within the multilingual settings that one typically finds in World Englishes contexts, metaphors are shaped through contact with local and culturally salient concepts.

2.3 Cognitive Sociolinguistics and Cultural Linguistics

Recent years have seen an increase in studies at the interface of Conceptual Metaphor Theory (CMT) (Lakoff and Johnson 1980) and World Englishes that explore the culture-specific nature and within-language variation of conceptual metaphor and their surface figurative expressions, including idioms and proverbs. This kind of research is typically grounded and framed in the fields of Cognitive (Socio-)Linguistics (e.g. Wolf and Polzenhagen 2009; Callies and Onysko 2017). Research on conceptual and linguistic variation in metaphor has long had a strong focus on cross-cultural differences in metaphorical mappings in different languages (e.g. by exploring the conceptualization of emotions through body parts, see for example Kövecses 2000; Sharifian et al. 2008), but variation in metaphor is also present in varieties of one language, especially in pluricentric languages that have been transplanted to diverse cultural contexts. First applications of CMT to World Englishes highlight the importance of cultural background knowledge and underlying cultural conceptualizations for the interpretation of lexical domains (e.g. Wolf and Polzenhagen 2007; Wolf and Chan 2016). A crucial question as to the locus and extent of variation in conceptual metaphor concerns universality: If so much in metaphorical mapping processes appears to be grounded in basic human (physical) experience (embodied cognition) as CMT claims, it should be possible to separate universal from culture-specific domain-mappings. However, experience that leads to the formation of metaphorical concepts is different in nature; it may relate to the physical (inanimate and animate things, especially human physiology), the geographical (i.e. topography and climate), and the socio-cultural environment (various kinds of interaction between human beings; traditions, customs, cultural values).

Research at the interface of CMT, culture and World Englishes is also frequently set within Cultural Linguistics (e.g. Wolf et al. 2017; Sharifian 2017; Sadeghpour and Sharifian 2021; Callies and Degani 2021). Cultural Linguistics, popularized by Sharifian (2017), is a multidisciplinary field of research that explores the relationship between language and cultural conceptualisations, and how such conceptualisations are entrenched in (features of) human languages and language varieties. It shares with Cognitive Linguistics the focus on the study of cognitive/conceptual processes and structures underlying language, but regards conceptualisation as predominantly culturally constructed. Cultural Linguistics meets with sociolinguistics in its principal concern with patterns and variation at the level of socio-cultural groups, but has an explicit focus on the group as the locus of cultural knowledge and hence the object of analysis.

Cultural conceptualizations are a key element in this theoretical framework. Culture is understood as an inter-subjectively shared cognitive system in the form of distributed cognition, heterogeneously shared by members of a speech community (Sharifian 2017: 6). Cultural conceptualisations embody group-level cognitive systems such as worldview and can take the form of cultural categories (classes for objects and events), cultural metaphors (cross-domain conceptualisations as in Cognitive Linguistics, but culturally grounded), and cultural schemas (cognitive schemas – aka frames, scripts) that are culturally constructed and serve as basis for communicating and interpreting cultural meanings (Sharifian 2017: 8). In the process of the localisation of English, cultural conceptualisations encoded in (indigenous) contact languages enter local Englishes to express cultural conceptualisations and world views.

An illustrative and often-cited example is the Ghanaian cultural schema of introducing a newborn to the local community. In a traditional ceremony a baby is brought outside for the first time, usually eight days after the birth. In the indigenous language and culture of the Ga this is lexicalised by the word *kpodziemo* 'going out'. In Ghanaian English this concept has been lexicalised through the noun *outdooring* that according to the *Oxford English Dictionary* (OED 2021a) was modelled on the lexical item in Ga and is first attested in 1954. Subsequently, this lead to the formation of a corresponding verb *outdoor* (first attested in 1962, OED 2021b). In the course of time, semantic widening has occurred in that the meaning of *outdoor(ing)* is extended to refer to the occasion of presenting someone (e.g. a person running for office) or something in public for the first time, see the following examples from the Ghanaian component of the *Global Web-based English* corpus (GloWbE = Davies 2013).

(1) Mobile telephone network, Tigo has **outdoored** the first ever unlimited time-based internet prepaid service at a short ceremony in Accra.
(2) With barely two weeks to the crunch 2012 general elections in the country, the only independent candidate in the race, Mr Jacob Osei Yeboah, has finally **outdoored** his running-mate, Mr Kelvin Nii Takie, 41, who hails from NII Teiko Tsuru We, of the Akropong Royal House.
(3) The launch marks the official **outdooring** of a series of Ghana Decides online and offline activities including the iRegistered campaign meant to propel young voters to go out in numbers, register and take videos or pictures of themselves doing so or after registering.

Brato (2018: 29) argues that this extended meaning is now deeply entrenched in the vocabulary of Ghanaian English and occurs even much more frequently than that of the traditional meaning. It seems unlikely that the corresponding term *kpodziemo* 'going out' in Ga has also participated in this semantic shift.

3 Nigerian English, Nigerian Pidgin English, and the social and cultural significance of proverbs in Nigeria

The history of English in mainland West Africa can be divided into two major phases: early contacts through trading between the 16th and 17th centuries (this phase includes the emergence and development of West African Pidgin English) and later contact through colonization and missionary activities from the 19th century to the 1960s with large-scale import of Western religion and education, and increasing contact with formal English. Ghana, Nigeria, and Cameroon are former British administrative colonies.

According to Schneider (2007: 199ff.) English was introduced in Nigeria with the establishment of British trading contacts on the West African coast in 16th and 17th centuries, but this contact was largely restricted to (slave) trade. Only in the 1880s were missionary stations ordered to teach English in their schools to Africans who would serve British colonial and trade interests. Colonization became formalized after the partitioning of Africa at the Berlin Conference of 1884, and Nigeria became a colony of Britain in 1914 with English being firmly established as the language of administration, education, commerce, and law. Nigeria gained its independence in 1960, and English was made the official language.

English is fully entrenched in social life and institutionalized across different linguistic domains of Nigerian society such as business, advertising, administration, education, mass media, science and technology, and law. While there are no accurate figures as to the number of speakers of English, going by the literacy level of the population (which is largely equated with the ability to use English), 57% of the 140 million people in Nigeria speak or understand English to some extent (Taiwo 2012: 410). English is considered an ethnically neutral language and thus serves as a tool for effective cross-cultural and inter-ethnic communication. Nigeria is a republic, a federation of separate regions based on tribal affiliations (the main ethnic groups are the Yoruba and the Igbo who both speak languages of the same name). Nigeria is a highly multilingual country with an enormous diversity of native languages, English operating side by side with these. While it is not exactly clear how many languages are spoken in Nigeria, the Ethnologue database of language resources (Ethnologue 2022) lists 520 for Nigeria. The three major indigenous languages are Hausa, Igbo, and Yoruba, and are also recognized as main provincial languages because they are spoken by a majority of people in regional parts.

While there is still a strong exonormative orientation towards British and American English in Nigerian society, in research on World Englishes Nigerian English (NigE) is considered a nativising variety of English that functions as a second language and that receives increasing recognition and codification (see, for example, Salazar 2020 on the recent update to the OED that included numerous innovations from NigE). However, there is no uniform proficiency and accent of English spoken throughout Nigeria because sociolinguistic parameters of variation are important, just as in other second-language varieties of English. Social lects are usually being correlated with levels of formal education. Udofot (2003) suggests a (post-creole) lectal continuum of degree of competence in English with three to four levels of proficiency in the use of English that broadly correspond to levels of education (see also Jowitt 2019: 28ff.):

- Level 1 (Pidgin): no formal education;
- Level 2: only primary education completed (basilect);
- Level 3: primary and secondary education completed (mesolect);
- Level 4: university education completed (upper mesolect / acrolect = local standard).

Even more widespread than English is Nigerian Pidgin English (NPE), a product of the contact between English and Nigerian languages. It has no official status but is estimated to be used by more than 50% of the population on official or semi-official occasions (at least in the south; see Schneider 2007: 204; Faraclas 2012). Faraclas (2012: 418) considers it "undoubtedly the most widely spoken, readily learned, practically useful, and fastest growing language in Nigeria today". NPE is locally perceived as an informal variant of English, used as a main language of daily communication in contact venues like schools and markets, but is at the same time stigmatized and associated with socially inferior strata. It is learned as a first language among the urban population especially in the south but also elsewhere in the country, a majority of the rural population of the southeast, and a minority of rural population elsewhere. Importantly, there are millions of users in the diaspora (see, for example, Honkanen 2020), thus, strictly speaking, a creolizing language with an estimate of 3–5 million native speakers.

Proverbs are a common speech strategy among Nigerians, and the frequent use of proverbs is a characteristic feature of both speakers of NigE and NPE. According to Nwachukwu-Agbada, the ethnic languages are particularly rich in proverbs, illustrating the linguistic impact of folk culture and traditional wisdom of the different groups (Nwachukwu-Agbada 1990, 1991): "[t]he ethnic languages will perforce influences its depth of imagery, color and metaphor. Locale, landscape, morals, norms and syntax will combine in appropriate amounts yielding meaning in Pidgin proverbs" (Nwachukwu-Agbada 1990: 39). Nwachukwu-Agbada (1990: 37) further argues that, in the urban context where the indigenous languages can no longer fulfil all communicative needs, the traditional speech strategy of the proverb has been carried over into the popular lingua franca, NPE. The distinguishing feature of the NPE stock of proverbs is that it draws on the traditions of different ethnic groups and also includes new proverbs which reflect the modern urban setting (Nwachukwu-Agbada 1991: 128).

Mensah (2013: 89) highlights the linguistic, literary, and ethnographic potential of proverbs which he describes as "unique forms of oral art that are detached somehow from the knowledge system of NP [Nigerian Pidgin, MC] superstrate and substrate languages and cultures". He also emphasises the important social functions of proverbs in NPE. For example, they can function as a social control mechanism to support moral instruction and sanction unethical and immoral behavior, foster the cultivation of positive societal values such as patience, circumspection, and (team)work (Mensah 2013: 92). Proverbs also play a major role in advertising and the music industry.

Deuber (2002) provides an analysis of NPE used in newstexts (radio broadcasts in the Pidgin Section of Radio Nigeria 3 and non-broadcast speech) to examine the nature and extent of English influences in NPE spoken by educated speakers, i.e. those who have completed at least secondary education. She observes that the newscasters add proverbs that are not part of the original English scripts to introduce each news item (Deuber 2002: 203). Apparently, these illustrate the impact of traditional West African culture by means of a discourse convention of putting the moral of a story up front which in a nutshell (and by using indigenous metaphors) spells out the core message of the news item (Schneider 2011: 147). Deuber further argues that by using the proverbs the newscasters seem to have found an ideal strategy for relating the news to folk culture and traditional wisdom.

NPE proverbs also feature prominently on the internet and in social media. In August 2017, the BBC launched a digital service in Pidgin English for West African audiences at https://www.bbc.com/pidgin. NPE proverbs seem to be one means by which this new service is popularised because proverbs frequently feature on the service's social media services on Twitter (https://twitter.com/ bbcnewspidgin) and especially on Instagram (https://www.instagram.com/ bbcnewspidgin/). This apparently supports the proliferation of Pidgin English proverbs, in particular through the hashtags #pidginproverb/s and #naijaproverb/s.

Honkanen (2020) studied the linguistic repertoires of Nigerians living in the United States who use African-American Vernacular English, Nigerian English, Nigerian Pidgin, and ethnic Nigerian languages in an online community. She found that proverbs are frequently used in online communication, and often so in the three main ethnic languages used in the forum (Igbo, Yoruba, Hausa). While reproducing them in the ethnic source language associated with the culture provides added value, users regularly provide a translation in English (Honkanen 2020: 261), because many of these proverbs are language- and culture-specific.

4 The cognitive motivations of idioms and proverbs and their potential role in linguistic acculturation

Idioms have long been thought to be frozen phraseological units of language that fall outside of metaphorical thought and linguistic creativity, and whose meaning is semantically non-compositional and thus, non-transparent (Gibbs 2007). Findings in psycholinguistics and Cognitive Linguistics, however, have shown that idioms as a particular kind of figurative language are in large numbers motivated by underlying conceptual metaphorical mappings (as summarized, for instance, in Gibbs 2007), thus reflect metaphorical thought and the culture-specific nature of figurative language, at the same time being subject to linguistic creativity and lexico-grammatical variability (Langlotz 2006).

Phraseology and idioms are promising starting points for the identification of possible conceptual, structurally nativised linguistic markers of World Englishes (Schneider 2007: 46, 86). For example, Bamgbose (1992: 155f.) claims that "most differences between Nigerian English and other forms of English are to be found in the innovations in lexical items and idioms and their meanings". In this spirit, several recent studies have been devoted to West African Englishes (e.g. Fiedler 2016; Callies 2017, 2021). Still, when compared to the field of lexico-grammar, there is relatively little research on idiomatic phraseology and figurative language use in varieties of English. Platt et al. (1984: 107) were the first to draw up a taxonomy of idioms in New Englishes which they at the time referred to as "learners' attempts to use a British English or American English idiom" that are not (yet) "true, stabilized idioms in the New English". Their taxonomy includes six types as follows:
1) blending of two existing idiomatic expressions into one new idiom (e.g. Singapore English *be in hot soup* 'be in trouble' from Standard (British) English *be in hot water* and *be in the soup*);

2) variants of existing idioms in speech or writing due to pronunciation differences in that particular variety (e.g. Singapore English *in lips and bounce* for British English *in leaps and bounds*);
3) lexico-grammatical variants of existing British or American English idioms (e.g. Singapore English *eat your cake and have it* instead of *have your cake and eat it*);
4) expressions combining elements from English with indigenous forms (e.g. Nigerian English *put sand in someone's gar(r)i* 'threaten someone's livelihood', 'interfere with someone's good fortune' [*gar(i)i* = according to the OED a borrowing from Igbo *gàrị* and Yoruba *gàrí*, designating a type of flour];
5) loan translations of idioms from indigenous languages (e.g. Malaysian English *shake legs* 'be idle' as a translation of Malay idiom *goyang kaki* 'rocking away');
6) true innovations (e.g. East African English idiom *be on the tarmac* 'seek a new job').

Obviously, types 4 and 5 are of utmost importance for the present discussion.

Lakoff and Turner (1989) suggest that proverbs have a conceptual basis, too. They argue that proverbs evoke schemas that are rich in images and information, such as knowledge of nature, common animals, objects, and situations. While proverbs thus specify a source domain, such as NATURE, ANIMALS, or OBJECTS, they often do not specify the target domain. Still, speakers intuitively know that the implied target is the HUMAN domain. Lakoff and Turner suggest a complex mechanism called the GREAT CHAIN METAPHOR for the comprehension of proverbs. The key components are 1) a single generic-level metaphor GENERIC IS SPECIFIC, which has variable source and target domains and provides a general cognitive mechanism for understanding the general in terms of the specific, one of the key features of proverbs; and 2) The Great Chain of Being, "a cultural model that concerns kinds of beings and their properties and places them on a vertical scale with "higher" beings [such as humans, MC] and properties above "lower" beings [such as animals, MC] and properties" (Lakoff and Turner 1989: 166f.).

As for proverbs and language contact, calquing / loan translation from indigenous languages has been identified as a frequent process in the literature on African Englishes, especially with a view to proverbs and idioms (see, for instance, Schmied 1991: 92f.; Skandera 2003: ch. 10). In NPE a substantial number of proverbs appear to be "sourced, word-for-word, from indigenous languages" such as Igbo and Yoruba (Mensah 2013: 104). Mensah (2013: 105) notes that about 15% of the proverbs in his corpus are actually rooted in indigenous languages according to his informants. An often cited example is *Water don pass garri*, literally 'Water has passed garri', metaphorically meaning 'The problem is beyond a solution' (Jowitt 2019: 136). Proverbs, and also idioms, can thus be assumed to be a rich source of culture-specific lexis and conceptualisations in African Englishes.

Importantly, to establish the link between proverbs and idioms, previous studies suggest that proverbs may serve as the basis for the emergence and formation of idioms and other types of figurative language (e.g. Fiedler 2016). Gibbs (2007: 713) notes that traditional proverbs and sayings are "truncated from their canonical or earliest forms to create lower-level grammatical units". In other words, proverbs may feed into the formation of new idioms in a language contact situation. One case in point is the NPE proverb *If life dey show you pepper, make pepper soup* ('If life shows you pepper, make pepper soup', meaning 'Make something good out of a bad experience'). This proverb is apparently the source of the Nigerian English idiom *show someone pepper* 'give someone a hard time' (see Callies 2017: 77). Kperogi (2015: 163) argues that the related, but less frequently attested forms *see/smell pepper* are direct translations from major native Nigerian languages like Igbo and Yoruba and were exclusively used in Nigerian Pidgin English but now also appear in educated Nigerian English. Callies (2017) shows that the transitively used and thus more conceptually flexible variant *show someone pepper* can be considered a variety-specific signature-idiom of Nigerian English.

5 Conclusion and outlook

Despite the enormous proliferation of research into World Englishes, the linguistic impact of pragmatic, cognitive and cultural features (as manifest e.g. in cultural keywords and different kinds of figurative language use) have largely been neglected. Questions of the role of the local linguistic ecologies in the evolution of New Englishes, and how they interact with sociolinguistic and cultural factors, are receiving increasing attention. Such research has a rich potential for exploring if and how the culturally diverse settings in which Englishes have formed and are developing enrich the local cultural phraseology.

The conceptual background and initial observations delineated in this contribution warrant and necessitate more systematic and comprehensive empirical research. A shortlist of frequently used Nigerian Pidgin proverbs can be drawn up on the basis of earlier collections (for example Nwachukwu-Agbada 1990, 1991; Mensah 2013). Importantly, the use of proverbs on social media, especially on Twitter and Instagram, provides large, very recent and thus valuable data for the study of linguistic innovations. Research on the use of World Englishes in digital media and on social media platforms is receiving increasing attention as well, see for instance the abovementioned study by Honkanen (2020) on the "Nairaland" web forum and the recent thematic issue on World Englishes and digital media edited by Lee (2020). Access to that kind of data makes it possible to identify recurrent themes and keywords in proverbs, such as those relating to food (eating and drinking) and animals (see Callies forthcoming). These can then serve as lexical anchors for searches in large-scale electronic corpora that aim at detecting patterns or fixed expressions that may be interpreted as innovations at the early stages of idiom formation (see e.g. Callies and Oyebola forthcoming).

Finally, in view of some strong parallels between English and other pluricentric languages such as Spanish and Portuguese, as well as the scarcity of research into the cognitive and culture-specific grounding of figurative language in these languages, future comparative research seems a fruitful undertaking.

Abbreviations

CL	Cognitive Linguistics
CMT	Conceptual Metaphor Theory
OED	Oxford English Dictionary
PCE	Postcolonial English
NigE	Nigerian English
NPE	Nigerian Pidgin English
STL	settler strand
IDG	indigenous population

References

Achebe, Chinua. 1996. *Things fall apart*. Portsmouth, NH: Heinemann.
Anchimbe, Eric A. 2018. *Offers and offer refusals: A postcolonial pragmatics perspective on World Englishes*. Amsterdam: Benjamins.
Bamgbose, Ayo. 1992. Standard Nigerian English: Issues of identification. In Braj B. Kachru (ed.), *The other tongue. English across cultures*, 148–161. Urbana, Ill: University of Illinois Press.

Bartens, Angela. 2013. Creole languages. In Peter Bakker & Yaron Matras (eds.), *Contact languages. A comprehensive guide*, 65–158. Berlin: De Gruyter Mouton.

Brato, Thorsten. 2018. 'Outdooring' the historical corpus of English in Ghana. *English Today* 34. 25–34.

Callies, Marcus. 2017. 'Idioms in the making' as evidence for variation in conceptual metaphor across varieties of English. *Cognitive Linguistic Studies* 4(1). 65–83.

Callies, Marcus. 2021. Comparing large electronic corpora and elicitation techniques in research on conceptual metaphor and idioms in world Englishes: Validating the "lexicon of corruption" in West African Englishes. In Marcus Callies & Marta Degani (eds.), *Metaphor in language and culture across world Englishes*, 33–52. London: Bloomsbury Academic.

Callies, Marcus. 2024. Cultural keywords in World Englishes. In Kingsley Bolton (ed.), *Wiley Blackwell Encyclopedia of World Englishes*.

Callies, Marcus. forthcoming. Cultural conceptualisations and phraseology in Nigerian Pidgin English proverbs. World Englishes.

Callies, Marcus & Marta Degani (eds.). 2021. *Metaphor in language and culture across world Englishes*. London: Bloomsbury Academic.

Callies, Marcus & Folajimi Oyebola. forthcoming. Pidgin English proverbs as a source of structural nativization in Nigerian English. World Englishes.

Callies, Marcus & Alexander Onysko (eds.). 2017. Metaphor variation in Englishes around the world. Special issue of the *Cognitive Linguistic Studies* 4(1).

Davies, Mark. 2013. *Corpus of global web-based English: 1.9 billion words from speakers in 20 countries*. https://www.english-corpora.org/glowbe/

Deuber, Dagmar. 2002. "First year of nation's return to government of make you talk your own make I talk my own". Anglicisms versus pidginization in news translations into Nigerian Pidgin. *English World-Wide* 23(2). 195–222.

Ethnologue. 2022. *Nigeria*. https://www.ethnologue.com/country/ng.

Faraclas, Nicolas. 2012. Nigerian Pidgin English. In Bernd Kortmann & Kerstin Lunkenheimer (eds.), *The Mouton world atlas of variation in English*, 417–432. Berlin: Mouton de Gruyter.

Fiedler, Astrid. 2016. Fixed expressions and culture. The idiomatic monkey in common core and West African varieties of English. *International Journal of Language and Culture* 3(2). 189–215.

Finzel, Anna & Hans-Georg Wolf. 2019. Conceptual metaphors as contact phenomena? The influence of local concepts on source and target domain. In Eline Zenner, Ad Backus & Esme Winter-Froemel (eds.), *Cognitive contact linguistics: Placing usage, meaning and mind at the core of contact-induced variation and change*, 187–211. Berlin: Mouton de Gruyter.

Gibbs, Raymond W. Jr. 2007. Idioms and formulaic language. In Dirk Geeraerts & Hubert Cuyckens (eds.), *The Oxford handbook of cognitive linguistics*, 697–725. Oxford: Oxford University Press.

Grant, Anthony (ed.). 2019. *The Oxford handbook of language contact*. Oxford: Oxford University Press.

Hickey, Raymond (ed.). 2020. *The handbook of language contact*. Hoboken, NJ: Wiley-Blackwell.

Honkanen. Mirka. 2020. *World Englishes on the web. The Nigerian diaspora in the USA*. Amsterdam: Benjamins.

Jowitt, David. 2019. *Nigerian English*. Boston & Berlin: De Gruyter Mouton.

Kirkpatrick, Andy. 2015. World Englishes and local cultures. In Farzad Sharifian (ed.), *The Routledge handbook of language and culture*, 460–470. London & New York: Routledge.
Kövecses, Zoltan. 2000. *Metaphor and emotion: Language, culture, and body in human feelings*. Cambridge: Cambridge University Press.
Kövecses, Zoltan. 2005. *Metaphor in culture. Universality and variation*. Cambridge: Cambridge University Press.
Kperogi, Farooq A. 2015. *Glocal English: The changing face and forms of Nigerian English in a global world*. New York: Peter Lang.
Kristiansen, Gitte, Karlien Franco, Stefano De Pascale, Laura Rosseel & Weiwei Zhang (eds.). 2021. *Cognitive sociolinguistics revisited*. Berlin & Boston: De Gruyter Mouton.
Lambert, James. 2020. Lexicography and world Englishes. In Daniel Schreier, Marianne Hundt & Edgar W. Schneider (eds.), *The Cambridge handbook of world Englishes*, 408–435. Cambridge: Cambridge University Press.
Lakoff, George & Mark Johnson. 1980. *Metaphors we live by*. Chicago: The University of Chicago Press.
Lakoff, George & Mark Turner. 1989. *More than cool reason. A field guide to poetic metaphor*. Chicago & London: The University of Chicago Press.
Langlotz, Andreas. 2006. *Idiomatic creativity. A cognitive-linguistic model of idiom-representation and idiom-variation in English*. Amsterdam: Benjamins.
Lee, Jamie Shinhee. 2020. Digital communication, social media, and Englishes. *World Englishes* 39. 2–6.
Levisen, Carsten & Sophia Waters. 2017. How words do things with people. In Carsten Levisen & Sophia Waters (eds.), *Cultural keywords in discourse*, 1–23. Amsterdam: Benjamins.
Mensah, Eyo O. 2013. Proverbs in Nigerian Pidgin. *Journal of Anthropological Research* 69(1). 87–115.
Mesthrie, Rajend. 2020. Contact and African Englishes. In Raymond Hickey (ed.), *The handbook of language contact*, 385–401. Hoboken, NJ: Wiley-Blackwell.
Mühleisen, Susanne & Bettina Migge (eds.). 2005. *Politeness and face in Caribbean creoles*. Amsterdam: Benjamins.
Mukherjee, Joybrato & Tobias Bernaisch. 2015. Cultural keywords in context. A pilot study of linguistic acculturation in South Asian Englishes. In Peter Collins (ed.), *Grammatical change in English world-wide*, 411–435. Amsterdam: Benjamins.
Nwachukwu-Agbada, Joseph O. J. 1990. Nigerian Pidgin proverbs. *Lore and Language* 9(1). 37–43.
Nwachukwu-Agbada, Joseph O. J. 1991. Wisdom in a melting-pot: Nigerian urban folk and Pidgin English proverbs. *International Folklore Review* 8. 125–129.
Oxford English Dictionary (OED) online. 2021a. *outdooring*, n. Oxford: Oxford University Press. https://www.oed.com/view/Entry/240646.
Oxford English Dictionary (OED) online. 2021b. *outdoor*, v. Oxford: Oxford University Press. https://www.oed.com/view/Entry/257552.
Palmer, Gary B. 1996. *Toward a theory of cultural linguistics*. Austin, TX: University of Texas Press.
Peters, Pam & Kate Burridge (eds.). 2021. *Exploring the ecology of world Englishes in the twenty-first century. Language, society and culture*. Edinburgh: Edinburgh University Press.
Platt, John, Heidi Weber & Ho Mian Lian. 1984. *The New Englishes*. London: Routledge.

Polzenhagen, Frank & Hans-Georg Wolf. 2021. Culture-specific conceptualisations of corruption in African English: Linguistic analyses and pragmatic applications. In Marzieh Sadeghpour & Farzad Sharifian (eds.), *Cultural linguistics and world Englishes,* 361–399. Singapore: Springer.

Sadeghpour, Marzieh & Farzad Sharifian (eds.). 2021. *Cultural linguistics and world Englishes.* Singapore: Springer.

Salazar, Danica. 2020. OED release notes: Nigerian English. https://public.oed.com/blog/nigerian-english-release-notes/

Salazar, Danica. 2021. Documenting world Englishes in the *Oxford English Dictionary*: Past perspectives, present developments, and future directions. In Alexander Onysko (ed.), *Research developments in world Englishes,* 271–294. London: Bloomsbury Academic.

Schmied, Josef. 1991. *English in Africa: An introduction.* London: Longman.

Schneider, Edgar W. 2007. *Postcolonial English. Varieties around the world.* Cambridge: Cambridge University Press.

Schneider, Edgar W. 2011. *English around the world.* Cambridge: Cambridge University Press.

Sharifian, Farzad. 2015. Cultural Linguistics and World Englishes. *World Englishes* 34(4). 515–532.

Sharifian, Farzad. 2017. *Cultural Linguistics. Cultural conceptualisations and language.* Amsterdam: Benjamins.

Sharifian, Farzad, Ning Yu, Réné Dirven & Susanne Niemeier (eds.). 2008. *Culture, body, and language: Conceptualizations of internal body organs across cultures and languages.* Berlin: Mouton de Gruyter.

Skandera, Paul. 2003. *Drawing a map of Africa: Idiom in Kenyan English.* Tübingen: Gunter Narr.

Soares da Silva, Augusto. 2013. *Pluricentricity: Language variation and sociocognitive dimensions.* Berlin & Boston: De Gruyter Mouton.

Soares da Silva, Augusto. 2021. Measuring the impact of (non)figurativity in the cultural conceptualization of emotions in the two main national varieties of Portuguese. In Augusto Soares da Silva (ed.), *Figurative Language: Intersubjectivity and usage,* 387–438. Amsterdam: John Benjamins.

Sridar, Kamal K. 2012. Acculturation in World Englishes. *The Encyclopedia of Applied Linguistics.* https://doi.org/10.1002/9781405198431.wbeal0005.

Stubbs, Michael. 1996. *Text and corpus analysis: Computer assisted studies of language and culture.* Oxford: Blackwell.

Stubbs, Michael. 2002. *Words and phrases. Corpus studies of lexical semantics.* Oxford: Blackwell.

Taiwo, Rotimi. 2012. Nigerian English. In Bernd Kortmann & Kerstin Lunkenheimer (eds.), *The Mouton world atlas of variation in English,* 410–416. Berlin: Mouton de Gruyter.

Udofot, Inyang. 2003. Stress and rhythm in the Nigerian accent of English. *English World Wide* 24. 201–220.

Wierzbicka, Anna. 1997. *Understanding cultures through their key words: English, Russian, Polish, German, and Japanese.* New York: Oxford University Press.

Williams, Raymond. 1976. *Keywords: A vocabulary of culture and society.* London: Croom Helm.

Wolf, Hans-Georg & Frank Polzenhagen. 2007. Fixed expressions as manifestations of cultural conceptualizations: Examples from African varieties of English. In Paul Skandera (ed.), *Phraseology and culture in English,* 399–435. Berlin: Mouton de Gruyter.

Wolf, Hans-Georg & Frank Polzenhagen. 2009. *World Englishes. A cognitive sociolinguistic approach*. Berlin: Mouton de Gruyter.
Wolf, Hans-Georg, Frank Polzenhagen & Arne Peters (eds.). 2017. Cultural linguistic contributions to World Englishes. Thematic issue of the *International Journal of Language and Culture* 4(2).
Wolf, Hans-Georg & Thomas Chan. 2016. Understanding Asia by means of cognitive sociolinguistics and cultural linguistics. The example of GHOSTS in Hong Kong English. In Gerhard Leitner, Azirah Hashim & Hans-Georg Wolf (eds.), *Communicating with Asia: The future of English as a global language*, 249–266. Cambridge: Cambridge University Press.
Zenner, Eline, Ad Backus & Esme Winter-Froemel (eds.). 2019. *Cognitive contact linguistics: Placing usage, meaning and mind at the core of contact-induced variation and change*. Berlin: Mouton de Gruyter.

Diana Forker and Ala Al Sheshani
Far beyond the Caucasus

Chechen in contact with Jordanian Arabic

Abstract: This paper examines the impact of Arabic on the East Caucasian (Nakh-Daghestanian) language Chechen in Jordan. Chechens settled down on the territory of today's Kingdom of Jordan around 120 years ago. All Jordanian Chechens are bilingual and use Chechen as an oral community language and Arabic for all other purposes on a daily basis. The paper provides an overview about influences of Jordanian Arabic on the lexicon and the morphosyntax of Chechen. The influence of Arabic on the Chechen lexicon is growing, especially among young speakers, and loan words are morphosyntactically integrated into the recipient language. With respect to syntax only little impact can be detected concerning constituent order in main clauses and complex sentences. The paper also briefly compares Jordanian Chechen with Caucasian Chechen and concludes that despite some sociolinguistic difference the linguistic impact of the genealogically and typologically diverse majority languages Arabic and Russian on one and the same minority language Chechen exhibits more commonalities than differences. Therefore, heritage language studies should be extended to oral languages such as Chechen and collaborate with studies on endangered minority languages.

Keywords: Chechen, Arabic, Jordan, language contact, borrowing, heritage language

1 Introduction

Though in recent years more and more Caucasian languages have been documented and studied in great detail, systematic studies of language contact are rare. We know little about the impact of Russian or Turkic languages, Arabic or Persian on the languages of the Caucasus and this knowledge is largely restricted to investigations of loan words, see, e.g. the studies on loan words in languages

---

Diana Forker, University of Jena, Department of Caucasus Studies, Jenergasse 8, 07743 Jena, Germany. E-mail: diana.forker@uni-jena.de
Ala Al Sheshani, Göttingen University, English Department, Käte-Hamburger-Weg 3, 37073 Göttingen, Germany.

https://doi.org/10.1515/9783111323756-003

of the northern Caucasus such as Comrie and Khalilov (2009), Chumakina (2009), Chechuro (2021), and Chechuro et al. (2021). There are only very few works with a broader focus that examine also other areas of the grammar in which contact-induced changes can be observed (e.g. Höhlig 1997; Forker 2019a, b). We know even less on those Caucasian languages whose speakers fled to the Ottoman Empire and whose descendants today live in Turkey, Jordan, Syria, Israel, or Lebanon. Published works are devoted to the sociolinguistic situation, mostly with respect to West Caucasian languages (e.g. Chirikba 1997; Al-Wer 1999; Dweik 2000; Abd-el-Jawad 2006; Rannut 2011; Kailani 2002; Alomoush 2015; Suleiman 2008). The only studies regarding the lexical and/or structural impact on Caucasian languages are Höhlig (1997), Kutscher (2008), Bağnıaçık et al. (2015), and Alagozlu (2007), and in all works the dominant language is Turkish. The impact of Arabic – one of the largest languages (or cluster of languages) in the world – on minority languages has also not been investigated in great detail. In particular there are almost no studies with Arabic as majority language and oral minority languages from other language families than Semitic, Iranian or Turkic such as, e.g., Caucasian languages (but see the studies in Part II of Lucas and Manfredi 2020: 351–550).

In this pilot study we want to contribute to language contact studies involving Arabic and Caucasian languages by highlighting the major traits of Chechen-Arabic language contact in Jordan. Thus, we want to pave the way for comparative investigations in which either the dominant language or the dominated language are kept constant. As Stolz (2008: 2) writes referring, among others, to Johanson (2000), "it makes good sense methodologically to work with one constant and several variables when comparing language contact situations". Today, the main contact language for Chechen in the Caucasus is Russian. For the Chechen minorities in Georgia, Turkey, Jordan, or Syria major contact languages are Georgian, Turkish, and Arabic. This makes the study of Chechen particularly interesting because we can compare the impact of dominant contact languages that differ genetically and typologically (Kartvelian, Turkic, Semitic) on one and the same (minority) language.

But our goal is not solely descriptive. We will also suggest that Chechen in Jordan is a heritage language that actually undergoes a similar process of language change as Chechen in the Caucasus.

Before coming to the data a few words on the problem of how to distinguish between borrowing and code-switching are in order. We follow the viewpoint of those linguists who maintain that there is no clear-cut distinction between the two processes (e.g. Gardner-Chloros 1987; Matras 2009: 110–114). In this paper, we will mainly speak of "borrowed" or "loan" items but we do not want to imply that all instances of Jordanian Arabic words used in Chechen conversations are fully integrated and clearly part of Chechen grammar. All Jordanian Chechens are bilingual and naturally switch between the two languages. There are no monolingual speakers of Jordanian Chechen who could serve as comparative group to bilingual Jordanian Chechens and we do not have a corpus that is representative of Jordanian Chechen in order to count for frequency and compare different speakers. Therefore, Arabic items should be interpreted as insertions. In order to facilitate the identification of Arabic words, they are indicated by [AR] in the glosses of the examples.

The data that we use for this paper has been gathered by Al Sheshani who is a member of the Jordanian Chechen community and a bilingual speaker of Arabic and Chechen. The data are mostly private conversations with another bilingual speaker of Arabic and Chechen from the same community that have partially been transcribed by Al Sheshani and complemented by data from some other community members (Al Sheshani 2020). These data will be marked as "data from Al Sheshani" and "Jordanian Chechen" in the paper. However, we do not have enough transcribed materials to make quantifications. In addition, we also use published literature on Chechen, which is restricted to the variety of Chechen spoken in the Northern Caucasus in the autonomous Republic of Chechnya (Russian Federation) and elicited examples from our colleague Zarina Molochieva, who is a native speaker of Caucasian Chechen.[1] Caucasian Chechen and Jordanian Chechen are mutually understandable and most of the constructions used in Caucasian Chechen are equally used in Jordanian Chechen. Therefore, it is not always possible or meaningful to attribute certain elicited or published examples which are grammatical in both varieties to Jordanian Chechen or Caucasian Chechen, and in those cases we will limit ourselves to the label "Chechen".

For Chechen items we use the transliteration system by Nichols (1994) and Komen et al. (2021). For the transliteration of Jordanian Arabic we follow Herin and Al-Wer (2022) and other works from the same authors. For two consonants that exist in both languages this leads to the somewhat unsatisfying situation of representing them with two different letters, depending on the language: /ħ/ is written as *ħ* in all Chechen words and as *ḥ* in Arabic loans; Arabic /ɣ/, written here as *ġ* largely corresponds to Chechen *gh*, but the Chechen sound can also be realized as the uvular allophone [ʁ].

---

1 By "Caucasian Chechen" we refer to Chechen in the Chechen Republic and in parts of Dagestan with a large Chechen population, but not to Chechen spoken in Georgia.

Our paper is structured as follows. In Section 2, we sketch the sociolinguistic background of Jordanian Chechen. We then provide linguistic profiles of Chechen and Jordanian Arabic that highlight major grammatical differences of the two languages (Section 3). In Section 4, we present our own data from Jordan, organized according to lexical classes and grammatical topics. We start with borrowed particles and adverbials, followed by adjectives, verbs and nouns. We also analyze constituent order and complex sentences. In Section 5, we define the concept of "heritage language" and compare Jordanian Chechen to Caucasian Chechen. Section 6 contains the conclusion.

2 Sociolinguistic background: The Chechens of Jordan

Chechens began to settle in Jordan in 1901/1902 in the aftermath of the Russian conquest of the Caucasus (Al-Wer 1999; Jaimoukha 2005: 238–239; Alomoush 2015: 83–84). They established a few settlements and today mainly live in four settlements (Zarqa, Sweileh, Al-Suhknah, and Al-Azraq), relatively close to the Circassian neighborhoods in and around Amman that were established some twenty years earlier. Estimations of the Chechen community in Jordan vary between around 9,000 (Alomoush 2015) and 15,000 (Jaimoukha 2005: 238). In a personal interview a member of the community from Amman estimated the number at about 12,000. Many Chechens of Jordan live in close neighborhood with other Chechens and only 30 to 40 years ago Chechen children still grew up mainly speaking Chechen with their family members, friends and neighbors.

Jordan is a country in which Caucasian diasporas enjoy the greatest freedom and the highest esteem (see Suleiman 2008 for an overview of the language ecology of Jordan). Chechens often work for the government, the army and public security. Together with Circassians, they have their own representatives in the Jordanian parliament and have traditionally a close relationship with the ruling Hashemite family. Chechens established their own cultural centers, associations and clubs, councils, magazines, etc. The only official language in Jordan is Arabic and Chechen is exclusively used as an oral language. Some Chechens organize private classes for teaching the Cyrillic alphabet that is used in the northern Caucasus.

The most detailed sociolinguistic study of the Chechen community in Jordan by Dweik (2000) is based on interviews with 100 Chechens (age 10 to 59) of the third- and fourth-generation. He shows that already at the time of his study around the year 2000 basically all Chechens were bilingual. Chechen is in a diglossic relationship with Arabic and almost exclusively used as an oral language. The major functional domains of Chechen are private situations within the family, among friends and relatives, in the neighborhood, at school and in the market place. In general, the Chechens of Jordan have largely maintained their language and culture (see also Alomoush 2015 for a more recent study that comes to a similar conclusion). According to Dweik (2000), this is due to the tight social networks among community members and residential closeness, which allows daily interactions, resistance to ethnically mixed marriages, and a positive attitude towards the Chechen language and culture, which serve as strong identity markers, and the original homeland. In her comparative study of Chechen and Circassian communities in Jordan from around the same period of time, Al-Wer (1999: 266) stresses the fact that the traditional social organization of the Chechens has an "egalitarian structure with a non-hereditary unified leadership, which helped to maintain the unity of the group in the new social and political contests." Language shift is generally favored by urbanization. In the case of the Jordanian Chechens we can state that a large part of them lived and continue to live in the rural areas of Al-Suhknah and Al-Azraq where networks are tighter than in Sweileh (today a district of Amman) and Zarqa, the second largest city of Jordan (Al-Wer 1999). Chechens generally have a higher education than other ethnic groups of Jordan and are economically and politically strong (Haddad and Kailani 2004). Therefore, despite being a minority, they are not marginalized or face a pressure to assimilate to the majority population. Kailani (2002) adds to this that the maintenance of an independent Chechen identity in Jordan has also been possible because the concepts of nation and national citizenship are not that important and established in the Middle East. Jordan is, in fact, a young state and Chechens have settled on today's Jordanian territory when it was still a part of the Ottoman Empire.

Our own observations, in particular Al Sheshani's personal links with the community which she is a member of, largely confirm these studies. Chechens often marry within their community or with Circassians. The majority of them speaks Chechen at home and with other Chechens. A large number of children still grow up acquiring Chechen as their first language and get introduced to Arabic when they start going to kindergarten.

Yet we have also observed indications that point towards a slow but continuous shift towards the dominant language. There are more and more families in which Arabic is used on a daily basis and children of those families are Arabic-dominant even before they enter kindergarten or school. On the other hand, English-Chechen code-switching may surface in the speech of these children due to the rapidly increasing exposure to English media. As predicted by Al-Wer (1999), we assume that language shift will happen faster in the urban settlements of Zarqa and Sweileh than in the rather rural settlements of Al-Suhknah and Al-Azraq.

3 Linguistic profiles of Chechen and Jordanian Arabic

The grammatical properties of Chechen and Jordanian Arabic are quite divergent, which comes as no surprise since the languages belong to different language families. Chechen (Glottolog chec1245, ISO 639-3 che) is an East Caucasian or Nakh-Daghestanian language from the Nakh branch. Arabic belongs to the Semitic languages. Jordanian Arabic (together with Palestinian Arabic) is a South Levantine Arabic variety (Glottolog sout3123, ISO 639-3 ajp).

The consonant inventory of Chechen is rich and the most obvious difference to the consonants of Jordanian Arabic are the ejective obstruents. The number of vowels is relatively high and includes long vowels. The language also has non-phonemic diphthongs and morphologically conditioned nasalization (that is not indicated in our transcription). It is an ergative language with agglutinating morphology, a preference for suffixing and a large inventory of genders.[2] In other words, there are plenty of differences to Jordanian Arabic. Major grammatical descriptions of Chechen in English that we have used for this study are Nichols (1994) and Komen et al. (2021). The main Chechen-Russian dictionary has been published by Maciev (1961) and Karasaev and Maciev (1978) is a comprehensive Chechen-Russian dictionary. An online version of Maciev (1961) created by Erwin Komen can be found at http://erwinkomen.ruhosting.nl/che/dict/lexicon/main.htm.

As is well known, Arabic is not a single language but rather a cluster of varieties (see, e.g., the discussion in Bassiouney 2009: 18–27). It is therefore important to base research on Arabic as a contact language on the very variety that is spoken in the respective area, which in our case is Jordanian Arabic / Amman Arabic. According to Al-Wer (2020), "there is no geographically neutral variety of spoken Jordanian Arabic. All speakers therefore use some form of local dialect." In her studies, Al-Wer shows that in Amman a new unique dialect has evolved as an outcome of the contact between Jordanian and urban Palestinian dialects. The

---

[2] In our paper, we use the term "nominative" for the unmarked case (instead of "absolutive"). Genders of nouns are given in brackets () in the glosses whenever the gender is relevant because the noun controls agreement. See Section 4.4 for nominal morphology.

new dialect is distinct from these input varieties, but all varieties are mutually understandable.

Amman Arabic has a comparatively rich consonant inventory that differs only very little from Modern Standard Arabic. A typical feature of Arabic are the so-called emphatic consonants /sˤ tˤ ðˤ/, transcribed with a dot below the letter <ṣ, ṭ, ḍ>. In Amman Arabic the voiceless uvular stop /q/ is frequently realized as glottal stop [ʔ], in particular among female speakers (Al-Wer 2007, 2020), but there are also other variants used, namely [k] and [g], depending on the dialectal background and gender of the speaker (Al-Wer and Herin 2011).

Arabic morphology is usually described in terms of consonantal roots and patterns of vowels (and sometimes certain other consonants) and differs significantly from the Chechen system. Colloquial urban Arabic varieties have undergone considerable simplification in comparison to Classical Arabic and MSA in terms of morphosyntax, e.g. case marking. Amman / Jordanian Arabic has accusative alignment and is head-marking. Subject arguments are expressed on the verb, but there is no case marking of nouns (Herin and Al-Wer 2022: 276–277).

A comprehensive description of Jordanian Arabic is Herin and Al-Wer (2022), and papers such as Herin (2014) and Al-Wer (2007, 2020) highlight particular aspects of Arabic varieties in Jordan. For Arabic items quoted in our paper we follow the transcription used in those works.

4 The linguistic impact of Arabic on Chechen in Jordan

Arabic as the language of Islam was (and is) a prestigious language in Chechnya (Jaimoukha 2005: 111), but there was no widespread bilingualism in the Caucasus.[3] Chechen has a number of older Arabic loanwords and these words are also found in other languages of the area, including even languages whose speakers are Christians such as the Georgians. Before the Cyrillic script was implemented in 1937/1938 Chechen was written with Arabic letters since the 18th century (Jaimoukha 2005: 204–208) and for a very short period with a Latin script. Thus, the

---

[3] For instance, during the North Caucasian Imamate, a theocratic state that was founded on the territory of the larger part of Daghestan and Chechnya and existed from 1840 to 1859, Arabic was the official language and large part of the official written and even oral communication was done in Arabic (Zelkina 2000). During Soviet times to practice the religion was largely forbidden, the Arabic scripts used to write Chechen and other languages were replaced first by Latin scripts and later by Cyrillic scripts and thus knowledge of Arabic also declined.

impact of Arabic on Caucasian Chechen was relatively limited. Loan words were mostly nouns related to religion and abstract terms and might also have reached Chechen via Persian or Turkic languages, and a few examples will be given below.

As we have explained in Section 2, in today's Jordan the situation is of course very different because all Chechens are bilingual in Arabic and Chechen and use both languages on a daily basis. In the following subsections we will describe the impact of Arabic on Jordanian Chechen. In this study we limit ourselves to morphosyntactic phenomena and the lexicon. The phonetic inventories of Chechen and Jordanian Arabic only partially overlap and we noticed some phonological adaptation, but we will leave phonetics / phonology for future research.

4.1 Discourse particles, focus particles and adverbials

The use of discourse and focus particles is extremely widespread in language contact and has been explained by the special function of discourse markers within the 'monitoring-and-directing apparatus' that speakers use to regulate the interaction with the hearer (Matras 1998, 2009). They are not predominantly used for reasons of prestige, but to monitor the hearer's reactions and assumptions, similarly to non-verbal behavior such as gestures.

In our data we find Arabic items that have frequently been borrowed by diverse languages in contact with Arabic (e.g. Domari, Matras 2007, Herin 2018; Kurdish, Haig 2007). (1) shows the filler item and hesitation marker *yaʕni* 'that is, that means' in clause-initial position. The sentence in (2) contains the morphologically complex discourse particle *ʕa fekra* 'by the way'. Other items are the scalar focus-sensitive particle *ḥatta* 'even' in (21) and the restrictive focus particle / coordinator *bas* 'but, only' (3), (21). In the function as focus particles they are placed to the left of the item in their scope in (21).

(1) [data from Al Sheshani]
yaʕni, suun ḥazim toxor deen v-awz
means[AR], 1SG.DAT Hazim long.ago since V-be_familiar_with
'**I mean**, I've known Hazim for a long time.'

(2) [data from Al Sheshani]
j-u ḥuun **ʕa-fekra** qeṭar-iš
J-be.PRS 2SG.DAT **by.the.way**[AR] train(J)[AR]-PL
'There are trains, **by the way**, (for your information).'

(3) [data from Al Sheshani]
 bas   *dug*   *eto-q*   *cuo*   *cergaš*   *čoh*
 but[AR] heart   crack.PRS-EMPH   3SG.ERG   tooth.PL   inside
 '**But** it is annoying between the teeth.' (lit. 'It cracks the heart.')

In our data, Arabic adverbs were not particularly frequent and limited to temporal adverbs (*awwal* 'first', *mabdaʔiyan* 'initially', *fağʔa* 'suddenly') and manner adverbials (*bel ʕagel* 'in mind, logically'). The temporal adverbs occurred in clause-initial in (4) and (5) and once in clause-final position (6), i.e. in the usual position for such items in Chechen.

(4) [data from Al Sheshani]
 henc   **mabdaʔiyan**   *xilla*   *meg*   *ešt*
 right.now   **initially**[AR] be.PRF   may   like.this
 'Right now. **Initially** it might be like this.'

(5) [data from Al Sheshani]
 fağʔa   *v-alx-iš*   *ʕaš*   *v-u*
 Suddenly[AR]   V-cry-CVB.SIM   stay.CVB.SIM   V-be.PRS
 '**Suddenly**, he is crying.'

(6) [data from Al Sheshani]
 ħuun   *laʔ-aħ,*   *fedēn-iš*   *d-axk*   ***awwal!***
 2SG.DAT   want-COND   silver[AR]-PL   D-put.IMP   **first**[AR]
 'If you want, put the silver ones **first**!'

The borrowing of numerals, in particular of higher numerals, is common in language contact even in those cases in which the borrowing language already has its own inherited numerals (Matras 2009: 201). In fact, the Caucasian Chechen word for 'thousand', *ezar*, has ultimately been borrowed from Persian. In Jordanian Chechen, numerals higher than thirty are very often inserted from Arabic, and also dates and annual figures are expressed in Arabic. The two languages vary in how they syntactically integrated numerals into noun phrases. In Arabic, such constructions are not unified. There is a dual used when the modifying numeral is two. Modification of a noun with cardinal numerals from three to ten requires plural marking on the noun and for all numerals from eleven onwards the modified noun remains in the singular (Table 1). In contrast, in Jordanian and Caucasian Chechen the noun always remains in the singular.

Table 1: Nouns modified with numerals.

Jordanian Arabic	Chechen	translation
toffaḥa (singular)	ʕaӡ	'(one) apple'
toffaḥten (dual)	ši ʕaӡ	'two apples'
talat tofaḥat (plural)	q'o ʕaӡ	'three apples'
eḥdaʕšar toffaḥa (singular)	čhaitt ʕaӡ	'eleven apples'

4.2 Adjectives

In Arabic adjectives agree in gender, number, case, and definiteness with the head noun and follow the noun that they modify. Agreement is expressed by suffixes. In Caucasian Chechen, only around ten adjectives show gender/number agreement by means of prefixes, but adjectives distinguish a direct from an oblique form as in (7) and (8). The direct form is used when the head noun occurs in the nominative case; the oblique form is used to modify head nouns in any other case. Adjectives precede the modified noun.

(7) [Komen et al. 2021: 330]
    d-ouxa   xi
    D-hot   water.D
    'hot water'

(8) [Komen et al. 2021: 330]
    d-ouxača   xunuo
    D-hot.OBL   water.D.ERG
    'hot water'

There are some examples of Arabic adjectives in our data. They are always used in the masculine singular form and never showed inflection for gender, number or case. The use of the masculine singular form with adjectives borrowed from Arabic has also been observed for Domari (Herin 2018: 24). The attested adjectives denote human properties but also other qualities, e.g. laṭēf 'nice', šērer 'evil', fateḥ 'light', ġamiʔ 'dark', mozʕiğ 'noisy', rahēb 'wonderful'. In the following examples the adjectives occur in copula clauses, which in the present tense in Chechen require the use of a copula whereas in Arabic no copula is used.

(9) [data from Al Sheshani]
 cħa **laṭēf** j-ac-q ħo
 PTCL **nice**[AR] J-be.NEG.PRS-EMPH 2SG.ABS
 'You (fem.) are not **nice**.'

(10) [data from Al Sheshani]
 sa koč **fateḥ** j-a-r, as **ġami?** j-ena
 1SG.GEN dress.J **light**[AR] J-be-WPST 1SG.ERG **dark**[AR] J-do.PRF
 'My dress was **light** colored, and I made it **dark**.'

In addition to these adjectives we also found the Jordanian Arabic item *nahfe* that is a noun of feminine gender but used as an adjective to modify nouns in Jordanian Arabic and Jordanian Chechen. In both languages its English translation is 'funny' and in Jordanian Chechen it does not show any inflection like the adjectives listed above.

(11) [data from Al Sheshani]
 cħa **nahfe** xilla i
 PTCL **funny**[AR] be.PRF DEM
 'She became **funny**.'

4.3 Verbs

In addition to combined gender / number agreement, Chechen verbs are inflected for tense, aspect, mood, modality. and evidentiality (Molochieva 2010). The language has a wide range of non-finite verbal forms: masdar (verbal noun), infinitive, participles, and converbs, which are used to form periphrastic tense-aspect forms and also widely occur in subordinate clauses. For example, clausal coordination and complementation usually do not employ coordinating or subordinating particles but special verb forms such as nominalized verbs, converbs or the subjunctive.

Chechen has a relatively small inventory of simple verbal stems (around 200), which constitute a closed class. The verbal lexicon can very productively be enriched by means of compound verbs that involve loans and Chechen light verbs (Komen et al. 2021). These constructions are characteristic for East Caucasian languages and allow for easy and fast integration of borrowed items, but in Chechen they are also used with certain native items (Nichols 2003). In these constructions we find Arabic, Persian, Turkic, and Russian loans that can be nouns, adjectives, or verbs and sometimes do not exist as independent words in Chechen. Chechen light verbs used in these constructions are *d-an* 'do, make', *d-ala* 'give', the copula *v-u/d-u* (PRS), and the verb *xilla* 'be, become' (PRF). Depending on the light verb the resulting compound verb is intransitive or transitive. Older Arabic loans used in compound verbs are, e.g. *ǧawab* 'answer' > *žop d-ala* 'to answer', *salaam* 'peace' > *salam d-ala* 'greet', *sabr* 'patience' > *sobar d-an* 'endure, tolerate, wait for', *qabul* 'acceptance' > *qobal d-an* 'approve, accept' (Khalidovna 2012). In many compounds with *d-an* 'do, make' as auxiliary the borrowed element does not have an independent syntactic status, i.e., it is not the direct object of the auxiliary, but the entire phrasal verb can take a direct object, which then controls the agreement on the verb.

In Jordanian Chechen we find more such verbs and there are not only compounds that contain nouns as the ones just listed, but compounds with inflected but frozen Arabic verbs, which are treated like an integral part of the compound verb (Table 2). The Arabic verb form is usually the third person masculine singular perfect. When used as part of a compound verb the Arabic verb does not show agreement and only the Chechen light verb is inflected for tense, mood, polarity, evidentiality, gender, and number and thus shows agreement with the nominative argument of the clause.

Table 2: Chechen compound verbs with Arabic items.

Arabic	Jordanian Chechen	translation
sabaġ	*sabagh d-an*	'dye'
ʕaṭal	*ʕaṭal xilla / v-u*	'take a vacation'
ǧarrab	*žarrab d-an*	'try'

For instance, in (12) the compound verb is transitive and the direct object at the end of the clause, which is a singular feminine noun in the nominative case controls the agreement prefix on the light verb *d-an* 'do, make', which for feminine singular nouns is *j-*.

(12) [data from Al Sheshani]
    ʕaqqad   ***j-e-na***   *cuo*   *i*   *joʕ*
    complicate[AR]   J-do-PRF   3SG.ERG   DEM   girl.J
    'She caused psychological problems for the girl.' (lit. 'She **complicated** the girl.')

(13) [data from Al Sheshani]
    as   *ho*   **qarrar**   *d-e-na*   *xaʔe*   *ḥuun?*
    1SG.ERG   what   **decide**[AR]   **D-do**-PRF   know.PRS   2SG.DAT
    'Do you know what I **have decided**?'

(14) [data from Al Sheshani]
    caar   *šaša*   **ḥağez**   *d-e-na*
    3PL.ERG   3PL.REFL.ERG   **book**[AR]   **D-do**-PRF
    'They **have booked** it themselves.'

(15) [data from Al Sheshani]
    cun   *ḥeqel*   *ešt*   **barmağ**   *xilla*
    3SG.GEN   brain   like.this   **program**[AR]   **be**.PRF
    'His brain **has been programmed** like this.'

The following example shows a syntactic minimal pair. The transitive verb *barmağ d-an* 'program' agrees with the object that is the loan word *computer* (gender J) and requires a subject in the ergative. In (17) the intransitive verb *barmağ xilla* 'was, became programmed' does not show agreement because the light verb *xilla* does not have a slot for an agreement affix.

(16) [data from Al Sheshani]
    as   *sa*   *computer*   **barmağ**   *j-e-q*
    1SG.ERG   1SG.GEN   computer.J   **program**[AR]   J-do-EMPH
    'I **programmed** my computer.'

(17) [data from Al Sheshani]
    sa   *computer*   **barmağ**   *xilla*
    1SG.GEN   computer   **program**[AR]   **be**.PRF
    'My computer **was programmed**.'

Light verb constructions with frozen Arabic verb forms are also attested in other languages, e.g. Kurdish (Haig 2007: 174; Öpengin 2020), Swahili, Harari, Gurage, Farsi, Persian, Hindi, Urdu (Versteegh 2001), Aiki and Fur (both Nilo-Saharan) (Güldemann 2005). Wohlgemuth (2009: 180) notes that in particular Turkic languages and Indo-Iranian languages which, in general, prefer to borrow verbs by means of the light verb strategy as we saw it in Chechen, mostly integrate Arabic verbs as frozen forms and add light verbs such as 'do' or 'be'. He concludes that this preference is not caused by the special morphological structure of the Semitic donor language but by the light verb constructions that are native to and common in the respective recipient languages. In other words, it is the structure of the recipient language and not the structure of the donor language that determines the preferred borrowing strategy. This conclusion also applies to Chechen. The integrated loan verbs come from genealogically and typologically differing languages.

4.4 Nouns

In Chechen, nouns are inflected for number (singular vs. plural) and case, and control gender agreement. Some nouns undergo ablaut and/or require stem extensions before the inflectional suffixes are added. Both ablaut and extensions are lexically conditioned and limited to simple native words and only occasionally found in older loanwords. Most nouns take a regular plural suffix -(i)š or -i in the nominative case, e.g *kor* 'window' > plural *koor-iš*. There are a few nouns with irregular plural forms, e.g. *maaxa* 'needle' > plural *maix-i / mexij*. The case inventory comprises ten cases: nominative (= absolutive), ergative, dative, genitive, instrumental, locative, ablative, lative, allative, and comparative.

Depending on the analysis, Chechen has two or three human genders and three or four non-human genders (Nichols 1994; Komen et al. 2021). We follow the tradition and label the genders by the form of their morphological gender markers (B, V, D, J), which are used as prefixes, infixes, and suffixes. Gender markers differ between singular and plural for many nouns, so gender agreement also encodes number agreement (Table 3). Gender marking for human referents is predictable based on sex (masculine, feminine); but for non-human nouns it is arbitrary.

Table 3: Gender and gender markers in Chechen.

Gender (& person)	Singular	Plural
1st & 2nd person (pronouns only)	V/J	D
human male	V	B
human female	J	B
various (animals, inanimates)	B	B/D
various (animals, inanimates)	D	D
various (animals, inanimates)	J	J

Gender mostly shows up through agreement on verbs and very few adjectives. Gender agreement on the clausal level is controlled by the argument in the nominative case, and on the level of the noun phrase by the head noun. Example (18) shows a predicative clause with an agreeing adjective and a copula, and (19) an existential / locational clause with an agreeing copula. Note that in (19) the Russian loan *stol* 'table', which is masculine in the donor language, has variable gender assignment in Caucasian Chechen, which means that some speakers assign gender D and other speakers gender J (see below for one more example).

(18) Caucasian Chechen [Zarina Molochieva, p.c.]
 hara *kaad* *b-oqqa* *b-u*
 this bowl.B B-big B-be.PRS
 'This bowl is big.'

(19) Caucasian Chechen [Zarina Molochieva, p.c.]
 kuxni *čoħ* *stol* *d-u* / *j-u*
 kitchen[R] inside table[R].D/J D-be.PRS / J-be.PRS
 'There is a table in my kitchen.'

Modern Standard Arabic has two genders, masculine and feminine, that are partially marked on nouns and otherwise show up through agreement of nouns with verbs or adjectives. Gender assignment for some animate nouns is based on semantics, i.e. biological sex; for all other nouns it is semantically arbitrary. Traditional Jordanian dialects have maintained a gender distinction in the second and third person plural pronouns, and pronominal, verbal, and nominal suffixes. In Amman Arabic, this distinction has been lost and only the masculine plural forms are used (Al-Wer 2020: 558), which is typical for other urban Arabic dialects of the area. Nouns are marked for definiteness by means of the prefixed article *el/il* and for number (singular vs. plural). The dialects of central and northern Jordan have a very productive dual suffix (Herin and Al-Wer 2022: 80). Plural marking is expressed by suffixes or by changing the consonant and vowel patterns of the noun. Classical Arabic had nominative, accusative, and genitive cases, and Classical and Modern Standard Arabic have accusative alignment, but in colloquial varieties including Jordanian / Amman Arabic case marking has been lost and grammatical functions are mostly expressed through subject agreement on verbs and word order (Ryding 2005: 166; Moutaouakil 2018: 213; Herin and Al-Wer 2022).

In short, morphosyntactic categories of Arabic nouns differ from those of the Chechen nouns in basically all areas, namely definiteness, number (with respect to marking), gender (number of genders and rules for the agreement systems), and case (number and function of cases).

Nouns, in particular those that denote technical, cultural, or religious objects and concepts, are easily borrowed in many languages of the world (e.g. Tadmor 2009). Older Arabic loan words in Chechen denote religious concepts such as *Allah*, *malik* 'angel' (D) < *malak* (masculine), *din* 'faith, belief, religion' (D) < *diin* (masculine) 'religion, debt, judgement, custom', moral and other abstract concepts such as *niʕmat* 'grace, beneficence, goodness' (D) < *niʿmāt* (feminine plural) 'blessing, grace, mercy, favor', *vesiet* 'testament, will, precept' (D) < *waṣiyyāt* (feminine plural) 'will, testament, legacy, precept', but also a few other nouns, e.g. *ḥajba* 'cattle, livestock' (D) < *ḥayawān* (masculine) 'animal', *havaʔ* 'atmosphere, air' (D) < *hawā'* (feminine) 'air'. These loans had already been borrowed in the Caucasus and therefore also exist in contemporary Caucasian Chechen. In Jordanian Chechen, their form has not changed, i.e. they have not been re-arabicized.

In our data, we found a number of Jordanian Arabic nouns from various semantic fields that are not used in Caucasian Chechen but in Jordanian Chechen. We cite them here in their Jordanian Arabic form and give in brackets their Arabic gender and their form in Modern Standard Arabic (MSA): *qanoon* (masculine) 'basic rule, law, norm, regulation' (MSA *qānūn*), *sodfe* (feminine) 'coincidence' (MSA *ṣudfa*), *markiz* (masculine) 'center' (MSA *markaz*), *ʕeleh* 'family' (MSA *ʕāʔila*), *ṭareeʔa* (feminine) 'recipe' (MSA *ṭarīqa*), *šaḥene* (feminine) 'truck' (MSA *šāḥina*), *foṭor* (masculine) 'breakfast' (MSA *faṭūr*), *dawam* 'work' (MSA *dawām* 'duration, continuance, permanence, endurance'), *mobarat* (feminine) 'game, match' (MSA *mubārāh*), *loʕbe* (feminine) 'toy' (MSA *luʿba*) , *wağbe* (feminine) 'meal' (MSA *wağba*), *moddeh* (feminine) 'period of time, interval, duration' (MSA *mudda*), and *ġorfe* (feminine) 'room' (MSA *ġurfa*).

Gender assignment in Nakh-Daghestanian has raised the interest of linguists because of the comparatively large number of genders and the seemingly arbitrary distribution of non-human nouns across them. Gender assignment in these languages is partially based on semantic criteria, in particular for nouns denoting humans, but formal criteria also play a role. One of the formal criteria that has been investigated for a number of languages is the word-initial segment. The hypothesis is that there is a correlation between the initial segment of a noun and the appropriate agreement prefix. Based on the dictionary by Maciev (1961), Nichols (1989) found for Chechen that nouns with initial *b*, *d* and *j* significantly often belong to the respective genders (B, D, J), and this tendency she calls 'articulatory harmony'. She also notes that articulatory harmony probably facilitates the acquisition of the gender system, but it is not a rule or a dominant principle. In her study, Nichols excluded Russian loans because for them gender assignment is more transparent than for native words. She also lists the example of the Arabic word *din* 'faith' (D) as instantiating articulatory harmony.

Gender assignment to loan words seems on the whole to be more transparent than gender assignment to native words. It is based on a variety of tendencies, including default gender, articulatory harmony and copying of the gender from a semantically similar or even identical native word or older loan word. In general, a large number of loan words in Chechen is assigned gender J. This applies to recent loan words from Russian into Caucasian Chechen and internationally used words from English or other languages such as *pineapple, sushi, burger, cappuccino, pizza, computer, telephone* (all gender J). Other examples from our data are *qeṭar* 'train' (MSA *qiṭār*, masculine), *aleyat* 'mechanisms, machineries, mechanics' (MSA *ālīya*, feminine), *maḥmeyə* 'forest reserve' (MSA *maḥmiyya*), *niḍam* 'system' (MSA *niẓām*, masculine), *ʕeleh* 'family' (MSA *ʕāʔila*), and *sodfe* 'coincidence' (MSA *ṣudfa*, feminine). All these nouns belong to gender J in Jordanian Chechen whereas in Jordanian Arabic they are feminine or masculine. These examples show that the original Arabic gender does not play a role when it comes to gender assignment in Jordanian Chechen.

There are only a few words in our data that are assigned to gender B or D, and it seems that semantically similar loan words from Russian are treated alike. Again the original gender in Arabic does not impact on the gender that is assigned to the noun in Jordanian Chechen (and the same applies to Russian loan words in Caucasian Chechen except for nouns that refer to human beings and whose gender is therefore semantically transparent). For instance, the Jordanian Arabic loan *qanoon* 'basic rule, law' is assigned gender D and the same is true for the Russian loan *zakon* 'law, rule', perhaps because the older Arabic loan *ʕaadat* 'customary law, traditions, norms' belongs to the same gender in Chechen. In Arabic, the noun *qanoon* is masculine whereas *ʕādāt* is a plural form of the feminine noun *ʕāda* that – as a rule – requires feminine singular agreement like all non-human plural nouns. The Russian noun *zakon* is also masculine. Another example is Jordanian Chechen (and Caucasian Chechen) *krem* 'cream' (D) (the borrowed items in Arabic and Russian are masculine in both languages). The English word *mouse* (for computer) is assigned gender B in Jordanian Chechen, perhaps because the Chechen word *daxka* 'mouse', which only refers to the animal, belongs to gender B. This might also apply to *ġorfe* 'room' (D) (from Arabic where it is feminine) which is semantically similar to the Chechen word *c'a* 'house' (gender D in Chechen). The loan *borġi* 'screw' (< Jordanian Arabic *borġi*, MSA *burġī*, masculine) falls into gender B, perhaps because it begins with the phoneme /b/ and it thus exemplifies articulatory harmony. Its Russian equivalent that is used in Chechnya – *drel'* – has initial /d/ and belongs to gender D in Caucasian Chechen (and feminine in the Russian donor word). There are also a few nouns that vary in their gender assignment from speaker to speaker and a similar variation has been observed in Russian loan words in Caucasian Chechen. For example, Jordanian Chechen *lamba* 'lamp'(B/J) (from Arabic *lamba*, feminine) and Caucasian Chechen *lampa* (B/J) (from Russian *lampa*, which is feminine in Russian.

In our data we find that Arabic loans are used without definite articles. They receive regular case marking from Chechen without any additional stem extension. For instance, in (20) the Arabic loan *markiz* 'center' is marked for the allative case with the suffix *-ie* and the locative suffix *-eħ* is used in (22) with the Arabic noun *dawam-eħ* 'work'. In example (21) the Arabic noun *foṭor* 'breakfast' bears the dative case suffix *-en*.

(20) [data from Al Sheshani]
Mama **markiz-ie** *j-ax-na?*
Mama.J **center[AR]-ALL** J-go-PRF
'Did mum go **to the center**?'

(21) [data from Al Sheshani]
ḥatta **foṭor-en,** *bas naxč eecer as*
even[AR] **breakfast[AR]-DAT,** only[AR] cheese buy.WPST 1SG.ERG
'Even **for breakfast**, I bought only cheese.'

(22) [data from Al Sheshani]
ḥamada **dawam-eħ** *xer v-u-q*
Hamada.V **work[AR]-LOC** be.FUT V-be.PRS-EMPH
'Hamadah (masculine) would be **at work**.'

As for number marking, there is a bit of variation in our data. We found one sentence in which the Arabic noun *tasarof* 'behavior, disposal, action' is used with the Arabic plural suffix *-at* while everything else in the example is Chechen.

(23) [data from Al Sheshani]
suun cun **tasarof-at** *xaz ca xet*
1SG.DAT 3SG.GEN **behavior[AR]-PL[AR]** beautiful NEG believe.PRS
'I don't like her **behavior**.' (lit. 'Her behavior does not seem beautiful to me.')

There are a number of examples of singular Arabic nouns with Chechen plural markers, e.g. (2). However, most commonly we find double plural marking by means of Arabic and Chechen morphology. The Arabic plural can be formed by means of suffixation or it can be a 'broken plural form'. E.g., in (24) *ǧawaneb-iš* 'sides' and in (25) *aleyat-iš* 'mechanisms, machineries', are marked twice for plural whereby the Arabic marking is a broken plural form.

(24) [data from Al Sheshani]
Ħažaħ! bas **ǧawaneb-iš** t'eħ i j-u
look.IMP.POL but[AR] **side.PL[AR]-PL** on DEM J-be.PRS
'Look! But on the **sides**, there is that.' (Referring to fat on the sides of a meat steak)

(25) [data from Al Sheshani]
ah bas Adi, haxerg-eħ j-ul ***aleyat-iš***
yes[AR] but[AR] Adi 3PL-LOC J-be.PTCP **machinery.PL[AR]-PL**
raheeb j-u!
amazing[AR] J-be.PRS
'Yes, but Adi, their **machines** are amazing!'

In Table 4 we list some nouns from our data with plural and case marking. The first two nouns have double plural marking whereas the last two nouns are only marked with the Chechen plural suffix. Similar double plural marking of nouns borrowed from Arabic is found in Domari (Matras 2007: 155; Herin 2018: 23) and Nubian (Rouchdy 1991: 27–28).

Table 4: Number and case inflection of some borrowed nouns.

Jordanian Chechen (SG)	Jordanian Arabic (PL)	plural form in our data	case marked form in our data	translation
markiz	*marākiz*	*marakiz-iš*	*markez-eħ* (LOC)	'center'
maktabeh	*maktabāt / makātib*	*makatab-iš*	*maktaba-neħ* (LOC)	'library'
niḍam	*anḍime / noḍom*	*niḍam-iš*	*niḍam-ic* (INS)	'system'
fondoq	*fanādiq*	*fondoq-iš*	*fondoq-en* (DAT)	'hotel'

Boumans (1998: 91) hypothesizes that "the likelihood of double marking appears to increase when each language marks the same feature in a different manner, for instance, by means of prefixes and suffixes." Another explanation is given by Myers-Scotton in her *Matrix Language Frame Model* and its extension, the *4-M Model* (Myers-Scotton 2002). Myers-Scotton divides morphemes into different categories. In code switching, content morphemes (nouns, verbs, adjectives, adverbials, certain adpositions, certain pronouns), "early system morphemes" and occasionally "bridge late system morphemes" can come from both languages. By contrast, "outsider late system morphemes" must come from what Myers-Scotton calls the "Matrix Language" (in our case Chechen) and cannot come from the other "Embedded Language" (i.e. Arabic in our data). Examples of early system morphemes are plural markers, determiners, derivational affixes, aspectual, and tense markers. Bridge late system morphemes express (hierarchical) relationships between phrases and clauses; these are, e.g., possessive markers and sentential complementizers. Outsider late system morphemes are those that realize the grammatical frame, namely verbal agreement markers and case markers and also certain adpositions and pronouns. According to the *Early System Morpheme Hypothesis*, in code switching early system morphemes such as plural markers may come from both languages and thus double (Myers-Scotton 2002: 92). By contrast, double agreement on verbs or double case marking is not possible because the outsider late system morphemes can only come from the matrix language. In sum, our data confirms the hypotheses of the *Matrix Language Frame Model*: we find double plural marking but no other doubling of grammatical morphemes.

4.5 Constituent order in phrases

At the phrasal level both languages sharply differ in constituent order. Chechen is head final, e.g. modifying adjectives or genitives precede the head noun. With respective to possessive constructions, in Arabic the so-called "construct state" construction is used in which the head noun (possessor) is in the "construct form" and cannot be marked for definiteness with the definite article but only the possessee can be marked. As an alternative to the construct state a linker such as *tabaʕ* can be employed (Herin and Al-Wer 2022: 212–218). In any case the dependent (=possessor) precedes the head (=possessee). The following example from our data is entirely in Arabic (code-switching) and illustrates the construct state construction (26).

(26) [data from Al Sheshani]
 ǧamb eš-šareʕ
 side[AR] the-street[AR]
 'the side of the street'

In our data, Arabic words in a possessive construction are often used according to Chechen syntax, i.e. possessees are marked with the Chechen case marker for the genitive and precede the possessor. As already stated, no Arabic articles are used:

(27) [data from Al Sheshani]
 fağʔa   loʕb-e   kabbas taʕe-č   ghar
 suddenly[AR] toy[AR]-GEN button[AR] press-CVB.TEMP sound.J
 j-uqq-eš   j-ac
 J-take-CVB.SIM J-be.NEG.PRS
 'Suddenly, the toy's button does not make sounds when clicked.'

Modifying adjectives precede the head noun as it is required in Chechen. As mentioned above, in Jordanian Arabic adjectives follow the noun and agree in definiteness with it. In the following example, the Arabic adjective *xafēf* 'light' precedes the indefinite pronoun *hum* 'something'.

(28) [data from Al Sheshani]
 xafēf   **hum**   j-oʔo-r j-u   vai
 light[AR] **something** J-eat-FUT J-be.PRS 1PL.INCL.ERG
 'We will eat **something light**'

(29) [data from Al Sheshani]
 xaz   **sodfe**   j-u-q
 beautiful **coincidence**[AR] J-be.PRS-EMPH
 'It is a **nice coincidence**'

Similarly, in (30) the Arabic adjective *ḍaki* 'smart' modifies the Arabic noun *niḍam* 'system', but both items follow the word order of Chechen rather than Arabic. In Arabic, the word order of this NP would be *niḍam ḍaki*.

(30) [data from Al Sheshani]
 cħa   **ḍaki**   **niḍam** j-eh-ħam…
 one **smart**[AR] **system**[AR] J-do-in.order.to…
 'in order to make a **smart system**…'

In the next example, *Ağloun* is the name of a city in Jordan, and the Jordanian Arabic word *maḥmeyə* means 'forest reserve' (MSA *maḥmiyya*). A Jordanian Arabic noun phrase would be constructed with reversed constituent order, namely *maḥmeyət Ağloun*. In our example (31), the two nouns are Arabic borrowings but they follow the word order of Chechen.

(31) [data from Al Sheshani]

Ağloun	**maḥmeyə**	vono	xaz	j-u
Ağloun[AR]	forest_reserve[AR]	very	beautiful	J-be.PRS

'**Ajloun Forest reserve** is very beautiful.'

Furthermore, Chechen has postpositions and local cases to express spatial and temporal relationships whereas Arabic makes use of prepositions. In our data, Arabic prepositions only occurred in inserted phrases that can be analyzed as lexicalized such as *bel ʕagel* 'in mind, logically' but have not been used with Chechen nouns.

4.6 Constituent order in the main clause

In Chechen, constituent order at the clausal level is frequently SOV, but other orders are also possible and attested in texts. According to Nichols (1994), OVS is not uncommon in elicited sentences (see also Komen (2007: 32) for a similar assessment). Komen and Bugenhagen (2017), based on counts in a corpus of Chechen, found that one third of Chechen subjects occur after the finite verb in main clauses, and of those post-verbal subjects one third are pronominal. Information structure impacts on the position of subjects. Postverbal subjects occur in utterances with presentational focus to introduce new referents by means of NPs, in existential clauses, to express paragraph-internal cohesion, i.e. with topical and pronominal subjects, and in reported speech constructions.

In Jordanian Arabic, SVO is the basic and most frequent word order (El-Yasin 1985), but other orders are possible as well, in particular VSO as in Classical Arabic (Herin and Al-Wer 2022: 277). Al-Shawashreh (2016) conducted sociolinguistic interviews with speakers from the city of Iribd and rural areas and counted the constituent orders in a selected subcorpus. Table 5 gives his results which are slightly different from what is usually stated in the literature because not VSO but VOS is the second most frequent pattern. In intransitive clauses VS is very common, and is particularly often used in presentational utterances when the subject denotes a discourse-new referent and when there is topic continuity over some clauses (Herin and Al-Wer 2022: 277–278). As just stated, a similar tendency has been observed for Chechen (Komen and Bugenhagen 2017). As written in the introduction, we are not able to make quantitative statements our own data such that a comparison of the frequencies of constituent order patterns in Jordanian Arabic and Jordanian Chechen must be left for future research (which ideally should also include Caucasian Chechen). In the following, we present examples of various patterns from our data and report Al Sheshani's impressionistic estimations of which constructions are used relatively commonly in Jordanian Chechen.

Table 5: Constituent order patterns in Jordanian Arabic (Al-Shawashreh 2016).

monovalent verbs order			bivalent verbs order		
	#	%		#	%
SV	983	65,30%	SVO	491	90,30%
VS	522	34,70%	VOS	31	5,70%
Total	1505	100%	VSO	19	3,50%
			OSV	1	0,20%
			OVS	1	0,20%
			SOV	1	0,20%
			Total	544	100%

In our data, we have intransitive clauses with SV and VS order. Examples (22), (24), and (32) show copula clauses with SV order. Both orders are common in Chechen and Jordanian Arabic.

(32) [data from Al Sheshani]
    sa   ġorfe   zemi   d-u
    1SG.GEN   room(D)[AR]   small   D-be.PRS
    'My room is small.'

In copula clauses with adjectives used as predicates the order adjective-copula-subject is common. In these examples the postverbal subjects are pronouns and they seem to be continuous topics (9), (11), (33). This type of construction exists in Chechen and Arabic.

(33) [data from Al Sheshani]
    mozʕiġ   b-u-q   üš
    noisy[AR]   B-be.PRS-EMPH   3PL.ABS
    'They are noisy.'

In transitive clauses, SOV, OVS and VSO are common. The first two patterns, SOV and OVS, are clearly native Chechen patterns that are almost absent from Jordanian Arabic (Table 5). Example (23) shows SOV with a dative subject.

In the following examples with OVS order all postnominal subjects are pronouns and either continuous topics or first person. In (34) the verb is transitive, the subject is marked with the ergative and the direct object is in the nominative case. In the second example (35), we have a bivalent intransitive verb with a nominative subject and a second goal-like argument in the allative case. In our data, OVS occurs relatively frequently (see also (21), (28)).

(34) [data from Al Sheshani]
    ešt   qanoon   d-aq-na-q   caar   šain
    like.this law.D[AR] D-take-PRF-EMPH 3PL.ERG 3PL.REFL.DAT
    'They imposed themselves a rule like that.'

(35) [data from Al Sheshani]
    mobarat-eg   ħež-iš   v-a-r-qe   i
    match[AR]-ALL look-CVB.SIM V-be-WPST-EMPH DEM
    'He was watching the match.'

In the next example, *gabel* is the colloquial Jordanian counterpart of the Standard Arabic adverbial *qabla* 'before' that precedes the noun *Ramadan*. The word order in the first clause is SV whereas in the second clause it is OVS.

(36) [data from Al Sheshani]
    gabel   Ramadan   ṭollab-iš   ʕaṭal   b-u
    before[AR] Ramadan[AR] student.PL[AR]-PL vacation[AR] B-be.PRS
    ghert-iš,   i   hum   d-o-q   caar
    try-CVB.SIM DEM   something D-do-EMPH 3PL.ERG
    'So the students go on a vacation before Ramadan, they do this.'

There are also a couple of examples with VSO order. In the second clause in (37) both subject and object are pronouns and follow the verb. Another example is (12) above. The comparatively frequent occurrence of this pattern could be due to Arabic influence since VSO is moderately often attested in Jordanian Arabic (Table 5). But in order to verify this hypothesis we would need to compare our data to data from Caucasian Chechen.

(37) [data from Al Sheshani]
    har   ʕeleh   j-ul   del,   j-et-na-q   as   i
    this   family.J[AR] J-be.PTCP because   J-leave-PRF-EMPH   1SG.ERG   DEM
    'Because it is a family, I left her.'

SVO order is apparently not very common in Jordanian Chechen. If Arabic had a clear influence on the constituent order in Chechen we would expect more clauses with this type of pattern since it is extremely frequent in Jordanian Arabic (Table 5). In example (38) the initial item is not used as complementizer but rather as a kind of adverbial with causal meaning.

(38) [data from Al Sheshani]
    le-innu   suun   k'oor<d>e-na   j-aʔ-hum
    because[AR]   1SG.DAT   get.bored.D-PRF   J-eat-food.J
    'Therefore, I got bored of eating.'

4.7 Complex sentences

To express complex sentences Chechen makes use of participles, a large range of converbs and other non-finite verb forms such as infinitive and masdar. For clause coordination a special chaining construction is used (Good 2003). For adversative coordination Chechen employs the old Arabic loan *amma* 'but', and for disjunction the loan *ja* 'or' of ultimately Persian origin (Jeschull 2004; Stolz and Levkovych 2022). In Jordanian Arabic, for conjunctive coordination the particle *w/u* is used and for adversative coordination the particles *bass* and *lākin/lakn* 'but' and *amma* 'whereas'. There are two monosyndetic disjunctive coordinators *aw* and *willa/walla*; the first is used in statements and the latter is preferred in questions, and one bisyndetic disjunction *yā … yā …* .

In our data, we did not find the older Arabic loan *amma*, but instead *bas* was frequently used (mainly as a pragmatic discourse marker with adversative meaning or as restrictive focus particle (21), (24), (25)). For the marking of disjunctions *willa* was employed (39).

(39) [data from Al Sheshani]
    har   tallağ   čoħ   j-a-r   **willa**   araħ?
    this   refrigerator[AR]   inside   J-be-WPST   **or**[AR] outside
    'Was this inside **or** outside of the refrigerator?'

In reported speech constructions, Chechen uses asyndetic conjunction (i.e. no grammatical marking of the quote) or quotative particles derived from the verb 'say', but no complementizers because Chechen does not have complementizers. In Jordanian Arabic, quotes can also be unmarked as in Chechen or introduced by means of the complementizer *innu* of which also inflected forms exist (Herin and Al-Wer 2022: 328–330). In our data, the variant *innu* is used.

(40) [data from Al Sheshani]
    *hu   boox   saig,   **innu**   "šereket   seyaḥa-c   ma   gho!"*
    what tell.ITER 1SG.ALL, **that**[AR] company[AR] tourism[AR]-INS PROH go.IMP
    'What (she) tells me "Don't go with a travel agency!"'

(41) [data from Al Sheshani]
    *as   ca   boox   ḥaig   **innu**   [i   šērer   j-u]!*
    1SG.ERG NEG tell.PRS 2SG.ALL **that**[AR] DEM evil[AR] J-be.PRS
    'I am not telling you **that** she is evil!'

As the borrowing of discourse particles and filler items, the borrowing of conjunctions and/or complementizers is common in situations of intense language contact such as it is the case for Chechen in Jordan, in particular when the recipient language does not have a rich inventory of those items (e.g. Stolz and Levkovych 2022). Arabic conjunctions and complementizers have been borrowed by a wide range of languages such Domari (Matras 2007), Kurdish (Haig 2007) Turkic languages, Caucasian languages and many others (Stolz 2022; see also Versteegh 2001).

5 Chechen in Jordan vs. Chechen in Russia and heritage language studies

In the previous sections we have described the sociolinguistic situation of Chechen and the linguistic impact of Arabic on it. Chechen in Jordan is a heritage language. By contrast, in the Chechen Republic that roughly corresponds with the original homeland Chechen is an indigenous language of the majority population. Yet, as for today it ended up to be a minority language in the wider context of the Russian national state.

In this section, we want to argue that heritage Chechen and its speakers in Jordan should be examined in comparison with Chechen and its speakers in the

Caucasus since the changes that we observe in Jordanian Chechen are very similar to the changes in Caucasian Chechen. Therefore, we suggest that heritage language studies should extend its objects (i.e. languages) of study to predominantly oral languages such as Chechen and cooperate with language documentation studies that focus on endangered indigenous minority languages and vice versa.

There are only very few studies that focus on heritage languages from smaller communities, and basically none that target languages that are themselves minority languages in their place of origin. In the special issue on "lesser-studied heritage languages" of the *Heritage Language Journal* (2020), the editors state that "there is a need of new inquiries that will bring to the forefront other immigrant languages as well as languages traditionally outside the scope of heritage studies: indigenous languages (and their HL varieties), ..." (Ivanova-Sullivan and Wilkinson 2020).

When comparing the sociolinguistic situation of Jordanian Chechen with Caucasian Chechen, we conclude that there are more similarities than differences. For both varieties it is true that:

- Chechen is not the dominant language of the surroundings or the country where the speakers grow up
- it is learned at home in a natural environment either concurrently or before with the dominant language
- it connects the speaker to her/his family roots
- except for a few individuals (who are either very young or very old) speakers are bilinguals
- an increasing number of speakers are asymmetrical or imbalanced bilinguals for which the dominant language of the surroundings/country became the stronger language
- language shift has had and continues to have an impact on the grammar of Chechen

These criteria are almost all criteria that apply to the definitions of "heritage speaker" and "heritage language" by Scontras et al. (2015) and Aalberse et al. (2019: 1–11). At the same time, they fully apply to indigenous minority languages in asymmetrical contact situations.

There are obviously also some differences that we sum up in Table 6.

Table 6: The sociolinguistic situation of Caucasian Chechen vs. Jordanian Chechen.

Caucasian Chechen	Jordanian Chechen
indigenous language	migrant language
official status	no official status
official financial support	no official financial support
regular use in education, language teaching, media	no such regular use[4]
partially used in official public situations	no such use

However, we claim that these differences are rather minor and have only very limited effect. The largest impact concerns, in our mind, the written mode in the sense that in Chechnya people learn how to write and read Chechen even though written Chechen is not very widely used. Otherwise the results of the asymmetrical contact situation are comparable.

In Caucasian Chechen as spoken today in the northern Caucasus a large proportion of the lexicon used on a daily basis originates from Russian, including, of course, more and more international loans from English (e.g. Khalidovna 2012; Guérin 2015). In two Chechen Wikipedia articles, one on Chechen history and the other one on Georgia, we counted the number of Russian loans.[5] Out of 531 words 86 were of Russian origin, i.e. around 16%.

Examples of borrowed Russian lexemes are:
- adverbs: *nikogda* 'never', *prosto* 'simply', *srazu* 'immediately', *obyčno* 'usually', *sliškom* 'too much', *isključitel'no* 'exclusively', *slučajno* 'accidentally'
- conjunctions and particles: *a* 'and, but', *no* 'but', *uže* 'already', *net* 'no'
- adjectives (in the masculine singular): *etničeski* 'ethnic', *normal'ni* 'normal', *graždanski* 'civic'
- nouns: days of the week, *komp'juter* 'computer', *raspisanie* 'schedule', *kurs* 'course', *stol* 'table', *lampa* 'lamp'
- verbs (in the infinitive, accompanied by one of the light verbs): *vključit' d-an* 'turn off', *otvečat' d-an* 'answer', *sostojat'sja d-an* 'take place', *zakaz d-an* 'order, make an order' …

---

4 Note, however, that Chechens in Jordan watch TV Channels from the Chechen Republic and also use websites from the Chechen Republic.

5 https://ce.wikipedia.org/wiki/%D0%9D%D0%BE%D1%85%D1%87%D0%B8%D0%B9%D1%87%D0%BE%D1%8C%D0%BD%D0%B0%D0%BD_%D0%B8%D1%81%D1%82%D0%BE%D1%80%D0%B8#%D0%A5%D1%8C%D0%B0%D0%B6%D0%BE%D1%80%D0%B3%D0%B0%D1%88

As was discussed in Section 4.4, the gender assigned to Russian loans is frequently J, but also D and occasionally B and there is no sign of erosion of the gender system. Nominal borrowings are inflected with Chechen cases. There is no regular double plural marking except for a few words that are normally used in the plural in Russian such as *noski* 'stockings, socks'. As for word order, in noun phrases the order is consistently head-final and this also includes Russian borrowings, e.g. modifying adjectives precede the nouns and genitives precede the head even if both items are Russian loans, e.g. *respubliki-n* (genitive) *konstituci* (nominative) vs. Russian *konstitucija* (nominative) *respublik-i* (genitive) 'the republic's constitution'. Borrowed adjectives do not agree in gender, number or case and are used in a form that corresponds to the masculine singular in Russian. Verbs are borrowed as infinitives as it is very typical for Russian verbs, in particular in situations of intense contact (Forker 2021). In sum, the linguistic outcome of the contact situation strongly resembles our data from Jordan. The only difference concerns plural marking of nouns, which is often doubled in Jordanian Chechen but not doubled in Caucasian Chechen. We lack data to examine constituent order at the clause level.

6 Conclusion

Asymmetrical contact situations between a minority language (often endangered) and a larger (often national) language represent a well-known situation in language contact. The linguistic outcomes of this type of situation are as diverse as the languages involved and their sociolinguistic circumstances and also range from mainly lexical borrowing to large structural changes, up to attrition, and language shift of the entire community to the larger language.

In this paper we have examined the influence of Arabic on spoken Chechen in Jordan. Despite its comparatively small size, the Chechen community in Jordan continues to use their language, in contrast to another Caucasian community, the Circassians. Nevertheless, Chechen speakers are all bilinguals and thus code switching and borrowing are regular features of linguistic behavior. Jordanian Arabic words come from all parts of speech and are morphosyntactically integrated. Nouns are inflected for case whereas plural marking shows some variation and can occur twice by means of Arabic and Chechen markers. Verbs are inserted in a frozen form and combined with Chechen light verbs. Adjectives are used in the form of the Arabic masculine singular and not further inflected. Syntax shows relatively little impact of Arabic. At the phrasal level constituent order is not affected, but in main clauses there might be some influence that favors a use of VSO. In complex clauses Arabic complementizers occur. For future research we invite other linguists to conduct comparative studies of language contact between Chechen and genealogically and typologically differing majority languages in addition to Arabic, in particular Turkish and Georgian, but also Russian that go beyond lists of loan words.

In the case of Caucasian Chechen, we have observed similar changes that we have been describing for Jordanian Chechen despite the genetic and typological differences of the dominant languages and the sociolinguistic differences. One variety is spoken in the homeland in a locally rather homogenous ethno-linguistic environment (95% of the population are Chechens) that, however, is part of a large national state with a strong national language and an increasingly restrictive language policy, and the other variety is a heritage language. Yet we need more data on both varieties to substantiate our observations, in particular natural conversations because written and oral usages diverge. Our paper has shown that the study of heritage languages and of endangered minority languages have more similarities than differences and should aim at fruitful cooperation in the future.

Acknowledgements: We thank our friends, colleagues and Al Sheshani's husband Ahmad Isam Bino, Zarina Molochieva, Peter Konerding, and Adam Ishaqat Halashta who have helped us with their knowledge of Chechen and Arabic and the editors of this volume for their insightful comments.

Abbreviations

1/2/3	first/second/third person
ABS	absolutive
ALL	allative
AR	Arabic
B	gender marker
COND	conditional
CVB.SIM	simultaneous converb
CVB.TEMP	temporal converb
D	gender marker
DAT	dative
DEM	demonstrative
EMPH	emphatic
ERG	ergative
FUT	future
GEN	genitive
IMP	imperative
INCL	inclusive

INS	instrumental
ITER	iterative
J	gender marker
LOC	locative
MSA	Modern Standard Arabic
NEG	negation
NP	noun phrase
OBL	oblique stem
PL	plural
POL	polite imperative
PRF	perfect
PROH	prohibitive
PRS	present
PTCL	particle
PTCP	participle
REFL	reflexive
R	Russian
SG	singular
V	gender marker
WPST	witnessed past

References

Aalberse, Suzanne. P., Ad Backus & Pieter C. Muysken. 2019. *Heritage languages: A language contact approach*. Amsterdam: Benjamins.

Abd-el-Jawad, Hassan R. 2006. Why do minority languages persist? The case of Circassian in Jordan. *International Journal of Bilingual Education and Bilingualism* 9(1). 51–74.

Alagozlu, Nuray. 2007. Code-switching between Kabardian and Turkish. Paper presented at the *6th International Symposium on Bilingualism* (ISB6), University of Hamburg, 30 May – 2 June. http://www.isb6.org/static/proceedings/alagozlu.pdf (checked 02/18/22).

Alomoush, Omar Ibrahim. 2015. *Multilingualism in the linguistic landscape of urban Jordan*. Liverpool: Liverpool University dissertation.

Al-Shawashreh, Ekab. 2016. *Aspects of grammatical variation in Jordanian Arabic*. Ottawa: University of Ottawa dissertation.

Al Sheshani, Ala. 2020. *Intra-sentential code-switching: A case study of the speech of chechen-Arabic bilinguals*. Göttingen: University of Göttingen MA thesis.

Al-Wer, Enam. 1999. Language and identity: the Chechens and the Circassians in Jordan. *Dirasat, Proceedings of F.I.C.A.E.C.C.S.* 253–268.

Al-Wer, Enam. 2007. The formation of the dialect of Amman: From chaos to order. In Catherine Miller, Enam Al-Wer, Dominique Caubet & Janet C. E. Watson (eds.), *Arabic in the city: Issues in dialect contact and language variation*, 55–76. London: Routledge.

Al-Wer, Enam. 2020. New-dialect formation: The Amman dialect. In Christopher Lucas & Stefano Manfredi (eds.), *Arabic and contact-induced change*, 551–566. Berlin: Language Science Press.

Al-Wer, Enam & Bruno Herin. 2011. The lifecycle of Qaf in Jordan. *Langage et société* 138. 59–76.

Bağrıaçık, Metin, Angela Ralli & Dimitra Melissaropoulou. 2015. Borrowing verbs from Oghuz Turkic: Two linguistic areas. In Francesco Gardani, Peter Arkadiev & Nino Amiridze (eds.), *Borrowed morphology*, 109–135. Berlin: De Gruyter.

Bassiouney, Reem. 2009. *Arabic sociolinguistics*. Edinburgh: Edinburgh University Press.

Boumans, Louis. 1998. *The syntax of code switching: Analysing Moroccan Arabic/Dutch conversation*. Tilburg: Tilburg University Press.

Chechuro, Ilia Y. 2021. Lexical convergence reflects complex historical processes. In Diana Forker & Lenore A. Grenoble (eds.), *Language contact in the territory of the former Soviet Union*, 35–57. Amsterdam: Benjamins.

Chechuro Ilia Y., Michael Daniel & Samira Verhees. 2021. Small-scale multilingualism through the prism of lexical borrowing. *International Journal of Bilingualism* 25(4). 1019–1039.

Chirikba, Viacheslav A. 1997. Distribution of Abkhaz Dialects in Turkey. In A. Sumru Özsoy (ed.), *Proceedings of the conference on Northwest Caucasian linguistics, 10–12 October 1994*, 63–88. Oslo: Novus Forlag.

Chumakina, Marina. 2009. Loanwords in Archi, a Nakh-Daghestanian language of the North Caucasus. In Martin Haspelmath & Uri Tadmor (eds.), *Loanwords in the world's languages: A comparative handbook*, 430–446. Berlin: De Gruyter.

Comrie, Bernard & Madžid Š. Khalilov. 2009. Loanwords in Bezhta, a Nakh-Daghestanian language of the North Caucasus. In Martin Haspelmath & Uri Tadmor (eds.), *Loanwords in the world's languages: A comparative handbook*, 416–429. Berlin: De Gruyter.

Dweik, Bader S. 2000. Linguistic and cultural maintenance among the Chechens of Jordan. *Language, Culture and Curriculum* 13(2). 184–195.

El-Yasin, Mohammed Khalid. 1985. Basic word order in Classical Arabic and Jordanian Arabic. *Lingua* 65. 107–122.

Forker, Diana. 2019a. The impact of language contact on Hinuq: Phonology, morphology, syntax, and lexicon. *Language Typology and Universals* 71. 29–62.

Forker, Diana. 2019b. Sanzhi-Russian code switching and the Matrix Language Frame Model. *International Journal of Bilingualism* 23(6). 1448–1468.

Forker, Diana. 2021. The late success of Soviet language policy: The integration of Russian verbs in languages of the former Soviet Union. *International Journal of Bilingualism* 25(1). 240–271.

Gardner-Chloros, Penelope. 1987. Code-switching in relation to language contact and convergence. In Georges Lüdi (ed.), *Devenir bilingue-parler bilingue*, 99–115. Tübingen: Niemeyer.

Good, Jeff. 2003. Clause combining in Chechen. *Studies in Language* 27(1). 113–170.

Guérin, Françoise. 2015. The evolution of Chechen in asymmetrical contact with Russian. In Christel Stolz (ed.), *Language empires in comparative perspective*, 183–189. Berlin: De Gruyter.

Güldemann, Tom. 2005. Complex predicates based on generic auxiliaries as an areal feature in Northeast Africa. In Erhard Karl Friedrich Voeltz (ed.), *Studies in African linguistic typology*, 131–154. Amsterdam: Benjamins.

Haddad, Mohanna & Wasfi Kailani. 2004. Chechen identity, culture, and citizenship in Jordan. In Moshe Ma'oz & Gabi Sheffer (eds.), *Middle Eastern minorities and Diasporas*, 243–261. Eastbourne: Sussex Academic Press.

Haig, Geoffrey. 2007. Grammatical borrowing in Kurdish (Northern Group). In Yaron Matras & Jeanette Sakel (eds.), *Grammatical borrowing in cross-linguistic perspective*, 165–183. Berlin: De Gruyter.

Herin, Bruno. 2014. The dialect of Salt (Jordan). In Lutz Edzard & Rudolf de Jong (eds.), *Encyclopedia of Arabic language and linguistics*. Leiden: Brill Online.
Herin, Bruno. 2018. The Arabic component in Domari. In Stefano Manfredi & Mauro Tosco (eds.), *Arabic in Contact*, 19–36. Amsterdam: Benjamins.
Herin, Bruno & Al-Wer, Enam. 2022. *A grammar of Jordanian Arabic*. Marseille: Diacritiques Éditions.
Höhlig, Monika. 1997. *Kontaktbedingter Sprachwandel in der adygeischen Umgangssprache im Kaukasus und in der Türkei*. Munich: Lincom.
Ivanova-Sullivan, Tanya & Erin Wilkinson. 2020. Introduction to the Special Issue on Lesser-Studied Heritage Languages. *Heritage Language Journal* 17(2). i–vi.
Jaimoukha, Amjad. 2005. *The Chechens: A handbook*. London: Routledge Curzon.
Jeschull, Liane. 2004. Coordination in Chechen. In Martin Haspelmath (ed.), *Coordinating Constructions*. Amsterdam & Philadelphia: John Benjamins.
Johanson, Lars. 2000. Linguistic convergence in the Volga area. In Dicky G. Gilbers, John Nerbonne & Jos Schaeken (eds.), *Languages in contact*, 165–177. Amsterdam: Rodopi.
Kailani, Wasfi. 2002. *Chechens in the Middle East: Between original and host cultures*. https://www.belfercenter.org/publication/chechens-middle-east-between-original-and-host-cultures (checked 02/18/22).
Karasaev, A. T. & Axmed. G. Maciev. 1978. *Russko-Čečenskij slovar'*. Moskva: Izdatel'stvo Russij jazyk.
Khalidovna, Petimat Al'murzaeva. 2012. *Zaimstvovannaja leksika Čečenskogo jazyka. Avtoreferat* [Loanwords in Chechen. Dissertation abstract]. Moscow: Russian Academy of Science.
Komen, Erwin. R. 2007. *Focus in Chechen*. Leiden: Leiden University MA thesis. http://media.leidenuniv.nl/legacy/komen_2007_focusinchechen-ma.pdf (checked 02/18/22).
Komen, Erwin. R. & Robert D. Bugenhagen. 2017. *Postverbal pronominal subjects in Chechen and Ingush*. Paper presented at SLE 50, University of Zürich, 10–13 September.
Komen, Erwin R., Zarina Molochieva & Johanna Nichols. 2021. Chechen and Ingush. In Maria Polinsky (ed.), *The Oxford Handbook of Languages of the Caucasus*, 317–368. Oxford: Oxford University Press.
Kutscher, Silvia. 2008. The language of the Laz in Turkey: Contact-induced change or gradual language loss?. *Turkic Languages* 12(1). 82–102.
Lucas, Christopher & Stefano Manfredi (eds.). 2020. *Arabic and contact-induced change*. Berlin: Language Science Press.
Maciev, Axmed. G. 1961. *Čečensko-Russkij slovar'*. Moskva: Gosudarstvennoe Izd-vo Inostrannyx i Nacional'nyx Slovarej.
Matras, Yaron. 1998. Utterance modifiers and universals of grammatical borrowing. *Linguistics* 36. 281–331.
Matras, Yaron. 2007. Grammatical borrowing in Domari. In Yaron Matras & Jeanette Sakel (eds.), *Grammatical Borrowing in Cross-Linguistic Perspective*, 151–164. Berlin: De Gruyter.
Matras, Yaron. 2009. *Language contact*. Cambridge: Cambridge University Press.
Molochieva, Zarina. 2010. *Tense, aspect, and mood in Chechen*. Leipzig: University of Leipzig dissertation.
Moutaouakil, Ahmed. 2018. Issues in functional Arabic linguistics. In Elabbas Benmamoun & Reem Bassiouney (eds.), *The Routledge handbook of Arabic linguistics*, 204–223. London: Routledge.
Myers-Scotton, Carol. 2002. *Contact linguistics, bilingual encounters and grammatical outcomes*. Oxford: Oxford University Press.

Nichols, Johanna. 1989. The Nakh evidence for the history of gender in Nakh-Daghestanian. In Howard I. Aronson (ed.), *The Non-Slavic languages of the USSR: Linguistic Studies*, 158–175. Chicago: Chicago Linguistic Society.

Nichols, Johanna. 1994. Chechen. In Rieks Smeets (ed.), The indigenous languages of the Caucasus, Volume 4: The North East Caucasian languages II, 1–77. Delmar: Caravan books.

Nichols, Johanna. 2003. A Bipartite Verb Stem Outlier in Eurasia: Nakh-Daghestanian. *Proceedings of the Twenty-Ninth Annual Meeting of the Berkeley Linguistics Society* 29.

Öpengin, Ergin. 2020. Kurdish. In Christopher Lucas & Stefano Manfredi (eds.), *Arabic and contact-induced change*, 459–487. Berlin: Language Science Press.

Rannut, Ulle. 2011. Maintenance of the Circassian Language in Jordan. *Journal of Multilingual and Multicultural Development* 30(4). 297–310.

Rouchdy, Aleya. 1991. *Nubians and the Nubian language in contemporary Egypt: A case of cultural and linguistic contact*. Leiden: Brill.

Ryding, Karin C. 2005. *A reference grammar of modern standard Arabic*. Cambridge: Cambridge University Press.

Scontras, Gregory, Zuzanna Fuchs, & Maria Polinsky. 2015. Heritage language and linguistic theory. *Frontiers in Psychology* 6. https://doi.org/10.3389/fpsyg.2015.01545.

Stolz, Thomas. 2008. Romanticisation worldwide. In Thomas Stolz, Dik Bakker & Rosa Salas Palomo (eds.), *Aspects of language contact: New theoretical, methodological and empirical findings with special focus on Romanticisation processes*, 1–42. Berlin: de Gruyter.

Stolz, Thomas. 2022. Entlehntes aber. Kontaktinduzierte Diffusion adversativer Konnektoren des konjunktionalen Typs. In Julia Nintemann & Cornelia Stroh (eds.), *Über Widersprüche sprechen: Linguistische Beiträge zu Contradiction Studies*, 145–177. Wiesbaden: Springer.

Stolz, Thomas & Nataliya Levkovych. 2022. On loan conjunctions: A comparative study with special focus on the languages of the former Soviet Union. In Nataliya Levkovych (ed.), *Susceptibility vs. resistance: Case studies on different structural categories in language-contact situations*, 259–392. Berlin: De Gruyter.

Suleiman, Yasir. 2008. The language ecology of the Middle East: Jordan as a case study. In Angela Creese, Peter Martin & Nancy H. Hornberger (eds.), *Encyclopedia of language and education, Volume 9: Ecology of Language*, 125–139. Boston: Springer.

Tadmor, Uri. 2009. Loanwords in the world's languages: Findings and results. In Haspelmath, Martin & Uri Tadmor (eds.), *Loanwords in the world's languages: A comparative handbook*, 55–75. Berlin: De Gruyter.

Versteegh, Kees. 2001. Linguistic contact between Arabic and other languages. *Arabica* 48. 470–508.

Wohlgemuth, Jan. 2009. *A typology of verbal borrowings*. Berlin: De Gruyter.

Zelkina, Anna. 2000. The Arabic linguistic and cultural tradition in Daghestan: An historical overview. In Jonathan Owens (ed.), *Arabic as a minority language*, 89–111. Berlin: De Gruyter.

Martin Haase
Scenarios of Basque Language Contact

Abstract: The paper compares the scenarios of Romance-Basque language contact in different parts of the Basque Country. In the South-West the predominant contact language is Spanish, which has gained some territory to the detriment of Basque, whereas on the French side of the border the extension of the Basque speaking area has not been reduced in the same way. Here the contact situation is more complex since an often overlooked language intervenes: Gascon. The different scenarios cause certain differences in loan word integration, phonetics and phonology, and even grammar.

Keywords: Basque, language contact, bilingualism, language shift, borrowing

1 Introduction: Basque and the Basque Country

Basque (*Euskara* or *Euskera*) is a language isolate, typologically very different from the Romance languages with which it is in contact (Haase 2011). It has, however, been heavily influenced by Romance languages through borrowing, mainly because almost all speakers of Basque living in the Basque Country are bilingual with Spanish or French as the contact language. With the exception of a typical intonation pattern, there is no distinctive regional Basque accent of Spanish, whereas in the French Basque Country, the contact language is spoken with a distinct accent, shared with non-Basque speakers of South-Western France.

Only former emigrants to North America that have come back to the Basque Country may have a poor knowledge of Spanish or French, although, at least to some degree, they cannot help learning the predominant contact language of their part of the Basque Country, i. e. Spanish or French, in the latter case with the typical regional accent. Map 1 (Sarasua Garmendia 2008) shows the major dialects. These are, starting West: Biscayan, Gipuzkoan, Navarrese on the Spanish side of the border between France and Spain and (in lighter colors) on the other side of the border: Navarro-Lapurdian and Souletin (the dialect of Zuberoa, or Soule in French). The gray area shows where Basque was still spoken in the

Martin Haase, University of Bamberg, Chair for Romance Linguistics, 96045 Bamberg, Germany.
E-mail: martin.haase@uni-bamberg.de

19th century (based on Bonaparte 1991). Shaded areas are areas of transition or, if shaded in gray, areas of partial loss. The map outlines the traditional provinces of the Basque Country, starting West: Biscay, Araba/Alava, Gipuzkoa, Navarre on the Spanish side and Lapurdi/Labourd, Lower Navarre, and Zuberoa/Soule on the French side.

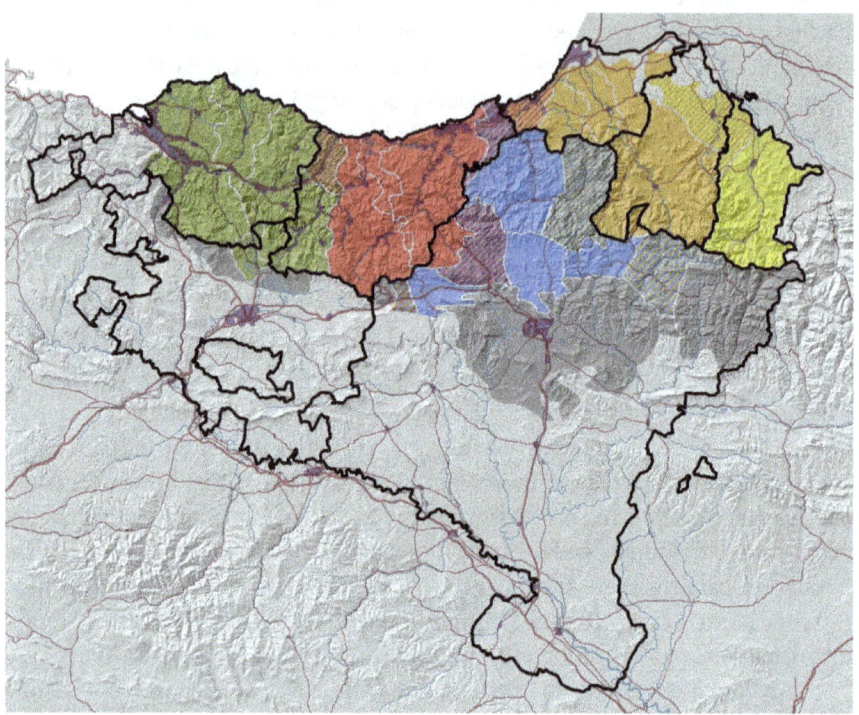

Map 1: Dialects

I distinguish between borrowing and substratum (or substrate) interference, following Thomason and Kaufman (1988). The scenarios described here are scenarios of borrowing into Basque. I will briefly mention substratum interference when it comes to Gascon, a Romance language heavily influenced by interference from Basque, since it came about when Basque speakers shifted from Basque to Latin or Romance (Haase 1997). The main focus is on loans taken over into Basque from the surrounding Romance languages (adstrata). I will start with concrete loan words (MATTER in the typology introduced by Sakel 2007), then treat more abstract grammatical borrowings (moving into the sphere of PATTERN according to

Sakel 2007). It will be obvious that PATTERN loans come about hand in hand with the borrowing of MATTER.

2 Simplistic assumptions

Outsiders and even speakers of Basque from the Spanish part of the Basque Country usually have a simplistic view of Basque language contact. They assume that the Basque Country is divided into a Spanish and a French part and that on the South-Western side of the border (commonly called *Hegoalde* 'South' in Basque) a more Spanish version of Basque is spoken, whereas on the North-Eastern side of the border (commonly called *Iparralde* 'North') the local varieties of Basque are influenced by French. While it is true that the Basque Country is still divided between the nation states of France and Spain, and Basque therefore borrows from the respective state language where this language is predominant, the Basque Country is not cut into two dialect areas along the state border, as a superficial approach (such as Schlaak 2014) might suggest. It goes without saying that French and Spanish play a role in their respective regions, but a closer look reveals a different division.

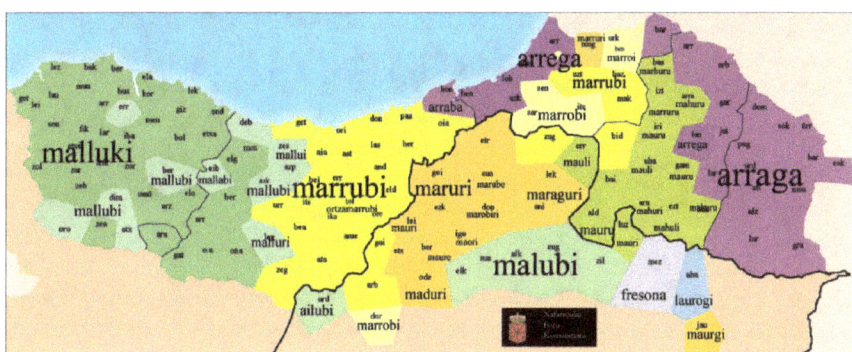

Map 2: *strawberry*, EHHA 572

Consider the data on Map 2 from the dialect atlas of the Basque Country (*Euskal Herriko Hizkeren Atlasa*[1] EHHA 572). It shows the different dialectal forms of the

---

[1] I will always refer to maps and comments in EHHA by the corresponding map number and not a page number, which makes it easier to consult the material online.

Basque word for 'strawberry' (*marrubi* in the Standard language *Euskara batua*). For the sake of simplicity, I will sum up dialectal variants with the help of lexical types enclosed in wedge-shaped brackets ⌐...⌐, as it is done in traditional dialectology. These types stand for a list of phonetically similar variants in an area.

With the exception of one place in Navarre where the Spanish loan word *fresón* is used there are two types of outcomes: (a) ⌐marrubi⌐ (with more or less obvious phonetic variants, ranging from *malluki* in Biscay to a heavily altered *laurogi* at the Navarrese outlayer village of Mezkiritz) and (b) ⌐arraga⌐ in part of Iparralde (with the variants *arrega* in Lapurdi and *arraga* in Zuberoa, and the variant *arraba*, just across the French border in Irún). The fact that both types cross the border between France and Spain already contradicts the idea that this frontier divides the Basque Country into two distinct dialectal areas. The colors of the two types suggest that ⌐arraga⌐ is an older form. The authors of the Atlas may have thought so, because words beginning with *m-/b-*, probably the only Basque phonemes that are (with one notable exception) unattested in Basque inflection, are probably loan words (cf. Michelena 1961 on the phonetic history of Basque loan words). In fact, *marrubi* is Latin MARRUBIUM 'horehound', a similar looking plant.

Map 3: *to hear*, EHHA 2073

The idea that the North-Eastern dialect of Zuberoa or Soule is archaic does not come as a surprise, since this region is a peripheral mountainous area that does not follow innovations of more progressive areas (linguistically and otherwise). In Romance linguistics such an area is called *area lateralis*, because the linguistically most conservative areas are usually peripheral (*lateralis* in Latin). Older Latin loan words do confirm the idea of the area lateralis. Map 3 (EHHA 2073) shows the distribution of the Latin loan *a(d)itu* (< AUDITU) 'to hear'. Only in the peripheral regions of the Basque Country the older indigenous form *entzun* is used on a dialectal level. Both words have been adopted by the standard language.

In his French-Basque dictionary the Basque priest and philologist Junes Casenave-Harigile (1989) systematically proposes Zuberoan vocabulary as archaic and thus preferable to words from *Euskara batua*, as in the case of *arraga*.

At first sight, this word does seem to have a more traditional consonance than *marrubi*, but things are not so simple. There is something strange about this word: Basque words cannot start with an *r* sound. In loan words an *e-* is inserted as in *errege* 'king' from Latin REGE(M), with one exception: Loan words from Gascon, a variety of Occitan in the South West of France, have a prosthetic *a-* as in *arrosa* 'rose'. The allegedly archaic Basque *arraga* is indeed a Gascon loan from *hraga* 'strawberry' (Gascon changes *f-* into *h-*, so the natural outcome of Latin FRAGA is *hraga* in Gascon). Since *hr-* is not pronounceable in Basque, the initial *h-* is lost and as in all Gascon loanwords with initial *r-* an *a-* is added, resulting in *arraga*.

The reason for these particularities in Gascon can be explained by the early history of this language: Since Basque cannot have words starting with *r-*, speakers shifting to Latin and later to Romance had a problem with such words and did not adopt the Basque solution, because they wanted to give up Basque. They found a "Romance" solution in adding *a(r)-*, modelled on the Romance prefix *a(d)-*. In the same way, these language shifters had a problem with *f-* and had to find a solution different to Basque. They had no difficulty in pronouncing *h*, since this is a Basque phoneme, so it comes in easily, because it had no functional load in Romance. It has been argued (critically reviewed by Penny 2014: 91) that the passage of *f-* to *h-* in Spanish could also be explained by substratum interference from Basque. This is difficult, as Penny points out, because the passage occurs rather late in the history of Spanish and in areas not directly in contact with Basque, and it does not concern all contexts of initial *f-*, which is unusual for substratum interference. Penny (2014: 92) comes up with the following compromise:

> This change may have been initiated by Frenchmen (speakers of French and Occitan) who entered Spain in large numbers in the twelfth and thirteenth centuries, sometimes occupying positions of great social prestige. (Penny 2014: 92)

These "Frenchmen" are, of course, speakers of Gascon who colonized the Basque country by creating fortified market towns (*Bastidas*), such as Bayonne, Bilbao, Labastide Clairence etc. and traded with people from neighboring regions. Thanks to their prestige, Castilian speakers imitated their speech, so the Spanish aspirated *h-* came into the language through borrowing.

Gascon is often overlooked, because it is a language nowadays without official status (with the exception of the Aran Valley in Spain). In France it is on the brink of language death. Philologists take an interest in the peculiar features of Gascon. Most of these features can be explained by substratum interference, as speakers of Basque switched from Basque to Latin and later Romance in a scenario of substituting one language for the other (Haase 1997). But Gascon has always played a role as a source of borrowing for Basque (adstratum) and probably Spanish too.

3 Romance influence

The North-Eastern part of the Basque Country, comprising the former provinces of Lower Navarre and Zuberoa, may be a conservative *area lateralis* in some respects (regarding *core* morphology and syntax, but there is more to say about this in this and the following section), however, where phonetics, phonology, and especially the lexicon is concerned, it is under heavy Gascon influence. It is a typical borrowing scenario. For a long time Gascon had been the more prestigious Romance language (used in administration in Navarre until shortly after the French revolution) and until very recently in bovine commerce. It has gradually been supplanted by French, esp. after World War II. Among elderly people, esp. in the Northern part of Lower Navarre, the so-called Pays-de-Mixe or Amikuze in Basque, and in Zuberoa, it is still common to be trilingual in Basque, Gascon, and French. This is especially true for people who get involved in bovine commerce (although their knowledge of Gascon may be limited to the necessities of their profession).

Bayonne is sometimes called capital of Iparralde (*Iparraldeko hiri nagusia*), but in spite of a certain presence of Basque, French seems to have supplanted Basque long ago. This is again a little simplistic, because in Bayonne French did not supplant Basque, but Gascon. Even nowadays some traces of Gascon can be found in street names and inscriptions. With respect to French, Gascon has had far less prestige, so it was easy for French to become the city's first language. Additionally, in the second part of the 20th century, Basque gained a lot of prestige, so that the idea of a bilingualism of French and Gascon in Bayonne was replaced by the idea of the Basque *hiri nagusia*, now speaking French.

But Gascon used to be more influential in former times, which explains the presence of Gascon borrowings in Lapurdi as well, passing even over the border into Spain. The intercalation of Gascon between French and Basque protected

Basque from French influences. After the disappearance of Aragonese and Navarrese (Neira Martínez 1982), an intermediary language did (and does) not exist between Spanish and Basque on the other side of the border. Here, Spanish could heavily influence Basque, on the one hand, and on the other, it started to gain territory to the detriment of Basque. The presence of Gascon is most obvious in the North of Lower Navarre (Amikuze) and in Zuberoa, the traditional areas of Gascon and Basque bilingualism. Most dialect maps reveal that the Basque Country is not cut into two by the state border, but by the presence or absence of this bilingualism.

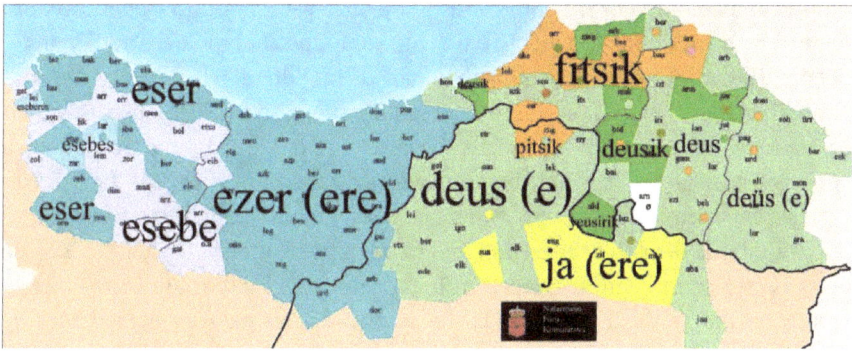

Map 4: *nothing*, EHHA 1743

The importance of Gascon does not stop there. As Ciérbide Martirena (1992/93) has pointed out, Gascon played a role in the Southern part of the Basque Country as well, although at an earlier time: Some cities in the Basque Country go back to Medieval Gascon settlements; these were (from West to East): Bilbao, San Sebastián (Donostia in Basque), Hondarribia, and Pamplona (Iruñ(e)a in Basque). Pamplona is particularly interesting, since it is situated in Navarre where Gascon was the language of the administration. This explains the presence of Gascon loanwords in Navarre as well, as is the case with *deus* 'nothing', going back to Gascon *degu(n)s* (<g> representing a lax fricative [ɣ]) with the same meaning. Map 4 (EHHA 1743) shows the distribution of the following types: the purely Basque ⸢ezer⸣ (a combination of *ez* 'not' and *zer* 'what'), the Gascon loan word ⸢deus⸣ (sometimes with the partitive ending -*ik*) and the expressive forms ⸢ja⸣ (probably a Romance cognate of Latin JAM 'already') and ⸢fitsik⸣. This form is found in Gascon too, *fich* is an expressive word to describe small quantities (in Basque always with the partitive ending). This word is unusual, because it conserves initial [f] which usually becomes [h] in Gascon and [p] in Basque. The strange conservation of [f] also appears in the opposite 'much' where *frango* (of obvious Romance origin) serves as an expressive variant of *hanitz* in Iparralde.

The negative is sometimes reinforced by *ere* 'also', if it is used emphatically. The map shows that Navarre together with Zuberoa opts for the Gascon loan word. It is interesting to see that in most of this area *deus* is rivaled by the more expressive forms – also of Romance origin. Since Gascon is still a (barely) living contact language (adstratum) only in Zuberoa and the North of Lower Navarre (Amikuze), it can be considered a superstratum in Upper Navarre. The long period of contact in Amikuze has led to a situation where we sometimes find more than one layer of borrowings as in the case of *fitsik* vs. *deus*.

At the beginning of the 16th century, Navarre was split into Upper Navarre, reigned by the Catholic Crown of Spain with some special privileges and an independent Lower Navarre which became part of the kingdom of France and Navarre. In Upper Navarre, Gascon was gradually replaced by Spanish as the main prestigious contact language (while Navarrese and Aragonese were Romance spoken varieties that kept on being used in rural settings, for the fate of Navarrese, cf. Neira Martínez 1982), whereas Gascon maintained its status as an important language of administration and trade in the Northern part of the Basque Country. By consequence, Gascon influence remained important in the North, whereas it gradually disappeared in the South, and Basque was pushed back by Spanish, gaining ground in Navarre. Moreover, Gascon served as a protective intermediary between Basque and French, after French became the language of post-revolutionary France.

Aragonese, the language with which Basque was also in contact in North-Eastern Upper Navarre (next to the neighboring provinces of Huesca and Saragossa), faced the same fate as Gascon in Spain. Consequently, Spanish started to push back Basque in the extreme North-East of Upper Navarre. Since some (scarce) documentation of these dialects has been preserved, it would be interesting to look for Aragonese influence. The early substitution of Aragonese by Spanish might explain the occasional appearance of Spanish loan words in the neighboring Basque dialects (cf. *fresona* < Spanish: *fresón* in Map 2). The contact situation of Basque can be summed up as follows:

– The current main contact languages (adstrata) of Basque are Spanish and French, and to a lesser degree Gascon (where it is still spoken),
– Gascon protects Basque against the advance of French in the Northern part of the Basque Country where the language border has not moved for centuries (with a zone of Basque and Gascon bilingualism in Amikuze in the North of Lower Navarre and the whole of Zuberoa). The go-between character of

Gascon between French and Basque can also explain why speakers of Basque speak the same form of regional French as their Gascon neighbors.
- At least historically, Aragonese and Gascon are contact languages in Navarre; in Amikuze and Zuberoa it is of utmost importance to take Gascon into account, even nowadays.
- Spanish has been pushing back Basque since early modern times in the Spanish Basque Country.
- Linguistically, the Basque Country is not so much divided by the border between France and Spain, but by the different impact of Gascon as an adstratum.

Or, to cut a long story short: Gascon is a largely neglected, but very important factor in the dialectalization of Basque.

4 Contact-induced change

It is interesting to take a closer look at loan word morphology. Map 5 shows how 'to stumble' is expressed in Basque. The extreme West shows direct Spanish influence: ⌈tropesau⌉ clearly is Spanish *tropezado,* which even preserves the Spanish participle (though in a spoken variant), the larger portion of Hegoalde has ⌈estrapozo (eg)in⌉ 'to make a stumble', where *estrapozo* probably goes back to a Latin or early Romance formation (*EXTRAPODIU or *EXTRAPEDIU?, which somewhat resembles Spanish *tropezón*, probably going back to *INTERPEDIU), Navarre has a Basque formation ⌈muturkatu⌉, which is based on *mutur* 'snout' ('to fall on one's snout', the form *muturketu* on the map seems to be a typo).

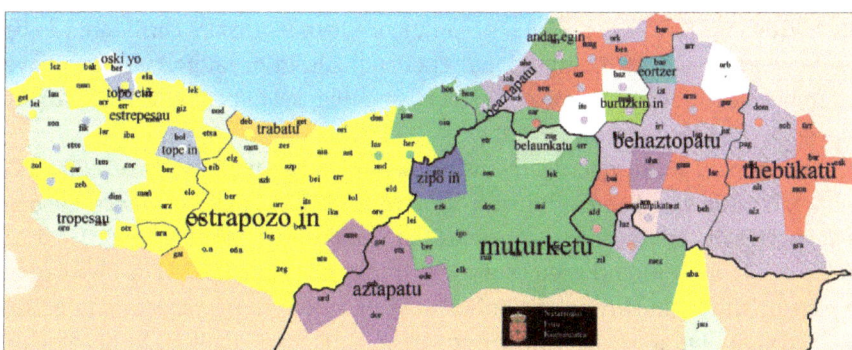

Map 5: *to stumble*, EHHA 381

Amongst other solutions Iparralde shows many instances of ⌈trebukatu⌉, which the EHHA editors consider a French loan (EHHA 381). It cannot be a Gascon borrowing, because in Gascon it is *trabucar*. But the French verb is *trebucher*. How do we get from there to *trebukatu*? It looks as if *trebucher* has passed through a Gascon filter, because *-cher* corresponds to Gascon *-car*, and Gascon [y], which corresponds to French [y] is generally pronounced [y] in Gascon loan words in Zuberoa and some places of Amikuze, but is adapted to [u] in the rest of the Basque Country. The borrowed *trebucatu* starts out French (*tre-*), then turns into Gascon (*-buka-*) and finishes with an ending originally borrowed from Latin (*-tu*).

This is by no means surprising. Loan word integration often works along the strategies acquired in older borrowing scenarios. Thus, for borrowing from French, strategies derived from Gascon loan words are employed, whereas these strategies depend on the structure of Latin loan words. Latin facilitates the introduction of Gascon loan words, and Gascon facilitates the introduction of French loan words. I call this phenomenon syphon effect (or "Schleuseneffekt" in German (Haase 1992: 51) the English translation was proposed by Bakker 1993). The syphon effect can be found in many borrowing scenarios. I have treated it in some detail for Maltese (Haase 2002), where Italian loan words look, as if they have passed through Sicilian, and English loan words look and sound Italian when integrated into Maltese.

Even from a general standpoint the difference between the borrowing scenarios of Biscay and Iparralde is striking: In Biscay, where Basque is under some pressure from Spanish, speakers go straight for a Spanish solution (⌈tropesau⌉), whereas in Iparralde a French loan word is integrated by sophisticated integration strategies, based on older loan strata (Gascon and Latin).

In an intensive borrowing scenario grammatical change comes about through lexical borrowing. We have seen an example on Map 4 above where a new negator is borrowed into the replica language. Negations are often affected by borrowings (Willis et al. 2013: 47–50), since loan words are considered to be more expressive than the traditional grammaticalized negators, and the above example clearly shows that even a first layer of loans will be innovated again by newer, more expressive borrowings.

Like Spanish, Basque distinguishes between the auxiliary 'have' (Spanish *haber*, Basque *ukan*) and a full verb 'to have/to possess' (Spanish *tener*, Basque *eduki*). This distinction is prescribed in Standard Basque, but from the EHHA data (Map 6, EHHA 1756), it becomes evident that this distinction is borrowed from Spanish, although *eduki* is certainly an old Basque verb (as *tener* is an old Romance verb), but in former times (and still in all Eastern dialects) forms of *ukan* can be used to express possession, just as the outcomes of HABERE can in most

Romance languages. The map shows how the distinction between *ukan* 'haber' (*badut* or *badet* in the first person singular Ergative) and *eduki* 'tener' (in the first person singular *daukat* 'tengo', or in English: 'I have') is pushing forward from the West. Even conservative places in Gipuzkoa that still use *badet* mostly have *daukat* as a second answer. And even across the French border the distinction can be made in some places, but never in Zuberoa or the Northern part of Lower Navarre. The prefix *ba-* corresponds to the Enunciative that is so typical of Gascon, compare ***qu'èi*** 'I have' in Gascon. I have argued elsewhere (Haase 1997) that this peculiar Gascon feature came about through substratum interference from Basque.

Map 6: *I have*, EHHA 1756

Map 7: *too much/many*, EHHA 1224

In addition to Comparative and Superlative, Basque has an Excessive ('too'), expressed by the ending *-egi*. The irregular stem *ge(h)i-* is used to form Comparative and Superlative forms of 'much, many': *ge(h)iago* 'more', *ge(h)ien* 'most', *ge(h)iegi* 'too much/many'. This is, of course, a place where expressive innovations can be expected. Map 7 (EHHA 1224) shows what is going on. The center of the Basque Country uses the traditional form. The West shows an innovation, the expressive adverb *lar* (possibly from *larri* 'big, pressing') is used, partly with the Excessive ending, but not so in most of the direct contact zone with Spanish, but the traditional form is still present in most places. The Eastern Basque Country opts for the Gascon loan word *sob(e)ra* (Gascon *sobra* < SUPRA). The modern Gascon pronunciation is [suβrɔ, suβrʊ] or [suβrɛ], but it is integrated following traditional integration strategies, corresponding to older pronunciations of Gascon (that are reflected in the "classic" Gascon orthography, used in this article). The *br* cluster is split by an epenthetic vowel and *r* is lost in Zuberoa. The Gascon borrowing is so successful that *ge(h)iegi* cannot be found in the Eastern part of the Basque Country anymore.

The case system is also under attack by (expressive) borrowings, as in Map 8 (EHHA 1173).

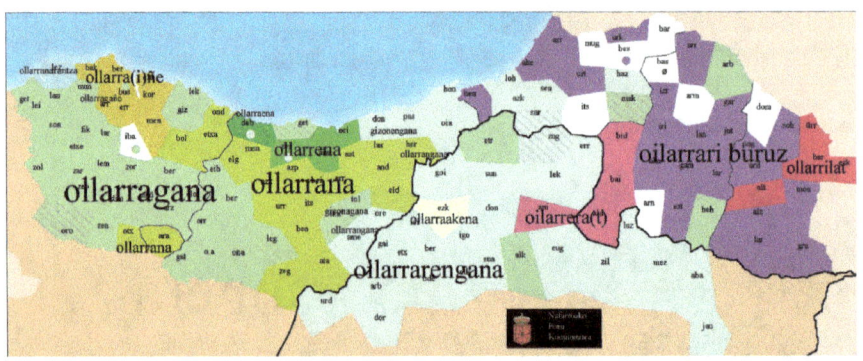

Map 8: *to the rooster*, EHHA 1173

The Standard Basque form *oilarrengana* 'to the rooster' is only present in the center of the Basque Country (surprisingly not so much in Gipuzkoa); *-rengan-* is normally used with animated nouns in locative cases (consisting of the Possessive/Genitive ending *-ren*, and the animated location suffix *-gan*). The Possessive/Genitive ending is left out in the West, so that *-gana* looks more like a postposition. This solution is sporadically found in the East too. Here another solution consists in adding the Allative case directly to the animated noun, as in *oilarrera(t)* and *ollarrilat*, but here another solution is more widespread: The noun is in the Dative case and followed by *bürü* 'head' in the Instrumental case. This construction is difficult to explain within Basque grammar because the Dative is normally not found under such circumstances. It can, however, be explained by Gascon: it is a calque of Gascon *cap a* '(with) head to', used to indicate a direction. The preposition *a* is normally used to express the Dative in Gascon, so the calque is very natural for bilingual speakers. Once established, it is used in the everyday language until efforts of language purism will eradicate it.

Map 9: Potential mode, EHHA 1775

Map 9 (EHHA 1775) shows changes in the verbal morphology of Basque. Possibility is normally expressed morphologically by the Potential mode. It is formed by changing the auxiliary stem and by adding the Potential marker *-ke* to the auxiliary. Romance languages would rather use an auxiliary construction with *poder* 'can' in Spanish or Gascon. It comes as no surprise that the morphological solution is maintained in the center of the Basque Country (mainly in Gipuzkoa again), whereas the peripheries opt for more Romance constructions.

Here the potential modal operator *a(h)al* is used. It is usually inserted between the full verb and the auxiliary (as can be seen in the East of the Basque Country). In the West, however, the order resembles Spanish word order *al zara joan* 'you can go' ~ 'puedes ir'. Instead of the nominalized verb in the Inessive (*joaten*), the use of the basic form *joan* seems to calque an infinitive construction. Whereas in Basque a form of 'to be' has to be used with an intransitive verb, *al* is coupled with 'to have' (*dozu*) in parts of Biscay, which makes the construction look even more like a modal auxiliary construction. In the Eastern part of the Basque Country 'to be' is used with the verb of movement (as is the case in French and Gascon), but the modal operator is also assimilated to an auxiliary, because it can take a future-tense marker (*-ko*). In my own research I have observed at least one case where the modal operator is fully transformed into a verb (Haase 1992: 114). An extreme case can be seen in Hondarribia where the whole construction is substituted by *posible duzu xuatia* [joatea] 'it is possible to go (*or rather:* you have it possible going)', based on the Romance (Gascon or Spanish) loan word *posible*.

Map 10: *(s)he helps him/her*, EHHA 1760

The full impact of Spanish language contact can be seen on Map 10 (EHHA 1760). Spanish has differential object marking: an animated object (human or animal) is put into the Dative. This should not be possible in Basque, because the Dative case always implies the presence of an Absolutive (the case for the direct object in a transitive clause), which would be empty, but still under Spanish influence this can be observed with the verb *lagundu* 'to help' which should have a direct object in Basque, but gets an indirect one in most dialects of Hegoalde, leaving the direct-object position empty (note that in German too, *helfen* is constructed with an indirect object without having a direct one).

The auxiliary *du* is transitive, referencing an Ergative and an Absolutive in the 3rd person singular. The auxiliary *dio* or *dotzo* references a Dative in the 3rd person singular in addition to Absolutive and Ergative. This is the closest we can get to the idea of the Basque Country split into two parts, one under Spanish and one under French, or rather Gascon, influence. We can still see that the distribution does not fully coincide with the Spanish-French border and that there are isolated cases of non-differential marking in Gipuzkoa (Aia) and in several places in Navarre.

It comes as no surprise that – together with loan words – phonemes can be borrowed from one language to another (Stolz and Levkovych 2021). A case in point is the [y] in Zuberoa and sporadically in Amikuze too. For the rest of the Basque Country Gascon [y] is rendered as [u], and so is French [y]. What is more surprising is that Basque word stress (tonic accent) seems to be a result of borrowing, as I have shown (Haase 2016: 70f.) with respect to the data by Aurrekoetxea et al. (2012). Most dialects of Basque have a syntagmatic accent and no word stress, but all Eastern dialects show word stress, as in Gascon. Standard Basque has word stress too, but this is probably due to the common misunderstanding that the dialects of Zuberoa and Lower Navarre represent an archaic form of Basque; moreover, when Standard Basque was set up, philologists may have thought that syntagmatic stress is the outcome of a decay of stress pattern, as was the case in the evolution of French. That can explain why the Basque Academy promulgated word stress for Standard Basque. The dialect distribution of stress patterns in Basque shows, however, that word stress is an innovation, stemming from the contact with Gascon.

5 Language change, language reform, and purism

A presentation of language contact in Basque cannot be complete without reference to the scenario of language reform and purism. I have already mentioned that the Basque Academy established word stress as a norm for Standard Basque and that case forms are preferred over constructions such as *-ri buruz*, calqued from Gascon *cap a* 'head to, in the direction of'. In a study on purism (Haase 2004: 128), I have treated causal constructions, showing that a more Romance looking sentential variant of the causal construction is suppressed by purists in favor of a more nominal construction type. This observation has been confirmed by dialect data.

Map 11 (EHHA 1794) shows the answer to the last part of the following sentence: "No se casó con Juan porque era rico, sino porque le amaba" or « Ce n'est pas parce qu'il était riche qu'elle s'est mariée avec Jean, mais parce qu'elle l'aimait », meaning: 'She did not marry John because he was rich, but because she loved him.' The sentence was included into the questionnaire, in order to distinguish different causal relations (wrong and true cause, subjective and objective cause). Basque uses constructions with *-lako(tz)* for true and objective cause and *-lakoan* for wrong or subjective cause. But the sentence has another pitfall: The true cause is added last, integrated into an adversative clause after the conjunction 'but'. So, in the translation, informants would prefer a construction where the causal part follows the matrix clause. This is impossible with *-lako*, which must precede the main clause (the Delimitative marker *-ko* cannot come at the end). The obvious solution is another causal construction in which the inflected verb is prefixed by the subordinator *b(a)it-*. This construction usually follows the main clause and can be introduced with *ze(r)en (eta)* an improvised conjunction, meaning 'for what (and)' (cf. Spanish *por qué*, French *pourquoi* or Gascon *perqué, per de qué, pr'amor de qué*, which even accounts for the Possessive/Genitive ending *-(r)en* in *ze(r)en eta*). This construction is heavily proscribed by purists. But since purists are mainly active on the Spanish side of the border, it comes as no surprise that the proscribed forms can be more easily found in France. Again, however, it is not the state border that cuts the Basque Country into two parts, but the presence of Gascon. Since the sentential variant is very close to the construction in the Gascon model language, Basque and Gascon bilingualism reinforces the use of this construction, and purists will have a hard time getting rid of it.

Map 11: *because she loved him*, EHHA 1794

6 Conclusion

The border between France and Spain did not play any role in the long-term dialectal development of Basque since the Middle Ages. Here other contact languages play a significant role, namely Gascon, Aragonese, and Navarrese. Navarrese (and later Aragonese) have gradually been substituted by Spanish as the main contact language in the South (Neira Martínez 1982). Then between the 19th and the 20th century Spanish has pushed back Basque in Hegoalde, and has contributed to the eradication of traditional Basque dialects in Spain. In Iparralde, there is still a significant amount of traditional, now elderly speakers of dialectal Basque, not influenced very much by the standard language, some of them (mainly in Amikuze and Zuberoa) being bilingual in Basque and Gascon (with the addition of French for most speakers). On the other hand, in Hegoalde, Basque is mainly maintained through the establishment of a standard language (E*uskara batua*), which brings about new speakers, a tendency towards purism and the imposition of normative grammar to the detriment of traditional dialects.

All in all, three contact scenarios can be observed in the Basque Country:
- Spanish is in direct contact with Basque in a scenario of language substitution. At the same time it has an impact as a model language on Basque, which is heavily borrowing from Spanish.
- Purism is avoiding Romance and especially Spanish borrowings in Basque. In this respect Spanish is a negative model language. Distance from Spanish is very important for purists. This can result in filtering out even genuinely Basque structures, as can be shown in the case of subordination.
- Although Basque is borrowing from French, the presence of Gascon on the Northern border of the Basque Country is protecting Basque from some pressure from French. At least the Northern Border has not been pushed back by the modern contact language, as has happened in the South of the Basque Country. Moreover, due to the extended contact between Gascon and Basque, Basque has integrated a lot of borrowings from Gascon. With lexical borrowings, phonological and other structural innovations have come about.

The importance of Gascon for Basque language contact has already been pointed out by French physician Paul Broca (1875) who was born in Gascony and studied the border between Gascon and Basque. It has since been often overlooked (recently once again by Schlaak 2014). Allières (1978) is probably the first who took the role of Gascon for the evolution of Basque seriously and inspired me to my own studies (Haase 1992). In the 1990s the Basque dialect atlas EHHA did not exist, and I had to rely on my own field work which often resulted in impressionistic evidence from few places in Lower Navarre and Zuberoa. Starting in 2008 the publication of EHHA began to confirm all of my results. Each volume of the atlas showed evermore clearly the overall impact of Gascon and the difference between the different language-contact scenarios in Iparralde and Hegoalde.

References

Allières, Jacques. 1978. Petit Atlas linguistique basque-français Bourciez (20 cartes commentées). *Fontes Linguae Vasconum* 27. 353–386.

Aurrekoetxea, Gotzon, Iñaki Gaminde, Leire Gandarias, Aitor Iglesias. 2012. *Stress accent in Basque from the traditional dialects to standard variety*. Vienne: Congrès de la Société de dialectologie et géolinguistique.

Bakker, Peter. 1993. Review of Haase 1992. *Language* 69. 624–625.

Bonaparte, Louis-Lucien. 1991. *Opera omnia vasconice*. 4 vols. Bilb(a)o: Euskaltzaindia.

Broca, Paul. 1875. Sur l'origine de la répartition de la langue basque (Basques français et Basques espagnols). *Revue d'Anthropologie*. 1–54.

Casenave-Harigile, Junes. 1989. *Hiztegia français-eüskara : Züberotar eüskalkitik abiatzez*, Ozaze i.e. Ossas-Suhare: Hitzak.

Ciérbide Martirena, Ricardo. 1992/93. La Lengua de los francos de Estella : intento de interpretación. *Archivo de filología aragonesa* 48–49. 9–45. https://ifc.dpz.es/recursos/publicaciones/12/72/01cierbide.pdf (checked 14.8.2022).

EHHA: Aurrekoetxea, Gotzon & Charles Videgain (eds.). 2008. *Euskal Herriko Hizkeren Atlasa*. Bilb(a)o: Euskaltzaindia. https://www.euskaltzaindia.eus/230-baliabideakarloka/dialektologia5/5445-euskal-herriko-hizkuntz-atlasa (checked 14.08.2022).

Haase, Martin. 1992. *Sprachkontakt und Sprachwandel im Baskenland: Die Einflüsse des Gaskognischen und Französischen auf das Baskische*. Hamburg: Buske.

Haase, Martin, 1997. Gascon et basque. Bilinguisme et substrat. *Sprachtypologie und Universalienforschung* 50. 189–228.

Haase, Martin. 2002. Mehrschichtiger Sprachkontakt in Malta. In Michael Bommes, Christina Noack & Doris Tophinke (eds.), *Sprache als Form. Festschrift für Utz Maas*, 101–107. Opladen: Westdeutscher Verlag.

Haase, Martin. 2004. Sprachpurismus im Baskischen. In Dónall ó Riagáin & Thomas Stolz (eds.), *Purism. Second Helping*, 121–130. Bochum: Brockmeyer.

Haase, Martin. 2011. Basque. In Bernd Kortmann & Johan van der Auwera (eds.), *The Languages and Linguistics of Europe. A Comprehensive Guide*, 209–221. Berlin & Boston: De Gruyter Mouton.

Haase, Martin. 2016. Les influences gasconnes en basque. In Calvo Rigual, Cesário, Laura Minervini & André Thibault (eds.), *Actes du XVIIe Congrès international de linguistique et de philologie romanes* (Nancy, 15–20 juillet 2013), *Section 11: Linguistique de contact*, 63–72. Nancy: ATILF. https://web-data.atilf.fr/ressources/cilpr2013/actes/section-11/CILPR-2013-11-Haase.pdf (checked 14.08.2022).

Michelena, Luis [Mitxelena, Koldo]. 1961. *Fonética histórica vasca*. Donostia & San Sebastián: Diputación de Guipúzcoa.

Neira Martínez, Jesús. 1982. La desaparición del romance navarro y el proceso de castellanización. *Revista Española de Lingüística* 12(2). 267–80.

Penny, Ralph J. 2014. *A history of the Spanish language*. Cambridge: Cambridge University Press.

Sakel, Jeanette. 2007. Types of loan: Matter and pattern. In Yaron Matras & Jeanette Sakel (eds.), *Grammatical borrowing in cross-linguistic perspective*, 15–29. New York & Berlin: Mouton de Gruyter.

Sarasua Garmendia, Asier. 2008. *Euskalkiak*. https://commons.wikimedia.org/wiki/File:Euskalkiak_koldo_zuazo_2008.png (checked 14.08.2022).

Schlaak, Claudia. 2014. *Das zweigeteilte Baskenland. Sprachkontakt, Sprachvariation und regionale Identität in Frankreich und Spanien*. Berlin: de Gruyter.

Stolz, Thomas & Nataliya Levkovych [in cooperation with Beke Seefried]. 2021. *Areal linguistics within the Phonological Atlas of Europe: Loan phonemes and their distribution*. Berlin & Boston: De Gruyter Mouton.

Thomason, Sarah Grey & Terrence Kaufman. 1988. *Language contact, creolization, and genetic linguistics*. Berkeley, Los Angeles & Oxford: University of California Press.

Willis, David, Christopher Lucas & Anne Breithbart. 2013. Comparing diachronies of negation. In David Willis, Christopher Lucas & Anne Breithbart (eds.), *The history of negation in the languages of Europe and the Mediterranean: Volume I Case studies*, 1–50. Oxford: Oxford University Press.

Maike Vorholt
The relevance of origin

Exploring the connection between the origin and frequency of Maltese prepositions

Abstract: This paper takes a closer look at the origin and token frequency of Maltese prepositions to describe a possible connection between the two. What is known about adposition borrowing in general is compared to the Maltese situation. The composition of the word class of prepositions is analyzed and the integration of borrowed prepositions into the language is described. Possible other factors influencing frequency are discussed. Regression analyses of origin and other factors are conducted to see which of them is best to model token frequency.

Keywords: frequency, language contact, Maltese, origin, prepositions

1 Introduction

This paper[1] takes a closer look at the origin and token frequency of Maltese prepositions[2]. To my knowledge, the possible interplay between frequency and origin has not been the subject of any empirical studies, yet. Similarly, prepositions in language contact situations have not been studied in connection with token frequency. It is investigated whether a connection between token frequency and origin exists in this word class. It is expected that the token frequency of a word is connected to its origin, primarily because core vocabulary is less likely to be borrowed. Therefore, if prepositions are borrowed, they are not expected to occupy core meanings and consequently have lower token frequencies (cf. Thomason 2001: 71; Matras 2007: 42; Matras 2011: 214; Haspelmath 2009: 36).

---

1 This study is part of the project *Präpositionen und ihre Grammatik im Maltesischen / Prepositions and their grammar in Maltese* (Grant STO 186/22-1) funded by the *Deutsche Forschungsgemeinschaft*.
2 One possible postposition in Maltese *ilu* 'ago' will not be included here since there is some debate about its status as a postposition (cf. Saari 2007; Stolz 2020: 440).

Maike Vorholt, University of Bremen, FB 10: Linguistics / Language Sciences, Universitäts-Boulevard 13, 28359 Bremen, Germany. E-Mail: vorholt@uni-bremen.de

Maltese is a perfect candidate for this study due to its long-lasting language contact with Italian, Sicilian, and English that led to a substantial number of Maltese prepositions being borrowed. There are studies on various aspects of language contact in connection with the Maltese language. However, there has not been much research in the area of token frequency in the context of language contact. Schmidt et al. (2020: 261) notice the importance of a closer analysis of frequency in connection with word origin but leave this question to following studies. Since the word class of prepositions is usually quite restricted, it makes it an excellent starting point for the study of token frequency in language contact situations. In addition, further descriptive studies are needed in the area of Maltese prepositions. Thus, this paper can shed some light on two thematic areas that have not been studied satisfactorily so far.

The paper is organized into six sections. Section 2 gives a brief review of relevant literature concerned with adposition borrowing in general. In Section 3 I describe the language contact situation in Malta and how the language is composed with regards to word origin. I take a closer look at Maltese prepositions and especially borrowed ones. The characteristics of Maltese prepositions and the integration of loan prepositions into the language will be analyzed in more detail. This is followed by a detailed description of the relationship between token frequency, origin, and possible other influencing factors to determine the relationship between these variables in Section 4. Prepositions that are borrowed and those of Semitic origin are compared. In Section 5 different regression models are generated using the factors analyzed in the previous section. The last section summarizes the results and a conclusion is drawn.

2 Adposition borrowing

For this paper I take Haspelmath and Tadmor's (2009a) definition of loanwords and borrowing: "Loanword (or lexical borrowing) is here defined as a word that at some point in the history of a language entered its lexicon as a result of borrowing (or *transfer*, or *copying*)." (Haspelmath and Tadmor 2009a: 36).

According to Libert (2002: 148), it is possible to borrow adpositions but this happens less often than with nouns. The words in the semantic field of spatial relations in the *World loanword database* by Haspelmath and Tadmor (2009b) show only very low borrowability scores. Many authors propose hierarchies of borrowability of different word classes or grammatical items. Field and Comrie (2002: 37) ascertain that nouns are the most likely to be borrowed, followed by verbs and adjectives and at last function words, like adpositions. Hekking et al.

(2010: 123) propose several borrowing hypotheses like the one in (1) which states that nouns are more easily borrowed than verbs leading to adpositions on the rightmost position.

(1) noun > verb > adjective > adverb > adposition

Matras (2007: 31) uses the term borrowability in the sense of the "likelihood of a structural category to be affected by contact-induced change". His hierarchy (2) is thus based on the frequency that the word classes are affected by contact in his sample of 27 languages:

(2) nouns, conjunctions > verbs > discourse markers > adjectives > interjections > adverbs > other particles, adpositions > numerals > pronouns > derivational affixes > inflectional affixes

Even though the definitions of borrowability differ, the reported hierarchies lead to the same grading of categories. Matras (2011: 214) also proposes the hierarchy in (3) for expressions of local relations. In his sample of 27 languages, Matras (2007: 42) notices that "[t]he preposition indicating 'between' is the most frequently borrowed". This is not the case in Maltese, though, where the preposition indicating 'between' – *bejn* – is of Semitic origin.

(3) peripheral local relations > core local relations

Adposition borrowing does not seem to be as unlikely as one might expect in hindsight of the hierarchies depicted above. Stolz and Stolz (1996: 105) provide a list of ten Spanish prepositions borrowed into several languages in Mesoamerica. Stolz (2008: 23) also observes in a paper about Romancisation that Romance prepositions are "rather successful in language contact". The preposition *contra* 'against' has been borrowed by many languages in contact with Italian or Spanish, Maltese being one of them with *kontra* 'against'[3] (Stolz 2008).

---

3 For each preposition an English translation will be given based on the first entry in Aquilina's (1987, 1991) Maltese-English dictionary.

3 Maltese language contact

The Maltese language has been in an intense language contact situation with Italian, Sicilian, and more recently English, which led to extensive borrowing. For a more thorough report see Brincat's (2018) description of the development of Maltese as the national language of Malta and the linguistic situation in Malta today. Lucas and Čéplö (2020) also present a comprehensive account of the history of Maltese language contact and give a detailed description of contact-induced changes that happened in the language.

There have been various studies on the proportion of words from different origins in the Maltese lexicon. I give a brief overview of some of their findings here to draw a general picture of the composition of Maltese that is compared to the word class of prepositions later on. Maltese prepositions are described in detail with a focus on the integration of borrowed prepositions, the distribution according to different origins, and their token frequencies in the Korpus Malti 3.0, which will be described in Section 3.2.3.

3.1 The composition of Maltese

Fenech (1978: 140) compared the composition of Maltese referring to the origin of words in journalistic texts with literary and spoken Maltese. First of all, he found that the proportions varied greatly across genres. In journalistic Maltese, 22.34% of words are of Romance origin compared to only 5.53% in literary and 9.19% in spoken Maltese. Words of English origin are represented with 4.74% in journalistic, 0.37% in literary, and 4.66% in spoken Maltese. Interestingly, Fenech (1978: 140) also analyzed the distribution of grammatical classes, among them prepositions, which are mostly of Semitic[4] origin in his sample.

Bovingdon and Dalli (2006) looked at a sample of 1000 words from the *Maltilex* corpus. They found that Italian as a donor language takes up the biggest proportions with 54% of their sample being of Italian origin, followed by Arabic 41% and English with 5%. They also list the etymological distribution for each word class. Only 2% of words of Semitic origin are function words (Bovingdon and Dalli 2006: 69) and there are no prepositions among the words of Italian or English origin (Bovingdon and Dalli 2006: 71). Only 1% of their sample of Maltese words

---

4 Some authors use the term "Semitic" while others use "Arabic" when referring basically to the same part of the Maltese lexicon. For the described studies I use the original terminology. For my own descriptions the term "Semitic" is used exclusively.

are prepositions (Bovingdon and Dalli 2006: 72). They conclude the following insight about prepositions among other word classes:

> Smaller word classes in the category of pronouns, prepositions and conjunctions are not favoured either from the Italian or the English lexicon. This trend attests to their stronger adherence to their older Arabic origins. (Bovingdon and Dalli 2006: 71)

Brincat (2011: 407) analyzes the composition of the Maltese lexicon based on Aquilina's Maltese-English dictionary (1987, 1991) and finds that 60.23% of the words are of non-Semitic origin. Those numbers were then compared to a concise version of the Lexicon where the proportion of non-Semitic words was about 10% higher (Brincat 2018: 215).

Comrie and Spagnol (2016: 325) find in their sample of 1500 lexical meanings translated into Maltese that 56% are of Arabic origin, 30.3% of Romance origin, 4.8% of English origin, and 8.9% what they label as other. They define Maltese as a "high borrower" in the sense of Tadmor (2009). They have also looked at the etymological distribution of word classes. In the category of function words, they find almost 85% are of Arabic origin while 6.2% are of Romance origin (Comrie and Spagnol 2016: 328), which they see as a confirmation of the "nearly, but not quite universal cross-linguistic tendency for function words to be less borrowable than content words" (Comrie and Spagnol 2016: 327).

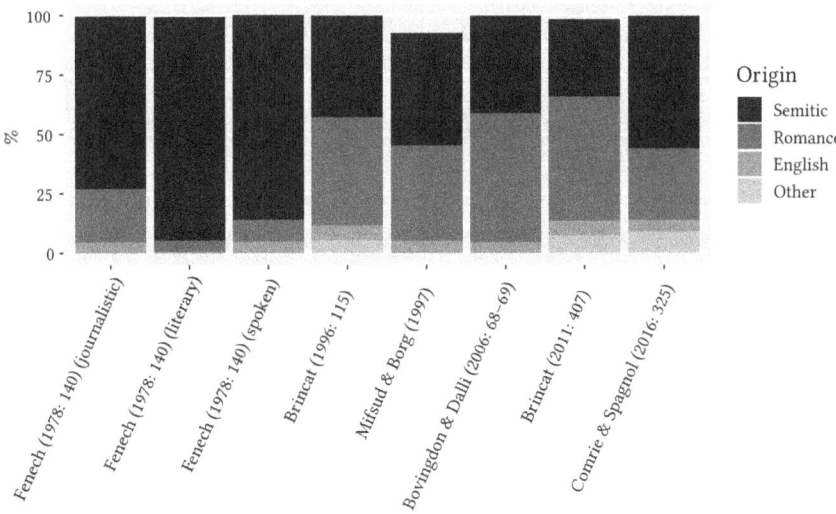

Figure 1: Previous studies of the composition of the Maltese lexicon (Lucas & Čéplö 2020: 288).

Lucas and Čéplö (2020: 288) compare previous studies concerned with the composition of the Maltese lexicon, including the ones just mentioned by Fenech (1978), Bovingdon and Dalli (2006), Brincat (2011), and Comrie and Spagnol (2016). These show great variance as shown in Figure 1. Lucas and Čéplö (2020: 288) conclude that the different compositions the studies report are mainly due to differences in methodology.

Most studies mentioned above include prepositions or the wider class of function words in their counts, the only paper that focusses exclusively on loan prepositions in Maltese though, is Saari (2009). He assumes the low number of only four prepositions of Romance origin in a system of altogether 44 prepositions[5]. He gives etymological information for them and describes how they were adapted phonologically into Maltese.

Stolz (2003) looks at various typologies of language contact and opts for a continuum when it comes to classifying contact languages. He examines where Chamorro and Maltese fit into this continuum between massive borrowing and mixed languages. He notes a high number of function words of Romance origin in both languages (Stolz 2003: 288). Besides relying on lexicon entries, Stolz (2003: 307) also states the need for analyzing text frequencies when describing and classifying the composition of languages. This paper takes on part of this endeavor for the word class of prepositions.

3.2 Maltese prepositions

To analyze the composition of the word class of prepositions, a list of its members is needed. I use the *Bremen List of Maltese Prepositions (BLOMP)*[6] for this purpose. *BLOMP* consists of 57 candidates for a complete list of Maltese prepositions (Stolz and Levkovych 2020: 217). For this study, I exclude two of its members, *sotta* 'under' and *oltri* 'besides', since they do not appear in the Korpus Malti 3.0 (Schmidt et al. 2020: 247) that is also used here (Section 3.2.3). Both prepositions are highly

---

[5] Saari (2009) does not say how many Maltese prepositions of Arabic origin he assumes but, in his dissertation (Saari 2003), a system of 44 prepositions is discussed for Maltese (cf. Stolz and Levkovych 2020: 204).
[6] In the course of the project *Präpositionen und ihre Grammatik im Maltesischen / Prepositions and their grammar in Maltese BLOMP* was revised and updated to *BLOMP* 2.0. For practical reasons this study is based on the original version of *BLOMP*.

restricted or even obsolete in Maltese today.[7] Interestingly, they are both of Romance origin.

Aquilina's dictionary of Maltese (1991, 1987) was used to gather information about the origin of each preposition. Only for one preposition, namely *sa* 'until', there is doubt about the accuracy of Aquilina's specifications regarding the preposition's origin. Procházka (1993) provides information about the origin of *sa* that is considered more plausible, so the preposition will consequently be classified as Semitic.

Maltese prepositions can be split up into the following four classes according to their origin:
(a) Semitic
(b) Romance
(c) Semitic and Romance
(d) unclear

There are 43 prepositions in class (a), listed under (4). Ten prepositions belonging to class (b) that are in use in Maltese today are listed under (5). Classes (c) and (d) are made up of only one member each. The preposition with mixed origin under (6) is made up of the Semitic components *minn* 'from' and *fi* 'in' and *lok* from the Sicilian *locu* 'place' (Aquilina 1987: 350). In (7) one preposition with unclear origin[8] (Aquilina 1987: 205) is provided. In the following, I refer to those Maltese prepositions with Romance origin as "Romance prepositions" and to the ones with Semitic origin as "Semitic prepositions". Prepositions in classes (b), (c), and (d) will be referred to as borrowed prepositions since they contain a least some foreign element or cannot clearly be assigned to the Semitic prepositions in the case of (d).

(4) *bejn* 'between', *bħal* 'like', *bħala* 'as', *bi* 'with', *biswit* 'facing', *bla* 'without', *dwar* 'about', *fejn* 'near', *fi* 'in', *fost* 'between', *fuq* 'on', *ġewwa* 'in', *ġo* 'in', *għajr* 'except', *għal* 'for', *għand* 'at s.o.'s place', *ħdejn* 'beside', *ħlief* 'except', *'il* 'to', *kif* 'as', *lejn* 'towards', *lil* OBJECT MARKER, *ma'* 'with', *madwar* 'around', *maġenb* 'close to', *minħabba* 'on account of', *minbarra* 'except', *mingħajr* 'without', *mingħala* 'in s.o.'s opinion', *mingħand* 'from s.o.', *minkejja* 'in spite of', *minn* 'from', *mnejn* 'from where', *qabel* 'before', *qalb* 'amongst',

---

7 According to Aquilina (1991: 1014), *oltri* is "of limited use amongst the educated class" and both are very rare in spoken language (p.c. Ray Fabri 17.12.2020).
8 Serracino-Inglott (1975: 19) argues that *daqs* is a univerbation of *ta' qies* 'of the measure' and rejects other Semitic or Greek origins because they are too distant from the Maltese meaning of the preposition. Nevertheless, *daqs* will remain in the class of unclear origin for this study.

qrib 'near', *quddiem* 'in front of', *sa* 'till', *ta'* 'of', *taħt* 'under', *matul* 'during', *waqt* 'at the time of', *wara* 'after'

(5) *apparti* 'apart from', *faċċata* 'opposite', *favur* 'on the side of', *kontra* 'against', *permezz* 'by means of', *rigward* 'concerning', *sforz* 'thanks to', *skont* 'according to', *versu* 'towards', *viċin* 'near

(6) *minflok*[9] 'instead of, in lieu of'

(7) *daqs* 'equal to'

3.2.1 Integration of borrowed prepositions

Several studies have focused on borrowing and the integration of loanwords in Maltese, e.g. on verbs (cf. Mifsud 1995), derivation (cf. Gatt and Fabri 2018; Saade 2020), or word formation in general (cf. Brincat and Mifsud 2016). When taking a closer look at the integration of Maltese loan prepositions several aspects are of importance: person suffixes, fusion with the definite article, deletion under coordination, and usage with other prepositions. These will be described in more detail below to show the degree of integration of prepositions of Romance origin into the Maltese morphology and syntax.

3.2.1.1 Person suffixes

In Maltese, some prepositions can be combined with person suffixes as in (8) when their complement is pronominal.

(8) Semitic preposition with person suffix   [Korpus Malti 3.0, literature20]
kien   ħabib   ġenwin   minkejja
be.PFV.3SG.M   friend   genuine   in_spite_of
d-*differenzi*   **bejn:iet-kom**
DEF-difference:PL   **between:PL-2PL**
'He was a genuine friend, despite the differences **between them**.'

---

9 Some Maltese prepositions have short and long forms (e.g. *minflok ~ flok* 'instead of, in lieu of'; *matul ~ tul* 'during'). These prepositions will be listed only in their frequent form but refer to all possible forms of that preposition.

Maltese prepositions with Romance origin are well integrated into the Maltese morphology and, just like Semitic ones, some of them can be combined with person suffixes. The three prepositions *favur* 'on the side of', *kontra* 'against', and *skont* 'according to' are such cases. An example is shown in (9) for *favur* parallel to the Semitic prepositions *dwar* 'about'. The mixed preposition *minflok* 'instead of, in lieu of' can also be combined with suffixes.

(9)   Romance preposition with person suffix   [Korpus Malti 3.0, news152214]
     mhux   hekk   il-Parlament   Ewropew   li   dejjem
     NEG   so   DEF-parlament   European   SUB   always
     kien   qawwi   dwar-ha   u
     be.PFV.3SG.M   strong.SG.M   about-3SG.F   and
     favur-ha
     on_the_side_of-3SG.F
     'Not so the European Parliament, which has always been strong about and **in favor of it**.'

3.2.1.2 Article fusion

Some Maltese prepositions fuse with the definite article when appearing adjacent to it. This is only possible for the ten prepositions *bi* 'with', *bħal* 'like', *fi* 'in', *għal* 'for', *ġo* 'in', *lil* OBJECT MARKER, *ma'* 'with', *minn* 'from', *sa* 'till', and *ta'* 'of', all of which are monosyllabic (Schmidt et al. 2020: 259). None of the prepositions of Romance origin can fuse with the article, although some of them are monosyllabic. They do not meet the phonological criteria found in Schmidt et al. (2020: 259) for article fusion.

3.2.1.3 Deletion under coordination

Maltese prepositions can be deleted under coordination (EQUI-P-deletion). However, when exactly deletion occurs and when two overt prepositions are placed with each complement instead, still needs to be analyzed in more detail (cf. Stolz and Ahrens 2017). This deletion is also possible for all prepositions of Romance origin, examples for both options are given in (10) and (11).

(10)   [Korpus Malti 3.0, news208812]
     ivvota   **kontra**   **l-ġenituri**   u   **kontra**   **t-tfal**
     vote.3SG.M   **against**   DEF-**parent:PL**   and   **against**   DEF-**child.PL**
     'They [the labor party] voted **against parents and children**.'

(11) [Korpus Malti 3.0, literature20]
The magic hour din **skont** *iċ-ċineasti*
the magic hour this:SG.F **according_to** DEF-filmmaker:PL
u ∅ l-fotografi
and ∅ DEF-photographer:PL
'This is the magic hour, **according to filmmakers and photographers**.'

3.2.1.4 Compound prepositions

Some Maltese prepositions can be combined with each other to form compound prepositions with mainly spatial meanings (Stolz 2020: 452; Fabri 1993: 187; Borg and Azzopardi-Alexander 1997: 297). Stolz (2020: 449) identifies four prepositions (*favur* 'on the side of', *rigward* 'concerning', *sa* 'till', *skont* 'according to') that are not attested in combination with other prepositions based on Saari (2003). Except for *sa* 'till' they are of Romance origin. Still, the Romance preposition *kontra* 'against' can occupy the second slot in combinations with *għal* 'for' (Stolz 2020: 448) as in (12).

(12) [Korpus Malti 3.0, literature11]
Denise sabet xi ġel **għal** **kontra**
Denise find.PFV.3SG.F some gel **for** **against**
l-infjammazzjoni u kienet qiegħda
DEF-inflammation:PL and be.PFV.3SG:F located.3SG.F
tapplika-h fuq il- minkeb ta' Josef
3SG.F.IPFV:apply-3SG.M on DEF-elbow of Josef
'Denise found an anti-inflammatory gel and was applying it to Josef's elbow.'

Stolz (2020) notices, however, that Saari did not include *ta'* in his observations. Nevertheless, Saari does mentions the possibility of using *ta'* 'for' with *kontra* 'against' in his paper on prepositions of Romance origin, while indicating, that it is much more common for *kontra* to occur without *ta'* (Saari 2009: 273). Stolz (2020: 462) additionally states that "[t]he second PREP *ta'* 'of' is mandatory with the Italian loan-PREP[osition] *permezz*"[10]. An example is given in (14). Examples

---

[10] A glance in the Korpus Malti 3.0 reveals that this is not entirely true. Although combinations of *permezz* 'by means of' with some form of *ta'* 'of' hold overwhelming majority in the Korpus Malti 3.0, there are 25 examples where *permezz* is directly followed by a noun. An example is given in (13):

(12) and (14) show that Romance prepositions can occupy the first and second slot in compound preposition, which is another indicator of the full integration of loan prepositions into the language.

(14) [Korpus Malti 3.0, academic12]

permezz	***ta'***	konferenzi	u	artikli	
by_means_of	**of**	conference:PL	and	article:PL	
huwa	bena		stampa ta'	Malta bħala	gżira
3SG	bulid.3SG.M.PFV		picture of	Malta as	island
ta'	storja	u	kultura fiċ- ċentru	tal- Mediterran	
of	history	and	culture in:DEF-center	of:DEF-Mediterranean	

'**Through** conferences and articles, he built a picture of Malta as an island with history and culture in the center of the Mediterranean.'

3.2.2 Distribution according to origin

The distribution of Maltese prepositions among the four classes of origin mentioned in 3.2 is listed in Table 1. The majority of Maltese prepositions, about three thirds, is of Semitic origin. Prepositions of Romance origin still reach quite a high proportion with 21.1%. Additionally, there is one preposition with mixed Semitic and Romance origin and one of unclear origin. All in all, the proportion of borrowed prepositions reaches almost 25%.

Table 1: Origin of Maltese prepositions.

Origin	Number of prepositions	%
Semitic	43	75.4
Romance	12	21.1
Semitic and Romance	1	1.8
unclear	1	1.8
Total	57	100.0

---

(13) [Korpus Malti 3.0, european9354]
*għandhom ikunu ddentifikati [**permezz** proċedura ta' ezaminazzjoni xieraq]*
'[...] must be identified [**by (means of)** an appropriate examination procedure].'

When looking at prepositions (types), the picture that emerges is significantly different from what previous studies have found about the composition of the Maltese lexicon. The proportion of Romance prepositions is much higher than what was expected due to former research discussed in 3.1 above. With almost a quarter of loan prepositions, borrowings in this word class are no isolated cases. Maltese does not seem to be opposed to borrowing prepositions as much as could be expected from the hierarchies described in Section 2.

3.2.3 Token frequency

Frequency data for each preposition was obtained from the Korpus Malti which contains about 250 million words (Gatt and Čéplö 2013, version 3.0). Prepositions were counted in all their forms (including person suffixes, fused forms, short and long forms). No part of speech tags were used since not all prepositions and their different forms are tagged as prepositions.

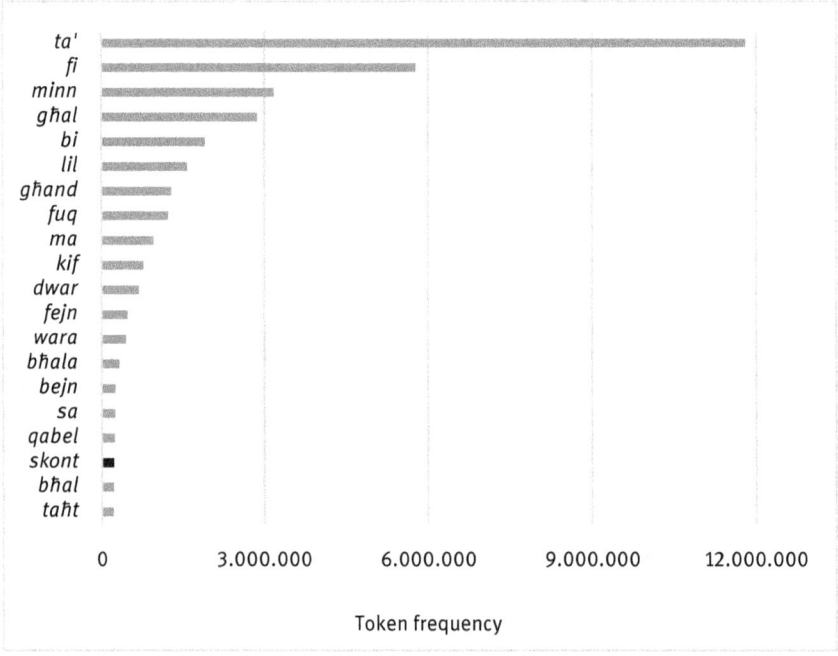

Figure 2: Token frequency of the 20 most frequent Maltese prepositions.

It does not come as a surprise that there are great differences in token frequencies among the members of this word class. The 20 prepositions with the highest token frequencies can be seen in Figure 2. Few prepositions show very high token frequencies. The most frequent preposition is *ta'* 'of' with about 11.8 million tokens. Due to this highly skewed distribution, frequency classes will be used for further analyses later on in Section 4.1. The Romance preposition *skont* 'according to' at place 18, indicated by a darker bar, is the only borrowed preposition among the 20 most frequent prepositions. All others are of Semitic origin.

4 A connection between frequency and origin

In this section, I will first give a description of frequency in combination with origin. Possible other factors that could have an impact on the frequency and/or origin will then be looked at more closely. These are the phonological length and the semantic domains the prepositions belong to.

4.1 Frequency and origin combined

The basic descriptive statistics for Maltese prepositions in the classes of Semitic and Romance origin are provided in Table 2. This includes the mean frequency of the class and the lowest and highest frequency of a preposition in the class. The mean frequency indicates that in general Romance prepositions have lower token frequencies. The lowest token frequency (besides not occurring in the corpus at all) is 228 and it belongs to a Romance preposition as well. The highest frequency is almost 12 million and reached by a Semitic preposition. However, in between these two extremes, there is also a large range where Romance and Semitic prepositions share the space frequency-wise, which I will take a closer look at later on.

Table 2: Descriptive statistics of token frequencies for Semitic and Romance prepositions.

Origin	Mean frequency	Lowest frequency	Highest frequency
Semitic	851,968	1,949	11,801,461
Romance	61,490	228	226,324

The token frequencies and consequent usage percentages for each class of origin are listed in Table 3. With 97.8%, Semitic prepositions hold the overwhelming majority of cases a preposition occurs in the Korpus Malti 3.0. Lucas and Čéplö (2020) find in their comparison of different studies on the Maltese lexicon (Section 3.1) that "[t]he high ratio of words of Semitic origin in token-based analyses is thus due to the prevalence of function words, which are overwhelmingly Arabic" (Lucas and Čéplö 2020: 288). Since prepositions are function words, the high proportion of Semitic prepositions is not surprising after all.

Table 3: Proportion of tokens with different origin.

Origin	Tokens	%
Semitic	36,634,611	97.8
Romance	737,655	2.0
Semitic and Romance	65,237	0.2
unclear	30,428	0.1
Total	37,467,931	100.0

The highly skewed distribution of token frequency with few high-frequency outliers, visible in Figure 2 above, led to a logarithmic transformation of the frequencies. The token frequency of each preposition in the Korpus Malti 3.0 was log-transformed using the natural logarithm, removing some of the skewness and making comparison easier. This led to ten frequency classes that are occupied by Maltese prepositions in the Korpus Malti 3.0.

Figure 3 illustrates the distribution among frequency classes in the sample. The distribution among frequency classes draws a different picture to the clear dominance of Semitic prepositions present in Table 3. The lowest frequency class is 5, the highest 16. Classes 6 and 7 are not represented. Class 12 is by far the biggest class, with 18 members. All other classes have fewer prepositions. Seven prepositions are in class 10 followed by class 11 and 14 with six members. Class 9 and 13 have four representatives and class 8 three. The classes with the lowest relative frequency in the sample are 15 and 16 with two members each and class 5 with only one member.

As a next step, the origin was mapped onto the frequency classes in Figure 4. Borrowed prepositions only appear in frequency class 12 and lower classes while the highest four classes are exclusively occupied by Semitic prepositions. The lowest frequency class 5, has one Romance preposition. Class 12 is the most common frequency class for Semitic and Romance prepositions alike. The mixed preposition is in class 11 while the prepositions of unclear origin is in class 10.

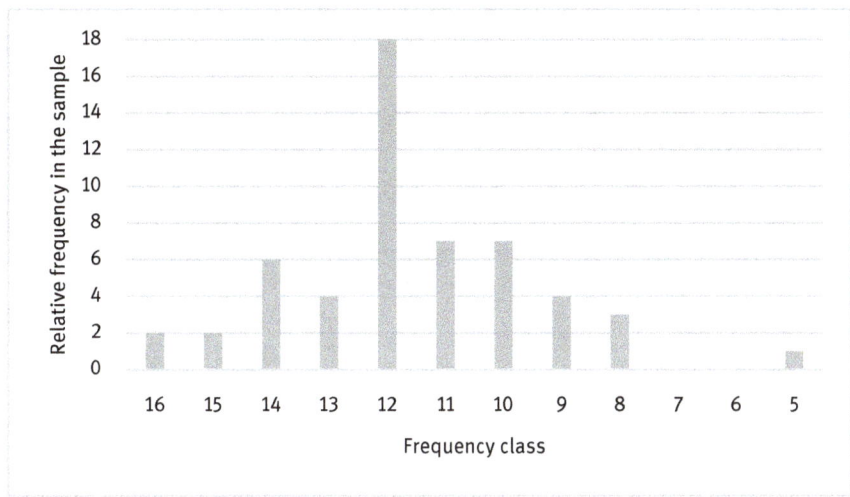

Figure 3: Relative frequencies of frequency classes.

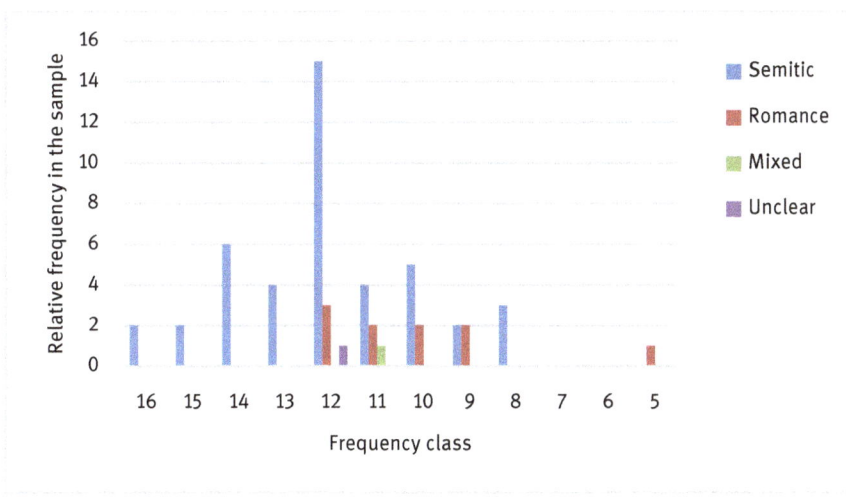

Figure 4: Distribution of origin among the frequency classes.

All Maltese prepositions are listed in Table 4 in the corresponding frequency class according to their origin. Classes 13 to 16 are exclusively made up of Semitic prepositions, most of which are short with two to four segments (cf. Section 4.2.1). The first Romance prepositions appear in class 12 and like classes 11, 10, and 9, these are shared with Semitic prepositions. The only mixed Semitic-Romance preposition is in class 11. Class 10 hosts, besides Semitic and Romance prepositions, the preposition *daqs* 'equal to' of unclear origin. Class 8 has only Semitic prepositions and class 5 is occupied only by one Romance preposition.

Table 4: Prepositions in frequency classes.

Frequency class	Semitic prepositions	Romance	Mixed or unclear origin
16	*ta'* 'of'		
	fi 'in'		
15	*minn* 'from'		
	għal 'for'		
14	*bi* 'with'		
	lil OBJECT MARKER		
	għand 'at one's place'		
	fuq 'on, upon'		
	ma' 'with'		
	kif 'as'		
13	*dwar* 'about'		
	fejn 'near'		
	wara 'after'		
	bħala 'as'		
12	*bejn* 'between'	*kontra* 'against'	
	qabel 'before'	*skont* 'according to'	
	bħal 'like'	*permezz* 'by means of'	
	taħt 'under'		
	matul 'during'		
	ġewwa 'in'		
	lejn 'towards'		
	quddiem 'in front of'		
	waqt 'instance'		
	minbarra 'except'		

Frequency class	Semitic prepositions	Romance	Mixed or unclear origin
11	*minħabba* 'on account of' *fost* 'between' *mingħajr* 'without' *madwar* 'around' *sa* 'until' *minkejja* 'in spite of' *bla* 'without' *qalb* 'amongst' *mingħand* 'from s.o.'	*rigward* 'concerning' *favur* 'on the side of'	*minflok* 'instead of'
10	*qrib* 'near' *ħlief* 'except' *ġo* 'in' *'il* 'to' *ħdejn* 'beside'	*apparti* 'apart from' *viċin* 'near'	*daqs* 'equal to'
9	*għajr* 'except' *mingħala* 'in someone's opinion'	*sforz* 'thanks to' *faċċata* 'opposite'	
8	*biswit* 'facing' *maġenb* 'close to' *mnejn* 'from where'		
5		*versu* 'towards'	

4.2 Other influencing factors

Other factors might be relevant and have some connection to the frequency of prepositions or are connected to a preposition's origin. I will look at two of them more closely in this paper: length and semantic function.

A link between frequency and length was found in Vorholt (2022) for Maltese prepositions, which makes it worth taking a closer look at length as a possible factor influencing variance in the frequency of Maltese prepositions of different origin.

Since "'[c]ore' relations ('in', 'at', 'on') are borrowed less frequently than 'peripheral' relations ('between', 'around', 'opposite')" (Matras 2007: 42), meaning and respectively semantic function are relevant factors for this study because 'core' relations are used with much higher token frequencies (cf. Hagège 2010: 129).

4.2.1 Length

First of all, I will take a look at the phonological length of Maltese prepositions in general and in combination with different classes of origin to explore a possible connection between the two variables. The segmental value attributed to different phonemes is based on Stolz et al. (2017: 57). According to their counting method, affricates and consonants with secondary articulation are treated as monosegmental units and thus have a value of one, and geminates, diphthongs, long vowels, and nasal vowels are bisegmental units with a value of two. If a preposition is used with different forms, e.g. *minflok ~ flok* 'instead of, in lieu of', the most frequent form according to the Korpus Malti 3.0 was analyzed.

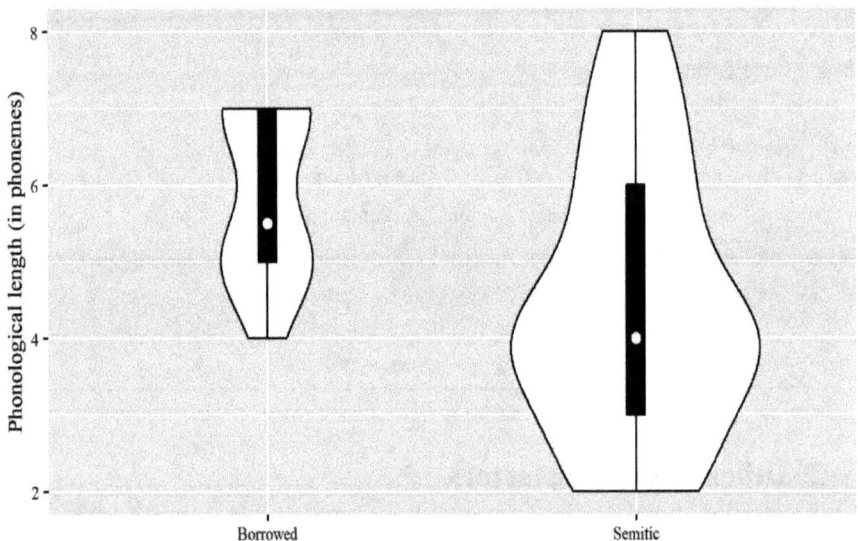

Figure 5: Distribution of phonological length.

The violin plot with overlaid box plot in Figure 5 visualizes the length distribution for borrowed and Semitic prepositions. Borrowed prepositions are between four and seven segments long, while the range for Semitic ones is larger with two to eight segments. Semitic prepositions have a mean length of 4.5 and the median, indicated by the white dot, is 4. The mean for borrowed prepositions is 5.8 and the median 5.5 segments. The density curve for Semitic prepositions on the right gets wider around the length of four which indicates that many Semitic prepositions have the corresponding length.

Vorholt (2022) took a closer look at the correlation between frequency and length for Maltese, among other European languages. The frequency data were restricted to news corpora or the news sections of larger corpora. For Maltese the subsection "Press: News" of the Korpus Malti 3.0 was used. The basic principle behind the study is Zipf's (1949) famous law, that there is an inverse relationship between word frequency and length. A regression analysis was conducted to determine how well phonological length could be predicted by token frequency. For Maltese, the regression analysis showed a significant model fit and almost 15% of the variation in length could be explained by frequency (Vorholt 2022). The same test will be conducted for Maltese using frequency data from the whole Korpus Malti 3.0 in Section 5, to see whether this leads to similar results.

4.2.2 Semantics

Brincat (2018: 216) observes that "the words derived from Arabic are more frequent because they denote the basic ideas and include the function words". In combination with Matras's (2007) statement above, that core relations are borrowed less frequently, we do not expect Maltese borrowed prepositions to express core relations.

All Maltese prepositions were classified according to Hagège's (2010) extensive classification of semantic domains. He distinguishes between "core" and "non-core" meanings, the second of which are than divided into "spatio-temporal" and "non-spatio-temporal" meanings (Hagège 2010: 261–262). "Spatio-temporal" meanings can either be "static" or "non-static" (Hagège 2021: 261). The distribution of Maltese prepositions over these domains is illustrated in Figure 6. A significant proportion of prepositions that denote non-spatio-temporal functions are borrowed, namely nine of 24, or 37.5%. In the other domains, borrowed prepositions have only a small proportion or are not present at all. As expected, none of the Maltese prepositions with Romance origin expresses a core meaning. However, there are only two Maltese prepositions that express core meanings at all (*ta'* 'of', *lil* OBJECT MARKER).

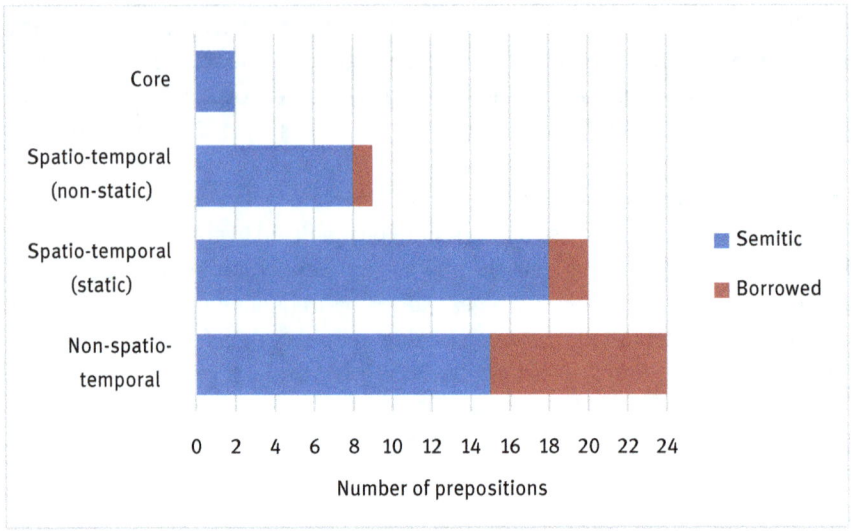

Figure 6: Distribution of semantic domains.

In Table 5 the semantic domains and functions are listed for all borrowed Maltese prepositions. Nine of the borrowed prepositions denote a non-spatio-temporal meaning and only three a spatio-temporal one. Of these three, two express a static and one a non-static meaning. This corresponds well to the proposed hierarchy for expressions of local relations in (3) in Section 2 which states that peripheral local relations are easier borrowed than core local relations. Matras (2011: 214) defines peripheral local relations as

> cognitively more complex, as they involve the creation of a conceptual relationship with reference to two or more rather than just one named object ('between'), or to movement rather than situation ('around', 'across'), or to a relation that is qualified (by attitude) rather than just spatial ('against', 'for the benefit of') [...] [or] which are more abstract and which deal with the negative processing of presuppositions concerning sets (e.g. 'without', 'instead of', 'except').

Borrowed prepositions in Maltese all fit well into this hierarchy, except for the two that express static spatio-temporal meaning: *viċin* 'near' and *faċċata* 'opposite'. Since Maltese was subjected to extensive language contact, it is not surprising, that not only peripheral local relations were borrowed.

Table 5: Semantic functions of borrowed prepositions.

Preposition	Semantic domain	Semantic function
apparti	non-spatio-temporal	exceptive
daqs	non-spatio-temporal	comparative, equative
faċċata	spatio-temporal, static	obessive
favur	non-spatio-temporal	motivative
kontra	non-spatio-temporal	adversative
minflok	non-spatio-temporal	substitutive
permezz	non-spatio-temporal	instrumentative
rigward	non-spatio-temporal	pertentive
sforz	non-spatio-temporal	instrumentive
skont	non-spatio-temporal	roborative
versu	spatio-temporal, non-static	allative
viċin	spatio-temporal, static	adessive

5 Regression analysis

The previous sections have shown that something is going on between token frequency and origin in combination with the length and semantic domain of the preposition. To determine whether there is a significant correlation between these variables, a series of regression analyses will be conducted. First of all, frequency and length will be analyzed, confirming whether Zipf's law holds for the whole Korpus Malti 3.0. Following that, the relationship between frequency and origin will be examined. First on its own and then length and semantic domain will be added to evaluate their impact on token frequency.

A regression analysis[11] of logarithmic frequency and length in the whole Korpus Malti 3.0 reveals that there is still a significant model fit ($F(1,53) = 10.11$, $p < 0.05$) and about 16% of the variation in length can be explained by frequency ($R^2 = 0.1602$). Thus, looking at the whole Korpus Malti 3.0 makes the fit of the regression model slightly better. The residuals are not normally distributed though, which can indicate that some explanatory variables are missing from the model[12].

---

[11] Detailed results and graphs for non-normal distributed residuals are provided in the Appendix.
[12] Another reason for non-normal distributions can be a small sample size (Field et al. 2013: 298).

Coming to the main focus of this paper, I measure a possible correlation between frequency and origin. A regression analysis of logarithmic token frequency and origin yields a significant model fit ($F(1,53) = 6.767$, $p < 0.05$). Nevertheless, origin can only explain about 11% of the variation in frequency ($R^2 = 0.1132$). When length and origin are both used as explanatory variables in the model, the results are significant ($F(2,52) = 6.794$, $p < 0.05$), and R^2 is higher (adjusted $R^2 = 0.1767$) than with only one of them. Thus, with a combination of length and origin we can explain more – almost 17.7% – variation in token frequency than length alone. However, the residuals of this model are not normally distributed.

As another step, it is determined whether a better prediction can be reached when semantic domains are added as an explanatory variable as well. Fitting semantic domains to a model of logarithmic frequency results in a significant model ($F(2,52) = 3.66$, $p < 0.05$) that can explain about 12% of variation in frequency ($R^2 = 0.1234$). A regression analysis of frequency with the explanatory variables length and semantic domain yields a significant fit ($F(3,51) = 5.578$, $p < 0.05$) and can explain about 20% of variation (adjusted $R^2 = 0.2028$). Again, the residuals are not normally distributed. When the origin and semantic domain are used to explain variation in token frequency, the model is also significant ($F(3,51) = 5.564$, $p < 0.05$) and the rate is about the same as before with about 20% (adjusted $R^2 = 0.2023$).

When all three explanatory variables – length, origin, and semantic domain – are fitted, the model can explain 26.4% of variation in length (adjusted $R^2 = 0.2649$, $F(4,50) = 5.841$, $p < 0.05$). Since the assumption of normally distributed residuals is also violated in this model, some important explanatory variables might still be missing.

The *Akaike information criterion* (AIC) measures the fit of the model while also penalizing for having more explanatory variables (Field et al. 2013: 263). The models with two explanatory variables have almost the same AIC-value of about 232. The model with all variables fitted has the smallest AIC-value (AIC = 228.6) and is thus indeed the best model to predict token frequency.

6 Conclusion

The detailed analysis of Maltese prepositions in Sections 3.2.2 and 4.1 have shown that the composition of the class of Maltese prepositions is not as would be predicted from previous studies on the composition of the language. The majority of Maltese prepositions are of Semitic origin, but, with about one-quarter, borrowed prepositions make up a significant amount when looking at types. These high shares of borrowed prepositions cannot be replicated when looking at tokens, though. The token frequency of borrowed prepositions does not reach the most frequent prepositions of Semitic origin and the first 17 ranks in token frequency are occupied by Semitic prepositions. All in all, only about 2% of tokens in the Korpus Malti 3.0 is made up by borrowed prepositions, so that Semitic ones make up almost all of prepositional usage in the Korpus Malti 3.0. Thus, prepositions of Semitic origin evidently dominate when it comes to overall token frequency. Semitic prepositions are present in all but the lowest frequency class and occupy the first four classes on their own whereas the highest frequency class a Romance preposition is present in is class 12. In class 8 there are only Semitic prepositions. But borrowed prepositions cannot be disregarded simply as low-frequency prepositions either, since there are Semitic prepositions that show lower frequencies than Romance ones as well.

Other factors that were expected to affect frequency were considered as well. Borrowed prepositions overall seem to be slightly longer than Semitic ones. Semitic prepositions on the other hand show a wider range in length than borrowed ones. Core meanings are not expressed by borrowed prepositions. They mostly convey non-spatio-temporal functions, which fits well with the proposed hierarchies for borrowing.

Borrowed prepositions are well integrated into the system of Maltese prepositions and cannot be identified by looking at their structure and usage patterns alone. The difference between borrowed prepositions and prepositions of Semitic origin is rather subtle.

A regression model has shown that the origin of prepositions can explain some variation in token frequency, but it is not enough on its own. Adding origin to a previously fitted model with just length as an explanatory variable leads to a slightly better prediction of token frequency. Origin is not the only relevant factor, though. Fitting semantic domain to the model led to an even higher value of R^2. A comparison of different regression models has shown, that adding all variables discussed in this paper is most suitable to explain variation in frequency. Still, the proportion of variation that can be explained with this model is not very high and residuals are not normally distributed. This indicates that more variables are needed for a better prediction of token frequency and that the model cannot be generalized and applied to other contexts.

Text genre might be one of the factors that should be looked at in follow-up studies. Fenech (1978) has shown with his study mentioned at the beginning of this paper, that the composition of Maltese texts when it comes to word origin can vary greatly across genres so that proportions in different registers in the Korpus

Malti 3.0 might not be the same. Further studies are needed especially with a focus on spoken Maltese.

Even though some aspects of borrowed prepositions in Maltese still need to be explored further, this study can provide a first methodological step for describing prepositions in language contact situations in connection with usage frequency in other languages as well. This could then be used as a next step to compare the usage of borrowed prepositions across languages.

Abbreviations

2/3	2nd/3rd person
DEF	definite article
F	feminine
IPFV	imperfective
M	masculine
NEG	negation
PFV	perfective
PL	plural
SG	singular
SUB	subordinator

References

Aquilina, Joseph. 1987. *Maltese-English dictionary: Volume one. A-L.* Malta: Midsea Books.
Aquilina, Joseph. 1991. *Maltese-English dictionary: Volume two. M-Z.* Malta: Midsea Books.
Borg, Albert & Marie Azzopardi-Alexander. 1997. *Maltese.* London: Routledge.
Bovingdon, Roderick & Angelo Dalli. 2006. Statistical analysis of the source origin of Maltese. In Andrew Wilson, Dawn Archer & Paul Rayson (eds.), *Corpus Linguistics Around the World*, 63–76. Amsterdam: Brill Academic Publishers.
Brincat, Joseph M. 2011. *Maltese and other languages: A linguistic history of Malta.* Santa Venera, Malta: Midsea Books.
Brincat, Joseph M. 2018. Maltese: blending Semitic, Romance and Germanic lexemes. *Lexicographica* 33. 207–224.
Brincat, Joseph M. & Manwel Mifsud. 2016. Maltese. In Peter O. Müller, Ingeborg Ohnheiser, Susan Olsen & Franz Rainer (eds.), *Word-Formation: An international handbook of the languages of Europe*, 3349–3366. Berlin: De Gruyter.
Comrie, Bernard & Michael Spagnol. 2016. Maltese loanword typology. In Gilbert Puech & Benjamin Saade (eds.), *Shifts and patterns in Maltese.* Berlin & Boston: De Gruyter.
Fabri, Ray. 1993. *Kongruenz und die Grammatik des Maltesischen.* Tübingen: Niemeyer.
Fenech, Edward. 1978. *Contemporary journalistic Maltese: An analytical and comparative study.* Leiden: Brill.

Field, Fredric & Bernard Comrie. 2002. *Linguistic borrowing in bilingual contexts*. Amsterdam & Philadelphia: John Benjamins Publishing Company.
Field, Andy, Jeremy Miles & Zoë Field. 2013. *Discovering statistics using R*. Los Angeles: Sage.
Gatt, Albert & Ray Fabri. 2018. Borrowed affixes and morphological productivity: A case study of two Maltese nominalisations. In Patrizia Paggio & Albert Gatt (eds.), *The languages of Malta*, 143–169. Berlin: Language Science Press.
Gatt, Albert & Slavomír Čéplö. 2013. Digital corpora and other electronic resources for Maltese. In Andrew Hardie & Robbie Love (eds.), *Proceedings of the International Conference on Corpus Linguistics*, 96–97. Lancaster: UCREL.
Hagège, Claude. 2010. *Adpositions*. Oxford: Oxford University Press.
Haspelmath, Martin. 2009. Lexical borrowing: Concepts and issues. In Martin Haspelmath & Uri Tadmor (eds.), *Loanwords in the world's languages: A comparative handbook*, 35–54. Berlin: De Gruyter Mouton.
Haspelmath, Martin & Uri Tadmor (eds.). 2009a. *Loanwords in the world's languages: A comparative handbook*. Berlin: De Gruyter Mouton.
Haspelmath, Martin & Uri Tadmor. 2009b. *World Loanword Database*. Leipzig: Max Planck Institute for Evolutionary Anthropology. (accessed on 15 March, 2021).
Hekking, Ewald, Dik Bakker & Jorge Gómez Rendón. 2010. Language contact and language typology: anything goes, but not quite. In Claudine Chamoreau (ed.), *A new look at language contact in Amerindian languages*, 119–148. München: Lincom.
Korpus Malti 3.0. assessable at https://mlrs.research.um.edu.mt/CQPweb/malti03/
Libert, Alan. 2002. On the range and variety of cases assigned by adpositions. In Mengistu Amberber & Peter Collins (eds.), *Language universals and variation*, 131–154. London: Praeger.
Lucas, Christopher & Slavomír Čéplö. 2020. Maltese. In Christopher Lucas & Stefano Manfredi (eds.), *Arabic and contact-induced change*, 265–302. Berlin: Language Science Press.
Matras, Yaron. 2007. The borrowability of structural categories. In Yaron Matras & Jeanette Sakel (eds.), *Grammatical borrowing in cross-linguistic perspective*, 31–74. Berlin & New York: Mouton de Gruyter.
Matras, Yaron. 2011. Universals of structural borrowing. In Peter Siemund (ed.), *Linguistic universals and language variation*, 204–234. Berlin: De Gruyter Mouton.
Mifsud, Manwel. 1995. *Loan verbs in Maltese: A descriptive and comparative study*. Leiden, New York & Köln: Brill.
Procházka, Stephan. 1993. *Die Präpositionen in den neuarabischen Dialekten*. Wien: VWGÖ.
Saade, Benjamin. 2020. Quantitative approaches to productivity and borrowing in Maltese derivation. *Morphology* 30(4). 447–467.
Saari, Rami. 2003. *Milot-ha-yahas ha-Maltaziyot* [The Maltese prepositions]. Jerusalem: Karmel.
Saari, Rami. 2007. Maltese *ilu* – The only postposition in a language of prepositions? In Tali Bar & Eran Cohen (eds.), *Studies in Semitic and general linguistics in honor of Gideon Goldenberg*, 75–88. Münster: Ugarit-Verlag.
Saari, Rami. 2009. Some remarks on Maltese prepositions of Italian origin. In Gidon Goldenberg & Ariel Shisha-Halevy (eds.), *Egyptian, Semitic and general grammar: Studies in memory of H. J. Polotsky*, 270–276. Jerusalem: The Israel Academy of Sciences and Humanities.

Schmidt, Emeli, Maike Vorholt & Nele Witt. 2020. Form and behavior of Maltese prepositions – A usage-based approach. In Slavomír Čéplö & Jaroslav Drobný (eds.), *Maltese linguistics on the Danube*, 241–270. Berlin & Boston: De Gruyter Mouton.

Serracino-Inglott, Erin. 1975. *Il-Miklem Malti. Volume 2.* Santa Venera: Klabb Kotba Maltin.

Stolz, Christel & Thomas Stolz. 1996. Funktionswortentlehnung in Mesoamerika Spanisch-amerindischer Sprachkontakt. *STUF – Language Typology and Universals* 49(1). 86–123.

Stolz, Thomas. 2003. Not quite the right mixture: Chamorro and Malti as candidates for the status of mixed language. In Yaron Matras & Peter Bakker (eds.), *The mixed language debate: Theoretical and empirical advances*, 271–316. Berlin & New York: De Gruyter Mouton.

Stolz, Thomas. 2008. Romancisation worldwide. In Thomas Stolz, Dik Bakker & Rosa Salas Palomo (eds.), *Aspects of language contact: New theoretical, methodological and empirical findings with special focus on romancisation processes*, 1–42. Berlin & New York: Mouton de Gruyter.

Stolz, Thomas. 2020. A chapter on compound prepositions in Maltese: prep-prep combinations and related issues. In Benjamin Fagard, José P. de Lima, Dejan Stosic & Elena Smirnova (eds.), *Complex adpositions in European languages: A micro-typological approach to complex nominal relators*, 439–470. Berlin & Boston: De Gruyter Mouton.

Stolz, Thomas & Carolin Ahrens. 2017. On prepositional ellipsis and the factors which block its application in Maltese. In Benjamin Saade & Mauro Tosco (eds.), *Advances in Maltese linguistics*. Berlin & Boston: De Gruyter Mouton.

Stolz, Thomas & Nataliya Levkovych. 2020. From variation towards the grammar of Maltese prepositions – first steps. In Slavomír Čéplö & Jaroslav Drobný (eds.), *Maltese linguistics on the Danube*, 199–240. Berlin & Boston: De Gruyter Mouton.

Stolz, Thomas, Nataliya Levkovych, Aina Urdze, Maja Robbers & Julia Nintemann. 2017. *Spatial interrogatives in Europe and beyond: where, whither, whence.* Berlin & Boston: De Gruyter Mouton.

Tadmor, Uri. 2009. Loanwords in the world's languages: Findings and results. In Martin Haspelmath & Uri Tadmor (eds.), *Loanwords in the world's languages: A comparative handbook*, 55–75. Berlin: De Gruyter Mouton.

Thomason, Sarah G. 2001. *Language contact.* Edinburgh: Edinburgh University Press.

Vorholt, Maike. 2022. Can frequency predict length?: A crosslinguistic investigation of Zipf's law for European adpositions. In Przemysław Turek & Julia Nintemann (eds.), *Maltese: Contemporary changes and historical innovations*, 197–228. Berlin & Boston: De Gruyter Mouton.

Appendix

Table I: lm(formula = logTokens ~ Length, data = data).

Residuals:					
	Min	1Q	Median	3Q	Max
	-6.0613	-1.5959	0.5721	1.2547	3.3192
Coefficients:					
	Estimate	Std. Error	t value	Pr(>|t|)	
(Intercept)	13.9443	0.7801	17.875	<2e-16***	
Length	-0.4899	0.1541	-3.179	0.00247**	

Signif. codes: 0 '***' 0.001 '**' 0.01 '*' 0.05 '.' 0.1 ' ' 1
Residual standard error: 1.961 on 53 degrees of freedom
Multiple R-squared: 0.1602, Adjusted R-squared: 0.1443
F-statistic: 10.11 on 1 and 53 DF, p-value: 0.002465
Shapiro-Wilk normality test: W = 0.94184, p-value = 0.01018

Table II: lm(formula = logTokens ~ Origin, data = data).

Residuals:					
	Min	1Q	Median	3Q	Max
	-4.8394	-1.3409	0.1625	1.3039	4.2996
Coefficients:					
	Estimate	Std. Error	t value	Pr(>|t|)	
(Intercept)	10.2731	0.5816	17.664	<2e-16***	
OriginSemitic	1.7110	0.6577	2.601	0.012*	

Signif. codes: 0 '***' 0.001 '**' 0.01 '*' 0.05 '.' 0.1 ' ' 1
Residual standard error: 2.015 on 53 degrees of freedom
Multiple R-squared: 0.1132, Adjusted R-squared: 0.0965
F-statistic: 6.767 on 1 and 53 DF, p-value: 0.01201
Shapiro-Wilk normality test: W = 0.97383, p-value = 0.272

Table III: lm(formula = logTokens ~ Length + Origin, data = data).

Residuals:

	Min	1Q	Median	3Q	Max
	-5.1705	-1.0869	0.4527	1.3806	3.3202

Coefficients:

	Estimate	Std. Error	t value	Pr(>|t|)
(Intercept)	12.5907	1.0863	11.591	4.98e-16***
Length	-0.3973	0.1601	-2.482	0.0163*
OriginSemitic	1.1674	0.6650	1.756	0.0850

Signif. codes: 0 '***' 0.001 '**' 0.01 '*' 0.05 '.' 0.1 ' ' 1
Residual standard error: 1.923 on 52 degrees of freedom
Multiple R-squared: 0.2072, Adjusted R-squared: 0.1767
F-statistic: 6.794 on 2 and 52 DF, p-value: 0.002391
Shapiro-Wilk normality test: W = 0.94545, p-value = 0.01454

Table IV: lm(formula = logTokens ~ Sem_domain, data = data).

Residuals:

	Min	1Q	Median	3Q	Max
	-5.8640	-1.2274	0.3284	1.0601	4.2715

Coefficients:

	Estimate	Std. Error	t value	Pr(>|t|)
(Intercept)	15.282	1.430	10.688	9.95e-15***
non-spatio-temporal	-3.599	1.488	-2.418	0.01913*
spatio-temporal	-3.985	1.478	-2.695	0.00945**

Signif. codes: 0 '***' 0.001 '**' 0.01 '*' 0.05 '.' 0.1 ' ' 1
Residual standard error: 2.022 on 52 degrees of freedom
Multiple R-squared: 0.1234, Adjusted R-squared: 0.08967
F-statistic: 3.66 on 2 and 52 DF, p-value: 0.03258
Shapiro-Wilk normality test: W = 0.98244, p-value = 0.598

Table V: lm(formula = logTokens ~ Length + Sem_domain, data = data).

Residuals:

Min	1Q	Median	3Q	Max
-5.644	-1.243	0.613	1.257	3.437

Coefficients:

	Estimate	Std. Error	t value	Pr(>|t|)
(Intercept)	16.4226	1.3949	11.773	3.71e-16***
length	-0.4560	0.1576	-2.894	0.00558**
non-spatio-temporal	-2.3453	1.4586	-1.608	0.11405
spatio-temporal	-3.0648	1.4196	-2.159	0.03558*

Signif. codes: 0 '***' 0.001 '**' 0.01 '*' 0.05 '.' 0.1 ' ' 1
Residual standard error: 1.892 on 51 degrees of freedom
Multiple R-squared: 0.2471, Adjusted R-squared: 0.2028
F-statistic: 5.578 on 3 and 51 DF, p-value: 0.002183
Shapiro-Wilk normality test: W = 0.9469, p-value = 0.01682

Table VI: lm(formula = logTokens ~ Origin + Sem_domain, data = data).

Residuals:

Min	1Q	Median	3Q	Max
-4.1642	-1.0364	0.4243	1.0347	4.0754

Coefficients:

	Estimate	Std. Error	t value	Pr(>|t|)
(Intercept)	13.3865	1.4909	8.979	4.44e-12***
OriginSemitic	1.8960	0.6565	2.888	0.00568**
non-spatio-temporal	-2.8884	1.4148	-2.042	0.04639*
spatio-temporal	-3.7886	1.3856	-2.734	0.00858**

Signif. codes: 0 '***' 0.001 '**' 0.01 '*' 0.05 '.' 0.1 ' ' 1
Residual standard error: 1.893 on 51 degrees of freedom
Multiple R-squared: 0.2466, Adjusted R-squared: 0.2023
F-statistic: 5.564 on 3 and 51 DF, p-value: 0.002215
Shapiro-Wilk normality test: W = 0.9628, p-value = 0.08668

Table VII: lm(formula = logTokens ~ Length + Origin + Sem_domain, data = data).

Residuals:

Min	1Q	Median	3Q	Max
-4.3477	-0.9559	0.4193	1.0861	3.3318

Coefficients:

	Estimate	Std. Error	t value	Pr(>|t|)
(Intercept)	14.6868	1.5400	9.537	7.74e-13***
Length	-0.3606	0.1570	-2.296	0.0259*
OriginSemitic	1.4971	0.6541	2.289	0.0264*
non-spatio-temporal	-2.0464	1.4076	-1.454	0.1523
spatio-temporal	-3.1025	1.3641	-2.274	0.0273*

Signif. codes: 0 '***' 0.001 '**' 0.01 '*' 0.05 '.' 0.1 ' ' 1
Residual standard error: 1.818 on 50 degrees of freedom

Multiple R-squared: 0.3185, Adjusted R-squared: 0.2639
F-statistic: 5.841 on 4 and 50 DF, p-value: 0.0006163
Shapiro-Wilk normality test: W = 0.93885, p-value = 0.007611

Julia Nintemann and Nicole Hober
On the morphosyntax of place names vs. common nouns in pidgins and creoles

The encoding of two types of Ground in Goal and Source constructions

Abstract: The paper explores the morphosyntax of place names (PNs) and common nouns (CNs) in Goal and Source constructions in pidgins and creoles. Based on 64 sample languages with different lexifiers located in four different macroareas, the coding strategies for the two types of Ground phrases are compared and assessed in both qualitative and quantitative terms. It is shown that spatial relations are not always coded in the same way with the different types of Ground, as differential coding of PNs vs. CNs frequently occurs. Overall, this study combines aspects of contact linguistics, typology, the grammar of space, and the grammar of names to account for the dynamics and complexity of coding two types of Grounds in two types of spatial relations.

Keywords: place names; common nouns; spatial relations; differential coding

1 Introduction

In this study, we explore the morphosyntax of place names (PNs) vs. common nouns (CNs) in pidgins and creoles.[1] The focus lies on the marking of Ground phrases in Goal and Source constructions. Some recent research suggests that spatial relations are not always coded in the same way in the languages of the

---

[1] Personal names (anthroponyms) are another category which would be interesting to include in this comparison. As our study heavily relies on the data represented in the APiCS (see Section 3) that does not feature personal names in Goal and Source constructions, a separate data collection would unfortunately have exceeded the scope of this study. The inclusion of personal names thus remains a topic for future research.

Julia Nintemann, University of Bremen, FB 10: Linguistics / Language Sciences, Universitäts-Boulevard 13, 28359 Bremen, Germany. E-Mail: jnintemann@uni-bremen.de
Nicole Hober, University of Bremen, FB 10: English-Speaking Cultures, Universitäts-Boulevard 13, 28359 Bremen, Germany. E-Mail: hober@uni-bremen.de

https://doi.org/10.1515/https://doi.org/10.1515/9783111323756-006

world, especially when comparing different types of Grounds (cf. e.g. Stolz et al. 2014, 2017a; Haspelmath 2019). We are, therefore, interested in differences in the marking of CNs vs. PNs as Ground in Goal and Source constructions. This study forms part of a larger project dedicated to the morphosyntax of PNs vs. CNs in the world's languages. The basics of this project are outlined in Stolz et al. (2017a, 2017b, 2018), Stolz and Levkovych (2019a, 2019b, 2020), and Stolz (2020).

The linguistics of space and motion has long been of interest to scholars of the various subdisciplines within the linguistic field. Research includes case studies (e.g. Levinson and Wilkins 2006), typological comparisons (e.g. Creissels 2006, 2009; Pantcheva 2009, 2010, 2011; Stolz et al. 2017c; Nintemann et al. 2020), psycholinguistic experiments (e.g. Feinmann 2020), and cognitive research (e.g. Levinson 2003). However, the encoding of PNs in contrast to CNs for the two dynamic relations Goal and Source in general, and with a view to contact languages in particular, presents largely uncharted territory. Exceptions include Features 79 and 80 in the APiCS (Michaelis et al. 2013; cf. Section 3) and the section on pidgins and creoles in the book-length study on the zero-marking of spatial relations by Stolz et al. (2014: 157–182).

The paper is structured as follows. In Section 2, we provide the theoretical background discussing the encoding of Grounds in Goal and Source constructions, and some properties of PNs as compared to CNs. Section 3 offers some information on the data and methodology of this study, including research questions and hypotheses, and a discussion of potential problems. In Section 4, we present the findings and provide a closer look at selected languages, before the data will be discussed in primarily quantitative terms in Section 5. The last section concludes this paper and addresses the afore-stated hypotheses.

2 Theoretical background

To describe motion events, we follow Talmy's (1983) nomenclature. Figure is the moving entity and Ground is the reference entity with respect to which the Figure is moving. Path specifies the direction of movement. Goal constructions are those where the Figure is moving toward the Ground. Source constructions are those where the Figure is moving away from the Ground. Grounds can be realized by different types of noun phrases. Moreover, Ground phrases in Goal and Source constructions can be coded by a number of strategies in the world's languages, i.e. through adpositions, case marking, serial verb constructions, and non-overt marking. Indeed, different strategies may be employed for these purposes in one and the same language. The selection seems to depend on several structural and non-structural factors, e.g. the type of spatial relation, the Ground's word class, the motion verb type, the degree of formality in the usage context, or pragmatic needs such as adding emphasis.

2.1 The encoding of Ground in Goal and Source constructions

To provide an overview of the possible coding patterns, we focus on Goal and Source relations with CNs involving go- and come-type verbs in 'unmarked' pragmatic contexts as reported for the standard variety of a language. English uses prepositions in both relations, *to* for Goal (1a) and *from* for Source (1b) as displayed in our first example[2].

(1) English
   a. *The man goes **to** <u>the store</u>.*
   b. *The man comes **from** <u>the store.</u>*

In Kharia, Ground phrases occur with the postposition *tay* in Source relations (2b) but they precede the motion verb without overt morphology in Goal constructions (2a).[3]

(2) Kharia   [Peterson 2006: 298; 2008: 496]
   a. babu   musa   iɲ   <u>kinir</u>   Ø   co=na   um=iɲ   pal=e
      child   today   1SG   forest   Ø   go=INF   NEG=1SG   be.able=ACT.IRR
      'Son, today I will not be able to go **to** <u>the forest</u>.'
   b. jhaɽi   mudui=ki   hathiyar   dhoʔ=ta   dhoʔta
      all   enemy=PL   weapon   take=CV   RPT
      <u>poʔda</u>   **tay**   muʔ=ki=may
      <u>village</u>   ABL   emerge=M.PST=3PL
      'All the enemies grabbed their weapons and set out **from** their <u>village</u>.'

Quechua employs case-marking on Ground phrases. The allative suffix *-man* occurs in Goal (3a) and the ablative suffix *-paq* in Source relations (3b).

---

2 In our examples, Goal and Source markers such as adpositions, affixes, or clitics are given in boldface, the Ground is underlined. For glossed examples, we tried to stick as close to the original sources as possible. For the sake of consistency and clarity, however, minor changes sometimes had to be made, e.g. changing some abbreviations or inserting Ø in zero-marked constructions. In some cases, we added the glosses by ourselves. Such cases are indicated by a footnote.
3 See also Stolz et al. (2014: 114–116) on the encoding of spatial relations in Kharia.

(3) Yauyos Quechua [Shimelman 2017: 230, 82]
  a. ri-nki   qaqa-**man**   tiya-ra-chi-shu-nki.
     go-2SG   cliff-ALL   sit-UNINT-CAUS-2OBJ-2
     'You'll go **to** the cliff and he'll make you sit and sit [stay] there.'
  b. ¿Imay-taq   llaqta-yki-**paq** lluqsi-mu-la-nki?
     when-SEQ   town-2-ABL   go.out-CISL-PST-2
     'When did you go out **from** your country?'

Serial verb constructions are common in Austronesian and Papuan languages (Crowley 2002; Senft 2004). These constructions are also employed for encoding motion events. In Paamese, the general spatial preposition *en* is used in Place, Goal, or Source contexts. The exact motion interpretation of example (4a) is thus ambiguous (Crowley 2002: 71–72). To disambiguate the reading, motion and posture verbs are serialized to the primary motion verb, i.e. a go-type motion verb *-vaa* to encode Goal (4b), a come-type motion verb *-mai* to mark Source (4c), and a posture verb *-mule* 'stay' to indicate Place (4d). Effectively, Paamese combines serial verbs and an adposition.

(4) Paamese [Crowley 2002: 70–72]
  a. na-muali   eni   leiai
     1SG.REAL-walk   SP   bush
     'I walked **to** the bush.' OR 'I walked **from** the bush.' OR 'I walked **in** the bush.'
  b. na-muali   nau-**vaa**   eni   leiai
     1SG.REAL-walk   1SG.REAL-**go**   SP   bush
     'I walked **to** the bush.'
  c. na-muali   nau-**mai**   eni   leiai
     1SG.REAL-walk   1SG.REAL-**come** SP   bush
     'I walked **from** the bush.'
  d. na-muali   na-**mule**   eni   leiai
     1SG.REAL-walk   1SG.REAL-**stay** SP   bush
     'I walked **in** the bush.'

This study demonstrates that while the different strategies to mark Ground in Goal and Source constructions are found among the here examined pidgins and creoles, adpositions are the most common coding strategy used.

2.2 The encoding of PNs vs. CNs

Outside the domain of onomastics (a discipline for which morphosyntax is of no interest), up until recently, PNs (aka toponyms) – like names in general – have received little attention by linguists in general and typologists in particular.[4] It has been noted that "proper names are missing in ordinary dictionaries" (Van Langendonck 2007: 3) and that "most grammatical descriptions do not include information on proper names" (Croft 1990: 268, fn. 24). Recently, however, PNs and their morphosyntactic behaviour have become a growing field of linguistic research and some recent publications on the grammar of names have appeared (e.g. Anderson 2007; Van Langendonck 2007). In grammatical descriptions, PNs are generally treated as a simple subcategory of CNs and are often only mentioned in passing, if at all. However, an example from German clearly shows that PNs cannot (always) be treated the same as CNs and can show some unique traits. Compare the examples in (5):

(5) German[5]
    a. *Der*   *Mann*   *geht*   ***zum***   *Laden*.
        DET   man   go:3SG.PRS   **to**:DEF.M.DAT   store
        'The man goes **to** the store.'
    b. *Der*   *Mann*   *geht*   ***nach***   *Berlin*.
        DET   man   go:3SG.PRS **to**   Berlin$_{PN}$
        'The man goes **to** Berlin.'

German uses prepositions to mark motion towards a Goal. In (5a), the CN *Laden* 'store' is used as Ground, whereas the PN *Berlin* serves as Ground in (5b). Depending on the Ground's properties, different prepositions are used. CNs occur with the preposition *zu* 'to'. In (5a), *zum* is a contraction of *zu* and the masculine definite article *dem*.[6] PNs, on the other hand, take *nach* as a preposition as exemplified in (5b). Definiteness is not grammatically specified in the case of PNs. The

---

[4] The category of PNs can be further divided into several subcategories, such as country names (choronyms), city or other settlement names (econyms), street names (dromonyms), names of islands (insulonyms), bodies of water (hydronyms), mountains or valleys (oronyms), and so forth. We mainly look at choronyms and econyms, as these are the two subcategories found most often in descriptive material.
[5] The examples are based on our own native speaker competence.
[6] Similar to CNs, personal names also take the preposition *zu* 'to' in Goal constructions, e.g. *Ich gehe zu Martin* 'I go to Martin'. In Standard German, personal names do not take a definite article. Thus, there are no contractions of the preposition and the definite article in these cases, e.g. *Ich

two prepositions are not interchangeable. Comparing examples (5a) and (5b) to their English equivalents, i.e. *The man goes to the store* vs. *The man goes to Berlin*, we can see that while in English the same preposition *to* is employed with both CNs and PNs, German uses distinct prepositions. The only difference for Grounds in English lies in the use of the definite article together with the CN. As PNs are mono-referential and thus inherently definite, there is no need for a definite article in combination with a PN in these examples (cf. Nübling et al. 2015: 17–20). With CNs, however, some kind of determiner – whether definite or indefinite – is used (*The man goes to store*).

Note, however, that in Kiezdeutsch, a (controversial) German variety mainly spoken by multilingual young adults in urban areas, PNs and CNs are not obligatorily marked by *nach* and *zu*, respectively, but can occur without a preposition, see (6) for examples of Goal constructions.

(6) Kiezdeutsch[7] [Wiese 2006: 257][8]
 a. *Klar, wir   gehen   wieder Ø Turmstraße*
    of.course 1PL go:1PL.PRS again Ø Turmstraße$_{PN}$
    'Of course, we go **to** <u>Turmstraße</u> again.'
 b. *Ey, wir   sollen   Ø Fahrstuhl gehen*
    DM   1PL   must:1PL.PRS Ø elevator   go:INF
    'Ey, we have to go **to** <u>the elevator</u>.'

There is also evidence of zero-marking of Ground in some varieties of English. For Indian South African English, for example, the CN occurs without a preposition in a Goal construction, see (7). We did not come across an example of zero-marking with a PN.

(7) Indian South African English [Mesthrie 2008: 510]
    I'm a man, I don't go Ø <u>church</u> an' all.
    'I'm a man who doesn't go **to** <u>church</u>, and so forth.'

The examples of German and English already show that it is worthwhile having a closer look at the morphosyntax of different Ground phrases in Goal and Source

---

gehe zum Martin. In colloquial German, especially in southern regions of Germany, however, definite articles are frequently used with personal names. The reader is referred to Helmbrecht (2020: 16) for more information on the use of the definite article with German personal names.
7 See also Stolz et al. (2014: 5–10) on Kiezdeutsch.
8 Glosses added by the authors.

constructions, as different varieties of the same language may use different strategies depending on, e.g., the type of motion event and the type of Ground involved. Moreover, it appears that especially in non-standard varieties, the option of zero-coding is more prominent.

What is more, Stolz et al. (2014) investigated the possibility of 'zero' in spatial relations generally and found a preference for zero with PNs in the languages of the world: "If in a given language zero-marking of spatial relations applies, it almost always applies to toponyms" (Stolz et al. 2014: 291). In their crosslinguistic sample of 116 languages, they found that PNs can be zero-marked in 90% of the sample languages, while zero-marking is an option for CNs only in approx. 40% of cases (Stolz et al. 2014: 287). Much like in its Yucatecan sister language Yucatec Maya, as reported in Stolz et al. (2014: 145–147), CNs are marked by a preposition in Goal constructions in Mopan Maya, i.e. *ti* 'to', see (8a); while PNs can occur without the preposition, see (8b).

(8) Mopan Maya [Hofling 2017: 728; Yasugi 2003: 53]
    a. *B'in-Ø-i*   *b'in*   ***ti***   <u>kol</u>
       go-CIS-B3.SG REP   **to**   milpa
       'They say he went **to** <u>the milpa</u>.'
    b. *u-p'ät-aj-Ø*   *a*   *t'an-a*   *ka'*   *xik-ech*   ***Ø***   <u>*Meerida*</u>
       A3-leave-COM-B3 DET word-TER that go.POT-B2 ***Ø***   Mérida_{PN}
       'He told you to go **to** <u>Mérida</u>.'

Similarly, in his survey on differential place and object marking, Haspelmath (2019) puts forward several universals, one of which directly relates to the present investigation: "If a language has asymmetric differential coding of place in common nouns and place names, the place-name marker will be shorter" (Haspelmath 2019: 319).

Thus, while we do not expect PNs to act differently from CNs in Goal and Source constructions in all pidgins and creoles in our sample, we expect that if there is differential coding, it will be asymmetric in that PNs are marked shorter and more likely to be zero-marked. The zero-marking of PNs in contrast to overt marking of CNs is one of the most prominent and best known features of the *Special Toponymic Grammar (STG)*, explored and documented in, among others, Stolz et al. 2014, 2017a, 2017b, 2018. Moreover, in line with the findings by Stolz et al. (2014: 281), we expect that if there is a zero option for Grounds in Source constructions, there will also be a zero option for Grounds in Goal constructions.

3 Data and methodology

To begin with, we consulted the *Atlas of Pidgin and Creole language structures online* database (APiCS; Michaelis et al. 2013). The database served to assemble the sample languages for this study. In the APiCS, 76 varieties are listed. All of the varieties listed in the APiCS are considered pidgins and creoles in this study. Due to data scarcity for some of these, however, we only included 64 languages, see Table 1.

Table 1: Global distribution of sample languages.

	English-based	Dutch-based	Spanish-based	Portuguese-based	French-based	Other	Total
Africa	5	1	0	7	3	6	22
Asia	2	0	3	4	0	3	12
Americas	12	2	2	0	5	1	22
Oceania	4	0	0	0	1	3	8
Total	23	3	5	11	9	13	64

Some data and examples could directly be taken from the APiCS. In many cases, however, we needed to consult grammars and other descriptive work to complete the picture. For each language, we collected data of PNs and CNs as Ground in Goal and Source constructions. If this was not possible, the language was excluded from our sample.

To shed light on the morphosyntax of PNs vs. CNs in Goal and Source constructions in pidgin and creoles, we addressed the following research questions:

> **RQ1:** How are Ground phrases marked in Goal and Source constructions in pidgins and creoles?
> **RQ2:** Is there variation between multiple coding strategies?
> **RQ3:** Is there differential coding of Ground phrases with PNs vs. CNs?
> **RQ4:** Is there an option of zero-marking of Ground phrases with PNs and/or CNs?

Based on the previous research outlined in Section 2.2, and grounded in the assumption that pidgins and creoles behave like other languages, we tested the following hypotheses:

HP1: If PNs and CNs are coded differentially, the PN marker will be shorter/zero.

HP2: If the marking of one spatial relation is shorter than the other, Goal will be shorter than Source. If zero-marking is an option in Source constructions, it will also be an option in Goal constructions.

Before moving on to the results of the study, a few words on the merits and drawbacks of the APiCS are in order. The APiCS contains two chapters that served as the starting point for our study on PNs, i.e. 'Feature 79 Going to named places' and 'Feature 80 Coming from names places', offering invaluable data on the otherwise often neglected category of PNs. Both chapters rely on grammars as well as the knowledge of various expert linguists and their field data. However, we frequently found discrepancies between the data in the APiCS and other published material.

Comparing the feature entries for Chinuk Wawa, for example, it appears that the language employs no adpositional or case marking in Goal constructions (9a), while there is a preposition *kapa* 'at' to mark Source (9b).

(9) Chinuk Wawa
    a. Goal   [Grant 2013, Ex. 74-127]

	náyka	tlatwa	Ø	Siyátl
	1SG	go	Ø	Seattle_PN

        'I go **to** Seattle.'

    b. Source   [Grant 2013, Ex. 74-128]

	náyka	čáku	**kapa**	Siyátl
	1SG	come	**at**	Seattle_PN

        'I come **from** Seattle.'

Both examples are marked as "constructed by linguist". The glosses of (9b) suggest that the preposition *kapa* is not a dedicated Source marker as it is glossed as 'at'. In fact, Powell (n.d.: 57) notes that *kopa*[9] is the most important preposition in Chinuk Wawa which "serves to denote any locational or attributive relationship" (Powell n.d.: 57). Powell cites Shaw (1909: 12) who gives the following meanings for *kopa*: "at; according to; around; about; concerning; to; into; with; towards;

---

9   All other sources we consulted on Chinuk Wawa (mostly found as Chinook Jargon) suggest the form *kopa* instead of *kapa*. We assume that *kopa* is derived from Chinook *kō'pa* 'there' (see Boas 1911: 648).

of; there; in that place; than; for; from; on; during; through; instead of". The exact meaning of the preposition depends on the context (Powell n.d.: 57). Compare the following examples:

(10) Chinuk Wawa [Powell n.d.: 57][10]
    a. Place
          Alki   nika   **kopa**   <u>Tumwata</u>   kopa   kwinnum   sun.
          FUT   1SG   PREP   <u>Tumwater</u>$_{PN}$ PREP   five   day
          'I will be **in** <u>Tumwater (Washington)</u> for five days.'
    b. Goal
          Mika   klatawa   **kopa**   <u>La Push</u>
          2SG   go   PREP   <u>La Push</u>$_{PN}$
          'You are going **to (or towards)** <u>La Push (Washington)</u>.'
    c. Source
          Mesika   chako   **kopa**   <u>makook</u>   house?
          you.PL   come   PREP   <u>buy</u>   house
          'Are you all coming **from** <u>the store</u>?'

The examples in (10) suggest that *kopa* is used as a general marker for different kinds of relations. The construction *kopa kwinnum sun* 'for five days' in (10a) shows that the preposition is not only used for spatial relations but also with temporal (and other) meanings. The example of Chinuk Wawa illustrates that the APiCS may sometimes not be enough to get the full picture. Instead of functioning as a Source preposition only, *kopa* is used as an all-purpose marker.

Moreover, in several cases, we found that the source of an example is given as 'own knowledge', and that examples given for 'Going to named places' or 'Coming from named places' actually involved a CN rather than a PN. It was therefore often necessary to consult additional data and carry out a more fine-grained analysis to obtain a clearer picture.

4 Results

To facilitate their presentation, we grouped the results according to lexifier. For each group, we provide an overview table with the coding strategies for PNs and CNs in Goal and Source constructions. If there are multiple coding strategies, they

---

[10] Glosses added by the authors.

are listed in the same cell with parentheses indicating the optionality of respective elements. Dark grey shading indicates definite differential coding for PNs and CNs (= strong split). Light grey shading indicates potential differential coding (= weak split), due to another additional coding option for either PNs or CNs (or both). As explained in Chapter 3, the APiCS served as the basis for our research. The rightmost column of our data tables indicates the sources consulted for each language. If there is more than one reference, the first one always refers to the respective structure dataset taken from the APiCS, while a second or even third one indicates that additional sources were consulted for that language. In addition to these overviews, we also give some illustrative examples and make some general observations.

4.1 English-based

As mentioned in 2.1, in Standard English, Goal and Source constructions take two different prepositions. But, there is no differential coding of PNs vs. CNs as Ground in these two relations. Goal is always expressed with the preposition *to*, while Source is always expressed with the preposition *from*. In Table 2, the results for 23 English-based pidgins and creoles of our sample are displayed.

Table 2: CNs and PNs in Goal and Source constructions in English-based pidgins and creoles.

Language	Goal CN	Goal PN	Source CN	Source PN	References
African American English	*to* CN	*to* PN	*from* CN	*from* PN	Green (2013)
Bahamian Creole	*to* CN	(*to*) PN	*from* CN	*from* PN	Hackert (2013)
Belizean Creole	(*tu/at/[d]a*) CN	(*tu/at/[d]a*) PN	*f(r)a* CN	*f(r)a* PN	Escure (2013); Greene (1999)
Bislama	*long* CN	*long* PN	*long* CN	*long* PN	Meyerhoff (2013)
Cameroon Pidgin	(*fo*) CN VV (*fo*) CN	(*fo*) PN VV (*fo*) PN	*fo* CN	*fo* PN	Schröder (2013); Ayafor and Green (2017)
Chinese Pidgin	(*to*) CN	(*to*) PN	(*from*) CN	(*from*) PN	Li and Matthews (2013)
Creolese	(VV) (*a*) CN	(VV) (*a*) PN	*from* CN	*from* PN	Devonish and Thompson (2013); Gibson (1992)

Language	Goal CN	Goal PN	Source CN	Source PN	References
Early Sranan	(VV) na CN	(VV) na PN	na/fu CN	na/fu PN	van den Berg and Bruyn (2013); van den Berg (2007)
Ghanaian Pidgin	(VV) (fɔ) CN	(VV) (fɔ) PN	frɔm CN	frɔm PN	Huber (2013, 1999)
Hawai'i Creole	(tu) CN	(tu) PN	fɹɔm CN	fɹɔm PN	Velupillai (2013)
Jamaican	(VV) (a) CN	(VV) (a) PN	fram/frahn CN	fram/frahn PN	Farquharson (2013); Durrleman (2008)
Krio	na CN	(na) PN	na/frɔm CN	na/frɔm PN	Finney (2013)
Kriol	la(nga) CN	(la[nga]) PN	from/brom CN	from/brom PN	Schultze-Berndt and Angelo (2013)
Nengee	VV a CN	VV a PN	VV na CN	VV na PN	Migge (2013)
Nicaraguan Creole	tu CN	Ø PN	fram CN	from PN	Bartens (2013b)
Nigerian Pidgin	(VV) (fɔ̀r) CN	(VV) (fɔ̀r) PN	(VV) (frɔ̀m) CN	(VV) (frɔ̀m) PN	Faraclas (2013, 1996)
Pichi	(VV) (na/fɔ) CN	(VV) (na/fɔ) PN	(VV) na/frɔn CN	(VV) na/frɔn PN	Yakpo (2013, 2019)
San Andres Creole	(da) CN	Ø PN	faan/fram CN	faan/fram PN	Bartens (2013a)
Saramaccan	(VV) a CN	(VV) a PN	a CN	a PN	Aboh et al. (2013); McWhorter and Good (2012)
Singlish	(to) CN	(to) PN	from CN	from PN	Lim and Ansaldo (2013)
Sranan	(VV) na CN	(VV) na PN	(VV) fu CN	(VV) fu PN	Winford and Plag (2013); Winford (1990, 2002)
Tok Pisin	(VV) long CN	(VV) long PN	long CN	long PN	Smith and Siegel (2013)
Vincentian Creole	(a) CN	(a) PN	fram CN	fram PN	Prescod (2013)

Out of the 23 English-based pidgins and creoles, only five show differential marking of PNs and CNs in Goal constructions, while there are no splits in any of the Source constructions. A strong split is found only in Nicaraguan Creole. Overall, it appears that differential coding is not very frequent among the English-based pidgins and creoles in our sample. The majority marks Ground via prepositions. But, especially among the Goal constructions we find frequent zero-coding. In several languages, there is also the option for serial verbs plus the preposition, as in Sranan. Interestingly, verb serialisation without prepositions is rarely found and, apart from Creolese, mostly occurs in English-based pidgins (rather than creoles), i.e. Nigerian Pidgin, Ghanaian Pidgin, and Cameroon Pidgin.

As far as the option of verb serialisation is concerned, based on the data from the APiCS and the data presented in grammars, it would appear that verb serialisation is sometimes not possible in Source constructions while it is an option in Goal constructions, e.g. Early Sranan. We remain cautious at this point as to whether this is indeed differential coding or whether this is due to scarcity in data and description. In what follows, we thus limit ourselves to discussing clear cases.

A candidate for a strong split is Nicaraguan Creole. The language seems to have definite differential coding of PNs and CNs in Goal constructions, with the former always being zero-marked (11a) and the latter always occurring with the preposition *tu* (11b). In Source constructions, by contrast, PNs and CNs are always marked by *from*.

(11) Nicaraguan Creole [Bartens 2013b: Ex. 11-252, 11-249]
    a. *From deer yu go rait ∅ Managua.*
        from DEM.LOC 2SG go right ∅ Managua$_{PN}$
        'From there you can go straight **to** Managua.'
    b. *wen yu gwain tu di maakit*
        when 2SG go.PROG to ART.DEF market
        'When you go **to** the market.'

The Goal constructions in Kriol are also in line with our expectations: If there is an additional option of zero, it will apply to the PN. PNs are either marked by the locative/allative preposition *la(nga)* (12a), or they are zero-marked (12b). Conversely, CNs do not appear to have a zero option and seem to always take the preposition (12c) – at least as far as the data available to us indicate. Note also that we did not find examples of *langa*, i.e. the long form of the preposition, together with PNs. This lends further support to the assumption that PNs take the shorter marker.

(12) Kriol [Hudson 1985: 31, 28; Sandefur and Sandefur 1982: 63]
    a. *I maitbi garra go la Debi.*
        3SG.S maybe POT go LOC Derby$_{PN}$
        'He might have to go **to** Derby.'

b. *Ai   bin   go   Ø   <u>Debi.</u>*
   1SG.S   PST   go   Ø   <u>Derby</u>_PN_
   'I went **to** <u>Derby</u>.'

c. *Brom   jea   mibala=n   kipgon,   raidap – kaman raidap*
   from   there   1PL.EXCL=PST   keep.going   right.up come   right.up
   ***langa*   *taun*   *na.*[11]**
   LOC   town   now
   'From there we kept going, [and] came straight **to** <u>the town</u> then.'

There is no definite evidence of splits in Source constructions that is conditioned by the type of Ground involved. The examples given in the APiCS (Bartens 2013b) for Nicaraguan Creole Source constructions show the preposition *fram* with CNs and *from* with PNs. We assume, however, that these are different realisations of the same preposition so that we do not consider this a split. Furthermore, it is asserted in the APiCS for Creolese that PNs in Source constructions can be zero-marked, but the examples given are Goal constructions (APiCS, Devonish and Thompson 2013). In Holbrook (2012), the Source preposition is given as *from*, and Gibson (1992) provides an example of *from* with a PN. No example with a zero-marked PN as Source can be found. Given this uncertainty, we do not discuss Creolese further.

Overall, the English-based pidgins and creoles only seldom show differential marking of PNs and CNs. If there are multiple coding strategies or the option of zero, these often apply to both PNs and CNs. Factors that determine which strategy is employed include, among others, the specific type of motion verb involved, as, e.g., in Pichi (Yakpo 2019: 291) or Nigerian Pidgin (Faraclas 1996).

4.2 Dutch-based

There are three Dutch-based pidgins and creoles in our sample. Dutch has a dedicated marker for Goal (preposition *naar*) and a dedicated marker for Source (preposition *van*). PNs, however, usually take the preposition *uit* '(lit.) out (of)' to express Source. There is thus a split between CNs, e.g. *van de winkel* 'from the store', and PNs, e.g. *uit Amsterdam* 'from Amsterdam'. With CNs, *uit* can be used for elative, e.g. *uit de winkel* 'out of the store', rather than ablative. Out of the three sample languages, Berbice Dutch shows a weak split in Goal constructions, and Afrikaans shows a weak split in Source constructions.

---

11 Glosses added by the authors.

Table 3: CNs and PNs in Goal and Source constructions in Dutch-based pidgins and creoles.

Language	Goal CN	Goal PN	Source CN	Source PN	References
Afrikaans	na CN (toe) CN toe	na PN (toe) PN toe	van CN (af)	van/uit PN van PN af	den Besten and Biberauer (2013); Donaldson (1993)
Berbice Dutch	CN (angga) VV CN	PN Ø VV PN	fa(n) CN VV CN	fa(n) PN VV PN	Kouwenberg (2013a, 1994)
Kreeol	a CN	a PN	fa(n) CN	fa(n) PN	van Sluijs (2013)

Berbice Dutch is one of the few languages in our sample that makes use of a postposition, viz. the general locative *angga*[12], to mark Grounds as either Place or Goal.[13] With CNs, the postposition is used optionally, while "toponyms have a tendency to being zero-marked" (Stolz et al. 2014: 177), see (13a). We did not come across an instance of *angga* in combination with a PN. (13b) shows an instance of the postposition – here encliticised to the noun and realised as *anga* – following a CN. Note that serial verb constructions with *mu* 'go' (Goal) or *kumu* 'come' (Source) are also options.

(13) Berbice Dutch [Kouwenberg 1994: 484, 643][14]
    a.   ju   oiti   mutɛ   <u>birbistati</u>   Ø
        2SG   ever   go.PFV <u>New Amsterdam</u>ₚₙ Ø
        'Have you ever gone **to** <u>New Amsterdam</u>?'
    b.   jə   drai   mu   di   <u>ʃap</u>=***anga***
        SG   COP   go   DEF <u>shop</u>=LOC
        'You go **to** <u>the shop</u>.'

Grounds in Source construction, irrespective of whether they are PNs or CNs, are also marked overtly, either by the preposition *fa(n)* or by means of a serial verb construction.

In Afrikaans, Source constructions with both PNs and CNs usually take the preposition *van* 'from', sometimes in a circumpositional construction with *af* following the Ground. However, just like in Dutch, PNs have an additional option,

---

[12] According to Kouwenberg (1994: 557), *angga* "is optionally encliticised to the noun" and "is often reduced to **ang** or **à**" (original boldface).
[13] See also Stolz et al. (2014: 176–177) on Berbice Dutch.
[14] Glosses added by the authors.

i.e. the preposition *uit* 'out, out of, from'. Donaldson (1993: 341) explains that "'[f]rom' a town or country is usually rendered by *van*, but *uit* is also possible". The following examples show the use of the preposition *van* with CNs (14a) and PNs (14b) as well as the use of the preposition *uit* with PNs (14c).

(14) Afrikaans Source constructions [Donaldson 1993: 276, 336, 340][15]
    a.   Die   honde   kom   **van**   die   huis   **af**   anngehol.
        DEF   dog:PL   come   **from**   DEF   house   **of**   run:PTCP
        'The dogs come running **from** the house.'
    b.   Hy   kom   **van**   Pole   *(af)*
        3SG.M   come   **from**   Poland_PN   (of)
        'He comes **from** Poland.'
    c.   Hy   kom   **uit**   Holland.
        3SG.M   come   **out**   Holland_PN
        'He comes **from** Holland.'

While the construction with *van ... (af)* is an option for both CNs and PNs, the preposition *uit* as a genuine Source marker seems to be mainly used with PNs. We found a number of instances of *uit* being used with CNs, e.g. *uit die perd se bek* (out DEF horse POSS mouth) 'from the horse's mouth' (Donaldson 1993: 341). We suspect, however, that – similar to Dutch – *uit* expresses an elative meaning rather than ablative. *Uit* can also be found in several constructions that do not express movement per se, e.g. *Die regter is uit sy amp ontslaan* (DEF judge COP out POSS office fired) 'The judge was sacked from his office.' (Donaldson 1993: 340) or *Kry meer uit die lewe* (get more out life) 'Get more out of life.' (Donaldson 1993: 340). We thus assume a weak split between CNs and PNs in Source constructions.

4.3 Spanish-based

Spanish uses different prepositions to mark Goal and Source constructions, viz. *a* for Goal and *de* for Source. There is an additional preposition *para* 'for, to', which is sometimes used in Goal constructions and can be understood as 'in the direction of'. These prepositions are used for both PNs and CNs alike. The five Spanish-based varieties in Table 4 behave very homogeneously when it comes to the marking of Goal and Source with PNs and CNs.

---

15 Glosses added by the authors.

Table 4: CNs and PNs in Goal and Source constructions in Spanish-based pidgins and creoles.

Language	Goal CN	Goal PN	Source CN	Source PN	References
Cavite Chabacano	*na* CN	*na* PN	*di* CN	*di* PN	Sippola (2013b); Perez (2015)
Palenquero	*aí/a* CN	*aí/a* PN	*ri* CN	*ri* PN	Schwegler (2013)
Papiamentu	(*na/pa*) CN	(*na/pa*) PN	(*for*) *di* CN	(*for*) *di* PN	Kouwenberg (2013b); Florenciano (2018)
Ternate Chabacano	*na* CN	*na* PN	*na/di* CN	*na/di* PN	Sippola (2013a, 2011)
Zamboanga Chabacano	(*para*) *na* CN	(*para*) *na* PN	*na* CN	*na* PN	Steinkrüger (2013)

Papiamentu shows a variety of options ranging from zero-marking in Goal constructions to obligatory overt marking in Source constructions. Generally, Goal constructions are zero-marked.[16] "The goal is conveyed by means of an NP because the verbs *bai/bay* ['go'] and *bini* ['come'] inherently express direction" (Florenciano 2018: 102). This is true for both CNs (15a) and PNs (15b).

(15) Papiamentu
    a. Zero-marked going to CN [Goilo 1972: 42, cited in Florenciano 2018: 102]
        Mi   ta   bai   Ø   <u>ciudad</u>   cu   auto.
        1SG TA go   Ø   <u>city</u>   with car
        'I go **to** <u>town</u> by car.'
    b. Zero-marked going to PN   [Florenciano 2018: 110]
        Nan   ta   bai   Ø   <u>Sürnam</u>.
        3PL   TA   go   Ø   Suriname$_{PN}$
        'They are going **to** <u>Suriname</u>'

However, there are some contexts in which prepositions are used. The preposition *na* indicates a movement towards an inanimate Ground[17] and may invoke a semantic difference as seen in (16).

---

16 See also Stolz et al. (2014: 166–167) on Papiamentu.
17 Similarly, the preposition *den* is used to expressed the movement into a room in a house and *serka/seka/cerca* to a person (Florenciano 2018: 102).

(16) Papiamentu
    a. Going to CN with *na*   [Goilo 1972: 42, cited in Florenciano 2018: 102]
        El   a   bai   **na**   <u>e</u>   <u>supermerkado</u>   <u>ei</u>.
        3SG PFV go   PREP DEF supermarket there
        'S/he went **to** <u>that supermarket</u>.' (but s/he did not enter)
    b. Going to CN without *na* [Muller 1989: 201, cited in Florenciano 2018: 103]
        El   a   bai   Ø   <u>e</u>   <u>supermerkado</u>   <u>ei</u>.
        3SG PFV go   Ø   DEF supermarket there
        'S/he went **to** <u>that supermarket</u>.' (and entered it)

Florenciano (2018: 103) explains that "while the insertion of the preposition *na* in [(16a)] conveys an allative reading, the omission of the preposition in [(16b)] entails an illative interpretation". Apart from that, the use of a preposition is obligatory when the semantics of the verb otherwise does not allow a Goal reading. In the examples in (17), the preposition *pa* 'to, for' (< Sp. *para* 'to, for') is used to induce a Goal reading.

(17) Papiamentu
    a. Going to PN   [van Putte and van Putte-de Windt 2014: 191,
                                                cited in Florenciano 2018: 191]
        El   a   sali   **pa**   <u>Hulanda</u>.
        3SG PFV leave **to** Netherlands$_{PN}$
        'He left **for** <u>the Netherlands</u>/he went **to** <u>the Netherlands</u>.'
    b. Going to CN   [Lauffer 2013: 59, cited in Florenciano 2018: 157]
        Si   mi   ke,   mi   por   sali   **pa**   <u>laman</u>   mesora.
        if   1SG want 1SG can exit **to** sea immediately
        'If I want, I can leave **for** <u>the sea</u> immediately.'

For Source constructions then, the Ground, whether CN or PN, is usually marked with the preposition *di* 'from, of'. In some cases, however, a combination of *for* 'from' and *di* is used.[18] The examples in (18) show the two types of constructions with PNs. CNs take the same prepositions *di* or *for di*.

---

18 Florenciano (2018: 121, fn. 28) explains that *for di* "originates from the Portuguese *fora de* 'out of (a close place)', which follows a motion verb. However, due to having direct contact with the African substrate or the Afro-Portuguese contact via the creole languages spoken in the Gulf of Guinea (São-Tomense, Principense, Anobonense and Angolar), the preposition extended its function to indicate the spatial and temporal source of an activity".

(18) Papiamentu [Florenciano 2018: 110, 121–122]
   a. *Nan   ta   bin   **di**   Ulanda*.
      3PL   TA   come **from** Netherlands_PN
      'They come **from** the Netherlands.'
   b. *Nos   tabata nuebe ora   den avion   **for** **di** Kòrsou*
      1PL   COP.PST nine   hour LOC plane   **from** **of** Curaçao_PN
      bai   Ø   Hulanda
      go   Ø   Netherlands_PN
      'We spent nine hours on the plane **from** Curaçao to the Netherlands.'

Papiamentu is just one example of a Spanish-based creole. Overall, similar strategies are used in all of the sample languages depicted in Table 4. There seems to be no differential coding of PNs vs. CNs in Goal and Source constructions in any of the Spanish-based varieties looked at in this study.

4.4 Portuguese-based

The eleven Portuguese-based varieties in our sample again behave quite homogeneously. Only two languages are candidates for a weak split between CNs and PNs in Goal constructions. Similar to Spanish, Portuguese makes use of the prepositions *a* or *para* to express Goal and *de* or *desde* for Source. The pidgins and creoles in Table 5 show some traces of the prepositions *para* and *de*. However, zero-marking is much more prominent.

Table 5: CNs and PNs in Goal and Source constructions in Portuguese-based pidgins and creoles.

Language	Goal CN	Goal PN	Source CN	Source PN	References
Angolar	Ø CN	Ø PN	VV CN	VV PN	Maurer (2013a); Lorenzio (1998)
Cape Verdean Creole of Sotavento[19]	(*pa/na*) CN	(*pa/na*) PN	*di* CN	*di* PN	Lang (2013); Baptista (2013, 2002)

---

19 We decided to represent the data we gathered for the Cape Verdean Creole varieties of Sotavento (= the islands of Brava, Santiago, Fogo, and Maio). The APiCS features the varieties of Santiago, Brava, and São Vicente. The structures found in these varieties are very similar, however, based on the data given in the APiCS, there remained some gaps for each of the varieties. We thus focused on the data given by Baptista (2002) for the Sotavento varieties, complemented by the APiCS data of the Brava and Santiago varieties.

Language	Goal CN	Goal PN	Source CN	Source PN	References
Casamancese Creole	(pa) CN	(pa) PN	di CN	di PN	Biagui and Quint (2013); Biagui (2012)
Diu Indo-Portuguese	(pə/nə) CN	(pə/nə) PN	də CN	də PN	Cardoso (2013, 2009)
Fa d'Ambô	Ø CN	Ø PN	(VV) CN (V)	(VV) PN (V)	Post (2013); Hagemeijer et al. (2020)
Guinea-Bissau Kriyol	(pa) CN	(pa) PN	di CN	di PN	Intumbo et al. (2013)
Korlai	(nə) CN	(nə/da) PN	CN (su/pasun)	PN (su/pasun)	Clements (2013, 1996)
Papiá Kristang	(VV) (na) CN	(VV) (na) PN	(di) CN	(di) PN	Baxter (2013, 1988)
Principense	Ø CN	Ø PN	VV CN	VV PN	Maurer (2013b)
Santome	Ø CN	Ø PN	VV CN	VV PN	Hagemeijer (2013)
Sri Lanka Portuguese	CN Ø	PN(-pa)	CN impa	PN impa	Smith (2013)

Sri Lanka Portuguese is one of the two languages that potentially have a (weak) split between CNs and PNs in Goal constructions. While zero-marking of Goal is an option with both CNs and PNs (19a–b), there is an example in which the PN is additionally marked by a dative suffix (19c).

(19) Sri Lanka Portuguese
    a. Zero-marked going to CN   [Smith 2013, Ex. 41-133]
        eev   jaa-andaa   Ø   maaket
        1SG   PST-go   Ø   market
        'I went **to** the market.'
    b. Zero-marked going to PN   [Smith 2013, Ex. 41-136]
        ɛla-su   fiija   jaa-foy-tu   Ø   tavnsvil   ɔstreeliya
        3SG.F-GEN daughter PST-go-PFV.PTCP Ø Townsville$_{PN}$ Australia$_{PN}$
        'Her daughter having gone **to** Townsville, Australia.' or 'Her daughter has gone **to** Townsville, Australia.'
    c. Overtly marked going to PN   [Smith 2013, Ex. 41-135]
        aartar   silva-su   fiiya-su   fiiya   uŋa   jaa-foy   teem
        Arthur   Silva-GEN   daughter-GEN daughter one   PST-go   PRS.PRF
        tavnsvil-**pa**   ɔstreeliya-**pa**
        Townsville$_{PN}$-DAT Australia$_{PN}$-DAT
        'One of Arthur Silva's daughter's daughters went **to** Townsville, Australia.'

As we did not come across any examples of a CN marked by the dative suffix -*pa*, there is a possibility that there is a (weak) split in Sri Lanka Portuguese. However, the data given by Smith (2013) suggests, that the zero-marked option is much more common also for PNs.

Korlai, another potential candidate for a weak split, is a more doubtful case. Both CNs and PNs show zero-marking in Goal constructions. Additionally, the general locative preposition *nə* may be used with both types of Ground. The general locative preposition *də* on the other hand appears to be used only with PNs. We assume, however, that CNs may in fact also take the preposition *də* as it is used in combination with CNs in other constructions, cf. (20).

(20) Korlai   [Clements 1996: 162]
     elo   tɛ   **(də)**   <u>kadz</u>.
     they be.PRS **(in)**   house
     'They are **at** <u>home</u>.'

We thus suspect that the split suggested in Table 5 is actually non-existent. The results show that Portuguese-based pidgins and creoles generally lack differential coding of CNs and PNs.

4.5 French-based

Nine languages in our sample have French as a major lexifier. Although French shows the use of dedicated prepositions for both Goal (*à*) and Source (*de*)[20], the majority of the French-based creoles have no adpositional or case marking for going to and coming from PNs. However, many French-based creoles make use of an (optional) general locative marker (GLM), especially with CNs, cf. Table 6.

---

20 However, Stolz et al. (2014: 188–224, 274–275) found that street names can – or in fact have to – be zero-marked in certain Place and Goal constructions, e.g. *il est allé Ø <u>rue Réaumur</u>* 'he has gone to rue Réaumur' (Stolz et al. 2014: 222). Zero-marking of street names in Place and Goal constructions is used when the exact place (or address) is known to the relevant participants in a speech situation, i.e. the Figure (here: *il* 'he') did not just go anywhere in *rue Réaumur*, but to a specific address. This phenomenon is a new discovery documented by Stolz et al. (2014) and only recently confirmed by Mel'čuk (2018) under the notion of *preposition zéro*.

Table 6: CNs and PNs in Goal and Source constructions in French-based pidgins and creoles.

Language	Goal CN	Goal PN	Source CN	Source PN	References
Guadeloupean Creole	*anba* CN	Ø PN	*anba* CN	Ø PN	Colot and Ludwig (2013a)
Guyanais	(*annan/adan*) CN	Ø PN	(*annan/adan*) CN	Ø PN	Pfänder (2013)
Haitian Creole	(*nan*) CN	Ø PN	(*nan*) CN	Ø PN	Fattier (2013); Valdman (1988); Phillips (1982)
Louisiana Creole	*dan/o* CN	(*a/kote*) PN	*dan/an* CN	(*a*) PN	Neumann-Holzschuh and Klingler (2013)
Martinican Creole	(*an/anba/o-*)CN	(*an-/ann-/o-/oz-*)PN	(*an/anba/o-*)CN	(*an-/ann-/o-/oz-*)PN	Colot and Ludwig (2013b); Zribi-Hertz and Jean-Louis (2017, 2018)
Mauritian Creole	(*dan*) CN	Ø PN	(*depi/depi dan*) CN	(*depi*) PN	Baker and Kriegel (2013); Baker (1972); Kriegel et al. (2008)
Reunion Creole	*dan* CN	Ø PN	*dan* CN	Ø PN	Bollée (2013)
Seychelles Creole	(*dan*) CN	Ø PN	(*dan*) CN	Ø PN	Michaelis and Rosalie (2013); Michaelis (2008)
Tayo	Ø CN	Ø PN	(*nde*) CN	(*nde*) PN	Erhart and Revis (2013)

As Table 6 suggests, many French-based creoles have different strategies for the encoding of Goal and Source with CNs on the one hand and PNs on the other. Only Tayo uses the same Goal and Source constructions for both CNs and PNs. Five varieties show a weak split. In these varieties, both Goal and Source constructions can be expressed the same for CNs and PNs, respectively. However, due to different optional prepositions, CNs and PNs may also be expressed differently. In Mauritian Creole, for example, both CNs and PNs can be zero-coded for Goal, cf. (21).

(21) Mauritian Creole [Police-Michel et al. 2012: 57, 108][21]
    a. Mo   finn   al   Ø   *Mahébourg*   yer.
       1SG COMPL go Ø Mahébourg[PN] yesterday
       'I've been **to** Mahébourg yesterday.'

---

[21] Glosses added by the authors.

b. Mo   ti   'nn   al   Ø   *bazar*   samedi [...]
    1SG   PST   ASP   go   Ø   market   Saturday
    'I went **to** the market on Saturday.'

In both (21a) and (21b), the Ground in the Goal construction is zero-coded. The verb *al* (< Fr. *aller* 'go') induces Goal reading so that no overt marker is needed. With CNs, however, there is an additional strategy involving the preposition *dan* (< Fr. *dans* 'in').

(22) Mauritian Creole   [Baker and Kriegel 2013, Ex. 55-140]
    mo   ti   al   **(dan)**   *lafore*
    1SG   PST   go   **(LOC)**   forest
    'I went **into** the forest.'

The example in (22) suggests that CNs may optionally take the preposition *dan*. However, the preposition is not used to overtly mark *lafore* 'forest' as the Goal of a movement. Instead, "*dan* refers to the local region of the reference object or Ground" (Kriegel et al. 2008: 183). The Goal reading in (22) is still induced by the motion verb *al*. The preposition can thus be classified as a GLM. We did not find any instances of *dan* being used in Goal constructions involving a PN. A similar picture is found for Source constructions, cf. (23).

(23) Mauritian Creole Source   [Kriegel et al. 2008: 179, 182]
  a. Mo   sorti   Ø   *Vakwa*
      1SG   come.from   Ø   Vacoas_PN
      'I'm coming **from** Vacoas.'
  b. Dadi   sort   Ø   *lakanpagn*.
      Grandma   come.from   Ø   countryside
      'Grandma comes **from** the countryside.'
  c. Mo   papa   sort   **depi**   *Sesel*,
      1SG   father   come.from   ABL   Seychelles_PN
      li   'nn   vini   pu   travay dan   *Moris*.
      3SG   ASP   come   for   work LOC   Mauritius_PN
      'My father comes **from** the Seychelles, he came to work in Mauritius.'
  d. Pyer   finn   zet   so   bann   vye   soulye   **depi**   *enn*   *pon*.
      Pyer   COMPL   throw   POSS.3SG PL   old   shoe   ABL   INDF   bridge
      'Pyer threw his old shoes **off** a bridge.'
  e. Mo   sorti   **depi**   **dan**   *lafore*.
      1SG   come.from   ABL   LOC   forest
      'I am coming **out of** the forest.'

Apart from the possibility of having zero-coded Source constructions with both CNs and PNs (23a–b), the preposition *depi* (< Fr. *depuis* 'since, from') can be used to overtly mark a Ground for Source. Additionally, the preposition *dan* may be used in combination with *depi* when a CN is involved. Again, we did not find any instances of *dan* being used in a Source construction involving a PN. The optional use of the GLM *dan* in combination with CNs only may be because PNs inherently refer to specific locations, while CNs can also denote other things, e.g. the concept of a forest, i.e. a place with a lot of trees and other kinds of flora and fauna. The preposition *dan* then marks the CN as a location or Ground rather than anything else. Without further insight into this matter, however, this remains speculative.

As Table 6 suggests, GLMs such as *dan* discussed above for Mauritian Creole are common in French-based creoles (cf. also Zribi-Hertz and Jean-Louis 2018: 152). Martinican Creole is one of the languages that make use of a GLM when CNs serve as Ground.

(24) Martinican Creole [Zribi-Hertz and Jean-Louis 2018: 152]
    a. Pòl   ka   alé   **an**   *maaché-a*
        Paul   IPFV   go   LOC   market-DEF
        'Paul is going **to** the market.'
    b. Pòl   sòti   **an**   *maaché-a*
        Paul   exit   LOC   market-DEF
        'Paul came (back) **from** the market.'[22]

The GLM *an* 'in'[23] is used in the Goal construction in (24a) and the Source construction in (24b). In both cases, the Ground is a CN. With PNs, however, the GLM is not needed.

---

[22] In addition to Goal and Source constructions, Place constructions with CNs similarly take the GLM *an* in Martinican Creole:
(i)   Martinican Creole Place construction   [Zribi-Hertz and Jean-Louis 2018: 152]
       Pòl   té   **an**   *maaché-a*
       Paul ANT LOC market-DEF
       'Paul was **at** the market.'

[23] The examples given by Colot and Ludwig (2013b) for Feature 81 'Motion-to and motion-from' suggest a construction using *anba* 'under': *Man ka alé/sòti* **anba** *marché*. (1SG PROG go/come.back under market) 'I am going **to**/coming back **from** the market.' We are unsure, if *anba* functions as a preposition in these examples, in which case it similarly functions as a GLM. Another possibility is that *anba* is used as a spatial adverb, i.e. *anba marché* would mean something like 'the market down there'.

(25) Martinican Creole [Zribi-Hertz and Jean-Louis 2018: 165]
    a. *Pòl*   *ay*   Ø   *Fòdfrans*
        Paul   go   Ø   Fort-de-France_PN
        'Paul went **to** Fort-de-France.'
    b. *Pòl*   *vini*   Ø   *Fòdfrans*
        Paul   come   Ø   Fort-de-France_PN
        'Paul came **from** Fort-de-France.'

As the examples in (25) illustrate, both Goal and Source constructions with a PN are zero-coded. The verb suffices to indicate whether the Ground is the goal or the source of a movement. Zribi-Hertz and Jean-Louis (2018: 171) show, however, that *an-* may be used as a prefix with a PN to evoke a specific reading of the verb *soti*, see the examples in (26).

(26) Martinican Creole [Zribi-Hertz and Jean-Louis 2018: 171]
    a. *Espion-an*   *soti*   Ø   *Tirki*   *bonmaten-an.*
        spy-DEF   exit   Ø   Turkey_PN   morning-DEF
        'The spy got out **from** Turkey this morning.'
    b. *Pòl*   *soti*   *an-Tirki*   *bonmaten-an.*
        Paul   exit   LOC-Turkey_PN   morning-DEF
        'Paul came/arrived **from** Turkey this morning.'
    c. *Sa fè lontan*   *Pòl*   *soti*   Ø   *Tirki.*
        it is a.long.time   Paul   exit   Ø   Turkey_PN
        'Pòl left Turkey a long time ago.'

The same verb *soti* is used in all three examples. The reading, however, is different in each sentence. Because of the locative prefix *an-* in (26b), the verb meaning changes from 'get out (from)' (Fr. *sortir*) to 'come (from), arrive (from)' (Fr. *venir, arriver*). Due to the adverbial phrase in (26c), *soti* has to be understood as 'leave (from)' (Fr. *partir*). Thus, a telic movement from one place to another is indicated in (26b) with the locative prefix: Paul left Turkey and arrived at the place where he is at the time of the utterance. In (26a) and (26c) on the other hand, the movement is atelic. We only know that the referents left the location.

Apart from that, certain country names also take a GLM. Zribi-Hertz and Jean-Louis (2017: 75–76) explain that there are three groups of country names:

(i)   those that have an initial element *l(a)-* or *lé(z)-* as a remainder from the French articles *le*, *la*, or *les* as non-locative arguments. If they serve as Ground, the initial elements change to one of the locative markers: *la* > *an* (< Fr. *en* 'in the'), *l* > *ann* (< Fr. *en* 'in the'), *lé* > *o* (< Fr. *au* 'to the'), *léz* > *oz*

(< Fr. *aux* 'to the (PL)'), e.g. *Lafrans* 'France' > *an-Frans* 'in/to/from France', *Léz-Etazini* 'United States' > *oz-Etazini* 'in/to/from the United States'.

(ii) those that may be used with the masculine definite article *le* in French, but did not inherit the article in Martinican Creole and are shorter than three syllables. These country names take the particle *o-* (< Fr. *au* 'to the') when used as locative arguments, e.g. *o-Tchad* 'in/to/from Chad' or *o-Maròk* 'in/to/from Morocco'.

(iii) those that do not take any article in French or take the masculine definite article *le* or the plural article *les* in French, but are longer than two syllables. These country names do not take a locative marker when used as locative arguments, e.g. *Panama*.

There are thus special rules for country names that trigger the use of one of the locative particles or zero-marking. As Zribi-Hertz and Jean-Louis (2018: 158) explain, these particles, "unlike the free prepositions […], show signs of morphological attachment to the noun on their right". They seem to be prefixed rather than used prepositionally.

As we have seen above, CNs in Martinican Creole usually take the GLM *an* 'in'. However, there are some exceptions for CNs as well. Compare the following examples.

(27) Martinican Creole   [Zribi-Hertz and Jean-Louis 2018: 165]
    a.   *Pòl*   *ay*   *o-<u>biro</u>.*
         Paul   go   LOC-office
         'Paul went **to** the office.'
    b.   *Pòl*   *ay*   Ø   *<u>lapisin</u>.*
         Paul   go   Ø   (the)swimming-pool
         'Paul went **to** the swimming-pool.'
    c.   *Pòl*   *ay*   *an*   *<u>pisin-nan</u>.*
         Paul   go   in   swimming-pool-DEF
         'Paul went **into** the swimming-pool.'

We can make several observations from the three examples depicted in (27). First of all, the CN *biro* 'office' in (27a) takes the locative prefix *o-* instead of the locative preposition *an*. In a chapter on locative morphology in Martinican Creole, Zribi-Hertz and Jean Louis (2018: 158–161) note that the oblique particle "*o-* further selects a subclass of bare nouns denoting institutionalised places ('office', 'market', 'doctor', etc.)" and that "[t]he nouns of this latter class share with proper names their syntactic bareness and their intrinsic 'semantic definiteness' (Löbner

1985)". The examples in (27b) and (27c) both have an expression for 'swimming-pool' as Ground. In (27b), the word is *lapisin* from French *la piscine* 'the swimming-pool' where the initial element *la* goes back to the French article. In this case, the construction is zero-marked and denotes that Paul went to the place where the swimming-pool is located. In (27c), the expression used is *pisin-nan*, similarly derived from French *piscine* but in this case without the initial element *la* and instead bearing the Martinican Creole definite article *-nan* which is suffixed to the stem. In this construction, the GLM *an* is used. Compared to (27b) the meaning is different in that Paul did not simply go to the place where the swimming-pool is located, but into the swimming-pool itself, i.e. into the water. With reference to Löbner (1985), Zribi-Hertz and Jean-Louis (2018: 160) state that "[t]he null locative marker occurs with polysyllabic city names and nouns denoting types of institutionalised places such as 'church', 'school', 'home', construed as individual concepts". In their work on the grammar of country names in Martinican and Haitian Creole, Zribi-Hertz and Jean-Louis (2017: 77) note that nouns with initial *l(a)-* may be used as bare nouns and that they, when used in zero-marked locative constructions, "dénote contextuellement un type de lieu fonctionnel présupposé unique, à la manière d'un nom propre"[24]. A second type of these nouns denote "un concept sortal" (a sortal concept) when used without the initial *l(a)-* and "un concept individuel" (an individual concept) when used with the initial *l(a)-* (Zribi-Hertz and Jean Louis 2017: 77).

Although there seems to be a preference for zero-marking with CNs with the initial *l(a)-* from the French definite article and overt marking with nouns without *l(a)-*, the examples in (28) show, that both strategies are not exclusively reserved for the two types of nouns.

(28) Martinican Creole
    a. Zero-marking of CN without initial *l(a)-* [Zribi-Hertz and Jean-Louis 2017: 77]
        Mari   enmen   alé   Ø   <u>sinéma</u>[25].
        Marie like   go   Ø   <u>cinema</u>
        'Marie likes to go **to** <u>the cinema</u>.'

---

[24] Our translation: (They) contextually denote a unique type of place with a unique presupposed function, just like a proper name.
[25] Note that Zribi-Hertz and Jean-Louis (2017: 160–161) mention that *sinéma* 'movies' is one of those institutionalised places that usually begin with *l(a)-*, but it is an exception in that it does not follow this morphological pattern.

b. Overt marking of CN with initial *l(a)*   [Colot and Ludwig 2013b]

Sé	kannot-la	ay	**an**	lanmè.
PL	ship-DEF	go	**LOC**	sea

'The ships have gone out **to** <u>sea</u>.'

The in-depth discussion of Martinican Creole reveals that there are additional factors that need to be considered when looking at Goal and Source constructions with CNs and PNs. Unfortunately, we were not able to gain as much insight into all of the sample languages. Guadeloupean Creole, which is said to be very similar to Martinican Creole (cf. Colot and Ludwig 2013b), looks much simpler in Table 6. In fact, just considering the respective chapters in the APiCS the Martinican Creole data looks just the same as Guadeloupean Creole. We thus assume that there may be more to Guadeloupean Creole (and several other varieties included here) than what we were able to gather at this point.

Overall, the French-based creoles unanimously confirm our HP1 as stated in Chapter 3. In all instances of differential coding of CNs and PNs, the PN marker – if there is one at all – is shorter than or has the same length as the CN marker. Most often, however, the constructions involving PNs are zero-coded, while CNs may at least optionally take a preposition. Furthermore, our HP2 is also confirmed by the data. If zero is an option in Source constructions, it is also an option in Goal constructions. Moreover, the French-based creoles show more splits compared to the varieties discussed in previous sections. This is mainly due to the use of the GLM with CNs and zero-marking with PNs.

4.6 Other lexifiers

4.6.1 Malay-based

Malay in its many dialects usually makes use of two different prepositions to mark a Ground as Goal and Source, i.e. *ke* 'to' (or sometimes *ka* as in Jambi Malay, see Yanti 2010) and *dari* 'from', see (29).[26]

---

[26] The prepositions *ke* 'to' and *dari* 'from' are used with PNs and locational nouns alike. Personal names and CNs describing a person, however, sometimes take a different preposition. Sneddon et al. (2010: 196) explain for Indonesian that "[w]hen the following noun refers to a person, either **ke** or **kepada** is used" and that "**[k]e** tends to occur in informal registers, whereas **kepada** is used mostly in formal registers" (original boldface). Furthermore, *pada* is sometimes used instead of the longer form *kepada* (Sneddon et al. 2010: 197).

(29) Malay [Nida Dusturia, p.c.]
   a. *lelaki   itu   pergi   **ke**   kedai / Kuala Lumpur*
       man   DEM   go   **to**   store / Kuala Lumpur$_{PN}$
       'The man goes **to** the store / Kuala Lumpur.'
   b. *lelaki   itu   datang   **dari**   kedai / Kuala Lumpur*
       man   DEM   come   **from**   store / Kuala Lumpur$_{PN}$
       'The man arrives **from** the store / Kuala Lumpur.'

Table 7: CNs and PNs in Goal and Source constructions in Malay-based pidgins and creoles.

Language	Goal CN	Goal PN	Source CN	Source PN	References
Ambon Malay	(*ka/di*) CN	(*ka/di*) PN	*dari* PN	*dari* PN	Paauw (2013, 2008)
Singapore Bazaar Malay	(*ke/ka*) CN	(*ke/ka*) PN	*dari* CN	Ø PN	Aye (2013, 2005)
Sri Lanka Malay	CN=*nang*/=*ka*	PN=*nang*/=*ka*	CN=*deri(ng)* CN=*ka (asà)duuduk* CN=*ka (a)sduuduk*	PN=*deri(ng)* PN(=*ka*) *(asà)duuduk* PN(=*ka*) *(a)sduuduk*	Slomanson (2013); Nordhoff (2009)

As Table 7 suggests, there are some remains of both prepositions in the Malay-based creoles considered in this study. While Singapore Bazaar Malay and Ambon Malay use almost the same prepositions, there is some more variation in Sri Lanka Malay.

There are two potential splits in the Malay-based varieties displayed in Table 7, viz. a strong split in Singapore Bazaar Malay Source constructions and a weak split in Sri Lanka Malay Source constructions. In Singapore Bazaar Malay, it seems that CNs are overtly marked for Source with the preposition *dari* 'from', while PNs are zero-marked, see (30).

(30) Singapore Bazaar Malay [Aye 2005: 459, 146]
   a. *Lagi   maybe   lu   minya   anak   prempuan   dating*
       moreover   maybe   2SG   POSS   child   female   come
       ***dari**   sekola   dan   minum*
       from   school   and   drink
       'Moreover, probably, your daughter came back **from** school and drank.'
   b. *Saya   datang   Ø   Chinese.*
       1SG   come   Ø   China
       'I came **from** China.'

Unfortunately, the example given in (30b) is the only instance of a Source construction with a PN as Ground in Aye (2005), and there are only two examples of a Source construction with a CN. Due to this scarcity of data (and a lack of descriptions), we cannot be certain that there actually is a strong split as suggested in Table 7. Aye's (2005: 83–84) explanations that "the use of prepositions is mostly optional in Bazaar Malay" and that "[t]he frequency of the use of prepositions varies contingent on the level of competence and fluency of Bazaar Malay speakers" and "on the discourse information that the speaker would like to convey" make it even more doubtful that there is a strong split between CNs and PNs. However, according to the few examples on hand, Singapore Bazaar Malay is at least a candidate for supporting our HP1: The PN is zero-marked, while CNs are overtly marked by the preposition *dari*.

4.6.2 Bantu-based

As observed by Michaelis (2019: 221), "in many West African and Bantu languages, which are substrates of the Atlantic and Indian Ocean contact languages, motion-to and motion-from in sentences relating to a situation like 'I go to/come from the market' are not overtly marked, but orientation is expressed through the semantics of the verb". However, some Bantu languages make use of a grammaticalised form of a come.from-verb as a preposition in Source constructions, e.g. Swahili *(ku)toka* 'from' < *ku-toka* (INF-come.from). The two Bantu-based varieties displayed in Table 8 show similar constructions.

Table 8: CNs and PNs in Goal and Source constructions in Bantu-based pidgins and creoles.

Language	Goal CN	Goal PN	Source CN	Source PN	References
Kikongo-Kituba	*(na)* CN	*(na)* PN	*(na)* CN *katuka (na)* CN	*(na)* PN *katuka (na)* PN	Mufwene (2013); Swift and Zola (1963)
Lingala	*(na)* CN	*(na)* PN	*(na)* CN	*(na)* PN	Meeuwis (2013)

Both Kikongo-Kituba and Lingala optionally make use of the GLM *na* in both Goal and Source constructions with both CNs and PNs. Whether the Figure is moving toward or away from the Ground is determined by the verb. In Kikongo-Kituba, however, it is possible to use *katuka*, a grammaticalised form of the verb *ku-katuka* (INF-depart-FV) 'to depart, leave, be from' (see Swift and Zola 1963: 187) as exemplified by (31).

(31) Kikongo-Kituba [Swift and Zola 1963: 329][27]
katuka <u>Isoki</u>, yandi ke kwenda na balabala
from <u>Isoki.street</u>_PN_ 3SG HAB go LOC street
ya Prince Baudoin
of Prince Baudoin
'**From** <u>Isoki street</u>, he goes to Prince Baudoin street.'

This preposition can be found with both PNs and CNs. Overall, the two Bantu-based creoles in our sample do not show differential coding of PNs and CNs.

4.6.3 Arabic-based

(Modern Standard) Arabic uses the preposition *'ilaa* to mark a Ground as the goal of a movement and the preposition *min* to mark a Ground as the source of a movement (see Ryding 2005). The regional Neo-Arabic varieties, however, usually attest to zero-marking in Goal constructions (cf. Stolz et al. 2014: 91–94), while Place relations are commonly marked with an overt preposition. In Sudanese Arabic, "[s]tatic predicates (= Place relations) always require the presence of a preposition (which is mostly *fi* 'in')" (Stolz et al. 2014: 92). We found some instances of *fi* being used also in Goal constructions in Sudanese Arabic (e.g. Trimingham 1946: 67, 89). For Darfur Arabic (spoken in Southwest Sudan), Roset (2018: 96) states that "[t]he preposition *fi* is not only used to express 'in' but also 'at', 'on' and 'to'". The preposition *fi* can be found in both varieties displayed in Table 9 (both spoken in Sudan) as a kind of GLM that is used in Goal and partly also Source constructions. Similar to both Modern Standard Arabic and Sudanese (and other) Arabic varieties, Source is expressed with the preposition *min* in both creoles.

Table 9: CNs and PNs in Goal and Source constructions in Arabic-based pidgins and creoles.

Language	Goal CN	Goal PN	Source CN	Source PN	References
Juba Arabic	(*fi*) CN	(*fi*) PN	*min* CN	*min* PN	Manfredi and Petrollino (2013)
Kinubi	*fi* CN	*fi* PN	*min* (*fi*) CN *fi* CN	*min* (*fi*) PN *fi* PN	Luffin (2013); Wellens (2003)

---

27 Glosses added by the authors.

In Kinubi, Goal constructions generally seem to take *fi*, which can mean 'in', 'at', or "movement towards or away from", while "the direction is implied in the verb" (Wellens (2003: 157)). For Source constructions, there are several possibilities. The use of only the preposition *min* 'from' seems to be the most common construction (32a). It is also possible to have a combination of both *min* and *fi* (32b), and, with some verbs, the semantics of the verb suffices to imply a Source reading (31c).

(32) Kinubi Source constructions [Wellens 2003: 97, 159, 158]
    a. 'keya   ke'bir   al   'jibu   Nubi'ya **min**   Su'dan
        army   big   REL   bring Nubi   **from** Sudan_{PN}
        'the big army that brought the Nubi **from** Sudan.'
    b. (...)   'ino   'gum   **min** **fi**   'Mirya, (...).
              1PL   get.up **from** LOC Mirya_{PN}
        '(...) we left (**from**) Mirya, (...).'
    c. (...), 'ana   'tala   **fi**   'samba, (...)
              1SG   leave   LOC   field
        '(...), I left (**from**) the field, (...).'

While there are different coding strategies, we did not discover a split between CNs and PNs, neither in Kinubi nor in Juba Arabic.

4.6.4 Other

Table 10 displays six varieties with six different lexifiers. Much like most of the languages treated in this study, differential coding of CNs vs. PNs is rarely found, and there is only one candidate for a weak split, i.e. Pidgin Hawaiian.

Table 10: CNs and PNs in Goal and Source constructions in pidgins and creoles with different lexifiers.

Language	Lexifier	Goal CN	Goal PN	Source CN	Source PN	References
Chinuk Wawa	Costal Chinook	(*kopa*) CN	(*kopa*) PN	(*kopa*) CN	(*kopa*) PN	Grant (2013); Powell (n.d.)
Gurindji Kriol	Gurindji, Kriol	CN-*(ng)kirri* CN-*jirri* CN-*ta* *langa* CN Ø CN	PN-*(ng)kirri* PN-*jirri* PN-*ta* *langa* PN Ø PN	CN-*nginyi* *brom* CN *brom* CN-*nginyi*	PN-*nginyi* *brom* PN *brom* PN-*nginyi*	Meakins (2013, 2011)

Language	Lexifier	Goal CN	Goal PN	Source CN	Source PN	References
Mixed Ma'a	Cushitic, Maasai	(na) CN	(na) PN	(na) CN	(na) PN	Mous (2013, 2004)
Pidgin Hawaiian	Hawaiian	ma CN	(ma) PN	ma CN mai CN mai	ma PN mai PN mai	Roberts (2013)
Pidgin Hindustanic	Fiji Hindi	Ø CN	Ø PN	CN se	PN se	Siegel (2013)
Sango	Ngbandi	na CN	na PN	na CN	na PN	Samarin (2013, 1967)

Following the examples given in Features 79–81 in the APiCS, the use of the general locative preposition *ma* (< Hawaiian *ma* 'at', see Elbert and Pukui 1979: 135) is obligatory in Goal constructions in which a CN serves as the Ground, while it is optional with PNs.

(33) Pidgin Hawaiian Goal constructions [Roberts 2013, Ex. 71-140, 71-141, 71-137]
   a. Kanaka   pauloa   hele   Ø   *Kauai*.
       person   all   go   Ø   Kauai_{PN}
       'Everyone went **to** <u>Kauai</u>.'
   b. Wau   makemake hele   *ma*   *Hanalei*.
       1SG   want   go   LOC   Hanalei_{PN}
       'I want to go **to** <u>Hanalei</u>.'
   c. Wau   hele   *ma*   *kela* *hale*   *wau*.
       1SG   go   LOC   DET   house   1SG.POSS
       'I went **to** <u>my house</u>.'

The Goal construction involving the PN *Kauai* in (33a) is zero-marked, while the GLM *ma* is used in (33b) and (33c) involving the PN *Hanalei* and the CN *kela hale wau* 'my house', respectively. Roberts (2013) states for the examples given in Feature 80: 'Coming from named places' that "zero marking may occur in motion-to constructions". It is not specified whether this applies to both PNs and CNs or to PNs only (as this statement has been made in a chapter concerning named places). As there is only one example of a CN in a Goal construction (see (33c) above), we are unsure if we are dealing with an actual instance of a weak split, or if this might be another case influenced by data scarcity.

Although no other split is indicated in Table 10, it is worthwhile to have a short look at Gurindji Kriol and its many options for Goal constructions. Four different options are available for both CNs and PNs:

(i) the use of an allative suffix -*(ng)kirri* after vowels (< Gurindji -*ngkurra*) or -*jirri* after consonants (< Gurindji -*jirri*),
(ii) the use of the locative suffix -*ta* (<Gurindji -*ta*[28]),
(iii) the use of the locative preposition *langa* (< Kriol *la(nga)*), and
(iv) zero-marking.[29]

These options are exemplified in (34) in the same order.

(34) Gurindji Kriol Goal constructions [Meakins 2011: 200]
  a. karu-walija   gon   motika-**ngkirri**   rarraj.
     child-PAUC   go   car-**ALL**   run
     'The children run **to** the car.'
  b. wan   jinek   bin   gon   Wave-hill-**ta**
     a   snake   PST   go   Kalkaringi_PN-**LOC**
     'A snake went **to** Kalkaringi.'
  c. jinek   bin   gon   **langa**   shop,   walyak
     snake   PST   go   **LOC**   shop   inside
     'The snake went **to** the shop, and went inside.'
  d. partaj   motika-ngka   wi-l   teik-im-bek   yu   Ø   hospel
     climb   car-LOC   3PL.S-FUT   take-TR-back   2SG   Ø   hospital
     'Climb into the car and we'll take you **to** the hospital.'

All of these options can be used with both CNs and PNs, however, there is a restriction for CNs. According to a table given by Meakins (2011: 201), only option (i) can be used for any kind of (inanimate) Ground. Options (ii)–(iv), however, are restricted to PNs, public buildings, and home. Thus, other CNs, apart from public buildings and home, only have option (i) for a Goal construction. Although there is no clear split between CNs and PNs, the category of CNs shows differential coding depending on the type of Ground denoted by the CN.[30]

---

[28] In Gurindji, the locative suffix -*ta* can only be used to mark Place, not Goal (Meakins 2011: 203).
[29] Animate Grounds on the other hand are marked with the dative suffix -*yu* or the dative preposition *bo*.
[30] Haspelmath (2019: 322–324) uses the notion of topo-nouns for these kinds of special CNs that are treated like PNs rather than CNs in a given language: "In addition to place names and human nouns, languages sometimes give special treatment to a diverse set of nouns that denote concepts which are commonly used as spatial landmarks, such as '(one's) house', 'village', 'school', 'church', 'beach'" (Haspelmath 2019: 322).

5 Discussion

After presenting our data qualitatively in the previous section, we will now discuss the data primarily in quantitative terms. In Section 5.1, the distribution of splits among the sample languages will be discussed. In Section 5.2, we will have a closer look at the average lengths of Goal and Source markers, while Section 5.3 provides an overview of possible zeros. Section 5.4 offers a short discussion on Goal=Source syncretism in our sample languages.

5.1 Distribution of splits

The tables presented in Section 4 indicated the (weak or strong) splits between the constructions employed for CNs and PNs as Ground, respectively. The results are presented quantitatively in Tables 11 (for Goal) and 12 (for Source). First of all, we will have a look at the distribution of splits between CNs and PNs in Goal constructions. The number on the top shows the absolute number of splits, while the number on the bottom gives the percentage, i.e. how many languages show no split, a weak split, or a strong split out of the total number of languages (per lexifier) considered in this study.

Table 11: Distribution of splits in Goal constructions per lexifier.

	English	Dutch	Spanish	Portuguese	French	Other	Total
No split	18	2	5	9	1	12	47
	78%	67%	100%	82%	11%	92%	74%
Weak split	4	1	0	2	5	1	13
	18%	33%	0%	18%	56%	8%	20%
Strong split	1	0	0	0	3	0	4
	4%	0%	0%	0%	33%	0%	6%
Total	23	3	5	11	9	13	64
	100%	100%	100%	100%	100%	100%	100%

As Table 11 shows, most sample languages do not have any splits between CNs and PNs as Ground in Goal constructions. The Spanish-based pidgins and creoles do not employ differential coding at all, while in all other groups, at least some weak splits can be found. Strong splits were found in only one English-based creole (Nicaraguan Creole, see Section 4.1 above) and three French-based creoles

(Guadeloupean, Louisiana, and Reunion Creole, respectively, see Section 4.5 above). Overall, out of 64 sample languages, 47 did not show any splits in Goal constructions, while we counted 13 weak splits and four strong splits.

The distribution of splits between CNs and PNs as Ground in Source constructions is displayed in Table 12.

Table 12: Distribution of splits in Source constructions per lexifier.

	English	Dutch	Spanish	Portuguese	French	Other	Total
No split	23	2	5	11	1	11	53
	100%	67%	100%	100%	11%	84%	83%
Weak split	0	1	0	0	5	1	7
	0%	33%	0%	0%	56%	8%	11%
Strong split	0	0	0	0	3	1	4
	0%	0%	0%	0%	33%	8%	6%
Total	23	3	5	11	9	13	64
	100%	100%	100%	100%	100%	100%	100%

Our sample languages show even fewer splits in Source constructions. There are no splits in the Source constructions of English-, Spanish-, and Portuguese-based pidgins and creoles. Weak splits were found in one Dutch-, five French-, and one Malay-based creole, while three French-based creoles (again Guadeloupean, Louisiana, and Reunion Creole) and one Malay-based creole (Singapore Bazaar Malay) have a strong split between CNs and PNs in Source constructions.

Overall, it is striking that the French-based creoles show the most splits overall. There is only one French-based creole (Tayo) that does not differentiate between CNs and PNs at all. All the other languages have at least different options for the two categories. Moreover, splits are most often due to (optional) zero-marking of PNs in contrast to (optional) overt marking of CNs. Of the 28 attested splits, 22 are at least partially due to PNs allowing for zero, or, the other way around, CNs allowing for overt marking.

5.2 Average length of overt Goal and Source markers

As our HP1 addresses the issue of shorter (or zero) markers for PNs in comparison to CNs, we calculated the average lengths of Goal and Source markers, i.e. adpositions and affixes, for CNs and PNs, respectively. For this, we counted the segments of each possible overt marker and divided the sum through the number of options with overt markers found in the respective group of languages.[31] The results are presented in Table 13.

Table 13: Average length of Goal/Source markers per lexifier

	English		Dutch		Spanish		Portuguese		French		Other		Total	
	CN	PN	CN	PN	CN	PN	CN	PN	CN	PN	CN	PN	CN	PN
Goal	2,07	2,04	3,0	2,75	2,38	2,38	2,0	2,0	3,0	2,17	2,79	2,79	2,54	2,35
Source	3,3	3,3	3,0	3,0	2,43	2,43	2,5	2,5	3,43	2,29	4,88	5,29	3,26	3,14

For Goal markers, it is noticeable that the average length of markers used in combination with PNs is shorter than the length of markers used with CNs in English-, Dutch-, and French-based pidgins and creoles. For the other lexifiers, the average length is the same, which can largely be explained by the fact that there are almost no splits. For Source markers, the average length in combination with PNs was found to be shorter in French-based pidgins and creoles, while there is no difference between CNs and PNs in English-, Dutch-, Spanish-, and Portuguese-based pidgins and creoles. The Source markers of the languages with other lexifiers are exceptional in that the average length of markers used in combination with PNs is longer than those used with CNs. However, this can be explained by the many long options in Sri Lanka Malay (cf. Table 7 in Section 4.6.1). Due to the enclitic =ka being optional with PNs, there are twice as many options for PNs.[32] As each of the options is longer than the average Source construction, the average is higher for PNs than it is for CNs, even though the optionality of the enclitic makes it possible to have shorter Source constructions with PNs as compared to CNs in Sri Lanka Malay. Apart from this outlier, the average length of markers used with PNs is always shorter or the same as the one of markers used with CNs.

---

31 For these calculations, both zeros and serial verb constructions were disregarded. For zero-marking, see Section 5.3.
32 The options for CNs are (i) CN=*deri*, (ii) CN=*dering*, (iii) CN=*ka asàduuduk*, (iv) CN=*ka asduuduk*, (v) CN=*ka sduuduk*, and (vi) CN=*ka duuduk*. The options for PNs are (i) PN=*deri*, (ii) PN=*dering*, (iii) PN=*ka asàduuduk*, (iv) PN=*ka asduuduk*, (v) PN=*ka sduuduk*, (vi) PN=*ka duduk*, (vii) PN *asàduuduk*, (viii) PN *asduuduk*, (ix) PN *sduuduk*, and (x) PN *duuduk*.

Another observation we can make here is that the average length of Source markers is always longer or the same length as the average length of Goal markers. This is very much in line with the markedness hierarchy as proposed in, among others, Stolz (1992), Stolz et al. (2014, 2017c), Lestrade (2010), and Nintemann et al. (2020) where it is assumed that Source constructions tend to be more complex (in terms of, e.g. the number of words, morphs and morphemes, syllables, and segments) and less often zero-marked than Goal constructions (which in turn are more complex than Place constructions). The results are also in line with Haspelmath's (2018) predictions on differential coding of allative and ablative markers that are based on the findings by Stolz et al. (2014), i.e. that "[w]ithin the oblique case-markers and adpositions, we find that allative and ablative are asymmetric, with allatives showing a much greater tendency to be zero than ablatives [...], and if both are overtly marked, the ablative tends to have a longer shape" (Haspelmath 2018: 612).

5.3 Zero-marking

As stated in HP1, we assume that the marking of PNs does not only tend to be shorter than the marking of CNs but that there are also more zeros. In Table 14, we give the number of possible zeros in Goal and Source constructions with CNs and PNs per lexifier.[33] In each cell, the number on the top shows the absolute number of zeros, while the number on the bottom shows the percentage, i.e. how many languages have an option for zero-marking Goal and Source constructions, respectively, out of the total number of languages (per lexifier) considered in this study.

Table 14: Number of possible zeros in Goal and Source constructions per lexifier.

	English		Dutch		Spanish		Portuguese		French		Other		Total	
	CN	PN	CN	PN	CN	PN	CN	PN	CN	PN	CN	PN	CN	PN
Goal	12 52%	16 70%	1 33%	1 33%	1 20%	1 20%	11 100%	11 100%	6 67%	9 100%	9 69%	10 77%	40 63%	48 75%
Source	2 9%	2 9%	0 0%	0 0%	0 0%	0 0%	3 27%	3 27%	6 67%	9 100%	4 31%	5 38%	15 23%	19 30%

---

[33] Serial verb constructions are not counted as zero here as a directional verb can be considered a directional marker.

	English		Dutch		Spanish		Portuguese		French		Other		Total	
	CN	PN	CN	PN	CN	PN	CN	PN	CN	PN	CN	PN	CN	PN
Total	14	18	1	1	1	1	14	14	12	18	13	15	55	67
	30%	39%	17%	17%	10%	10%	64%	64%	67%	100%	50%	58%	43%	52%

Goal constructions in English- and French-based pidgins and creoles as well as pidgins and creoles with other lexifiers are less often zero-marked with CNs than they are with PNs. In Dutch-, Spanish-, and Portuguese-based languages, the number of zeros is the same for both CNs and PNs. Zeros are much less common for Source than for Goal. This is, again, in line with the markedness hierarchy mentioned above. Even though zeros are much less common in Source constructions, there is still a discrepancy between CNs and PNs: In French-based pidgins and creoles as well as pidgins and creoles with a different lexifier, PNs are more often zero-marked than CNs.

In fact, no language in our sample has zero-marking in Source constructions but not in the respective Goal constructions. That means that the option of zero-marking the Ground in Source constructions automatically implies the option of zero-marking the Ground also in Goal constructions (HP2).

Compared to the lexifier languages, more zeros are employed. In all of the Indo-European lexifiers, both Goal and Source are overtly marked with a preposition. Other lexifiers, e.g. Malay or Arabic, have (at least optionally employed) overt markers as well. In pidgins and creoles, however, zero-marking is a recurring option especially for Goal. About half (52%) of the English-based pidgins and creoles allow for a CN to be zero-marked in a Goal construction, even more allow for zero-marked PNs (70%). Two-thirds of the French-based creoles at least optionally zero-mark CNs in both Goal and Source constructions. With PNs, all of the nine sample languages allow for zero-marking. Zero-marking is found more often in pidgins and creoles than in their (mostly Indo-European) lexifier languages. This does not come as a surprise, as the "degree of overt signalling of various phonetic, morphological, syntactic, and semantic distinctions beyond communicative necessity" is said to be generally low for pidgins and creoles (McWhorter 2001: 125). That means, that more zero-marking and less distinctive morphology is likely to occur in the marking of spatial relations in these languages. Several explanations can be found for individual languages. In Bahamian Creole, for example, the absence of a preposition is considered more basilectal (Hackert 2013). As discussed in Section 4.6.1 on Singapore Bazaar Malay, the level of competence and fluency as well as the wish to emphasise a location may influence the use of prepositions as well (see Aye 2005: 451). In Ghanaian

Pidgin English, on the other hand, "[i]t seems that the use of the preposition *fɔ* (< *for*) is predominantly found in older speakers" (Huber 1999: 211–215), i.e. age plays a role, and younger speakers tend to zero-mark the Ground in Goal constructions more often. The reasons for the occurrence of zero-marking are manifold and investigating them exceeds the scope of this study. Nevertheless, it is to be noted that zero-marking is a frequent occurrence in pidgins and creoles and is one of the major features found in the differential coding of PNs and CNs.

5.4 Goal=Source syncretism

A number of sample languages do not employ distinct marking of Goal and Source, i.e. there is Goal=Source syncretism. This has been observed before by Michaelis (2019: 217), who states that "it is striking to see that many European-based creoles do not follow the Western European lexifier patterns and instead mark goal and source identically". Previous studies on the (a)syncretism of spatial relations, usually of Place, Goal, and Source (e.g. Creissels 2006, 2009; Pantcheva 2009, 2010, 2011; Lestrade 2010; Stolz et al. 2017c; Nintemann et al. 2020), found that the logically possible patterns[34] are unevenly distributed over the world's languages (see Stolz et al. 2017c: 11). For the sample languages of this study, there are mainly two reasons why there is no distinction between the two spatial relations: (i) a GLM that is employed for both Goal and Source (and possibly also for Place), or (ii) there is zero-marking of both Goal and Source (and possibly also of Place).[35] Table 15 provides an overview of how many languages allow for Goal=Source syncretism due to the use of a GLM or zero-marking.

---

34 The five logically possible patterns are I Place≠Goal≠Source, II (Place=Goal)≠Source, III Place≠(Goal=Source), IV Goal≠(Place=Source), V Place=Goal=Source (see Stolz et al. 2017c: 11).
35 Serial verbs were again not taken into consideration for this. They combine properties of both zero-marking and overt marking, as the distinction is made by verbs only, but one verb usually serves as a directional that unambiguously induces a Goal or Source reading, respectively. If we counted serial verbs as zero-marking, the number of Goal=Source syncretism would actually increase.

Table 15: Goal=Source syncretism per lexifier

	English		Dutch		Spanish		Portuguese		French		Other		Total	
	CN	PN	CN	PN	CN	PN	CN	PN	CN	PN	CN	PN	CN	PN
GLM	7	7	0	0	2	2	0	0	7	2	7	7	23	18
	30%	30%	0%	0%	40%	40%	0%	0%	78%	22%	54%	54%	36%	28%
Zero	2	2	0	0	0	0	3	3	6	9	4	5	15	19
	9%	9%	0%	0%	0%	0%	27%	27%	67%	100%	31%	38%	23%	30%
n of languages	9	9	0	0	2	2	3	3	9	9	7	8	30	31
	39%	39%	0%	0%	40%	40%	27%	27%	100%	100%	54%	62%	47%	48%

The bottom row indicates the number of languages in which either GLMs or zero-marking occur. As some languages have an optional GLM (the other option being zero-marking), it is important to distinguish between the number of options that allow for Goal=Source syncretism (GLM+Zero) and the number of languages. In each cell, the number on the top shows the absolute number of languages, while the number on the bottom gives the percentages.

Of the 64 languages in our sample, 31 languages (~48%) at least partly allow for Goal=Source syncretism. While 30 languages allow for Goal=Source syncretism with both CNs and PNs, Singapore Bazaar Malay is the only language that has optional Goal=Source syncretism only with PNs due to the lack of an overt marker in Source constructions. The French-based creoles again show the most variation: The use of a GLM is more common with CNs, while zero-marking is more prominent with PNs. In most other languages, both CNs and PNs have the same options. This is not surprising considering that splits have been found most often in French-based creoles, while those with other lexifiers show much fewer splits between CNs and PNs.

Of the 30 or 31 languages, respectively, 50% may disambiguate the constructions by a distinct marker for either of the spatial relations (or both). Conversely, this means that the other 50% do not use formal (morphosyntactic) means to distinguish Goal and Source. In these cases, the verb usually disambiguates the construction.

Similar to zero-marking discussed above, at least the Indo-European lexifier languages do not allow for Goal=Source syncretism at all. Malay and Arabic similarly make formal distinctions between the two spatial relations, while only few other lexifier languages, mainly from Sub-Saharan Africa, do not formally distinguish Goal and Source. That means that Goal=Source syncretism is found much more often in pidgins and creoles than in their (mostly Indo-European) lexifier languages. Michaelis (2019: 217–222) provides some evidence that the substrate language(s) rather than the lexifiers serve as a model for motion-to and motion-from constructions. She admits, however, that "[i]t is not clear to [her] why so many English-based Atlantic creoles with West-African substrates do not show the identity pattern" (Michaelis 2019: 222, fn. 21), i.e. why Goal and Source are not coded identically in these languages. As stated above, West African and Bantu languages usually do not code Goal and Source differentially. We would thus assume that, if the substrate(s) are most influential when it comes to the coding of Goal and Source, these creoles would not differentiate between the two types of spatial relations. Although we follow Michaelis's (2019: 222) generalization that "motion-to/motion-from constructions mirror the substrate patterns instead of the lexifier patterns of the creoles", we assume that there is always room for variation.

6 Conclusions

This study combined aspects of contact linguistics, typology, the grammar of space, and the grammar of names to account for the dynamics and complexity of the morphosyntax of Goal and Source constructions with CNs vs. PNs. It was shown that the pidgins and creoles in our sample mostly do not employ differential coding of CNs vs. PNs. However, most groups, i.e. pidgins and creoles with the same lexifier language, have some exceptions that show weak or even strong splits. The French-based pidgins and creoles are exceptional in that almost all of them have at least a weak split between CNs and PNs. The languages are spoken in different macro-areas and different types of substrates (and adstrates) were involved. At this point, we are unable to explain why the French-based varieties in particular show this behaviour. Nevertheless, this is an interesting find that invites further research.

Our hypotheses can be divided into two major topics: HP1 deals with differential coding of CNs vs. PNs, while HP2 concerns differential coding of Goal vs. Source. Both issues have been addressed in the previous sections. We consider both of our hypotheses confirmed.

As formulated in HP1, we found that the average PN marker is shorter than the average CN marker. This is the case with both types of Grounds as shown in Table 13. Moreover, PNs allow for zero-marking more often than CNs, see Table 14. Many languages have an (optional) overt marker (or GLM) that is used with CNs, whereas PNs are zero-marked. This is particularly common in French-based pidgins and creoles, but other varieties show similar behaviour, e.g. San Andres

Creole, Berbice Dutch, or Singapore Bazaar Malay, to name a few. Counterexamples can be found, too. In Sri Lanka Portuguese, for example, PNs may optionally take the dative suffix -*pa*, while this is not attested for CNs.

Turning to Goal vs. Source as addressed in HP2, we found that the average length of Goal constructions is shorter than the average length of Source constructions, see Table 13. There are many examples in line with these results, e.g. several English-based pidgins and creoles that adopted the English prepositions *to* and *from*, or the Portuguese-based Korlai that has the preposition *pasun* (or *su*) as a Source marker in contrast to the GLM *nə* (or *də*) used in Goal constructions. A few counterexamples exist. In Zamboanga Chabacano, for example, the GLM *na* is used in both Goal and Source constructions. Goal, however, may be further specified by the preposition *para* used in addition to *na*. Nevertheless, the results discussed in Section 5.2 clearly show that Goal constructions are shorter on average than Source constructions. Moreover, it was shown in Section 5.3 that the Ground is more often zero-marked in a Goal construction than it is in a Source construction (see also Stolz et al. 2014: 182–183). As stated before, we did not find a single example of a language allowing zero-marking for Source but not for Goal.

Taken together, we assume the following markedness hierarchy, inspired by previous studies as discussed in Section 5.2.

<Goal PN; Goal CN; Source PN; Source CN>

Figure 1: Markedness hierarchy of CNs and PNs in Goal and Source constructions.

The markedness hierarchy presented in Figure 1 indicates an increase in markedness from a Goal construction with a PN as Ground to a Source construction with a CN as Ground. That means that a PN in a Goal construction is more likely to be zero-marked and/or have a shorter marker than a CN in a Goal construction, which in turn is more likely to be zero-marked and/or have a shorter marker than a PN in a Source construction, and so forth. Future research will show if the same markedness hierarchy can be confirmed for non-pidgin-and-creole languages.

Acknowledgements: We would like to thank Thomas Stolz for piquing our interest in the differential coding of place names vs. common nouns and for his comments on the first version of this paper. Nataliya Levkovych similarly deserves our thanks for her comments and advice as well as for providing relevant literature. We are also grateful to Nida Dusturia for sharing her insight into Malay. The responsibility for the contents of this paper including any errors lies with us. This study forms part of the project *Morphosyntaktische Typologie der Toponyme / Morphosyntactic typology of toponyms (TYPTOP)* (STO 186/27-1; eBer-22-55215) which is financed by the *Deutsche Forschungsgemeinschaft (DFG)* from 1st of April 2023 until 31st of March 2026.

Abbreviations

1/2/3	first/second/third person
A	set A
ABL	ablative
ACT	active
ALL	allative
ANT	anterior
ART	article
ASP	aspect
B	set B
CAUS	causative
CISL	cislocative, translocative
CIS	completive intransitive status
CN	common noun
COM	comitative
COMPL	complementizer
COP	copula
CV	converb
DAT	dative
DEM	demonstrative
DEF	definite
DET	determiner
DM	discourse marker
EXCL	exclusive
F	feminine
Fr.	French
FUT	future tense
FV	final vowel
GEN	genitive
GLM	general locative marker
HAB	habitual
INDF	indefinite
INF	infinitive
IPFV	imperfective
IRR	irrealis
LOC	locative
M	masculine
NEG	negation
OBJ	object

PAUC	paucal
PFV	perfective
PL	plural
PN	place name
PRF	perfect
POSS	possessive
POT	potential
PREP	preposition
PROG	progressive
PRS	present tense
PST	past tense
PTCP	participle
REAL	realis
REL	relativiser
REP	reportative
RPT	repetition
SEQ	sequential
S	subject
SG	singular
SP	spatial
Sp.	Spanish
TA	tense-aspect
TER	terminal suffix
TR	transitive
UNINT	uninterrupted action
V	verb
VV	serial verb construction

References

Aboh, Enoch O., Tonjes Veenstra & Norval S. H. Smith. 2013. Saramaccan structure dataset. In Susanne Michaelis, Philippe Maurer, Martin Haspelmath & Magnus Huber (eds.), *Atlas of Pidgin and Creole language structures online*. http://apics-online.info/contributions/3 (checked 08/05/22).

Anderson, John M. 2007. *The grammar of names*. Oxford: Oxford University Press.

Ayafor, Miriam & Melanie Green. 2017. *Cameroon Pidgin English: A comprehensive grammar*. Amsterdam & Philadelphia: John Benjamins.

Aye, Daw Khin Khin. 2005. *Bazaar Malay: History, grammar and contact*. National University of Singapore dissertation.

Aye, Khin Khin. 2013. Singapore Bazaar Malay structure dataset. In Susanne Michaelis, Philippe Maurer, Martin Haspelmath & Magnus Huber (eds.), *Atlas of Pidgin and Creole language structures online*. http://apics-online.info/contributions/67 (checked 08/05/22).

Baptista, Marlyse. 2002. *The syntax of Cape Verdean Creole: The Sotavento varieties*. Amsterdam &Philadelphia: John Benjamins.
Baptista, Marlyse. 2013. Cape Verdean Creole of Brava structure dataset. In Susanne Michaelis, Philippe Maurer, Martin Haspelmath & Magnus Huber (eds.), *Atlas of Pidgin and Creole language structures online*. http://apics-online.info/contributions/31 (checked 08/05/22).
Baker, Philip. 1972. *Kreol: A description of Mauritian Creole*. London: C. Hurst/Company.
Baker, Philip & Sibylle Kriegel. 2013. Mauritian Creole structure dataset. In Susanne Michaelis, Philippe Maurer, Martin Haspelmath & Magnus Huber (eds.), *Atlas of Pidgin and Creole language structures online*. http://apics-online.info/contributions/55 (checked 08/05/22).
Bartens, Angela. 2013a. San Andres Creole English structure dataset. In Susanne Michaelis, Philippe Maurer, Martin Haspelmath & Magnus Huber (eds.), *Atlas of Pidgin and Creole language structures online*. http://apics-online.info/contributions/10 (checked 08/05/22).
Bartens, Angela. 2013b. Nicaraguan Creole English structure dataset. In Susanne Michaelis, Philippe Maurer, Martin Haspelmath & Magnus Huber (eds.), *Atlas of Pidgin and Creole language structures online*. http://apics-online.info/contributions/11 (checked 08/05/22).
Baxter, Alan N. 1988. *A grammar of Kristang (Malacca Creole Portuguese)*. Canberra: The Australian National University.
Baxter, Alan N. 2013. Papiá Kristang structure dataset. In Susanne Michaelis, Philippe Maurer, Martin Haspelmath & Magnus Huber (eds.), *Atlas of Pidgin and Creole language structures online*. http://apics-online.info/contributions/42 (checked 08/05/22).
Biagui, Noël Bernard. 2012. *Description générale du Créole Afro-Portugais parlé à Ziguinchor (Sénégal)*. Institut National des Langues et Civilisations Orientales/Université Cheikh Anta Diop de Dakar dissertation.
Biagui, Noël Bernard & Nicolas Quint. 2013. Casamancese Creole structure dataset. In Susanne Michaelis, Philippe Maurer, Martin Haspelmath & Magnus Huber (eds.), *Atlas of Pidgin and Creole language structures online*. http://apics-online.info/contributions/34 (checked 08/05/22).
Boas, Franz. 1911. Chinook. In Franz Boas (ed.), *Handbook of American Indian languages 1*, 559–678. Washington, D.C.: Government Printing Office.
Bollée, Annegret. 2013. Reunion Creole structure dataset. In Susanne Michaelis, Philippe Maurer, Martin Haspelmath & Magnus Huber (eds.), *Atlas of Pidgin and Creole language structures online*. http://apics-online.info/contributions/54 (checked 08/05/22).
Cardoso, Hugo C. 2009. *The Indo-Portuguese language of Diu*. Utrecht: LOT.
Cardoso, Hugo C. 2013. Diu Indo-Portuguese structure dataset. In Susanne Michaelis, Philippe Maurer, Martin Haspelmath & Magnus Huber (eds.), *Atlas of Pidgin and Creole language structures online*. http://apics-online.info/contributions/39 (checked 08/05/22).
Clements, Clancy J. 1996. *The genesis of a language. The formation and development of Korlai Portuguese*. Amsterdam & Philadelphia: John Benjamins.
Clements, Clancy J. 2013. Korlai structure dataset. In Susanne Michaelis, Philippe Maurer, Martin Haspelmath & Magnus Huber (eds.), *Atlas of Pidgin and Creole language structures online*. http://apics-online.info/contributions/40 (checked 08/05/22).
Colot, Serge & Ralph Ludwig. 2013a. Guadeloupean Creole structure dataset. In Susanne Michaelis, Philippe Maurer, Martin Haspelmath & Magnus Huber (eds.), *Atlas of Pidgin and*

Creole language structures online. http://apics-online.info/contributions/50 (checked 08/05/22).

Colot, Serge & Ralph Ludwig. 2013b. Martinican Creole structure dataset. In Susanne Michaelis, Philippe Maurer, Martin Haspelmath & Magnus Huber (eds.), http://apics-online.info/contributions/51 (checked 08/05/22).

Creissels, Denis. 2006. Encoding the distinction between location, source and direction: A typological study. In Maya Hickman & Stephane Robert (eds.), *Space in languages*, 19–28. Amsterdam & Philadelphia: John Benjamins.

Creissels, Denis. 2009. Spatial cases. In Andrej Malchukov & Andrew Spencer (eds.), *The Oxford handbook of case*, 609–625. Oxford: Oxford University Press.

Croft, William. 1990. *Typology and universals.* Cambridge: Cambridge University Press.

Crowley, Terry. 2002. *Serial verbs in Oceanic: A descriptive typology.* Oxford: Oxford University Press.

den Besten, Hans & Theresa Biberauer. 2013. Afrikaans structure dataset. In Susanne Michaelis, Philippe Maurer, Martin Haspelmath & Magnus Huber (eds.), *Atlas of Pidgin and Creole language structures online.* http://apics-online.info/contributions/29 (checked 08/05/22).

Devonish, Hubert & Dahlia Thompson. 2013. Creolese structure dataset. In Susanne Michaelis, Philippe Maurer, Martin Haspelmath & Magnus Huber (eds.), *Atlas of Pidgin and Creole language structures online.* http://apics-online.info/contributions/5 (checked 08/05/22).

Donaldson, Bruce C. 1993. *A grammar of Afrikaans.* Berlin: Walter de Gruyter.

Durrleman, Stephanie. 2008. *The syntax of Jamaican Creole: A cartographic perspective.* Amsterdam & Philadelphia: John Benjamins.

Elbert, Samuel H. & Mary Kawena Pukui. 1979. *Hawaiian Grammar.* Honolulu: University of Hawaii Press.

Erhart, Sabine & Melanie Revis. 2013. Tayo structure dataset. In Susanne Michaelis, Philippe Maurer, Martin Haspelmath & Magnus Huber (eds.), *Atlas of Pidgin and Creole language structures online.* http://apics-online.info/contributions/57 (checked 08/05/22).

Escure, Geneviève. 2013. Belizean Creole structure dataset. In Susanne Michaelis, Philippe Maurer, Martin Haspelmath & Magnus Huber (eds.), *Atlas of Pidgin and Creole language structures online.* http://apics-online.info/contributions/9 (checked 08/05/22).

Faraclas, Nicholas. 1996. *Nigerian Pidgin.* London & New York: Routledge.

Faraclas, Nicholas. 2013. Nigerian Pidgin structure dataset. In Susanne Michaelis, Philippe Maurer, Martin Haspelmath & Magnus Huber (eds.), *Atlas of Pidgin and Creole language structures online.* http://apics-online.info/contributions/17 (checked 08/05/22).

Farquharson, Joseph T. 2013. Jamaican structure dataset. In Susanne Michaelis, Philippe Maurer, Martin Haspelmath & Magnus Huber (eds.), *Atlas of Pidgin and Creole language structures online.* http://apics-online.info/contributions/8. (checked 08/05/22).

Fattier, Dominique. 2013. Haitian Creole structure dataset. In Susanne Michaelis, Philippe Maurer, Martin Haspelmath & Magnus Huber (eds.), *Atlas of Pidgin and Creole language structures online.* http://apics-online.info/contributions/49 (checked 08/05/22).

Feinmann, Diego. 2020. Language and thought in the motion domain: Methodological considerations and new empirical evidence. *Journal of Psycholinguistic Research* 49. 1–29.

Finney, Malcolm Awadajin. 2013. Krio structure dataset. In Susanne Michaelis, Philippe Maurer, Martin Haspelmath & Magnus Huber (eds.), *Atlas of Pidgin and Creole language structures online.* http://apics-online.info/contributions/15 (checked 08/05/22).

Florenciano, Lloret. 2018. *Syntactic variation in Papiamentu/o: Directional and resultative serial verb constructions*. Universität Hamburg dissertation.
Gibson, Kean. 1992. Tense and aspect in Guyanese Creole with reference to Jamaican and Carriacouan. *International Journal of American Linguistics* 58(1). 49–95.
Goilo, E. R. 1972. *Papiamentu textbook*. Aruba: De Wit Stores.
Grant, Anthony P. 2013. Chinuk Wawa structure dataset. In Susanne Michaelis, Philippe Maurer, Martin Haspelmath & Magnus Huber (eds.), *Atlas of Pidgin and Creole language structures online*. http://apics-online.info/contributions/74 (checked 08/04/22).
Green, Lisa. 2013. African American English structure dataset. In Susanne Michaelis, Philippe Maurer, Martin Haspelmath & Magnus Huber (eds.), *Atlas of Pidgin and Creole language structures online*. http://apics-online.info/contributions/14 (checked 08/05/22).
Greene, Laurie A. 1999. *A grammar of Belizean Creole*. New York: Peter Lang.
Hackert, Stephanie. 2013. Bahamian Creole structure dataset. In Susanne Michaelis, Philippe Maurer, Martin Haspelmath & Magnus Huber (eds.), *Atlas of Pidgin and Creole language structures online*. http://apics-online.info/contributions/12 (checked 08/05/22).
Hagemeijer, Tjerk. 2013. Santome structure dataset. In Susanne Michaelis, Philippe Maurer, Martin Haspelmath & Magnus Huber (eds.), *Atlas of Pidgin and Creole language structures online*. http://apics-online.info/contributions/35 (checked 08/05/22).
Hagemeijer, Tjerk, Philippe Maurer-Cecchini & Armando Zamora Segorbe. 2020. *A grammar of Fa d'Ambô*. Berlin & Boston: De Gruyter.
Haspelmath, Martin. 2018. Explaining grammatical coding asymmetries: Form-frequency correspondences and predictability. *Journal of Linguistics* 57. 605–633.
Haspelmath, Martin. 2019. Differential place marking and differential object marking. *STUF* 72(3). 313–334.
Helmbrecht, Johannes. 2020. Form and function of personal names: Dimensions of the morphosyntactic diversity. In Nataliya Levkovych & Julia Nintemann (eds.), *Aspects of the grammar of names. Empirical case studies and theoretical topics*, 1–24. München: LINCOM.
Hofling, Charles Andrew. 2017. Comparative Maya (Yucatec, Lacandon, Itzaj, and Mopan Maya). In Judith Aissen, Nora C. England & Roberto Zavala Maldonado (eds.), *The Mayan languages*, 687–759. London & New York: Routledge.
Holbrook, David Joseph. 2012. *The classification of the English-lexifier Creole languages spoken in Grenada, Guyana, St. Vincent, and Tobago: Using a comparison of the markers of some key grammatical features: A tool for determining the potential to share and/or adapt literary development materials* (SIL eBooks 25). Dallas: SIL International. https://www.sil.org/resources/archives/43481 (checked 08/05/22).
Huber, Magnus. 1999. *Ghanaian Pidgin English in its West Afrixan context: A socio-historical and structural analysis*. Amsterdam & Philadelphia: John Benjamins.
Huber, Magnus. 2013. Ghanaian Pidgin English structure dataset. In Susanne Michaelis, Philippe Maurer, Martin Haspelmath & Magnus Huber (eds.), *Atlas of Pidgin and Creole language structures online*. http://apics-online.info/contributions/16 (checked 08/05/22).
Hudson, Joyce. 1985. *Grammatical and semantic aspects of Fitzroy Valley Kriol*. Darwin: Summer Institute of Linguistics, Australian Aborigines Branch.
Intumbo, Incanha, Liliana Inverno & John Holm. 2013. Guinea-Bissau Kriyol structure dataset. In Susanne Michaelis, Philippe Maurer, Martin Haspelmath & Magnus Huber (eds.), *Atlas*

of Pidgin and Creole language structures online. http://apics-online.info/contributions/33 (checked 08/05/22).

Kouwenberg, Silvia. 1994. *A grammar of Berbice Dutch Creole.* Berlin & New York: De Gruyter.

Kouwenberg, Silvia. 2013a. Berbice Dutch structure dataset. In Susanne Michaelis, Philippe Maurer, Martin Haspelmath & Magnus Huber (eds.), *Atlas of Pidgin and Creole language structures online.* http://apics-online.info/contributions/28 (checked 08/05/22).

Kouwenberg, Silvia. 2013b. Papiamentu structure dataset. In Susanne Michaelis, Philippe Maurer, Martin Haspelmath & Magnus Huber (eds.), *Atlas of Pidgin and Creole language structures online.* http://apics-online.info/contributions/47 (checked 08/05/22).

Kriegel, Sybille, Ralph Ludwig & Fabiola Henri. 2008. Encoding path in Mauritian Creole and Bhojpuri: Problems of language contact. In Susanne Michaelis (ed.), *Roots of Creole structures: Weighing the contribution of substrates and superstrates*, 169–196. Amsterdam & Philadelphia: John Benjamins.

Lang, Jürgen. 2013. Cape Verdean Creole of Santiago structure dataset. In Susanne Michaelis, Philippe Maurer, Martin Haspelmath & Magnus Huber (eds.), *Atlas of Pidgin and Creole language structures online.* http://apics-online.info/contributions/30 (checked 08/05/22).

Lauffer, Pierre. 2013. *Kuenta pa kaminda.* Curaçao: Fundashon Pierre Lauffer/Fundashon pa Planikifashon di Idioma.

Lestrade, Sander. 2010. *The space of case.* Nijmegen: Radboud Universiteit.

Levinson, Stephen C. 2003. *Space in language and cognition: Explorations in cognitive diversity.* Cambridge: Cambridge University Press.

Levinson, Stephen C. & Davin P. Wilkins (eds.). 2006. *Grammars of space: Explorations in cognitive diversity.* Cambridge: Cambridge University Press.

Li, Michelle & Stephan Matthews. 2013. Chinese Pidgin English structure dataset. In Susanne Michaelis, Philippe Maurer, Martin Haspelmath & Magnus Huber (eds.), *Atlas of Pidgin and Creole language structures online.* http://apics-online.info/contributions/20 (checked 08/05/22).

Lim, Lisa & Umberto Ansaldo. 2013. Singlish structure dataset. In Susanne Michaelis, Philippe Maurer, Martin Haspelmath & Magnus Huber (eds.), *Atlas of Pidgin and Creole language structures online.* http://apics-online.info/contributions/21 (checked 08/05/22).

Löbner, Sebastian. 1985. Definites. *Journal of Semantics* 4. 279–326.

Lorenzio, Gerardo A. 1998. *The Angolar Creole Portuguese of São Tomé: Its grammar and sociolinguistic history.* Ann Arbor: UMI.

Luffin, Xavier. 2013. Kinubi structure dataset. In Susanne Michaelis, Philippe Maurer, Martin Haspelmath & Magnus Huber (eds.), *Atlas of Pidgin and Creole language structures online.* http://apics-online.info/contributions/63 (checked 08/05/22).

Manfredi, Stefano & Sara Petrollino. 2013. Juba Arabic structure dataset. In Susanne Michaelis, Philippe Maurer, Martin Haspelmath & Magnus Huber (eds.), *Atlas of Pidgin and Creole language structures online.* http://apics-online.info/contributions/64 (checked 08/05/22).

Maurer, Philippe. 2013a. Angolar structure dataset. In Susanne Michaelis, Philippe Maurer, Martin Haspelmath & Magnus Huber (eds.), *Atlas of Pidgin and Creole language structures online.* http://apics-online.info/contributions/36 (checked 08/05/22).

Maurer, Philippe. 2013b. Principense structure dataset. In Susanne Michaelis, Philippe Maurer, Martin Haspelmath & Magnus Huber (eds.), *Atlas of Pidgin and Creole language structures online.* http://apics-online.info/contributions/37 (checked 08/05/22).

McWhorter, John H. 2001. The world's simplest grammars are creole grammars. *Linguistic Typology* 5. 125–166.
McWhorter, John H. & Jeff Good. 2012. *A grammar of Saramaccan Creole*. Berlin & Boston: De Gruyter.
Meakins, Felicity. 2011. *Case-marking in contact: The development and function of case morphology in Gurindji Kriol*. Amsterdam & Philadelphia: John Benjamins.
Meakins, Felicity. 2013. Gurindji Kriol structure dataset. In Susanne Michaelis, Philippe Maurer, Martin Haspelmath & Magnus Huber (eds.), *Atlas of Pidgin and Creole language structures online*. http://apics-online.info/contributions/72 (checked 08/05/22).
Meeuwis, Michael. 2013. Lingala structure dataset. In Susanne Michaelis, Philippe Maurer, Martin Haspelmath & Magnus Huber (eds.), *Atlas of Pidgin and Creole language structures online*. http://apics-online.info/contributions/60 (checked 08/05/22).
Mel'čuk, Igor. 2018. Les prépositions zéro en français. *Lingvisticae Investigationes* 41(2). 269–283.
Mesthrie, Rajend. 2008. Indian South African English: Morphosyntax and syntax. In Rajend Mesthrie (ed.), *Varieties of English, Vol. 4: Africa, South and Southeast Asia*, 501–520. Berlin & Boston: De Gruyter.
Meyerhoff, Miriam. 2013. Bislama structure dataset. In Susanne Michaelis, Philippe Maurer, Martin Haspelmath & Magnus Huber (eds.), *Atlas of Pidgin and Creole language structures online*. http://apics-online.info/contributions/23 (checked 08/05/22).
Michaelis, Susanne. 2008. Valency patterns in Seychelles Creole: Where do they come from?. In Susanne Michaelis (ed.), *Roots of creole structures: Weighing the contribution of substrates and superstrates*, 225–251. Amsterdam & Philadelphia: John Benjamins.
Michaelis, Susanne. 2019. World-wide comparative evidence for calquing valency patterns in Creoles. *Journal of Language Contact* 12(1). 191–231.
Michaelis, Susanne, Philippe Maurer, Martin Haspelmath & Magnus Huber (eds.). 2013. *Atlas of Pidgin and Creole language structures online*. https://apics-online.info/ (checked 08/04/22).
Michaelis, Susanne & Marcel Rosalie. 2013. Seychelles Creole structure dataset. In Susanne Michaelis, Philippe Maurer, Martin Haspelmath & Magnus Huber (eds.), *Atlas of Pidgin and Creole language structures online*. http://apics-online.info/contributions/56 (checked 08/05/22).
Migge, Bettina. 2013. Nengee structure dataset. In Susanne Michaelis, Philippe Maurer, Martin Haspelmath & Magnus Huber (eds.), *Atlas of Pidgin and Creole language structures online*. http://apics-online.info/contributions/4 (checked 08/05/22).
Mous, Maarten. 2004. *The making of a mixed language: The case of Ma'a/Mbugu*. Amsterdam & Philadelphia: John Benjamins.
Mous, Maarten. 2013. Mixed Ma'a/Mbugu structure dataset. In Susanne Michaelis, Philippe Maurer, Martin Haspelmath & Magnus Huber (eds.), *Atlas of Pidgin and Creole language structures online*. http://apics-online.info/contributions/62 (checked 08/05/22).
Mufwene, Salikoko S. 2013. Kikongo-Kituba structure dataset. In Susanne Michaelis, Philippe Maurer, Martin Haspelmath & Magnus Huber (eds.), *Atlas of Pidgin and Creole language structures online*. http://apics-online.info/contributions/58 (checked 08/05/22).
Muller, Enrique A. F. 1989. *Inleiding tot de syntaxis van het Papiamentu*. Universiteit van Amsterdam dissertation.
Neumann-Holzschuh, Ingrid & Thomas A. Klingler. 2013. Louisiana Creole structure dataset. In Susanne Michaelis, Philippe Maurer, Martin Haspelmath & Magnus Huber (eds.), *Atlas of*

Pidgin and Creole language structures online. http://apics-online.info/contributions/53 (checked 08/05/22).

Nintemann, Julia, Maja Robbers & Nicole Hober. 2020. *Here – Hither – Hence and related categories: A cross-linguistic study.* Berlin & Boston: De Gruyter.

Nordhoff, Sebastian. 2009. *A gramar of Upcountry Sri Lanka Malay.* Utrecht: LOT.

Nübling, Damaris, Fabian Fahlbusch & Rita Heuser. 2015. *Namen: Eine Einführung in die Onomastik.* Tübingen: Narr.

Paauw, Scott H. 2008. The Malay contact varieties of Eastern Indonesia: A typological comparison. Ann Arbor: UMI.

Paauw, Scott. 2013. Ambon Malay structure dataset. In Michaelis et al. (eds.), *Atlas of Pidgin and Creole language structures online.* http://apics-online.info/contributions/68 (checked 08/05/22).

Pantcheva, Marina. 2009. Directional expressions cross-linguistically: Nanosyntax and lexicalization. *Nordlyd* 36(1). 7–39.

Pantcheva, Marina. 2010. The syntactic structure of locations, goals, and sources. *Linguistics* 48(5). 1043–1081.

Pantcheva, Marina. 2011. *Decomposing path. The nanosyntax of directional expressions.* University of Tromsø dissertation.

Perez, Marilola. 2015. *Cavite Chabacano Philippine Creole Spanish: Description and typology.* University of California, Berkeley dissertation.

Peterson, John. 2006. *Kharia. A South Munda language.* Unpublished "Habilitation"-Thesis, Universität Osnabrück, Volume I: Grammatical Analysis.

Peterson, John. 2008. Kharia. In Gregory D.S. Anderson (ed.), *The Munda Languages*, 434–507. London & New York: Routledge.

Pfänder, Stefan. 2013. Guyanais structure dataset. In Susanne Michaelis, Philippe Maurer, Martin Haspelmath & Magnus Huber (eds.), *Atlas of Pidgin and Creole language structures online.* http://apics-online.info/contributions/52 (checked 08/05/22).

Phillips, Judith Wingerd. 1982. *A Partial grammar of the Haitian Creole verb system: Forms, function and syntax.* Ann Arbor: UMI.

Police-Michel, Daniella, Arnaud Carpooran & Guilhem Florigny. 2012. *Gramer kreol morisien.* Phoenix & Mauritius: Akademi Kreol Morisien.

Post, Marike. 2013. Fa d'Ambô structure dataset. In Susanne Michaelis, Philippe Maurer, Martin Haspelmath & Magnus Huber (eds.), *Atlas of Pidgin and Creole language structures online.* http://apics-online.info/contributions/38 (checked 08/05/22).

Powell, J. V. n.d. Chinook Jargon. *The language of Northwest Coast History: Lessons, dictionary, & historical introduction.* Unpublished manuscript provided by the U.B.C. Museum of Anthropology.

Prescod, Paula. 2013. Vincentian Creole structure dataset. In Susanne Michaelis, Philippe Maurer, Martin Haspelmath & Magnus Huber (eds.), *Atlas of Pidgin and Creole language structures online.* http://apics-online.info/contributions/7 (checked 08/05/22).

Roberts, Sarah J. 2013. Pidgin Hawaiian structure dataset. In Susanne Michaelis, Philippe Maurer, Martin Haspelmath & Magnus Huber (eds.), *Atlas of Pidgin and Creole language structures online.* http://apics-online.info/contributions/71 (checked 08/05/22).

Roset, Caroline. 2018. *A grammar of Darfur Arabic.* Utrecht: LOT.

Ryding, Karin C. 2005. *A reference grammar of Modern Standard Arabic.* Cambridge: Cambridge University Press.

Samarin, William J. 1967. *A grammar of Sango.* The Hague & Paris: De Gruyter.

Samarin, William J. 2013. Sango structure dataset. In Susanne Michaelis, Philippe Maurer, Martin Haspelmath & Magnus Huber (eds.), *Atlas of Pidgin and Creole language structures online*. http://apics-online.info/contributions/59 (checked 08/05/22).

Sandefur, John & Joy Sandefur. 1982. *An introduction to conversational Kriol*. Darwin: Summer Institute of Linguistics, Australian Aborigines Branch.

Schröder, Anne. 2013. Cameroon Pidgin English structure dataset. In Susanne Michaelis, Philippe Maurer, Martin Haspelmath & Magnus Huber (eds.), *Atlas of Pidgin and Creole language structures online*. http://apics-online.info/contributions/18. (checked 08/05/22).

Schultze-Berndt, Eva & Denise Angelo. 2013. Kriol structure dataset. In Susanne Michaelis, Philippe Maurer, Martin Haspelmath & Magnus Huber (eds.), *Atlas of Pidgin and Creole language structures online*. http://apics-online.info/contributions/25 (checked 08/05/22).

Schwegler, Armin. 2013. Palenquero structure dataset. In Susanne Michaelis, Philippe Maurer, Martin Haspelmath & Magnus Huber (eds.), *Atlas of Pidgin and Creole language structures online*. http://apics-online.info/contributions/48 (checked 08/05/22).

Senft, Gunter. 2004. What do we really know about serial verb constructions in Austronesian and Papuan languages? In Isabelle Bril & Françoise Ozanne-Rivierre (eds.), *Complex predicates in Oceanic languages*, 49–64. Berlin: De Gruyter.

Shaw, George C. 1909. *The Chinook Jargon and how to use it: A complete and exhaustive lexicon of the oldest trade language of the American continent*. Washington: Rainier Printing Company.

Shimelman, Aviva. 2017. *A grammar of Yauyos Quechua*. Berlin: Language Science Press.

Siegel, Jeff. 2013. Pidgin Hindustani structure dataset. In Susanne Michaelis, Philippe Maurer, Martin Haspelmath & Magnus Huber (eds.), *Atlas of Pidgin and Creole language structures online*. http://apics-online.info/contributions/70 (checked 08/05/22).

Sippola, Eeva. 2011. *Una gramática descriptive del Chabacano de Ternate*. Helsinki: Unigrafia.

Sippola, Eeva. 2013a. Ternate Chabacano structure dataset. In Susanne Michaelis, Philippe Maurer, Martin Haspelmath & Magnus Huber (eds.), *Atlas of Pidgin and Creole language structures online*. http://apics-online.info/contributions/44 (checked 08/05/22).

Sippola, Eeva. 2013b. Cavite Chabacano structure dataset. In Susanne Michaelis, Philippe Maurer, Martin Haspelmath & Magnus Huber (eds.), *Atlas of Pidgin and Creole language structures online*. http://apics-online.info/contributions/45 (checked 08/05/22).

Slomanson, Peter. 2013. Sri Lankan Malay structure dataset. In Susanne Michaelis, Philippe Maurer, Martin Haspelmath & Magnus Huber (eds.), *Atlas of Pidgin and Creole language structures online*. http://apics-online.info/contributions/66 (checked 08/05/22).

Smith, Geoff. P. & Jeff Siegel. 2013. Tok Pisin structure dataset. In Susanne Michaelis, Philippe Maurer, Martin Haspelmath & Magnus Huber (eds.), *Atlas of Pidgin and Creole language structures online*. http://apics-online.info/contributions/22 (checked 08/05/22).

Smith, Ian R. 2013. Sri Lanka Portuguese structure dataset. In Susanne Michaelis, Philippe Maurer, Martin Haspelmath & Magnus Huber (eds.), *Atlas of Pidgin and Creole language structures online*. http://apics-online.info/contributions/41 (checked 08/05/22).

Sneddon, James Neil, Alexander Adelaar, Dwi Noverni Djenar & Michael C. Ewing. 2010. *Indonesian Reference Grammar*. Sydney: Allen & Unwin.

Steinkrüger, Patrick O. 2013. Zamboanga Chabacano structure dataset. In Susanne Michaelis, Philippe Maurer, Martin Haspelmath & Magnus Huber (eds.), *Atlas of Pidgin and Creole language structures online.* http://apics-online.info/contributions/46 (checked 08/05/22).

Stolz, Thomas. 1992. *Lokalkasussysteme. Aspekte einer strukturellen Dynamik*. Weinberg: Egert.

Stolz, Thomas. 2020. Is there anything wrong with *iya*? On morphosyntactic issues connected to place names in Chamorro. In Nataliya Levkovych & Julia Nintemann (eds.), *Aspects of the grammar of names. Empirical case studies and theoretical topics*, 53–145. München: LINCOM.

Stolz, Thomas, Sander Lestrade & Christel Stolz. 2014. *The crosslinguistics of zero-marking of spatial relations*. Berlin: De Gruyter.

Stolz, Thomas & Nataliya Levkovych. 2019a. Toponomastics meets linguistic typology: Glimpses of Special Toponymic Grammar from Aromanian and sundry languages. *Onomastica Uralica* 11. 43–61.

Stolz, Thomas & Nataliya Levkovych. 2019b. Absence of material exponence. *Language Typology and Universals – STUF* 72(3). 373–400.

Stolz, Thomas & Nataliya Levkovych. 2020. Zwischen Ortsnamenbildung und Relationsmarkierung. Strukturelle Ambiguitäten, Grauzonen und Übergänge. *Beiträge zur Namenforschung* 55(1). 1–25.

Stolz, Thomas, Nataliya Levkovych & Aina Urdze. 2017a. When zero is just enough… In support of a Special Toponymic Grammar in Maltese. *Folia Linguistica* 51(2). 453–482.

Stolz, Thomas, Nataliya Levkovych & Aina Urdze. 2017b. Die Grammatik der Toponyme als typologisches Forschungsfeld: Eine Pilotstudie. In Johannes Helmbrecht, Damaris Nübling & Barbara Schlücker (eds.), *Namengrammatik*, 121–146. Hamburg: Buske.

Stolz, Thomas, Nataliya Levkovych & Aina Urdze. 2018. La morfosintassi dei toponimi in prospettiva tipologica. In Giuseppe Brincat & Sandro Caruana (eds.), *Tipologia e 'dintorni': il metodo tipologico alla intersezione di piani d'analisi*, 307–324. Roma: Bulzoni.

Stolz, Thomas, Nataliya Levkovych, Aina Urdze, Julia Nintemann & Maja Robbers. 2017c. *Where – whither – whence: Spatial interrogatives in cross-linguistic perspective*. Berlin & Boston: De Gruyter Mouton.

Swift, Lloyd Balderston & Emile W.A. Zola. 1963. *Kituba: Basic course*. Washington: Foreign Service Institute.

Talmy, L. 1983. How language structures space. In Herbert L. Pick & Linda P. Acredolo (eds.), *Spatial orientation: Theory, research, and application*, 225–282. New York & London: Plenum Press.

Trimingham, J. Spencer. 1946. *Sudan Colloquial Arabic*. London: Oxford University Press.

Valdman, Albert. 1988. *Ann pale kreyòl: An introductory course in Haitian Creole*. Bloomington: Indiana University.

van den Berg, Margot. 2007. *A grammar of Early Sranan*. Manta: Zetten.

van den Berg, Margot & Adrienne Bruyn. 2013. Early Sranan structure dataset. In Susanne Michaelis, Philippe Maurer, Martin Haspelmath & Magnus Huber (eds.), *Atlas of Pidgin and Creole language structures online.* http://apics-online.info/contributions/1 (checked 08/05/22).

Van Langendonck, Willy. 2007. *Theory and typology of proper names*. Berlin: De Gruyter.

van Putte, Florimon & Igma van Putte-de Windt. 2014. *Grammatica van het Papiaments: Vormen en communicatieve strategieën*. Zutphen: Walburg Pers.

van Sluijs, Robbert. 2013. Negerhollands structure dataset. In Susanne Michaelis, Philippe Maurer, Martin Haspelmath & Magnus Huber (eds.), *Atlas of Pidgin and Creole language structures online*. http://apics-online.info/contributions/27 (checked 08/05/22).

Velupillai, Viveka. 2013. Hawai'i Creole structure dataset. In Susanne Michaelis, Philippe Maurer, Martin Haspelmath & Magnus Huber (eds.), *Atlas of Pidgin and Creole language structures online*. http://apics-online.info/contributions/26 (checked 08/05/22).

Wellens, Inneke Hilda Werner. 2003. *An Arabic creole in Africa: The Nubi language of Uganda*. PhD Thesis, Universiteit Nijmegen.

Wiese, Heike. 2006. "Ich mach dich Messer": Grammatische Produktivität in Kiez-Sprache ("Kanak Sprak"). *Linguistische Berichte* 207. 245–273.

Winford, Donald. 1990. Serial verb constructions and motion events in Caribbean English Creoles. *Ohio State University Working Papers in Linguistics* 39. 109–48.

Winford, Donald. 2002. Tense and aspect in Sranan and the creole prototype. In John McWhorter (ed.), *Language change and language contact in pidgins and creoles*, 383–442. Amsterdam & Philadelphia: John Benjamins.

Winford, Donald & Ingo Plag. 2013. Sranan structure dataset. In Susanne Michaelis, Philippe Maurer, Martin Haspelmath & Magnus Huber (eds.), *Atlas of Pidgin and Creole language structures online*. http://apics-online.info/contributions/2 (08/05/22).

Yakpo, Kofi. 2013. Pichi structure dataset. In Susanne Michaelis, Philippe Maurer, Martin Haspelmath & Magnus Huber (eds.), *Atlas of Pidgin and Creole language structures online*. http://apics-online.info/contributions/19 (checked 08/05/22).

Yakpo, Kofi. 2019. *A grammar of Pichi*. Berlin: Language Science Press.

Yanti. 2010. *A reference grammar of Jambi Malay*. University of Delaware dissertation.

Yasugi, Yoshiho. 2003. *Materiales de lenguas mayas de Guatemala*. Osaka: ELPR.

Zribi-Hertz, Anne & Loïc Jean-Louis. 2017. Les grammaires des noms de pays en martiniquais et en haïtien et la question du "prototype créole". *Études Créoles* XXXV(1&2). 64–91.

Zribi-Hertz, Anne & Loïc Jean-Louis. 2018. General locative marking in Martinican Creole (Matinitjè): A case study in grammatical economy. *Working Papers in Linguistics and Oriental Studies* 4. 151–176.

Thomas Stolz and Nataliya Levkovych
Places, manners, and the areal phonology of Europe

Abstract: In this study, the validity of several parameters relating to places and manners of articulation is assessed in connection with the distribution of phonological properties across the languages of Europe. It is shown that the results reflect patterns which are interesting both for areal typology and phonological typology. Language contact is assumed to be at least partly responsible for similarities between genetically unrelated neighbouring languages. It is argued that these and similar parameters should be tested on a grand scale in the format of phonological atlases dedicated to individual macro-areas.

Keywords: Places of articulation, manners of articulation, areal typology, Europe, borrowing, language contact

1 Introduction

In language-contact studies, phonological issues are in the centre of attention only unsystematically (a notable exception being Matras (2009: 221–233)). Similarly, phonologists seldom venture to address cases of historical contact (Hyman 2018: 14). Loan phonology focuses very strongly on aspects of bilingualism and loanword adaptation involving binary contact situations (Calabrese and Wetzels 2009). The possibility of studying the behaviour of phonologies under the conditions of language contact on a wider scale has not yet been inquired into sufficiently. Blevins (2017) and Stolz and Levkovych (2017) show that indirect proof of contact-induced phenomena in the domain of phonology can be provided by way of determining the areal distribution of properties. This paper takes up this issue. It is argued that relatively abstract analogies in the architecture of phonological systems can be the result of everyday language-contact processes such as material borrowing.

Thomas Stolz, University of Bremen, FB 10: Linguistics / Language Sciences, Universitäts-Boulevard 13, 28359 Bremen, Germany. E-Mail: stolz@uni-bremen.de
Nataliya Levkovych, University of Bremen, FB 10: Linguistics / Language Sciences, Universitäts-Boulevard 13, 28359 Bremen, Germany. E-Mail: levkov@uni-bremen.de

https://doi.org/10.1515/9783111323756-007

In his paper on the (lack of) relationships between typology and phonology, Plank (2018: 22) mentions "contacts between speech communities" only in passing whereas areal typology is not at issue at all. However, the paragraph devoted to reviewing the achievements of EUROTYP and the underrepresentation of phonology in this research program (Plank 2018: 32) can be taken as indirect evidence of the necessity to also include areal typology in the general discussion about the past, present, and future of phonological typology. The neglect of phonological issues within the framework of EUROTYP is symptomatic of the persistence of preconceived ideas according to which Europe is of no particular interest phonologically. The detailed history of thought behind this prejudice is traced in Stolz and Levkovych (2021). We agree with Haspelmath (2001: 1493) that phonologists have probably not looked hard enough to uncover the rich phenomenology of the areal phonology of Europe. There is thus a gap in the otherwise very detailed knowledge about the structural properties of the languages of Europe. This is an untenable state of affairs for the areal typology of Europe – and to some extent at least for phonological typology and language-contact studies if it comes to comparing macro-areas.

Bickel's (2007: 239) oft-cited dictum to propagate distributional typology requires of the typologist to answer the triple question "what's where why." In our interpretation of this assignment, the task can be fulfilled also without adopting the global perspective. Inspired by Clements and Rialland (2008) and their work on Africa as a phonological area, we try to get a better understanding of what is there in Europe and why – without, however, presupposing that there is a homogenous phonological *Sprachbund* in the first place. To this end, we are preparing the Phonological Atlas of Europe whose aim it is to take stock of, systematize, and evaluate as many aspects of the (primarily) synchronic segmental phonology of the languages of Europe as possible and thus create a tool that can be used to the benefit of future studies in the domains of areal typology, language-contact studies, and phonological typology. To our mind, macro-areal atlases of this kind will help getting phonological typology on the right track. It makes sense therefore to engage in similar projects focusing on other continents or large geographical regions to create an empirically robust basis for the purpose of cross-linguistic research.

The little that has been done so far in connection with the areal phonology of Europe is by far too insufficient to serve as reliable foundation for our project. We have to start from scratch by way of collecting the data directly from the extant descriptive linguistic sources. The primary reason why we do not exploit the accessible electronic repositories (Plank 2018: 35) is that the European data which can be extracted from the online resources are generally to scarce to meet the standards of areal typology. What is required is an ideally full coverage of the languages which are situated in the area under scrutiny. As Kiparsky (2018: 97) argues "linguistic descriptions [] cannot be theory-neutral or atheoretical" so that working with literally hundreds of different descriptive grammars and phonological treatises might mean that we are running the risk of comparing like with unlike. According to Kiparsky (2018: 54–61), this problem is especially acute in regard to the concept of phoneme. To avoid the pitfalls of comparing differently defined phonemes, we take generally acknowledged principles of organization of phonological systems as our point of departure (Stolz and Levkovych 2017: 128–147). Maddieson (2018: 107) alludes to places and manners of articulation which belong to "a set of categories [] largely common to all humans." In this study, we focus on selected aspects of the horizontal and vertical dimensions of the ordered inventory of consonantal phonemes in the languages of Europe.

We draw upon a sample of 210 European languages (aka: doculects (Plank 2018: 51 footnote 25)) which were alive or in the process of being revitalized at some point during the 20th century. The members of the sample are identified in the appendix. The composition of the sample in terms of genealogy is disclosed in Figure 1.

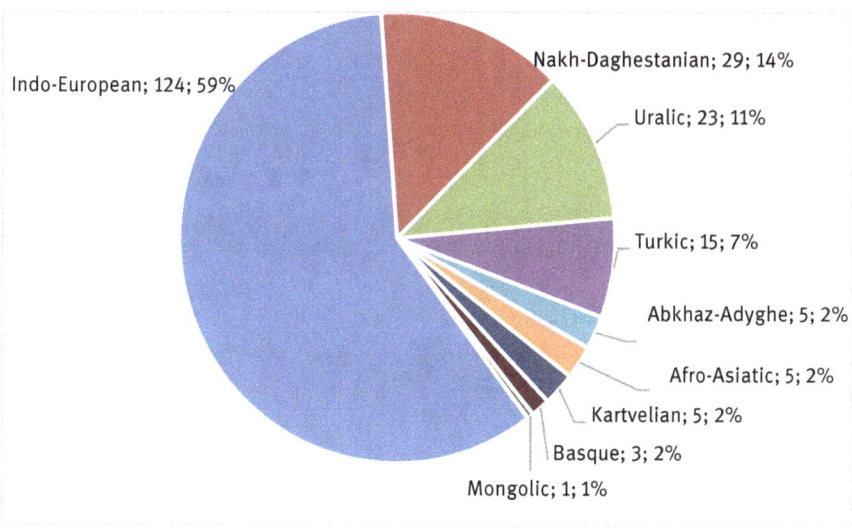

Figure 1: Genealogical composition of the sample.

The sample includes three varieties of Basque to which we refer for convenience as phylum and not as isolate. The sole representative of Mongolic is Kalmyk. The quantitative differences reflect the contemporary representation of the phyla in Europe. Thus, Indo-European is by no means overrepresented but its share of the sample is justified by the numerical dominance of Indo-European languages in Europe.

As to the continent itself, we follow the lead of EUROTYP in the sense that the entire national territory of Turkey, the trans-Caucasian region north of the Iranian border, and Malta as well as Cyprus are considered to belong to Europe (König and Haspelmath 1999: 112–114). To avoid relying on ideas about possible intra-European linguistic areas, we have divided Europe into nine geographic sectors (henceforth: nonant(s)) of equal size irrespective of how many and which languages are situated in a given nonant. The nonants are identified by the following abbreviations: NW = north west, NC = north centre, NE = north east, MW = middle west, MC = middle centre, ME = middle east, SW = south west, SC = south centre, and SE = south east. Figure 2 reveals how densely the nonants are populated.

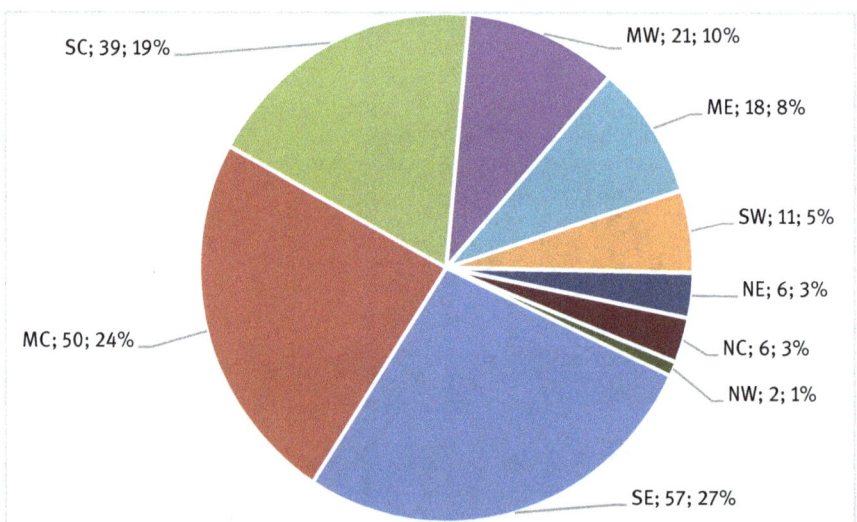

Figure 2: Distribution of sample languages over nonants.

The distribution of languages over nonants is uneven. With about a quarter of all languages each SE and MC together are responsible for slightly more than half of the sample. As in the case of the phyla, this is a direct reflex of the actual geolinguistic situation in Europe.

The phenomena we address are scrutinized from two different perspectives in turn, namely genealogy and geography. According to Hyman (2018: 14), these are two "aspects of typology in which most phonologists have expressed little interest." The question is raised whether the genetic affiliation or the location of a given language correlates to any extent with the selected phonological properties, if at all. In this way, we test not only whether genealogy and/or geography are determining factors in the domain under scrutiny but also whether the concepts employed in this study make sense linguistically in the first place. To this end, we make very simple and basic calculations to see whether already on this low level of sophistication linguistically meaningful patterns emerge. If this is the case, dedicated in-depth follow-up studies are called for.

In the subsequent sections, we define and quantitatively evaluate the following concepts which are inspired by and large by Maddieson's (1984: 7–19) ideas about the relationship of size and structure of inventories:

– Place-Manner Space (= PMS) (Section 2),
– Place-Manner Quotient (= PMQ) (Section 3),
– Sequences of Places (= SEQP) (Section 4),
– Sequences of Manners (= SEQM) (Section 5),
– Interruptions on the level of Places (= INTERP) (Section 6),
– Interruptions on the level of Manners (= INTERM) (Section 7),
– most densely populated Place (= PHONP) (Section 8),
– most densely populated Manner (= PHONM) (Section 9).

The impact of borrowing is discussed in Section 10. Section 11 contains the conclusions. The phenomena are studied quantitatively by way of employing basic mathematical operations (explained for each concept separately below) whose results can be characterized as "simple-minded phonological [] scores" (Maddieson 2018: 116). At this early stage of the project, the lack of sophistication is fully justified because we only aim at determining whether the above parameters are promising enough to be worth studying in-depth with the full series of measures of advanced statistical methodology. Exclusively for the purpose of the calculations executed in this study, we rely on the 2018 version of the IPA which, on account of our empirical findings within the European sample, we have modified to include ALVEOLO-PALATAL, EPIGLOTTAL, LABIAL-VELAR, and LABIAL-PALATAL as additional places of articulation (Maddieson 1984: 18) and AFFRICATE as well as LATERAL AFFRICATE as additional manners of articulation. This choice of places and manners is not meant to be mandatory for likeminded investigations. The experimental conditions are only temporary and can be revised at any time. In contrast to prior work pertinent to our topic (Maddieson 1984; Ladefoged and Maddieson

1995: 370; Gordon 2016: 44–48), we do not approach our research object only from the perspective of the manners of articulation but check each phenomenon for each of the two dimensions separately.

In each section, to make things as easy as possible for us, a binary distinction is made between HIGH and LOW values. Values are HIGH if they belong to the upper half of the calculated results whereas LOW characterizes those values which form part of the lower half of the results. In case of uneven numbers of values, the cut-off line between HIGH and LOW changes so that the LOW-category comprises one member in excess of the HIGH-category. For convenience, we often refer to H[IGH]-languages and L[OW]-languages – a practice that should not be mistaken as an attempt at doing holistic typology (Hyman 2009: 214–215). For each of the categories HIGH and LOW, it is checked to what extent there are genealogical and/or geographic preferences. This is achieved by way of determining
(a) how many members of a given phylum can be categorized as either HIGH or LOW,
(b) whether a given phylum has a share of either HIGH or LOW which exceeds or falls below the share the same phylum has of the sample,
(c) which nonant hosts how many H-languages and L-languages,
(d) whether a given nonant has a share of either HIGH or LOW which exceeds or falls below the share the same nonant has of the sample.

We start from the intuitively plausible working hypothesis that phyla and nonants yield shares for HIGH and LOW which are identical to their shares of the sample. Without giving away too much in advance, we nevertheless anticipate one of the results of this study, namely that the working hypothesis does not stand the test.

2 PMS

PMS is an abstract category which covers a virtual bidimensional area whose size is determined by the potential number of (virtual IPA) cells it covers. The potential number of cells is the product of the multiplication of the number of activated places of articulation and the number of activated manners of articulation of a given system of consonantal phonemes. A place or manner of articulation counts as activated if there is at least one phoneme which occupies a cell in the appropriate column or row of the (modified) IPA grid. There are thus fifteen places of articulation (= multiplicands) and ten manners of articulation (= multipliers). According to the simple formula [P x M = PMS], we get a maximum PMS of (15 x 10

=) 150. The vast majority of these 150 cells remains unoccupied mostly for general articulatory reasons. The PMS does not serve to determine how many and which cells of the grid host fillers but it is indicative of the size of the frame within which phonological density and richness might occur (Nikolaev and Grossman 2018: 565). The languages can systematically be ordered and classified according to their different PMSs. It is then possible to control for possible correlations with genealogical and/or geographic factors. This is exactly what this section is dedicated to.

With reference to the members of our European sample, the PMSs range from 30 to 99. There are twenty-one different PMSs which form two groups, namely the eleven PMSs from 30 to 60 are classified as LOW whereas the ten PMSs from 61 to 99 are considered to be HIGH. The characterization as HIGH applies to fifty-three languages (= 25% of the sample); 157 languages (= 75%) associate with the label LOW. Figure 3 shows the absolute numbers in combination with the relative shares of H/L-languages per phylum.

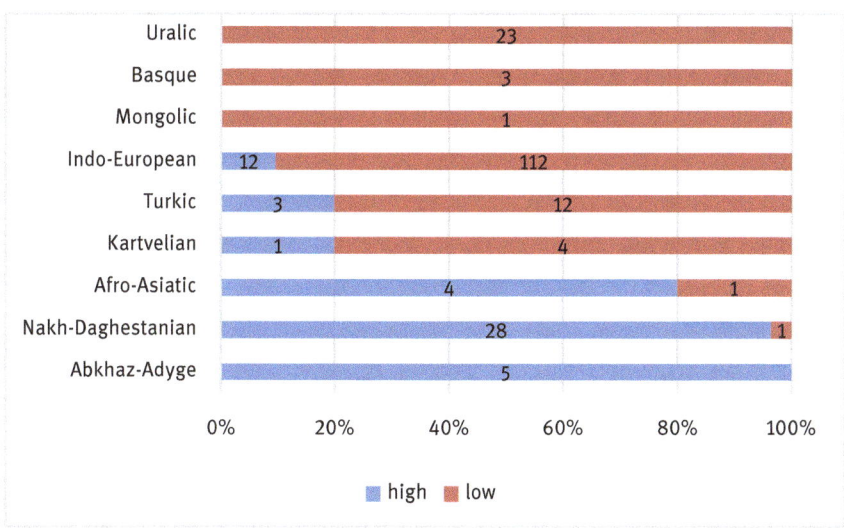

Figure 3: PMSs (absolute numbers and shares) per phylum.

What we see immediately is that the phyla behave differently. At the two extremes of the continuum, entire multi-member phyla are classified as either LOW (e.g. Uralic) or HIGH (e.g. Abkhaz-Adyghe). Five phyla allow for both options albeit with clear preferences for the one over the other.

To better understand the significance of the above differential behaviour, it is necessary to look at the quantities from a different vantage point. Figure 4 confronts the shares the phyla have of three different categories, namely
(a) the class of languages with the feature HIGH,
(b) the sample, and
(c) the class of languages with the feature LOW.

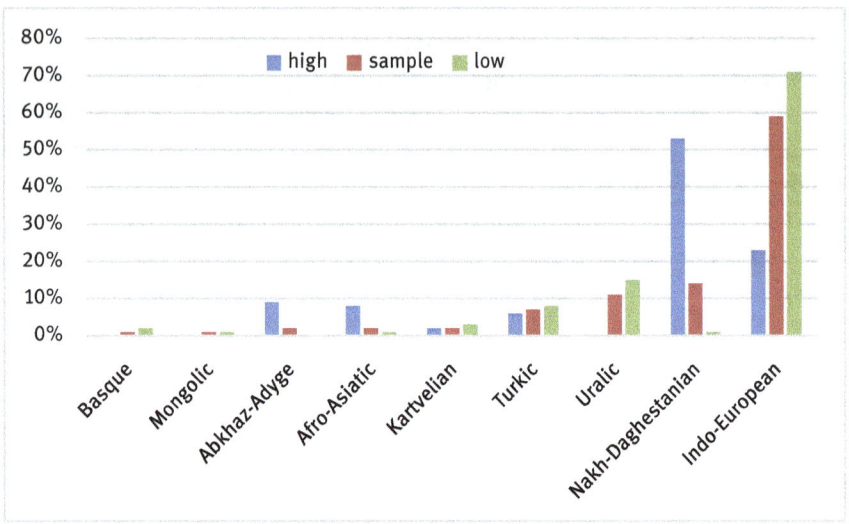

Figure 4: Phyla and their shares of HIGH PMS, sample, and LOW PMS.

If we take the share a phylum has of the sample as our yardstick, it is easy to detect striking discrepancies. For Abkhaz-Adyghe, Afro-Asiatic, and Nakh-Daghestanian, the shares of HIGH exceed by far the shares which these phyla boast within the sample. At the same time (and not surprisingly), these three phyla yield negligible results as to the category LOW. This is especially different with Uralic and Indo-European and to a lesser degree also with Basque, Kartvelian, and Turkic. For these phyla, the bar for LOW stands out from the two competing bars. It is tempting to interpret these differences as genealogically rooted preferences.

Since several phyla are heterogeneous on the PMS-parameter, the possibility comes to mind that the spatial coordinates of languages might be responsible for part of the intra-phylum variation. To ascertain the interference of geographic factors, we first look at the distribution of H- and L-languages over the different nonants (see Figure 5).

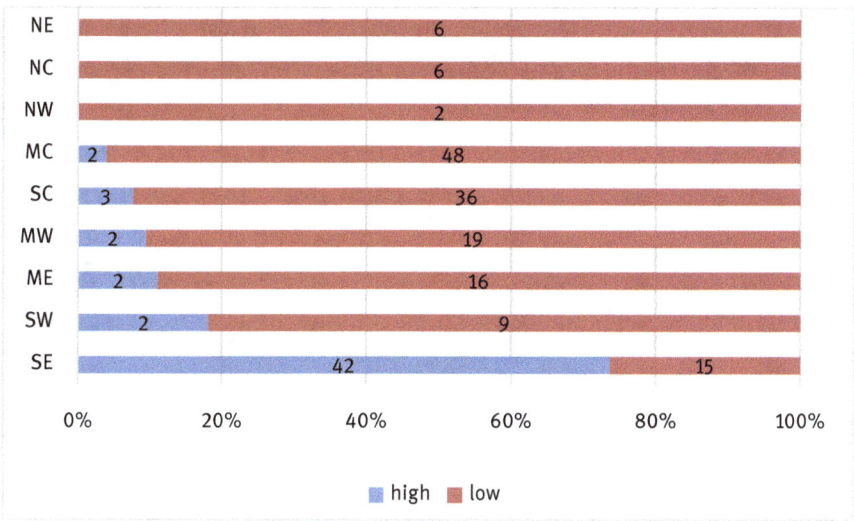

Figure 5: Absolute numbers and shares of H- and L-languages per nonant (PMS).

The numerical dominance of HIGH in SE is hardly surprising because this is the nonant which hosts all members of the Abkhaz-Adyghe and Nakh-Daghestanian phyla as well as four of five Afro-Asiatic languages which have been shown above to prefer HIGH over LOW to a considerable extent. However, these three phyla cover only 36 of the 42 languages in SE which attest to HIGH. In point of fact, the six missing HIGH languages of this nonant belong to different phyla, namely Armenian (Eastern), Kurmanji, Zaza (Northern), and Zaza (Southern Dimili) which are members of Indo-European, Noghay which is a Turkic language, whereas Laz is a Kartvelian language. According to Figures 3–4, Indo-European, Turkic, and Kartvelian display a preference for LOW. Indo-European is in inverse proportion to its representatives in SE. Armenian (Eastern), Kurmanji, Zaza (Northern), and Zaza (Southern Dimili) behave strikingly similar to their local but genealogically unrelated neighbours whereas they are dissimilar to their closest relatives as to PMS. If we consider the complete absence of HIGH from all three northerly nonants, we have to concede the possibility of a strong geographic factor interacting with genealogy to determine the distribution of a given phonological property.

Figure 6 largely corroborates this assumption. What we see here is the parallel behaviour of the bulk of the nonants in the sense that except NW and SE, the share of LOW surpasses that the same nonant has of the sample. HIGH, however, is generally disfavoured. Therefore, the 79%-share of all H-languages attributed to

SE is not only exceptional in the European perspective but also a strong indicator of the areality of certain phonological properties since the feature HIGH is not confined to a single genealogical group.

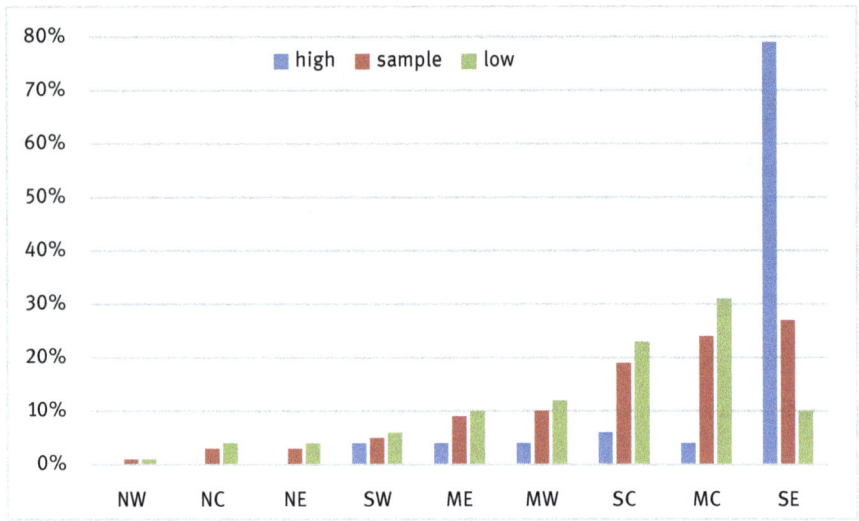

Figure 6: Nonants and their shares of HIGH PMS, sample, and LOW PMS.

On the basis of these observations, we provisionally assume that PMS has been proved to be a useful parameter which should be developed further to become a fully-fledged item in the toolbox (not only) of areally oriented phonological typology.

3 PMQ

The previous section has presented PMS as a suitable parameter for the classification of languages. What impairs the usefulness of PMS to some extent at least is the fact that identical values can arise from the multiplication of different multiplicand values and multiplier values. A PMS of 42 is attested forty-four times in the sample. In exactly 50% of the cases there are seven places of articulation (multiplicand) and six manners of articulation (multiplier) (e.g. Bulgarian) whereas in the other half of the cases the multiplicand is 6 and the multiplier 7 (e.g. Aromanian). The situation recurs with PMS 72 albeit less often. All in all, ambiguities of this kind are infrequent. Nevertheless, it makes sense to determine the quantitative relation between places and manners of articulation.

This relation is calculated by way of dividing the number of activated places of articulation (dividend) by the number of activated manners of articulation (divisor) to yield the quotient. In the above cases, we get (7 / 6 =) PMQ 1.2 for Bulgarian as opposed to (6 / 7 =) PMQ 0.9 for Aromanian. If two neighbouring and distantly related languages differ as to their PMQs, the question can be posed whether there is a general split of the sample languages into those with PMQs n > 1 and those with a PMQ n < 1 – and whether their distribution over phyla and nonants is (not) random.

There is indeed a division into a majority of 175 languages (= 83% of the sample) which attest to PMQs between 0.6 and 1.0 (= LOW) and a minority of 35 languages (= 17%) with PMQs of 1.1 to 1.4 (= HIGH). Their distribution over the phyla is interesting. Figure 7 follows the same principles as Figure 3 above.

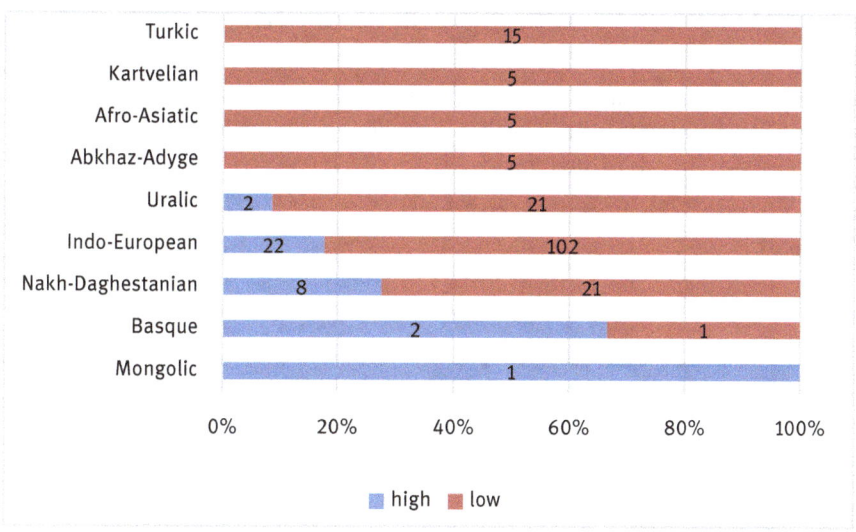

Figure 7: PMQs (absolute numbers and shares) per phylum.

Except Basque and Mongolic, all phyla prefer LOW over HIGH (even to the complete exclusion of the latter). Moreover, it results from Figure 8 that Nakh-Daghestanian and Indo-European are overrepresented among H-languages.

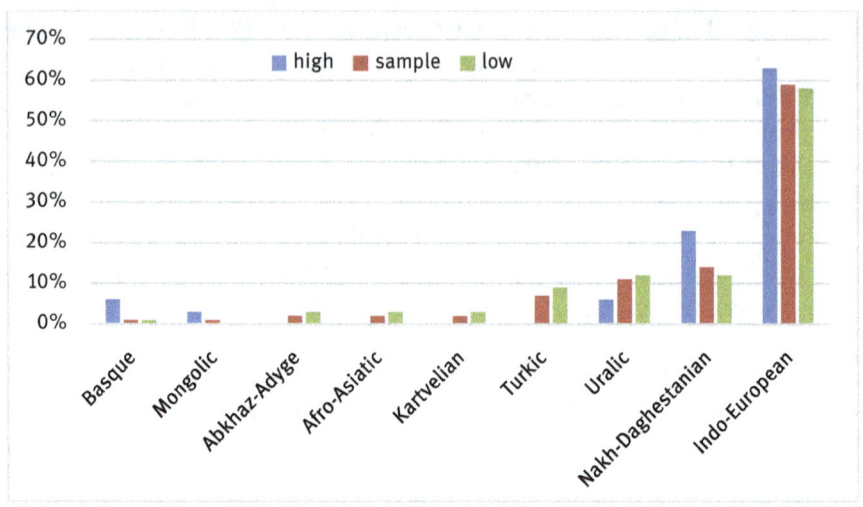

Figure 8: Phyla and their shares of HIGH PMQ, sample, and LOW PMQ.

Both Indo-European and Nakh-Daghestanian boast a clear majority of L-languages. It is legitimate to ask whether their parallel strong involvement with HIGH is explicable in terms of areality, too.

Figure 9 disenchants us because none of the nonants hosts a majority of H-languages.

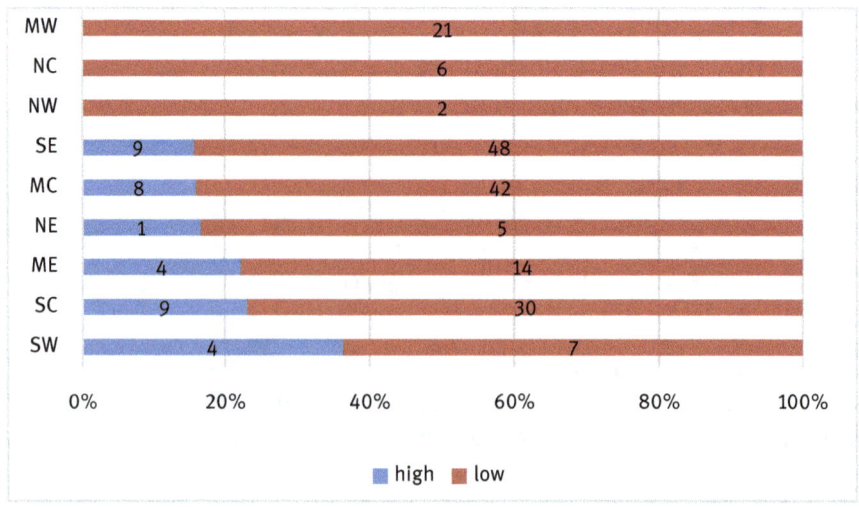

Figure 9: Absolute numbers and shares of H- and L-languages per nonant (PMQ).

The most one can get from these facts is that all southerly and easterly nonants allow for a minority of H-languages. In contrast, there are northerly, westerly, and also central and middle nonants which lack any evidence of HIGH. If one is allowed to speak of areality at all, the geographic factor is severely limited as to the PMQs. Figure 10, however, is suggestive of a slightly different interpretation.

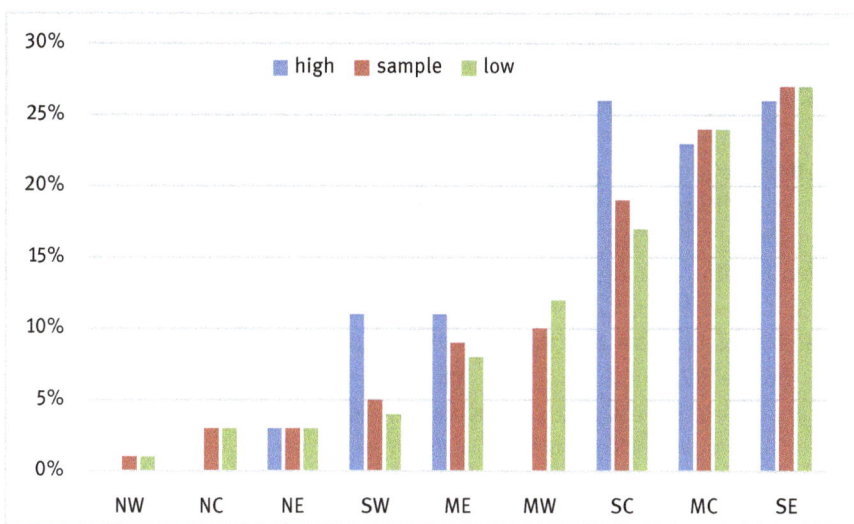

Figure 10: Nonants and their shares of HIGH PMQ, sample, and LOW PMQ.

The relatively meagre turnouts of H-languages notwithstanding, it is clearly visible from Figure 10 that SW, ME, and especially SC claim considerably bigger shares of the H-languages than they are entitled to according to their shares of the sample. It strikes the eye, that in SW Basque (Bátua) and Basque (Lekeitio) agree with their genealogically unrelated Ibero-Romance neighbours Galician and Spanish. In SC too genealogical boundaries do not hinder neighbouring languages to produce similar PMQs. This is the case with the Slavic languages Bulgarian, Bulgarian (Dimitrovgrad), Macedonian, Macedonian (Kostur-Korča), Slovene, as well as the Kalderash variety of Romani, Greek, Greek (Sternatia), and the Romance language Ladino. Except for the Italo-Greek variety of Sternatia, these languages are situated in a Southeast European (and more narrowly defined, in a Balkanic) neighbourhood. Last but not least, the four H-languages in ME involve three varieties of Russian and the North-Russian variety of Romani.

These parallels are not hard proof of contact-induced diffusion of properties. Still, they set us thinking about the possibility that we are not dealing with coincidence. This means that irrespective of the hardly impressing absolute numbers and shares presented above, PMQ too should not be discarded sweepingly as a potential parameter for future studies in the domain of areally-minded phonological typology.

4 SEQP

PMS and PMQ together provide us with a very basic and still largely incomplete idea about the internal organization of the phonological inventory in the domain of consonants. The different values we have seen in the previous sections do not tell us anything as to the relative compactness of the systems. A system displays a high degree of compactness if immediately adjacent columns, rows, and cells are activated. In the case of the places of articulation, this means that a phoneme with the specification [DENTAL] and another with the specification [ALVEOLAR] – independent of the manners of articulation – constitute a binary sequence and thus contribute to the compactness of the system.

In this section, we take account of the maximal length of sequences involving places of articulation. The length of a sequence is determined by the uninterrupted chain of activated places of articulation. The number of places of articulation which form part of the chain is identical to SEQP. In our sample, SEQPs range from minimally 2 to maximally 8. The seven length types do not enjoy the same popularity among the European languages. SEQPs of 2–5 are LOW. This is the majority option which is attested in 202 languages (= 96%) whereas only eight languages (= 4%) display HIGH SEQPs of 6–8. Figure 11 shows that HIGH is confined to three phyla only two of which allow for a noticeable minority of H-languages. These phyla are Nakh-Daghestanian and Abkhaz-Adyghe. Everywhere else the dominance of LOW is uncontested.

Places, manners, and the areal phonology of Europe — 263

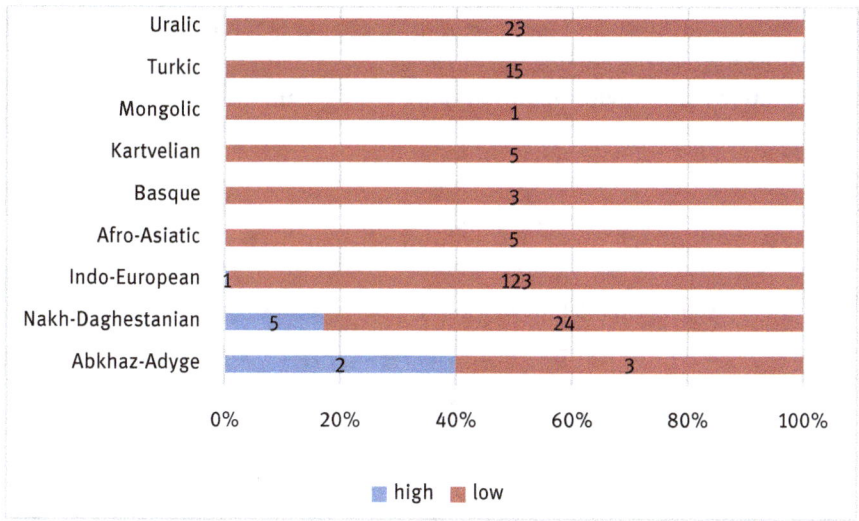

Figure 11: SEQPs (absolute numbers and shares) per phylum.

The outstanding role the two phyla from the Caucasian region play with regards to HIGH SEQPs comes nicely to the fore also Figure 12.

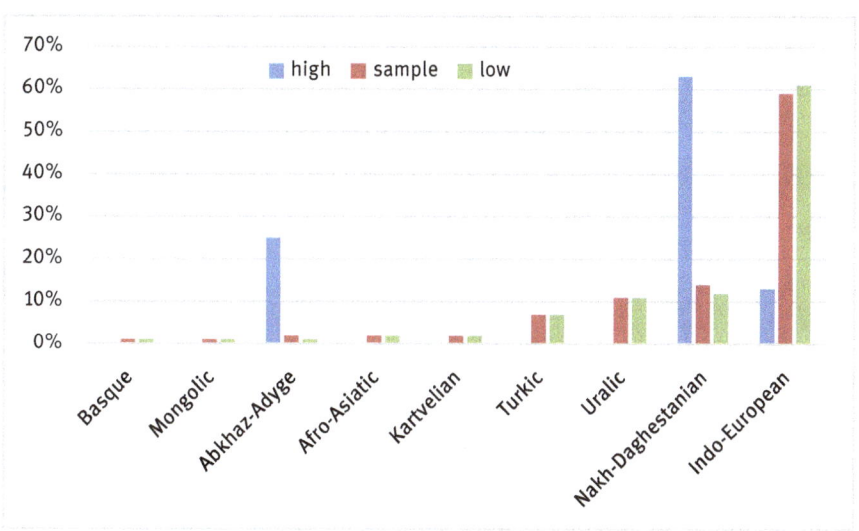

Figure 12: Phyla and their shares of HIGH SEQP, sample, and LOW SEQP.

Since the two phyla which host the most H-languages in this category are located in the same geographic region, it is to be expected that their nonant will reflect this situation accordingly. Figures 13–14 corroborate this hypothesis.

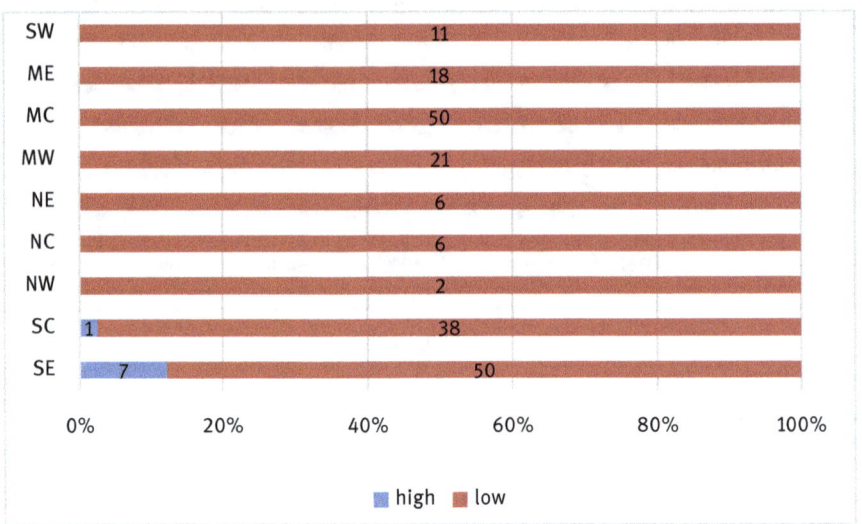

Figure 13: Absolute numbers and shares of H- and L-languages per nonant (SEQP).

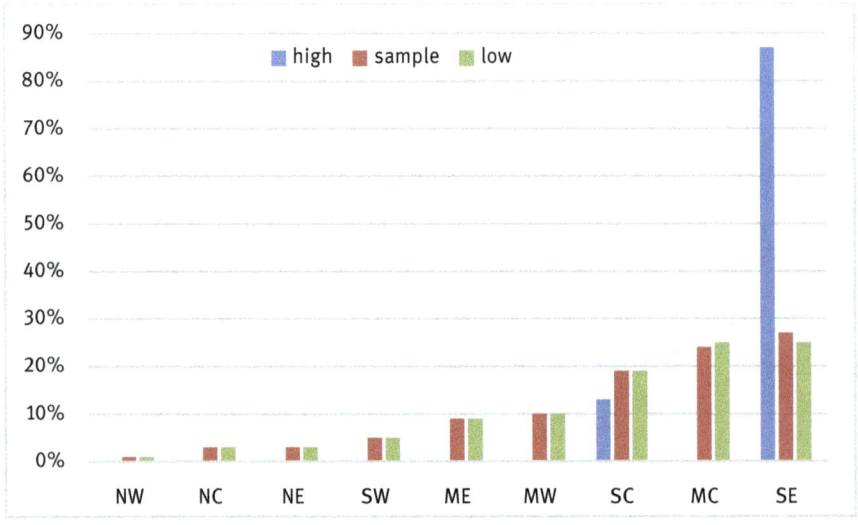

Figure 14: Nonants and their shares of HIGH SEQP, sample, and LOW SEQP.

The only language outside SE which displays a HIGH SEQP is Sardinian (Nuorese), a Romance language. The occurrence of HIGH SEQPs is thus almost exclusively restricted to two phyla which are neighbours of each other in one and the same nonant. It is interesting to see whether a similar partition of the sample can be observed with regards to the manners of articulation.

5 SEQM

To determine the SEQM the same principles as laid down in the foregoing section are applied the only difference being that vertical chains of activated manners of articulation are counted. The SEQMs range from 2–7. SEQMs of 2–4 are labelled LOW. LOW SEQMs are found in 180 languages (= 86%). The label HIGH is attached to SEQMs from 5–7. Only 30 languages (= 14%) belong to this class. According to Figures 11 and 15, five of the phyla which only allow for LOW SEQPs also tolerate only LOW SEQMs. In contrast, the two phyla which are characterized by sizable shares of languages with HIGH SEQPs also host relatively many languages with HIGH SEQMs.

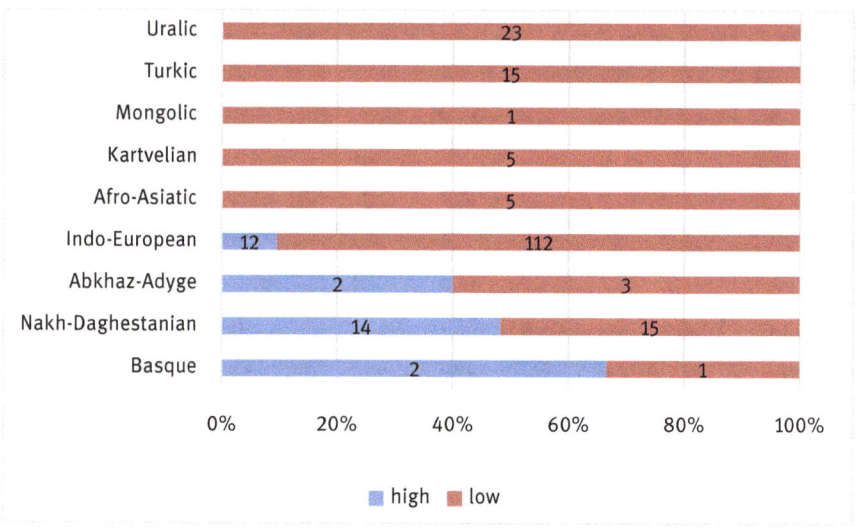

Figure 15: SEQMs (absolute numbers and shares) per phylum.

Abkhaz-Adyghe and Nakh-Daghestanian are the two phyla which allow for comparatively many H-languages both in the domain of SEQPs and SEQMs. In contrast to the picture that arises from the distribution of HIGH SEQPs, however, these two phyla do not monopolize HIGH SEQMs. It is therefore necessary to have a look at Figure 16 which reveals the relative importance of the different phyla for the categories of HIGH and LOW.

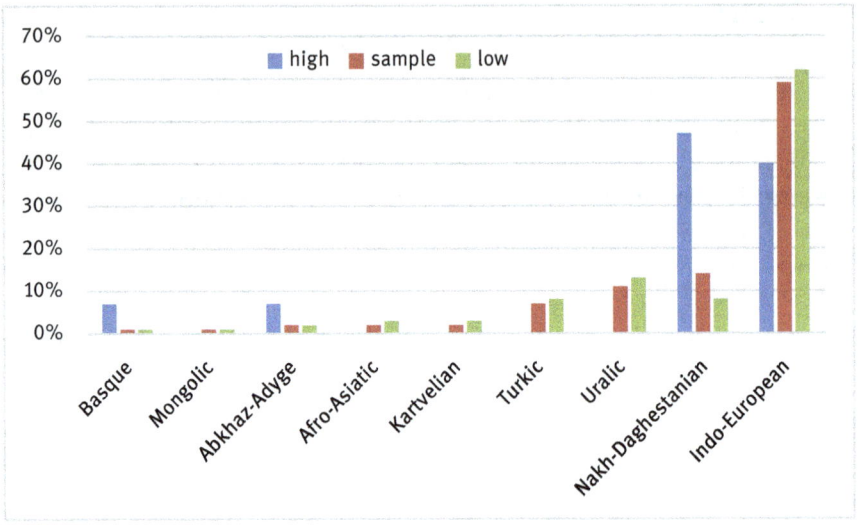

Figure 16: Phyla and their shares of HIGH SEQM, sample, and LOW SEQM.

The twelve Indo-European languages with HIGH SEQMs notwithstanding, the share of this phylum within the class of H-languages is considerably smaller than the Indo-European share of the sample. In contrast, Abkhaz-Adyghe, Nakh-Daghestanian, and Basque are overrepresented in the class of H-languages. Yet, the Indo-European H-languages should not be tacitly passed over. Where are they located? Figure 17 shows that languages with HIGH SEQMs are exclusively attested in southerly nonants.

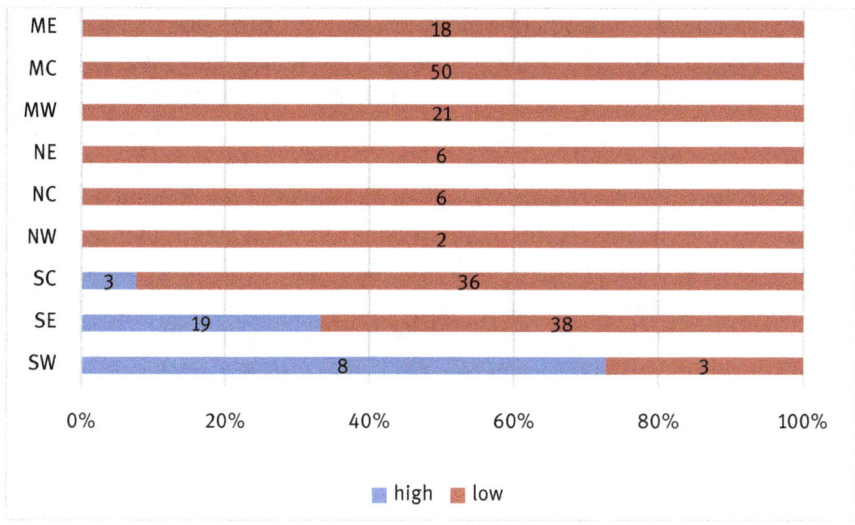

Figure 17: Absolute numbers and shares of HIGH and LOW languages per nonant (SEQM).

What is more, Figure 18 identifies SW and SE as the only nonants which are overrepresented in connection to the class of H-languages.

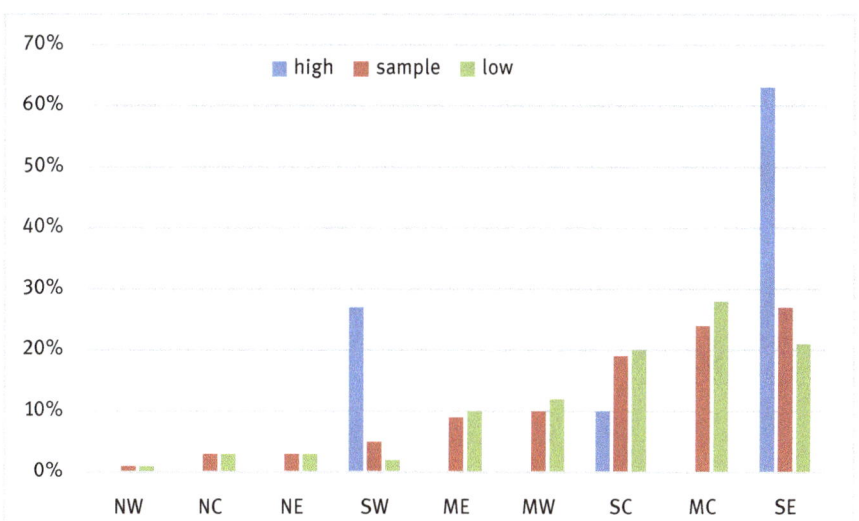

Figure 18: Nonants and their shares of HIGH SEQM, sample, and LOW SEQM.

We have identified 19 H-languages in SE. The majority of 16 goes to the credit of Abkhaz-Adyghe and Nakh-Daghestanian. However, the remaining three languages – Armenian (Eastern), Zaza (Northern), and Zaza (Southern Dimili) – belong to different branches of Indo-European. These Indo-European languages display HIGH SEQMs which correspond to those of their genealogically unrelated (distant) neighbours. We know this pattern already from the discussion of HIGH PMSs in SE. The situation is similar in SW where the HIGH SEQMs of Basque (Batúa) and Basque (Lekeitio) agree with the HIGH SEQMs of their Romance neighbours Asturian, Catalan, Galician, Occitan (Gascon), Occitan (Languedocien), and Spanish. This distribution is reminiscent of that described for HIGH PMQs in SW. We therefore register the instances of HIGH SEQMs in SE and SW as candidates for the status of areal convergence phenomena.

6 INTERP

LOW SEQPs and SEQMs – especially in combination – are suggestive of loosely packed grids, in a manner of speaking. In contrast, HIGH SEQPs and SEQMs invoke the image of a high degree of compactness. To verify whether these assumptions can be upheld, we carry out a crosscheck. The crosscheck focuses on the number of gaps in columns and rows of the grid. Gaps interrupt potential sequences. For the places of articulation, this means that if the column between activated dental and activated postalveolar is empty, there is a gap. Gaps can only occur between activated places of articulation. The number of gaps on the horizontal plane yields the INTERP value (= interruptions with places of articulation).

In the sample languages, there are up to four gaps in the domain of the places of articulation. Three to four gaps are overwhelmingly common since they are reported for 151 languages (= 72% of the sample). These are the H-languages. At the opposite end, we find 59 L-languages (= 28%) which allow for one to two gaps. There is no language without gaps. As Figure 19 teaches us INTERP is not simply the inverse of SEQP.

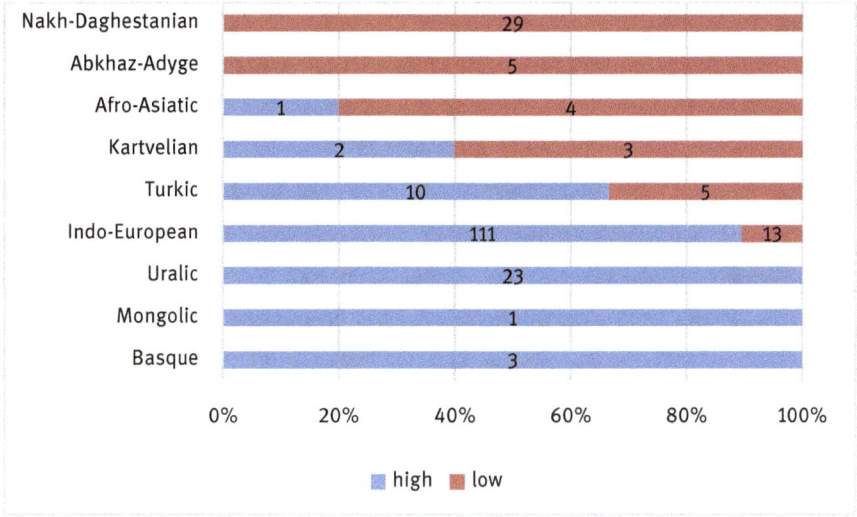

Figure 19: INTERPs (absolute numbers and shares) per phylum.

It is true that the behaviour of Abkhaz-Adyghe and Nakh-Daghestanian is not entirely unexpected on account of their tolerance towards HIGH SEQPs. Similarly, the absence of LOW INTERPs from Uralic, Mongolic, and Basque is not surprising either since these phyla only allow for LOW SEQPs. However, we find LOW INTERPs also with phyla which give no evidence of HIGH SEQPs, namely Afro-Asiatic, Kartvelian, and Turkic. Thus, INTERP cannot be filed away as the mirror image of SEQP.

Figure 20 reveals that Abkhaz-Adyghe, Afro-Asiatic, Kartvelian, Turkic, and Nakh-Daghestanian are overrepresented under the rubric of languages with LOW INTERPs. This enumeration of phyla involves all three of the phyla which are autochthonous in the Caucasian region.

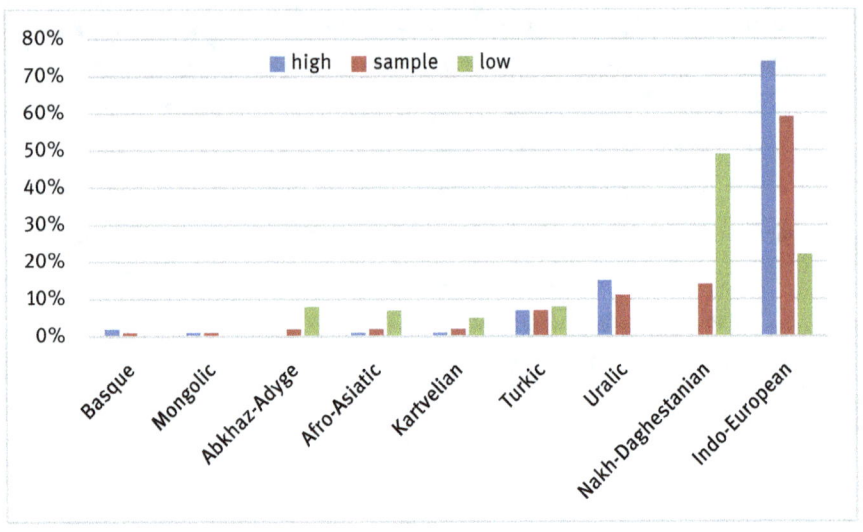

Figure 20: Phyla and their shares of HIGH INTERP, sample, and LOW INTERP.

This geographic cluster is reflected in Figure 21 according to which the vast majority of the L-languages is situated in SE where they outnumber the H-languages by far.

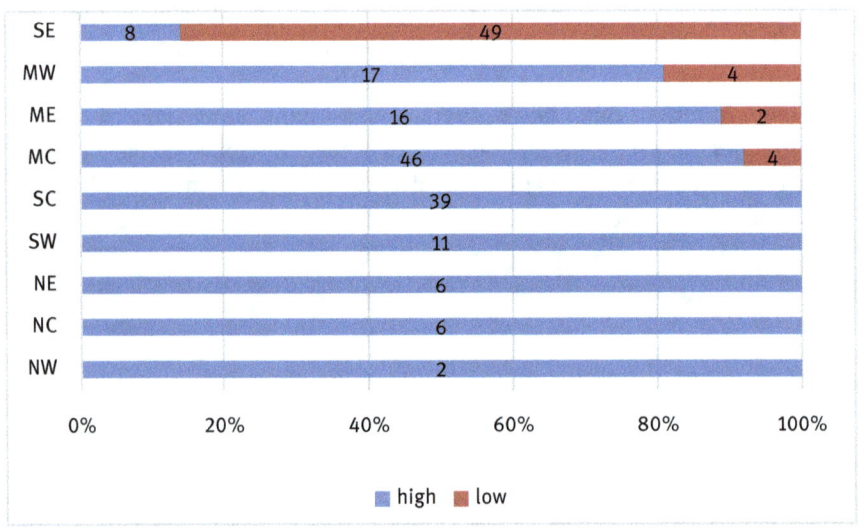

Figure 21: Absolute numbers and shares of H- and L-languages per nonant (INTERP).

According to Figure 22, SE is the only nonant in which languages with LOW IN-
TERPs are significantly overrepresented.

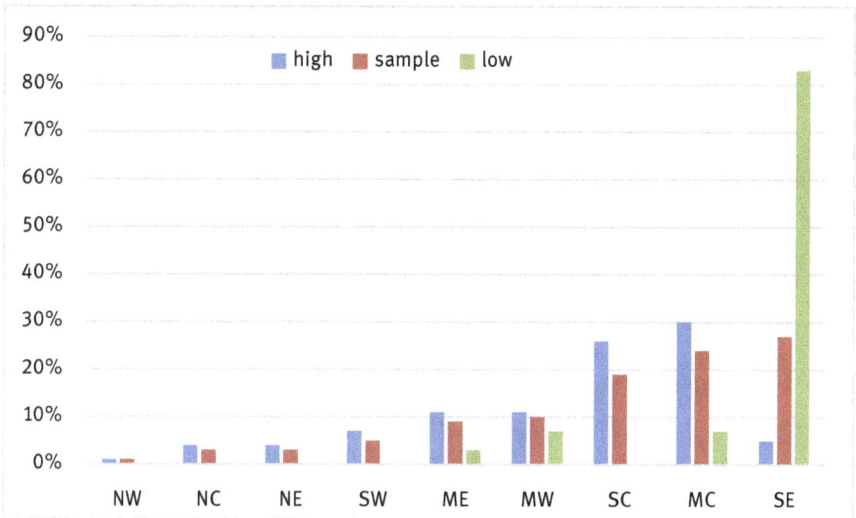

Figure 22: Nonants and their shares of HIGH INTERP, sample, and LOW INTERP.

The three phyla Abkhaz-Adyghe, Kartvelian, and Nakh-Daghestanian are responsible for 37 of the 49 L-languages in SE. The remaining dozen comprises the Afro-Asiatic languages Arabic (Çukurova), Arabic (Cypriot/Kormakiti), Aramaic (Cudi), and Aramaic (Hertevin), the Turkic languages Azerbaijani, Crimean Tatar, and Noghay as well as the Indo-European languages Armenian (Eastern), Armenian (Western), Kurmanji, Zaza (Northern), and Zaza (Southern Dimili). These languages behave differently from the bulk of their relatives spoken outside SE. The neighbourhood relation to the phyla in the Caucasus seems to be a crucial factor for this divergence from the genealogical patterns.

7 INTERM

In analogy to INTERP, it is possible to take account of the gaps vertically, meaning: the number of empty rows between two activated manners of articulation yields the INTERM. No language of our sample is exempt from vertical gaps. The INTERMs range from 1 to 4. One to two gaps are associated with LOW. With 150 languages (= 71% of the sample), LOW is the majority option. The remaining 60 H-languages cover 29% of the sample. Figure 23 is indicative of the absence of H-languages from four phyla whereas two phyla attest exclusively to H-languages. Three phyla are mixed as to HIGH and LOW with the latter always forming the majority.

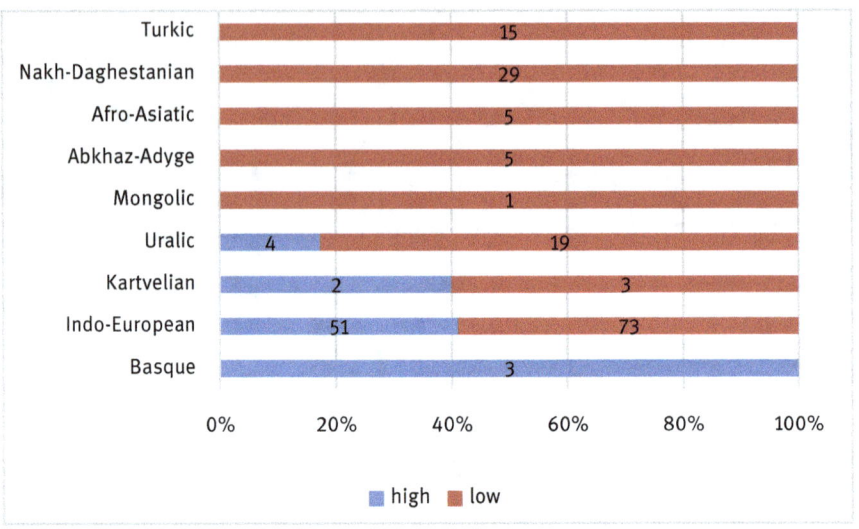

Figure 23: INTERMs (absolute numbers and shares) per phylum.

Note that Nakh-Daghestanian has only LOW INTERMs whereas half of its members display HIGH SEQMs. This means that, at least potentially, a sizable proportion of the Nakh-Daghestanian languages is characterized by considerable compactness. This also holds to some extent for Abkhaz-Adyghe. In Figure 24, Indo-European clearly stands out from the rest of the phyla.

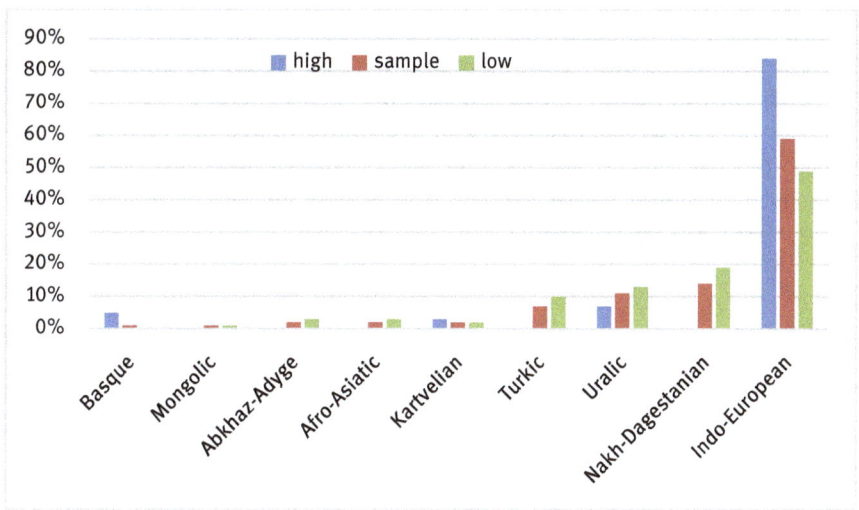

Figure 24: Phyla and their shares of HIGH INTERM, sample, and LOW INTERM.

Indo-European is responsible for 84% of all H-languages. HIGH is typical of 41% of the Indo-European languages. These HIGH INTERMs square with the preponderance of LOW SEQMs in Indo-European. In contrast to the relatively compact Nakh-Daghestanian systems, many Indo-European languages boast systems with a lesser degree of compactness.

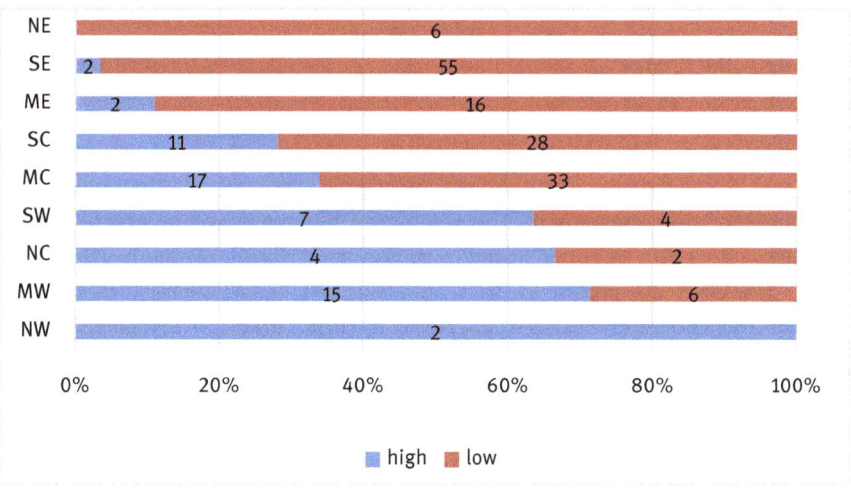

Figure 25: Absolute numbers and shares of HIGH and LOW languages per nonant (INTERM).

Geographically, the distribution of H-languages and L-languages over the nonants can be depicted as a continuum as shown in Figure 25.

Both extremes are located in the north. NE exclusively hosts L-languages whereas NW is populated only by H-languages. NC which forms the bridge between the other two northerly nonants attests to the co-presence of both types of languages. In Figure 26, we see that all three easterly nonants are overrepresented in the domain of LOW.

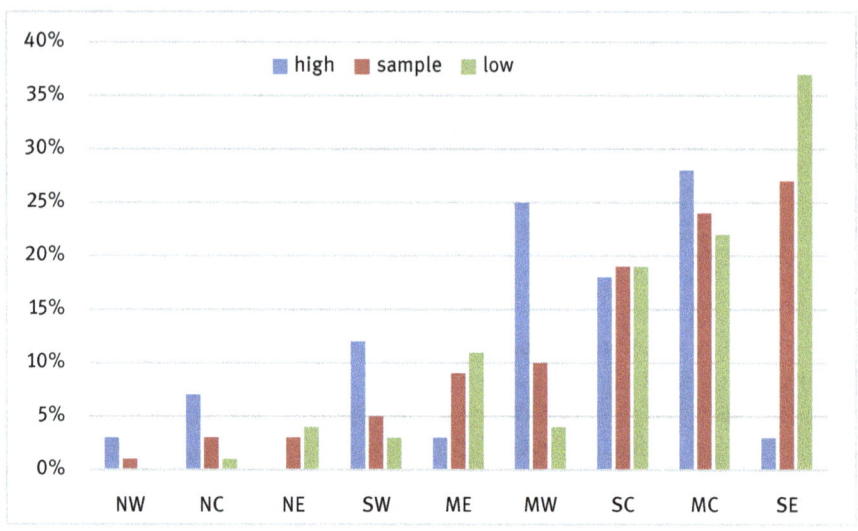

Figure 26: Nonants and their shares of HIGH INTERM, sample, and LOW INTERM.

In contrast, the overrepresentation in connection with HIGH occurs in the three nonants in the west and in MC. There are 55 languages marked as LOW in SE. Only 37 of these L-languages belong to the Caucasian phyla Abkhaz-Adyghe, Kartvelian, and Nakh-Daghestanian. The remaining eighteen languages are Arabic (Çukurova), Arabic (Cypriot/Kormatiki), Aramaic (Cudi), Aramaic (Hertevin) from Afro-Asiatic, Azerbaijani, Crimean Tatar, Karachay-Balkar, Karaim (Eastern), Kumyk, Noghay, and Turkish (Trabzon) from Turkic, Armenian (Eastern), Armenian (Western), Kurmanji, Ossetic, Zaza (Northern), and Zaza (Southern Dimili) from Indo-European, and the Mongolic language Kalmyk. Languages with different genealogical backgrounds display identical properties. Superficially, this seems to suggest that we are dealing again with a potential case of areal diffusion. However, LOW is also attested for many Indo-European outside SE. Moreover, the entire Turkic and Afro-Asiatic phyla consist only of L-languages, i.e. LOW is not a monopoly of SE. Since the five Indo-European languages in ME are L-languages too, LOW can be considered a general trait of easterly Indo-European languages although it is also attested elsewhere.

8 PHONP

The next step leads us to functional load that is associated with a given place of articulation. We determine the functional load by way of adding up the phonemes which are produced at the same place of articulation. In this section, we exclusively look at the highest PHONP, i.e. the place of articulation which yields the biggest turnout of phonemes per language. The sample languages clearly favour the alveolar place of articulation. In 202 languages (= 96% of the sample), the highest number of phonemes bears the place specification [ALVEOLAR]. Add to this number the three languages which have equal numbers of phonemes at the alveolar and the palatal or retroflex places of articulation, the dominance of alveolar increases further to cover 98% of the sample. The five languages which give preference to other places of articulation are located in SE, namely three members of Abkhaz-Adyghe: Abaza (velar), Abkhaz (velar), and Ubykh (uvular), and two Nakh-Daghestanian languages: Aghul (post-alveolar) and Rutul (uvular).

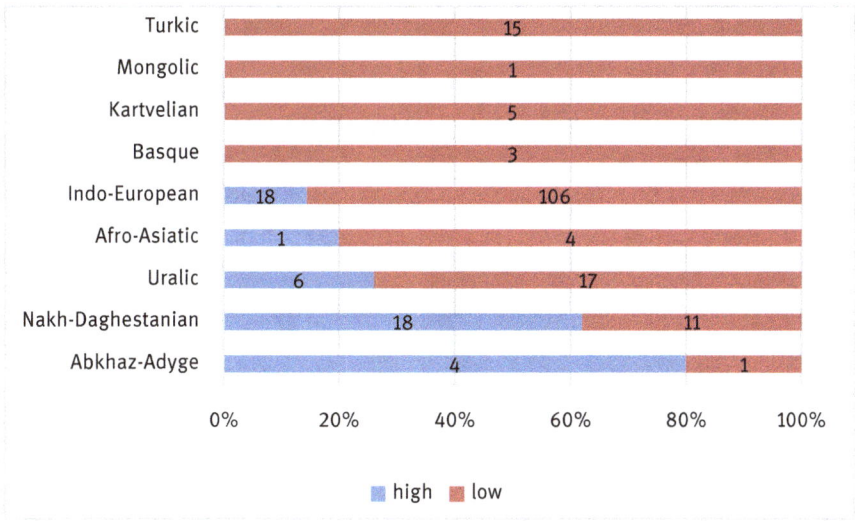

Figure 27: PHONPs (absolute numbers and shares) per phylum.

In terms of quantities, the maximal number of phonemes per place of articulation ranges from 5 to 30. The label LOW is given to turnouts between 5 to 13. This is the case in 163 languages (= 78% of the sample). The H-languages number 47 (= 22%); they have 14 to 30 phonemes at a given place of articulation. According to Figure 27, there are four phyla whose members do not privilege any place of articulation to exceed the threshold of 14 phonemes. No phylum hosts only H-languages. Nakh-Daghestanian and Abkhaz-Adyghe are phyla which host a majority of H-languages.

Overrepresentation in connection with HIGH applies to Abkhaz-Adyghe, Nakh-Daghestanian, and Uralic as can be gathered from Figure 28. Interestingly, the contributions of Nakh-Daghestanian and Indo-European to the number of H-languages are identical but Indo-European is nevertheless clearly underrepresented.

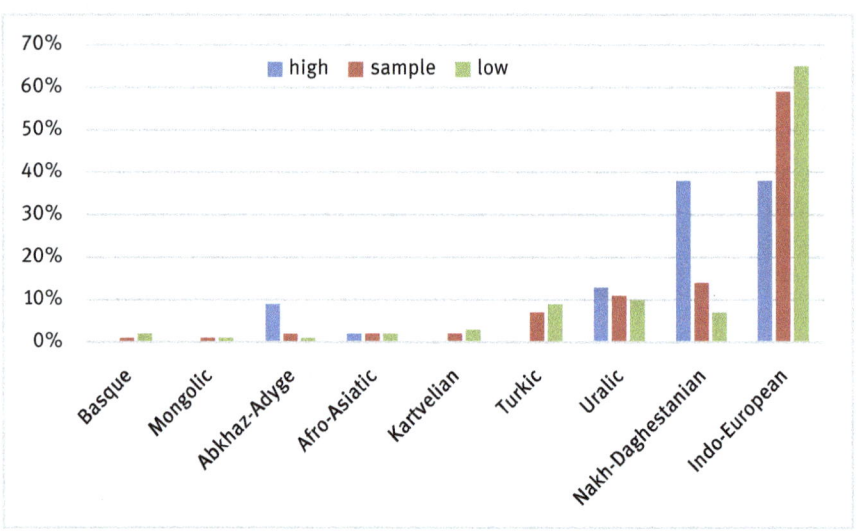

Figure 28: Phyla and their shares of HIGH PHONP, sample, and LOW PHONP.

The three overrepresented phyla invoke an easterly basis of HIGH. This is corroborated by Figure 29.

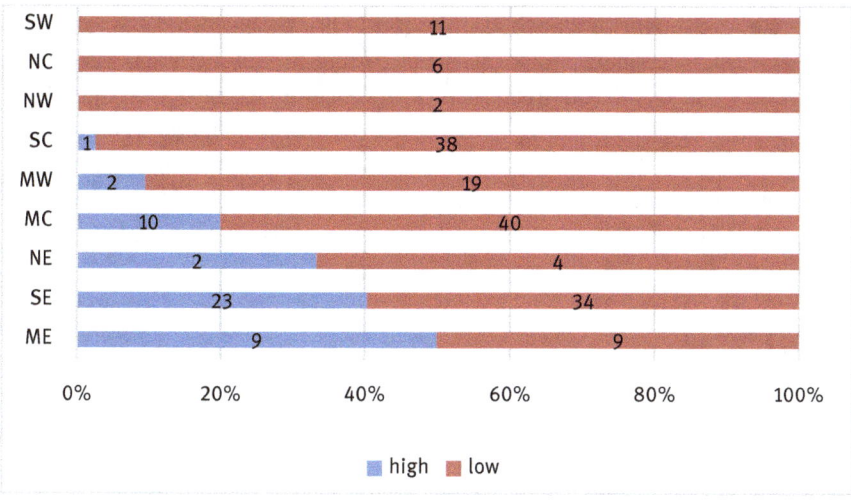

Figure 29: Absolute numbers and shares of H- and L-languages per nonant (PHONP).

NE, SE, and ME are overrepresented in the domain of H-languages. Further to the west, the importance of HIGH diminishes considerably. Figure 30 shows that overrepresentation in the domain of HIGH is especially pronounced in the case of SE.

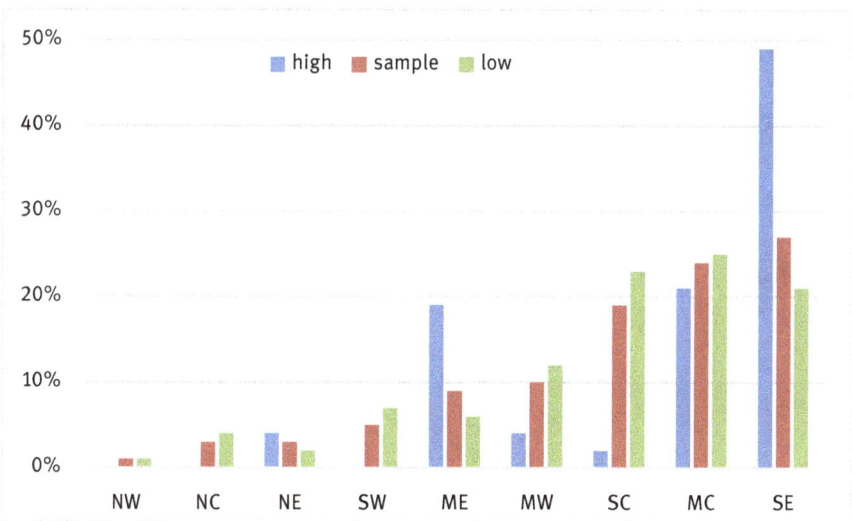

Figure 30: Nonants and their shares of HIGH PHONP, sample, and LOW PHONP.

In SE, the Afro-Asiatic language Aramaic (Cudi) is the sole example among 23 H-languages of the nonant which does not belong to either Abkhaz-Adyghe or Nakh-Daghestanian. Except Irish, Irish (Southern), and Bulgarian, all Indo-European H-languages are located in MC or ME (Baltic, Slavic, and Indo-Iranian). Most of these are co-territorial with Uralic languages all of which are marked as HIGH. However, co-territoriality cannot explain everything because the Turkic languages in ME and SE are unaffected by the preferences of their neighbours.

9 PHONM

This section takes up the issue of the previous one by way of looking at the highest number of phonemes per manner of articulation. The top results are termed PHONM in shorthand. In stark contrast to the places of articulation, there are two contenders for the status of favourite manner of articulation. At the top of the scale, we find fricative with 96 languages (= 46% of the sample) followed by plosive with 79 languages (= 38%). In addition, there are 32 languages (= 15%) which display the same number of phonemes for fricative and plosive. Two languages put both fricative and affricate on top whereas one language opts for affricate. The latter three languages belong to the Andic branch of Nakh-Daghestanian, namely Andi, Botlikh, and Karata. We come back to this competition between fricative and plosive in Section 10.

In terms of quantities, there is a 90% majority of the sample languages which attest to LOW PHONMs, i.e. 188 languages display a maximum of 3 to 15 phonemes for their favourite manner of articulation. This is the group of L-languages. Only 22 languages (= 10%) deserve the label HIGH because they have 16 to 28 phonemes with the favourite manner of articulation. Figure 31 shows that HIGH is absent from four phyla whereas it is the majority option only in Abkhaz-Adyghe.

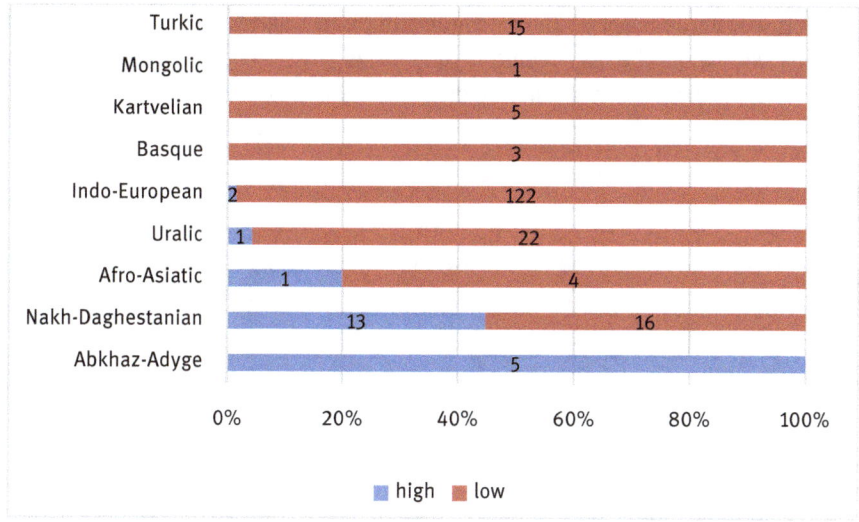

Figure 31: PHONMs (absolute numbers and shares) per phylum.

Abkhaz-Adyghe, Nakh-Daghestanian, and Afro-Asiatic are clearly overrepresented in the domain of HIGH whereas LOW dominates in most of the other phyla. These differences are visible in Figure 32.

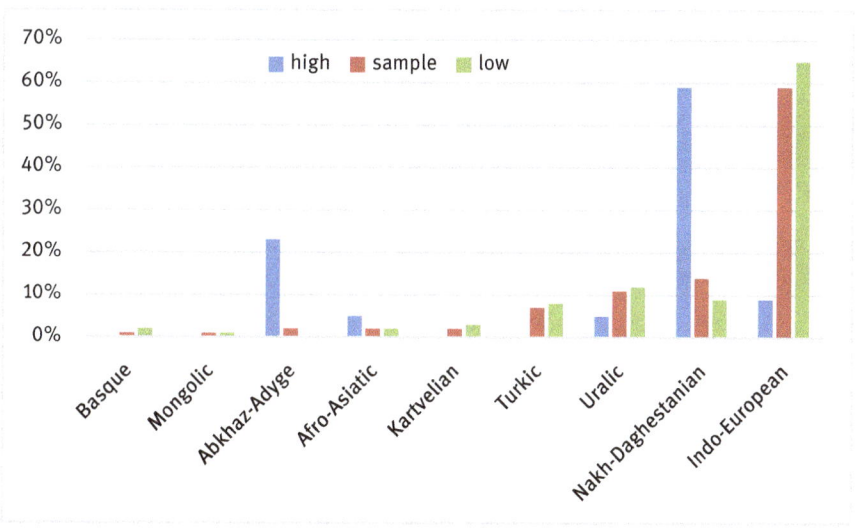

Figure 32: Phyla and their shares of HIGH PHONM, sample, and LOW PHONM.

Given the prominence of Abkhaz-Adyghe and Nakh-Daghestanian in the domain of HIGH, we expect the SE nonant to reflect this status. Figure 33 confirms this insofar as H-languages have their biggest share exactly in SE.

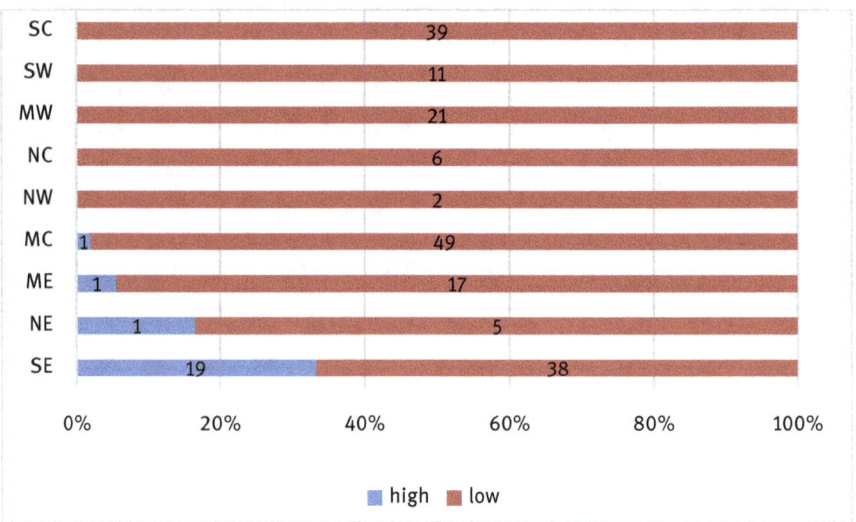

Figure 33: Absolute numbers and shares of HIGH and LOW languages per nonant (PHONM).

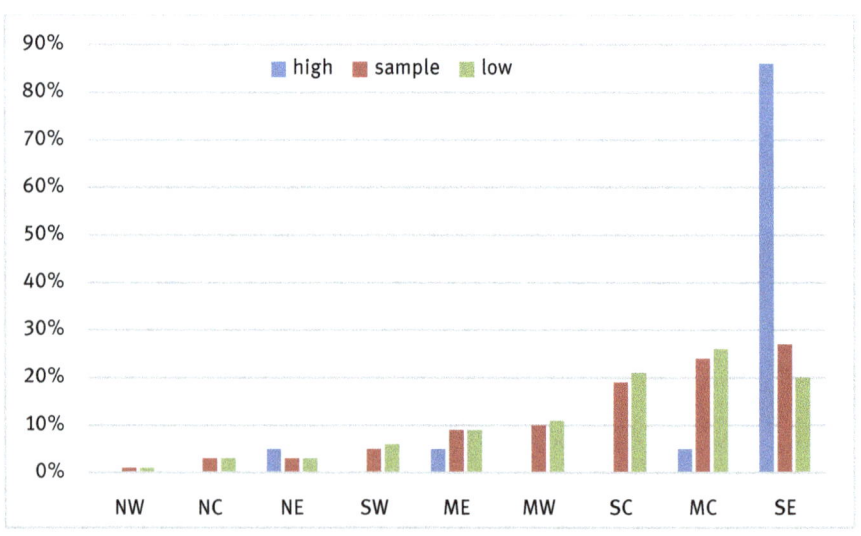

Figure 34: Nonants and their shares of HIGH PHONM, sample, and LOW PHONM.

Figure 33 also tells us that the feature HIGH is relatively well-established in the easterly nonants whereas it is lacking from those in the west. Moreover, ME and NE cannot compete with SE when overrepresentation is taken account of. The exceptional status of SE is evident from Figure 34 although NE is also slightly overrepresented.

Of the 19 H-languages in SE, 18 belong to either Nakh-Daghestanian or Abkhaz-Adyghe. The Afro-Asiatic language Aramaic (Cudi) is the sole exception.

10 Borrowing

In several of the above cases, the geographic distribution of the phenomena is suggestive of the possibility of contact-induced diffusion along the lines of the areal sound pattern hypothesis and the *perceptual magnet effect* (Blevins 2017: 98–99). Since these phenomena are relatively abstract in the sense that they are related mostly to quantitative relations of very general phonological classes, it is hard to prove the contact-borne nature of the observed facts. To give more substance to the hypothesis that language contact might be responsible for the parallel behaviour of genealogically unrelated but geographically close languages (Eisen 2019), we focus on the impact loan phonemes have on the systems of consonants in our sample languages (Stolz and Levkovych 2021). To this end, we take up an issue we already touched upon at the beginning of the foregoing section, namely the competition of the fricative and plosive manners of articulation for the highest PHONM.

To keep in line with the binary structure of the previous comparisons of HIGH and LOW, we take account only of those 175 languages which either opt for FRICATIVE (n = 96; 55% of 175) or PLOSIVE (n = 79; 45% of 175) as a favourite manner of articulation. Synchronically, there is thus a majority of FRICATIVE-languages although the class of PLOSIVE-languages is by no means small. In point of fact, the situation was different in the past. How do we know that without going into the diachronic details of language history? We assume that loan phonemes are innovations within the systems and if we strip the consonant system of these loan phonemes the picture changes dramatically. Of the above 96 FRICATIVE-languages only 56 remain because in 40 languages the prominent position of fricative is secondary in the sense that it results from the integration of loan phonemes. In 19 languages, FRICATIVE has been promoted to PHONM to the detriment of PLOSIVE.

In 20 languages of our sample, the two manners of articulation shared the same status prior to the advancement of FRICATIVE. Figure 35 shows how many members of a given phylum assign the PHONM status to FRICATIVE on the basis of their inherited inventory of consonants as opposed to those of their relatives which are FRICATIVE-languages only if the loan phonemes are counted in. Only those phyla are included in Figure 35 which attest to FRICATIVE-borrowing. In numerous cases (but by no means always), it is the voiceless labiodental fricative /f/ which is borrowed (Hockett 1985) whereby a new manner of articulation and/or a new place of articulation is established in the replica language; these processes mostly belong to Maddieson's (1986: 6–9) Classes 2 or 4–6 for the integration of borrowed sounds.

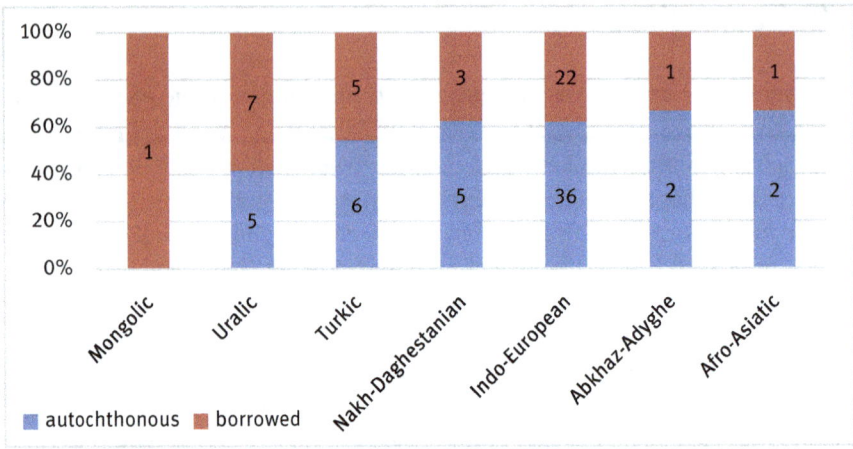

Figure 35: Primary FRICATIVE-languages vs secondary FRICATIVE-languages (absolute numbers and shares) per phylum.

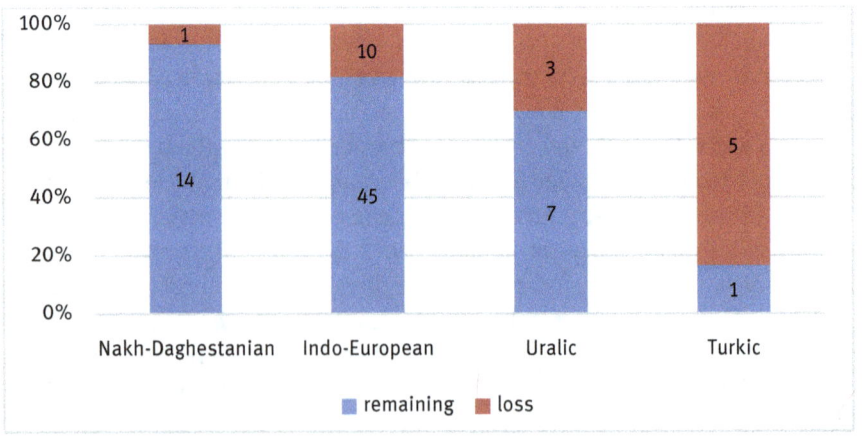

Figure 36: Loss of PHONM status for PLOSIVE per phylum.

It is a remarkable fact that borrowing has the opposite effect with PLOSIVE. This manner of articulation is never promoted to PHONM status via borrowing. To the contrary, PLOSIVE has lost this status frequently as shown in Figure 36.

Four phyla are affected by a change at the PHONM-level which goes to the detriment of PLOSIVE. In all of these cases, FRICATIVE has ousted PLOSIVE because of the integration of loan phonemes.

Since Nakh-Daghestanian, Turkic, and Uralic are featured (alongside Indo-European) in Figures 35–36, it makes sense to crosscheck the genealogically based results against the geographic parameter. Figure 37 reveals that borrowing is irrelevant for the PHONM status of fricative in NW and NC.

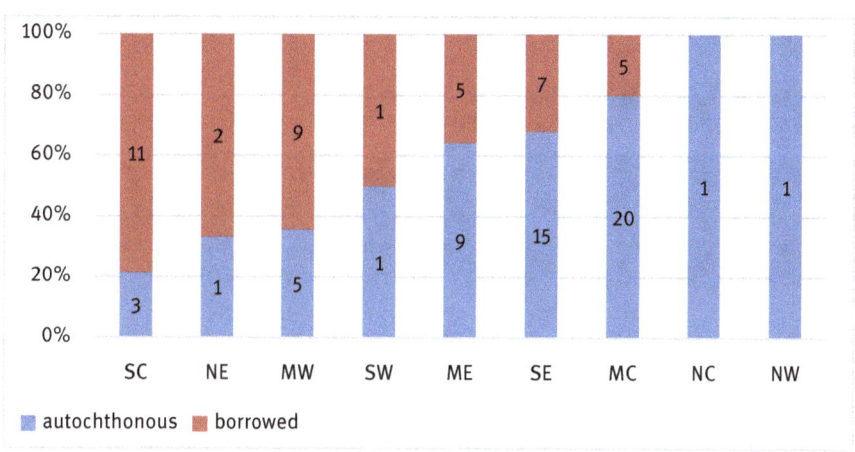

Figure 37: Absolute numbers and shares of primary FRICATIVE-languages vs secondary FRICATIVE-languages per nonant.

Borrowing has contributed substantially to the promotion of FRICATIVE to PHONM status in SC, NE, and MW. Figure 38 shows that in the same nonants, PLOSIVE has suffered losses owing to borrowing.

The increase of the number of FRICATIVE-languages is responsible to a high degree for the recession of the number of PLOSIVE-languages. If language contact has repercussions on the parameter of PHONM, one might want to know whether other parameters experience changes too under the impact of language contact.

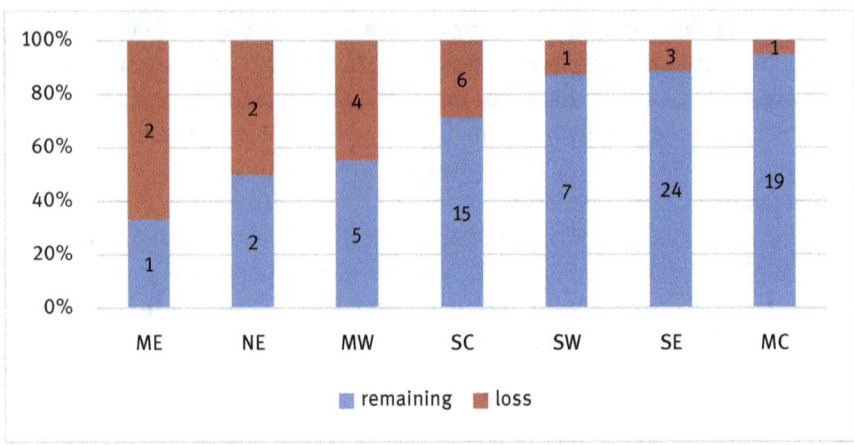

Figure 38: Loss of PHONM status for PLOSIVE per nonant.

We only mention those cases in which a language moves from LOW to HIGH or vice versa. As to PMS, for eleven languages, it makes a difference if loan phonemes are taken account of or not. Languages which are situated in the northern nonants are absent from Table 1.

Table 1: From LOW PMS to HIGH PMS.

language	nonant	phylum	with LP	without LP	difference
Aramaic (Hertevin)	SE	Afro-Asiatic	70	54	16
Bashkir	ME	Turkic	70	60	10
Khinalug	SE	Nakh-Daghestanian	63	54	9
Laz	SE	Kartvelian	63	56	7
Maltese	SC	Afro-Asiatic	63	56	7
Noghay	SE	Turkic	63	49	14
Sardinian (Nuorese)	SC	Indo-European	63	56	7
Sorbian Lower	MC	Indo-European	63	56	7
Sorbian Upper	MC	Indo-European	63	56	7
Tatar	ME	Turkic	70	42	28
Welsh (Southern)	MW	Indo-European	72	56	16

The change from LOW to HIGH means that in the course of borrowing the number of places of articulation and/or that of manners of articulation increased at least by one. These changes in the domain of PMS notwithstanding, there seems to be hardly any noticeable contact-borne effect on PMQ. Greek [SC, Indo-European] is the only case of a language which changes from LOW PMQ (= 1.00) to HIGH PMQ (= 1.20).

Contact-induced changes from LOW to HIGH SEQP can be assumed for Hinukh [SE, Nakh-Daghestanian] and Sardinian (Nuorese) [SC, Indo-European] which share the LOW SEQP 4 which rises to the HIGH SEQP 6 if loan phonemes are admitted to the count. The only language which moves from LOW to HIGH SEQM is Abaza [SE, Abkhaz-Adyghe] which yields the LOW SEQM 3 without loan phonemes but the HIGH SEQM 6 with loan phonemes.

With INTERP and INTERM, borrowing has the opposite effect in the sense that a language replaces its HIGH values with LOW values. In Table 2, we register five languages whose HIGH INTERP diminished under contact to yield a LOW INTERP.

Table 2: From HIGH INTERP to LOW INTERP.

language	nonant	phylum	with LPs	without LPs	difference
Breton	MW	Indo-European	2	3	-1
Crimean Tatar	SE	Turkic	2	3	-1
Noghay	SE	Turkic	2	3	-1
Tatar	ME	Turkic	2	4	-2
Welsh (Northern)	MW	Indo-European	2	3	-1

In the case of INTERM, the languages which change from HIGH to LOW number eight as shown in Table 3. It is worth noting that Tatar is the only language to be mentioned in Tables 1, 2, and 3. Noghay and Sardinian (Nuorese) show up in two different tables.

Table 3: From HIGH INTERM to LOW INTERM.

language	nonant	phylum	with LPs	without LPs	difference
Arabic (Cypriot/Kormakiti)	SE	Afro-Asiatic	2	3	-1
Aramaic (Hertevin)	SE	Afro-Asiatic	2	3	-1
Bashkir	ME	Turkic	2	3	-1
Dutch	MC	Indo-European	2	3	-1

language	nonant	phylum	with LPs	without LPs	difference
Estonian	MC	Uralic	2	3	-1
Kazakh	ME	Turkic	2	3	-1
Livonian	MC	Uralic	2	3	-1
Tatar	ME	Turkic	2	3	-1

The final parameter on which a change of class can be stated is PHONM. Two languages change from a LOW PHONM to a HIGH PHONM, namely Lithuanian [MC, Indo-European] with LOW PHONM 13 > HIGH PHONM 16 and Saami (Kildin) [NE, Uralic] with LOW PHONM 12 > HIGH PHONM 16. To conclude this section, we emphasize that in many cases the effects noted in Tables 1–3 are causally related to the integration of fricatives – most notably /f/ – into the replica languages, i.e. the changes on the different parameters are not absolutely independent of each other. We assume that this means that although "not EVERYTHING [will] turn out to cohere with EVERYTHING else" (Plank 2018: 27) there is still something that coheres with something else.

11 Conclusions

The tentative application of the above parameters to the sample languages is revealing in terms of the areal typology of Europe. On the one hand, our initial working hypothesis receives some support in the sense that in several of the sections Nakh-Daghestanian and Abkhaz-Adyghe could be shown to behave markedly different from the majority of the other phyla. This result only states the obvious, in a manner of speaking. Ternes (1998) for instance excludes the languages of the Caucasus from his survey of European phonologies on account of their striking differences in comparison to the typical representative of Standard Average European. At the same time, we also see that it is not possible to sweepingly subsume all phyla of the Caucasian region under one heading because Kartvelian frequently disagrees with its next-door neighbours. Moreover, properties which are associated with Nakh-Daghestanian and/or Abkhaz-Adyghe are repeatedly attested in unrelated languages in SE for which the presence of these properties is difficult to justify on genealogical grounds. This pattern fits in with Haig's (2017: 401–403) observations as to East Anatolia as a transition zone and Grawunder's (2017: 387–388) conclusions as to the diffusion of phonological properties throughout the Caucasus and beyond. In SW and to a lesser extent also in SC and ME, we find similar parallels among neighbouring and not necessarily closely related languages. This additionally confirms the working hypothesis because both genealogy and geography have a say in the shaping of the European phonological landscape.

Eisen (2019) proves convincingly that loan phonemes are cross-linguistically very common and that their borrowing is subject to inhibiting and facilitating factors. In Europe too, material borrowing can be held responsible for the levelling of many differences between languages not the least because the integration of a (single) loan phoneme can have repercussions on several of the above parameters so that the consonantal systems of languages which previously differed from each other throughout become similar to each other not only selectively but on the whole.

However, the phenomena investigated in Sections 2–9 more often than not come in the shape of continua. This means that there is no one-to-one correspondence between parameter values and affiliation or location of a given language. The shares phyla and nonants have of a given phenomenon very frequently diverge from the share they have of the sample. It is therefore impossible to generalize about a genealogically or geographically circumscribed group of languages only on the limited basis of one or two representatives. To put it succinctly, if a global sample hosts only a handful of European languages or hides them away indistinguishably in a Eurasian macro-area, the phonological reality of the continent will be distorted – and this also to the detriment of a globally oriented phonological typology. This is why we strongly plead for the coordinated planning and realization of phonological atlases of all macro-areas under the proviso that the atlases do not only comprise maps but also phonologically well-informed thematic chapters.

This study has neither solved any problem of phonological typology nor has it exhausted the phenomenology of subject matters which are worthwhile looking into. The methodology needs to be refined substantially. The binary distinction of HIGH/LOW is probably too simplistic to guide us much further. The choice of the modified IPA as frame of reference should be revised in the future. For reasons of space, the necessary test of the behaviour of phyla, individual languages, and nonants across different parameters must be developed further. These many aspects which need tidying up notwithstanding, we are confident that the ideas expressed in the foregoing paragraphs can be useful for (areal-)typological phonology and/or phonological (areal-)typology (Plank 2018). Furthermore, the still preliminary results of this study are already indicative of what the intensified investigation of phonological issues holds in store for the theory of language contact.

Abbreviations

INTERM	Interruptions on the level of Manners
INTERP	Interruptions on the level of Places
LP	loan phoneme
M	manner of articulation
MC	middle centre nonant
ME	middle east nonant
MW	middle west nonant
NC	north centre nonant
NE	north east nonant
NW	north west nonant
P	Place of articulation
PHONM	most densely populated Manner
PHONP	most densely populated Place
PMQ	Place-Manner Quotient
PMS	Place-Manner Space
SC	south centre nonant
SE	south east nonant
SEQM	Sequences of Manners,
SEQP	Sequences of Places
SW	south west nonant

References

Bickel, Balthasar. 2007. Typology in the 21st century: major current developments. *Linguistic Typology* 11. 239–251.

Blevins, Juliette. 2017. Areal sound patterns: from perceptual magnets to stone soup. In Raymond Hickey (ed.), *The Cambridge handbook of areal linguistics*, 88–121. Cambridge: Cambridge University Press.

Calabrese, Andrea & W. Leo Wetzels (eds.). 2009. *Loan phonology*. Amsterdam & Philadelphia: Benjamins.

Clements, G.N. & Annie Rialland. 2008. Africa as a phonological area. In Bernd Heine & Derek Nurse (eds.), *A linguistic geography of Africa*, 36–85. Cambridge: Cambridge University Press.

Eisen, Elad. 2019. *The typology of phonological segment borrowing*. Unpublished MA-thesis. The Hebrew University of Jerusalem: Department of Linguistics.

Gordon, Matthew K. 2016. *Phonological typology*. Oxford: Oxford University Press.

Grawunder, Sven. 2017. The Caucasus. In Raymond Hickey (ed.), *The Cambridge handbook of areal linguistics*, 356–395. Cambridge: Cambridge University Press.

Haig, Geoffrey. 2017. Western Asia: East Anatolia as transition zone. In Raymond Hickey (ed.), *The Cambridge handbook of areal linguistics*, 396–424. Cambridge: Cambridge University Press.

Haspelmath, Martin. 2001. The European linguistic area: Standard Average European. In Martin Haspelmath, Ekkehard König, Wulf Oesterreicher & Wolfgang Raible (eds.), *Language typology and language universals. An international handbook,* 1492–1510. Berlin: de Gruyter.
Hockett, Charles F. 1985. Distinguished lecture: F. *American Anthropologist* 87. 263–281.
Hyman, Larry M. 2009. How (not) to do phonological typology: the case of pitch-accent. *Language Sciences* 31. 213–238.
Hyman, Larry M. 2018. What is phonological typology? In Larry M. Hyman & Frans Plank (eds.), *Phonological typology*, 1–20. Berlin & Boston: De Gruyter Mouton.
Kiparsky, Paul. 2018. Formal and empirical issues in phonological typology. In Larry M. Hyman & Frans Plank (eds.), *Phonological typology,* 54–106. Berlin & Boston: De Gruyter Mouton.
König, Ekkehard & Martin Haspelmath. 1999. Der europäische Sprachbund. In Norbert Reiter (ed.), *Eurolinguistik. Ein Schritt in die Zukunft*, 111–128. Wiesbaden: Harrassowitz.
Ladefoged, Peter & Ian Maddieson. 1995. *The sounds of the world's languages.* Oxford: Blackwell.
Maddieson, Ian. 1984. *Patterns of sounds.* Cambridge: Cambridge University Press.
Maddieson, Ian. 1986. Borrowed sounds. In Joshua A. Fishman, Andrée Tabouret-Keller, Michael Clyne, Bh. Krishnamurti & Mohamed Abdulaziz. (eds.), *The Fergusonian impact. In honor of Charles A. Ferguson on the occasion of his 65th birthday. Volume 1: From phonology to society*, 1–16. Berlin, New York & Amsterdam: Mouton de Gruyter.
Maddieson, Ian. 2018. Is phonological typology possible without (universal) categories? In Larry M. Hyman & Frans Plank (eds.), *Phonological typology*, 107–125. Berlin & Boston: De Gruyter Mouton.
Matras, Yaron. 2009. *Language contact.* Cambridge: Cambridge University Press.
Nikolaev, Dmitry & Eitan Grossman. 2018. Areal sound change and the distributional typology of affricate richness in Eurasia. *Studies in Language* 42(3). 562–599.
Plank, Frans. 2018. An implicational universal to defy: typology $\supset \neg$ phonology $\equiv$ phonology $\supset \neg$ typology $\equiv \neg$ (typology $\wedge$ phonology) $\equiv \neg$ typology v $\neg$ phonology. In Larry M. Hyman & Frans Plank (eds.), *Phonological typology*, 21–53. Berlin & Boston: De Gruyter Mouton.
Stolz, Thomas & Nataliya Levkovych. 2017. Convergence and divergence in the phonology of the languages of Europe. In Raymond Hickey (ed.), *The Cambridge handbook of areal linguistics*, 122–160. Cambridge: Cambridge University Press.
Stolz, Thomas & Nataliya Levkovych. 2021. *Areal linguistics within the Phonological Atlas of Europe. Loan phonemes and their distribution.* Berlin & Boston: De Gruyter Mouton.
Ternes, Elmar. 1998. Lauttypologie der Sprachen Europas. In Winfried Boeder, Christoph Schroeder, Karl Heinz Wagner & Wolfgang Wildgen (eds.), *Sprache in Raum und Zeit: Beiträge zur empirischen Sprachwissenschaft*, 139–152. Tübingen: Narr.

Appendix

Table I: Languages without contact-induced changes of values.

Grey shading indicates that a given language has integrated loan phonemes nevertheless. The languages are presented according to phylum. af = affricate, fr = fricative, pl = plosive; al = alveolar, pa = palatal, rf = retroflex, uv = uvular, vl = velar.

Language (n = 95)	Nonant	PMS	PMQ	SEQP	SEQM	INTERP	INTERM	PHONP	Place	PHONM	Manner
Abkhaz-Adyge											
Abkhaz	SE	77	0.6	8	3	2	2	15	vl	21	pl
Ubykh	SE	88	0.7	7	5	2	1	20	uv	28	pl
Indo-European											
Albanian											
Albanian	SC	56	0.9	5	6	3	3	11	al	9	fr
Albanian (Mandrica)	SC	56	0.9	5	3	3	2	10	al	9	fr
Baltic											
Latgalian	MC	49	1.0	2	3	4	2	17	al	12	pl
Latvian	MC	49	1.0	2	3	3	2	10	al	8	pl
Latvian (Skrunda)	MC	42	1.2	2	3	4	2	9	al	8	pl
Lithuanian (Dieveniškės)	MC	42	1.2	2	3	4	2	16	al	12	pl

Language (n = 95)	Nonant	PMS	PMQ	SEQP	SEQM	INTERP	INTERM	PHONP	Place	PHONM	Manner
Celtic											
Irish	MW	36	1.0	2	3	4	3	17	al	12	pl, fr
Irish (Northern)	MW	30	0.8	2	2	3	4	12	al	12	pl
Irish (Southern)	MW	36	1.0	2	3	3	3	18	al	13	fr
Manx	MW	42	0.9	2	3	3	3	11	al	10	pl
Scottish Gaelic	MW	40	0.6	3	3	2	4	11	al	10	pl
Scottish Gaelic (Applecross)	MW	48	0.8	3	3	2	3	12	al	15	pl
Germanic											
Danish	MC	40	0.6	4	2	3	3	5	al	6	pl, fr
Danish (Brøndum)	MC	35	0.7	3	2	3	3	5	al	6	pl
Dutch (Drente)	MC	42	0.9	2	3	3	3	6	al	6	pl
Dutch (Flemish Oostduinkerke)	MW	42	0.9	2	3	3	3	7	al	6	fr
Faroese	NW	35	0.7	2	2	3	3	6	al	6	pl
Frisian Eastern (Seeltersk)	MC	42	0.9	2	3	3	3	6	al	6	fr
Frisian Northern (Weesdring)	MC	42	0.9	2	3	3	3	13	al	10	pl
Frisian Western	MW	42	0.9	2	3	3	3	7	al	7	fr
German (Brig)	SC	49	1.0	2	3	3	2	7	al	5	pl, fr
German (Ladelund Danish)	MC	36	1.0	2	3	3	3	6	al	6	pl

Language (n = 95)	Nonant	PMS	PMQ	SEQP	SEQM	INTERP	INTERM	PHONP	Place	PHONM	Manner
German (urban Kölsch)	MC	56	0.9	3	3	2	2	7	al	7	fr
Icelandic	NW	35	0.7	4	3	3	4	9	al	10	fr
Low German (North Saxon)	MC	35	0.7	2	3	3	4	8	al	8	fr
Norwegian (Central East Tromsø)	NC	42	0.9	2	2	3	3	6	al, pa	10	pl
Norwegian (Nynorsk)	NC	36	1.0	2	3	3	3	6	al	6	pl
Norwegian (Østnorsk)	MC	48	0.8	2	2	3	3	6	al, rf	8	pl
Swedish	MC	30	0.8	2	3	3	4	6	al	7	fr
Swedish (Österbotten)	NC	56	0.9	3	3	3	2	9	al	11	pl
Greek											
Greek (Italo-Greek Sternatia)	SC	35	1.4	2	3	4	2	8	al	5	pl
Indo-Iranian											
Kurmanji	SE	63	0.8	3	3	2	2	7	al	8	fr
Ossetic	SE	56	0.9	3	3	3	2	11	al	10	pl
Romani (Burgenland)	MC	49	1.0	2	3	3	2	8	al	9	pl
Zaza (Northern)	SE	72	0.9	3	6	2	2	9	al	9	fr
Zaza (Southern Dimili)	SE	80	0.8	4	6	2	2	11	al	12	fr
Romance											
Asturian	SW	49	1.0	5	6	4	3	7	al	5	pl, fr

Places, manners, and the areal phonology of Europe — 293

Language (n = 95)	Nonant	PMS	PMQ	SEQP	SEQM	INTERP	INTERM	PHONP	Place	PHONM	Manner
Corsican	SC	49	1.0	2	3	4	2	13	al	9	pl
Franco-Provençal (Faetar)	SC	36	1.0	2	3	4	3	7	al	5	pl, fr
French	MW	54	0.7	3	3	3	3	6	al	6	pl, fr
Friulian (Udine)	SC	36	1.0	2	3	4	3	7	al	6	pl
Galician	SW	56	1.1	5	6	4	2	7	al	6	pl
Istriot	SC	36	1.0	2	3	4	3	8	al	7	pl
Italian (Genovese)	SC	49	1.0	3	3	4	2	7	al	6	pl, fr
Ladin	MC	42	0.9	2	3	3	3	8	al	7	fr
Norman (Jersey)	MW	42	0.9	5	3	4	3	13	al	12	fr
Occitan (Aranese)	SW	42	0.9	2	3	3	3	9	al	6	pl, fr
Occitan (Gascon)	SW	64	1.0	2	6	3	2	12	al	8	pl
Occitan (Languedocien)	SW	64	1.0	2	6	4	2	9	al	6	pl
Portuguese	SW	48	0.8	3	2	3	3	7	al	7	fr
Romansch (Puter)	SC	42	0.9	2	3	3	3	8	al	8	pl, fr
Romansch (Surmeiran)	MC	42	0.9	2	3	3	3	8	al	8	pl
Romansch (Sursilvan)	MC	42	0.9	2	3	3	3	8	al	8	pl
Romansch (Sutselvan)	MC	42	0.9	2	3	3	3	8	al	8	pl
Romansch (Vallader)	MC	42	0.9	2	3	3	3	8	al	8	pl

Language (n = 95)	Nonant	PMS	PMQ	SEQP	SEQM	INTERP	INTERM	PHONP	Place	PHONM	Manner
Sardinian (Limba Sarda)	SC	49	1.0	3	3	4	2	9	al	7	pl
Sardinian (Campidanese)	SC	56	0.9	3	3	4	2	8	al	7	pl
Spanish	SW	56	1.1	5	6	4	2	7	al	6	pl
Slavic											
Croatian (Burgenland)	MC	42	1.2	3	3	4	2	8	al	8	pl
Russian (Meščera)	ME	42	1.2	2	3	4	2	15	al	11	fr
Kartvelian											
Laz (Mutafi Turkey)	SE	36	1.0	2	3	3	3	10	al	9	pl
Mingrelian	SE	56	0.9	3	3	2	2	11	al	11	pl
Svan	SE	56	0.9	3	3	2	2	11	al	11	pl
Nakh-Daghestanian											
Aghul	SE	70	0.7	4	3	2	2	14	pa	19	fr
Akhvakh	SE	72	1.1	2	6	2	1	19	al	14	fr
Andi	SE	72	1.1	3	6	2	1	17	al	13	af
Archi	SE	90	0.9	6	6	2	1	30	al	24	pl
Avar	SE	81	1.0	4	6	2	1	17	al	13	pl, fr
Bagvalal	SE	72	1.1	3	6	2	1	13	al	12	fr
Bezhta (Tlyadal)	SE	81	1.0	4	6	2	1	13	al	10	pl, fr

Language (n = 95)	Nonant	PMS	PMQ	SEQP	SEQM	INTERP	INTERM	PHONP	Place	PHONM	Manner
Botlikh	SE	72	1.1	3	6	2	1	16	al	11	fr, af
Budukh	SE	70	0.7	6	3	2	2	9	al	14	pl
Chamalal	SE	72	1.1	3	6	2	1	16	al	9	pl, fr
Dargwa (Icari)	SE	63	0.8	3	3	2	2	13	al	16	pl
Godoberi	SE	72	1.1	3	6	2	1	15	al	11	fr
Ingush	SE	70	0.7	6	3	2	2	12	al	12	pl
Karata	SE	72	1.1	3	6	2	1	17	al	11	fr, af
Kryts	SE	63	0.8	4	3	2	2	11	al	19	pl
Kryts (Alyk)	SE	63	0.8	4	3	2	2	9	al	13	pl
Lak	SE	63	0.8	4	3	2	2	13	al	16	pl
Lezgian	SE	63	0.8	3	3	2	2	20	al	26	pl
Rutul	SE	56	0.9	3	3	2	2	18	uv	25	pl
Tindi	SE	72	1.1	3	6	2	1	15	al	11	fr
Tsova-Tush	SE	72	0.9	4	4	2	1	16	al	16	pl
Udi (Nidž)	SE	63	0.8	3	3	2	2	16	al	11	pl, fr
Turkic											
Karaim (Eastern)	SE	49	1.0	2	3	3	2	7	al	9	fr
Karaim (Galits)	MC	49	1.0	2	3	3	2	9	al	8	fr

Language (n = 95)	Nonant	PMS	PMQ	SEQP	SEQM	INTERP	INTERM	PHONP	Place	PHONM	Manner
Uralic											
Estonian (Rõngu)	MC	42	1.2	2	3	3	2	6	al	3	pl
Komi-Zyrian (Udora)	NE	49	1.0	3	3	4	2	7	al, pa	8	pl
Mari (Meadow)	ME	49	1.0	5	3	4	2	6	al	7	fr
Nenets (Tundra)	NE	42	1.2	2	3	3	2	14	al	10	pl
Saami (Central-South)	NC	56	0.9	2	3	3	2	8	al	6	pl
Saami (Northern Enontekiö)	NC	48	0.8	5	3	3	3	11	al	9	fr

Table II: Languages with contact-induced changes of values.

Grey shading indicates different values with and without loan phonemes in a given category.
pl = plosive, ns = nasal, fr = fricative; al = alveolar, pa = palatal, vl = velar.

EDL (n = 115)	Nonant	PMS without LP	PMS with LP	PMQ without LP	PMQ with LP	SEQP without LP	SEQP with LP	SEQM without LP	SEQM with LP	INTERP without LP	INTERP with LP	INTERM without LP	INTERM with LP	Place PHON without LP	Place PHON with LP	Manner PHON without LP	Manner PHON with LP
Abkhaz-Adyge																	
Abaza	SE	99	88	0.8	0.7	5	5	3	6	1	1	1	1	15 vl	15 vl	21 pl, fr	23 fr
Adyghe	SE	70	70	0.7	0.7	5	5	3	3	1	1	1	1	14 al	14 al	20 fr	22 fr
Kabardian	SE	77	77	0.6	0.6	5	5	3	3	2	2	1	1	13 al	13 al	19 fr	20 fr
Afro-Asiatic																	
Arabic (Çukurova)	SE	70	70	0.7	0.7	4	4	3	3	1	1	2	2	10 al	10 al	10 fr	11 fr
Arabic (Cypriot/Kormakiti)	SE	56	48	0.9	0.8	5	5	3	3	2	2	3	2	6 al	6 al	10 fr	10 fr
Aramaic (Cudi)	SE	70	63	0.7	0.8	4	4	3	3	2	2	2	2	18 al	18 al	16 pl	16 pl
Aramaic (Hertevin)	SE	70	54	0.7	0.7	4	4	3	3	2	2	3	2	9 al	9 al	9 pl	10 pl

EDL (n = 115)			Maltese	Indo-European Albanian Albanian (Salamis)	Armenian Armenian (Eastern)	Armenian (Western)	Baltic Lithuanian	Celtic Breton	Breton (Léonais)	Breton (Trégorrois)
Manner PHON	without LP		pl,fr	pl,fr	pl	fr	fr	pl	pl	pl,fr
			5	8	9	8	13	6	6	6
Manner PHON	with LP		fr	fr	pl,fr	fr	fr	fr	fr	fr
			9	11	9	9	16	7	7	8
Place PHON	without LP		al	al	al	al	al	al	al	al
			7	10	12	9	18	5	9	7
Place PHON	with LP		al	al	al	al	al	al	al	al
			9	11	12	9	18	5	9	7
INTERM	without LP		2	2	2	2	2	3	3	3
	with LP		2	2	2	2	2	3	3	3
INTERP	without LP		3	3	2	2	4	3	4	3
	with LP		3	3	2	2	4	2	4	3
SEQM	without LP		3	6	6	3	3	3	3	3
	with LP		3	6	6	3	3	3	3	3
SEQP	without LP		2	5	3	3	2	3	2	2
	with LP		5	5	3	3	2	3	2	2
PMQ	without LP		0.9	1.0	1.0	0.9	1.2	0.7	1.0	0.9
	with LP		0.8	1.0	1.0	0.9	1.2	0.6	0.9	0.8
PMS	without LP		56	64	64	56	42	54	36	42
	with LP		63	64	64	56	42	60	42	48
Nonant			SC	SC	SE	SE	MC	MW	MW	MW

EDL (n = 115)		Breton (Vannetais)	Cornish	Welsh (Northern)	Welsh (Southern)	*Germanic*	Dutch	English	English (Bolton Area)	English (Cannock)	English (Cockney)	German	Low German (East Frisian)	Low German (Westphalian)
Manner PHON	without LP	pl	pl, fr	fr	pl, fr		fr	pl, fr	pl	pl	pl, fr	fr	fr	fr
		8	6	7	6		7	6	6	6	6	8	8	7
Manner PHON	with LP	pl	fr	fr	fr		fr	fr	fr	fr	fr	fr	fr	fr
		8	7	8	8		9	9	8	8	9	9	8	8
Place PHON	without LP	al	al	al	al		al	al	al	al	al	al	al	al
		9	7	9	7		7	6	6	6	6	8	6	7
Place PHON	with LP	al	al	al	al		al	al	al	al	al	al	al	al
		9	7	9	8		7	7	7	7	7	8	7	7
INTERM	without LP	3	2	1	1		3	2	2	2	3	2	2	3
	with LP	3	2	1	1		2	2	2	2	3	2	2	3
INTERP	without LP	3	3	3	3		3	3	4	4	3	3	2	3
	with LP	3	3	2	3		3	3	4	4	3	3	2	3
SEQM	without LP	3	3	3	3		3	2	2	2	2	3	3	3
	with LP	3	3	3	3		3	2	2	2	2	3	3	3
SEQP	without LP	2	2	4	4		2	5	5	5	5	2	3	2
	with LP	2	2	5	5		2	5	5	5	5	2	3	2
PMQ	without LP	0.9	0.9	0.8	0.9		1.0	0.7	0.8	0.8	0.6	1.0	0.9	1.0
	with LP	0.8	0.9	0.8	0.9		1.0	0.7	0.8	0.8	0.6	1.0	0.9	1.0
PMS	without LP	42	56	63	56		36	54	48	48	45	49	56	36
	with LP	48	56	80	72		49	54	48	48	45	49	56	42
Nonant		MW	MW	MW	MW		MC	MW	MW	MW	MW	MC	MC	MC

EDL (n = 115)			Luxembourgish	Yiddish	*Greek*	Greek	*Indo-Iranian*	Romani (Ajia Varvara)	Romani (Bugurdži)	Romani (Kalderash)	Romani (Lithuanian)	Romani (North Russian)	Romani (Sepecides)	*Romance*	Aromanian
Manner	without LP	PHON	fr / 8	fr / 7		fr / 8		pl / 12	pl / 9	pl / 9	pl / 15	pl / 17	pl / 9		pl / 8
Manner	with LP	PHON	fr / 9	fr / 8		fr / 8		pl / 12	pl / 9	pl / 9	pl / 15	pl / 17	pl, fr / 9		fr / 12
Place	without LP	PHON	al / 10	al / 7		al / 6		al / 8	al / 10	al / 9	al / 16	al / 15	al / 8		al / 8
Place	with LP	PHON	al / 10	al / 7		al / 9		al / 9	al / 11	al / 10	al / 16	al / 17	al / 8		al / 9
INTERM	without LP		3	3		4		2	2	2	2	2	2		3
INTERM	with LP		3	3		3		2	2	2	2	2	2		3
INTERP	without LP		3	2		4		4	3	4	4	4	4		4
INTERP	with LP		3	2		4		3	3	4	4	4	3		4
SEQM	without LP		3	3		3		3	3	6	3	3	3		3
SEQM	with LP		3	3		3		3	3	6	3	3	3		3
SEQP	without LP		2	3		4		2	2	2	2	2	2		2
SEQP	with LP		2	3		4		5	2	2	2	2	2		5
PMQ	without LP		1.0	0.8		1.0		1.2	1.0	1.3	1.2	1.2	1.2		1.0
PMQ	with LP		1.0	0.8		1.2		0.9	1.0	1.3	1.0	1.2	1.0		0.9
PMS	without LP		36	48		25		42	49	48	42	42	42		36
PMS	with LP		36	48		30		56	49	48	49	42	49		42
Nonant			MC	MC		SC		SC	SC	SC	MC	ME	SC		SC

Places, manners, and the areal phonology of Europe — 301

EDL (n = 115)	Nonant	PMS with LP	PMS without LP	PMQ with LP	PMQ without LP	SEQP with LP	SEQP without LP	SEQM with LP	SEQM without LP	INTERP with LP	INTERP without LP	INTERM with LP	INTERM without LP	Place with LP PHON	Place without LP PHON	Manner with LP PHON	Manner without LP PHON
Catalan	SW	49	42	1.0	1.2	5	2	6	6	4	4	3	3	al 8	al 8	fr 7	pl 6
Istro Romanian	SC	36	36	1.0	1.0	2	2	3	3	4	4	3	3	al 9	al 8	pl,fr 8	pl 8
Italian	SC	49	49	1.0	1.0	2	2	3	3	4	4	2	2	al 9	al 9	pl,fr 6	pl 6
Ladino	SC	42	42	1.2	1.2	2	2	3	3	4	4	2	2	al 9	al 6	fr 7	pl 6
Megleno-Romanian (Greece)	SC	42	36	0.9	1.0	5	2	3	3	4	4	3	3	al 9	al 8	fr 12	pl 8
Romanian	SC	49	49	1.0	1.0	2	2	3	3	3	3	2	2	al 8	al 7	fr 7	pl 6
Romanian (Megleno)	SC	42	36	0.9	1.0	5	2	3	3	4	4	3	3	al 9	al 8	fr 12	pl 8
Sardinian (Nuorese)	SC	63	56	0.8	0.9	6	4	3	3	4	4	2	2	al 8	al 8	pl 7	pl 7
Slavic																	
Belarusian	MC	49	49	1.0	1.0	2	2	3	3	4	4	2	2	al 15	al 14	fr 14	fr 13
Belarusian (Gervjaty)	MC	42	42	1.2	1.2	2	2	3	3	4	4	2	2	al 15	al 14	fr 13	fr 12
Bosnian	SC	56	49	0.9	1.0	3	3	3	3	4	4	2	2	al 8	al 8	pl,fr 6	pl 6
Bulgarian	SC	42	42	1.2	1.2	2	2	3	3	4	4	2	2	al 17	al 16	pl,fr 12	pl 12

EDL (n = 115)	Manner without LP		Manner with LP		Place without LP		Place with LP		INTERM		INTERP		SEQM		SEQP		PMQ		PMS		Nonant
		PHON		PHON		PHON		PHON	without LP	with LP	without LP	with LP	without LP	with LP	without LP	with LP	without LP	with LP	without LP	with LP	
Bulgarian (Dimitrovgrad)	pl	8	pl	8	al	10	al	11	2	2	4	4	3	3	2	2	1.2	1.2	42	42	SC
Croatian	pl, fr	6	fr	7	al	8	al	8	2	2	3	3	3	3	3	3	0.9	0.9	56	56	SC
Czech	pl, fr	7	pl, fr	8	al	9	al	8	2	2	3	3	3	3	2	2	1.0	1.0	49	49	MC
Czech (Moravian-Slovak)	pl, fr	7	pl, fr	8	al	9	al	9	2	2	3	3	3	3	2	2	1.0	1.0	49	49	MC
Kashubian	pl, fr	6	fr	7	al	10	al	10	2	2	4	4	3	3	2	2	1.0	1.0	49	49	MC
Macedonian	pl	8	pl	8	al	8	al	9	2	2	4	4	3	3	2	2	1.2	1.2	42	42	SC
Macedonian (Kostur-Korča)	pl	8	pl	8	al	8	al	9	2	2	4	4	3	3	3	3	1.2	1.2	42	42	SC
Polish	fr	8	fr	9	al	9	al	9	2	2	4	4	3	3	2	3	0.9	0.9	56	56	MC
Polish (Lazduny)	pl, fr	10	fr	11	al	15	al	15	2	2	4	4	3	3	2	2	1.2	1.2	42	42	MC
Russian	fr	13	fr	14	al	15	al	15	2	2	4	4	3	3	2	2	1.2	1.2	42	42	ME
Russian (Ostrovcy)	pl	12	pl, fr	12	al	15	al	15	2	2	4	4	3	3	2	2	1.2	1.2	42	42	MC
Russian (Permas)	fr	12	fr	13	al	15	al	15	2	2	4	4	3	3	2	2	1.2	1.2	42	42	ME
Serbian	pl, fr	6	fr	7	al	8	al	8	2	2	4	4	3	3	3	3	1.0	1.0	49	49	SC

Places, manners, and the areal phonology of Europe — **303**

EDL (n = 115)		Slavomolisano	Slovak	Slovene	Slovene (Resia)	Sorbian Lower	Sorbian Lower (Vetschau)	Sorbian Upper	Ukrainian	Ukrainian (Middle-Dnieper)	Ukrainian (North Hutsul)	Basque	Basque (Lekeitio)
Manner PHON	without LP (type)	fr	pl,fr	pl,fr	pl	pl,fr	pl	fr	fr	fr	fr	pl	pl
	without LP (n)	7	7	7	6	8	8	8	9	9	11	8	6
Manner PHON	with LP (type)	pl,fr	pl,fr	fr	pl	fr	pl,fr	fr	fr	fr	fr	pl	pl
	with LP (n)	8	8	7	8	10	8	10	10	10	12	8	6
Place PHON	without LP (type)	al	al	al	al	al	al	al	al	al	al	al	al
	without LP (n)	8	9	8	8	10	10	10	17	17	17	10	8
Place PHON	with LP (type)	al	al	al	al	al	al	al	al	al	al	al	al
	with LP (n)	9	9	8	9	10	10	10	18	18	18	10	8
INTERM	without LP	3	2	2	2	2	2	2	2	2	2	3	3
	with LP	3	2	2	2	2	2	2	2	2	2	3	3
INTERP	without LP	4	3	4	4	3	4	2	3	3	3	4	4
	with LP	4	3	4	4	3	4	2	3	3	3	4	4
SEQM	without LP	3	3	3	3	3	3	3	3	3	3	6	6
	with LP	3	3	3	3	3	3	3	3	3	3	6	6
SEQP	without LP	2	2	2	2	3	3	4	2	2	2	2	2
	with LP	2	2	2	2	3	3	4	2	2	2	2	2
PMQ	without LP	1.0	1.0	1.2	1.0	0.9	1.0	0.9	1.0	1.0	1.0	1.4	1.8
	with LP	1.0	1.0	1.2	1.0	0.8	0.9	0.8	1.0	1.0	1.0	1.2	1.2
PMS	without LP	36	49	42	49	56	49	56	49	49	49	35	28
	with LP	36	49	42	49	63	56	63	49	49	49	42	42
Nonant		SC	MC	SC	SC	MC	MC	MC	MC	ME	MC	SW	SW

Isolate: Basque, Basque (Lekeitio)

EDL (n = 115)		Basque (Zuberoa)	**Kartvelian** Georgian	Laz	**Mongolic** Kalmyk	**Nakh-Daghestanian** Chechen	Hinukh	Hunzib	Khinalug	Khwarshi	Tabasaran
Manner PHON	without LP	pl / 11	pl / 10	pl / 10	pl,fr / 6	pl,fr / 11	pl / 17	pl / 12	pl / 21	pl / 20	pl,fr / 17
Manner PHON	with LP	pl / 11	pl / 10	pl / 10	fr / 8	fr / 13	pl / 18	pl / 12	pl / 21	fr / 21	fr / 19
Place PHON	without LP	al / 10	al / 11	al / 11	al / 8	al / 11	al / 13	al / 13	al / 16	al / 20	al / 14
Place PHON	with LP	al / 13	al / 11	al / 11	al / 8	al / 13	al / 13	al / 13	al / 17	al / 20	al / 14
INTERM	without LP	3	3	2	2	2	1	1	2	1	2
INTERM	with LP	3	3	2	2	2	1	1	2	1	2
INTERP	without LP	3	3	2	4	2	2	2	2	2	2
INTERP	with LP	3	3	2	4	2	2	2	2	2	2
SEQM	without LP	3	3	3	3	3	6	6	2	7	3
SEQM	with LP	3	3	3	3	3	6	6	3	7	3
SEQP	without LP	2	2	3	2	6	4	3	3	4	3
SEQP	with LP	2	2	3	2	6	6	4	3	4	4
PMQ	without LP	1.0	1.0	0.9	1.2	0.6	1.0	1.1	0.7	1.1	0.8
PMQ	with LP	0.9	0.9	0.8	1.2	0.6	0.8	1.0	0.8	1.0	0.7
PMS	without LP	36	36	56	42	77	81	72	54	72	63
PMS	with LP	42	42	63	42	77	99	81	63	81	70
Nonant		SW	SE	SE	SE	SE	SE	SE	SE	SE	SE

Places, manners, and the areal phonology of Europe — **305**

EDL (n = 115)			Tsakhur	**Turkic** Azerbaijani	Bashkir	Chuvash	Crimean Tatar	Gagauz	Karachay-Balkar	Karaim (Trakai)	Kazakh	Kumyk	Noghay	Tatar
	Manner	without LP	pl	pl	fr	fr	pl	pl	pl	fr	pl	pl	pl	pl
	PHON		27	7	9	5	8	6	7	8	6	7	7	6
	Manner	with LP	pl	fr	fr	fr	pl, fr	fr	pl, fr	fr	fr	pl, fr	fr	fr
	PHON		27	9	11	8	11	8	7	9	9	9	10	12
	Place	without LP	al	al	al	al	al	al	al	al	al	al	al	al
	PHON		17	7	7	7	8	7	7	7	7	7	7	7
	Place	with LP	al	al	al	al	al	al	al	al	al	al	al	al
	PHON		17	8	8	10	13	8	8	7	8	8	8	8
	IN-TERM	without LP	2	2	2	3	2	2	2	2	2	3	2	3
		with LP	2	2	2	2	2	2	2	2	2	2	2	2
	IN-TERP	without LP	2	2	2	2	4	3	4	3	3	4	4	3	4
		with LP	2	2	2	2	4	2	3	3	3	3	4	2	2
	SEQM	without LP	3	3	3	3	3	3	3	3	3	3	3	3
		with LP	3	3	3	3	3	3	3	3	3	3	3	3
	SEQP	without LP	3	3	5	3	3	2	3	2	2	2	3	3
		with LP	3	3	5	3	3	2	3	2	2	2	3	4
	PMQ	without LP	0.8	1.0	0.6	1.0	1.0	1.2	1.0	1.0	1.0	1.2	1.0	0.9
		with LP	0.7	0.9	0.7	1.0	0.9	1.0	0.9	1.0	0.9	1.0	0.8	0.7
	PMS	without LP	63	49	60	49	49	42	49	49	36	42	49	42
		with LP	70	56	70	49	56	49	56	49	56	49	63	70
	Nonant		SE	SE	ME	ME	SE	SC	SE	MC	ME	SE	SE	ME

EDL (n = 115)		Turkish	Turkish (Trabzon)	**Uralic** Estonian	Finnish	Hungarian	Karelian (Archangelsk)	Karelian (Tichvin)	Karelian (Valdai)	Komi-Permyak (Jaźva)	Komi-Zyrian	Komi-Zyrian (Pečora)	Livonian
Manner	without LP	pl	fr	pl, ns, fr	pl	pl	pl, fr	pl	pl, fr	pl	pl	pl	pl
PHON		8	7	4	4	8	4	12	6	8	8	8	9
Manner	with LP	pl	fr	fr	pl	pl	pl, fr	pl, fr	fr	pl, fr	fr	fr	pl
PHON		8	8	8	6	8	4	12	8	8	9	9	9
Place	without LP	al	al	al	al	al	al	al	al	al, pa	al, pa	al, pa	al
PHON		8	6	9	6	8	9	14	7	7	7	7	11
Place	with LP	al	al	al	al	al	al	al	al	al	al	al	al
PHON		8	7	10	6	9	10	15	8	9	8	8	13
INTERM	without LP	2	2	3	3	2	2	2	2	2	2	2	3
	with LP	2	2	2	3	2	2	2	2	2	2	2	2
INTERP	without LP	4	3	3	3	3	3	3	3	4	4	4	3
	with LP	3	3	3	3	3	3	3	3	4	4	4	3
SEQM	without LP	3	3	3	3	3	3	3	3	3	3	3	3
	with LP	3	3	3	3	3	3	3	3	3	3	3	3
SEQP	without LP	2	2	2	2	2	2	2	2	3	3	3	2
	with LP	2	2	2	2	2	2	2	2	3	3	3	2
PMQ	without LP	1.2	1.0	1.0	1.0	1.0	1.0	1.0	1.0	1.0	1.0	1.0	0.9
	with LP	1.0	1.0	1.0	0.8	1.0	1.0	1.0	1.0	1.0	1.0	1.0	1.0
PMS	without LP	42	49	36	36	49	49	49	49	49	49	49	42
	with LP	49	49	49	48	49	49	49	49	49	49	49	49
Nonant		SC	SE	MC	NC	MC	NE	ME	ME	ME	NE	NE	MC

		Mari (Hill)	Mordvin (Erzya)	Mordvin (Moksha)	Saami (Kildin)	Udmurt	Veps	Votic
Manner PHON	without LP	fr / 7	pl,fr / 8	fr / 10	fr / 12	pl / 8	pl,fr / 10	pl / 5
Manner PHON	with LP	fr / 9	fr / 10	fr / 11	fr / 16	pl,fr / 8	fr / 12	fr / 8
Place PHON	without LP	al / 7	al / 16	al / 20	al / 21	al / 7	al / 15	al / 8
Place PHON	with LP	al / 7	al / 16	al / 20	al / 23	al / 8	al / 15	al / 8
INTERM	without LP	2	3	3	2	2	2	2
INTERM	with LP	2	3	3	2	2	2	2
INTERP	without LP	4	4	4	3	4	3	3
INTERP	with LP	4	4	4	3	4	3	3
SEQM	without LP	3	3	3	3	3	3	3
SEQM	with LP	3	3	3	3	3	3	3
SEQP	without LP	5	2	2	2	3	2	2
SEQP	with LP	5	2	2	2	3	2	2
PMQ	without LP	1.0	1.0	1.0	1.0	1.0	1.0	1.0
PMQ	with LP	1.0	1.0	1.0	1.0	1.0	1.0	1.0
PMS	without LP	49	36	36	49	49	49	49
PMS	with LP	49	36	36	49	49	49	49
Nonant		ME	ME	ME	NE	ME	ME	MC

EDL (n = 115)

Table III: Sample languages and sources.

Language – nonant, phylum (branch)	Source
Abaza – SE, Abkhaz-Adyge (Abkhaz-Abaza)	Lomtatidze, Ketevan & Rauf Klychev. 1989. Abaza. In B. George Hewitt (ed.), *The indigenous languages of the Caucasus. Volume 2: The Northwest Caucasian languages*, 89–154. Delmar & New York: Caravan Books.
Abkhaz – SE, Abkhaz-Adyge (Abkhaz-Abaza)	Hewitt, George B. 1989. Abkhaz. In George B. Hewitt (ed.), *The indigenous languages of the Caucasus. Vol. 2: The North West Caucasian languages*, 39–88. Delmar & New York: Caravan Books.
Adyghe – SE, Abkhaz-Adyge (Circassian)	Paris, Catherine. 1989. West Circassian. In B. George Hewitt (ed.), *The indigenous languages of the Caucasus. Vol. 2: The North West Caucasian languages*, 155–260. Delmar & New York: Caravan Books.
Aghul – SE, Nakh-Daghestanian (Lezgic)	Magometov, Aleksandr Amarovič. 1970. *Agul'skij jazyk: Issledovanie i teksty*. Tbilisi: Mecniereba.
Akhvakh – SE, Nakh-Daghestanian (Andic)	Magomedbekova, Zagidat Magomedovna. 1967. *Axvaxskij jazyk. Grammatičeskij analiz, teksty, slovar'*. Tbilisi: Mecniereba.
Albanian – SC, Indo-European (Albanian)	Buchholz, Oda & Wilfried Fiedler. 1987. *Albanische Grammatik*. Leipzig: Verlag Enzyklopädie.
Albanian (Mandrica) – SC, Indo-European (Albanian)	Sokolova, Bojka Borisova. 1983. *Die albanische Mundart von Mandrica*. Wiesbaden: Harrassowitz.
Albanian (Salamis) – SC, Indo-European (Albanian)	Haebler, Claus. 1965. *Grammatik der albanischen Mundart von Salamis*. Wiesbaden: Harrassowitz.
Andi – SE, Nakh-Daghestanian (Andic)	Gudava, Togo. 1964. *Konsonantizm andijskix jasykov: Istoričesko-sravnitel'nyi analiz*. Tbilisi: Izdatel'stvo Akademii Nauk gruzinskoj SSR.

Language – nonant, phylum (branch)	Source
Arabic (Çukurova) – SE, Afro-Asiatic (Semitic)	Procházka, Stephan. 2002. *Die arabischen Dialekte der Çukurova (Südtürkei)*. Wiesbaden: Harrassowitz.
Arabic (Cypriot/Kormakiti) – SE, Afro-Asiatic (Semitic)	Borg, Alexander. 1985. *Cypriot Arabic*. Stuttgart & Wiesbaden: Steiner.
Aramaic (Cudi) – SE, Afro-Asiatic (Semitic)	Sinha, Jasmin. 2000. *Der neuostaramäische Dialekt von Bespən (Provinz Mardin, Südosttürkei). Eine grammatische Darstellung*. Wiesbaden: Harrassowitz.
Aramaic (Hertevin) – SE, Afro-Asiatic (Semitic)	Jastrow, Otto. 1988. *Der neuaramäische Dialekt von Hertevin (Provinz Siirt)*. Wiesbaden: Harrassowitz.
Archi – SE, Nakh-Daghestanian (Lezgic)	Chumakina, Marina, Oliver Bond & Greville G. Corbett. 2016. Essentials of Archi grammar. In Oliver Bond, Greville G. Corbett, Marina Chumakina & Dunstan Brown (eds.), *Archi: Complexities of agreement in cross-theoretical perspective*, 17–42. Oxford: Oxford University Press.
Armenian (Eastern) – SE, Indo-European (Armenian)	Dum-Tragut, Jasmine. 2009. *Armenian*. Amsterdam & Philadelphia: Benjamins.
Armenian (Western) – SE, Indo-European (Armenian)	Vaux, Bert. 1998. *The phonology of Armenian*. Oxford: Clarendon.
Aromanian – SC, Indo-European (Romance)	Kramer, Johannes. 1989. Rumänisch: Areallinguistik II. Aromunisch. Les aires linguistiques II. Aroumain. In Günter Holtus, Michael Metzeltin & Christian Schmitt (eds.), *Lexikon der romanistischen Linguistik. Vol. 3. Die einzelnen romanischen Sprachen und Sprachgebiete von der Renaissance bis zur Gegenwart: Rumänisch, Dalmatisch / Istroromanisch, Friaulisch, Ladinisch, Bündnerromanisch*, 423–435. Tübingen: Max Niemeyer.
Asturian – SW, Indo-European (Romance)	Academia de la Llingua Asturiana. 1999. *Gramática de la Llingua Asturiana*. Uviéu: Academia de la Llingua Asturiana.
Avar – SE, Nakh-Daghestanian (Avar)	Charachidzé, Georges. 1981. *Grammaire de la langue avar. Langue du Caucase Nord-Est*. Saint-Sulpice de Favières: Jean-Favard.
Azerbaijani – SE, Turkic (Oghuz)	Širalijev, M. Š. & E. V. Sevortjan. 1971. *Grammatika azerbajdžanskogo jazyka. Fonetika, morfologija, sistaksis*. Baku: ĖLM.

Language – nonant, phylum (branch)	Source
Bagvalal – SE, Nakh-Daghestanian (Andic)	Gudava, Togo. 1964. *Konsonantizm andijskix jasykov: Istoričesko-sravnitel'nyi analiz.* Tbilisi: Izdatel'stvo Akademii Nauk gruzinskoj SSR.
Bashkir – ME, Turkic (Kipchak)	Juldašev, A. A. 1981. *Grammatika sovremennogo baškirskogo literaturnogo jazyka.* Moskva: Nauka.
Basque – SW, Isolate (Isolate)	Hualde, José Ignacio & Jon Ortiz de Urbina. 2003. *A Grammar of Basque.* Berlin & New York: De Gruyter Mouton.
Basque (Lekeitio) – SW, Isolate (Isolate)	Hualde, José Ignacio, Gorka Elordieta & Arantzazu Elordieta. 1994. *The Basque dialect of Lekeitio.* Bilbo, Donostia: Universidad del País Vasco.
Basque (Zuberoa) – SW, Isolate (Isolate)	Hualde, José Ignacio & Jon Ortiz de Urbina. 2003. *A grammar of Basque.* Berlin & New York: De Gruyter Mouton.
Belarusian – MC, Indo-European (Slavic)	Burlyka, I. R. & A. L. Padlužny. 1989. *Fanetyka belaruskaj litaraturnaj movy.* Minsk: Navuka i tèchnika.
Belarusian (Gervjaty) – MC, Indo-European (Slavic)	Sudnik, T. M. 1975. *Dialekty litovsko-slavjanskogo pograničʼja: očerki fonologičeskix sistem.* Moskva: Nauka.
Bezhta (Tlyadal) – SE, Nakh-Daghestanian (Tsezic)	Bokarev, E. A. 1967. Bežitinskij jazyk. In E. A. Bokarev & K. V. Lomtatidze (eds.), *Iberijsko-kavkazskie jazyki,* 66–109. Moskva: Nauka.
Bosnian – SC, Indo-European (Slavic)	Jahić, Dževad, Senahid Halilović & Ismail Palić. 2000. *Gramatika bosanskoga jezika.* Zenica: Dom Štampe.
Botlikh – SE, Nakh-Daghestanian (Andic)	Gudava, Togo. 1964. *Konsonantizm andijskix jasykov: Istoričesko-sravnitel'nyi analiz.* Tbilisi: Izdatel'stvo Akademii Nauk gruzinskoj SSR.
Breton – MW, Indo-European (Celtic)	Ternes, Elmar. 1992. The Breton language. In D. MacAulay (ed.), *The Celtic Languages,* 371–452. Cambridge: Cambridge University Press.
Breton (Léonais) – MW, Indo-European (Celtic)	Jackson, Kenneth Hurlstone. 1967. *A historical phonology of Breton.* Dublin: The Dublin Institute for Advanced Studies.

Language – nonant, phylum (branch)	Source
Breton (Trégorrois) – MW, Indo-European (Celtic)	Jackson, Kenneth Hurlstone. 1967. *A historical phonology of Breton*. Dublin: The Dublin Institute for Advanced Studies.
Breton (Vannetais) – MW, Indo-European (Celtic)	Jackson, Kenneth Hurlstone. 1967. *A historical phonology of Breton*. Dublin: The Dublin Institute for Advanced Studies.
Budukh – SE, Nakh-Daghestanian (Lezgic)	Alekseev, Mikhail E. 1994. Budukh. In Rieke Smeets (ed.), *The indigenous languages of the Caucasus. Volume 4: North East Caucasian languages part 2*, 259–296. Delmar & New York: Caravan.
Bulgarian – SC, Indo-European (Slavic)	Feuillet, Jack. 1996. *Grammaire synchronique du bulgare*. Paris: Institut d'études slaves.
Bulgarian (Dimitrovgrad) – SC, Indo-European (Slavic)	Bozkov, Rangel. 1984. *Dimitrovgradskijat (caribrodskijat) govor*. Sofija: Izdatelstvo na Bălgarskata Akademija na naukite.
Catalan – SW, Indo-European (Romance)	Hualde, José Ignacio. 1992. *Catalan*. London & New York: Routledge.
Chamalal – SE, Nakh-Daghestanian (Andic)	Gudava, Togo. 1964. *Konsonantizm andijskix jasykov: Istoričesko-sravnitel'nyi analiz*. Tbilisi: Izdatel'stvo Akademii Nauk gruzinskoj SSR.
Chechen – SE, Nakh-Daghestanian (Nakh)	Dešeriev, Junus Dešerievič. 1960. *Sovremennyj čečenskij literaturnyi jazyk. Čast' 1. Fonetika*. Groznyj: Čečeno-ingusškij NII istorii, jazyka i literatury.
Chuvash – ME, Turkic (Bolgar)	Krueger, John R. 1961. *Chuvash manual: Introduction, grammar, reader, and vocabulary*. The Hague: Mouton & Co.
Cornish – MW, Indo-European (Celtic)	Wmffre, Iwan. 1998. *Late Cornish*. München & Newcastle: Lincom Europa.
Corsican – SC, Indo-European (Romance)	Dalbera-Stefanaggi, Marie José. 1978. *Langue corse. Une approche linguistique*. Paris: Klincksieck.
Crimean Tatar – SE, Turkic (Kipchak)	Kavitskaya, Darya. 2010. *Crimean Tatar*. München: LINCOM EUROPA.
Croatian – SC, Indo-European (Slavic)	Barić, Eugenija. 2005. *Hrvatska gramatika*. Zagreb: Školska Knjiga.
Croatian (Burgenland) – MC, Indo-European (Slavic)	Benčić, Nikola. 2003. *Gramatika gradišćanskohrvatskoga jezika*. Željezno: Znanstveni Inst.

Language – nonant, phylum (branch)	Source
Czech – MC, Indo-European (Slavic)	Short, David. 1993. Czech. In Bernard Comrie & Greville G. Corbett (eds.), *The Slavonic languages*, 455–532. London & New York: Routledge.
Czech (Moravian-Slovak) – MC, Indo-European (Slavic)	Skulina, Josef. 1964. *Severní pomezí moravskoslovenských nářečí*. Praha: Naklad. Československé Akad. Věd.
Danish – MC, Indo-European (Germanic)	Basbøll, Hans. 2005. *The phonology of Danish*. Oxford: Oxford University Press.
Danish (Brøndum) – MC, Indo-European (Germanic)	Ejskjær, Inger. 1954. *Brøndum-Mälet. Lydsystes met i en Sallingdialekt*. København: Schulz.
Dargwa (Icari) – SE, Nakh-Daghestanian (Dargwic)	Sumbatova, Nina R. & Rasul O. Mutalov. 2003. *A grammar of Icari Dargwa*. München: LINCOM.
Dutch – MC, Indo-European (Germanic)	Booij, Geert. 2012. *The phonology of Dutch*. Oxford: Oxford University Press.
Dutch (Drente) – MC, Indo-European (Germanic)	Kocks, Geert Hendrik. 1970. *Die Dialekte von Südostdrente und anliegenden Gebieten: Eine strukturelle Untersuchung*. Groningen: Rijksuniversiteit te Groningen.
Dutch (Flemish Oostduinkerke) – MW, Indo-European (Germanic)	Sercu, Aurel. 1972. *Het dialect van Oostduinkerke en omgeving*. Gent: Koninklijke Vlaamse Academie voor Taal- en Letterkunde.
English – MW, Indo-European (Germanic)	Gramley, Stephan & Michael Pätzold. 2004. *A survey of modern English*. London & New York: Routledge.
English (Bolton Area) – MW, Indo-European (Germanic)	Shorrocks, Graham. 1998. *A grammar of the dialect of the Bolton area*. Frankfurt am Main: Lang.
English (Cannock) – MW, Indo-European (Germanic)	Heath, Christopher D. 1980. *The pronunciation of English in Cannock, Staffordshire. A socio-linguistic survey of an urban speech-community*. Oxford: Blackwell.
English (Cockney) – MW, Indo-European (Germanic)	Sivertsen, Eva. 1960. *Cockney phonology*. Oslo & New York: University Press; Humanities Press.
Estonian – MC, Uralic (Finnic)	Hasselblatt, Cornelius. 2001. *Grammatisches Wörterbuch des Estnischen*. Wiesbaden: Harrassowitz.

Language – nonant, phylum (branch)	Source
Estonian (Rõngu) – MC, Uralic (Finnic)	Hint, Mati & Heikki Paunonen. 1984. On the phonology of the Southern Estonian Tartu Dialect. In Péter Hajdú & László Honti (eds.), *Studien zur phonologischen Beschreibung uralischer Sprachen*, 275–284. Budapest: Akadémiai Kiádó.
Faroese – NW, Indo-European (Germanic)	Thráinsson, Höskuldur, Hjalmar P. Petersen, Jógvan í Lon Jacobsen & Zakaris Svabo Hansen. 2004. *Faroese. An overview and reference grammar*. Tórshavn: Føroya Fróðskaparfelag.
Finnish – NC, Uralic (Finnic)	Fromm, Hans. 1982. *Finnische Grammatik*. Heidelberg: Winter.
Franco-Provençal (Faetar) – SC, Indo-European (Romance)	Kattenbusch, Dieter. 1982. *Das Frankoprovenzalische in Süditalien*. Tübingen & Münster: Narr.
French – MW, Indo-European (Romance)	Meisenburg, Trudel & Maria Selig. 2006. *Phonetik und Phonologie des Französischen*. Stuttgart: Klett.
Frisian Eastern (Seeltersk) – MC, Indo-European (Germanic)	Fort, Marron C. 2001. Das Saterfriesische. In Horst Haider Munske (ed.), *Handbuch des Friesischen*, 409–422. Tübingen: Niemeyer.
Frisian Northern (Weesdring) – **MC, Indo-European (Germanic)**	Walker, Alastair & Ommo Wilts. 2001. Das Saterfriesische. In Horst Haider Munske (ed.), *Handbuch des Friesischen*, 284–304. Tübingen: Niemeyer.
Frisian Western – MW, Indo-European (Germanic)	Hoekstra, Jarich F. 2001. Standard West Frisian. In Horst Haider Munske (ed.), *Handbuch des Friesischen*, 83–98. Tübingen: Niemeyer.
Friulian (Udine) – SC, Indo-European (Romance)	Haiman, John & Paola Benincà. 1992. *The Rheato-Romance languages*. London & New York: Routledge.
Gagauz – SC, Turkic (Oghuz)	Pokrovskaja, L. A. 1964. *Grammatika gagauzskogo jazyka: Fonetika i morfologija*. Moskva: Nauka.
Galician – SW, Indo-European (Romance)	Carballo Calero, Ricardo. 1979. *Gramática elemental del Gellego Común*. Vigo: Galaxia.
Georgian – SE, Kartvelian (Georgic)	Hewitt, George B. 1995. *Georgian. A structural reference grammar*. Amsterdam & Philadelphia: J. Benjamins Pub. Co.
German – MC, Indo-European (Germanic)	Wiese, Richard. 1996. *The phonology of German*. Oxford: Oxford University Press.

Language – nonant, phylum (branch)	Source
German (Brig) – SC, Indo-European (Germanic)	Werlen, Iwar. 1976. *Zur Phonologie der Mundart von Brig*. Bern: Institut für Sprachwissenschaft der Universität.
German (Ladelund Danish) – MC, Indo-European (Germanic)	Willkommen, Dirk. 1977. *Ladelunder Dänisch: Phonologie eines Schleswiger Dialekts*. Kiel: Universität Kiel.
German (urban Kölsch) – MC, Indo-European (Germanic)	Heike, Georg. 1964. *Zur Phonologie der Stadtkölner Mundart*. Marburg & Bonn: Elwert.
Godoberi – SE, Nakh-Daghestanian (Andic)	Saidova, P. A. 2004. Ghodoberi. In Michael Job (ed.), *The indigenous languages of the Caucasus. Vol. 3: The North East Caucasian languages*. Part 1, 69–112. Ann Arbor: Caravan.
Greek – SC, Indo-European (Greek)	Holton, David, Peter Mackridge & Irene Philippaki-Warburton. 2012. *Greek: A comprehensive grammar*. London: Routledge.
Greek (Italo-Greek Sternatia) – SC, Indo-European (Greek)	Italia, Gemma Gemma & Georgia Lambroyorgu. 2001. *Grammatica del dialetto greco di Sternatia (Grecia Salentina)*. Galatina: Congedo editore.
Hinukh – SE, Nakh-Daghestanian (Tsezic)	Forker, Diana. 2013. *A grammar of Hinuq*. Berlin & Boston: De Gruyter Mouton.
Hungarian – MC, Uralic (Hungarian)	Kenesei, István, Robert Michael Vago & Anna Fenyvesi. 1998. *Hungarian*. London: Routledge.
Hunzib – SE, Nakh-Daghestanian (Tsezic)	van den Berg, Helma. 1995. *A grammar of Hunzib (with texts and lexicon)*. München & Newcastle: Lincom Europa.
Icelandic – NW, Indo-European (Germanic)	Thráinsson, Höskuldur. 1994. Icelandic. In Ekkehard König & Johan van der Auwera (eds.), *The Germanic languages*, 142–189. London: Routledge.
Ingush – SE, Nakh-Daghestanian (Nakh)	Nichols, Johanna. 1994. Ingush. In Rieke Smeets (ed.), *The indigenous languages of the Caucasus. Volume 4: North East Caucasian languages part 2*, 79–146. Delmar & New York: Caravan.
Irish – MW, Indo-European (Celtic)	Ó Dochartaigh, Cathair. 1992. The Irish language. In D. MacAulay (ed.), *The Celtic languages*, 11–99. Cambridge: CUP.

Language – nonant, phylum (branch)	Source
Irish (Northern) – MW, Indo-European (Celtic)	Ní Chasaide, Ailbhe. 1999. Irish. In International Phonetic Association (ed.), *Handbook of the International Phonetic Association: A guide to the use of the international phonetic alphabet*. 111–116. Cambridge: Cambridge University Press.
Irish (Southern) – MW, Indo-European (Celtic)	Ó Cuív, Brian. 1975. *The Irish of West Muskerry, Co. Cork*. Dublin: Dublin Institute for Advanced Studies.
Istriot – SC, Indo-European (Romance)	Cernecca, Domenico. 1967. Analisi fonematica del dialetto di Valle d'Istria. In *Studia Romanica et Anglica Zagrabiensia: Revue publiée par les Sections romane, italienne et anglaise de la Faculté des Lettres de l'Université de Zagreb* 23, 137–160.
Istro Romanian – SC, Indo-European (Romance)	Dahmen, Wolfgang. 1989. Rumänisch: Areallinguistik IV. Istrorumänisch. In Günter Holtus, Michael Metzeltin & Christian Schmitt (eds.), *Lexikon der romanistischen Linguistik. Vol. 3. Die einzelnen romanischen Sprachen und Sprachgebiete von der Renaissance bis zur Gegenwart: Rumänisch, Dalmatisch / Istroromanisch, Friaulisch, Ladinisch, Bündnerromanisch*. 448–460. Tübingen: Max Niemeyer.
Italian – SC, Indo-European (Romance)	Dardano, Maurizio & Pietro Trifone. 2008. *La lingua italiana: morfologia, sintassi, fonologia, formazione delle parole, lessico, nozioni di linguistica e sociolinguistica*. Bologna: Zanichelli.
Italian (Genovese) – SC, Indo-European (Romance)	Toso, Fiorenzo. 1997. *Grammatica del genovese. Varietà urbana e di koinè*. Recco: Le Mani.
Kabardian – SE, Abkhaz-Adyge (Circassian)	Colarusso, John. 1989. East Circassian (Kabardian dialect). In George B. Hewitt (ed.), *The indigenous languages of the Caucasus. Vol. 2: The North West Caucasian languages*, 261–355. Delmar & New York: Caravan Books.
Kalmyk – SE, Mongolic (Oirat)	Street, John C. 1959. *Structure of Kalmyk*. American Council of Learned Societies. Research and Studies in Uralic and Altaic Languages. Project No. 1.
Karachay-Balkar – SE, Turkic (Kipchak)	Seegmiller, Steve. 1996. *Karachay*. Unterschleissheim: Lincom Europa.

Language – nonant, phylum (branch)	Source
Karaim (Eastern) – SE, Turkic (Kipchak)	Musaev, K. M. 1997. *Karaimskij jazyk*. In Ėdgem R. Tenišev & Viktorija Nikolaevna Jarceva (eds.), *Jazyki mira: Tjurkskie jazyki*, 254–264. Moskva: Indrik.
Karaim (Galits) – MC, Turkic (Kipchak)	Musaev, K. M. 1997. *Karaimskij jazyk*. In Ėdgem R. Tenišev & Viktorija Nikolaevna Jarceva (eds.), *Jazyki mira: Tjurkskie jazyki*, 254–264. Moskva: Indrik.
Karaim (Trakai) – MC, Turkic (Kipchak)	Musaev, K. M. 1997. *Karaimskij jazyk*. In Ėdgem R. Tenišev & Viktorija Nikolaevna Jarceva (eds.), *Jazyki mira: Tjurkskie jazyki*, 254–264. Moskva: Indrik.
Karata – SE, Nakh-Daghestanian (Andic)	Gudava, Togo. 1964. *Konsonantizm andijskix jasykov: Istoričesko-sravnitel'nyi analiz*. Tbilisi: Izdatel'stvo Akademii Nauk gruzinskoj SSR.
Karelian (Archangelsk) – NE, Uralic (Finnic)	Leskinen, Heikki. 1984. Über die Phonemsysteme der karelischen Sprache. In Péter Hajdú & László Honti (eds.), *Studien zur phonologischen Beschreibung uralischer Sprachen*, 247–257. Budapest: Akadémiai Kiadó.
Karelian (Tichvin) – ME, Uralic (Finnic)	Rjagoev, Vladimir. 1977. *Tixvinskij govor karel'skogo jazyka*. Leningrad: Nauka.
Karelian (Valdai) – ME, Uralic (Finnic)	Palmeos, Pauline Jur'evna. 1962. *Karjala valdai murrak*. Tallinn.
Kashubian – MC, Indo-European (Slavic)	Stone, Gerald. 1993. Cassubian. In Bernard Comrie & Greville G. Corbett (eds.), *The Slavonic languages*, 759–794. London & New York: Routledge.
Kazakh – ME, Turkic (Kipchak)	Muhamedowa, Raihan. 2016. *Kazakh. A comprehensive grammar*. London & New York: Routledge.
Khinalug – SE, Nakh-Daghestanian (Dargwic)	Dešeriev, Junus Dešerievič. 1959. *Grammatika xinalugskogo jazyka*. Moskva: Izdatel'stvo Akademii Nauk SSSR.
Khwarshi – SE, Nakh-Daghestanian (Tsezic)	Khalilova, Zaira. 2009. *A grammar of Khwarshi*. Utrecht: LOT.
Komi-Permyak (Jaźva) – ME, Uralic (Permian)	Lytkin, Vasilij Il'ič. 1961. *Komi-jaz'vinskij dialekt*. Moskva: Izdatel'stvo Akademii Nauk SSSR.
Komi-Zyrian – NE, Uralic (Permian)	Rédei, Károly. 1978. *Syrjänische Chrestomathie*. Wien: Verband der wissenschaftlichen Gesellschaften Österreichs.

Language – nonant, phylum (branch)	Source
Komi-Zyrian (Pečora) – NE, Uralic (Permian)	Saxarova, Marfa Aleksandrovna, Nikolaj Nikitič Sel'kov & Nina Andreevna Kolegova. 1976. *Pečorskij dialekt komi jazyka*. Syktyvkar: Komi Knižnoe Izdatel'stvo.
Komi-Zyrian (Udora) – NE, Uralic (Permian)	Sorvačeva, Valentina Aleksandrovna & Ljucija Michajlovna Beznosikova. 1990. *Udorskij dialekt komi jazyka*. Moskva: Nauka.
Kryts – SE, Nakh-Daghestanian (Lezgic)	Saadiev, Sh. M. 1994. Kryts. In Rieke Smeets (ed.), *The indigenous languages of the Caucasus. Volume 4: North East Caucasian languages part 2*, 407–446. Delmar & New York: Caravan.
Kryts (Alyk) – SE, Nakh-Daghestanian (Lezgic)	Authier, Gilles. 2009. *Grammaire kryz (langue caucasique d'Azerbaïdjan, dialecte d'Alik)*. Leuven & Paris: Peeters.
Kumyk – SE, Turkic (Kipchak)	Abdullaeva, A. Z., N. É. Gadžiaxmedov, K. S. Kadyradžiev, I. A. Kerimov, N. X. Ol'mesov & D. M. Xangišiev. 2014. *Sovremennyj kumykskij jazyk*. Maxačkala: IjaLI DNC RAN.
Kurmanji – SE, Indo-European (Indo-Iranian)	Aygen, Gülşat. 2007. *Kurmanjî Kurdish*. München & Newcastle: Lincom Europa.
Ladin – MC, Indo-European (Romance)	Valentini, Erwin. 2001. *Gramatica dl ladin standard*. Urtijei: SPELL.
Ladino – SC, Indo-European (Romance)	Hetzer, Armin. 2001. *Sephardisch. Judeo-Español, Djudezmo. Einführung in die Umgangssprache der südosteuropäischen Juden*. Wiesbaden: Harrassowitz.
Lak – SE, Nakh-Daghestanian (Lak)	Anderson, Gregory D. S. 1997. Lak phonology. In Alan S. Kaye (ed.), *Phonologies of Asia and Africa. Vol. 2*, 973–997. Winona Lake, Indiana: Eisenbrauns.
Latgalian – MC, Indo-European (Baltic)	Nau, Nicole. 2011. *A short grammar of Latgalian*. München: Lincom Europa.
Latvian – MC, Indo-European (Baltic)	Muižniece, Lalita. 2002. *Latviešu valodas praktiskā fonoloģija*. Rīga: Rasa ABC.
Latvian (Skrunda) – MC, Indo-European (Baltic)	Pīrāga, Mirdza. 2006. *Skrundas izloksnes apraksts*. Liepāja: LiePA.
Laz – SE, Kartvelian (Zan)	Holisky, Dee Ann. 1991. Laz. In Alice C. Harris (ed.), *The indigenous languages of the Caucasus. Vol. 1: The Kartvelian languages*, 395–472. Delmar & New York: Caravan Books.

Language – nonant, phylum (branch)	Source
Laz (Mutafi Turkey) – SE, Kartvelian (Zan)	Stathi, Ekaterini. 1995. Phonetik und Phonologie des Lazischen. In Silvia Kutscher (ed.), *Das Mutafi-Lazische*, 7–20. Köln: Institut für Sprachwissenschaft der Universität zu Köln.
Lezgian – SE, Nakh-Daghestanian (Lezgic)	Haspelmath, Martin. 1993. *A grammar of Lezgian*. Berlin & New York: De Gruyter Mouton.
Lithuanian – MC, Indo-European (Baltic)	Ulvydas, Kazys. 1965. *Lietuvių kalbos gramatika: Fonetika ir morfologija*. Vilnius: Mintis.
Lithuanian (Dieveniškės) – MC, Indo-European (Baltic)	Sudnik, T. M. 1975. *Dialekty litovsko-slavjanskogo pograničʼja: Očerki fonologičeskix sistem*. Moskva: Nauka.
Livonian – MC, Uralic (Finnic)	Moseley, Christopher. 2002. *Livonian*. München: LINCOM EUROPA.
Low German (East Frisian) – MC, Indo-European (Germanic)	Reershemius, Gertrud. 2004. *Niederdeutsch in Ostfriesland. Zwischen Sprachkontakt, Sprachwandel und Sprachwechsel*. Wiesbaden: Steiner.
Low German (North Saxon) – MC, Indo-European (Germanic)	Keller, Rudolf E. 1961. *German dialects: Phonology and morphology*. Manchester: Manchester University Press.
Low German (Westphalian) – MC, Indo-European (Germanic)	Keller, Rudolf E. 1961. *German dialects: Phonology and morphology*. Manchester: Manchester University Press.
Luxembourgish – MC, Indo-European (Germanic)	Keller, Rudolf E. 1961. *German dialects: Phonology and morphology*. Manchester: Manchester University Press.
Macedonian – SC, Indo-European (Slavic)	Lunt, Horace Gray, Victor A. Friedman & Ljudmil Jordanov Spasov 2003. *Dve amerikanski gramatiki na sovremeniot makedonski standarden jazik*. Skopje: Makedonska Akademija na Naukite i Umetnostite.
Macedonian (Kostur-Korča) – SC, Indo-European (Slavic)	Šklifov, Blagoj. 1973. *Kosturskijat t govor. Prinos kăm proučvaneto na jugo zapadnite bălgarski govori*. Sofija: Izdatelstvo na Bălgarskata Akademija na naukite.
Maltese – SC, Afro-Asiatic (Semitic)	Borg, Albert & Marie Azzopardi-Alexander. 1997. *Maltese*. London & New York: Routledge.
Manx – MW, Indo-European (Celtic)	Broderick, George. 1986. *A handbook of late spoken Manx. Vol. 3: Phonology*. Tübingen: Niemeyer.

Language – nonant, phylum (branch)	Source
Mari (Hill) – ME, Uralic (Mari)	Alhoniemi, Alho. 1993. *Grammatik des Tschermissischen (Mari)*. Hamburg: Buske.
Mari (Meadow) – ME, Uralic (Mari)	Alhoniemi, Alho. 1993. *Grammatik des Tschermissischen (Mari)*. Hamburg: Buske.
Megleno Romanian (Greece) – SC, Indo-European (Romance)	Dahmen, Wolfgang. 1989. Rumänisch: Areallinguistik III. Meglenorumänisch. Les aires linguistiques III. Meglonoroumain. In Günter Holtus, Michael Metzeltin & Christian Schmitt (eds.), *Lexikon der romanistischen Linguistik. Vol. 3. Die einzelnen romanischen Sprachen und Sprachgebiete von der Renaissance bis zur Gegenwart: Rumänisch, Dalmatisch / Istroromanisch, Friaulisch, Ladinisch, Bündnerromanisch*, 436–447. Tübingen: Max Niemeyer.
Mingrelian – SE, Kartvelian (Zan)	Harris, Alice C. 1991. Mingrelian. In Alice Harris (ed.), *The indigenous languages of the Caucasus. Vol. 1: The Kartvelian languages*, 313–394. Delmar & NY: Caravan Books.
Mordvin (Erzya) – ME, Uralic (Mordvin)	Keresztes, László. 1990. *Chrestomathia Morduinica*. Budapest: Tankönyvkiadó.
Mordvin (Moksha) – ME, Uralic (Mordvin)	Keresztes, László. 1990. *Chrestomathia Morduinica*. Budapest: Tankönyvkiadó.
Nenets (Tundra) – NE, Uralic (Samoyedic)	Nikolaeva, Irina. 2014. *A grammar of Tundra Nenets*. Berlin & Boston: De Gruyter Mouton.
Noghay – SE, Turkic (Kipchak)	Csató, Éva Ágnes & Birsel Karakoç. 1998. Noghay. In Lars Johanson & Éva Csató-Johanson (eds.), *The Turkic languages*, 333–343. London & New York: Routledge.
Norman (Jersey) – MW, Indo-European (Romance)	Liddicoat, Anthony. 1994. *A grammar of the Norman French of the Channel Islands*. Berlin & New York: De Gruyter Mouton.
Norwegian (Central East Tromsø) – NC, Indo-European (Germanic)	Nordli, Ingrid C. 2008. Tromsø. In Olaf Husby & Tore Høyte (eds.), *An introduction to Norwegian dialects*, 25–38. Trondheim: Tapir Academic Press.
Norwegian (Nynorsk) – NC, Indo-European (Germanic)	Beito, Olav T. 1970. *Nynorsk grammatikk. Lyd- og ordlære*. Oslo: Det Norske Samlaget.
Norwegian (Østnorsk) – MC, Indo-European (Germanic)	Kristoffersen, Gjert. 2000. *The phonology of Norwegian*. Oxford: Oxford University Press.
Occitan (Aranese) – SW, Indo-European (Romance)	Carrera, Aitor. 2006. *Gramatica aranesa*. Lhèida: Pagès editors.

Language – nonant, phylum (branch)	Source
Occitan (Gascon) – SW, Indo-European (Romance)	Romieu, Maurice & André Bianchi. 2005. *Gramatica de l'occitan gascon contemporanèu*. Pessac: Presses Universitaires de Bordeaux.
Occitan (Languedocien) – SW, Indo-European (Romance)	Romieu, Maurice & André Bianchi. 2005. *Gramatica de l'occitan gascon contemporanèu*. Pessac: Presses Universitaires de Bordeaux.
Ossetic – SE, Indo-European (Indo-Iranian)	Abaev, Vasilij I. 1964. *A grammatical sketch of Ossetic*. Bloomington: Indiana University.
Polish – MC, Indo-European (Slavic)	Strutyński, Janusz. 1997. *Gramatyka polska*. Kraków: Wydawnictwo Tomasz Strutyński.
Polish (Lazduny) – MC, Indo-European (Slavic)	Sudnik, T. M. 1975. *Dialekty litovsko-slavjanskogo pograničʹja: Očerki fonologičeskix sistem*. Moskva: Nauka.
Portuguese – SW, Indo-European (Romance)	Azevedo, Milton Mariano. 2005. *Portuguese. A linguistic introduction*. Cambridge: Cambridge University Press.
Romani (Ajía Varvara) – SC, Indo-European (Indo-Iranian)	Igla, Birgit. 1996. *Das Romani von Ajía Varvara. Deskriptive und historisch-vergleichende Darstellung eines Zigeunerdialekts*. Wiesbaden: Harrassowitz.
Romani (Bugurdži) – SC, Indo-European (Indo-Iranian)	Boretzky, Norbert. 1993. *Bugurdži. Deskriptiver und historisches Abriß eines Romani-Dialekts*. Wiesbaden: Harrassowitz.
Romani (Burgenland) – MC, Indo-European (Indo-Iranian)	Halwachs, Dieter W. 2002. *Burgenland-Romani*. München, Newcastle: Lincom Europa.
Romani (Kalderash) – SC, Indo-European (Indo-Iranian)	Čerenkov, L. N. & R. S. Demeter. 1990. Kratkij grammatičeskij očerk kėldėrarskogo dialekta cyganskogo jazyka. In R. S. Demeter & P. S. Demeter (eds.): *Cygansko-russkij i russko-cyganskij slovar' (kėldėrarskij dialekt)*. 285–306. Moskva: Russkij jazyk.
Romani (Lithuanian) – MC, Indo-European (Indo-Iranian)	Tenser, Anton. 2005. *Lithuanian Romani*. München & Newcastle: Lincom Europa.
Romani (North Russian) – ME, Indo-European (Indo-Iranian)	Wentzel, Tatjana W. & Erika Klemm. 1980. *Die Zigeunersprache (nordrussischer Dialekt)*. Leipzig: Verlag Enzyklopädie.
Romani (Sepečides) – SC, Indo-European (Indo-Iranian)	Cech, Petra & Mozes F. Heinschink. 1996. *Sepečides-Romani*. München & Newcastle: Lincom Europa.

Language – nonant, phylum (branch)	Source
Romanian – SC, Indo-European (Romance)	Beyrer, Arthur, Klaus Bochmann & Siegfried Bronsert. 1987. *Grammatik der rumänischen Sprache der Gegenwart*. Leipzig: Enzyklopädie.
Romanian (Megleno) – SC, Indo-European (Romance)	Atanasov, Petăr. 1990. *Le mégléno-roumain de nos jours. Une approche linguistique*. Hamburg: Buske.
Romansch (Puter) – SC, Indo-European (Romance)	Haiman, John & Paola Benincà. 1992. *The Rheato-Romance Languages*. London & New York: Routledge.
Romansch (Surmeiran) – MC, Indo-European (Romance)	Haiman, John & Paola Benincà. 1992. *The Rheato-Romance Languages*. London & New York: Routledge.
Romansch (Sursilvan) – MC, Indo-European (Romance)	Haiman, John & Paola Benincà. 1992. *The Rheato-Romance Languages*. London & New York: Routledge.
Romansch (Sutselvan) – MC, Indo-European (Romance)	Haiman, John & Paola Benincà. 1992. *The Rheato-Romance Languages*. London & New York: Routledge.
Romansch (Vallader) – MC, Indo-European (Romance)	Haiman, John & Paola Benincà. 1992. *The Rheato-Romance Languages*. London & New York: Routledge.
Russian – ME, Indo-European (Slavic)	Švedova, Natal'ja Jul'evna. 1980. *Russkaja grammatika. Tom 1: Fonetika, fonologija, udarenie, intonacija, slovoobrazovanie, morfologija*. Moskva: Nauka.
Russian (Meščera) – ME, Indo-European (Slavic)	Sidorov, V. N. 1949. Nabljudenija nad jazykom odnogo iz govorov rjazanskoj meščery. In S. P. Obnorskij et al. (eds.), *Materialy i issledovanija po russkoj dialektologii. Tom I*, 93–134. Moskva & Leningrad: Izdatel'stvo AN SSSR.
Russian (Ostrovcy) – MC, Indo-European (Slavic)	Honselaar [Xonselaar], Zep. 2001. *Govor derevni Ostrovcy Pskovskoj oblasti*. Amsterdam & Atlanta: Rodopi.
Russian (Permas) – ME, Indo-European (Slavic)	Orlova, V. G. 1949. O govore sela Permas Nikol'skogo rajona Vologodskoj oblasti. In S. P. Obnorskij et al. (eds.), *Materialy i issledovanija po russkoj dialektologii. Tom I*, 45–70. Moskva, Leningrad: Izdatel'stvo AN SSSR.

Language – nonant, phylum (branch)	Source
Rutul – SE, Nakh-Daghestanian (Lezgic)	Alekseev, Mikhail E. 1994. Rutul. In Rieke Smeets (ed.), *The Indigenous Languages of the Caucasus. Volume 4: North East Caucasian Languages Part 2*, 213–258. Delmar & New York: Caravan.
Saami (Central-South) – NC, Uralic (Saami)	Hasselbrink, Gustav. 1965. *Alternative analyses of the phonemic system in Central South-Lappish*. Bloomington: Indiana University.
Saami (Kildin) – NE, Uralic (Saami)	Kert, Georgij Martynovič. 1971. *Saamskij jazyk (kil'dinskij dialekt). Fonetika, morfologija, sintaksis*. Leningrad: Nauka.
Saami (Northern Enontekiö) – NC, Uralic (Saami)	Sammallahti, Pekka. 1998. *The Saami languages. An introduction*. Kárášjohka: Davvi Girji.
Sardinian (Limba Sarda) – SC, Indo-European (Romance)	Puddu, Mario. 2008. *Grammàtica de sa limba sarda*. Cagliari: Condaghes.
Sardinian (Campidanese) – SC, Indo-European (Romance)	Jones, Michael. 1988. Sardinian. In Martin Harris & Nigel Vincent (eds.), *The Romance Languages*, 314–350. London & Sydney: Croom Helm.
Sardinian (Nuorese) – SC, Indo-European (Romance)	Jones, Michael. 1988. Sardinian. In Martin Harris & Nigel Vincent (eds.), *The Romance Languages*, 314–350. London & Sydney: Croom Helm.
Scottish Gaelic – MW, Indo-European (Celtic)	Lamb, William. 2003. *Scottish Gaelic*. München: LINCOM Europa.
Scottish Gaelic (Applecross) – MW, Indo-European (Celtic)	Ternes, Elmar. 2006. *The phonemic analysis of Scottish Gaelic based on the dialect of Applecross, Ross-shire*. Dublin: School of Celtic Studies.
Serbian – SC, Indo-European (Slavic)	Klajn, Ivan. 2005. *Gramatika srpskog jezika*. Beograd: Zavod za Udžbenike i Nastavna Sredstva.
Slavomolisano – SC, Indo-European (Slavic)	Breu, Walter & Giovanni Piccoli. 2000. *Dizionario croato molisano di Acquaviva Collecroce*. Campobasso: Associazione Culturale Naš Grad.
Slovak – MC, Indo-European (Slavic)	Short, David. 1993. Slovak. In Bernard Comrie & Greville G. Corbett (eds.), *The Slavonic languages*, 533–592. London & New York: Routledge.
Slovene – SC, Indo-European (Slavic)	Priestly, T. M. S. 1993. Slovene. In Bernard Comrie & Greville G. Corbett (eds.), *The Slavonic languages*, 388–451. London & New York: Routledge.

Language – nonant, phylum (branch)	Source
Slovene (Resia) – SC, Indo-European (Slavic)	Steenwijk, Han. 1992. *The Slovene dialect of Resia: San Giorgio*. Amsterdam: Rodopi.
Sorbian Lower – MC, Indo-European (Slavic)	Stone, Gerald. 1993. Sorbian (Upper and Lower). In Bernard Comrie & Greville G. Corbett (eds.), *The Slavonic languages*, 593–685. London & New York: Routledge.
Sorbian Lower (Vetschau) – MC, Indo-European (Slavic)	Faßke, Helmut. 1964. *Die Vetschauer Mundart*. Bautzen: Domowina-Verlag.
Sorbian Upper – MC, Indo-European (Slavic)	Schaarschmidt, Gunter. 2004. *Upper Sorbian*. München: LINCOM Europa.
Spanish – SW, Indo-European (Romance)	Blaser, Jutta. 2007. *Phonetik und Phonologie des Spanischen. Eine synchronische Einführung*. Tübingen: Niemeyer.
Svan – SE, Kartvelian (Svan)	Tuite, Kevin. 1997. *Svan*. München: LINCOM EUROPA.
Swedish – MC, Indo-European (Germanic)	Lindqvist, Christer. 2007. *Schwedische Phonetik für Deutschsprachige*. Hamburg: Buske.
Swedish (Österbotten) – NC, Indo-European (Germanic)	Wiik, Barbro. 2002. *Studier i de österbottniska dialekternas fonologi och morfologi*. Helsingfors: Svenska litteratursällskapet i Finland.
Tabasaran – SE, Nakh-Daghestanian (Lezgic)	Magometov, Aleksandr Amarovič. 1965. *Tabasaranskij jazyk. (Issledovanie i teksty)*. Tbilisi: Mecniereba.
Tatar – ME, Turkic (Kipchak)	Comrie, Bernard. 1997. Tatar (Volga Tatar, Kazan Tatar) Phonology. In Alan S. Kaye & Peter T. Daniels (eds.), *Phonologies of Asia and Africa*, 899–925. Winona Lake, Indiana: Eisenbrauns.
Tindi – SE, Nakh-Daghestanian (Andic)	Gudava, Togo. 1964. *Konsonantizm andijskix jasykov: Istoričesko-sravnitel'nyi analiz*. Tbilisi: Izdatel'stvo Akademii Nauk gruzinskoj SSR.
Tsakhur – SE, Nakh-Daghestanian (Lezgic)	Talibov, B. B. 2004. Tsakhur. In Michael Job (ed.), *The Indigenous Languages of the Caucasus. Volume 4: North East Caucasian Languages Part 1*, 347–419. Delmar & New York: Caravan.
Tsova-Tush – SE, Nakh-Daghestanian (Nakh)	Holisky, Dee Ann & Rusudan Gagua. 1994. Tsova-Tush (Batsbi). In Rieks Smeets (ed.), *The indigenous languages of the Caucasus. Vol. 4: North East Caucasian languages*, 147–212. Delmar & New York: Caravan Books.

Language – nonant, phylum (branch)	Source
Turkish – SC, Turkic (Oghuz)	Göksel, Aslı & Celia Kerslake. 2005. *Turkish. A comprehensive grammar*. London & New York: Routledge.
Turkish (Trabzon) – SE, Turkic (Oghuz)	Brendemoen, Bernt. 2002. *The Turkish dialects of Trabzon. Their phonology and historical development*. Wiesbaden: Harrassowitz.
Ubykh – SE, Abkhaz-Adyge (Ubykh)	Charachidze, Georges. 1989. Ubykh. In B. George Hewitt (ed.), *The indigenous languages of the Caucasus. Volume 2: The Northwest Caucasian languages*, 357–459. Delmar & New York: Caravan Books.
Udi (Nidž) – SE, Nakh-Daghestanian (Lezgic)	Schulze-Fürhoff, Wolfgang. 1994. Udi. In Rieke Smeets (ed.), *The indigenous languages of the Caucasus. Volume 4: North East Caucasian languages Part 2*, 447–514. Delmar & New York: Caravan.
Udmurt – ME, Uralic (Permian)	Winkler, Eberhard. 2011. *Udmurtische Grammatik*. Wiesbaden: Harrassowitz Verlag, in Kommission.
Ukrainian – MC, Indo-European (Slavic)	Bilodid, I. K. 1969. *Sučasna ukrajins'ka literaturna mova. Vstup. Fonetyka*. Kyjiv: Naukova dumka.
Ukrainian (Middle Dnieper) – ME, Indo-European (Slavic)	Martynova, G. I. 2009. Fonologična systema mišanoї govirky. In G. I. Martynova (ed.), *Movoznavčyj visnyk: zbirnyk naukovyx prac' na pošanu profesora Kateryny Gorodens'koji z nagody jiji 60-riččja*, 27–37. Čerkasy: Čerkas'kyj nacional'nyj universytet.
Ukrainian (North Hutsul) – MC, Indo-European (Slavic)	Kalnyn', L. É. 1992. Fonetičeskij stroj odnogo gucul'skogo govora. In L. É. Kalnyn' & G. P. Klepikova (eds.), *Issledovanija po slavjanskoj dialektologii*, 7–74. Moskva: RAN.
Veps – ME, Uralic (Finnic)	Zajceva, Marija Ivanovna. 1981. *Grammatika vepsskogo jazyka. Fonetika i morfologija*. Leningrad: Nauka.
Votic – MC, Uralic (Finnic)	Ariste, Paul. 1968. *A Grammar of the Votic Language*. Bloomington: Indiana University.
Welsh (Northern) – MW, Indo-European (Celtic)	Hannahs, S. J. 2013. *The phonology of Welsh*. Oxford: Oxford University Press.
Welsh (Southern) – MW, Indo-European (Celtic)	Hannahs, S. J. 2013. *The phonology of Welsh*. Oxford: Oxford University Press.

Language – nonant, phylum (branch)	Source
Yiddish – MC, Indo-European (Germanic)	Jacobs, Neil G. 2005. *Yiddish. A linguistic introduction*. Cambridge: Cambridge University Press.
Zaza (Northern) – SE, Indo-European (Indo-Iranian)	Selcan, Zülfü. 1998. *Grammatik der Zaza-Sprache, Nord-Dialekt (Dersim-Dialekt)*. Berlin: Wissenschaft & Technik.
Zaza (Southern Dimili) – SE, Indo-European (Indo-Iranian)	Todd, Terry Lynn. 1985. *A grammar of Dimili*. Stockholm: Iremet.

Thomas Stolz and Nataliya Levkovych
Travellers in time and space

Tracing loan conjunctions in the replica languages of the Arabo-Persian sphere of linguistic influence (with special focus on the shores of the Indian Ocean)

Abstract: In language-contact theory, it is hypothesized that conjunctions are not borrowed randomly but in a predictable and universally valid order. Empirical proof in support of this hypothesis is strong but by no means fully comprehensive in terms of the cross-linguistic coverage of cases. This study focuses on the still unexplored success of Arabic, Persian, and Arabo-Persian conjunctions by way of tracing their diffusion over the vast landmass between Iran and Indonesia and the many replica languages populating this area. In this way, the Arabo-Persian sphere of linguistic influence and its internal structure is revealed. The attestations of loan conjunctions originating from Arabic or Persian are registered language by language, compared to other cases of conjunction borrowing in the Arabo-Persian sphere of linguistic influence, and evaluated for language-contact theory. It is shown that indirect borrowing via intermediaries applies frequently in our sample.

Keywords: conjunctions, coordination, subordination, borrowing, Arabic, Persian

Dedicated to Martin Haspelmath on occasion of his 60th birthday

1 Introduction

The point of departure of this study is a summary statement by Matras (2020: 210) who claims that

> Arabic-derived markers for contrast (*ama/amma/lākin/lakini* etc.) are found across a vast area from west Africa to the Caucasus and on to Southwest Asia, including in Hausa, Fula, Somali, Swahili, Lezgian, Turkish, Uzbek, Hindi, and Punjabi. Many of these languages also

---

Thomas Stolz, University of Bremen, FB 10: Linguistics / Language Sciences, Universitäts-Boulevard 13, 28359 Bremen, Germany. E-Mail: stolz@uni-bremen.de
Nataliya Levkovych, University of Bremen, FB 10: Linguistics / Language Sciences, Universitäts-Boulevard 13, 28359 Bremen, Germany. E-Mail: levkov@uni-bremen.de

https://doi.org/10.1515/9783111323756-008

use the Arabic-derived disjunction marker *ya*, and some also an Arabic-derived addition marker *u/w*.

This study is not only meant to empirically substantiate the claim but also to prove that the (geographically even much wider) diffusion of many of these Arabisms is inextricably connected to that of Persian (and at times Turkish) loan conjunctions (= LC). This and similar cases of indirect transmission of LCs can be shown to be of interest for the theory of language contacts. For the point we are going to make, it is crucial to understand which reading of Arabic-derived is the correct choice in a given case of borrowing. Albalá Hernández (2000) distinguishes between *lenguas emisoras*, *lenguas transmisoras*, and *lenguas receptoras* to put names to the different stops itinerant words can take on their way from the distant donor (= D-donor) via the intermediate donor (= I-donor) and the near-donor (= N-donor) to a given replica language (= replica). In what follows we will use the bracketed terms for the same purpose.

The cross-linguistically recurrent patterns of conjunction borrowing form the centerpiece of several strong hypotheses of Matras's with regards to
(a) the pragmatic-cognitive motivation of discourse-operator borrowing (Matras 1998),
(b) the differential markedness and
(c) borrowability hierarchies of connectors (and their tacitly presupposed universality) (Matras 2007: 54–56) which seem to be strong enough to guarantee a high degree of predictability of what can happen in the domain of conjunctions of replicas under the influence of a given N-donor language.

Paradigm cases of conjunction borrowing have been reported in great numbers for language-contact situations which involve Spanish as N-donor and indigenous languages in the Americas, Micronesia, and the Philippines as replicas (Stolz and Stolz 1996, 1998). The prominent role played by adversative conjunctions in function-word borrowing (Matras 1998, 2020: 209–210) is reflected in many contributions to the field. Stolz et al. (2021) discuss the ubiquity of Spanish *pero* 'but' as LC in dozens of languages in Mesoamerica and beyond. Stolz (2022) argues that it makes sense to broaden our horizon by way of investigating cases of adversatives which are borrowed from languages other than Spanish to test whether the assumed primacy of adversatives is valid universally. In the same vein, Stolz and Levkovych (2022) survey LCs in the 141 languages of the former Soviet Union. The results overwhelmingly confirm the extant hypotheses which means that the patterns are cross-linguistically recurrent independent of the languages and the regions involved in the language-contact situation. As the scarcity of evidence for borrowing of English *but* (Hober 2022) suggests, however, there is no compelling reason to already stop taking stock of the empirical facts at this point.

Especially the two last-mentioned studies reveal that

(a) Russian, Arabic, and Persian are at least as prolific donors of LCs as Spanish is, so that, when it comes to drawing conclusions for language-contact theory, these three and probably other languages need to be taken account of to the same extent as Spanish,

(b) different donors might become competitors in situations where a given replica experiences influence from different sides at different stages in the course of its history so that multiple borrowing of functionally identical but etymologically different LCs is possible, and

(c) indirect borrowing in the sense of transfer from D-donor via one or several I-donors to a given replica is a very frequent phenomenon so that on the one hand, the LCs become itinerant elements and, on the other hand, the interpretation of a LC as being borrowed from the D-donor by the final replica in a chain of previous replicas (= I-donors + N-donor) fails to capture the complexity of the situation.

To prove that (a)–(c) do not refer to marginal phenomena but are of general interest for language-contact studies, we check whether the behaviour of LCs with an Arabic and/or Persian etymology observed, for instance, in replicas situated in the former Soviet Union finds parallels in other regions where Arabic and/or Persian were/are linguistically powerful with special focus on the languages spoken along the northern shore of the Indian Ocean and in the Indonesian archipelago. To this end, we propose the working hypothesis (1) which serves as our guidance throughout the empirical part of the paper (cf. Sections 2–3).

(1) Working hypothesis

Many supposed Arabic (or Persian) LCs can be shown not to be borrowed directly from Arabic (or Persian) but from a different N-donor and thus belong in a different category from that of genuine Arabisms (or Persisms).

If (1) can be proved right, the initial quote from Matras (2020) must be interpreted with caution since, for non-native speakers of English, the original formulation might be suggestive of a plethora of direct borrowings from Arabic – a reading which Matras (2020) certainly does not intend and with which we take issue in this study.

To achieve our goal, we adopt a qualitative methodology (Sections 2–3) which is further inspired by the approaches of the cross-linguistic project on grammatical borrowing (Matras and Sakel 2007) and the *Loanword Typology Project* (Haspelmath and Tadmor 2009). The *Loanword Typology meaning list* (Haspelmath and Tadmor 2009: 22–34) hosts only four entries which can be associated with LCs, viz. in Section 17 *Cognition*: 17.51 *and*, 17.52 *because*, 17.53 *if*, 17.54 *or*. The absence of an entry for *but* is worth noting. There is thus an urgent need to determine how the majority of other conjunctions fare in language contact. Our project contributes to filling these gaps. We exclusively discuss instances of MAT-borrowing (Sakel 2007). The data are taken mostly from extant descriptive-linguistic studies with additional data from pedagogical grammars, electronic corpora, and sundry sources. Apart from the occasional language from outside the area of interest, the sample comprises nineteen replicas from the Indian Ocean region whose glossonyms and genetic affiliation are unveiled on the fly in Section 3. A systematic overview over the sample languages and the LCs can be found in the appendix. No attempt at synchronizing the data is undertaken. This means that the LCs featured in this study may be typical only of a certain register, style, genre, epoch, (regional) variety, etc. The presence of identical LCs in different replicas does not imply that they are equally made use of. As to the donors, unless otherwise specified, we refer to Classical Arabic (CA) and the contemporary standard varieties Modern Standard Arabic (MSA) and Modern Persian. Only at a later stage of our project will it be possible to also involve other documented stages of the two major donors. The coexistence of autochthonous conjunctions or other means of clause-combining in the replicas is not systematically taken account of but needs to be addressed in a dedicated follow-up study.

Arabic, Persian, and Arabo-Persian loanwords in general in individual replicas of the region under inspection have already been studied in prior philologically oriented research such as Bausani (1964). For reasons of space, we refrain from discussing these earlier approaches to our topic in any detail. However, a systematic linguistic account in comparative perspective is still wanting. In this sense, our paper is a first and as such can only scratch the surface of the phenomenon hoping that further dedicated in-depth studies will follow soon to fill the many gaps that remain.

The paper is organized as follows. In Section 2, we explain the most relevant concepts and the terminology we employ by way of determining – on the basis of examples from a variety of unrelated languages – the size of the Arabo-Persian sphere of linguistic influence (= APSLI) which stretches over (parts of) three continents. Thereby the pitfalls of dealing with several competing donors are identified. Section 3 contains the linguistically annotated presentation of the pieces of evidence of borrowed Arabic, Persian, and Arabo-Persian conjunctions in Middle East and South(east) Asia. The evaluation of these data in the spirit of the theory of language contacts is the topic of Section 4 where we conduct very simple frequency counts to systematize the results. Conclusions are drawn in Section 5.

2 The Arabo-Persian sphere of linguistic influence – and what happens on its inside

The circum-Indian Ocean region forms part of the much larger APSLI. With special focus on the situation past and present in North Africa, Tosco (2015: 22–24) speaks of an Arabic language empire in which co-territorial languages have been exposed to Arabization for centuries. In Asia, however, Persian gained prominence and prestige as second language of Islam (Fragner 2006: 47). Since Persian itself underwent massive Arabization it could serve as intermediary in the diffusion of originally Arabic elements including conjunctions.

As is shown below, the role of intermediary is not the exclusive privilege of Persian. Other languages have also contributed substantially to the transfer of Arabic conjunctions into regions far away from the heartland of Arabic. Moreover, not only genuinely Arabic conjunctions are involved in these processes but also Persian conjunctions and etymological hybrids. It is therefore necessary to distinguish terminologically between Arabic LCs, Persian LCs, and Arabo-Persian LCs. Why this differentiation makes sense linguistically transpires from the following discussion of concrete data. The intricacies of the language-contact situations in the APSLI requires us to spend considerable time in the more westerly area before we enter the circum-Indian Ocean region. The long detour is worth taking since it helps clarifying many issues which otherwise would burden the presentation of the empirical data in Section 3.

2.1 Four replicas – one LC

Sentences (2)–(5) from four different languages feature four etymologically identical LCs on which we comment subsequently.[1]

---

[1] The sentential examples are glossed according to the *Leipzig Glossing Rules*. Original glosses – where necessary – are modified to correspond to these rules. Boldface marks out the LCs, their glosses, and their equivalent in the translation. Marked elements are consistently glossed according to the meaning the LC has in the N-donor. Unless otherwise stated the English translations are ours. We have not homogenized the at times strongly diverging graphic representations of the object-language data.

(2) Central Albanian (Indo-European, Albanian) [Dizdari 2005: 1083]
goca me vërtë ka nji çike faj
girl with truth have.3SG.PRS INDEF small fault
gand gjymtim në trup
scar mutilation in body
***velaqim** s' e ka shoqen*
but NEG 3SG.F.ACC have.3SG.PRS girl_friend:ACC
për punë e sifate xhinsi
for work:ACC and property:ACC.PL race:GEN
'The girl has a little fault (a scar, a bodily mutilation), **but**, as to her performance at work and the good manners of her family, nobody compares to her.'

(3) Bashkir (Turkic, Kipchak) [Landmann 2015: 109]
*min heðð̆e anlajym **läkin** irken höjläšä almajym*
1SG 2PL.ACC understand:1SG **but** free converse take:NEG:1SG
'I understand you **but** I cannot converse freely.'

(4) Swahili (Niger-Congo, Bantu) [Möhlig and Heine 1999: 103]
Upepo ukavuma sana
CL6.SG:wind CL6.SG:PST:blow very
***lakini** mzee akalishika koti*
but CL1.SG:old_man CL1.SG:PST:hold_fast coat
'The wind blew strongly then, **but** the old man held fast to the coat [...].'

(5) Indonesian (Austronesian, Sundic) [Indonesian corpus][2]
Saya berucap makasih pada dia juga
1SG INTR:say thanks ACC 3SG too
***lakin** pertemuan kami diawali salam sedang*
but NMZL:meeting 1PL.EXCL PASS:beginning:TR greet while
perpisahan kami tidak salam
NMZL:farewell 1PL.EXCL NEG greet
'I also said 'thanks' to him, although our meeting began with a handshake **but** ended without a handshake [...].'

---

[2] https://corpora.uni-leipzig.de/en/res?corpusId=ind_mixed_2013&word=lakin, consulted on 17 February, 2023.

The replica languages share an adversative conjunction which ultimately goes back to Arabic as reflected in CA *lākinna* = MSA *laakinna* 'but' whose contemporary use in MSA is illustrated in (6). Henceforth, we use this MSA form when we refer generally to LCs which derive from *laakinna* 'but' no matter how they are realised phonologically in a given language.

(6) MSA (Afro-Asiatic, Semitic)   [Ryding 2005: 427]
    lays-at   *lubnaaniyyat-an*
    not_be-3SG.F   Lebanese:F-ACC
    wa-laakinna-*haa*   *saʕid-at*   *fii*   *lubnaan-a*
    and-but-POSS.3SG.F   be_happy-3SG.F.PST   in   Lebanon-ACC
    'She is not Lebanese, **but** she was happy in Lebanon.'

Example (6) involves the MSA coordinating conjunction *wa* 'and' which is a typical (and often untranslated) "sentence starter" (Ryding 2005: 409) that frequently combines with other conjunctions to form a clause-initial collocation such as *wa-laakinna* 'but' (Ryding 2005: 423). This collocation is reflected in Central Albanian *velaqim* in (2) whose initial syllable /ve/ corresponds to MSA *wa* without, however, claiming morpheme status. Dizdari (2005: 1083) notes that in the Albanian variety of Elbasan, the initial *ve-* is usually dropped so that the conjunction comes in the shape of *lakin* 'but', i.e. this reduced dialectal form corresponds more closely to the LCs in the other three replicas which show no sign of a reflex of Arabic *wa*. The absence of the final *-na* in the replica corresponds to the truncation of the adversative in CA if it is followed by elements other than nouns or pronouns (Fischer 2006: 158).

Central Albanian *velaqim*, Bashkir *läkin*, Swahili *lakini*, and Indonesian *lakin* fulfil the criteria of being classified as LCs because
(i) they serve the purpose of clause linkage,
(ii) they occupy the inter-clausal position, and
(iii) they consist of borrowed matter (independent of phonological adjustments).

For phrase-level LCs, the criteria (i)–(ii) refer to phrase linkage and the inter-phrasal position. Simplifying, we also subsume complementizers under the umbrella of conjunctions. Note that it is the grammar of the replica language that determines whether a given borrowed item is a LC independent of its status in the N-donor. To be counted as a LC, it suffices that a given element takes on clause-combining functions in inter-clausal position at least occasionally or occurs clause-initially in the subordinate clause. As transpires from Section 3, there are also replicas which assign LCs to a clause-internal position (mostly in the

Wackernagel slot). Many of the LCs in our database may also and sometimes predominantly function as discourse markers. LCs may be simple or complex (polymorphic or even multi-word expressions). The borrowed matter may cover only part of the segments which together constitute the conjunction of the replica.

Examples (2)–(5) stem from four languages from four different language families whose typological properties differ from each other and which are spoken in four different geographical regions. Therefore, it seems highly unlikely that Central Albanian in the Balkans, Bashkir bridging the border between Europe and Siberia, Swahili in East Africa, and Indonesian in Southeast Asia have something materially in common. Yet, they have. Superficially, this similarity seems to be unpredictable and coincidental. On closer scrutiny, however, the occurrence of one and the same LC in several languages which otherwise differ widely from each other meets the expectations in the sense that

(a) adversative conjunctions are especially prone to being borrowed (Matras 1998) and
(b) the four languages have been direct or indirect partners in contact with one and the same donor, namely Arabic.

Since several of the replicas in (2)–(5) are not and have never been spoken in the immediate vicinity of Arabic, the question arises how the LCs have found their way from Arabic into the replicas. Cultural loans within the context of societies heavily influenced by Islam are taken for granted. Except Swahili, the replicas have been exposed predominantly to Persian (or Turkish) influence. Example (7) from Persian involves the same Arabic LC as in the previous cases.

(7) Persian (Indo-European, Iranian) [Alavi and Lorenz 1988: 92]
 u šouhar-e xub-i-st **walikan** pul nadārad
 he husband-LK good-INDEF-be.3SG **but** money NEG:have:3SG
 'He is a good husband, **but** he has no money.'

Persian *walikan* is a bona fide Arabic LC. It contains initial *va* = <wa> 'and' (< Arabic *wa* 'and') which is characterized as typical for colloquial style when combined with other conjunctions (Yousef 2018: 139). The adversative conjunction *vali* 'but' is the truncated form of *valikan*. At the end of the 19th century, Horn (1898: 166) recorded the alloforms *valēkīn* ~ *lēkīn* ~ *lēk* ~ *valēk* ~ *vale*.[3] It is from this set of forms that other languages have borrowed their adversative LCs.

---

3 Horn (1898: 166) translates the conjunction as German *doch* which is probably short for *jedoch* 'however'.

2.2 Ottoman Turkish and two competing donors

In Ottoman Turkish, *lā́kin* 'but' (as in (8)) as well as *wä* 'and' were widely used (Weil 1917: 208–209) but the former fell victim to the anti-Arabic/anti-Persian language reform which started in 1928 (Brendemoen 1998). A synopsis of LCs in Turkish is presented in Johanson (1996).

(8) Ottoman Turkish (Turkic, Oghuz) [Weil 1917: 208]
    Aḥmäd   gälmädi   lākin   Ḥusēin
    Ahmed   come:NEG:PST   **but** Hussein
    'Ahmed did not come **but** Hussein did.'

Today, it is only marginally attested in the stylistically marked collocation *amma ve lakin* 'but, however' as in (9) whose internal composition is especially interesting for the topic of this section. Both *am(m)a* 'but' and *ve* 'and' are still frequently used in post-reform Turkish.

(9) Turkish (Turkic, Oghuz) [Ersen-Rasch 2012: 124]
    İşim   iyi   **amma** ve   **lakin** yorucu
    work:POSS.1SG   good   **but**   and   **but**   tiring
    'My work is good **but also** tiring.'

What is remarkable about this residual collocation is that it consists of three LCs each of which can be traced back to Arabic, namely to the discontinuous topic-change marker CA *'ammā...fa-* = MSA *'ammaa...fa-* '(but) as for' (Fischer 2006: 157; Ryding 2005: 420), the copulative conjunction *wa-* 'and', and the above adversative conjunction *laakinna* 'but'. At the same time, all three of them are also attested as Arabic LCs in Persian two of which have been introduced in the previous paragraph already. Persian *ammā* 'but' is a synonym of *vali* 'but' (Yousef 2018: 139). Either Arabic or Persian could be the donor of the three LCs in (9).

To decide the issue, we have to take stock of the inventory of LCs of Ottoman Turkish and relate them to their equivalents in Persian and Arabic. To tell the donors Arabic and Persian apart it would be necessary to conduct a separate and philologically well-informed diachronic study for which issues of historical phonology are important (Stein 2006). There is already a venerable tradition of research dedicated to the Arabic and Persian influence on (Ottoman) Turkish (e.g. Bittner 1900). Brendemoen (2006: 230) argues that the oldest layer of Arabisms in Turkish dates back to the 9th–11th centuries when it was acquired via Persian by Turkish-speaking groups during their migration south-westwards through

Iran. We do not pretend to answer the many open questions of this strand of research. What the subsequent paragraphs are meant to show is that not everything that outwardly looks Arabic needs to be borrowed directly from Arabic.

Weil (1917: 208) claims that "[a]us dem Arabischen sind nur nebenordnende, aus dem Persischen außer einigen neben- vor allem unterordnende Konjunktionen übernommen worden."[4] There are thus structural implications characterizing the Arabic LCs as easy to integrate and those borrowed from Persian as difficult to accommodate with the Turkic language structure. Tables 1–2 are based on information given by Horn (1898) and Weil (1917). In Table 1, we include those Ottoman Turkish LCs which might be traced back to Arabic.

Table 1: LCs in Ottoman Turkish with a possible Arabic origin.

MSA	19th century Persian	Ottoman Turkish
wa- 'and'	va 'and'	wä 'and'
laakinna 'but'	(va)lēk(īn) ~ valēk ~ vale 'but'	lākin 'but'
'ammaa...fa- '(but) as for'	ammā 'but'	ama 'but'
waqt 'time'	vaqt-ī (ke) 'when'	waktā́-ki 'when'
faqaT 'only, solely'		fakat 'however'

In Persian, the Arabism *faqat* 'only' exists but has not acquired clause-combining functions. It remains in the adverbial domain. The temporal conjunction *waktā́-ki* 'when' which is characterized as being rarely used at the time of 1st World War is the only non-adversative item in Table 1. Etymologically, this now obsolete conjunction is a hybrid in the sense that it contains both an Arabic component (= the noun *waqt* 'time') and a replica of the Persian complementizer (= *ke*). The presence of the latter suggests that the conjunction was transferred to Ottoman Turkish via Persian. Since *waktā́-ki* 'when' is made up of two etymologically distinct components, it is a true Arabo-Persian LC of the hybrid kind in Ottoman Turkish. There are further hybrids in the inventory of Ottoman Turkish conjunctions, namely

(i) disjunctive (*wä*)*jaḫod* 'or' < Arabic *wa-* 'and' 19th century Persian *yāxvaδ* 'or (rather)' (Horn 1898: 165),

---

4 Our translation: 'from Arabic only coordinating conjunctions have been transferred whereas from Persian, except a few coordinating conjunctions, mostly subordinating conjunctions have been transferred.'

(ii) causal *mā-dā́m-ki* 'since' < Arabic *mā dāma* 'as long as it continues' + Persian *ki* 'that' (Eyuboğlu 2017), and
(iii) concessive *ḫāl-bú-ki* 'although' < Arabic *ḥāl* 'situation' + Turkish *bu* 'this' + Persian *ki* (Eyuboğlu 2017).

Compound cases of this kind strongly suggest that they were borrowed from Persian or, in the case of (iii), coined within Ottoman Turkish itself.

Table 2 features those LCs for which the Persian origin is unquestionable.

Table 2: LCs in Ottoman Turkish originating from Persian.

19th century Persian	Ottoman Turkish
ham…ham 'both…and'	*hä̂m…hä̂m (dä)* 'both…and'
na…na 'neither…nor'	*nä…nä (dä)* 'neither…nor'
yā…yā 'either…or'	*jā… (wä-)jā* 'either…or'
čūnki 'when, since, because'	*čű́nki* 'because'
zērā 'because'	*zirắ* 'because'
sān-ki 'like'	*şan-ki* 'as if'
magar 'if not''	*mäjär(- ki)* 'although, unless'
(a)garči ~ (v)arči 'although'	*gä́rči* 'although'
((v)a)gar ~ (v)ar 'if'	*ägär ~ äjär* 'if'
šāyad '(be) fitting'	*šāyäd* 'if (perhaps)'
(tā)ki ~ tā(k) 'so that'	*(tā)ki* 'so that'
ki 'that'	*ki* 'that'

The bulk of the LCs attested in Ottoman Turkish can be attributed directly to the N-donor Persian. Except one, all LCs with an Arabic etymology are also present as Arabic LCs in Persian. It is therefore tempting to assume that Ottoman Turkish borrowed several if not all of the Arabic LCs via Persian, too. They are Persisms in Ottoman Turkish whereas they are Arabisms in Persian. This ultimately makes them Arabo-Persian LCs in Ottoman Turkish. In contrast to the abovementioned hybrid Arabo-Persian LCs, those adversatives registered in Table 1 are of a different kind since they cannot be decomposed morphologically into constituents with different etymology. They are Arabo-Persian LCs nevertheless because of their historical itinerary.

2.3 Buffers and intermediaries

In the foregoing section Persian has been depicted as intermediary in the contact between Arabic and Ottoman Turkish. Ottoman Turkish in turn assumed the role of intermediary for the propagation of Arabic, Persian, and Arabo-Persian LCs both in Anatolia and further westwards into the Balkans. For Cappadocian Greek for instance, Grant (2012: 332–339) identifies *ama* 'but', *lekin* 'but', *ya* 'or', *çünkü* 'because', and the complementizer *ki* 'that' as LCs which were borrowed directly from Turkish and indirectly from Persian with the two adversative conjunctions ultimately going back to Arabic. The chain of donor-replica relations becomes too long to be adequately reflected by our terminology which would otherwise create overlong attributes like Arabo-Perso-Turkish.

The further west we move on the map of the former Ottoman Empire the less likely it becomes that Persian and/or Arabic were directly involved in the borrowing process. This is why Boretzky (1975: 246) classifies the following eleven LCs in Albanian as borrowings from Turkish although none of them is an autochthonous Turkish element (cf. (10)).[5]

(10) Supposed Turkish LCs in Albanian
    (a) adversative:
        (i) Albanian *ama* 'but' < Turkish *am(m)a* 'but' < Persian *ammā* 'but' < Arabic *'ammaa* 'but (as for)',
        (ii) Central Albanian *vel(l)akin* 'but' < Turkish *lâkin* 'but' < Persian *laken* 'but' < MSA *laakinna* 'but';
    (b) causal:
    Albanian *çynqi* / *çimçi* 'because' < Turkish *çünkü* 'because' < Persian *čūn ke* 'when, since, because';
    (c) correlative:
        (i) Albanian *hem...hem* 'both...and' < Turkish *hem...hem* 'both...and' < Persian *ham...(va) ham* 'both...and',
        (ii) Albanian *ja...ja* 'either...or' < Turkish *ya...ya (da)* 'either...or' < Persian *(yā...)yā* '(either...)or'.

Not all of the LCs listed in (10) are tolerated by the standard language which was created in the 1970's. Albanian's neighbours – sometimes only in the colloquial

---

[5] Genuine Turkish LCs also exist in Albanian such as *anxhak* 'but, however' < Turkish *ancak* 'but, however, only' (Boretzky 1975: 246).

register – display similar behaviour as can be gathered from Table 3. The meanings given for these LCs in (10) are preserved throughout Table 3.

Table 3: LCs in Balkan languages acquired via Ottoman Turkish (Stolz and Levkovych 2022: 269–270).

Turkish	replicas			
	Bulgarian	Megleno-Romanian	Macedonian	Aromanian
ama	ami	ama	ama	ama
hem…hem	xem…xem	hem…hem		
ya…ya	ja…ja		ja…ja	

We are facing proper subsets of the inventory of LCs attested in Albanian. As could almost be expected all five of the Balkan replicas borrow the adversative *ama* 'but' whereas the synonymous *velakin* 'but' seems to be restricted to Albanian. In the absence of an Arabic or Persian speech-community in the Balkans during the time of Ottoman hegemony, the N-donorship of the above LCs can only be claimed for Ottoman Turkish. Thus, Ottoman Turkish served both as intermediary and as buffer.

As to the latter function, the territory occupied by the Turkish speech-community separated the western parts of the Ottoman Empire from the Arabic-speaking parts in the south and Persia in the east. Similarly, the Arabic-speaking regions formed an impenetrable border to the south so that Africa became the hinterland of Arabic linguistic expansion. No sizable bilingual communities with Turkish or Persian as part of their repertoire were reported for Africa in the past. At the same time, the Persian-speaking area buffered off Turkish and Arabic from directly exerting influence on the languages to the north and to the east. Turkic languages from the Caucasus through Central Asia underwent strong Iranisation. The same happened to Nakh-Daghestanian languages and those languages which we address in Section 3. Smaller Arabic-speaking islands in Uzbekistan and Afghanistan were not powerful enough to influence their neighbourhood thoroughly.

There are four facts which support the buffer hypothesis:
(a) The replicas in Europe and Asia only attest to those Arabic LCs which also form part of the Persian LC inventory.
(b) In Asia, in addition to these Arabo-Persian LCs, there is also a plethora of genuinely Persian LCs.

(c) No Persian or Turkish LCs are reported from Africa.[6]
(d) In Africa, in addition to the adversatives, some replicas have borrowed further conjunctions from Arabic none of which are attested in the European and Asian parts of the APSLI.

A case in point is Swahili. From (4) we already know that *lakini* 'but' is attested in this language. However, there are also further borrowings as shown in (11).

(11) Arabic LCs in Swahili [Ashton 1944: 197–198]
  (a) disjunctive:
      au 'or' = CA *'aw* = MSA *'aw* 'or' (Fischer 2006: 156; Ryding 2005: 418);
  (b) adversative:
      (i) *bali* 'but' = CA *bal* = MSA *bal* 'but (actually)' (Fischer 2006: 154; Ryding 2005: 411),
      (ii) *ila* 'but, unless' = CA *'illā* 'except' = MSA *'ilaa* 'but, except' (Fischer 2006: 148; Ryding 2005: 651);
  (c) consecutive:
      illi 'so that' = Cairene Arabic *illi* 'that, because' (Woidich 2006: 161);
  (d) correlative:
      (i) *ama...ama* 'either...or',
      (ii) *wala...wala* 'neither...nor' = MSA *wa-* 'and' + *la* NEGATION (Ryding 2005: 646).

It strikes the eye that Arabic is the N-donor of the Swahili correlative constructions. Outside Africa, correlative LCs are usually borrowed from Persian.

In Europe and Asia, Arabic is credited only for being the D-donor of coordinating LCs whereas in Africa, it is also the source of subordinating conjunctions. Africa differs from the European and Asian parts of the APSLI insofar as it has

---

[6] Matras (2020: 210) assumes the widely spread disjunctive LC *ya* 'or' to be of Arabic origin as claimed in the initial quote from his work. As a matter of fact, *ya* is of Persian origin (< Middle Persian *ayâ* < *ayōw* 'or' (Salemann 1895: 322)) at least in the area in focus in this volume whereas the disjunctives of CA and MSA are *'aw* 'or' and *'am* 'or' (Fischer 2006: 156; Ryding 2005: 418). However, Syrian Arabic gives evidence of disjunctive *yā* 'or' (Cowell 2005: 395). Can it be a Persism? What is striking, however, is the presence of the correlative *ya...ya* 'either...or' for instance, in Cairene Arabic (Woidich 2006: 160) whereas singleton *ya* is not reported to exist in the regional varieties of Arabic in Egypt and Sudan. Note that the correlative has been borrowed from Sudanese Arabic into the co-territorial Fulfulde (Abu-Manga 1986: 162). To determine in what way, if at all, these correlatives are connected to their Persian equivalent a separate diachronic investigation is required.

been the home of large arabophone speech-communities for many centuries in the north and east of the continent. The presence of huge numbers of native speakers, the high degree of bilingualism with (regional varieties of) Arabic, and the prestige of Arabic as language of Islam have contributed to the diffusion of Arabic LCs in the replicas from Morocco down to Zanzibar. However, in Africa too, intermediaries had their share in this process – most notably Hausa which has passed on the ubiquitous adversative *àmmá* 'but' to several other Chadic languages such as Goemai. Examples (12)–(13) illustrate this relationship.

(12) Hausa (Afro-Asiatic, Chadic) [Wolff 1993: 450]
 naa tàfi Kanòo **ʔàmmaa** bàn gan shì ba
 1SG go Kano **but** NEG see 3SG NEG
 'I went to Kano, **but** I did not see him.'

(13) Goemai (Afro-Asiatic, Chadic) [Hellwig 2019: 444]
 ní góe mís **àmmá** ní góe jáp bá
 3SG COM man **but** 3SG COM child.PL NEG
 '[...] she has a husband **but** she doesn't have children.' [original translation]

Hellwig (2019: 444) considers the Goemai case to involve a borrowing from Hausa – and not from Arabic, i.e. the N-donor is mentioned but not the D-donor.

The findings of Section 2 are summarized in Figure 1 which schematically represents the directionality of linguistic influence among the major forces within the APSLI. The possibility of minor direct influence on the part of a donor is indicated by the grey arrows. The triangle (dotted line) marks out the zone of overlap on the border between the three donor languages. In this zone of overlap all kinds of language-contact situations are located where Turkish functions as N-donor inter alia for local Arabic varieties, the latter may influence other minority languages in the same zone, some of which in turn serve as N-donors for yet other languages on the local level. For reasons of space, we cannot elaborate on this intricate network of partly superimposed language contacts.[7]

---

[7] Haig (2001) characterizes East Anatolia as a zone of extremely and intertwined intensive language contacts so that it is by no means too far-fetched if we classify the region as a Contact Superposition Zone (Koptjevskaja-Tamm and Wälchli 2001: 624–625). Procházka (2002: 144–145) assumes that five of six coordinating conjunctions of the Arabic variety spoken at Çukurova are borrowings from Turkish. They are Turco-Persian and Arabo-Persian LCs including the originally Arabic *ama(n)* 'but'. The borrowing process has gone almost full circle: Arabic1 > Persian > Turkish > Arabic2. Northeastern Neo-Aramaic has borrowed *bas* 'but' from Iraqi Arabic *bass* 'but' perhaps via the I-donor Kurmanji (Coghill 2019: 507), etc. Grant (2012) mentions a number

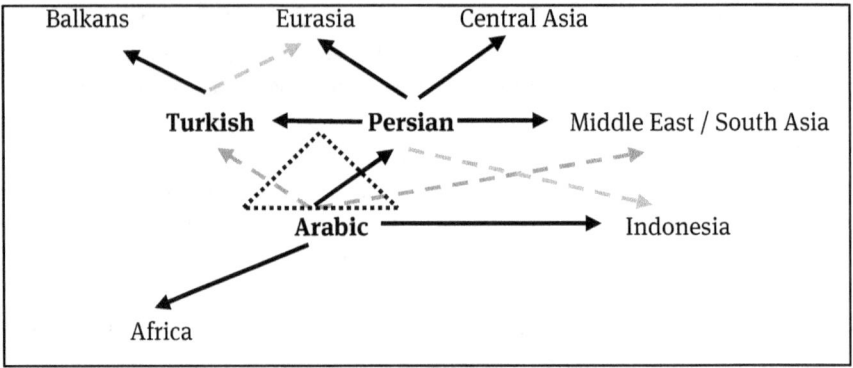

Figure 1: The directionality of influence.

Arabic has the monopoly for Africa and a strong position in Indonesia. Everywhere else, however, it is helped along by Persian and/or Turkish with the former claiming the biggest part of the APSLI. What we expect to find when we turn our attention to the Asian shores of the Indian Ocean is that, on the mainland, Persian LCs are the rule with the occasional Arabo-Persian and Arabic addition. How the languages of the Indonesian archipelago fit into the picture is discussed in Section 3.6.

3 Between Bagdad and Jakarta

Thanks to Section 2, we are prepared to find similar intricacies in the Middle Eastern and South(east) Asian language-contact scenarios. We expect to find evidence for the wide distribution of Persian LCs. Wherever LCs stem originally from Arabic we are dealing with Arabo-Persian LCs. These generalisations of necessity gloss over many aspects of the enormously colourful contact zone in which languages other than Arabic and Persian also exert linguistic influence on their neighbours albeit on a smaller scale. The Munda language Juang for instance, has borrowed the coordinating conjunction *au* 'and' from Indo-Aryan Oriya (Patnaik 2008: 545).

---

of supposed Arabisms in Turoyo at least some of which are probably better explained as Turco-Persian LCs, etc.

The sources frequently disagree as to the presence/absence of LCs in a given replica. Since this is a first and preliminary data collection whose goal is to facilitate future investigations, we accept each piece of evidence of conjunction borrowing for fact at least for the time being. We proceed from here as follows. The replicas are ticked off language family by language family according to a (loosely interpreted) geographical order starting in Iran moving eastwards with a detour via the Pamir Mountains and through India to come to a stop in Southeast Asia. In the subsequent sections, sentential examples are provided only for cases of
(a) borrowed *laakinna* 'but' because of its connection to the D-donor Arabic and
(b) borrowed *agar* 'if' because it is the prototypical representative of a genuinely Persian LC throughout Asia.

The Persian reflex of *laakinna* 'but' is illustrated in (7) above. Example (14) features the conditional conjunction *agar* (= *æge*) 'if' as it is used in contemporary Persian.

(14) Persian (Indo-European, Iranian) [Mahootian 1997: 40]
æge bahæm kar-kon-im zud tæmum-mi-š-e
if together work-SUBJ.do-1PL fast finish-DUR-become-3SG
'**If** we work together it'll get done quickly.'

All other LCs are illustrated summarily by single-word examples.

3.1 Indo-European

3.1.1 Iranian

Persian's immediate neighbours to the east belong to the same branch of the Indo-European language family, namely Iranian. They are thus relatively close relatives of Persian. This genetic relation does not imply that all Iranian languages have identical sets of conjunctions. What we see instead is that several of them have borrowed extensively from Persian and/or Tajik.[8]

A case in point is Balochi. Jahani and Korn (2009: 678) argue that

---

8 According to Payne (1989: 442) "[a] large number of subordinating conjunctions in the Pāmir languages are Tājikī loans, for example *agar* 'if'." Thus, on closer inspection, some of the cases discussed in this section might turn out not to be borrowed directly from Persian but from Tajiki which generally shares many properties with Persian.

[a]s Balochi is primarily a spoken language the syntax is fairly simple. Subordination closely follows the basic pattern of Persian, and several conjunctions have been borrowed from neighbouring languages (e.g. *agar* 'if', *lēkin* 'but').

The use of adversative *lēkin* 'but' is stylistically highly marked. This LC is exclusively attested in Balochi poetry where it does not show up frequently enough to be considered a fully integrated borrowing. However, *lēkin* 'but' has a far more popular competitor, namely the adversative LC *ammaʿ* 'but'. Examples of the employment of the conditional LC are easier to come by as shown in (15).

(15) Balochi (Indo-European, Iranian) [Jahani and Korn 2009: 683]
age be bāzār rapt-ō čīz-ē ger-ō
if to market go.PST-1SG thing-INDEF take-1SG
'I will buy a little something **if** I go to the market.'

Table 4 is the synopsis of the Persian and Arabo-Persian LCs we have identified in Iranian replica languages.

Table 4: (Arabo-)Persian LCs in Iranian replicas.[9]

Persian		replicas				
		Balochi	Pashto	Wakhi	Parachi	Shugni
agar 'if'		*agar ~ age*			*aga(r)*	*aga*
(wa)lakin 'but'		*lēkin*	*lékin ~ låkin*	*lōkin*		
ammā 'but'		*ammā*	*ammā́*			
yā...yā 'either...or'		*yā...yā*	*jā... jā*			
ham...ham 'both...and'		*ham...ham*	*ham...ham*			
na...na 'neither...nor'		*na...na*	*nə...nə*			
yā 'or'			*jā*	*yā*		
vali 'but'		*balē*				
magar 'if not'			*magár* 'but'			
balke 'but'			*balki*			
ke 'that'		*ki*				

---

9 The data are taken from Jahani and Korn (2009: 678–679) for Balochi, Lorenz (1982: 79) for Pashto, Bashir (2009: 849) for Wakhi, Kieffer (2009: 714) for Parachi, and Edelman and Dodykhudoeva (2009: 813) for Shugni.

Balochi and Pashto are frequent borrowers whereas in the other three replicas, LCs are attested only to a limited extent. Interestingly, both *agar* 'if' and *laakinna* 'but' are borrowed by three languages so that no clear preference for either of the two candidates can be postulated. There is only a single instance of meaning change (highlighted in grey in Table 4). Several of the LCs in Table 4 have parallels in Tables 1–2. The sets of (Arabo-)Persian LCs in Turkish and those of the Iranian languages largely overlap. The little differences there are might disappear if the investigation can be continued on the basis of an enlarged data-base set.

3.1.2 Indo-Aryan

In his list of borrowers of Arabic adversative conjunctions, Matras (2020: 210) explicitly mentions Punjabi and Hindi. It goes almost without saying that Urdu can be added to this list, too. Evidence for (Arabo-)Persian LCs is also available for Kashmiri, Sindhi, and Gujarati.

Both Punjabi in (16)–(17) and Hindi in (18)–(19) make frequent use of the borrowed adversative and conditional.

(16) Punjabi (Indo-European, Indo-Aryan)   [Bhatia 1993: 106]
 mãi   sardaar ãã   **lekan** meraa pràà   monaa ai
 1SG   Sikh   be.1SG **but**   my   brother Hindu be.3SG
 'I am a Sikh **but** my brother is a Hindu.' [original translation]

(17) Punjabi (Indo-European, Indo-Aryan)   [Bhatia 1993: 77]
 agar ó   aaiaa   te   mãi   páRããgaa
 if   he   come:3SG.M then I   read:FUT.1SG.M
 '**If** he comes, I will read.' [original translation]

(18) Hindi (Indo-European, Indo-Aryan)   [McGregor 1977: 172]
 cāhe   āp   yahāṁ raheṁ   **lekin** maiṁ nahīṁ rahūṁga
 one_may_wish   you here   stay:SUBJ   **but**   I   NEG   stay:1SG:FUT
 'You can stay if you like, **but** I shan't.' [original translation]

(19) Hindi (Indo-European, Indo-Aryan)   [McGregor 1977: 123]
 agar mehnat karoge   to   saphal   hoge
 if   effort do:2PL.M.FUT then successful   be:2PL.M.FUT
 '**If** you make an effort you will be successful.' [original translation]

In contrast, Kashmiri only attests to borrowed *agar* 'if' as shown in (20).

(20) Kashmiri (Indo-European, Indo-Aryan) [Koul 2007: 943]

agar	rūd	peyi	teli	bani	jãn	phasil
if	rain	fall.FUT	then	get	good	crop

'**If** it rains, then the crops will be good.' [original translation]

Table 5 reveals that the catalogue of (Arabo-)Persian LCs in the six Indo-Aryan replicas is remarkably rich. Note that the only meaning difference between LC and original Persian conjunction involves *magar* 'if not' which has adversative function in Hindi, Urdu, Kashmiri, and Punjabi just as in Pashto.

Table 5: (Arabo-)Persian LCs in Indo-Aryan replica languages.[10]

Persian	replicas					
	Hindi	Urdu	Punjabi	Kashmiri	Sindhi	Gujarati
yā 'or'	ya	ya	ja	yā	yā	
agar 'if'	agar	agar	agar	agar		
magar 'if not'	magar 'but'	magar 'but'	magar 'but'	magar 'but'		
(wa)lakin 'but'	lekin	lekin	lekan			
čun ke 'because'	cūṁki	coonkeh	cüüki			
balke 'but'	balki	balkeh				bəlke
agar-če 'although'	agarce	agarceh		agarči		
(tā) ke 'so that'	(tā) ki		(taa) ki			
yā...yā 'either...or'	yā...yā			yā...yā		
na...na 'neither...nor'	na...na			na...na		
va 'and'	va					
ke 'that'	ki					

None of the LCs is attested in all replicas. Disjunctive *ya* 'or' occurs in five out of six replicas. It is particularly difficult to judge the status of the complementizer *ke/ki* 'that' properly. Future research might reveal that it is a LC in all of the Indo-

---

10 The data are taken from McGregor (1977: 123–128 and 182–184) for Hindi, Young (2014: 86–87) for Urdu, and Bhatia (1993: 67–79 and 106) for Punjabi, Khubchandani (2007: 650) for Sindhi, Cardona and Suthar (2007: 693) for Gujarati, and Koul (2007: 943–944) for Kashmiri.

Aryan replicas – a conclusion we dare not draw in this study. Hindi boasts the longest list of LCs. It is worth noting that there are also subordinating conjunctions of the causal, concessive, and consecutive types.

3.2 Dravidian

Since the foregoing replicas belong to closely related branches of Indo-European, the integration of Persian LCs into the replicas is hardly surprising because the basic morphosyntactic structure of donor and replica are sufficiently similar to facilitate transfer. However, in the geographical vicinity of Balochi and Punjabi, we encounter languages which are members of a different language family – Dravidian – whose structural differences with Persian have not blocked the integration of the LCs.

According to Andronov (2003: 105) "[c]onjunctions, which are mostly borrowed from Indo-Aryan or Iranian, too, are on the whole uncharacteristic of Dravidian". The author adds that

> [c]onjunctions as a part of speech are not typical of the Dravidian languages, so that even in those languages which possess them their use frequently is optional. [] Conjunctions proper are attested only in the languages of the North-Western, North-Eastern and Gondwana groups. They are [] borrowings (Andronov 2003: 297).

For the purpose of clause-linkage, Dravidian languages resort to completely different means such as nominalizations and subordinate verbal inflection. It is telling that proper conjunctions exist only in those Dravidian languages whose speech communities are linguistic minorities surrounded by unrelated languages which make ample use of conjunctions. These similarities can only be explained by convergence and/or direct material borrowing.

At a considerable distance from the bulk of the Dravidian languages situated in southern India, Brahui is spoken on both sides of the border between Iran and Pakistan. It is a neighbour of Balochi's from which Brahui has borrowed some of its LCs, the D-donor being Persian (Elfenbein 2020: 462). Among these LCs we again find a reflex of *agar* 'if' as shown in (21). Note that Brahui *aga* 'if' is placed clause-medially, i.e. the criterion of the clause-initial or inter-clausal position is not fulfilled.

(21) Brahui (Dravidian, North Dravidian) [Andronov 1980: 91]
nī **aga** kāsa ī nētō barēva
you **if** go:FUT.2SG I you:COM come:FUT.1SG
'**If** you are going, l shall go with you.' [original translation]

In Malto, another outlier member of the North Dravidian branch spoken on the border between India and Bangladesh, borrowed *agar* 'if' is mostly positioned clause-internally as in (22) but may also occur clause-initially.

(22) Malto (Dravidian, North Dravidian) [Steever 2020: 463]
*ilko   nīm   **agar**   ortno   manēner*
this_way   2PL.NOM   **if**   one_person:LOC be:SUBJ:2PL
tān   to   nimen   berbād   nallānar
then   TOP   2PL:ACC   destruction   do:NEG.FUT:3PL
'**If** you live together as one, then they will not destroy you.' [original translation]

Malto attests to a number of other loans from Indo-Aryan but not from Persian except indirectly the complementizer *ki* 'that'. Steever (2020: 462) assumes that the N-donor of the LCs could be Bangla, Oriya, Sadri or other unidentified Indo-Aryan languages. However, we have not been able to find evidence of borrowed *agar* 'if' in any of these potential N-donor languages. For Kurux, the third member of the North Dravidian branch, Mishra (1996: 88 and 96) mentions the LCs *agar* 'if' and *magar* 'but' without providing sentential examples. In (23), we enumerate the Persian LCs in Brahui.

(23) Persian LCs in Brahui [Andronov 2003: 297]
maga(r) 'but', *ya* 'or', *aga(r)* 'if', *ney ... ney* 'neither...nor', *ki* 'that'

The absence of borrowed *laakinna* 'but' is noteworthy.

3.3 Burushaski

The genetic isolate Burushaski has no autochthonous conjunctions since clause combining is again mostly a matter of nominalizations and dedicated verbal inflections. The language is spoken in the border region between Pakistan and India (Kashmir) where linguistic influence from Iranian and Indo-Aryan languages is particularly strong. Like its Dravidian neighbours, Burushaski has borrowed the Persian conditional *agar* 'if' (cf. (24)) although clause combining by means of inter-clausal free morphemes does not form part of the inherited grammatical patterns of the replica.

(24) Burushaski (isolate) [Berger 1974: 55]
agár khené ílji galí ka mumkín dúa
if DEM.M back go:3SG.M and possible be.3SG.INAN
'**If** this one goes back it will become difficult.'

The list of Persian LCs in (25) resembles that given for Brahui in (23). The resemblance holds also for the absence of borrowed *laakinna* 'but'.

(25) Persian LCs in Burushaski [Berger 1974: 125–189]
magám ~ magár 'but', *yâ* 'or', *yâ...yâ* 'either...or', *na...na* 'neither...nor', *táke* 'so that', *ke* 'that'

Berger (1974: 1) emphasizes that in recent years, Burushaski has borrowed heavily from Urdu but that there are also older layers of Persian and Arabic loans. Whether the latter can be considered direct borrowing is irrelevant for our study since (25) contains no item with an Arabic origin.

3.4 Mongolic

Moghol, a member of the Mongolic language family, spoken in Afghanistan owes its hypotactic sentence structure to the massive remodelling on the Persian pattern (Weiers 1972: 150). Accordingly, we also find instances of matter borrowing in the domain of conjunctions. In (26), the conditional *agar* 'if' is involved which, however, occupies a clause-internal position in lieu of occurring at the left edge of the subordinate clause (cf. Section 3.2).

(26) Moghol (Mongolic) [Weiers 1972: 127]
či **agar** ómši čini ogúmbi
2SG **if** sing 2SG:ACC hit:1SG
'**If** you sing I will hit you.'

There is no trace of borrowed *laakinna* 'but' in this replica language. In contrast to the absent adversative LC, Moghol attests to an array of LCs which are not common across the replicas in our sample (cf. (27)).

(27) (Arabo-)Persian LCs in Moghol [Weier 1972: 150–153]
u 'and' (< Arabo-Persian *va*),
jɔ 'or',
(h)ʌm...(h)ʌm 'both...and',

k(j)ɛ ~ ki '(so) that',
mʌgʌr 'although',
bʌdʌsu kɛ 'after, as soon as' (< Arabo-Persian *ba'da az ūn ki* 'after, as soon as' = Persian *ba'd-az ān-ke* 'after' (Yousef 2018: 283) involving MSA *ba'd-a 'an* 'after' (Ryding 2005: 415)),
bʌɔdʃudi kɛ 'although' (< Arabo-Persian *bā wuǧud-i ki* 'although' = Persian *bā vojud-e in* 'however' (Yousef 2018: 297)),
wʌqtɛ kɛ 'when' (< Arabo-Persian *waqt-i ki* 'when' = Persian *vaghti ke* 'when' (Yousef 2018: 282)).

Most notably, there are three multi-word (or periphrastic) LCs all of which are Arabo-Persian hybrids. These periphrases also exist in Persian.

3.5 Austroasiatic

The Munda languages form the western branch of Austroasiatic and are scattered over the eastern part of the Indian sub-continent. Conjunctions are not absolutely unknown in this phylum. However, many of the conjunctions are borrowed from Indo-Aryan. In Kharia, the adversative *lekin* 'but' (28) and *magar* 'but' have entered the replica language's system via Hindi – the same holds for *agar* 'if' (29) (Peterson 2008: 485). Direct contacts between Kharia and Persian or Arabic can be ruled out. An intermediary was responsible for the spread of these conjunctions.

(28) Kharia (Austroasiatic, Munda) [Peterson 2011: 441–442]
 aba=ḍom=kiyar   um=kiyar   batay=oʔ   no   i   jinis
 father=POSS.3=HON NEG=HON tell=ACT.PST CMPL what animal
 heke   i   jhãut   heke
 QUAL.PRS what   animal   QUAL.PRS
 lekin   *muda   ḍan   goṭh=oʔ   sou'b=te=ga*
 but   but   send   C.TEL=ACT.PST all=OBL=FOC
 'Their father didn't tell them which animal it is, which animal it is, **but** he sent them all off.' [original translation]

Example (28) is especially interesting because as Peterson (2011: 441 footnote 5) explains the speaker autocorrects himself when he notices that he made use of the LC *lekin* 'but'. This is why the second adversative *muda* 'but' follows immediately after the LC. Peterson (2011: 408) assumes that Sadri is not only the N-donor of *lekin* 'but' but also of *je* (< Persian *yā* 'or') employed in correlative constructions.

(29) Kharia (Austroasiatic, Munda) [Peterson 2011: 394]
    agar   *am=aʔ*   *bhabru*   *onḍor=kon*   *kiɽoʔ*   *ḍe=na*
    if   2SG=GEN   bark   hear=SEQ   tiger   come=MID.IRR
    laʔ   *boriya=te=ga*   *tar*   *ɲog=e*
    then   both=OBL=FOC   kill   eat=ACT.IRR
    '**If**, having heard your barking, the tiger will come, he will kill and eat us both.' [original translation]

We repeat that since Kharia is spoken in eastern central India direct contacts with Persian are unlikely although we do not deny that the use of Persian during the Moghol administration cannot be ruled out as a factor in the diffusion of the LCs. Nevertheless, the LCs were most probably borrowed indirectly from Persian.

3.6 Austronesian

The situation in the Indonesian archipelago differs markedly from that described in the previous sections. First of all, both Arabic and Persian are said to have enormously influenced the major languages of this region. Their contributions to the lexicon of the replicas are at times indistinguishable as is acknowledged in Jones (1978: v–vi) who states that

> [f]or centuries Malay has been exposed to the influence of these two languages, one being the language of Islam and the other having occupied an important position in India, which has always influenced the Archipelago. Moreover, a very large number of words of Arabic origin has become naturalised in Persian. It is for this reason that both languages have been treated in one list, and no attempt has been made to decide which of the two languages was the *direct* [original italics] donor of a particular word to Malay/Indonesian.

This quote calls to mind the difficulties of determining the donor of LCs in Ottoman Turkish as discussed in Section 2.2. Travellers from the Near East arrived in Indonesia during the second half of the first millennium CE. Eventually, Arabic and Persian were to have a strong impact on Malay-Indonesian. However, this did not take place until centuries later, when local inhabitants began converting to Islam (Tadmor 2009: 689). Since Indonesian emerged via standardization only in the 1920's most if not all of its LCs must have been inherited from traditional Malay. Tadmor (2007: 319) argues that

> [t]he fact that so many adverbial clause markers in Indonesian are borrowed or based on loanwords may be an indication that this category of function words did not exist in early Malay, and its presence in modern Indonesian is due to borrowing.

We already know from example (5) that *laakinna* 'but' is attested as *lakin* 'but' in Indonesian. The presence of *agar* in the same replica can be gathered from (30). However, the conditional meaning of the Persian conjunction has been replaced with a purposive function in Indonesian.

(30) Indonesian (Austronesian, Sundic)   [Krause 1994: 117]

Aminah	selalu	berlatih	**agar**	menjadi
Aminah	always	train	**in_order_to**	become
murid	terbaik	dalam	kelasnya.	
pupil	SUP:good	in	class:POSS.3SG	

'Aminah rehearses all the time **to** become the best pupil in her class.'

For Malay, Winstedt (1952: 151) assumes the existence of the Arabic LC *(wa-) laakinna* 'but'. Jones (1978: 50 and 96), too, counts this as an Arabic element in both Malay and Indonesian. The search for this LC in the Malay corpus provided by the University of Leipzig (https://corpora.uni-leipzig.de/en?corpusId=msa) was unsuccessful. In contrast to the adversative LC, it is by no means difficult to find examples of borrowed *agar* in Malay. Example (31) reflects the same meaning change of the LC as stated for the above Indonesian equivalent.

(31) Malay (Austronesian, Sundic)   [Mintz 1994: 210]

Tapisan	oli	digunakan	dalam	mobil			
filter	oil	PASS:use:INS	in	car			
agar	benda~benda	kecil	tidak	masuk	ke	mesin.	
in_order_to	thing~RED	small	NEG	enter	to	engine	

'An oil filter is used in cars **so that** small particles don't enter the engine.' [original translation]

The question arises whether this meaning change is a local development independent of the rules of the N-donor. Is it possible that the conjunction had a wider functional domain in earlier stages of the N-donor from which only the segment has been copied which has afterwards disappeared from the N-donor? Or is an I-donor responsible for the functional change?

In point of fact, *agar* is the only LC whose N-donor can clearly be identified as Persian. In all other cases Arabic must be considered the N-donor (cf. (32)).

(32) Arabic LCs in Malay and Indonesian [Jones 1978: passim]
bada 'after' (= CA = MSA *baʻd-a ʼan* 'after' (Fischer 2006: 160; Ryding 2005: 415)),
in 'if' (= CA *ʼin* 'if' / MSA *wa-ʼin* 'even if' (Fischer 2006: 203; Ryding 2005: 655)),
(ka)lau 'if' (= CA *law* 'if' / MSA *law-laa* 'if it were not' (Fischer 2006: 204; Ryding 2005: 655)),
sebab 'because' (< Arabic *sabab* 'reason'),
wa 'and' (< Arabic *wa-* 'and').

In (32), subordinating conjunctions of the conditional and causal kind stand out. None of these conjunctions are registered as LCs in any of the replica languages on the mainland. Moreover, *in*, *lau*, and *sabab* are also absent from the Persian and Turkish inventories of Arabic LCs. On this basis, we conclude that the Indonesian archipelago belongs to the Arabic sphere of influence with only a modicum of additional influence from Persian. Thus, the APSLI is not homogeneous but constitutes an agglomeration of geographically adjacent subareas in which different donors have contributed their share to shaping this sphere. On account of the issues discussed throughout Section 2, one might even want to speak of APTSLI – the Arabo-Perso-Turkish sphere of linguistic influence.

4 Evaluation

Apart from revealing the internal partition in three of the APSLI, what do the above data tell us? Any attempt at evaluating them quantitatively can be taken only with a grain of salt because of the huge differences in the documentation of the replicas and the many languages which are not included in the sample. The preliminary character of our study notwithstanding, we take the risk of determining certain frequencies but only for a first orientation. Future research has to put our calculations to the test.

First of all, the replicas can be ordered on a scale according to the number of LCs they attest to. Figure 2 shows that Hindi borrows twelve times as many conjunctions as Sindhi, Gujarati, Shugni, or Parachi.

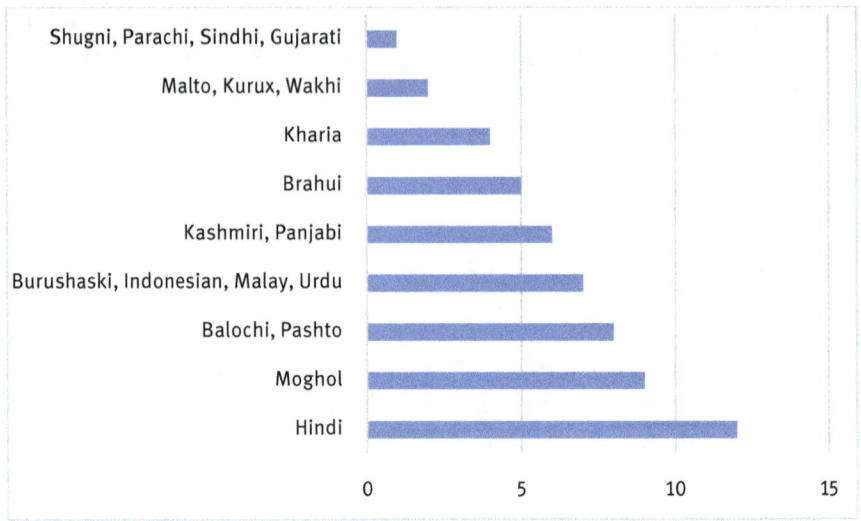

Figure 2: Number of LCs across replicas.

Whether these pronounced differences are causally connected to literacy and register differentiations or time of exposure to Arabo-Persian influence cannot be determined satisfactorily in this study. The genetic relation between donor and replica does not seem to be a crucial factor. The same largely seems to hold for geographical distance from the centre of diffusion.

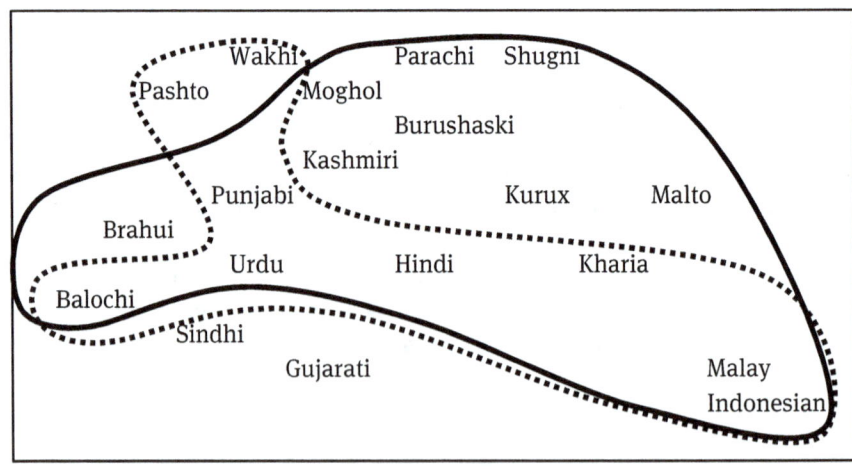

Figure 3: Isoglosses *agar* and *laakinna*.

The schematic map in Figure 3 shows, however, that neighbourhood does play a role when it comes to representing the parallel borrowing behaviour of replicas in the shape of isoglosses. The map features only two isoglosses, namely that of borrowed Persian *agar* 'if' (= uninterrupted line) and that of Arabic *laakinna* 'but' (= dotted line).

The isoglosses overlap without covering the same set of replicas. Seven languages take part in both isoglosses forming a kind of geographical nucleus. The two languages in Afghanistan which are excluded from the *agar*-isogloss are next-door neighbours of each other. Similarly, seven of the ten languages which do not take part in the *laakinna*-isogloss form an area of their own in the northern section of the map. Sindhi and Gujarati borrow neither *agar* 'if' nor *laakinna* 'but', thus they lie outside of both isoglosses and at the same time are geographical neighbours in the southern part of the area. This means that languages tend to behave like those in their vicinity. Whether comparable results can be achieved if further LCs are included in the cartography of borrowings has to be determined in a follow-up study.

Matras (2007: 54–56) proposes two borrowing hierarchies which we reproduce as (33)–(34).

(33) Borrowing hierarchy I: coordinating conjunctions
    but > or > and = ADVERSATIVE > DISJUNCTIVE > CONJUNCTIVE

(34) Borrowing hierarchy II: subordinating conjunctions

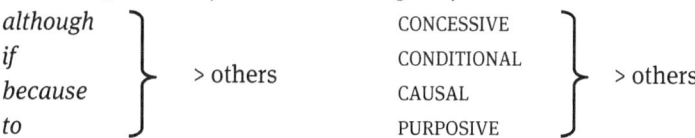

According to these hierarchies, LCs are not randomly borrowed but in accordance with a pragmatic-cognitively motivated chronology. To verify the validity of this hypothesis we first determine how many replicas borrow a given conjunction as Figure 4 shows.

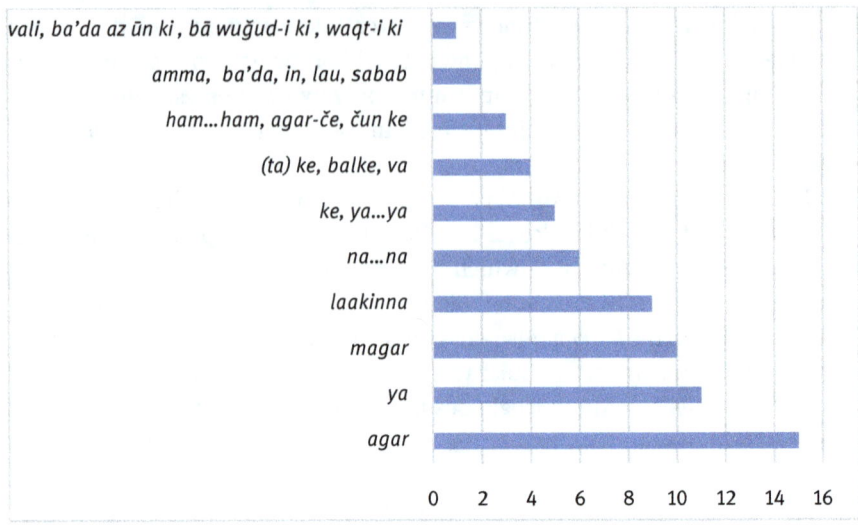

Figure 4: Number of replicas per LC.

The quantitative discrepancy between the most frequently borrowed LC *agar* 'if' and the four LCs at the opposing end of the scale are again striking. Fifteen replicas attest to the borrowing of conditional/purposive *agar* but only one to that of adversative *vali*, temporal *ba'da az ūn ki*, concessive *bā wuğud-i ki*, and temporal *waqt-i ki*. If we subsume the different LCs with similar function under the same label,[11] the picture is as follows. Since only four languages have borrowed CONJUNCTIVE[12] AND the Borrowing Hierarchy I in (33) cannot be confirmed because in one replica (Hindi) borrowed CONJUNCTIVE AND coexists with borrowed DISJUNCTIVE OR and ADVERSATIVE BUT whereas another two languages (Indonesian and Malay) display both borrowed CONJUNCTIVE AND and borrowed ADVERSATIVE BUT but lack evidence of borrowed DISJUNCTIVE OR. A noteworthy exception is Moghol with borrowed AND and OR in the absence of borrowed BUT. However, this inconclusive result is partly compensated for by the fact that nine languages which borrow DISJUNCTIVE OR also borrow ADVERSATIVE BUT. DISJUNCTIVE OR without borrowed ADVERSATIVE BUT occurs twice in the sample (in Sindhi and Moghol) whereas there

---

[11] Note that the identical phonological shape of LCs does not automatically mean that they are employed with the same functions in the replicas. This applies e.g. to borrowed *agar* in Malay and Indonesian which has purposive function instead of conditional. Similarly, *magar* in Moghol is concessive instead of adversative.

[12] The labels in small caps cover several functionally similar conjunctions.

are eleven instances of ADVERSATIVE *BUT* being borrowed without conjunctive *AND* being borrowed too. Borrowed DISJUNCTIVE *OR* is absent from five languages which have borrowed ADVERSATIVE *BUT*. There are three languages with borrowed ADVERSATIVE *BUT* without any other coordinating LC. The special status of ADVERSATIVE *BUT* is (weakly) corroborated. Borrowing Hierarchy I is not fully confirmed although the evidence lends some support to it. As to Borrowing Hierarchy II in (34), the only possible candidate for the category of OTHERS is the TEMPORAL function. Only three LCs are situated in this domain none of which is borrowed by more than two replicas. There are altogether four cases to account for. In all four cases, the TEMPORAL LC co-occurs with a CONDITIONAL LC so that the expectations of Borrowing Hierarchy II are met. In contrast, CONDITIONAL LCs are independent of the presence of a TEMPORAL LC since there are twelve replicas which only borrow the former but not the latter. Thus, Borrowing Hierarchy II is confirmed. We may even go a step further and claim that CONDITIONAL is the unmarked case in the domain of subordination since all replicas which borrow CAUSAL, CONCESSIVE, and/or PURPOSIVE conjunctions also borrow a CONDITIONAL conjunction but not vice versa. Note that CONDITIONAL is also the highest ranking function of subordinating LCs on the borrowing scale in Stolz and Levkovych (2022: 354).

On the basis of a sample of 22 languages from different parts of the world, Grant (2012: 350) puts forward hierarchies similar to those in (33)–(34) and additionally assumes that the borrowing of coordinating conjunctions presupposes the borrowing of at least one subordinating conjunction. Simple copulative *wa* 'and' corroborates this assumption since it is borrowed only by replicas which also borrow subordinating conjunctions. As to disjunctive *ya* 'or', Pashto, Wakhi, and Sindhi are the replicas which do not also borrow a subordinating conjunction. Pashto is also exceptional in the sense that it borrows correlative conjunctions in the absence of borrowed subordinators. Like in our prior study on the language contacts in the former Soviet Union (Stolz and Levkovych 2022: 357), Grant's hypothesis is not fully confirmed.

5 Conclusion

This study has proved the working hypothesis (1) right insofar as the data from outside Africa and Indonesia involve LCs whose D-donor is Arabic but whose diffusion across the Asian (and European) mainland is largely owed to I-donors and N-donors of different genetic affiliation. Accordingly, the initial quote from Matras (2020) should not be understood as the summary of many binary contacts between Arabic and various replicas. The LCs undergo diffusion not because they have an Arabic etymology but because they form part of the grammatical system of a (for whatever reason) dominant language the replica is in contact with. With reference to the shared "oriental lexicon" of languages of different stock in the Caucasian region Chirikba (2008: 76) states that "many of such words have entered individual languages not through the direct contacts with Arabs, Persians or Turks, but via the neighbouring idioms." It is likely that this scenario captures also much of what happened in the APSLI. For an Arabic or Persian or Arabo-Persian LC to be borrowed direct contacts with either Arabic or Persian are not mandatory. The conjunctions are borrowed not so much on account of their history but most probably because of their functions and structural properties.

We have also learned that the APSLI is considerably larger than Matras's observations as to the diffusion of Arabic-derived adversatives suggest. The presence of adversatives of this kind in Africa, Europe, and Asia, notwithstanding, the APSLI is by no means monolithic but displays an internal structure which reflects the co-existence of three major contributors to the diffusion of LCs, viz. Arabic, Persian, and Turkish. As to the situation in the Indian Ocean region, Persian claims the mainland part as its linguistic backyard, in a manner of speaking, whereas Arabic dominates both in Africa and the Indonesian Archipelago. This division of sub-spheres of linguistic influence must have historical reasons. Adequately taking account of the cultural, religious, and political history of the area under scrutiny is far beyond the scope of this study and must therefore be relegated to future research. That the propagation of Islam forms the backdrop of the success of the LCs addressed above is absolutely uncontroversial. However, the presence of Arabic in Koranic schools and mosques can neither fully explain the borrowing of conjunctions into languages whose speech-communities largely remained faithful to their pre-Islamic religion (Hinduism in India, Christian in parts of the Balkans) nor can it be held responsible for the notable presence of Persian LCs. We therefore assume an at best reinforcing role for Arabic-based Islamic religious instruction in the diffusion of LCs. Exactly when happened what linguistically during the culture-historical processes around the Indian Ocean can only be determined in the course of a detailed philological in-depth study of older documents.

We have shown that more often than not the adversative LCs come in a package with other LCs – like the parallel borrowing of coordinating LCs in the former USSR (Stolz and Levkovych (2022: 358–362)) – so that it is futile to concentrate exclusively on translation equivalents of English *but*. We emphasize that the prominence of conditional LCs needs to be paid more attention in language-contact studies if we want to refine the extant borrowing hierarchies.

The to-do-list resulting from this study is long. Not only do we need to considerably enlarge the sample of replicas – for instance, by way of including the understudied variety of Malayalam (Dravidian) in the Laccadive islands and the Indo-Aryan Dhivehi as spoken in the Maldives (both supposedly heavily Arabicized) as well as the Philippine languages spoken south of Luzon (Nikolaus Himmelmann p.c.). It is also a must to reduce the exclusive dependence on the information provided in grammars and dictionaries by way of additionally working with (not necessarily electronic) corpora although only a small subset of the sample languages is privileged in the sense that written texts are available. Another demanding task requires the differentiation of our findings according to parameters such as style, register, sociolect, etc. The role played by the LCs can only be fully understood if the other means of clause-combining and phrase-combining of the replicas are taken account of, too. Moreover, the comparison must look beyond the area under inspection. To the benefit of the theory of language contact the new insights gained on the basis of the data from the Indian Ocean region call for being compared to those from other geographical regions and different donor-replica combinations. To reach this ultimate goal we still need to do a lot of empirical work.

Acknowledgements: We gratefully acknowledge the kind help offered by Norbert Boretzky (Bochum) and Bardhyl Demiraj (Munich) with tracking down suitable Albanian examples. Uri Tadmor (Boston) and Paolo Miccoli (Naples) gave us access to useful resources documenting the Arabic influence on Indonesian and Malay. Nikolaus Himmelmann (Cologne) commented on the possibility of Arabo-Persian loans in Philippine languages. A word of thanks goes to our audiences for sharing their point of view with us at Bremen and Potsdam where nuclear versions of our research were presented on 15 July, 2022 and 3 March, 2023, respectively. On these occasions, Hugo Cardoso, Michael Cysouw, Michael Daniel, Holger Diessel, Tom Güldemann, Martin Haspelmath, Bernd Kortmann, Ekkehard König, Ralph Ludwig, Stefano Manfredini, Barbara Stiebels, and Bernhard Wälchli kindly discussed our preliminary ideas. We also like to thank the members of the Bremen research team – Kevin Behrens, Julia Nintemann, and Maike Vorholt – for commenting on the draft version of this paper. The pre-final version was painstakingly scrutinized by Tabea Salzmann who deserves an especially heartfelt word of thanks for her efforts. Her comments have helped us immensely to improve the quality of this paper. All remaining errors remain our own responsibility.

Abbreviations

1/2/3	first/second/third person
ACC	accusative
ACT	active voice
APSLI	Arabo-Persian sphere of linguistic influence
APTSLI	Arabo-Perso-Turkish sphere of linguistic influence
CA	Classical Arabic
C.TEL	culminatory telicity
CL	class
CMPL	complementizer
COM	comitative
D-donor	distant donor
DEM	demonstrative
DUR	durative
EXCL	exclusive
F	feminine
FOC	focus
FUT	future tense
GEN	genitive
HON	honorific
I-donor	intermediate donor
INAN	inanimate
INDEF	indefinite
INS	instrumental
INTR	intransitive
IRR	irrealis mood
LC	loan conjunction
LK	linker
LOC	locative
M	masculine
MID	middle voice
MSA	Modern Standard Arabic
N-donor	near donor
NEG	negation
NMZL	nominalizer
NOM	nominative
OBL	oblique
PASS	passive
PL	plural
POSS	possessive
PRS	present
PST	past
RED	reduplication
QUAL	qualitative predication
SEQ	sequential

SG	singular
SUBJ	subjunctive
SUP	superlative
TOP	topic marker
TR	transitive

References

Abu-Manga, Al-Amin. 1986. *Fulfulde in the Sudan. Process of adaptation to Arabic*. Berlin: Reimer.
Alavi, Bozorg & Manfred Lorenz. 1988. *Lehrbuch der persischen Sprache*. Leipzig: Enzyklopädie.
Albalá Hernández, Paloma. 2000. *Americanismos en las Indias del Poniente. Voces de origen indígena americano en las lenguas del Pacífico*. Frankfurt/Main: Vervuert.
Andronov, M[ikhail] S. 1980. *The Brahui language*. Translated by V. Korotky. Moscow: Nauka.
Andronov, Mikhail S. 2003. *A comparative grammar of Dravidian languages*. München & Newcastle: LINCOM Europa.
Ashton, E. O. 1944. *Swahili grammar (including intonation)*. London: Longman.
Bashir, Elena. 2009. Wakhi. In Gernot Windfuhr (ed.), *The Iranian languages*, 825–862. London & New York: Routledge.
Bausani, Alessandro. 1964. Note sui vocaboli persiani in malese-indonesiano. *Annali dell'Istituto Universitario Oriientale di Napoli, Nuova Serie* XIV. 1–32.
Berger, Hermann. 1974. *Das Yasin-Burushaski (Werchikwar)*. Wiesbaden: Harrassowitz.
Bhatia, Tej K. 1993. *Punjabi. A cognitive-descriptive grammar*. London & New York: Routledge.
Bittner, Maximilian. 1900. *Der Einfluß des Arabischen und Persischen auf das Türkische*. Wien: Gerold.
Boretzky, Norbert. 1975. *Der türkische Einfluss auf das Albanische. Teil 1: Phonologie und Morphologie der Turzismen*. Wiesbaden: Harrassowitz.
Brendemoen, Bernt. 1998. The Turkish language reform. In Lars Johanson & Éva Á. Csató (eds.), *The Turkic languages*, 242–247. London & New York: Routledge.
Brendemoen, Bernt. 2006. Ottoman or Iranian? An example of Turkic-Iranian language contact in East Anatolian dialects. In Lars Johanson & Christiane Bulut (eds.), *Turkic-Iranian contact areas. Historical and linguistic aspects*, 226–237. Wiesbaden: Harrassowitz.
Cardona, George & Babu Suthar. 2007. Gujarati. In George Cardona & Dhanesh Jain (eds.), *The Indo-Aryan languages*, 659–698. London & New York: Routledge.
Chirikba, Viacheslav A. 2008. The problem of the Caucasian Sprachbund. In Pieter Muysken (ed.), *From linguistic areas to areal linguistics*, 25–94. Amsterdam & Philadelphia: Benjamins.
Coghill, Eleanor. 2019. Northeastern Neo-Aramaic and language contact. In Anthony B. Grant (ed.), *The Oxford handbook of language contact*, 494–518. Oxford: Oxford University Press.
Cowell, Mark W. 2005. *A reference grammar of Syrian Arabic*. Washington/DC: Georgetown University Press.

Dizdari, Tahir N. 2005. *Fjalor i orientalizmave në gjuhën shqipe. (rreth 4500 fjalë me prejardhje nga gjuhët turke, arabe dhe perse)*. Tiranë: Instituti Shqiptar i Mendimit dhe Qytetërimit Islam (AIITC).

Edelman, D.I. & Leila R. Dodykhudoeva. 2009. Shugni. In Gernot Windfuhr (ed.), *The Iranian languages*, 787–824. London & New York: Routledge.

Elfenbein, Josef. 2020. Brahui. In Sanford B. Steever (ed.), *The Dravidian languages*, 495–519. London & New York: Routledge.

Ersen-Rasch, Margarete I. 2012. *Türkische Grammatik*. Wiesbaden: Harrassowitz.

Eyuboğlu, İsmet Zeki. 2017. *Türk dilinin etimoloji sözlüğü*. İstanbul: Say Yayınları.

Fischer, Wolfdietrich. 2006. *Grammatik des klassischen Arabisch*. Wiesbaden: Harrassowitz.

Fragner, Bert G. 2006. Das Persische als Hegemonialsprache in der islamischen Geschichte: Überlegungen zur Definition eines innerislamischen Kulturraums. In Lars Johanson & Christiane Bulut (eds.), *Turkic-Iranian Contact Areas. Historical and Linguisticl*, 39–48. Wiesbaden: Harrassowitz.

Grant, Anthony P. 2012. Contact, convergence, and conjunctions: a cross-linguistic study of borrowing correlations among certain kinds of discourse, phasal adverbial, and dependent clause markers. In Claudine Chamoreau & Isabelle Léglise (eds.), *Dynamics of contact-induced language change*, 311–358. Berlin & Boston: De Gruyter Mouton.

Haig, Geoffrey. 2001. Linguistic diffusion in present-day East Anatolia: from top to bottom. In Alexandra Y. Aikhenvald and R.M.W. Dixon (eds.), *Areal diffusion and genetic inheritance. Problems in comparative linguistics*, 195–224. Oxford: Oxford University Press.

Haspelmath, Martin & Uri Tadmor. 2009. The Loanword Typology project and the World Loanword database. In Martin Haspelmath & Uri Tadmor (eds.), *Loanwords in the world's languages. A comparative handbook*, 1–34. Berlin: De Gruyter Mouton.

Hellwig, Birgit. 2019. Language contact in the West Chadic language Goemai. In Anthony B. Grant (ed.), *The Oxford handbook of language contact*, 431–448. Oxford: Oxford University Press.

Hober, Nicole. 2022. On the borrowing of the English adversative connector *but*. In Nataliya Levkovych (ed.), *Susceptibility vs. resistance: Case studies on different structural categories in language-contact situations*, 283–258. Berlin: De Gruyter.

Horn, Paul. 1898. Neupersische Schriftsprache. In Wilhelm Geiger & Ernst Kuhn (eds.), *Grundriss der iranischen Philologie. Band I, Abteilung 2*, 1–200. Straßburg: Trübner.

Jahani, Carina & Agnes Korn. 2009. Balochi. In Gernot Windfuhr (ed.), *The Iranian Languages*, 634–692. London & New York: Routledge.

Jones, Russell. 1978. *Indonesian etymological project III: Arabic loanwords in Indonesian. A check-list of words of Arabic and Persian origin in Bahasa Indonesia and Traditional Malay, in the reformed spelling*. London: School of Oriental and African Studies.

Johanson, Lars. 1996. Kopierte Satzjunktoren im Türkischen. *Sprachtypologie und Universalienforschung* 49(1). 1–11.

Khubchandani, Lachman M. 2007. Sindhi. In George Cardona and Dhanesh Jain (eds.), *The Indo-Aryan languages*, 622–658. London & New York: Routledge.

Kieffer, Charles M. 2009. Parachi. In Gernot Windfuhr (ed.), *The Iranian languages*, 693–720. London & New York: Routledge.

Koptjevskaja-Tamm, Maria & Bernhard Wälchli. 2001. The Circum-Baltic languages: an areal-typological approach. In Östen Dahl and Maria Koptjevskaja-Tamm (eds.), *Circum-Baltic languages. Volume 2: Grammar and typology*, 615–749. Amsterdam & Philadelphia: Benjamins.

Koul, Omkar N. 2007. Kashmiri. In George Cardona and Dhanesh Jain (eds.), *The Indo-Aryan languages*, 895–952. London & New York: Routledge.
Krause, Erich-Dieter. 1994. *Lehrbuch der indonesischen Sprache*. München & Leipzig: Langenscheidt Enzyklopädie.
Landmann, Angelika. 2015. *Baschkirisch. Kurzgrammatik*. Wiesbaden: Harrassowitz.
Lorenz, Manfred. 1982. *Lehrbuch des Pashto (Afghanisch)*. Leipzig: Enzyklopädie.
Mahootian, Shahrzad. 1997. *Persian*. London & New York: Routledge.
Matras, Yaron. 1998. Utterance modifiers and universals of grammatical borrowing. *Linguistics* 36. 281–331.
Matras, Yaron. 2007. The borrowability of structural categories. In Yaron Matras & Jeanette Sakel (eds.), *Grammatical borrowing in cross-linguistic perspective*, 31–74. Berlin & New York: Mouton de Gruyter.
Matras, Yaron. 2020. *Language contact*. Cambridge: Cambridge University Press.
Matras, Yaron & Jeanette Sakel (eds.). 2007. *Grammatical borrowing in cross-linguistic perspective*. Berlin & New York: Mouton de Gruyter.
McGregor, R.S. 1977. *Outline of Hindi grammar*. New Delhi: Oxford University Press.
Mintz, Malcom W. 1994. *A student's grammar of Malay Indonesian*. Singapore: EPB Publishers.
Mishra, Awadesh K. 1996. *Word formation and language change in Kuṟux*. Varanasi: Tara Book Agency.
Möhlig, Wilhelm J. G. & Bernd Heine. 1999. *Swahili Grundkurs*. Köln: Köppen.
Patnaik, Manideepa. 2008. Juang. In Gregory D. S. Anderson (ed.), *The Munda languages*, 508–556. London & New York: Routledge.
Payne, John. 1989. Pāmir languages. In Rüdiger Schmitt (ed.), *Compendium linguarum iranicarum*, 417–444. Wiesbaden: Reichert.
Peterson, John. 2008. Kharia. In Gregory D. S. Anderson (ed.), *The Munda languages*, 434–507. London & New York: Routledge.
Peterson, John. 2011. *A grammar of Kharia. A South Munda language*. Leiden & Boston: Brill.
Procházka, Stephan. 2002. *Die arabischen Dialekte der Çukurova (Südtürkei)*. Wiesbaden: Harrassowitz.
Ryding, Karin C. 2005. *A reference grammar of Modern Standard Arabic*. Cambridge: Cambridge University Press.
Sakel, Jeanette. 2007. Types of loan: matter and pattern. In Yaron Matras & Jeanette Sakel (eds.), *Grammatical borrowing in cross-linguistic perspective*, 15–29. Berlin & New York: Mouton de Gruyter.
Salemann, C. 1895. Mittelpersisch. In Wilhelm Geiger & Ernst Kuhn (eds.), *Grundriss der iranischen Philologie. Band I, Abteilung 1*, 249–332. Straßburg: Trübner.
Steever, Sanford B. 2020. Malto. In Sanford B. Steever (ed.), *The Dravidian languages*, 433–468. London & New York: Routledge.
Stein, Heidi. 2006. Palatal-velar vocalism of Arabic-Persian loanwords. In Lars Johanson & Christiane Bulut (eds.), *Turkic-Iranian contact areas. Historical and linguistic aspects*, 143–157. Wiesbaden: Harrassowitz.
Stolz, Christel & Thomas Stolz. 1996. Funktionswortentlehnung in Mesoamerika. Spanisch-amerindischer Sprachkontakt (Hispanoindiana II). *Sprachtypologie und Universalienforschung* 49. 86–123.
Stolz, Christel & Thomas Stolz. 1998. Universelle Hispanismen? Von Manila über Lima bis Mexiko und zurück: Muster bei der Entlehnung spanischer Funktionswörter in die indigenen Sprachen Amerikas und Austronesiens. *Orbis* 39(1). 1–77.

Stolz, Thomas. 2022. Entlehntes ABER. Kontaktinduzierte Diffusion adversativer Konnektoren des konjunktionalen Typs. In Julia Nintemann & Cornelia Stroh (eds.), *Über Widersprüche sprechen: Linguistische Beiträge zu Contradiction Studies*, 145–177. Wiesbaden: Springer.

Stolz, Thomas, Deborah Arbes & Christel Stolz. 2021. Pero – Champion of Hispanization? On the challenges of documenting function word borrowing in Mesoamerican languages. In Danae Maria Perez & Eeva Sippola (eds.), *Postcolonial language varieties in the Americas*, 17–54. Berlin & Boston: De Gruyter.

Stolz, Thomas & Nataliya Levkovych. 2022. On loan conjunctions: A comparative study with special focus on the languages of the former Soviet Union. In Nataliya Levkovych (ed.), *Susceptibility vs. resistance: Case studies on different structural categories in language-contact situations*, 259–392. Berlin: De Gruyter.

Tadmor, Uri. 2007. Grammatical borrowing in Indonesian. In Yaron Matras & Jeanette Sakel (eds.), *Grammatical borrowing in cross-linguistic perspective*, 301–328. Berlin & New York: Mouton de Gruyter.

Tadmor, Uri. 2009. Loanwords in Indonesian. In Martin Haspelmath & Uri Tadmor (eds.), *Loanwords in the world's languages. A comparative handbook*. Berlin: De Gruyter Mouton, 686–716.

Tosco, Mauro. 2015. Arabic, and a few good words about empires (but not all of them). In Christel Stolz (ed.), *Language empires in comparative perspective*, 17–40. Berlin, München & Boston: De Gruyter.

Weiers, Michael. 1972. *Die Sprache der Moghol der Provinz Herat in Afghanistan*. Opladen: Westdeutscher Verlag.

Weil, Gotthold. 1917. *Grammatik der osmanisch-türkischen Sprache*. Berlin: Reimer.

Winstedt, R. O. 1952. *Malay grammar*. Oxford: Clarendon.

Woidich, Manfred. 2006. *Das Kairenisch-Arabische. Eine Grammatik*. Wiesbaden: Harrassowitz.

Wolff, H. Ekkehard. 1993. *Referenzgrammatik des Hausa*. Münster: LIT.

Young, David James. 2014. *Urdu grammar*. Leeds: Createspace Independent Publishing Platform.

Yousef, Saaed. 2018. *Persian. A comprehensive grammar*. London & New York: Routledge.

Appendix

language	ADVERSATIVE	CAUSAL	CMPL	CONCESSIVE	CONDITIONAL	CONJUNCTIVE	CORRELATIVE	DISJUNCTIVE	PURPOSIVE	TEMPORAL	total
Hindi	lekin balki magar	cũṁki	ki	agarce	agar	va	na...na yā...yā	ya	(tā) ki		12
Moghol				mʌgʌr bɔɔʃudi kɛ	agar	u	(h)ʌm...(h)ʌm	jɔ	k(i)ɛ~ki	bʌdʌsu kɛ wɑqtɛ kɛ	9
Balochi	lēkin ammā balē		ki		agar~age		na...na yā...yā ham...ham				8
Pashto	lékin~lǻkin balki ammã́ magár						na...na jā...jā ham...ham	jā			8
Burushaski	magám ~ magár		ke		agár		na...na yā...yā	yā	táke		7
Indonesian	lakin	sebab			in (ka)lau	wa			agar	bada	7
Malay	(lekin)	sebab			in (ka)lau	wa			agar	bada	7
Urdu	lekin balkeh magar	coonkeh		agarceh	agar			yā			7

language	ADVERSATIVE	CAUSAL	CMPL	CONCESSIVE	CONDITIONAL	CONJUNCTIVE	CORRELATIVE	DISJUNCTIVE	PURPOSIVE	TEMPORAL	total
Kashmiri	magar			agarči	agar		yā...yā na...na	yā			6
Panjabi	lekan magar	cüüki			agar			ja	(taa) ki		6
Brahui	maga(r)		ki		aga(r)		ney...ney	ya			5
Kharia	lekin magar				agar			je			4
Malto			ki		agar						2
Kurux	magar				agar						2
Wakhi	lōkin							yā			2
Parachi					aga(r)						1
Shugni					aga						1
Sindhi								yā			1
Gujarati	balke										1
sum LCs	25	5	5	5	17	4	14	11	6	4	
sum replicas	14	5	5	4	15	4	7	11	6	3	

Part II

Yaron Matras
The city as multilingual utopia

Creating decolonial spaces for language in an urban setting

Abstract: In this paper I examine how multilingual spaces emerge within institutions across a number of sectors in the city. Drawing on their repertoires of linguistic resources actors (institutional agents and clients) assume agency to change practice and forge ideological justifications for new practice routines. Repertoires of linguistic resources comprise not just linguistic forms but also experiences and encounters in the multilingual city and the ability to find creative solutions drawing on multimodal resources. The ideological stances that accompany practice and reflection on multilingual spaces represent notions of pluralism and transnational identities. They embrace symbols of belonging to a variety of places and practice communities. In this way the city as an organic network of de-centralised institutions accommodates practices and ideologies that differ from the prevailing one-language nation-state position. It develops its own city language narrative. That narrative is supported and in part shaped by a university-based research project – Multilingual Manchester – which introduced a new epistemology into the study of urban multilingualism, many of its elements echoing the decoloniality agenda. There is, however, a risk that the activist agenda might become unsustainable as the neoliberal corporate university environment adopts 'diversity' as a commodity and defaults to a stance that is shaped by colonial legacies.

Keywords: decoloniality, multilingualism, neoliberalism, language policy

1 Introduction: Linguaphobic nation, multilingual city

Speaking in September 2016 at the first Conservative Party Conference after the referendum in which UK voters decided by a narrow margin to leave the European Union, British Prime Minister Theresa May said that Britain's success on the

Yaron Matras, Aston Institute for Forensic Linguistics, Birmingham and Department of Hebrew Language, University of Haifa. Email: y.matras@aston.ac.uk

global stage was guaranteed because "our language is the language of the world"[1].[2] Just a few weeks before he succeeded her as Conservative prime minister in July 2019 Boris Johnson declared that there were "too many parts of the country" where immigrants "did not speak English as their first language"[3]. These statements demonstrate two aspects of a colonial legacy: the aspiration to maintain global hegemony for the benefit of the homeland and its prosperity and the view of immigrants as a market commodity brought in to help build the homeland while refusing to accept that their mobility has created a multilingual reality in that very place.[4]

Paradoxically a similar premise appears in some public statements by academics, who seek to promote interest in other languages in a bid to counteract the decline of enrolment in language subjects and the consequent closure of university language departments. After the 2016 EU referendum statements began to foreground even more intensely the benefits of learning languages as a way of protecting British interests in international trade, diplomacy and security.[5] A recent study even purports to be able to calculate the monetary value of investment in language learning for Britain's GDP[6]. Such interventions have been targeting policymakers committed to the proposition that releasing the UK from the constraints of the EU will unleash its economic and diplomatic potential. They often conclude with the phrase "now more than ever" suggesting that learning languages has become more necessary and urgent in the wake of Britain's voluntary renunciation of its unrestricted access to European markets (cf. Kelly 2018). Some have suggested that the study of foreign languages contributes to British 'soft power'[7] – understood as a way to dominate others with minimal use of force – while others have gone as far as to argue that it should be part of a political programme of 'progressive patriotism'[8], a concept that has since been criticised as

---

1 https://www.bbc.co.uk/news/av/uk-politics-37563510
2 All websites cited were last accessed in November 2022.
3 https://www.theguardian.com/politics/2019/jul/05/johnson-pledges-to-make-all-immigrants-learn-english
4 For 'the case against linguaphobia' see https://blog.policy.manchester.ac.uk/posts/2016/09/the-case-against-linguaphobia/
5 And see already British Academy report 'Lost for Words' from 2013: https://www.thebritishacademy.ac.uk/documents/199/British_Academy_report_Lost_for_words_report.pdf
6 https://www.rand.org/pubs/research_reports/RRA1814-1.html
7 See Cambridge University conference report on 'The value of languages' from 2016. https://www.publicpolicy.cam.ac.uk/system/files/documents/value-of-languages.pdf
8 See http://projects.alc.manchester.ac.uk/cross-language-dynamics/cultural-diplomacy-linguistic-diversity-and-the-softening-of-power-towards-a-progressive-patriotism/index.html

associated with a covert form of white supremacy (cf. Bhattacharyya et al. 2021: 68ff.).[9]

Statements in support of languages in this context have focused primarily on the study of Western European languages – coined 'Modern Foreign Languages' (MFL) – with some attention given to Mandarin Chinese and recently also to Arabic (cf. McLelland 2017). The languages of (other) immigrant populations – labelled 'Community Languages' in British public discourse – tend to receive only marginal attention if any.[10] They are taught almost exclusively outside of mainstream school curricula and, with the exception of Chinese and Arabic, they are given practically no space in the country's higher education programmes. In July 2020 the British Academy along with the British Council and three other leading academic organisations published a proposal for a 'National Languages Strategy'[11]. Its recommendations focus exclusively on investment in language skills in an effort to reverse the decline in enrolment in language subjects, which, the paper argues, will help "strengthen our relationships across the world". They hardly address domestic multilingualism, regulation of interpreting and translation services, accessibility of services, the importance of multilingualism for intergenerational relations and wellbeing or its role in cultural production. In fact the word 'multilingual' appears in the 25-page document just seven times, five of which are citations of the titles of other documents and projects.

Language policy in the UK is an aggregate of several different strands[12]. The devolved governments in Wales and Scotland have policies to protect and promote their indigenous regional languages (Welsh, Gaelic and Scots, respectively) while in Northern Ireland political power sharing stalled in 2018 in part due to controversies around proposals for an Irish Language Act. Education policies regulate the position of 'Modern Foreign Languages' in the school curriculum along with a limited offer of accredited extra-curricular examinations in other languages. Beyond the education system Britain's language policy often assumes a

---

9 See also https://www.opendemocracy.net/en/oureconomy/step-aside-progressive-patriotism-intergalactic-humanism-has-arrived/
10 An exception is the Times Education Commission report from June 2022 which called to "encourage pupils who speak English as a second language to gain a qualification in their native tongue", and the efforts of Baroness Jean Coussins on behalf of the All Party Parliamentary Group on Languages to acknowledge the language skills of young people with migration background.
11 https://www.thebritishacademy.ac.uk/documents/2597/Towards-a-national-languages-strategy-July-2020_R0FHmzB.pdf
12 For an overview of policy in English as a subject of teaching see Rampton et al. (2020).

gatekeeping function. The government relies on language analysis for the determination of origin (LADO) to verify claims for political asylum of applicants from certain countries (cf. Patrick 2012; Matras 2018b). Citizenship language tests link naturalisation to English proficiency (measures to support the instruction of English as additional or other language are devolved to local authorities). In 2011 a question on language was introduced into the national Census. It asks 'What is your main language?' but only gives respondents a choice between English (or Welsh) and indicating a single language linked to a self-assessment of their proficiency in English. There is no indication that the data are used to plan accessibility or language provisions. Only some government departments issue translations of selective information into immigrant languages. This tends to be limited to domains in which immigrant populations are deemed to pose a potential risk to themselves and to the most vulnerable members of their own communities in connection with practices such as forced or arranged marriage, female genital mutilation and religious extremism, while no multilingual information is available, for example, on immigration or citizenship procedures. After the outbreak of the Covid pandemic in 2020 government agencies were slow to produce guidance notes in immigrant languages relying instead on voluntary sector initiatives.[13] Concern for the wellbeing and safety of minority communities thus does not seem to be a key factor guiding translation policy at national level. On the whole it would not be inaccurate to say that language policy in the UK (with the exception of support for regional languages in the devolved nations) aims to ensure compliance and cultural uniformity while equipping an elite minority with skills to promote British interests abroad.

In this contribution I examine attitudes to multilingualism in a major UK city through the lens of decoloniality debates. I draw on arguments and insights from the fields of cultural and heritage studies, diaspora studies, urban studies and critical sociolinguistics, exploring links between notions of superdiversity, civic identity, linguistic repertoires, plurilingualism, translanguaging and linguistic citizenship. I show how everyday experiences and encounters with multilingualism shape actors' ideologies and in some cases prompt them to adopt practical solutions and strategies in response to the multilingual reality around them. I discuss how these practices have opened up multilingual spaces within a number of institutions in the city. Having gathered my observations in the context of an ambitious outreach programme launched as part of a university project that

---

[13] https://blog.policy.manchester.ac.uk/growth_inclusion/2020/05/a-tale-of-cities-local-diasporas-hold-a-key-to-strengthening-international-outreach/

aimed to develop a new epistemology for participatory research on urban multilingualism I conclude with a critical reflection on the concept of the 'civic university' as a catalyst for social change.

My principal argument is that the city as a site of cross-cultural and multilingual encounters is challenged to provide its own responses to multilingualism. It does that in order to meet its statutory commitment to equality of access to services and in order to maintain a workable level of community cohesion where different population sectors partake in key economic, social and political activities. The one-nation-one-language rhetoric loses much of its purpose and utility in the local constituency where in some districts more than half of the population is of immigrant or minority background and maintains distinct traditions and community-specific social and economic networks. Rather than rally behind nationalistic slogans or engage in overt confrontation with national policy by challenging it head-on, the city develops an alternative ideology: a civic identity narrative that embraces local diversity which it uses to brand itself as an entity that is open to the world.

When referring to 'the city' I address not just the agencies of local government: it is instead an organic network of institutions in a variety of sectors and the various individual actors that participate in them in the roles of agents and clients. The city language narrative embraces multilingualism and legitimises local practices that respond to the needs of the multilingual reality. It helps empower actors, encouraging them to reflect on their personal experiences and their own repertoires of multilingual practice routines and to draw upon them to find local solutions to practical challenges. I identify four dimensions in which these reflections take shape in the city: facilitating *access* to services, promoting *heritage*, cultivating and harnessing *skills*, and the overarching dimension of *celebration* that incorporates personal encounters and experiences into a display of togetherness around the theme of multilingualism (cf. Matras 2017b).

For actors of minority language background, multilingual practices and ideologies constitute what Brubaker (2005) calls a 'diasporic stance,' one that sets them apart from the majority population that is the primary target of neo-colonial, nationalist rallying. The city language narrative embraces these manifestations of diasporic identity. They become an emblem around which local constituents are mobilised to adopt a sense of co-ownership of measures for local support and outreach, which are becoming ever more devolved and de-centralised as austerity forces local government to downsize. This involves delegating a sense of agency: the right to subvert established routines and to introduce new ways of doing things and new solutions to problems. It forges an ideology of civic belonging that implicitly if not overtly challenges the colonial and neo-colonial positions propagated at national level – those that advocate linguistic and cultural uniformity and which have a place for foreign languages only as a way of strengthening the nation's hegemonic position in the world. This constellation of agency, ownership, local responses at civic level and pluralism of practice routines can be regarded as a decolonial enterprise, notwithstanding the absence of an overtly formulated statement of aims that brands it as such.

2 Conceptual anchoring: Decoloniality, diasporas, and urban multilingualism

Discussions around decolonising cultural policy, research and the education curriculum have been flourishing since the late 1990s, with a trajectory targeting the symbolic decolonising of public spaces gaining momentum post-2020 through the Black Lives Matters movement. Decoloniality seeks to undo what is perceived as Western hegemony over knowledge and, deriving from it, the shaping and legitimation of practice deemed culturally oppressive. Following Said (1978), Stuart Hall (1992) regards the West as a historical concept that emerged in the Enlightenment and is used for comparison among societies. It forges a binary distinction between the Self and the Other giving rise to a discourse representation that oversimplifies difference. At the heart of the decolonising agenda is the view that there are privileged narratives that dominate at the expense of other perspectives and which are the direct outcome of historical power relations between nations and the economic divisions that these power relations create and perpetuate (cf. Mignolo 2011). For Smith ([1999] 2021) decolonising means redefining privileges. That includes doing away with the representation of indigenous cultures through the prism of Western cultural norms and challenging the concept that the Other must accommodate to the norms of the colonial power.

2.1 The university setting

Universities are regarded in the context of this discussion as sites in which colonial knowledge is produced and perpetuated. This is partly expressed through the division among disciplines, which reproduces pre-defined epistemologies (cf. Bhambra et al. 2018). Holmwood (2018) points out that the rise of the neoliberal university and the view of higher education as the responsibility of individuals rather than a social right limits the space available for new and critical knowledge production yet further. Similarly, Lorenz (2012) argues that as the societal relevance of universities is defined more and more in terms of its economic relevance to business and industry, Neoliberal Public Management principles produce an environment in which research becomes a commodity. The mass production of knowledge to satisfy league tables and rankings is then accompanied by managerial regimes of permanent control, which Lorenz compares to the power of the Party in Communist regimes. Neary (2020) critiques contemporary concepts of the 'civic university' and 'university social responsibility' as merely serving that same neoliberal marketing agenda. He calls for an "intellectual insurgency" where genuine civic engagement relies on progressive social movements and political struggles. For Mignolo and Walsh (2018) decoloniality is linked to civil resistance and social movements as well as to the recognition of cultural diversity and the idea of a plurinational state. Critiquing Modernity as the basis of an ontological classification that postulates entities, they see the purpose of decoloniality as introducing a different epistemology, one that foregrounds the experience of relations – or Relationality – and which entails breaking away from established discipline boundaries that shape and create knowledge. Smith ([1999] 2021: 261) however notes that in an environment in which research is increasingly measured in order to assess the researcher's performance, those who choose to research with and fight for marginalised communities often find themselves in the margins of their own institutions and disciplines.

Since 2018 several UK universities have released statements of intent around decolonising the curriculum promising to use the university space to critique colonial legacies and the notion that Western knowledge is universal and superior and to include other philosophies and knowledge systems. At the time of writing no comprehensive information is available about the implementation of such declarations of intent in UK higher education. Attempts to implement strategic models of decolonial teaching and research in other parts of the world have so far taken a variety of shapes. Auto-ethnographic essays by scholars of non-Western and ethnic minority backgrounds adopt the notion of decolonising as a personal strategy to navigate intercultural encounters and power relations in the Western academic environment (e.g. Joseph 2008; Bhattacharya 2016; Batac 2022). That includes tackling interpersonal styles of communication as well as dominant epistemological stances that deem certain scholarly agendas to be unworthy or fail to take into account research mobility and the transnational identities of those involved in it. For Luke and Heynen (2021) decolonising the university entails using the university as a site for political engagement and anti-racist activism outside the university as well as a teaching and learning platform to critique colonial history and include disadvantaged and racially marginalised populations. Woldeyes and Offord (2018) describe how the teaching of human rights can be turned into a practical engagement space, moving beyond mere juridical aspects of human rights law and shifting the focus to responding to the voices of those who seek justice and articulate demands for social change. For Pidgeon (2016) taking the commitment to inclusivity beyond "tokenised checklist responses" requires system transformations that allow participants to 'indigenise' the academy by embracing what is referred to as "indigenous knowledges and ways of being". Such structural changes range from the inclusion of indigenous people in leadership positions and advisory committees to the drafting of Aboriginal strategic plans and policies, setting up Aboriginal student services, taking into consideration cultural expectations when drafting ethics protocols for research with Aboriginal communities and the internationalisation of indigenous movements to strengthen exchange and broaden perspectives. Brear and Tsotetsi (2021) discuss an example of structural transformation of research ethics protocols showing how researchers can obtain informed consent by engaging communities verbally and in their own language and without the conventional constraints on confidentiality of personal data, though such accommodation necessarily disrupts procedural norms giving rise to friction with university administrations.

Brooks et al. (2022) address a more wholesale approach to the decolonising of a programme of studies drawing an interim assessment of Romani studies at the Central European University (CEU) in Budapest. According to the authors the programme prioritised hiring staff of Romani background and engaging in advocacy and critique of what was seen as traditional methods of research in the field. Those were deemed to have neglected to articulate the Romani perspective. In particular, the programme's content is said to have moved away from that of a predecessor summer course in Romani studies. The authors maintain that that course had focused on the Roma as an "impoverished underclass" and sought solutions for their "economic integration". They state that the new, successor programme shifted the focus to discrimination, segregation and inequalities as well as studying the Romani political movement and forms of Roma resistance as a way of empowering Romani students. In fact the earlier Romani studies summer school programme at CEU did engage with Romani advocacy and gave Romani activists a regular platform. What Brooks et al. (2022) promote as an alternative, 'critical' model is one that gives Romani people a voice by being able to showcase a faculty group that is composed entirely of people who identify as Roma and so can be seen as representing Romani interests (cf. Stewart 2017; Matras 2017a). Nonetheless, the analogy drawn between the Romani people as a non-territorial minority in Europe and colonised nations is pertinent in demonstrating how decoloniality relates to values and methods of engagement that challenge power relations and cultural Eurocentrism. It is not confined to a pre-defined set of historical settings associated specifically with European overseas colonial expansionism.

2.2 Decoloniality and language

Decoloniality approaches are thus concerned with a number of issues including
a) re-defining the beneficiaries of research,
b) shifting the focus from reproducing what is considered to be Eurocentric knowledge to content that seeks to empower those who have been disadvantaged by historical colonialism and the ideologies that it produced,
c) incorporating an advocacy agenda into research, teaching and learning that aims to be directly responsive to the needs of participants outside of academia, particularly those considered to be 'colonised subjects', and
d) working beyond academic discipline boundaries toward internationalising a movement to mobilise for a change in power relations.

These are accompanied by an effort to bring about structural transformations within institutions: greater inclusivity of personnel and more diversity of procedures and norms of interaction. In some cases they may even seek to ensure that all or most staff on a programme of studies identify as members of the populations that are being studied. That approach is based on the view that academic programmes and disciplines constitute instruments of power and representation of interests. In this way decoloniality seeks to create new forms of knowledge by diversifying styles and the content of learning as well as using the academic space for activism to bring about social change. That very experience offers an opportunity to derive new knowledge through reflection on the decolonial project itself, which in turn enriches the enquiry agenda.

Applications of the decoloniality paradigm to language have involved a critique of the notion of languages as fixed and self-contained systems and the adoption instead of a view of language as practice that takes on fluid and hybrid forms. Veronelli (2015) regards the coloniality of language as the construction of hierarchies among languages. The latter are associated with the racialisation of speakers of languages considered to be inferior: coloniality links language to civilisation, writing, grammar and knowledge and thus treats it as a representation of power. The decolonial paradigm replaces this view of language by the notion of 'languaging' as a communal act, an activity that is attached to the materiality of everyday life, forging and negotiating relations. Stroud (2001, 2008, 2018) introduces the concept of 'linguistic citizenship' to capture the idea that language is a site of political and economic struggle and that debates around language should serve to give political voice and agency. Linguistic citizenship entails a critique of the 'essentialising' links between language and identity promoting instead awareness and respect for diversity and difference. Stroud and Kerfoot (2021) discuss how acts of linguistic citizenship can resist the hegemony of colonial languages. They understand citizenship as a set of interwoven acts of engagement that make subjects and their claims visible and audible, lending legitimacy to political actorhood. Such acts of language are performed outside the institutional status quo in order to create alternative relationships with Others, engage with voices on the margin and create conditions for transformative agency. Using marginalised languages in new spaces as tools to make audible neglected subjectivities can constitute a decolonial act of citizenship, rethinking and engaging new knowledge and reclaiming public space. Heugh (2022) links linguistic citizenship directly to decolonial epistemologies describing how the inclusion of indigenous voices in research and policy drafting serves to counteract historical practices of erasure and to question ownership of knowledge.

2.3 Language, community and dynamic repertoires

These ideas of language are connected to an emerging paradigm that reconsiders links between language, place and identity. It seeks to re-conceptualise language by taking account of the layered and dynamically changing configurations brought about by postcolonial mobility and globalisation. In many respects this direction of 'critical sociolinguistics' follows a path set by critical theory and cultural studies. It involves the appreciation of 'diaspora' as an alternative to constructivist notions of 'identity'. Stuart Hall (1990) refers to diaspora as an act of 'positioning' amidst a 'creolisation' of features. Anderson's (1983) notion of 'imagined communities' and Brubaker's (2004) position on 'ethnicity without groups' highlight 'community' as a category of practice rather than a collectivity that implies sameness. The dissolution of the link between culture and territoriality is regarded as a key feature of globalisation (cf. Tomlinson 1999) allowing individuals to partake in practices independently of location and across different dimensions, coined 'ethnoscapes' in Appadurai's (1992) influential work. In the paradigm of 'transnationalism' (Panayi 2010) diasporas are understood as forming what Werbner (2002) calls 'communities of co-responsibility' that act beyond locations and maintain a distinctive life within the host countries, particularly in cities (cf. Cohen 2008).

Vertovec's (2007) concept of 'superdiversity' has been influential in capturing the complexity and dynamism of relations between groups especially in cities, where diasporas exhibit multiple forms of local and global participation. It has been argued that the presence of economically active diasporas with transnational links allows cities to capitalise on a 'diversity dividend' (cf. Glick Schiller 2011; Syrett and Sepulveda 2011) with 'diversity' replacing multiculturalism as a policy paradigm by including the dimension of profitability of difference (Schiller 2015). Urban diversity has been argued to facilitate equality as cities are in a position to support the welfare and development of citizens irrespective of origin (White 2018). Much attention has been given to cities as spaces of cultural convergence. Gilroy (2004) speaks of 'conviviality' as a bottom-up process in urban areas, which can defend multiculturalism against what he calls "revivalist colonialist accounts", while Suzanne Hall (2012) discusses how conviviality is expressed through direct encounters requiring a critical analytical approach to 'community'. Such approach is offered by Blokland (2017) who defines urban communities as spaces of public familiarity in which people congregate around shared narratives of belonging.

Post-colonial, critical sociolinguistics connects to these notions of globalisation and the central role of cities as spaces in which diaspora communities are constantly redefining themselves through a plurality of encounters. Mac Giolla Chríost (2007) and Heller (2010) consider processes of identity formation in cities as 'post-national': they give rise to language policy and planning activities that are best characterised as reciprocal action in an eco-system of different actors rather than under the influence of constitutional prescriptivism. This echoes theorising in urban studies around the ideas of the 'right to the city' (e.g. Purcell 2013, following Lefebvre 1968) where inhabitants engage in meaningful networking to achieve aims that cannot be provided by the state, and notions of 'urban conviviality' (Douglass 2008) where participatory planning takes on an approach to governance that embraces inclusivity and multiculturalism. Case study descriptions of such processes around multilingual policy and practice in UK cities are offered by Matras and Robertson (2015) for city-based actors in Manchester and by Cadier and Mar-Molinero (2012) for a number of institutions and smaller outlets in Southampton.

Blommaert and Rampton (2011) and Blommaert (2010, 2013) address the wider methodological implications of superdiversity (see also Arnaut et al. 2016; Arnaut et al. 2017) calling to move away from the postulation of static correlations between linguistic variables and extra-linguistic descriptors and instead to explore communicative contexts through the lens of linguistic ethnography (cf. also Redder et al. 2013; Stevenson 2017). This has theoretical implications for the study of multilingual practices. Rampton (1995) discusses 'crossing' of boundaries as users adopt linguistic features that are associated with others' origins (see also Wiese and Kerswill 2022). Jørgensen (2008) calls for a focus on the fluidity of 'features' approaching users' linguistic resources as a wholesale repertoire rather than sets of discrete languages (see also Matras 2009 for a view of language change in multilingual settings as the product of pragmatic repertoire management and re-shaping of practice routines). Blommaert and Backus (2013) and Busch (2012) define repertoires in multilingual urban settings as consisting not just of language skills but also of experiences of encounters with language. This idea of fluidity of language resources and their flexible deployment by users is captured by concepts such as 'translanguaging' (Li 2018b) and 'metrolingualism' (Pennycook and Otsuji 2015). It also features in descriptions of pedagogical practice in multilingual settings as explicitly embracing the complexity and fluidity of linguistic resources rather than adhering strictly to prescriptivist notions of language (García and Li 2014; Blackledge and Creese 2010).

2.4 An agenda for social change

A sociolinguistic agenda that is decolonial in the sense of some of the works referred to above is presented at least as an aspiration in the introductory remarks to a collection of articles compiled by Creese and Blackledge (2018). Emphasising the need to recognise the new conditions that are created by global migrations and population change, they flag preoccupation with language and superdiversity as an "ideology" that is "equipped to critique forces of discrimination" (Creese and Blackledge 2018: xxiii) and call for an analytical and conceptual framework that requires academic researchers to "communicate effectively with those who can make a difference to policy and practice" and to forge alliances across disciplines in order to "contribute to the creation of more equal societies" (Creese and Blackledge 2018: xxvii).

In the following sections I discuss discourse representations and practices around multilingualism in several sectors and institutions in the city, drawing on the example of Manchester. I show how they present alternative ideologies to nation-state narratives around language and identity, particularly those that have gathered momentum in the public debate in the UK since the Brexit referendum. I show how actors feel empowered to engage in practices that build on their individual repertoires of experiences and exposure to multilingualism in the city, how such practices can constitute emerging micro-level policy changes, and how they are accompanied by an overarching city language narrative that is shaped and broadcast through celebratory events. A contributor to that narrative was the

Multilingual Manchester project, which I founded at the University of Manchester in 2010 and led until I left that institution in 2020. I show how the programme piloted a new epistemology that addressed key elements of the decoloniality agenda. I conclude by briefly addressing the potential contradictions of a civic engagement model that pursues a decolonial agenda while situated within a neoliberal higher education environment. As a result of historical circumstances, Eurocentric norms, values and approaches to knowledge prevail in that environment. When nationalist positions such as the association of languages with 'soft power' compete with the decolonial project over material resources and the authority to determine the content of public messages, there is a risk that the decolonial project might run out of favour with the corporate management structure. Civic engagement for social justice and equality might then have to yield to the commodification of diversity for the sake of corporate branding.

3 The setting: Manchester's multilingualism

Manchester has a current population of over half a million. In the 2021 Census some 18 per cent of residents stated that they had a 'main language' other than English – twice the national average. Even this figure probably underestimates the number of multilingual households. For one there was lack of clarity as to whether the term 'main language' represents personal preference, proficiency, or frequency of use (cf. Matras and Robertson 2015). In addition, respondents who would attribute the same or similar importance to English as they do to another language did not have the opportunity to indicate this on the census form. That puts the likely proportion of households that use languages other than or in addition to English at anywhere between 30–40 per cent, or roughly 150,000–200,000 of the city's residents. This figure does not include the many residents who have acquired foreign language skills through formal studies or periods of residence abroad. Annual school census data since 2012 indicate that between 30–40 per cent of pupils have a 'first language' other than English. In five of the city's thirty-two wards (administrative units with an average population of around 16,000) more than 60 per cent of children speak a language other than English in the home and in another eight the figure is higher than 40 per cent. In over twenty Manchester schools pupils who have a first language other than English make up more than 70 per cent of the school population. Around forty-five Manchester schools identify more than thirty different first languages that are spoken among their pupils. The most frequent are Urdu, Arabic, Somali, Panjabi, Bengali, Polish, French, Yoruba, Portuguese, Chinese, Pashto and Kurdish.

Again the figures are likely to under-report multilingualism as they tend not to take into account children who speak English at home with one parent and another language with another parent. The realistic proportion of pupils with a multilingual background is probably upwards of 50 per cent.

Statistics on the number of languages spoken in the city also vary. The 2021 Census named around 90 individual 'main languages' that were reported by respondents and grouped additional languages by region of origin. The annual School Census tends to report upwards of 150 different languages as pupils' 'first languages'. Interpreter requests in the health care sector show regular demand for around 120 languages. Many languages remain under-reported since they are regional or minority languages in the countries of origin or are used primarily for oral communication with family and friends, often alongside English. They are therefore not typically identified by speakers as their preferred 'main language' or as the principal 'first language' of school pupils. Nor do they figure in the list of languages for interpreting requests, either because their speakers also know English or because they ask for interpreters in a third language (often the state language of the country of origin). This is the case for many African languages, for regional varieties of various South Asian and East Asian languages, for non-territorial minority languages such as Romani and Yiddish, and for non-written languages such as Caribbean Creoles and West African Pidgins. Languages that are closely related are sometimes grouped together in the statistics under a single heading. That is the case, for example, for Potwari and Mirpuri, for Kurmanji, Badini and Sorani (Kurdish varieties), for various Chinese languages and sometimes even for unrelated languages such as English Romanes and Shelta (both referred to as 'Gypsy languages').

Languages other than English with large numbers of speakers in Manchester include Urdu, Arabic, Chinese, Polish, Panjabi, Spanish, Bengali, Somali, Italian, Persian and Kurdish. French and Portuguese are widespread among communities of both African and European origins. Greater Manchester has the country's highest speaker concentrations outside of London for a number of languages including Yiddish, Somali, Kurdish, and Romani. There are long established speaker communities of languages from different parts of the world including African languages such as Yoruba, Shona, Akan, Nigerian Pidgin English, Hausa, Swahili and Tigrinya, Caribbean languages such as Jamaican Patwa, eastern European languages such as Slovak, Czech, Lithuanian, Latvian, Ukrainian, Romanian and Hungarian, western European languages including German, Spanish and Greek, West Asian languages including Turkish, Armenian, Dari and Pashto, South Asian languages such as Gujarati, Telugu, Malayalam and Tamil and regional languages such as Sylheti and Pahari, and East Asian languages including

Korean, Vietnamese, Malay and Thai. Various languages are used by Manchester residents for liturgical purposes and religious study, among them Classical Arabic, Sanskrit, Biblical Hebrew, Biblical Greek, Armenian and Panjabi. Around 265 Manchester residents declared British Sign language (BSL) to be their 'main language' on the 2021 Census. Altogether around 16,000 persons or 3.3 per cent of the city's total population declared in 2011[14] that they had low or very low proficiency in English, with higher percentages (over 5 per cent) in some areas of the city. Around 10 per cent of households declared that they had no member who had English as their 'main language', that figure rising to up to 20 per cent in some districts.

Over fifty languages are represented in the city's public spaces on signs of local businesses and cultural and religious institutions, adverts and noticeboards, landmarks, parks, health and safety notices and on websites that are managed by Manchester residents and local commercial and cultural organisations (Gaiser and Matras 2016b). The most frequently encountered languages on public signage are Arabic and Chinese, followed by Polish, Urdu, Bengali, Kurdish, Somali, Persian, Romanian, Russian, Lithuanian, Hindi, Gujarati and Vietnamese, as well as, particularly in cultural and religious institutions, Hebrew, Ukrainian and Panjabi.

The city hosts a variety of language provisions.[15] Manchester libraries stock over 25,000 titles in more than twenty languages other than English with a high volume of stock for Urdu and Chinese as well as for Polish, Bengali, Arabic and Vietnamese. Public services maintain provisions for interpreting and translations. The city council's translation and interpreting service M-Four Translations has around eleven contracted staff and around 200 freelance vendors who respond annually to over 12,000 requests for interpreting and translation in more than 70 different languages. Central Manchester Hospitals, now also known as Manchester University NHS Foundation Trust (MFT), maintain an in-house translation and interpreting department with around ten full-time and additional ten part-time staff who are supported by external contractors. Together they respond to around 50,000 annual face-to-face and telephone requests for interpreting in around 100 different languages. Other hospitals and the city's emergency services rely on a number of local contractors for interpreting and translation who often draw on the language skills of local residents. Manchester's GP (General

---

14 The breakdown on English proficiency by 'main language' for the 2021 census is not yet available at the time of writing.
15 See 'MLM Digest': https://www.kratylos.org/~raphael/multilingual/wp-content/uploads/2015/12/MLMDigest.pdf

Practice) clinics register upwards of 15,000 interpreting requests annually. Languages with a high demand for interpreting services are generally those that are most widespread in the city, including Urdu, Panjabi, Arabic, Polish, Bengali, Persian, Kurdish, Cantonese, and Somali, as well as Romanian.[16]

A large number of weekend (supplementary) schools operated by part-time staff who are often volunteers offer children and young people instruction in speaking and writing skills in a variety of languages (see below). It is estimated that upwards of 5,000 children from the Greater Manchester area are enrolled in such programmes.

4 The Multilingual Manchester project

Multilingual Manchester[17] (MLM) emerged in the academic year 2009–2010 and developed into a new model for high impact and participatory research (for introductory overviews see Matras and Robertson 2017 and Matras 2018a). Its initial objective was to create an overarching and sustainable framework that would offer opportunities to archive the digital outcomes of a series of research projects in languages and linguistics in the absence of dedicated institutional resources to continue to maintain such outputs. The pilot shift to digital submission of undergraduate student coursework in that same year offered an opportunity to archive student work for a new course unit on Societal Multilingualism in which students were directed to explore multilingual needs and provisions in the city. This followed a series of postgraduate research projects that since 2005 had looked at various aspects of the city's multilingualism including city council language provisions (Donakey 2007) and multilingual communities and families (Lo 2007; Osman 2006). From these and other similar works we drew inspiration to encourage local students with various language backgrounds to explore communities to which they had an attachment, and use introspection opportunities to develop new insights, all on the one hand, while on the other hand to open up opportunities for immersion in multilingual communities for those students who had hardly had such opportunities. The project was formally inaugurated in October 2010 in the shape of a website that archived student research on local multilingualism and which soon attracted interest from local institutions including

---

16 For an overview and sources of data see various MLM publications: http://kratylos.org/~raphael/multilingual/publications/index.html
17 http://mlm.humanities.manchester.ac.uk/, also archived on https://archive.org and https://kratylos.org

the National Health Service (NHS), schools, community groups and the local authority seeking information and data to guide their own provisions.

4.1 A changing higher education environment

In the same year a new coalition government led by the Conservative party introduced a significant increase in student tuition fees. For humanities subjects this amounted to a threefold increase to around £9,000 per year. Public statements defended the move by linking university degrees to earning potential, a rationale that was soon to become embedded into university league tables, which captured the reported earnings of graduates within several months of graduation as a measure of the quality of their programmes of study. By 2012 pressure on universities grew to also demonstrate a 'return' on government investment in research in the form of 'demonstrable impact on society, economy and policy' and to show 'value for money' in the form of a unique 'student experience' and employability prospects. This was incorporated structurally into the national evaluation of universities in 2014 in the form of so-called 'impact case studies'. Scores were linked to financial rewards.

As we reported (Matras and Robertson 2017) the University of Manchester adopted in response a 'social responsibility' agenda. Managers entrusted with delivering on that agenda were on the search for university activities that could be flagged as 'making a difference' to society. It was in this context that MLM first received recognition within the institution. In 2013 modest resources were provided for a temporary position to support public engagement activities, particularly the running of a student volunteer scheme. Further resources were secured through small grants from a variety of external sources to address specific problems such as language provisions in the health care sector, the application of insights from multilingualism in judicial procedures, supporting so-called 'new arrivals' and lesser-known communities such as the Roma, exploring interdisciplinary approaches to superdiversity and running a series of events with public service providers and local authority agencies on the challenges of addressing the needs of multilingual communities. An interactive exhibition on the city's multilingualism was piloted at a histories festival at the local museum in early 2012 and was subsequently expanded and displayed at schools, hospitals, seminars and workshops and community events. Undergraduate student research continued to be published on the website[18] making original contributions

---

18 See https://www.kratylos.org/~raphael/multilingual/reports/index.html

to describing language use in local communities and neighbourhoods, first-hand surveys of multilingualism among school pupils, examining multilingual library resources and digital platforms, and more.

A major game changer was the setting up of a student volunteer scheme, the first of its kind in the university hosted at the level of a local programme unit. The first activity was launched at Central Manchester Hospitals in 2013. University students accompanied hospital interpreters to interview patients who did not speak English about their hospital experience and coded the information in a database. The hospital was able to fill a gap that existed in covering the full diversity of its client population when responding to its duty to evaluate patient experience. The volunteer scheme was then expanded to support a variety of organisations including schools seeking information on pupils' language backgrounds, the local police force seeking feedback on communications with victims of crime, speech and language therapists seeking information on language diversity and multilingual upbringing, and community organisations offering English language learning support to refugees and new arrivals.

4.2 A new non-linear model of teaching, research and impact

By 2013 a model had emerged that involved students and junior researchers in interaction with key local institutions across several sectors. Students carried out research to identify needs and volunteered in various sectors to respond to some of those needs. The objective was to promote awareness of and engagement with multilingualism within the local community and to use the university as a space to bring together practitioners and clients of key service providers. The terms 'knowledge transfer' and 'knowledge exchange' adopted in the university environment to denote interaction with non-academics and stakeholders outside the university took on a new practical meaning for MLM: A permanent dialogue was set up involving representatives of different sectors within the university (research staff at different levels, undergraduate and research students and support staff) and external partners and participants to create new forms of knowledge driven by a need to find practical responses to immediate challenges. We described the model as 'non-linear' (Matras and Robertson 2017) since it did not involve the mere 'transfer' of knowledge from the university to external audiences. Instead it acted on prompts from outside the university to engage with problems and develop solutions, reflecting critically on the partnerships and exchange modalities themselves, and then returned to the external partners with proposals for solutions to those problems. Of key importance was the fact that the various partners who engaged in the process retained ownership of their contributions: University students owned their research developed under guidance and through access to research sites; host institutions owned the objectives and deliverables of student volunteer engagement and of co-produced research and public events; and the stability of partnerships based on such revolving ownerships opened up unique opportunities for the research team to develop insights of its own.

By 2020 the MLM activity portfolio included a dedicated undergraduate course unit on the city's multilingualism; it was the first and only lecture from the School of Arts, Histories and Cultures to be opened to students of all university programmes. It had created the largest online archive of research on multilingualism in a given city and the largest archive of undergraduate student research, with around 150 reports authored by over 500 students. It included the first local student volunteer scheme in which around 200 students from various programmes across the university enrolled every year to work. It developed a package of interactive exhibits on languages and multilingualism that were deployed at events and festivals, public libraries, hospitals and schools, and a series of videos that showcased the project's activities and events and provided guidance for multilingual families and an introduction to the city's languages and language practices.

During its lifetime MLM hosted well over two-dozen workshops and conferences bringing together international academics from a variety of disciplines (linguistics, translation and interpreting studies, education, sociology, anthropology, history, modern languages, international relations, general practice and more) with local practitioners from communities, local government and public service providers. It pioneered the public celebration of multilingualism in the form of Language Days – local festivals with stalls, performances, language tutorials, lectures and panel discussions around the theme of languages. These were first piloted in one of the city's neighbourhoods as 'Levenshulme Language Day'[19], prompting the adoption in 2018 of UNESCO International Mother Language Day on 21 February as an official, annual city council celebration. MLM researchers co-produced reports with public service providers including the National Health Service, the police and the city council with recommendations for provisions for interpreting and translation, and for written communication with clients and English as second or other language (ESOL). These were accompanied by a number of direct policy interventions including an initiative to amend the question on languages in the national census, interventions in city council scru-

---

19 https://www.youtube.com/watch?v=IOfhRbxeHWI

tiny committees on behalf of language supplementary schools and local community groups and the drafting of a City Language Strategy for the city council. The project set up a support platform for the city's language supplementary schools that held regular networking and training events for staff and discussions with policy makers about the public image of supplementary schools and recognition of their contribution to society.

4.3 Innovating concepts, networks and resources

MLM also championed the development of digital resources. LinguaSnapp[20] was the University of Manchester's very first smartphone application and the first to offer a crowd-sourcing tool to document multilingual signage (linguistic landscapes) by uploading annotated images along with GPS location data to an interactive database and online map. Localised versions of the app have been produced for Jerusalem, Melbourne, St Petersburg, Hamburg, Birmingham and Tallinn. Another online resource, the Multilingual Manchester Data Tool, stores and maps different datasets on languages in Manchester from a variety of sources including the national census, the school census, data on interpreting and translation in the health care sector and more, accompanied by profiles of individual languages and language profiles of city districts (wards). Associated with MLM were also a number of online databases documenting dialects of three of the city's community languages – Romani, Kurdish, and Arabic. These formed the basis for the University of Manchester's first commercial consultancy enterprise in the arts and cultures 'MLM-Analysis' – a forensic linguistic service. It provided expert support mainly to immigration and asylum lawyers representing appellants whose applications for asylum had been rejected by the UK government based on language analyses carried out by government contractors. Counter-expertise reports by MLM-Analysis submitted to the courts helped determine the outcome of over two-dozen court decisions with the courts following the recommendations of each and every report (cf. Matras 2021). The service incorporated contributions from native speaker postgraduate students in linguistics offering paid part-time training in the practical application of linguistic analysis, supporting potential career paths of people of minority language background.

MLM also made a contribution to the internationalisation of research and public engagement. It partnered with a number of university-based projects that replicated key components of the model and embraced a number of its research

---

20 http://www.linguasnapp.manchester.ac.uk/

methods and research technologies. The programme served directly as a model and inspiration for projects that combined teaching, research and public engagement at the universities of Graz, Queen Mary and Metropolitan University (London), Melbourne, Sydney, Bremen, Hamburg, Oxford, Higher School for Economics (Moscow) and others. At a conference in early 2019 attended by many international partners a manifesto was published calling for the formation for a 'Multilingual Cities Movement' as a way of organising collaborative public engagement with academics, students, practitioners and officials to protect and promote multilingualism. The very framing of the initiative as a 'Movement' pointed to the aspiration for research and teaching to have a mobilising momentum in an effort to bring about social and policy change.

While not directly situated in a setting where historical colonialism impacted the lives of an indigenous population, MLM can nevertheless claim to have incorporated key aspects of the decoloniality agenda:[21] It sought to re-define the beneficiaries of research placing a focus on local diaspora communities which require support to access key services, protect cultural heritage, obtain recognition of their multilingualism and find a voice as citizens. Branding the city around its multilingualism and language diversity through public celebrations and work with practitioners it aimed to empower actors – practitioners, students and city residents – to draw on their multilingual experience in day-to-day institutional practice. The project adopted an advocacy agenda through direct interventions with local and national government proposing solutions to policy dilemmas around language provisions in interpreting, data collection and sharing and promoting good practice. Its participatory model was thus much more than what Schiller (2016) describes as 'research in return', where the researcher contributes analysis in return for access to an observation opportunity. Instead MLM tailored the very agenda of research activities to the need to find practical policy solutions.

Working across discipline boundaries MLM developed an international outlook aspiring not just to create new forms of knowledge but also to mobilise for change in policy and practice. By involving students as both researchers and active contributors to social change in the local community and integrating a body of staff and students from different subject areas and from different backgrounds it created new and diverse styles and content of learning. In various articles and opinion blog posts we directly challenged the colonial 'English-first' narrative as

---

21 As de Sousa Santos (2012: 51) comments, treating the terms North and South metaphorically: "a South... also exists in the global North, in the form of excluded, silenced and marginalized populations".

well as the one put forward by academics who advocated selective language learning as a way to strengthen British power and global dominance while paying little or no attention to the domestic needs of the UK as a multilingual society. We also called for an open and equal form of civic partnership.

In the following sections I provide snapshots from some of these activities showing how the research helped document the voices of actors and their experiences around multilingualism bringing to the fore reflection as well as innovative practices and prompting the formulation of needs, solutions and ideologies of multilingualism.

5 Access: The institutional agenda for equality

In the health care sector language provisions are vital for accessibility, managing risks and ensuring the quality of service. They are also seen as a way of avoiding over-reliance on emergency services (cf. Bischoff and Hudelson 2010; Bührig et al. 2012; Ngai et al. 2016; Schuster et al. 2016). The latter consideration prompted the local National Health Service in Manchester in 2015 to approach MLM and commission a study on the accessibility of primary care and preventive care to patients who rely on interpreting (Gaiser and Matras 2016a). This collaboration built on a relationship that had been developing since 2010. Following the publication of student reports on Manchester's languages on the MLM website we were approached by the NHS to help prioritise languages for an online video health care information campaign 'Choose Well Manchester'. The student volunteer scheme began to work at Central Manchester Hospitals (CMFT)[22] in early 2013. The relationship was further strengthened through regular participation of staff from local hospital trusts and the service's Clinical Commissioning Groups in a series of consultations on language provisions that MLM hosted since 2012. For this particular study we were given access to data on interpreter requests at Central Manchester Hospitals and in GP practices for the period between 2013–2016. We also carried out semi-structured interviews and focus group conversations with health care professionals and interpreters and with patients representing different communities about their experience of accessing healthcare and their engagement with language provisions. We found no evidence to suggest that lack of adequate interpreter provisions was driving patients with lower levels of English to turn to

---

[22] At the time 'Central Manchester Hospitals NHS Foundation Trust', since re-named 'Manchester University NHS Foundation Trust' (MFT).

emergency or other hospital services rather than to primary care. Our findings did suggest however that patients with limited English proficiency often encountered difficulties in communicating with administrative staff, causing potential obstacles for registration and booking appointments. While in the hospital environment guidelines were applied strictly to ensure that interpreter-mediated communication was carried out by registered professionals, in GP practices a more lax approach was generally adopted often relying on casual interpreting by patients' friends or family members without full awareness of the risks (Gaiser and Matras 2016a).

5.1 Interpreting provisions in the health care sector

Our research suggested that Manchester's interpreting provisions, particularly those managed by CMFT were among the most comprehensive of any documented health care system. The reliance on language provisions is derived from the NHS's commitment to ensure equal access to its services. In the absence of national legislation on language (apart from the Welsh Language Act) NHS policy documents usually reference national and international frameworks such as the Equality Act 2010, the Human Rights Act 1998, the European Convention for the Protection of Human Rights and Fundamental Freedoms 1950, and the UN Convention on the Rights of Persons with Disabilities 2005. Individual hospital trusts have their own policy documents on provision and use of language services. While principles tend to overlap, implementation guidelines sometimes differ. At CMFT internal guidelines placed the responsibility to book an interpreter on staff if they felt that the patient's knowledge of English was insufficient to communicate effectively with clinical staff even if the patient or their family felt otherwise. By contrast guidelines issued at the time by the University Hospitals of South Manchester stated that patients should decide whether an interpreter was needed. Micro-level policy thus varied across individual institutions even within the same sector.

CMFT set up a face-to-face interpreting service in 1989. At the time of our observations it operated a tiered system: Its in-house interpreting department comprised managerial and administrative staff as well as nine in-house permanent staff who handled face-to-face interpreting, of whom seven provided services for more than one language. Ten so-called 'bank staff' supported the in-house team but were not contracted to a fixed number of hours. Between them, permanent and bank staff handled nineteen different languages and sub-varieties including Urdu/Hindi, Arabic, Chinese (Mandarin and Cantonese), Panjabi/Mirpuri, Bengali/Sylheti, Polish, Persian/Dari, Somali, Bravanese/Swahili, Gujarati, and

Kurdish, covering around 20 per cent of all interpreting jobs during the observation period. To support high demand and cover additional languages CMFT contracted two private agencies that engaged part-time free-lance face-to-face interpreters and two additional companies to provide telephone interpreting. These contractors usually recruited among a population of first-generation immigrants. For telephone interpreting, free-lance staff were recruited from all across the country and even abroad. The telephone service was usually used for brief interactions such as confirmation of appointments rather than clinical sessions. This planning approach was anchored in local knowledge and monitoring of data collected via the digital booking system. Core staff covered the most frequently needed languages. Coverage of languages that were less frequently in demand ('rare languages' in the internal jargon) was outsourced. This meant that quality monitoring for some languages (around 80 per cent of languages for which interpreting was requested) and for some types of interaction was less strict and sometimes non-existent. The tiered system was thus also a system that instituted a hierarchy among languages as well as a prioritisation of quality assurance while at the same time allowing the hospital to cover an impressive range of languages. This still seems to be an exceptional setup not reported on within or outside the UK. But it is also noteworthy as a case of bottom-up or micro level language policy embedding first-hand knowledge and experience of the multilingual setting rather than scripted directives or legislation on language rights to maintain an effective albeit differentiated system.

In contrast to the hospital environment Manchester's GP practices relied exclusively on external providers for face-to-face and telephone interpreting. Procurement was at the time of the study arranged centrally by an organisation called 'Manchester Integrated Care Gateway' on behalf of the NHS Clinical Commissioning Groups. Some practices preferred the instant telephone interpretation service to save administration time and the effort required to pre-book face-to-face interpreters. While patients were not expected to bring their own interpreter GPs often relied on family members or friends and tended not to insist on booking a professional interpreter to replace them.

Overall, individuals in a variety of roles were involved in making decisions on how to respond to patients' language needs. In the hospital setting clinical staff and managers relied on their encounters with patients to assess needs while the Patient Experience Director assumed responsibility for the in-house delivery of the service and the Procurement Director was responsible for external contractors. The contractors in turn relied on free-lance staff who were in effect sub-contractors engaged based on their self-reported experience rather than a formal vetting of qualifications. At GP surgeries and in some hospital environments patients had a say about the need for interpreting. There were thus many opportunities for a range of participants to assume proactive roles in the process and to co-manage or shape the organisation of individual encounters.

5.2 Agency and policy enactment through local practice

In Matras et al. (2023) we draw on testimonials to show how the ability of actors (health care professionals or institutional agents, and patients or clients) to take decisions relies on local knowledge and personal experiences gained in the multilingual urban setting. That experience constitutes a resource that informs and empowers them in institutional contexts. In activating that resource, actors assume agency, which in the case of practitioners contributes in effect to policy enactment within their institution (cf. Hornberger et al. 2018; Johnson and Johnson 2015). Interviews with patients and practitioners illustrate how such experiences are processed and how actions are explained and justified: A patient who is an Urdu speaker described how sometimes she would go on her own but preferred to take one of her daughters with her to help communicate since she could only speak basic English. But she found collecting from the pharmacy an easy process as there was a worker there with whom she was familiar and who spoke Urdu. She reported that at the Accident and Emergency service the waiting process was long and she relied on her daughter to help with communication. The daughter of a Mirpuri speaker described how her mother's doctor speaks Panjabi and understands Urdu, which is similar to her mother tongue, so she can communicate with him, but someone usually goes with her. But when her mother went to the hospital she described it as 'a must' for someone to go with her. A patient who is a Romanian Romani speaker reported that her GP left it to her discretion whether she needed translation for Romanian, but also accepted when she preferred to use her phone to look up translations.

The testimonials demonstrated that patients were aware and made use of a range of options to overcome potential language barriers: direct communication, professional translation, reliance on family members and on technical support. In some settings they felt empowered to make choices among those options. These choices were often complementary, made in response to different types of institutional settings. Among the considerations were the local knowledge and awareness of the language skills of particular institutional agents (practitioners). Navigating access to the service and its various outlets thus involved a mapping of the multilingual repertoires and resources of local actors and those present in routine encounters.

A similar picture emerged from the testimonials of institutional agents or practitioners. An optician reported that when translators were not there it was very difficult to communicate. But the same optician also acted as a casual translator for her mother, who was not fluent in English. She reported how very few notices were written in her native language, and while those were helpful, she didn't have anyone there to help interpret her questions. A GP told us that she could "cover all ground" when it came to South Asian languages, and had some familiarity with African languages. After seeing many patients from Romania, she said she started picking up words. Another GP offered explanations about various languages used by patients: "There is three Kurdish languages. There is Kurmanji, Sorani, and Badini. There is two Farsi languages, Afghani and Persian. There is two types of Chinese, Mandarin and Cantonese". We see how personal multilingual experiences intertwine with and inform practice approaches in professional, institutional roles and how the institutional experience serves to develop and expand personal views and knowledge about languages.

The local multilingual setting is mapped and recognised in order to serve as a guide to shape practice (Matras et al. 2023). Actors assume what various authors define as 'agency' (cf. Emirbayer and Mische 1998; Ahearn 2001; Liddicoat and Taylor-Leech 2020): They feel empowered to take decisions at key decision nodes in communicative interactions in institutional settings: compartmentalising settings and types of encounter, selecting among different options to manage them, enriching provisions and sometimes overriding scripted procedures at their own discretion. They do so drawing on local knowledge and their own history of encounters in the multilingual city. Such knowledge can be said to represent the linguistic repertoires in the broader sense of experiences, as described by Busch (2012) and by Blommaert and Backus (2013): The multilingual urban setting is a source of knowledge about language practices, provisions, options for support and about language itself. This adds a new dimension to observations on the manner in which professionals draw on their own individual language skills (e.g. Cadier and Mar-Molinero 2012; Keshet and Popper-Giveon 2019; Gaibrois 2019). The engagement of researchers with actors (patients and practitioners) for the sake of identifying needs and possible solutions helps to bring such experiences to the fore.

6 Multilingualism as heritage

Museums and other cultural institutions have the remit to produce and strengthen identity narratives in addition to being custodians of general knowledge. As Deumert (2018) notes heritage is the outcome of a process of choosing inheritance. Local multiculturalism is not typically regarded as part of that inheritance. Presentation of cultural diversity through exhibits typically offers snapshots of overseas communities that are not or no longer easily accessible. In this context 'translation' refers not just to the transfer of content from one language into another but also to the process of interpretation in cross-cultural comparison (Sturge 2007; Silverman 2015). Multilingualism has been addressed in the museum setting as a way of ensuring accessibility and broadening audiences (Martin and Jennings 2015). Noting that the motivation to reach wider audiences often has commercial motivations for the museum as a creative industry, Liao (2018) offers a typology of functions according to which text translation in museums can be informative (giving guidance to visitors), interactive (making visitors feel welcome), political (reinforcing an ideological commitment to inclusivity), social-inclusive (increasing awareness of multilingualism) and exhibitive (displaying translation as an object) (see also Kelly-Holmes and Pietikäinen 2016). Others have noted the position of the museum as a space that can offer opportunities to engage audiences with multilingualism by embedding multilingual practices into its mission statement (Garibay et al. 2015; Soto Huerta and Huerta Migus 2015). Neather (2012) problematises the notion of professional translation and shows how the museum can offer a space in which multilingual community stakeholders can interact with curators. Different forms of expertise are negotiated to co-produce translation and to transform the museum into a community of practice in which both professional expertise and community identities can be interrogated.

6.1 The idea of a 'Multilingual Museum'

Since 2015 MLM had been approaching Manchester Museum to promote a multilingual agenda. In 2018 the museum announced an inclusivity policy. Highlights involved re-opening plans for a new South Asia Gallery to consultation with local stakeholders as well as the symbolic repatriation of artefacts from the museum's collections and their return to Aboriginal communities in Australia. These and other actions were branded in public as 'indigenising' and 'decolonising'.[23] In late 2018 a comprehensive collaboration plan was developed that included plans to

---

[23] https://www.museum.manchester.ac.uk/about/thetideofchange/; https://natsca.blog/2021/01/06/decolonising-manchester-museums-mineral-collection-a-call-to-action/

hold events on multilingualism at the museum, carry out museum tours in heritage languages for pupils of language supplementary schools, introduce language taster sessions for museum staff as a way of supporting staff consolidation and wellbeing and more. As the museum launched its refurbishment programme its renewal banner with the motto 'hello future' was translated into 50 languages. In February 2020 the museum hosted an evening event organised by MLM to launch UNESCO International Language Day celebrations.

In the spring of 2020, as the museum closed its doors to visitors due to the Covid outbreak, it set up a digital platform offering online access to exhibits from its collection. This was taken up as an opportunity to set up a multilingual platform, branded 'The Multilingual Museum'. The idea of the platform was to offer a space in which audiences could engage with objects (displayed as digital images accompanied by an English interpretation) in a language of their choice. To that end we introduced the concept of 'storied translation'[24], defined as a range of approaches from more literal translations to looser texts including reflections on the objects themselves and on various translation options. It was to be inclusive of a wide range of language forms such as regional dialects and family language repertoires.

6.2 Experiences of 'storied translation'

We understood storied translation as dynamic, fluid, imaginative and a product of individual agency and creativity. It embraced multilingualism as a repertoire of linguistic features rather than a juxtaposition of named languages with strict boundaries. Rather than produce a single definitive translation the goal of the platform was to promote engagement with the museum and its collections. It invited multiple translations of the same object to appear side-by-side even into the same language, as text, audio or visuals. Language was regarded as heritage in its own right. We assumed that the translation process would engage individuals with various levels of language proficiency as well as individuals with various degrees of experience in writing their own spoken language (as some languages were regional or minority languages that are not frequently written). The process would serve different functions. It would help make some artefacts accessible to new audiences. It would also offer a space for interactive learning and doing about language and culture and an opportunity to showcase the city's language

---

24 https://mmhellofuture.wordpress.com/2021/03/12/the-multilingual-museum/; https://mmhellofuture.wordpress.com/2021/09/30/a-story-of-storied-translation/

diversity and to connect different generations and community members around discussions about language.

While the online platform was open to all through a simple registration process targeted efforts were made to approach language supplementary schools and mainstream secondary schools. These put together collaborative contributions to the platform as part of classroom activities. The team also approached individuals and families who made voluntary contributions. The process was documented in the form of recorded interviews about contributors' experiences. A Romanian speaker who worked at a nursing home remarked:

> Some of my colleagues were saying that while doing this they learnt many new words in English. We also compared words in our languages at work, they were saying how some words are so long in a language and then we started asking so how do you say that in your language and how do you say that in yours. This actually took over our lives. It was impressive... One of the ladies was saying that it would be good for her to do something with her grandchild who is learning English in school. She said they could be then learning together, the grandchild would be learning her language and she could learn more English ... Now that I know how involved Manchester Museum are and how much they care about us, it will be such a pleasure to go [there].

A Somali speaker, born in France, who is a law graduate, said:

> I found some words difficult since I did not study in Somali in school and so I wasn't familiar with some of the words like 'circus' and 'zoological'. So I just used English words. ... Once I really got started I was using Google Translate for some words I wasn't familiar with and my knowledge of grammar and sentence structure in Somali to make it work. ... I wanted my native language to be represented. I wanted people to be familiar with written Somali because there aren't many Somali books out there.

A Luganda speaker who is a trained health care professional, said:

> To see something like this where there is an interest in my language is exciting. ... We didn't know some of the English terms and so we looked them up online. We also checked some terms in Luganda online. ... I whatsapped my sister in Uganda to check some words. ... Some terms were harder to translate, like 'springtime ', for example. We don't have four seasons like here ... So for 'springtime' we kept the English word 'spring'. We also kept the English word for 'science' as we use the English term in our language. ... It was also an opportunity to teach the children how to reflect on our language. ... Having all these languages at the museum, and your own language there, makes you feel included. It shows value for different backgrounds.

And a Romani (Romanes) speaker from Romania reported:

> My daughter was proud to see her language at the museum and know she had done this. It was also important for her to discover ways of spelling and writing in Romanes. She had to create her own way of writing in Romanes ... I wanted her to feel proud knowing that her language is known by other people and used by other people. I wanted to show her that non-Roma also want to see our language represented next to other languages ... We never learnt how to write in Romanes. My daughter used letters from Romanian and English to write it the way she pronounces it. I noticed that sometimes she used 'sh' from English and sometimes 'ş' from Romanian.

Several themes emerge from these testimonials: First, contributors report on feeling proud and empowered to be supporting a major and prestigious local institution in the city. They feel that the presence of their language on the museum's platform is a token of recognition and valorisation of their culture and identity. They feel that it is symbolic of the recognition of their contribution to the city's social and cultural fabric. One might say that they view the incorporation of their language contribution as an institutional act of recognition of their local citizenship, i.e. their belonging to a local civic identity collective. One of the interviewees even acknowledges that this recognition will motivate her to grant the museum recognition in return by visiting more often. This demonstrates how reaching out to audiences to be active contributors (rather than using in-house translation) can widen participation.

Second, the testimonials show how the task opened up opportunities for a dedicated intergenerational dialogue around language heritage (a notion of the family's past, memories, particular traditions that are shared with co-ethnics in the local diaspora, as well as a continuing affinity to their place of origin through family and other connections). Indeed in one of the interviews we learn how the activity prompted a dialogue within the work place among colleagues of different backgrounds where the theme of language and the motivation to complete a language-based task turned into an opportunity to strengthen inter-personal bonds and to develop a local collective identity – a micro-level practice community – around multilingualism.

Third, the task motivates and empowers contributors to act creatively in regard to the design of their own language outputs. Most contributors reported to have aspired to stay as close to the original content of the English model test. Their creativity is identified mainly in regard to the choice of lexical terminology and, in the case of minoritised[25] and regional languages, in the choice of orthography. Some language users have had little or no schooling in their family language and they possess no writing routine in that language. They turn to their overall repertoire of linguistic resources in order to set or improvise parameters that allow them to introduce a new practice routine into the set of practices for which they have so far used their family language. On the whole they feel empowered to embrace variation in form as well as to take an integrative approach to their language resources. They employ words and writing conventions from the set of features that they have at their disposal rather than aspire to set strict and consistent boundaries between named languages. The symbolism of making a choice in favour of a particular named language identified as the 'target' (and representing family heritage, memory and historical belonging) does not stand in contradiction to embracing a multiplicity of forms and features including those that are associated with other named languages. This is what others have referred to as 'translanguaging' or 'metrolingualism'. But here the principle guides the completion of a pre-set task broadly speaking within an institutional framework (or the expectations and parameters set by an institution) involving writing rather than oral conversation.

6.3 Co-curating language

We can look at the Multilingual Museum experience both from the perspective of the hosting institution and from that of the contributors. As a cultural institution Manchester Museum can boast another activity as part of its declared postcolonial portfolio, though in this case decoloniality would refer not to the relations with former overseas colonies but to the domestic multiculturalism that has come about in the aftermath of colonialism and often as a result of postcolonial displacement. The local, domestic post-colonialism is a pledge towards inclusivity. For the neoliberal cultural institution inclusivity is part of a business model to widen participation and attain better value on investment.

In terms of cultural policy the Multilingual Museum breaks the traditional mode of displaying 'foreign' cultures as primarily overseas exhibits[26] as well as

---

25 I adopt this term here as it seems appropriate for languages such as Luganda, which are not necessarily spoken by a numerical minority but have the socio-political status of a minority language in a given state or region.
26 At the time of writing Manchester Museum is preparing to open new galleries devoted to South Asia and China, both of which also represent the cultures of local migrant communities of significant size.

the traditional format of displaying 'cultures' as discrete entities that are separated from one another. Instead it recognises language as heritage; it embraces the notion of pluralism as a heritage experience, i.e. an inherited memory and package of practice in its own right.

Equally ground breaking for the institution is the invitation to community members (targeting individuals as well as schools and for the first time also community-run supplementary schools) to engage with the museum creatively by contributing content. It is also an invitation to contribute to the curation of a new form of heritage, through the flexibility in choice of form and multi-modality and the inclusion of reflections on the process itself. Traditionally the museum has recruited volunteers for pre-set support tasks involving its own collections and not as co-curators of content.

From the perspective of the contributors the opportunity to partake in this initiative strengthens a feeling of belonging as well as a new feeling of being a collective constituted around the local experience of multilingualism. This brings about an element of a distinct civic identity and communality; they are bound together by a feeling of responsibility and co-ownership of a platform that is hosted by one of the city's most prestigious institutions. As we saw from the testimonials, the prompt coming from an institution allows participants to open new multilingual spaces at their places of work and even at home, engaging in new conversations and in creative design around multilingualism, enriching existing practices and introducing new ones.

7 From heritage to skills

The offer of foreign languages at England's secondary schools has been declining since the early 2000s. As a result, enrolment has equally been declining both in secondary schools and in higher education. This has been the subject of numerous reports produced by and for academies, research councils and government[27]. They show a dramatic drop of around 50 per cent in the uptake of languages in general, particularly French and German, in the decade between 2000 and 2010, accompanied by a gradual rise in the uptake of Spanish (cf. also McLelland 2017: 33) and for community languages, in particular Arabic, Chinese and Polish. Burnage Academy for boys is a secondary school in what is considered a deprived

---

27 E.g. House of Commons briefing on Language Teaching in Schools from January 2020 https://researchbriefings.files.parliament.uk/documents/CBP-7388/CBP-7388.pdf

area of Manchester. In the 2020 school census 82 per cent of pupils in the school were recorded as having a home language other than English, with Urdu (40%), Bengali (13%), Arabic (9%) and Panjabi (7.5%) topping the list followed by Pashto, Somali, Italian, Kurdish, Persian, and Spanish. Those who identified Italian and Spanish were mainly of South Asian and Middle Eastern backgrounds and had lived in Italy and Spain before migrating on to the UK. Altogether thirty languages were recorded in the school among ca. 860 pupils.

The school has a Modern Languages department that employs at the time of writing five staff members and which offers classes in French (taught by three members of staff) and Urdu (taught by two) to GCSE level specifications (General Qualification of Secondary Education), the lower of two secondary school qualification levels. It is one of just four secondary schools in the city that offer Urdu as an exam subject, the others being two state schools for girls and one independent school run by an Islamic education trust. The school also hosts afternoon and evening classes through which pupils can prepare to take GCSE exams in other languages, particularly Arabic and Italian, led by teachers who are brought in from outside the school. The offer changes from year to year according to demand but the school maintains it as part of a commitment to recognising students' knowledge of heritage languages as a valuable skill and as a way of showing high achievement rates by promoting subjects in which pupils can perform well at examinations.

French is taught mainly by teachers who are non-native speakers to pupils who are non-native speakers. Lessons follow the scripted curriculum that is set by the examination board, which also produces the teaching materials and offers teacher training. Lessons cover primarily preparation for the examination format. By contrast Urdu is taught by teachers who are native speakers to pupils who have had at least some exposure to the language at home. They include pupils whose home languages are Panjabi and related varieties (e.g. Potwari and Mirpuri) as well as speakers of Pashto and Bengali. Urdu lessons draw on materials prepared by the teachers or obtained from a variety of sources including books from Pakistan and audio-visual materials. They are much more interactive than the French classes, relying considerably on pupils' own language experiences.

7.1 Valorising language experiences: Multilingual Streets

MLM's engagement with the school began in 2016 in the form of class visits to the university for dedicated sessions around the LinguaSnapp online platform of images of multilingual signs. Participants aged 12–13 were given an induction to the use of online databases, filtering images of multilingual signs by language, outlet and location. They discussed the implications of a linguistically diverse locality. Pupils took particular interest in exploring signs in languages with which they were familiar as well as exploring the presence of multilingual signs in their own neighbourhood. Through this collaboration the school was prompted to join an initiative to train 'young interpreters' giving interested students the opportunity to use their language skills to support school open days and parents' evenings. These activities were then showcased at a public event on multilingualism and language diversity hosted by MLM at Manchester Cathedral in 2019. The objective was to turn home language skills into a source of pride and confidence.

In the spring of 2019 we launched the Multilingual Streets activity. The school classified the activity as part of its citizenship and social engagement curriculum strand. Its aim was to offer pupils opportunities to explore institutions and areas of the city outside their immediate neighbourhood. The visit day started with a session in a university teaching room. We used as stimuli photos of multilingual signs, the LinguaSnapp online map and bespoke worksheets. We encouraged pupils to look at more photos and answer questions about languages they can identify, the reasons that signs might display different languages and what that might tell us about the way we use languages. The discussion raised issues such as the value of languages for identifying the background of shop owners and connecting them with customers of similar backgrounds as well as the visual representation of languages – the sharing of scripts across different languages (which makes some signs accessible to readers even if they did not know the language of the sign) and the difference between spoken language and writing systems.

The workbook also included guiding questions for the second stage: the walk around a multilingual neighbourhood in the vicinity of the university campus. The objective was to transfer the reflection from the earlier session into observations based on street experience. Working in groups of 4–5 the young people were prompted to identify signs in different languages, to take photos or draw pictures of them and to record a short meta-data inventory to accompany each sign stating the languages and script and the outlet to which the sign was attached. For the next session the group moved to the nearby Whitworth Art Gallery. Surrounded by art displays they were provided with a kit of materials for cutting and pasting paper in different colours and were asked to create an artwork poster based on their workbook and street observations. In this way observations were transferred into a multi-modal visual representation using scripts, colour and material shapes to identify themes that appeared to the participants as salient.

In the final activity stage the groups were filmed on video showing and discussing their posters. This offered a 2–3 minute discursive engagement that typically contained the elements of description, explanation and justification through which different sources of knowledge were drawn upon, activated and integrated. In this way the filming rendered an interpretation of observations, conveyed through art, through the lens of pre-formed pieces of knowledge and ideologies by means of narrating the experience and reasoning. It constituted the final 'output'. This method of blending observation, artwork and presentation to represent experiences of multilingualism is anchored in a series of works that bring together active pedagogy with multilingualism research (cf. Busch 2015, 2018; Purkarthofer 2016; Bradley 2017; Bradley et al. 2018; Purkarthofer and Flubacher 2022). Its art-based multimodal component drew on earlier work described by Bradley and Atkinson (2020) about the use of bricolage techniques with young people to explore the multilingual city landscape.[28]

7.2 Knowledge resources and ideologies

Multilingual Streets was carried out with Burnage Academy pupils on four separate days involving altogether 155 Year 9 pupils aged 12–13. Observations were collected in the form of notes taken by the researchers on pupils' responses to the preparatory session, pupils' workbooks, their selection of images, themes and material for the artwork and the filmed performances which were later transcribed and annotated.

In one of those a group reported on how they used their mobile phones to find translations of the word 'hello' into various languages. In the extract below they portray the notion of plurality of cultures associated with the city picking up the term 'communities'. They also connect to the school's annual celebration of European Day of Languages (one of its posters issued by the Council of Europe shows 'hello' in different languages). The experience of observations and discussions on the day is matched through the artwork to relevant knowledge and experienced gained in the institutional context of the school, where the ideology of pluralism is forged through celebratory events:

Boy 1:   We worked as a group to capture the many communities within Manchester. As we can see (*gestures to poster*), we've used 'hello' in all different languages to show how many cultures are within Manchester
Boy 2:   We took inspiration from the European Day of Languages ...

---

[28] See https://issuu.com/jessicamarybradley/docs/mls_burnage_final_issuu

In the next extract the group members relate directly to the street observations and convey how they chose the contrast and plurality of colours to represent diversity. The saliency of the latter as an ideological concept is expressed through repetition of the keyword 'diverse' and the construction of a plural form 'diversities' – in effect a double reinforcement of the notion of plurality. When explaining the distribution of colours the narrative contrasts the concept of plurality with that of isolation and discrimination, taking sides while juxtaposing ideologies. Boy 2 reinforces this through an explicit expression of pride and appraisal for the pluralism of the locality:

Boy 1: The white represents Manchester and this (*points to black tape around the white area*) represents every-everywhere else. The orange represents all the different language diversities inside of Manchester which shows that this is a very diverse place compared to other places. As we see we see different languages as we walked around town looking at it. (…) There's black scribbles here well not actually scribbles but in fact they are different em shops and buildings I would explain that how it's like proper and spread out. Not all languages are in one place being isolated and discriminated in fact it's all spread out, that's why these oranges are spread out across the whole thing.

Boy 2: And it shows how like Manchester is a more diverse place and is really good for people who come from other countries. That's it.

The next extract illustrates how the taught experience of language diversity is interpreted as an ideological stance. That in turn is associated with another ideological stance acquired in the school setting which equally has diversity and pluralism as its salient theme: The pupils report how they connected language plurality with what they learned from teachers about the LGBT community and how they chose to represent language diversity through colours in a similar way to the display of colours on the LGBT flag. The keywords 'different' and 'multi' represent the saliency of plurality while the choice of colours for the 'language flag' is explained through the association of colours with various national flags with which the pupils are familiar through their personal experience and family history (hence the mention of Bangladesh, Pakistan and Italy):

Boy 1: So basically we drew we drew this flag (*points to flag on poster*) because we were inspired when today morning, we have to go outside and look at all the different shops and they were all in different languages, so we (…)

and uh (...) And then the teachers talk about the uh LGBT flag so we thought why not doing a multi- (...) multi-language flag
Boy 2: And LGBT (*points to poster*) has different colours in it so we got we got that idea but used it in a different way, put random colours in different places, which made it look very (...) vibrant
Boy 1: 'Cause different lang- 'cause different flags have different colours so like make it colourful and everything
Boy 2: So for example, red (*points to colour on poster*) and green uh technically stand for Bangladesh
Boy 1: Or it could stand for Italy
Boy 2: Pakistan
Boy 1: Different countries

In the final extract the speaker is explaining a poster inspired by the image of a local restaurant front that displays the outlet name and menu highlights in English and Arabic. On the poster itself the boys inserted the name of the outlet in English along with word 'halal' in Arabic script. They also added the word 'Bangla' in Bengali script along with a colour combination based on the Bangladeshi flag, although the outlet itself does not contain any Bengali writing or imagery. The boys are thus responding to the task by connecting to a real outlet encountered during the street observation while at the same time adjusting it to convey their own personal knowledge gained in the family setting. As justification for that adaptation the speaker reverts to the ideological stance that the city as a whole is multicultural:

> Um (...) our poster shows how multicultural Manchester really is. Um, this particular culture is Bangladesh and Bengali is (*points to Bengali writing on poster*) um some Bengali words and (*points to flag*) that's the flag ... Um it also has Arabic [0.18 inaudible] It says [0.20 inaudible] here and (*laughs*) (...) yeah (...) The shop's name the takeaway's name is Al Bukhari and it's in a very busy part of Manchester and it's also (...) a very like (...) um multicultural place a whole as a whole.

The performance on camera to an imaginary audience prompts the pupils to engage in a speech event that serves several functions and combines several different actions of speech: It is a *description* of an artefact (the poster) accompanied by an *explanation* of the choice of objects depicted and the choice of materials used to represent them. It also offers a *justification* for the choice of themes, which in turn is anchored in an ideological stance. The recurring theme is that of plurality, conveyed by the keywords 'diverse', 'multicultural' and similar, and this appears to be what the pupils perceive as most salient from the content that was communicated by their instructors on the day. The pupils also appear to associate successful completion of the task with active embracing of an ideological stance. In doing so they create a synthesis of various sources of knowledge. As in the school learning routine they draw on the day's workshop discussion and the observations they were instructed to record. But they also incorporate elements of knowledge acquired through other school activities that are deemed relevant to the theme of plurality as well as their own personal knowledge and experience, in particular elements of their own multilingual repertoires.

As a method of engagement this shows how guided observation and recording of observations can valorise personal knowledge and experience, which comes to the fore in the form of a performance. From the school's perspective the activity offers an educational experience that helps pupils attach value to their personal knowledge and experience as a marketable skill. That skill can be used to obtain formal qualifications and so it and be deployed as career boosting capital. But it can also help pupils build confidence as equal members of the local civic community with rights and obligations – an explicit goal of the citizenship curriculum. All this is achieved by bringing a group of students out of their everyday environment and into a place that they have not previously visited prompting them to observe and reflect on that environment through a familiar lens. The school documented the activity through a permanent display within the school building of text and images including a 'zine' produced by artist Louise Atkinson based on the collages that the pupils created on the day. It became in this way a permanent multilingual space in the physical sense, and symbolic and an acknowledgement of the multilingual spaces that pupils experience in their daily lives and which are often excluded from the institutional environment of schools.

The engagement strategy pursued through Multilingual Streets was to create a setting that is equipped to accommodate a university-external audience for a bespoke activity. This contributes to breaking down barriers between the university as an institution and a population that is otherwise unlikely to connect with it. However, the direct and short term marketing value in terms of potential student recruitment (which is normally the target behind such visit days to the university) remains questionable both in light of the age group involved and their educational background (only some pupils from this school continue to acquire the higher secondary school qualification that is a prerequisite for admission to university). The value to the university must therefore be measured in a different way. Bradley et al. (2018) suggest that collaborative arts-based research can allow voices to be audible. This captures a key ambition of the decoloniality agenda to use the higher education environment as a platform for those who have been marginalised. Activities like Multilingual Streets could be seen as a contribution to long-term capacity building in citizenship. The university's stake in this activity is not to strengthen its own capacity but instead to act as a responsible contributor to the civic community around it.

McLelland (2017: 201) discusses how lobbying in favour of teaching languages in British schools has partly been driven by a consideration of social equity, aspiring to make available to all pupils offers that had earlier only been made in private sector schools. A further lobbying rationale cited as gaining momentum is one that regards languages as skills and attributes an economic value to language learning, arguing that it is necessary to facilitate trade and economic growth (cf. Holmes 2018; and see above). The importance of language learning is attributed to the individual's set of skills and the opportunity to draw on those skills for economic prosperity.

The dimension of citizenship and belonging is rarely addressed; it is not mentioned in McLelland's (2017) overview or in the contributions to a collection by Kelly (2018). Identity is more widely discussed in connection with community-based supplementary (or complementary) schools that teach the languages of diaspora communities outside the mainstream state curriculum. Blackledge and Creese (2010) observe that while teachers often reproduce and promote ideologies of nationalism in relation to the origin countries as part of the intergenerational transmission of community languages, pupils sometimes question these ideologies and act to 'disinvent the national' (Blackledge and Creese 2010: 194). Huang (2020) argues that heteroglossic awareness penetrates ideological stances rendering a 'stratified ideological ecology' where the value of the Standard language of the origin country is recognised but also contested in regard to certain contexts of interaction. In Matras et al. (2022) we showed how supplementary school staff justify new ideological dispositions that embrace multilingual repertoires relying on juxtapositions of types of language practices on the axes of time and space: In the Here and Now of the diaspora reality it is seen as legitimate, practical and sometimes vital to recognise linguistic variation actively.

7.3 Language supplementary schools as a diasporic stance

Well over fifty supplementary schools operate in the Manchester area catering for a diverse range of languages that include Chinese, Arabic, Polish, Russian, Ukrainian, Finnish, Bengali, Panjabi, French, Greek, German, Farsi, Kurdish, Armenian, Czech, Turkish, Lithuanian, Greek, Amharic, Uyghur, Tamil, Japanese, Somali, and more. Madrasahs offer instruction in Quranic Arabic often through the medium of Urdu and Yeshivas and 'Sems' (Jewish religious schools for boys and girls, respectively) teach Biblical and Mishnaic Hebrew often through the medium of Yiddish. MLM's engagement with supplementary schools began soon after the project was launched. Supplementary school staff members were invited to attend networking events and contribute information to a Digest report and video about the city's multilingualism[29]. In early 2017 we launched a Support Platform that offered regular networking and training events to supplementary school staff including workshops on how to address regional and dialect variation. Statements and scenes from supplementary schools were featured in a number of MLM video productions[30] and the project hosted end of year celebrations for schools and invited local politicians to attend. In a number of events and conferences we gave supplementary school staff a platform together with international academics and representatives of public services and the local authority. Supplementary schools were invited to take part in Language Day celebrations and to contribute to the Multilingual Museum platform. We published a number of research and policy reports on supplementary schools and initiated an event hosted by Afzal Khan, Member of Parliament for Manchester-Gorton, at the Houses of Parliament in 2019 which featured contributions from Manchester's supplementary schools and from supplementary school staff and pupils from other parts of the country. In late November 2018 we were invited to attend a meeting of Manchester City Council's Children and Young People Scrutiny Committee to make recommendations in regard to a possible municipal policy on supplementary schools and some recommendations were included in a draft City Language Strategy that we compiled by invitation of the City Council in the summer of 2018.

The local authority's statutory responsibility around supplementary schools is limited to monitoring safeguarding issues – from the adequacy of infrastructure through to ascertaining child protection provisions such as background checks on staff. The relevant children's services unit is also entrusted with supporting the delivery of the government's Prevent Strategy launched in 2011, which means maintaining a level of alertness toward any indications of radicalisation and extremism. This targets in particular establishments that serve the Muslim population. Staff members at supplementary schools generally feel unease in respect of visits by the city council's children's services unit and regard them as a form of surveillance while on the other hand they are keen to enjoy any benefits that cooperation and good relations with the local authority might bring. That ambivalence is at the heart of the relationship between the local government and supplementary schools. Government authorities do not intervene with or

---

29 https://www.youtube.com/watch?v=pmTDzsPrBp8
30 https://www.kratylos.org/~raphael/multilingual/manchester-arabic-school/index.html

support language supplementary schools and there are few government statements that relate to them. In March 2019 the government published an 'Integrated Communities Strategy'[31] in which it acknowledged that respondents to a survey noted "the value of supplementary schools in improving educational attainment" though the government responded to that by expressing concern about safeguarding and the risk of "harmful practices" (p. 14–15).

In 2019–2020 we carried out a questionnaire and interview-based survey speaking to 32 staff members in 24 different supplementary schools that teach altogether 21 different languages (cf. Matras et al. 2022) and we collected questionnaire responses from over 120 parents associated with 11 schools with the purpose of documenting parents' motivations to send children to supplementary schools and staff experiences and attitudes to challenges, relationships with external organisations, classroom practices and more. Asked about their motivation to send children to the supplementary schools 91 per cent of respondents answered 'to understand family and cultural heritage better' while only 40 per cent stated that they wanted their children to attain a further UK qualification based on their language skills. Asked more specifically about the language skills that are most important for their children to develop at supplementary schools over 80 per cent identified reading, writing and understanding conversation, while only 38 per cent named obtaining a formal qualification. Just under half of respondents indicated that their children intend to take a GSCE qualification in the language. The sample thus tends to show some hesitation in regard to expectations for the skills aspect of heritage languages, which might be interpreted in light of the fact that supplementary schools operate on the fringe of the education system and lack the formal recognition that is normally associated with skills qualifications. However, the following statement from the head teacher of one of the Chinese schools indicates that attitudes are shifting at least in regard to languages that are more seen as having global economic value:

> Some parents, they think that it is very important for their children to understand their heritage and all that, but I'd say for most of the parents the qualification is the most important thing and [the most] useful thing. It helps when you apply to university.

Families equally see a benefit in supplementary schools for languages that are offered at mainstream schools, such as French, as expressed by a teacher from a school that caters to the Cameroonian community:

---

[31] https://assets.publishing.service.gov.uk/government/uploads/system/uploads/attachment_data/file/777160/Integrated_Communities_Strategy_Government_Response.pdf

> Yeah, I have some children who have been attending the lessons for several years and the best thing about it is that they choose French at school and they do their GCSEs in French.

For other languages staff members tend confirm that the principal motivation is related to heritage and maintaining a community support network, as the following statements from the head teachers of the Armenian and Polish schools demonstrate:

> First of all they want to learn, that children learn Armenian, and then they want to keep the Armenian community close together, and learn Armenian culture, and that's it.

> When we first started it was as I said previously to maintain the Polish language with a view of going back to Poland ... From 2004 it changed again because we had the new economic immigration from Poland ... so we became a support mechanism basically ... there was quite a significant amount of bullying going on of the children in the mainstream school, ... So we were there to support the children, support the parents.

Beyond the view of language as a practical skill for communication with family relations and friends, partaking in language lessons and maintaining a dedicated institution to provide them is seen as a form of resilience, one that provides and promotes confidence and strengthens a sense of belonging in the diaspora setting.

The testimonials also suggest that supplementary schools contribute to forging a new ideological stance to language and through that also to the diasporic reality of 'community' as one that brings together people of different backgrounds. This is particularly apparent in the Arabic speaking community that includes populations from different countries in which Standard Arabic is the official language but different vernaculars are spoken. For pupils these vernaculars constitute their spoken home languages. They bring them into the supplementary school environment, prompting recognition of dialect variation in the institutional setting, something that is absent from the educational system in Arab countries, as describes by a teacher from one of the Arabic schools:

> I mean, I have a lot of variety in my class, like people from all different backgrounds, they speak different dialects and sometimes I don't understand a word myself, so I ask them to explain more, you know. I feel like this would help communication between me and the students, because you know, they would think about another word, another way to say this word which I can't understand, so that would really help them learning I think.

Active engagement in the classroom with regional variation is also reported from other supplementary schools (Matras et al. 2022), such as the head teacher of the German school:

> We have Standard German as the main language, but sometimes we do bring this into play and we have one child, he only spoke Swiss German ... The mother of this boy came in and she did Swiss and I did Bavarian,.. and we said 'yes, this is what we are fluent speakers of', another language – nearly – because the grammar is different, the vocabulary.

This indicates that supplementary schools are offering what Li (2018a) describes as a 'tanslanguaging space', one in which exhaustive use of the multilingual repertoire is accepted and supported; that, despite the fact that the mission statement of supplementary schools is to promote and support particular languages that are associated with the national heritage of particular diaspora communities. The reality is one of accommodation to the local multilingual setting using classroom engagement with language as a new action routine through which a novel, complex and integrated sense of belonging to a pluralistic community is forged. While the ideology that questions monolingual language norms has been described for the supplementary school setting more widely (Huang 2020; Blackledge and Creese 2010, and others), MLM's engagement with the schools contributed directly to valorising ideologies of pluralism. In partnership with other researchers we held a series of conferences and training workshops with supplementary school staff on language variation. Their aim was to sensitise teachers to issues of language variation and help them gain confidence in addressing vernacular and regional language forms in the classroom. Our observations and conversations with staff informed a policy report that called for more consideration to be given to non-standard varieties (Matras and Karatsareas 2020).

7.4 Local citizenship as pluralism

The sense of pluralism emerges from the testimonials also in regard to regional languages of the countries of origin as well as the reality of families of mixed backgrounds as a feature of the diaspora setting, as described by the head teacher of the Persian (Farsi) school and by a teacher from the Russian school:

> Yeah, in fact this gentleman we tell you the little one is speaking 3–4 [languages], because the dialect of the father and the dialect of the mother is a Kurd but then of course the national language is Persian, Iranian or Farsi that's why they bring them here – but they are quite proud that the kids can speak the other languages.

> You can see a lot of backgrounds, like a Pakistani dad and a Lithuanian mum, but the Lithuanian mum decided to carry on with the Russian language, because parents come – my mum just arrived yesterday – so she speaks Russian with my kids, so it is very important to carry on with the language. But a lot of people are actually going to Arabic school and continue to go to Russian school as well. So if family are supportive … so we are happy too.

Skills are normally regarded as the ability and confidence to use knowledge effectively and readily in order to execute performance. Most policy reports on languages in the UK from recent years use the collocation 'language skills' without offering a specific breakdown of the element of knowledge that is cited, implying that the default understanding of skill is proficiency in the use of language structures and the ability to follow and produce texts and conversation. McLelland (2017: 48ff.) discusses how language attitudes in Britain are a legacy of the late medieval and Enlightenment periods where the nobility learned languages as an emblem of cultivated fashion but also as practical knowledge to support foreign travel while the middle classes learned languages to support their profession. In 2021 the Silenced Voices report published by the think tank 'Global Future'[32] addressed what it called the "secret bias against community languages that is holding back students and the UK" and made an emphatic case for supporting the teaching of community languages. It pointed out the effect of the Covid lockdown in 2020 on attainment of qualifications reporting that in 2020 there was a 41 per cent drop in the uptake of A-level (higher secondary school qualifications) for community languages and a 28 per cent drop in GCSE qualifications due to the lack of accessibility of supplementary school learning facilities. It calculated that this led to 12,000 fewer qualifications than in the year before, which damaged young people's chances of gaining entry to university and to well-paid jobs. The report repeated familiar arguments about the need for investment in skills for the benefit of the economy in general and for international trade post-Brexit; but it also pointed out that in the case of young people of migrant and ethnic minority background, recognising their home language skills could serve as an instrument of social mobility.

The attitudes expressed by supplementary school staff members and the evidence from 'performances' by secondary school pupils from Burnage Academy indicate that the study of heritage languages can be used as knowledge – a skill – to understand the complexity of society and promote adaptability by embracing values of pluralism. It is a cultivation of heritage not necessarily just in the form

---

[32] https://ourglobalfuture.com/wp-content/uploads/2021/03/global-future-silenced-voices-report.pdf

of assessed language proficiency but as what Deumert (2018) describes as an "array of features".

Conscious exploration of the multilingual reality that is present particularly in 'global cities' offers a pathway to build confidence and assertiveness when acting in a pluralistic society, not just economic gain or measurable personal capital. Here it is necessary to embrace a definition of 'global cities' that goes beyond Sassen's (1991) widely cited understanding of an international economic centre, accepting instead that captured by of the notion of the 'worlding' of cities as a "nexus of transnational ideas" (Ong 2011: 4) with an emphasis on a wider set of relations that follow a vision of 'being in the world'. Müller (2021) applies the 'worlding' concept to a critique of linguistic privilege suggesting an "opening up of knowledge production to the world" (Müller 2021: 1454). This reminds us of Pratt's (1991) notion of 'contact zones' as spaces where cultures come into contact, often with unequal power relations. In such spaces community must be viewed as horizontal cooperation across cultures rather than a hierarchical identification with an idealised notion of homogeneity. This instigates reflection on the multilingual environment and on multilingual experiences and encounters. It offers an opportunity to explore the disconnect between language and place, and between language and pre-defined 'community' boundaries. It prompts instead acceptance of variation and multiple belongings.

Such experiences build knowledge that can be drawn upon to negotiate the pluralistic reality. Language skills seen from this perspective are not just about attaining qualifications and having the proficiency to use the structures of a given language. They are about the ability to take a differentiated approach to heritage and a confident and informed – 'skilled' – approach to one's own position in a diverse urban community. They help build civic identity or local citizenship. It is a perspective that foregrounds the benefits of language learning, language cultivation and multilingual awareness for individuals and their community and thus for society as a whole rather than primarily for the state's economy and national security. Instead of being driven by the quest for 'soft power' – essentially the ambition to control others without having to use force – multilingual awareness is about developing skills to interact and exchange outside and beyond a hierarchical, hegemonic structure.

8 Celebration: building a belonging

Since the early 2000s various Manchester schools have been putting on events to mark the Council of Europe's European Day of Languages. They are usually organised by the schools' modern languages departments to encourage and showcase the teaching of French, German, Spanish and sometimes other languages. Some schools use the occasion to encourage pupils with home languages other than English to contribute by showcasing their own languages. For example, an event that I attended at a secondary school in 2019 included performances by pupils taking Spanish and German reading out lines and acting out a sketch, and one by a group of children of Romanian background who put on an act entitled 'Romania has got talent' (mimicking a famous British television show) in Romanian. For many years Manchester Metropolitan University has been running a city-wide annual event in local schools called Mother Tongue Other Tongue that features a poetry competition where pupils are encouraged to use their home or heritage languages. The Council of Europe brands European Day of Languages as a 'celebration of language diversity'. MLM adopted the notion of 'celebration' on a few occasions when partnering with other organisations. For example, in the spring of 2019 we organised a 'Celebration of faith and language diversity' at Manchester Cathedral which, following the template of church ceremonies included readings from scriptures in different languages and musical and dance performances as well as an exhibition (of books and scriptures in different languages). The event also included workshops featuring Burnage Academy young interpreters' experience, deaf people's use of sign language, personal language biographies, conversations on the benefits of bilingualism and on language and scriptures.

8.1 Language days

The first city-wide public event pitched as a celebration of Manchester's language diversity was Levenshulme Language Day, organised by MLM in October 2015. Levenshulme is a residential ward with a mixed population of lower and middle-income families. It includes a sizeable population of South Asian and Eastern European backgrounds and a growing number of White professionals. It is a city council priority regeneration and development area due to its geographical proximity to the universities and city centre. MLM had a good relationship with the elected city councillors who represented the ward as well as with the ward coordinator, a city council officer. The idea was to use the location and contacts to make a public statement about the city's multilingualism. Community groups, artists, and supplementary schools were invited to make contributions in the form of stalls, music and dance performances, language taster sessions, workshops and films. They were able to reclaim public spaces to perform and showcase their languages and cultural heritage.

The event took place on a Saturday across three venues in close proximity to one another: the Saturday neighbourhood market, a community centre and a youth centre located on the district's high street. Local politicians were invited and used the occasion for photo opportunities, widely circulated on social media. Ahead of the event the city council used its weekly column 'Be Proud' in the local newspaper Manchester Evening News to print a text that MLM staff composed but was attributed to the Deputy Leader of the City Council, carrying her picture. It presented the event as a joint initiative of MLM and the city council and referred to Manchester's language diversity as one of the city's unique assets. Several months later, in February 2016, the Deputy Leader attended the launch event of LinguaSnapp at the University. In her speech at the event she mentioned how languages can be a bridge to bring people together and how they offer opportunities for the city's economy.[33] The speech had been prepared by the city council's Equality team based on briefings that MLM provided.

8.2 A city language narrative

By this point the city council had adopted an explicit position on the city's multilingualism that was informed by MLM research and the positions drafted by the project. Research and recommendations were forming the basis of an emerging policy approach. We continued to work with the elected councillors for Levenshulme and in late 2016 we drafted together with them a resolution to the city council's assembly calling for the adoption of UNESCO International Mother Language Day as an official, annual city event. For technical and procedural reasons that resolution could not be put on the assembly's agenda but it was widely circulated. In February 2017 MLM organised the first official event to mark UNESCO International Mother Language Day in Manchester in the form of a panel discussion held at the Central Library in the city centre. The panel included practitioners from several city council departments as well as the Lord Mayor and the Executive Member for Culture, Leisure and Skills. The latter two, representing the

---

33 http://mlm.humanities.manchester.ac.uk/wp-content/uploads/2016/07/Speech-23rd-Feb-2016.pdf

city's leadership, read out statements prepared by MLM, and by MLM via the council's Equality team, respectively. These statements were then published on the MLM website[34] documenting an emerging city council policy direction on languages, scripted largely by the project and made public through events instigated and hosted by the project.

This emerging policy narrative included a reference to the number of languages spoken in the city. In a university press release accompanying the publication of census data on languages in January 2013 I was quoted as saying that at least 153 languages were identified in the city (the census had only listed around 70). That figure was based on the latest school census for Manchester which surveyed pupils' reported 'first languages'. A number was included mainly because the university's media relations officer, a former political activist who became enthusiastically engaged with MLM, was of the opinion that citing a number would lend the press statement the news-item edge that it required to obtain media attention. The statement was cited by the BBC[35] as well as other media outlets. Then, in the spring of 2013 we engaged a group of assistants and final year students to carry out a survey of language provisions in Manchester. The outcome was a report entitled 'Multilingual Manchester: A Digest'[36]. The launch of the report in August 2013 at a public meeting with stakeholders from a variety of service providers was accompanied by another University press release[37] that carried the headline 'Manchester is Britain's City of Languages'. It reported that we estimated that there could be up to 200 languages spoken by long-term residents in the Greater Manchester area. Thanks to the proactive work of the media relations officer the story was featured in The Independent newspaper with the headline "200 languages: Manchester revealed as most linguistically diverse city in Western Europe"[38]. Several other daily newspapers also carried the story. In March 2015, the UK's Association of Chief Police Officers launched the #WeStandTogether campaign to promote solidarity among groups of different faiths and cultures. The initiative was a response to the rise of far-right extremist attacks targeting in particular Muslim communities in the aftermath of a wave of terrorist attacks by individual Muslim extremists across Europe. At the launch event Manchester's Chief of Police referred to Manchester as a city of 200 languages. The statement

---

34 http://mlm.humanities.manchester.ac.uk/living-in-a-city-of-languages/
35 https://www.bbc.co.uk/news/uk-england-manchester-21278437
36 http://mlm.humanities.manchester.ac.uk/wp-content/uploads/2015/12/MLMDigest.pdf
37 https://www.manchester.ac.uk/discover/news/manchester-is-britains-city-of-languages/
38 https://www.independent.co.uk/news/uk/home-news/200-languages-manchester-revealed-as-most-linguistically-diverse-city-in-western-europe-8760225.html

was repeated many times on social media and became emblematic of the campaign's ethos and objectives to bring together people of various backgrounds and to acknowledge and safeguard the city's multicultural fabric.

In May 2017 a suicide bomber attacked a music event at Manchester Arena, killing 22 people. The fact that the attacker, of Libyan background, was raised in Manchester added to the shock of what was one of Britain's worst terrorist attacks. The city united in expressions of grief, which quickly embraced the motto of cross-community and inter-faith solidarity. The Guardian newspaper's report on the day following the attack[39] cited in its second paragraph the fact that "200 languages are spoken in Manchester". In the online edition it inserted a hyperlink to the University of Manchester press release from August 2013. The message about the city's language diversity was repeated many times on social media as residents linked to the article and to the original University press release. In October 2017, MLM held its second Levenshulme Language Day. This time local politicians coordinated their visit to the event and broadcast it widely on social media. They connected the theme of multilingualism to their commitment to support local community groups and community cohesion in general. In 2018 the city council's Libraries department decided to adopt UNESCO International Mother Language Day (IMLD) as a regular annual event. It invited MLM to participate in a planning group for activities across the city. The template for that year's activities largely replicated the format of Levenshulme Language Days: interactive stalls at three neighbourhood library venues across the city targeted families, as the day (21 February) typically falls during a school mid-term holiday week. At our initiative the day was uniquely branded 'International Mother (and Father) Language Day' in order to prompt critical reflection on the ambiguity of the term 'mother tongue' and to equally acknowledge and encourage the contribution of male parents to the transmission of home and heritage languages.

8.3 Performing multilingualism

In the spring of 2018 the city council's Executive Member for Culture, Leisure and Skills commissioned a local poet to write a 'multilingual poem' celebrating the city. It was called 'Made in Manchester' and was launched as a crowd-sourcing project with the aim of prompting residents to add their own lines in their own home languages. Schools were invited to make contributions but the response

---

[39] https://www.theguardian.com/uk-news/2017/may/23/i-heart-manchester-thousands-gather-at-attack-vigil

rate was relatively low. MLM was approached to support the project and a student assistant collected around half of the fifty contributions to the first batch. Some of the contributions from schoolchildren were documented in a video released in the spring of 2019[40]. It was accompanied by an artwork that featured notes with schoolchildren's writings in numerous languages and a digital exhibit of the multilingual lines along with translations, both displayed at the Central Library foyer. The poem featured Fulani, Swahili, Somali, German, Italian, Cantonese, Albanian, Hindi, Latvian, Twi, Irish, Yiddish, Arabic and other languages. It used a crowd-sourced artistic performance and multi-modal promotion to make a public statement of belonging: it uses multilingualism as an emblem of belonging to the city and flags the participation of multiple co-creators as a symbol of plurality and democracy. Its emphasis is on contributors' emotional attachment to languages rather than on skills, qualifications or 'high culture'. In that respect it contrasts with a production released a year later, in June 2019, by the Creative Multilingualism project at Oxford University. That project commissioned a composer, a musical director and professional musicians to create a song 'We are children of the world'.[41] A children's choir performed the song in Arabic, Mandarin, Polish, Portuguese, Punjabi, Swahili and Urdu. The producers decided to include the languages spoken by children in the city's schools rather than the modern languages subjects that are taught in those schools and pitched a connection between language diversity and universality. The Manchester poem on the other hand addressed belonging to the locality. It kept the contribution of professional artists to a minimum and maximised the number of contributors featured in the video in the form of individuals reading out lines that they had written themselves. It combined diversity with individuality and the branding of a local civic identity, aspiring in that way to have a mobilising and rallying effect.

In 2018 a consortium of Manchester City Council, the University of Manchester and Manchester Metropolitan University successfully submitted a bid for the city to become recognised as a UNESCO City of Literature. The bid drew heavily on MLM's activities and highlighted the city's multilingualism as a unique feature promising to build cultural engagement around it. The consortium launched Manchester City of Literature run by a board of trustees and funded by the three organisations, which then took over the organisation of UNESCO International Mother Language Day. The branding of the day reverted to the official UNESCO

---

[40] https://literacytrust.org.uk/news/made-manchester-manchester-launches-multilingual-community-poem/
[41] https://www.youtube.com/watch?v=32HSJ-pIqY8

format and the unique Manchester title (with reference to the 'fathers') was withdrawn. As in the previous year, IMLD 2019 featured interactive stalls at several neighbourhood libraries including a larger festival-like exhibition of stalls and performances at the Central Library. Following the template of Levenshulme Language Day they were run by community groups and supplementary schools. The event was supported by the MLM public engagement team and student volunteers.

Coinciding with the IMLD 2019 events was a conference hosted by MLM and devoted to 'university public engagement with multilingualism'. It brought together academics and local practitioners, public service representatives and city council officers. For IMLD 2020 MLM organised an opening evening event at Manchester Museum which included around twenty stalls and activities, and a further daytime festival-like event at the Central Library. Other institutions also embraced IMLD celebrations. At Central Manchester Hospitals a Language Day briefing and information event was held for clinical and support staff organised by the Equality & Diversity Unit during a lunch hour with short presentations from the Interpreting unit including demonstrations of phrases from some of the more common languages of hospital patients.

In the following year (February 2021) events were held online due to the Covid outbreak. Manchester City of Literature, by now a registered charity organisation with several paid staff, took the lead again and hired a public relations firm to promote and market the series of online events. An online platform was created documenting the history of Language Day and IMLD celebrations in Manchester, featuring some of the activities going back to Levenshulme Language Day 2015.[42] Promotion of the various online events once again highlighted the figure of "200 languages" and the claim that the city was "one of the most linguistically diverse in the UK" or indeed "in Europe". A city language narrative had emerged by this point: the iteration of declarations of recognition of the city's multilingualism as a distinctinctive and defining feature.

The narrative's credibility continued to draw on its acknowledged provenance in academic research. Its active propagation was now embedded into an institutional context, allocated institutional resources and adopted as an institutional practice implemented by institutional agents as part of a scripted action plan. IMLD 2022 took on a hybrid format though most events were held online.

---

42 https://www.manchestercityofliterature.com/project/international-mother-language-day/a-virtual-tour-of-manchesters-language-celebrations/

On the occasion Manchester City of Literature appointed three 'multilingual poets' to work for a year across local schools and other venues to encourage creative writing and performances and discussions about heritage languages.

8.4 The interactive grassroots experience

A salient feature of the various Language Day and IMLD events that took place in the city until 2021 was their reliance on grassroots contributions. Participating groups usually presented stalls and posters (some also offering performances) in which they disseminated information about their organisation and their language. For example, at the 2020 event a local Amazigh initiative presented a talk and slide show about the geographical distribution of Tamazight and related languages, the Armenian supplementary school displayed kits to learn some of the letters of the Armenian alphabet, one of the Arabic schools offered instruction in calligraphy and a Pakistani cultural centre created a poster on the 'languages of Pakistan' drawing attention exceptionally to that country's multilingualism.

Over the years MLM had created an extensive portfolio of interactive exhibits on multilingualism. They included a 'language map' of Manchester where visitors were invited to write down the names of languages they use on a card and pin it to a location on the city map or write down words in their languages and attach them to a bunting banner. This kind of activities prompted contributions from visitors. They resulted in a public display of personal statements representing plurality. They also triggered conversations between parents and children around the choice of words and how to represent them in writing. Often, families with parents of mixed backgrounds deliberated on which languages to choose and in the case of regional languages and dialects, how to represent them in writing. The spontaneity attested through segments such as *como stass* for Spanish 'como estas' testifies to the way in which young visitors in particular felt empowered to represent their linguistic repertoire without feeling bound by institutional knowledge and norms, relying instead on their own personal knowledge. Many parents, speakers of regional and minoritised languages such as African languages, Azeri from Iran, Romani, and others reported feeling heartened by the opportunity to convey to their children at a public venue a sense of confidence in their heritage languages. The occasion thus contributed to a feeling of linguistic empowerment and confidence in elements of heritage and identity that are rarely acknowledged in public or institutional settings.

MLM's exhibit portfolio also included a board with pictures of animals. It invited visitors to write down and attach cards with the sounds associated with those animals in their languages. This exercise was particularly symbolic of notions of universality and plurality since animal sounds are usually regarded as onomatopoetic imitations. Yet in reality when compared across languages they show symbolic representations that are culture specific and at the same time often playful. The animal sounds activity thus addresses the core of 'languageness' and structural diversity pitched at the simplest and most intuitive common denominator.

Another unique activity was a stall co-curated by MLM and local Romani community activists. It gave information about the Romani language including a word-match game constructed to help identify inherited Indo-Aryan vocabulary and its similarities to present-day South Asian languages that are widely spoken in Manchester and Greek-derived loanwords with universal familiarity such as *drom* 'road' and *foro* 'town'. Visitors' most frequent questions at the stall were 'What the country is Romani spoken in?' and 'How it is written'. Both required answers that were intrinsically pluralistic, since Romani is a geographically dispersed minority language and since it has no uniform written Standard. The Romani stall served to interrogate and critique some of the most common (colonial) notions about language: its association with a nation-state territory and a standard writing system.

MLM's 'multilingual shop' presented small items purchased in shops across the city with labels in different languages and invited visitors to identify the languages and the areas within the city where those items might be on sale, prompting reflection on the geographical distribution of languages in the city. At some venues the shop was accompanied by a computer display of the LinguaSnapp online platform on which visitors could search for signs in different languages around the city.

8.5 Celebration as stepping stone to policy

The history of language day events in Manchester offers an opportunity to reflect on the connection between public celebration and linguistic citizenship as the inclusion of new voices in public discussions, empowerment and the use of language as a site to negotiate relations (cf. Stroud 2001, 2008)[43]. Celebrations are widely regarded as a way of upholding the social order and building a sense of shared belonging. Discussing peasant societies Wolf (1966: 7ff., 98) describes

---

43 See also https://blog.policy.manchester.ac.uk/growth_inclusion/2021/02/celebration-public-policy-international-mother-language-day-as-civic-identity-badge/

how ceremonials consist of public performances in which participants act out social relations and offer a public exhibition of their ideal model of such relations. Ceremonials are so essential to the social order that they are allocated a portion of the production surplus, which Wolf calls 'ceremonial expenditures'. Rappaport (1999: 115ff.) dwells on the communicative functions of celebrations as performative action. Rituals serve to deem a condition or to change it. They often have a perlocutionary function, as the ritual performance brings a commitment or a state into effect. Celebration is thus a communicative event that aims to bring about a certain social order. Manning (1983) considers celebrations as cultural performances and therefore symbolic action, and points out their participatory element as well as their use for ideological instrumentation. For Rusu and Kantola (2016) celebrations support the temporal framing of activities, imposing a cyclical pattern but also disrupting and suspending daily life while bringing about a sense of togetherness. Festivals are seen as community feasts cast through joyful events with the participation of the community but they can also be ideological instruments to boost status quo. Societies usually reserve special places for celebration, which are transformed during celebrations into festive locations.

Many of these features are recognisable in the language celebrations of Levenshulme Language Days and IMLD in Manchester. They are recurring annual or bi-annual events, often claiming spaces such as Levenshulme Market, Central Library and Manchester Museum. The wider dispersion of additional events at local neighbourhood libraries and community centres further strengthen the participatory aspect. They are performative actions where participants put their language resources on display, showcasing diverse backgrounds while demonstrating a common belonging to the locality. They convey the social order message around acceptance of plurality and sharing local space. They also convey an ideological commitment to equality and a message of togetherness. That is used to boost a sense of belonging to the city and confidence in its institutions including its community organisations. This is in line with Manchester City Council's key policy theme of many years of de-centralising services, particularly advice and support services, and relying on community initiatives to deliver them. The celebrations are also perlocutionary acts: By stating that Manchester is a 'city of languages' it becomes a city of languages in the minds of audiences, participants and observers.

Finally, the celebrations are entertaining events but also learning opportunities: intellectual curiosity is triggered and harnessed through interactive exhibits, discussion forums and presentations. These offer an educational experience, equally a contributor to recognising and accepting the social order of plurality.

From the linguistic citizenship perspective language celebrations offer individuals, families and organisations opportunities to perform their own heritage and reclaim public spaces. They become an integral and indeed a defining part of the emerging, collective city language narrative. The iteration of such practice in the form of regular events supports the emergence of a performative collective: a community of participants that meet regularly to enact the celebration ritual and become united around its ideological message. This offers participants the opportunity to feel as co-owners of the civic brand and to regard their contribution to it as essential and formative.

Consistent with Stroud's (2001, 2008) view of language as a site of political and economic struggles, the Manchester experience shows a direct pathway from reclaiming public space for celebration to the instigation of political interventions. In the spring of 2018 the city council's Executive Member for Culture, Leisure and Skills invited MLM to draft a City Language Strategy. It was emphasised in conversations with city council officials that this would be a 'city' rather than a 'council' strategy. It would avoid listing targets and deliverables that the local authority would be held accountable for. Instead it was to draw up principles based on which the local authority would lead a network of local institutions and actors. This was in line with the observation on the non-centralised, network-based provisions and policy for language described for Manchester by Matras and Robertson (2015). City council officers then held a series of consultations based on the draft Strategy with representatives of key public services providers. This resulted in the adoption by the council's Communities and Equalities Scrutiny Committee of a report on 'Manchester's Language Diversity'[44] that outlined work carried out "at local level". Following our draft Strategy document it linked multilingualism to the declared objectives of the city's existing development strategy on supporting sustainability and diversity, home grown talent, unlocking the potential of communities and ensuring equity and connectivity. The report also flagged the work of MLM to raise awareness of multilingualism using the term 'celebrate' multiple times in connection with language diversity and multilingualism.

The city council also supported an approach to the Office for National Statistics in 2018 suggesting an amendment to the question on languages in preparation of the 2021 Census. A letter drafted by MLM was signed by the city council's Chief Executive. It said that "researchers have expressed some concerns that the

---

44 https://democracy.manchester.gov.uk/documents/s9767/Manchesters%20Language%20Diversity.pdf

question 'What is your main language?' may not have allowed the census to collect all relevant data"[45]. It argued that a slight amendment to the census question could help map languages more accurately and that this would be helpful to the city council as it would "greatly improve our ability to assess the outreach potential of community based initiatives such as supplementary schools and advice and support groups that target particular language-based communities". It added that a change would also help the council and key public services assess requirements for interpreting and translation and survey the pool of language skills as an important asset on which the city draws for growth and development. The amendment that we had proposed to the government was to allow the listing of more than one 'main language'.[46] The step was to my knowledge a rare example of a university project taking on the role of an advocacy and lobbying group and acting via a major local authority. While the government did not accept a change to the wording, it invited us to help re-draft the guidance notes. These were changed to advise users that when thinking about 'main language' they should think of the one other than English that is 'most natural', which could be 'the language used at home'.[47]

The experience shows how the local authority took a stance that is opposed to that of the national government on an issue surrounding language, identity and the implications for public policy and public services. Afzal Khan, Labour MP for Manchester-Gorton, also supported the initiative and raised the matter in the House of Commons. In 2019 he hosted a public consultation at the Houses of Parliament on 'Recognising our citizens' many languages', organised by MLM in partnership with the National Resource Centre for Supplementary Education, the Speak for the Future charity and the British Academy. In March and April 2020 he repeatedly challenged the government on the absence of translation of Covid guidance into community languages. The iteration and gradual institutionalisation of celebrations around multilingualism provided a mandate to key political actors in Manchester toward recognising multilingualism as a public policy issue and making representations that challenged national policy. A pathway was established from the local to the national.

---

[45] http://mlm.humanities.manchester.ac.uk/wp-content/uploads/2018/04/MCCLetter.pdf
[46] See https://blog.policy.manchester.ac.uk/growth_inclusion/2019/04/improving-the-census-question-on-language-could-help-repair-community-relations-and-britains-international-image-post-brexit/;
http://projects.alc.manchester.ac.uk/cross-language-dynamics/what-is-your-main-language-in-order-to-engage-with-policy-modern-linguists-need-a-vision-for-society/
[47] See discussion as part of REF 2021 Impact Case Study: https://yaronmatras.files.wordpress.com/2022/07/impact-4-2021.pdf

As a result of these developments Manchester became widely regarded in circles of academic experts, practitioners and policymakers as a leading hub in the drafting of policy on domestic multilingualism. At the international conference hosted by MLM in February 2019 delegates decided to draft a Manifesto that called for the formation of a Multilingual Cities Movement[48]. The text was published on the MLM website in May 2019 along with a list of the first batch of signatories representing both individuals and organisations. It called for academics, practitioners, students and officials to build sustainable collaborations. It identified cities as sites where languages, plurality and difference are accepted. It alluded to complex linguistic repertoires and pointed out that language difference can be seen as a source of insecurity and conflict but also as connection and enrichment. It explained the use of the term 'Movement' as an ambition to create an umbrella of diverse models and initiatives and called for the formation of a networking platform "based in and around universities" that are committed to the principles outlined in the manifesto. The manifesto enshrined the idea that university projects should a) engage non-academics in the development of knowledge and outreach, b) serve as sites that actively initiate and lead advocacy work for social and political change, and c) seek to internationalise their exchange and mobilisation efforts. At the same time it chose not to address arguments that many UK academic bodies embraced when lobbying for more resources for language teaching and learning, namely the role of language in creating wealth and protecting national security. The message was instead explicitly internationalist and humanistic.

9 Conclusion and outlook

In Matras (2017b) I introduced a provisional typology of the domains of supplementary practice brought about through the city's engagement with its multilingual reality, referring to the dimensions of access, heritage and skills. To those I have now added the domain of celebration. In Manchester a number of institutions acknowledge an obligation to ensure equal access to public services by maintaining provisions for interpreting and translation. Interpreter-mediated communication in public services constitutes a communicative practice in its

---

[48] https://yaronmatras.files.wordpress.com/2022/07/call-for-a-multilingual-cities-movement.pdf

own right rather than mere duplication of institutional interaction in other languages (cf. Tipton and Furnamek 2016). Recognition of the multilingual reality in interaction between practitioners and clients also opens up spaces for individual creativity and agency subverting routines and giving rise to new practices (cf. Matras et al. 2023).

The cultivation of heritage is the mission statement and principal purpose of dozens of language supplementary schools that operate in Manchester. As their name suggests they provide a service that enriches existing provisions and offers participants an institutional framework that engages them in a distinct practice. A new dimension of practice is also added to the portfolio of major cultural institutions like the museum once they decide to dedicate spaces to develop multilingual exhibits and engage multilingual audiences. The crossover of heritage and skills was demonstrated for supplementary schools and mainstream schools that teach home or heritage languages. Turning heritage to skills often requires a dedicated institutional pathway, one that can produce qualifications that become part of an individual's formally recognised personal capital. Alternatively, it is embedded into a pedagogical approach that seeks to harness personal knowledge in order to build confidence and assertiveness. Celebrations introduce new practices backed by an overarching narrative of local belonging that embraces heritage cultivation, harnessing of skills and provisions of access measures.

The multilingual reality thus gives rise to new practices that make language difference and language identity an object and an objective in its own right. These practices empower actors to draw on a variety of knowledge resources including linguistic features, experiences, impressions and encounters as well as digital literacy and inter-personal resources. They are accompanied by an ideological discourse of communality that helps define the city and its citizenship.

This echoes Rehbein's (2013) discussion of what he gently calls a 'utopia' of multilingualism. Rehbein proposes that global migrations give rise to new communicative functions. The linguistic changes they bring about are therefore not only quantitative but qualitative. They require responses that aim not just to ensure smooth cooperation and coherence of existing structures but which take account of the complex situations that bring about new communicative action structures. These involve the potential deployment of multilingualism across a patchwork of multilingual spaces spread through society. Urbanisation means that such domains are no longer separated but co-exist in fluctuating spaces that constitute interactive contact zones.

Rehbein sees the multiplicity of languages in a society (for which he uses the term "community languages") as knowledge resources. Institutions are micro-spaces of multilingualism. They are challenged to integrate different knowledge resources into the various determinants of institutional talk including the social justification of the institution, the structure of sequences of talk within the institutional setting and relations between groups of agents and clients with diverse types of knowledge. Rehbein notes how monolingual ideology stands in the way of recognising and facilitating such change in institutional settings. He concludes by suggesting that research institutions can play an important part in counteracting nationalistic ideologies that are averse to multilingualism by creating models of multilingual practice and internationalisation and facilitating cross-sector spaces that work as a 'movement' to promote multilingualism.

A number of multilingual institutional practices, actions and multilingual spaces discussed in this paper are the direct product of the intervention of a university-based research project: The creation of a city language narrative and a platform to develop and promote it in the form of public celebrations; introduction of a dedicated multilingual practice into the agenda of a major cultural institution; creation of school activities that prompt reflection on personal multilingual knowledge and experience; networking and developing of a collective agenda giving a voice to supplementary schools; monitoring of language access provisions in a key public service provider (Central Manchester Hospitals); mobilisation of key actors in the city in support of language policy reforms at national level and the formulation and articulation of a policy direction on multilingualism at local level; and the initiative to internationalise exchange with a view toward mobilising actors on a larger scale in the form of a call for a Multilingual Cities Movement.

At various levels these initiatives have created new opportunities for agency, or for reflection on agency: The involvement of researchers helped valorise the experience of actors and turn it into a collective ideology articulated through expressions of belonging to the civic community. Rymes (2020) uses the term 'citizen' to denote the non-expert who claims the right to articulate opinion and experience-based expertise, but also to denote the subject or local inhabitant. She regards 'citizen sociolinguistics' as the acknowledgement of the linguistic expertise of members of the community. Contrasting with action that is organised and systematic, citizenship 'acts' are seen as 'momentary ruptures' that reveal assumptions about languages (Rymes 2020: 170). In our discussion they can be seen as acts of assertiveness anchored in a reflection about multilingual experience that position actors in what Brubaker (2005) calls a 'diasporic stance'. Through celebrations and the emergence of a city language narrative, multilingual practices become for some actors and institutions a part of the foundation of the urban community. In Blokland's (2017) terms, the city's multilingualism is acknowledged as part of its public familiarity and contributes to a shared sense of belonging.

The decoloniality paradigm emerged in order to lend intellectual resilience to indigenous populations that were disenfranchised economically and spiritually by European colonialism. As an intellectual paradigm it has opened up a new lens through which to discuss and understand cross-cultural encounters, particularly those that are embedded into asymmetrical power relations. Bhabha (1994), Stuart Hall (1990) and Spivak (1990, 1999) all emphasise the transnational character of culture and the need for the postcolonial perspective to enable agency and representation of the diasporic in the historical context of postcolonial displacement. As such the paradigm is applicable in principle to the question of culture and agency in a Western metropolis. The position of language as a particularly tangible representation of culture is indisputable.

A university-based project devoted to multilingualism can adopt and implement key elements of the decolonial paradigm in various ways: It can re-define the beneficiaries of research to include language users, practitioners and policy-makers. It can lend a voice to populations that are in the margins of power. It can create new forms of knowledge through exchange with stakeholders. It can break down traditional barriers among academic disciplines. It can adopt an agenda to bring about social and political change and counteract discrimination; and it can try to reclaim public space to challenge colonial discourses of what Bhabha (1994: 94) calls 'fixitiy' or the ideological construction of Otherness. It can also internationalise its work to create a mobilising momentum.

In Matras and Robertson (2017: 10–11) we identified a number of risks facing the model. First, the university is limited in the extent to which it can empower actors in other institutions. Consequently a university project cannot always meet the expectations of external stakeholders, particularly those relating to the sustainability of practical support. Within the university itself we mentioned uncertainties as the project is "caught up in volatile processes of prioritisation and internal competition for resources". We concluded by saying: "The major challenge remains the need to reconcile continuity and stability, which is a pre-requisite for the reputational capital on which the partnerships rest, with the institution's ability to maintain its practical commitment to the civic university vision". Rampton et al. (2018: 77–78) acknowledge MLM as a "spectacular model" of promoting sociolinguistic citizenship. At the same time they decry the absence of government support for such projects in the UK. They point out the need to rely on short term funding and considerable tactical energy and ingenuity to use university spaces to forge alliances with external stakeholders. They also comment on how the conditions that opened up opportunities – the drive to show impact and to score points on the student experience and employability metrics – pose a risk that makes the long term commitment volatile.

As described above, since the early 2000s a trend emerged to portray language learning as serving national interests in trade, security and diplomacy – coined 'soft power', implying the power to dominate others with minimal use of force. That trend took on a new momentum in late 2016 following the Brexit decision. Some researchers embraced those positions within the Open World Research Initiative (OWRI), a four-year scheme funded by the Arts and Humanities Research Council. Key figures in OWRI campaigned for the government to appoint a 'Chief Linguist' who would coordinate the teaching of languages among departments with an emphasis on the benefits to civil servants, foreign policy and security. In the conversations with officials the emerging idea was to accommodate the Chief Linguist within GCHQ, the country's spy agency, rather than in the departments for Education, Culture, or Communities, for example. The initiative was launched in November 2018 at an event at the Houses of Parliament hosted by Stephen Kinnock MP, who soon after the referendum expressed his opinion that "uncontrolled immigration can lead to racism".[49]

MLM was one of OWRI's dedicated research strands and it received some of its funding from that scheme.[50] Yet our call to add support of community languages to the prospective remit of the Chief Linguist was actively resisted, as were requests to devote space on the OWRI platform to positions articulated within MLM which emphasised bottom-up multilingualism as an issue of human rights, pluralism and citizenship and which called for a domestic language policy. There was also reluctance among some to support our efforts to call publicly for a change to the wording of the census question on language, with key actors within OWRI adopting the position that one should not "antagonise civil servants" but instead wait to be called upon if and when one's expertise was needed. At the same time attempts were made to flag MLM as a potential contributor to enhancing post-Brexit trade with India and to counteracting "extremism and radicalisation", usually understood as referring to certain ideologies among Muslim populations – both of which we declined. Some of these disagreements might be seen

---

49 https://www.theguardian.com/commentisfree/2016/sep/19/cure-divided-britain-managed-immigration-work-permits
50 For an optimistic view at the beginning of the scheme's lifetime see: http://projects.alc.manchester.ac.uk/cross-language-dynamics/open-world-research-aesthetics-practicalities-crossing-boundaries/

to revolve around what Gilroy (2004) called "revivalist colonialist accounts". They also reflected different understandings of academic freedom and the freedom to adopt advocacy agendas as opposed to the corporate privilege to control such agendas.

As these debates intensified MLM's activities came to a halt. The Covid outbreak brought about limitations on outreach work, a tightening of resources and discontinuation of staff positions. The student volunteer scheme came to an end, as did a number of external partnerships. The MLM web page was re-cast as a 'legacy site' and its narrative transposed into the past tense. Various activities are no longer showcased, among them the 'Call for a Multilingual Cities Movement', the report on the event at the Houses of Parliament on 'Recognising our citizens' many languages' hosted by the multilingual Member of Parliament from Manchester Afzal Khan, and my blog post 'Do Modern Languages include Community Languages? A plea for a domestic language policy agenda'.[51] The dialect databases that supported appeals in asylum cases are no longer accessible on the university's website, either.

Elements of the city language narrative are likely to stay. But inevitably not all those involved will embrace wholesale the values that guided MLM. As Rehbein (2013) notes, 'multilingualism' implies active recourse to a repertoire of multiple languages (in society in general and in institutional contexts). By contrast, 'linguistic diversity' represents difference including functional specialisations and hierarchical ordering. Schiller (2015, 2016) describes how 'diversity' is employed as a "neoliberal catchword" to increase productivity while avoiding recognition of the rights of population groups to maintain distinctive cultural practices. Campbell and Hwa (2015) even warn of the dangers of objectifying communities as part of a public engagement agenda.

Whether an experiment like MLM can be replicated will depend on the general direction in which the sector will move. Some voices are sceptical. Neary (2020) has suggested that higher education institutions that function as corporate enterprises use concepts like 'civic university' and 'social responsibility' merely as reputational devices. Others have described the neoliberal university as one that exercises "thought control" (Lorenz 2012) and as a "ruthless corporation" where institutional racism remains unchanged and unchallenged (Sian 2019: 186) and is addressed only through mechanistic procedures to show a balanced demography for reputational purposes (Beattie 2013). Some suggest that in such an environment there is a permanent risk that decoloniality initiatives linked to

---

51 Now archived here: https://yaronmatras.files.wordpress.com/2022/03/ymatras-do-modern-languages-include-community-languages.pdf

civil resistance and social movements are erased (Mignolo and Walsh 2018) and replaced by "tokenised checklist responses" (Pidgeon 2016). In the extreme, there is a risk that the "intellectual insurgency" that Neary (2020) calls for is harshly suppressed; that as Sian (2019: 32ff.) describes, those challenging "liberal racism" are viewed as "troublemakers" who deliberately disrupt the social order; and that, as Smith ([1999] 2021: 261) warns, those persons become marginalised who choose to research with and fight for marginalised communities.

Acknowledgements: In developing some of the ideas presented here and the activities to which they relate I have benefited from discussions and collaboration with Louise Atkinson, Jessica Bradley, Stephanie Connor, Andrea Donakey, Leonie Gaiser, Kathleen Easlick, László Fosztó, Katie Harrison, Petros Karatsareas, Viktor Leggio, Sandy Lo, Louise Middleton, Caitlin Morrissey, Eva-Maria Mosser, Ben Rampton, Gertrud Reershemius, Jochen Rehbein, Alex Robertson, Mirela Sutac and Rebecca Tipton. Alex Harman and Helen Hanna contributed to some of the data transcriptions. The work of MLM was partly funded by the Arts and Humanities Research Council through the Open World Research Initiative (2016–2021) and by a grant from the British Academy Wolfson Professorial Fellowship scheme (2017–2022). An earlier version of this paper was published in January 2023 in the online series Working Papers in Urban Languages and Literacies no. 307.

References

Ahearn, Laura. M. 2001. Language and agency. *Annual Review of Anthropology* 30(1). 109–137.
Anderson, Benedict. 1983. *Imagined communities: Reflections on the origin and spread of nationalism*. Brooklyn, NY: Verso Books.
Appadurai, Arjun. 1992. Global ethnoscapes: Notes and queries for a transnational anthropology. In Richard G. Fox (ed.), *Interventions: Anthropologies of the present*, 191–210. Santa Fe: School of American Research.
Arnaut, Karel, Jan Blommaert, Ben Rampton & Maximilian Spotti (eds.). 2016. *Language and Superdiversity*. New York & London: Routledge.
Arnaut, Karel, Martha Sif Karrebæk, Maximilian Spotti & Jan Blommaert (eds.). 2017. *Engaging superdiversity. Recombining spaces, times and language practices*. Bristol: Multilingual Matters.
Batac, Monica Anne. 2022. "Failing" and finding a Filipina diasporic scholarly "Home": A De/Colonizing Autoethnography. *Qualitative Inquiry* 28(1). 62–69.
Beattie, Geoffrey. 2013. *Our racist heart? An exploration of unconscious prejudice in everyday life*. London: Routledge.
Bhabha, Homi. 1994. *The location of culture*. London: Routledge.
Bhambra, Guminder K., Dalia Gebrial & Kerem Nişancıoğlu (eds.). 2018. *Decolonising the university*. London: Pluto Press.

Bhattacharya, Kakali. 2016. The vulnerable academic: personal narratives and strategic de/colonizing of academic structures. *Qualitative Inquiry* 22(5). 309–321.

Bhattacharyya, Gargi, Adam Elliott-Cooper, Sita Balani Kerem Nişancıoğlu, Kojo Koram, Dalia Gebrial, Nadine El-Enany & Luke de Noronha. 2021. *Empire's endgame*. London: Pluto Press.

Bischoff, Alexander & Patricia Hudelson. 2010. Access to healthcare interpreter services: Where are we and where do we need to go? *International Journal of Environmental Research and Public Health* 7(7). 2838–2844.

Blackledge, Aadrian & Angela Creese. 2010. *Multilingualism: A critical perspective*. London: Continuum International.

Blokland, Tala. 2017. *Community as urban practice*. Cambridge: Polity Press.

Blommaert, Jan. 2010. *Sociolinguistics of globalization*. Cambridge: Cambridge University Press.

Blommaert, Jan. 2013. *Ethnography, superdiversity and linguistic landscapes: Chronicles of complexity*. Bristol & Blue Ridge Summit: Multilingual Matters.

Blommaert, Jan & Ad Backus. 2013. Superdiverse repertoires and the Individual. In Ingrid de Saint-Georges & Jean-Jaques Weber (eds.), *Multilingualism and multimodality. The future of education research*, 11–32. Rotterdam: SensePublishers.

Blommaert, Jan & Ben Rampton. 2011. Language and superdiversity. *Diversities* 132. 1–21.

Bradley, Jessica. 2017. Translanguaging engagement: Dynamic multilingualism and university language engagement programmes. *Bellaterra Journal of Teaching & Learning Language & Literature* 10(4). 9–31.

Bradley, Jessica & Louise Atkinson. 2020. Translanguaging beyond bricolage: Meaning making and collaborative ethnography in community arts. In Emilee Moore, Jessica Bradley & James Simpson (eds.), *Translanguaging as transformation. The collaborative construction of new linguistic realities*, 135–154. Bristol & Blue Ridge Summit: Multilingual Matters.

Bradley, Jessica, Emilee Moore, James Simpson & Lousie Atkinson. 2018. Translanguaging space and creative activity: theorising collaborative arts-based learning. *Language and Intercultural Communication* 18(1). 54–73.

Brear, Michelle R. & Cias T. Tsotetsi. 2021. (De)colonising outcomes of community participation – a South African ethnography of 'ethics in practice'. *Qualitative Research* 4. 1–18.

Brooks, Ethel, Colin Clark & Iulius Rostas. 2022. Engaging with decolonisation, tackling antigypsyism: Lessons from teaching Romani Studies at the Central European University in Hungary. *Social Policy & Society* 21(1). 68–79.

Brubaker, Rogers. 2004. *Ethnicity without groups*. Cambridge, MA: Harvard University Press.

Brubaker, Rogers. 2005. The 'diaspora' diaspora. *Ethnic and Racial Studies* 28(1). 1–19.

Bührig, Kristin, Ortrun Kliche, Bernd Meyer & Birte Pawlack. 2012. Explaining the interpreter's unease. Conflicts and contradictions in bilingual communication in clinical settings. In Kurt Braunmüller & Christoph Gabriel (eds.), *Multilingual individuals and multilingual societies*, 407–418. Amsterdam: Benjamins.

Busch, Brigitte. 2012. The linguistic repertoire revisited. *Applied Linguistics* 33(5). 503–523.

Busch, Brigitte. 2015. Linguistic repertoire and Spracherleben, the lived experience of language. *Applied Linguistics* 38(3). 340–358.

Busch, Brigitte. 2018. *The language portrait in multilingualism research: Theoretical and methodological considerations*. Working Papers in Urban Language & Literacies 236.

Cadier, Linda & Clare Mar-Molinero. 2012. Language policies and linguistic super-diversity in contemporary urban societies: The case of the city of Southampton, UK. *Current Issues in Language Planning* 13(3). 149–165.
Campbell, James & Yen Siew Hwa. 2015. The spirit of community engagement. *International e-Journal of Community & Industry Engagement* 2(1). 1–10.
Cohen, Robin. 2008. *Global diasporas. An introduction*. Hoboken: Taylor & Francis.
Creese, Angela, & Adrian Blackledge. 2018. *The Routledge handbook of language and superdiversity*. London Routledge.
de Sousa Santos, B. 2012. Public sphere and epistemologies of the South. *Africa Development* 37(1). 43–67.
Deumert, Ana. 2018. The multivocality of heritage: Moments, encounters and mobilities. In Angela Creese & Adrian Blackledge (eds.), *The Routledge handbook of language and superdiversity*, 149–164. London: Routledge.
Donakey, Andrea. 2007. *Language Planning and Policy in Manchester*. University of Manchester dissertation.
Douglass, Mike. 2008. Livable Cities: Neoliberal v. Convivial Modes of Urban Planning in Seoul. *The Korea Spatial Planning Review* 59. 3–36.
Emirbayer, Mustafa & Ann Mische. 1998. What is agency? *American Journal of Sociology* 103(4). 962–1023.
Gaibrois, Claudine. 2019. From resistance to 'bricolage': Forms of power to get active and create possibilities in multilingual organizations. *Revista Internacional de Organizaciones* 23. 125–147.
Gaiser, Leonie & Yaron Matras. 2016a. *Language provisions in access to primary and hospital care in central Manchester. Multilingual Manchester*. The University of Manchester. http://mlm.humanities.manchester.ac.uk/wp-content/uploads/2016/09/Language-provisions-in-access-to-primary-and-hospital-care-Sept-2016.pdf
Gaiser, Leonie & Yaron Matras. 2016b. *The spatial construction of civic identities: A study of Manchester's linguistic landscapes*. http://mlm.humanities.manchester.ac.uk/wp-content/uploads/2016/12/ManchesterLinguisticLandscapes.pdf
García, Ofelia & Wei Li. 2014. *Translanguaging: Language, bilingualism and education*. New York: Palgrave Macmillan.
Garibay, Cecilia, Steven Yalowitz & Guest Editors. 2015. Redefining multilingualism in museums: a case for broadening our thinking. *Museums & Social Issues* 10(1). 2–7.
Gilroy, Paul. 2004. *After empire. Melancholia or convivial culture?*. London: Routledge.
Glick Schiller, Nina. 2011. Cities and transnationality. In Gary Bridge & Sophie Watson (eds.), *The new Blackwell companion to the city*, 179–192. Oxford: Blackwell.
Hall, Stuart. 1990. Cultural identity and diaspora. In Jonathan Rutherford (ed.), *Identity: community, culture, difference*, 222–237. London: Lawrence & Wishart.
Hall, Stuart. 1992 [2019]. The West and the rest: Discourse and power. In David Morley (ed.), *Essential Essays*, 141–184. Durham: Duke University Press.
Hall, Suzanne. 2012. *City, street and citizen. The measure of the ordinary*. London: Routledge.
Heller, Monica. 2010. *Paths to post-nationalism a critical ethnography of language and identity*. New York & Oxford: Oxford University Press.
Heugh, Kathleen. 2022. Linguistic citizenship as a decolonial lens on southern multilingualisms and epistemologies. In Quentin Williams, Ana Deumert & Tommaso M. Milani (eds.), *Struggles for multilingualism and linguistic citizenship*, 35–58. Bristol: Multilingual Matters.

Holmes, Bernardette. 2018. Speaking to a global future: The increasing value of language and culture to British business post-Brexit. In Michael Kelly (ed.), *Languages after Brexit. How the UK speaks to the world*, 61–74. Cham: Palgrave Macmillan.

Holmwood, John. 2018. Race and the neoliberal university: Lessons from the public university. In Guminder K. Bhambra, Dalia Gebrial & Kerem Nişancıoğlu (eds.), *Decolonising the university*, 37–52. London: Pluto Press.

Hornberger, Nancy H., Also Anzures Tapia, David H. Hanks, Frances Kvietok Dueñas & Siwon Lee. 2018. Ethnography of language planning and policy. *Language Teaching* 512. 152–186.

Huang, J. 2020. A shifting standard: a stratified ideological ecology in a Birmingham Chinese complementary school. *Journal of Multilingual and Multicultural Development* 42(2). 1–13.

Johnson, David Cassels & Eric J. Johnson. 2015. Power and agency in language policy appropriation. *Language Policy* 14(3). 221–243.

Jørgensen, J. Normann. 2008. Polylingual languaging around and among children and adolescents. *International Journal of Multilingualism* 5(3). 161–176.

Joseph, Cynthia. 2008. Difference, subjectivities and power: (de)colonizing practices in internationalizing the curriculum. *Intercultural Education* 19(1). 29–39.

Kelly, Michael (ed.). 2018. *Languages after Brexit. How the UK speaks to the world*. Cham: Palgrave Macmillan.

Kelly-Holmes Helen & Sari Pietikäinen. 2016. Language: A challenging resource in a museum of Sámi culture. *Scandinavian Journal of Hospitality and Tourism* 16(1). 24–41.

Keshet, Yael & Ariela Popper-Giveon. 2019. Language practice and policy in Israeli hospitals: the case of the Hebrew and Arabic languages. *Israel Journal of Health Policy Research* 8(1). 1–11.

Lefebvre, Henri. 1968. *Le droit à la ville*. Paris: Anthropos.

Li, Wei. 2018a. Linguistic (super-)diversity, post-multilingualism and translanguaging moments. In Angela Creese & Adrian Blackledge (eds.), *The Routledge handbook of language and superdiversity*, 16–29. London Routledge.

Li, Wei. 2018b. Translanguaging as a practical theory of languages. *Applied Linguistics* 39(1). 9–30.

Liao, Min-Hsiu. 2018. Museums and creative industries: The contribution of translation studies. *The Journal of Specialised Translation* 29. 45–62.

Liddicoat, Anthony J. & Kerry Taylor-Leech. 2020. Agency in language planning and policy. *Current Issues in Language Planning* 22(1–2). 1–18.

Lo, Sandy. 2007. *Cantonese-English code-switching in the Manchester Chinese immigrant community*. Manchester University of Manchester dissertation.

Lorenz, Chris. 2012. If you're so smart, why are you under surveillance? Universities, neoliberalism, and new public management. *Critical Inquiry* 38(3). 599–629.

Luke, Nikki & Nik Heynen. 2021. Abolishing the frontier: (De)colonizing 'public' education. *Social & Cultural Geography* 22(3). 403–424.

Mac Giolla Chríost, Diarmait. 2007. *Language and the city*. Basingstoke: Palgrave Macmillan.

Manning, Frank E. 1983. Cosmos and chaos: Celebration in the modern world. In Frank E. Manning (ed.), *The celebration of society: perspectives on contemporary cultural performances*, 3–30. Bowling Green, OH: Bowling Green University Press.

Martin, Jenni & Marilee Jennings. 2015. Tomorrow's museum: multilingual audiences and the learning institution. *Museums & Social Issues* 10(1). 83–94.

Matras, Yaron. 2009 [2020]. *Language contact*. Cambridge: Cambridge University Press.

Matras, Yaron. 2017a. From Journal of the Gypsy Lore Society to Romani Studies: Purpose and essence of a modern academic platform. *Romani Studies* 27(2). 113–123.

Matras, Yaron. 2017b. Can global cities have a language policy? *Society, Languages & Policy* 1(1), https://doi.org/10.17863/CAM.9800.

Matras, Yaron. 2018a. The Multilingual Manchester research model: An integrated approach to urban language diversity. *Acta Linguistica Petropolitana* 14(3). 248–274.

Matras, Yaron. 2018b. Duly verified? Language analysis in UK asylum applications of Syrian refugees. *International Journal of Speech, Language and the Law* 25(1). 53–78.

Matras, Yaron. 2021. Process, tools and agenda in LADO: A rejoinder. *International Journal of Speech, Language and the Law* 28(2). 233–250.

Matras, Yaron, Katie Harrison, Leonie Gaiser & Stefannie Connor. 2022. Actors' discourses on language supplementary schools: diaspora practices and emerging ideologies. *Journal of Multilingual and Multicultural Development*. https://doi.org/10.1080/01434632.2021.2020801

Matras, Yaron & Petros Karatsareas. 2020. *Non-standard and minority varieties as community languages in the UK. Towards a new strategy for language maintenance*. https://westminsterresearch.westminster.ac.uk/download/3fa4be6ef42c8897c1313da52024ca921b795d3453b99449306ba3ff983182f5/1137378/Non-Standard-and-Minority-Varieties-as-Community-Languages-in-the-UK-Position-Paper.pdf

Matras, Yaron & Alex Robertson. 2015. Multilingualism in a post-industrial city: Policy and practice in Manchester. *Current Issues in Language Planning* 16(3). 296–314.

Matras, Yaron & Alex Robertson. 2017. Urban multilingualism and the civic university: a dynamic, non-linear model of participatory research. *Social Inclusion* 5(3). 1–9.

Matras, Yaron, Rebecca Tipton & Leonie Gaiser. 2023. Agency and multilingualism in public health care: How practitioners draw on local experiences and encounters. In Betty Beeler, Claudine Gaibrois, Philippe Lecomte & Mary Vigier (eds.), *Understanding the dynamics of language and multilingualism in professional contexts: Advances in language-sensitive management research*, 26–60. Cheltenham: Edward Elgar.

McLelland, Nicola. 2017. *Teaching and learning foreign languages. A history of language education, assessment and policy in Britain*. London: Routledge.

Mignolo, Walter D. 2011. *The dark side of Western modernity. Global futures, decolonial options*. Durham: Duke University Press.

Mignolo, Walter D. & Catherine E. Walsh. 2018. *On decoloniality. Concepts, analytics, praxis*. Durham, N.C.: Duke University Press.

Müller, Martin. 2021. Worlding geography: From linguistic privilege to decolonial anywheres. *Progress in Human Geography* 45(6). 1440–1466.

Neary, Mike. 2020. Civic university or university of the earth? A call for intellectual insurgency. *Civic Sociology* 1(1). https://doi.org/10.1525/001c.14518.

Neather Robert. 2012. 'Non-Expert' translators in a professional community, identity, anxiety and perceptions of translator expertise in the chinese museum community. *The Translator* 18(2). 245–268.

Ngai, Ka Ming, Corita R. Grudzen, Roy Lee, Vicky Y. Tong, Lynne D. Richardson & Alicia Fernandez. 2016. The association between limited English proficiency and unplanned emergency department revisit within 72 hours. *Annals of Emergency Medicine* 68(2). 213–221.

Ong, Aihwa. 2011. Introduction: Worlding Cities, or the art of being global. In Ananya Roy & Aihwa Ong (eds.), *Worlding cities: Asian Experiments and the art of being global*, 1–26. Oxford: Blackwell.

Osman, Mohamed Fathi. 2006. *Language choice among Arabic-English bilinguals in Manchester*. Manchester: University of Manchester MA dissertation.

Panayi, Panikos. 2010. *An immigration history of Britain. Multicultural racism since 1800.* London: Routledge
Patrick, Peter L. 2012. Language analysis for determination of origin: Objective evidence for refugee status determination. In Lawrence Solan & Peter Tiersma (eds.), *The Oxford handbook of language and law*, 533–546. Oxford: Oxford University Press.
Pennycook, Alistair & Emi Otsuji. 2015. *Metrolingualism: Language in the city.* Abingdon: Routledge.
Pidgeon, Michelle. 2016. More than a checklist: meaningful indigenous inclusion in higher education. *Social Inclusion* 4(1). 77–91.
Pratt, Mary Louise. 1991. Arts of the contact zone. *Profession* 91. 33–40.
Purcell, Mark. 2013. Possible worlds Henri Lefebvre and the right to the city. *Journal of Urban Affairs* 36(1).141–154.
Purkarthofer, Judith. 2016. *Sprachort Schule. Zur Konstruktion von mehrsprachigen sozialen Räumen und Praktiken in einer zweisprachigen Volksschule.* Klagenfurt: Drava.
Purkarthofer, Judith & Mi-Cha Flubacher. 2022. *Speaking subjects in multilingualism research: biographical and speaker-centred approaches.* Bristol: Multilingual Matters.
Rampton, Ben. 1995. *Crossing: Language and identity among adolescents.* Manchester: St. Jerome Publishing.
Rampton, Ben, Mel Cooke & Sam Holmes. 2018. Sociolinguistic citizenship. *Journal of Social Science Education* 17(4). 68–83.
Rampton, Ben, Constant Leung & Mel Cooke. 2020. *Education, England and users of languages other than English.* Working Papers in Urban Language & Literacies 275.
Rappaport, Roy A. 1999. *Ritual and religion in the making of humanity.* Cambridge: Cambridge University Press.
Redder, Angelika, Julia Pauli, Roland Kießling, Kristin Bührig, Bernhard Brehmer, Ingrid Breckner & Jannis Androuttsopoulos. 2013. *Mehrsprachige Kommunikation in der Stadt.* Münster: Waxman.
Rehbein, Jochen, 2013. The future of multilingualism: Towards a HELIX of societal multilingualism and global auspices. In Kristin Bührig & Bernd Meyer (eds.), *Transferring linguistic know-how into institutional practice*, 43–80. Amsterdam: Benjamins.
Rusu, Mihai Stelian & Ismo Kantola. 2016. A time of meta-celebration: celebrating the sociology of celebration. *Journal of Comparative Research in Anthropology and Sociology* 7(1). 1–22.
Rymes, Betsy. 2020. *How we talk about language: exploring citizen sociolinguistics.* Cambridge: Cambridge University Press.
Said, Edward. 1978. *Orientalism.* London: Penguin
Sassen, Saskia. 1991. *The global city.* New York: Princeton University Press.
Schiller, Maria. 2015. Paradigmatic pragmatism and the politics of diversity. *Ethnic and Racial Studies* 38(7). 1–17.
Schiller, Maria. 2016. *European cities, municipal organizations and diversity: The new politics of difference.* London: Palgrave Macmillan.
Schuster, Michal, Irit Elroy & Ido Elmakais. 2016. We are lost: Measuring the accessibility of signage in public general hospitals. *Language Policy* 1(16). 23–38.
Sian, Katy P. 2019. *Navigating institutional racism in British universities.* Cham: Palgrave Macmillan.
Silverman, Raymond Aaron (ed.). 2015. *Museum as process: translating local and global knowledges.* London: Routledge.
Smith, Linda Tuhiwai. [1999] 2021. *Decolonising methodologies.* London: Zed books.

Soto Huerta, Mary Esther & Laura Huerta Migus. 2015. Creating equitable ecologies: broadening access through multilingualism. *Museums and Social Issues* 10(1). 8–17.
Spivak, Gayatri. 1990. Poststructuralism, marginality, postcoloniality, and value. In Peter Collier & Helga Geyer-Ryan (eds.), *Literary theory today*, 219–244. Ithaca: Cornell University Press.
Spivak, Gayatri. 1999. *A critique of postcolonial reason*. Cambridge, MA: Harvard University Press.
Stevenson, Patrick. 2017. *Language and migration in a multilingual metropolis. Berlin lives*. Houndmills: Palgrave Macmillan.
Stewart, Michael. 2017. Nothing about us without us, or The dangers of a closed society research paradigm. *Romani Studies* 27(2). 125–146.
Stroud, Christopher. 2001. African mother-tongue programmes and the politics of language: linguistic citizenship versus linguistic human rights. *Journal of Multilingual and Multicultural Development* 22(4). 339–355.
Stroud, Christopher. 2008. Bilingualism: Colonialism and post-colonialism. In Monica Heller (ed.), *Bilingualism: a social approach*, 25–49. Basingstoke: Palgrave.
Stroud, Christopher. 2018. Linguistic citizenship. In Lisa Lim, Christopher Stroud & Lionel Wee (eds.), *The multilingual citizen: Towards a politics of language for agency and change*, 17–39. Bristol: Multilingual Matters.
Stroud, Christopher & Caroline Kerfoot. 2021. Decolonizing higher education. Multilingualism, linguistic citizenship and epistemic justice. In Zannie Bock & Christopher Stroud (eds.), *Language and decoloniality in higher education: reclaiming voices from the south*, 19–46. London: Bloomsbury.
Sturge, Kate 2007. *Representing others: translation, ethnography, and the museum*. Manchester: St. Jerome.
Syrett, Stephen & Leandro Sepulveda. 2011. Realising the diversity dividend: Population diversity and urban economic development. *Environment and Planning* 43. 487–504.
Tipton, Rebecca, & Olgierda Furmanek 2016. *Dialogue interpreting. A guide to interpreting in public services and the community*. London: Routledge.
Tomlinson, J. 1999. *Globalization and culture*. Chicago: University of Chicago Press.
Veronelli, G. A. 2015. The coloniality of language: race, expressivity, power, and the darker side of modernity. *Wagadu: A Journal of Transnational Women's & Gender Studies* 13. 108–34.
Vertovec, Stephen. 2007. Super-diversity and its implications. *Ethnic and Racial Studies* 30(6). 1024–1054.
Werbner, Pnina. 2002. The place which is diaspora: citizenship, religion and gender in the making of chaordic transnationalism. *Journal of Ethnic and Migration Studies* 28(1). 119–133.
Wiese, Heike & Paul Kerswill (eds.). 2022. *Urban contact dialects and language change: insights from the Global North and South*. London: Routledge.
White, Bob W. (ed.). 2018. *Intercultural cities. Policy and practice for a new era*. Cham: Palgrave Macmillan.
Woldeyes, Yirga Gelaw & Baden Offord. 2018. Decolonizing human rights education: critical pedagogy praxis in higher education. *The International Education Journal: Comparative Perspectives* 17(1). 24–36.
Wolf, Eric R. 1966. *Peasants*. Englewood Cliffs, N.J.: Prentice Hall.

Magnus Fischer, Andreas Jäger, Carolin Patzelt and Ingo H. Warnke
Fluid registers and fixed language concepts in postcolonial spaces

Abstract: Postcolonial spaces are characterized by socioculturally heterogeneous societies with widespread multilingualism, where languages of erstwhile colonial powers co-exist with indigenous and immigrant languages as well as mixed codes that have emerged during and after the colonial period, often competing for recognition and dominance. Fluid linguistic practices on the discursive level are common and often contrast with fixed metapragmatic concepts of language. This paper explores this apparent contradiction exemplified by two decolonized societies, Australia and Mauritius, aiming at a reassessment of what is meant by *colonial language* in the light of contemporary social dynamics in postcolonial spaces.

Keywords: fluid registers, metapragmatic concepts, postcolonial spaces, colonial language

1 Introduction

In modern sociolinguistic theory, the *additive* conception of independent monolingual competences has been largely replaced by the idea of an integrated multilingual or polylectal competence (cf. Lüdi and Py 2003; Blommaert 2010).[1] It has

---

[1] See also Matras (2020: 340), who argues that although multilingual speakers may become experienced in separating communication routines and demarcating sub-components of their overall linguistic repertoire, that repertoire remains active at all times during a communicative interaction.

Magnus Fischer, University of Bremen, FB 10, Universitäts-Boulevard 13, 28359 Bremen, Germany.
E-Mail: fischerm@uni-bremen.de
Andreas Jäger, University of Bremen, FB 10, Universitäts-Boulevard 13, 28359 Bremen, Germany.
E-Mail: anjaeger@uni-bremen.de
Carolin Patzelt, University of Bremen, FB 10, Universitäts-Boulevard 13, 28359 Bremen, Germany.
E-Mail: cpatzelt@uni-bremen.de
Ingo H. Warnke, University of Bremen, FB 10, Universitäts-Boulevard 13, 28359 Bremen, Germany.
E-Mail: iwarnke@uni-bremen.de

https://doi.org/10.1515/9783111323756-010

been demonstrated that multilingual repertoires often show a great deal of fuzziness or reorganization of language boundaries in discourse (e.g. Migge and Léglise 2013), with speakers dynamically using linguistic resources from their multilingual repertoires as stances or acts of identity. As a result, the traditionally fixed concept of *language*[2] has increasingly been replaced by that of *linguistic repertoires* or even *feature pools* (cf. Cheshire et al. 2011; Matras 2020) in recent studies.

However, while the assumption of fluid registers has been broadly accepted in sociolinguistics and contact linguistics, the use of fixed categories still seems to dominate when it comes to what Agha (2007) labels the *metapragmatic* level. A good example of this are the fixed conceptions of *colonial language* as metapragmatic ideologies, which seems to contradict the pragmatics of fluid registers in postcolonial contexts. Recent discussions in France regarding French documented in Emmanuel Macron's vision of a future collaboration with Africa, which he developed in 2017 at the University of Ouagadougou in Burkina Faso and which continues to develop the ideas of the Francophonie, show that the critical evaluation of languages as *colonial* (languages) seems to be highly dependent on their current communicative value; the usefulness of a *colonial language* for social upward mobility seems to complement collective historical experiences as a basis of social valuation.

The aim of this paper is to discuss the contradictory treatment of fluidity on the discursive vs. the metapragmatic level and to demonstrate the need for empirical work on postcolonial spaces where fluid registers and several colonial languages (co-)exist. The paper is structured as follows: It starts off by exposing the concept of *colonial language* as employed here and the crucial premises it is based on (Section 2). Section 3 then contrasts the ideological conception of *languages* as monolithic entities with the dynamic, heterogeneous uses social actors make of linguistic resources in (postcolonial) spaces marked by multilingualism and multiculturalism. It outlines a treatment of fluidity in modern sociolinguistics which is largely absent on the metapragmatic level. The tension between colonial

---

[2] We adopt a constructionist approach to the term 'language' in this contribution, i.e., whenever we speak of a 'language', we refer not to a monolithic system, but to a pool of linguistic structures that is socially recognized as 'language X'. This pool is by no means static, since the integrated repertoire of 'features' made up by a user's inventory of linguistic structures is activated according to different communicative routines, i.e., speakers align particular forms and structures with certain interaction routines. While this means a selection of context-appropriate stylistic variants in the case of speakers considered to be monolingual, in the case of multilingual speakers it means the ability to select among a pool of structures that are socially recognized as different 'languages' (cf. Matras 2020: 336).

languages and fluid registers is then empirically discussed drawing on two case studies: Section 4 analyzes Australia as a postcolonial space which is characterized by a contradiction between the use of fluid registers and lingering conceptions of English as the codified colonial language. Section 5 applies the contradiction of translingual practices and metapragmatic notions of fixed language concepts to a different postcolonial society, since Mauritius has more than one colonial language.

2 Initial considerations on the concept of *Colonial Language*

In a paper on German as an academic language, Eichinger (2017: 53–54) writes that German has contributed significantly to the unfolding of the concept of modern scholarship; this would also and undoubtedly be true for French and English. There is, however, a downside to these traditions that is spoken about rather less frequently. German, French, and English, among a number of other European languages, are implicated in the history of colonialism, and this certainly has something to do with their visibility and functionality. The international spread of English, French, and German, among other, in recent linguistic history, especially since the 19th century, is inconceivable without colonialism; here, reference should also be made to Ibero-Roman colonialism and, above all, to linguistic empires in general (cf. Ostler 2005; Stolz 2015). For English, Eichinger (2017: 51) mentions this when he associates the Anglophone sphere with the colonial past. For French, this can also hardly be overlooked in view of Francophonie. However, the (formerly) international position of German must also be considered in the context of colonialism. Ammon (2014: 80) has emphasized this clearly in his remarkable book on the position of German in the world: global colonial policy, in addition to economic power, was decisive for the expansion of English, but also for the expansion of other European languages. Colonial language policy, according to Ammon, has contributed to a considerable international position of French, especially in diplomacy, and of German in scholarship; he sums this up prosaically with respect to German: "Schließlich trug auch [...] die deutsche Kolonialpolitik zur Verbreitung der deutschen Sprache in der Welt bei" (Ammon 2014: 101).[3] It could be noted, however, that no German colonial language policy in a

---

[3] Translation IHW: "And, not least, [...] German colonial policy also contributed to the spread of the German language throughout the world".

narrow sense existed for the dissemination of German (that the colonizers might have deemed successful). One could also argue that German has never found a comparable international spread and functional relevance as English and French. This is true. But interestingly, this is also related to European colonial history, which we consider particularly worthy of consideration. With respect to the global spread of the ten most important international languages as official languages, Ammon shows that English has official language status on five continents, French on four, and German, since the independence of Namibia, on only one, Europe. This overview is followed by an interpretation that is important for the contexts of our reflections:

> Der Überblick über die Größe und weltweite Verbreitung der Amtssprachterritorien der internationalen Sprachen gleicht einer Projektion der Geschichte ihrer „Mutterländer" auf die Gegenwart: Hier die erfolgreichen Kolonialmächte (Großbritannien, Frankreich, Portugal, Spanien, „Arabien", Russland und auch China), dort die mit ihren kolonialen Ambitionen Gescheiterten (Deutschland, Italien und Japan). (Ammon 2014: 254)[4]

The Netherlands, Belgium and Denmark could also be mentioned here. It is obvious that this has considerable consequences for the international functionality of German. To put it polemically, one could say that regretting the lack of international dissemination of German as an academic language is tantamount to complaining about the lack of Germany's colonial successes. One does not have to be that polemical, but a perspective on the colonial layers of European languages must be part of the appropriate assessment of their international status.

We are interested in precisely this dimension of colonial history in European languages, and especially in the consequences of this history in the present. In a first exemplary perspective, which results from our specializations, we focus on English, French, and German and consider their current international status against the backdrop of (i) colonial history, (ii) their instrumental character in colonial expansion, and especially (iii) in their ties to decolonization and postcolonial diffusion. We are not interested in monocausal explanations or a prioritization of colonialism for assessments in recent language history, but in looking more closely and by way of example at the colonial legacy of internationally disseminated languages in terms of specific effects. In this context, the classification

---

4 Translation IHW: "The overview of the size and worldwide distribution of the official language territories of the international languages resembles a projection of the history of their "mother countries" onto the present: On the one hand the successful colonial powers (Great Britain, France, Portugal, Spain, "Arabia", Russia, and also China), on the other hand those that failed with their colonial ambitions (Germany, Italy, and Japan)".

of English, German, and French as *colonial languages* is the starting point of our considerations. We define a *colonial language* as
(i) a national variety,
(ii) which has had functions in colonial expansion,
(iii) the (continuing) global spread of which (also) results from colonial history,
(iv) and which is still perceived as being anchored in colonial history by colonial language speakers today.

When we speak of *colonial languages*, however, this does not mean that we consider languages to be sufficiently described by this. It would not do justice to German, English, French, and other *colonial languages* to regard them as sufficiently defined if they are marked as *colonial languages*. This is evident and does not really necessitate a separate remark, but we want to prevent a possible misunderstanding here. It is not our intention to stigmatize languages and certainly not speakers, but to illuminate languages in their present, taking into account important and less seen historical layers. We thus assume for *colonial languages* that their dissemination and polyfunctionality is interdependent with colonialism. This fact itself can hardly be denied and is also well established. The link between language policy and colonialism, historically anchored in France, has already been dealt with in detail by Calvet (1974). For French, reference can also be made to Judge's (2005) account of the function of French as a tool of colonization 1830 to 1946. As she summarizes: "The French did indeed use their language as a tool of colonialism during the 2nd colonial empire, their linguistic and educational policies varying from the generously paternalistic to the cruelly self-seeking" (Judge 2005: 31). In detail, however, the circumstances are quite complex, so that one must be cautious against making hasty conclusions. Judge (2005: 32) also states that "[m]any of the elite in the ex-colonies have embraced French not only as a means of international communication, but as the expression of a universal if mythic civilization, an ideal to be aspired to". At the same time, a critical postcolonial reflection on such mythifications has long been taking place, for example when Diagne (2019) discusses the connection between African philosophy and African languages.

For English, too, its status as a *colonial language* is evident; but here the picture is complex as well. Pennycook (2007), for example, points out that "the massive expansion in the global use of English [...] occurred in the context of decolonization, the decline of Britain as an imperial power, and the rise of the US as the new global power" and that "in spite of the expansion in the number of English users by 1900, it is important to understand that British colonial language policy was not massively in favor of spreading English". This could also be stated for the German and the Dutch case.

Thus, for reasons of due differentiation, we consider it advisable not to address the supposed colonial roots of European languages in a wholesale way, but rather to scrutinize more closely current and specific constellations of colonial languages in the defined sense. One of our preliminary assumptions is that it is part of the realities of a postcolonial world with its decolonial dynamics that the shaping of colonial-referential discourses does not lie solely with those who once acted as the colonial aggressor, the de facto colonizer, but that colonial-referential works must always reckon with a plurality of voices that do not necessarily merge into polyphonic euphony. We refer here, for instance, to the prominent voice of Sarr (2016), who, with his call for absolute intellectual sovereignty in contemporary thinking about Africa, highlights clearly recognizable limitations to a Euro-perspectival project on colonialism and its persistences. The second chapter of the book, entitled *Contre la marée*, opens with the sentence: "Pour être féconde, une pensée du continent porte en elle l'exigence d'une absolue souveraineté intellectuelle" (Sarr 2016: 17).[5] Consequently, this also means that a colonial-critical perspective on European languages from a European perspective must reckon with evaluations that may deviate from one's own stance. We would like to refer here to a paper by Edjabou (2016) on the current enthusiasm about Germany in Togo. The text states: "Die gegenwärtig zu beobachtende Begeisterung für Deutschland kann größtenteils als Folge von zweckorientierter Verklärung der kolonialen Fakten angesehen werden, die sowohl von togoischer als auch von deutscher Seite betrieben wurde" (Edjabou 2016: 278).[6] Especially the ambivalences in the field of tension between contradictory attitudes of idealization and critique from different perspectives for us underlines the necessity of micro-analyses in order to be able to answer questions about the current status of colonial languages. Language evaluation and metapragmatic discourses (cf. Spitzmüller 2013) are an important object of research in this regard.

In particular, we assume that *colonial language* is not a static concept, but that features, classifications, and functions of colonial languages are negotiated in a purpose-driven way. Thus, Schwörer (1916) already drafted what he called "Kolonial-Deutsch", and explicitly uses the term *colonial language* in the subtitle

---

[5] Translation IHW: "To be prolific, a thought of the continent carries in it the requirement of an absolute intellectual sovereignty".
[6] Translation IHW: "The current enthusiasm for Germany can largely be seen as the result of a purpose-driven idealization of colonial facts, which has been pursued by both the Togolese and the Germans".

of his book; however, its meaning differs widely from what we understand by that term. *Colonial language* is a historically variable terminology, it should be noted. To our knowledge, however, a diachronic, European-oriented conceptual history of colonial language has yet to be written. In this context, the temporal extent of the establishment and effectiveness of colonial languages should by no means be clearly limited. For German colonialism, for example, one would have to ask in a diachronic project about the early modern colonial undertakings and their significance for the formation of German as a colonial language and one should not overlook the emigration of Germans.

Our discussion of the concept of *colonial language* is based on a number of premises. In particular, we are interested in the significance of fixed language concepts, theories, and practices of fluid repertoires for the conceptualization of colonial languages. Before we discuss fluidity in modern sociolinguistic theory, we formulate our premises in the form of three hypotheses (H1–3):

H1 Fixed and historically shaped notions of colonial languages, as metapragmatic ideologies, are at odds with the pragmatics of fluid registers in postcolonial spaces.
H2 In postcolonial spaces, different colonial languages are independently evaluated and dynamically assessed from perspectives of collective memory.
H3 The evaluation of the usefulness of a colonial language for social upward mobility is complementary to the collective historical experience of colonization.

From these hypotheses, we derive the fundamental need for empirical research on postcolonial spaces and their fluid registers in tension with one or more colonial languages.

3 Fluidity in modern sociolinguistic theory

3.1 Recent approaches to multilingual spaces and practices

Sociolinguistics is devoted to describing and explaining the relationship of linguistic variation to social factors. The core of the discipline is commonly referred to as *variationist* sociolinguistics and has traditionally concentrated on mostly quantitative studies of speech differences across socially-defined groups within one and the same community (cf. Hinrichs 2014: 236). However, the past two decades have witnessed a shift in focus: from macro-social categories such as social class, age, or sex towards a rather micro-social level with an expansion of interest in the connection between linguistic performance and individual identity. As a result, the discipline has experienced a considerable increase in qualitative studies which take into account individual patterns of variation, patterns which are often sociopragmatic in nature and motivated by social and cultural variables which traditional sociolinguistics did not explicitly consider, such as identity construction and indexicality (cf. Bürki and Patzelt 2020: 4).

Since the theoretical structure of the traditional variationist paradigm is based on empirical work in communities commonly defined as *monolingual* (cf. Labov 1966), a continuum between standard and vernacular varieties of the same language has long been at the center of sociolinguistic investigation. However, language contact and variation under the conditions of modern mobility and migration is characterized by complex and heterogeneous forms of contact, involving multilingual practices and switches among historically unrelated language varieties (cf. Hinrichs 2014: 236).

The linguistic forms or *resources* arising from this kind of contact are naturally heterogeneous, which means that they can be socioculturally linked to different languages, diatopic varieties, accents, or other forms of linguistic variation. Furthermore, it is obviously not always and only native speakers who are involved in such linguistic practices. Instead, and with reference to conditions such as linguistic diversity, mixed languages, and multilingual interactions, more recent studies in sociolinguistics have contested the idealization of the *native speaker* (cf. Migge and Léglise 2013; Rampton 2018), working with notions such as linguistic *repertoires* (cf. Blommaert and Backhus 2011; Pennycook 2018). This notion avoids establishing fixed links between origins, upbringing, proficiency, and types of language use. Instead, it refers to individuals' variable (and often rather fragmentary) grasp of a plurality of linguistic resources, styles or registers which are picked up in the course of biographical trajectories (cf. Blommaert and Rampton 2016: 26).

The social practices which display the dynamic use of such heterogeneous linguistic resources, according to the social context in which an interaction takes place, are what Léglise (2018) defines as *pratiques langagières hétérogènes* ['heterogeneous language practices']. Other concepts which have been coined to account for practices marked by multilingualism are *Crossing* (cf. Rampton 2018), *Superdiverse Linguistic Repertoires* (cf. Blommaert and Backus 2011; Blommaert and Rampton 2011), *Polylanguaging* (cf. Jørgensen et al. 2011), or *Translanguaging* (cf. Garcia and Li 2013), with *Translanguaging* currently being the most debated concept.

The interest in *Translanguaging* was initiated by Ben Rampton's empirical work in which he studied communication among adolescents in a UK neighborhood. Rampton views language crossing as involving "code alternation by people who are not accepted members of the group associated with the second language that they are using" (Rampton 1995: 485), i.e., code-switching into varieties that are not generally thought to belong to them. In examples such as the following, for instance, Rampton (2018: 18) detected the use of Creole influenced language by young people of Anglo and – in the case of Asif – Panjabi descent within a multiethnic neighborhood in the South Midlands of England as in (1).

(1) Ms J: *I'll be back in a second with my lunch*
      Asif: *NO dat's sad man (.) I had to miss my play right I've gotta go*
      (Ms J must now have left the room)
      Asif: **ll:unch** *(.) you don't need no lunch* **not'n grow**[7] *anyway*

This kind of switching across social or ethnic boundaries raises issues of legitimacy which participants need to negotiate in the course of their encounter. Generally speaking, studies based on the concept of *Translanguaging* are less interested in what distinct codes people fall back on and what affiliations these codes refer to than in how different communicative resources are employed to create meaning and what such a heteroglossic language practice means to speakers (cf. Rampton 2011).

Such an approach also implies challenging the traditionally widespread notion of *speech community*. This notion implies that the researcher is able, from the outset, to define a given (speech) community or some smaller, well-defined social entities (cf. Migge and Léglise 2013: 10). Obviously, this is not always the case in heterogeneous multilingual and multiethnic contexts. Therefore, Migge and Léglise (2013) suggest to adopt a constructionist approach to concepts such as *language* or *community*, both of which must be regarded as ideological constructions:

> [...] due to the differences in people's social practices, networks and ideologies, the systems of linguistic practices of members who consider themselves to belong to the same social entity [...] tend to be subject to a fair degree of variation (Migge and Léglise 2013: 330).

---

7 Both the stretched, heavily emphasized 'L' in *ll:unch* and the double negation in *not'n grow* [= not gonna grow] are associated with typical features of Creole or Black English (cf. Rampton 2018).

The general shift which can be observed in modern sociolinguistics is to replace the concept of *speech community* by a more empirically anchored and differentiating vocabulary that includes *communities of practice* or *networks* as "the often mobile and flexible sites and links in which representations of groups emerge, move and circulate" (Blommaert and Rampton 2016: 25).

During the last decade, Li (2011) developed a repertoire-like concept called *translanguaging space*, which he defines as "a space for the act of translanguaging as well as a space created through translanguaging" (Li 2011: 1222). With reference to Bhabha (1994), he defines this space as one in which different identities, values, and practices do not simply co-exist, but generate new identities, values, and practices. Thus, *Translanguaging*, according to Li, creates a social space for multilingual language users "by bringing together different dimensions of their personal history, experience and environment, their attitude, belief and ideology, their cognitive and physical capacity" (Li 2011: 1223).

All of the conceptual approaches mentioned above mark a shift away from assigning sets of linguistic structures to neatly separated languages and speech communities toward approaches that acknowledge fluidity and creativity in linguistic practices. There is consent among sociolinguists who deal with *Translanguaging* or related concepts that a significant revision of fundamental ideas about languages, (native) speakers, speech communities, and communicative practices is needed, and that the focus of interest should shift from *languages* to *speech* and *repertoire*. As a result, individual languages should not be unquestioningly regarded as set categories, a claim which is further elaborated on in the following paragraph.

3.2 Languages as ideologically constructed entities

A central assumption in modern sociolinguistics is that *languages* cannot be regarded as monolithic entities which are characterized as a set of fixed linguistic forms. Thus, instead of *languages*, the focus is placed on the *speakers* and the creative, variable uses they make of the linguistic resources and features available in their repertoire (cf. Bürki and Patzelt 2020: 4).

Especially over the last couple of years, quite a number of studies in Linguistic Anthropology, Critical Sociolinguistics and Applied Linguistics have centered around the assumption that languages should no longer be regarded as sociocultural (and ideological) entities that are easy to identify and assign a name to (cf. Léglise 2018; Makoni and Pennycook 2005; Heller 2007; Otheguy et al. 2015). These works present a critical discussion of the concept of *language*, which not only leads to a de-construction of *languages* as autonomous and clearly separable entities, but also criticizes the way in which *language* as a concept has been constructed on the basis of normative, political, and sociohistorical ideologies (cf. Sánchez Moreano 2020).

Makoni and Pennycook (2005: 138), for instance, regard the concept of *language* as a European invention which was imposed on colonized areas, where European colonizers rather arbitrarily assigned names to the ways of speaking of autochthonous speakers they came into contact with. Simultaneously, the idea of languages as separable, clearly definable entities, which were characteristically associated with the concept of *Nation-State*, arose (cf. Sánchez Moreano 2020). In this sense, as Makoni and Pennycook (2005) point out, both *languages* like English, Spanish, or French as such as well as the concept of *Nation-State* are, eventually, mere sociocultural and sociohistorical constructs.

In line with such considerations, researchers like Otheguy et al. (2015) also argue that the so-called *named languages* cannot, in fact, be linguistically defined as such, since there are no criteria that would justify the definition of a language as English, Spanish, or French.

This means that any language or linguistic variety could fundamentally be defined on the basis of external sociocultural criteria, such as social, political, or ethnic affiliations of its speakers, or on the basis of language policies implemented in a given territory on national and/or regional scales (cf. Jørgensen et al. 2011: 28). All of these criteria are obviously socioculturally and ideologically motivated and have contributed to the implementation of frontiers between languages and the disciplines that study them.

As a result, Jørgensen et al. (2011: 27) consider the concept of languages as neatly delimited systems insufficient for capturing and understanding the dynamic and heterogeneous use speakers make of linguistic resources in societies characterized by mobility and multilingualism – not only, but particularly in the 21st century, where an intense diversification of migration flows is accompanied by new digital language practices (cf. Creese and Blackledge 2018). The following example, representing a short extract from a Facebook conversation between three Danish girls, illustrates the creative use of linguistic resources dealt with by Jørgensen et al. (2011):

(2) Ayhan: *gracias muchas gracias!! jeg wenter shpæændt gardash:-)) love youuu...*

In (2), Ayhan first uses words associated with Spanish (*gracias, muchas gracias* 'thank you, thank you very much'), before continuing with words spelled in a way that reflects young Copenhagen speech (*jeg wenter shpæændt* 'I am waiting excitedly'). She then uses the word *gardash*, an adapted version of the Turkish word *kardeş* 'sibling'. Among young urban speakers in Denmark, though, it means 'friend' (cf. Jørgensen et al. 2011: 24) As Jørgensen et al. point out, it is difficult to categorize the linguistic features employed in (2) in one or more given "languages".[8]

In order to really capture what speakers do in social interactions, thus, the researchers suggest that more attention should be paid to the selection and situational – if not indexical – use of linguistic elements or *features* in interactions, rather than studying the use of and possible switches between *languages*. In terms of methodological approaches, this means that, instead of departing from the assumption of fixed categories (*languages*), the analysis of interactions in modern, multilingual, and multicultural societies is based on the different and variable uses speakers make of linguistic elements which constitute what is socio-culturally known as *English*, *Spanish*, or any other *language*. In other words, to communicate, speakers do not use *languages*, but *linguistic features* which are at their disposal and which can be – and actually are – associated with specific categories that receive a specific denomination as *language x* (cf. Jørgensen et al. 2011: 28–29).[9]

In sum, adopting the concept of *linguistic features* means being able to a) study the real use of multilingual repertoires which do show a great deal of fuzziness and reorganization of language boundaries in discourse, and b) study the use of linguistic resources from these repertoires as stances or acts of identity. These two goals, essential to modern sociolinguistic theory, seem to provide a valuable approach to the study of postcolonial societies as socioculturally heterogeneous spaces where new, complex webs of identity construction and group boundaries arise and are largely negotiated by the creative use of linguistic resources available to the social actors.

In the following sections, two case studies will exemplify a contradiction between the fluid linguistic practices treated in 3) and fixed metapragmatic concepts of language in decolonized societies, raising awareness for the need of further empirical work on the subject.

---

[8] For instance, would "youth Danish" be one language, separate from "standard Danish"? (Jørgensen et al. 2011: 25).
[9] Blommaert and Backus (2011), for instance, prefer the term *linguistic resources* to refer to *linguistic features*.

4 Australia as a contact zone

In the centuries following the establishment of the first British penal colony on the fifth continent in 1788 English has become the dominant language encompassing all aspects of colonial and subsequently postcolonial life in Australia. As a modern, postcolonial space it is still characterized by contrasts between the cultures of anglophone and indigenous people as well as more recent post-war immigrants and their descendants from Europe and around the world, resulting in a highly multilingual society. A distinct variety[10] of English has emerged in the course of the last two hundred years, which presently serves a variety of identificational and indexical purposes beyond merely signifying the colonial past. Similar to other postcolonial spaces there is also a considerable array of indigenous languages, most of which are under threat of extinction. In addition, we find numerous immigrant languages as well as some codes that would traditionally be labelled pidgins, creoles, and mixed languages, respectively (cf. Vaughan and Loakes 2020: 721 for an overview). Each of these are representative of different speaker groups with often divergent conceptions of English as the overarching means of communication.

A further contrast specifically owed to Australian geography as such is that between urban as well as agriculturally cultivated rural spaces and the outback. Whereas the former mainly represents the dominant anglophone culture as well as minority immigrant societies, the latter is the chief locus of indigenous speakers and their often remarkably different communicative practices. Generally speaking, the degree of urbanization is high and the distances are vast. The remainder of this section reflects on language contact between Aboriginal languages and English as well as on the diverging and changing views and attitudes by anglophone as well as indigenous members of modern, post-colonial Australian society.

The country's history of colonization is special in that the indigenous population was never recognized as such at all during the colonial period, which effectively lasted until the emergence of an independent nation in 1901 – the Commonwealth of Australia. As with every other newly formed country in the

---

10 In accordance with the definitions in footnote 2 also the terms 'variety' and 'dialect' are to be understood as pools of linguistic structures. They specifically comprise subsections of those that speakers deem representative of a given socially recognized 'language'. Acknowledging the overall dynamic nature of such repertoires, these terms and associated traditional glossonyms still have a descriptive value on some level of granularity and will be used for practical purposes.

postcolonial world the relationship between descendants of European immigrants and the indigenous population has been and still is difficult. Against the British legal doctrine of the 18th century, which prescribed that land could be taken for the crown only when uninhabited or else with the consent of the native inhabitants, James Cook laid claim to the territory in 1770 as if it was uninhabited despite evident encounters with indigenous people (Cook's journal entry of April 22, 1770, cf. Turnbull et al. 2004; Wallace-Bruce 1989; Nugent 2008). This effectively marks the beginning of the massive oppression suffered by Australia's indigenous population during the colonial and well into the postcolonial period. It is probably fair to say that the struggle for recognition as full-fledged members of modern multifaceted and multilingual Australian society is still not settled, even though the Aboriginal people's legal status as citizens has been established in 1967.

4.1 Australian English – a colonial dialect

If we analyze English as a colonial language, it should be noted that the distinct dialect spoken in Australia today that has amalgamated since the early days of immigration from various parts of Great Britain has a long history of emancipation from British varieties (cf. Collins and Blair 2001: 3). It signifies a noticeable difference between the erstwhile colonial periphery and the imperial center, bringing about an identity on its own.

Having developed as a geographically distinct variety relatively recently, it shows comparatively little internal variation among the anglophone descendants of British settlers. However, due to contact with the indigenous population as well as immigrants from other countries numerous lects have developed over time. Cox and Palethorpe (2007: 341) characterize Australian English as follows:

> It is a salient marker of national identity, and is used in broadcasting and in public life. The Aboriginal and Ethnocultural varieties are minority dialects allowing speakers to express their cultural identity within the multicultural Australian context.

Collins (2012: 75) uses the term *English in Australia* to encompass all these varieties and contrasts it with *Australian English* as the main code of non-indigenous native-born Australians. This dialect-internal variation of the spoken variety has traditionally been illustrated by a continuum *broad > general > cultivated*, where the latter bears the greatest resemblance to Received Pronunciation. While Broad Australian is somewhat emblematic of the lower classes and associated values that hark back to colonial times of convicts, peasants and laborers, the use of

Cultivated Australian indicates closer cultural ties with the former Imperial center. Even though Broad Australian is only used by a small percentage of the population, it serves as a stereotypical linguistic representation of Australia, even a cultural marker inside as well as outside the country. It is here, where we can perhaps detect a collective memory of the colonial past and conjecture that the active use of features from Broad Australian English showcases indirect identification with aspects of the working class, which reveals itself in what is however diffusely perceived as iconic Australian virtues such as egalitarianism and anti-authoritarianism.

Cox and Palethorpe (2007: 341) point out that internal variation of Australian English has indeed been reduced in recent decades, as younger Australians select resources from the General middle ground of the spectrum. According to the authors this circumstance reflects "post-colonial independence and sociopolitical maturity". General or Standard Australian English today is the regular variety used by the vast majority of Australians. However, the aforementioned emancipation of Australian English manifests itself in a noticeable increase of acceptance accompanied by the incorporation of linguistic features from the broad end of the spectrum into the mainstream media as well as politics and intellectual discourse since the 1980s. It seems as if the cultural cringe that had Australian society – and particularly the descendants of British settlers – in its grasp for a long time has been overcome and the Australian variety is evaluated positively and on a par with other varieties of the same colonial language such as British or American English (cf. Bradley and Bradley 2001: 274–275; Willoughby et al. 2013).

4.2 The ideological construction of English as the sole colonial language in Australia

In each of the European colonial languages introduced in Section 2 writing has propelled their codification and with it the inevitably ensuing asymmetry of prestige that commonly emerges wherever there is a contrast between a standardized written variety representing the ruling class on the one hand and a plethora of spoken lects on the other hand. Assessing the current situation of English in Australia with respect to producing written texts we find that in lieu of strict adherence to the rules of a singular high prestige variety there is a continuum of Australian Indigenous English sociolects ranging from acrolectal varieties closely resembling standard Australian English to basilectal Australian Kriol (cf. Eades 1992: 21; Russo 2007: 56).

In her study of appropriation in the Australian contact zone Russo (2007) notes that modern indigenous writers use different lects from the aforementioned continuum for different situationally defined purposes (cf. also Lenz 2017), so the metapragmatic conception of language as fluid repertoires as opposed to clearly delineated entities is being transposed wholesale to what may originally have been perceived as the overarching colonial language, but now comprises merely a fraction of the multilingual repertoire that expressions are drawn from as seen fit. In (3), a passage from Kim Scott's 1993 novel *True country* illustrates a „disruption of the Standard English language as the normative and prestigious narrative language" as cited by Russo (2007: 61). Russo describes this opening of the novel as two voices greeting the protagonist, one in what she calls *Standard English* and one in Indigenous English.

(3) [Russo 2007: 61]
You might stay that way, maybe forever, with no world to belong to   and belong to you. You in your many high places, looking over, looking over, waiting for a sign [....]
You listen to me. We're gunna make a story, true story. You might find it's here you belong. A place like this. And it is a beautiful place,   this   place. Call it our country, our country all 'round here. We got river, we got sea. Got creek, rock, hill, waterfall. We got bush tucker [...].

As a result, one may argue that the erstwhile colonial language has become integrated into the array of linguistic choices available to the individual speaker and thus provides an extension of the pool of linguistic expressions that can be reverted to in any given situation encountered in Australia today.

Indigenous people are faced with the dilemma that in order to be recognized and acknowledged the use of English as the most wide-spread medium permeating virtually all aspects of social life is inevitable, while at the same time it has not only been the language representative of the oppressive colonial system from the beginning of European settlement, but also the code in which all theoretical considerations of decolonization are being communicated. As such it is a "signifier of the British claims of superiority and civilization and as a technology for the construction of colonial consent" (Russo 2007: 22).

As Vaughan and Loakes (2020: 718) point out, "traditional languages in Aboriginal Australia are ideologized by their speakers as primordially connected to particular tracts of land". If this conception prevails, the same might apply to English. According to Russo (2007) the English language, writing and visual art, which have "assumed the connotation of 'colonial property'", are challenged by indigenous Australians through appropriation:

It is argued that the appropriation of the English language by Indigenous Australian peoples has resulted in the eruption of diversity and difference, which unveil the ideological nature of the assumption that the English language is a "neutral", "simple" and "essential" medium of communication (Russo 2007: 15).

As a consequence of this appropriation of the English language we now have a notion of an indigenous alterity. The widespread assumption that English is a "neutral" or even "essential" code is demasked as ideological (cf. Russo 2007: 20). The establishment of the monologism of English, grounded in the claim of possessing the "correct" meaning and syntax to which everybody must abide in order to communicate, is questioned by indigenous appropriations of English (cf. Russo 2007: 22–23).

If appropriation by indigenous peoples as a descriptive tool appears feasible to capture the linguistic situation of today's postcolonial Australia with respect to the status of English this shows that the term *colonial language* as a metapragmatic ascription is still suitable despite the fluidity of registers available to multilingual speakers. However, as opposed to the seemingly clearer functional delineation between English and other languages that prevailed throughout the colonial period, it is now not only the language in which all these concepts are being construed, negotiated, and often discussed controversially, but it has broadened significantly to accommodate the need of all inhabitants of the postcolonial contact zone that is modern Australia.

4.3 Fluid registers and the emergence of multiple-source languages

At the time of the first contact there were about 250 indigenous Australian languages, of which less than half have survived to this day, albeit many of them moribund. Currently less than 20 indigenous languages are being actively taught to children (cf. Vaughan and Loakes 2020: 717). In recent times there is a noticeable awareness among the indigenous population as well as Australian society in general of the importance of maintaining traditional languages and embracing an all-Australian history (cf. Lowe 2011 and references therein for a discussion of Aboriginal people's increasing assertion of their right to cultural and linguistic heritage), which has paved the way for language revitalization programs (cf. Walsh 2012; Baker and Wigglesworth 2017; Vaughan and Loakes 2020). The notion that Aboriginal languages as such reveal intricate ties between speakers, tradition, and land (cf. Rumsey 2018; Vaughan and Loakes 2020) is now commonplace even in predominantly Anglo-European Australian society.

Aboriginal communities have been in contact with English for over two hundred years to various extents. The present-day situation of multilingualism in Australia as a post-colonial space can be characterized in broad terms as follows:

> Aboriginal peoples' linguistic repertoires are typically complex, often including traditional languages and English alongside such contact varieties, combined in diverse patterns of multilingualism which are responsive to shifts in domain, interlocutor and other sociocultural factors (Vaughan and Loakes 2020: 718).

Vaughan and Loakes (2020: 718) furthermore point out that pre-colonial contact between indigenous languages is often different from that between indigenous languages and English.

Many indigenous languages today have dwindling numbers of native or otherwise competent speakers, but at the same time new mixed codes are developing that are all characterized by fluid repertoires incorporating English to various extents. While in some areas traditional indigenous languages remain the primary code, several multiple-source languages have already emerged, which show extensive borrowing and diffusion of features on both on the grammatical as well as the lexical level (cf. McConvell and Meakins 2005; O'Shannessy and Meakins 2016).

An example of a recently emerged mixed language is Gurindji Kriol (see (4) and (5)), which is the result of intensive contact between Kriol, an already established and rather wide-spread English-based creole[11] in the Northern Territory, and Gurindji (Ngumpin-Yapa, Pama-Nyungan), a local traditional language (in bold face):

(4) [McConvell and Meakins 2005: 11]
Kamon **warlaku** *partaj* **ngayiny** *leg-ta*
come.on **dog** go.up 1SINGULAR.DATIVE leg-LOCATIVE
'Come on dog jump up on my leg.'

(5) [McConvell and Meakins 2005: 11]
Ngali *plei-bat* **nyawa-ngka**.
1SINGULAR.INCLUSIVE play-CONTINUOUS **this-LOCATIVE**
'You and me can play here'

---

11 Kriol is the Aboriginal language with the most speakers (ca. 20.000) (cf. Vaughan and Loakes 2020: 721).

What is relevant for the present survey is that Gurindji Kriol serves as the main code of today's younger speakers in the community. McConvell and Meakins (2005: 9) report that while the previous generation of speakers were fluent in both source languages and fully aware of their respective social indexicality, which was manifest in frequently occurring code-switching, younger speakers born after ca. 1960 have decreasing command over traditional Gurindji and instead use a truly mixed language with each source language providing distinct parts of the grammar and the lexicon, respectively. The Gurindji Kriol situation lends itself to an evaluation in terms of Li's (2011) concept of *translanguaging space*, where new voices forge their own communicative code in an interesting merger of the colonial and the traditional.

Likewise of particular interest for the present discussion of fluidity and fixed language concepts is the on-going long-term contact between Jingulu (Mirndi, non-Pama-Nyungan) and Mudburra (Ngumpin-Yapa, Pama-Nyungan), both spoken in the Northern Territory. The two languages still have distinct grammatical systems after several centuries of contact but show intensive bi-directional borrowing to the effect that more than half of the lexicon is shared by both (R. Pensalfini p.c., May 4, 2021; cf. also Meakins and Pensalfini 2021; Meakins et al. 2020). Some of these exact matches are exemplified in Table 1.

Table 1: Examples of exact matches between Jingulu and Mudburra (Meakins et al. 2020: 7).

English	Jingulu	Mudburra
'all together'	warrb	warrb
'lie down'	manyan	manyan
'previously'	larrba	larrba
'lift'	wird	wird

This contact scenario is a counterexample to the frequent diffusion of grammatical markers in other contact situations involving Aboriginal languages, as can be observed amongst the Wororran languages of Western Australia (cf. Rumsey 2018), for instance.

Australia has been a place of extensive language contact for millennia (cf. O'Shannessy and Meakins 2016 for an overview). It can be assumed that some version of what we may currently describe metapragmatically as accessing fluid registers in contemporary English-based linguistic discourse has in fact been common practice long before the first contact with speakers of English and their often ill-informed conceptions of the indigenous social fabric, cultures, and languages.

The linguistic diversity of indigenous Australia can almost be conceived of as a continuum of codes, which has enabled efficient long-distance communication for eons without the written medium. Notwithstanding this observation, however, older multilingual speakers are usually very aware which resource they take from which language (R. Pensalfini p.c., May 4, 2021). In addition, in some places with a particularly high degree of multilingualism speakers regularly employ multilingual receptive practices, whereby they address others in one language, but receive responses in another. As an example for this, one may consider the Warruwi community in the Northern Territory, where no less than nine languages are currently being spoken, of which English is one. Singer (2018) claims that Warruwi can in fact be characterized as a speech community and that it is not a single, distinct code but the shared interpretations of indexicality ascribed to each of the languages in use that are constitutive for the speech community as a whole. Example (6) is an excerpt from a Warruwi resident reporting about the linguistic situation by accessing several codes.

(6) [Singer and Harris 2016: 183]
Ngapi ngungpanunma *as I was growing up. Because my mother was a Kunwinjku speaker but* **ja** *my* **father, naka Mawng.** *And I had* **ngarrkarrk ta ngaralk.**
'I'll tell you about how as I was growing up my mother was a Kunwinjku speaker but my father was a Mawng speaker. So I had two languages.'

Another example is the multilingual Maningrida community is characterized by "'hybrid spaces' (i.e. spaces shaped by the interaction of diverse groups, institutions and ways of speaking)" (Vaughan 2018: 125):

(7) [Vaughan 2018: 130]
Yaw, good afternoon **gu-ngarda yerrcha!** **Mun-guna** *book launching* **nguburrni barra** *– it's the most powerful dreamtime creation story. Wisdom* **arrbuwuna** *from our old people. And we're very lucky, recording* **burr-negarra** *our old people,* **aburr-ngayburrpa** *Gun-nartpa clan group,* **aburr-ngayburrpa** *family.*
'Yes, good afternoon all the kids! This book we will be launching, it's the most powerful dreamtime creation story. Wisdom they gave us from our old people. And we're very lucky that she recorded our old people, our Gun-nartpa clan group, our family.'

Vaughan (2018: 130) notes that while the recorded person's main language is Djinang, in this situation he switches to Burarra.

Interestingly, this circumstance presents us with an apparent contradiction that warrants further investigation: While the examples of fluidity encountered so far seem to confirm the considerations presented in Section 3.2 in regards to the concepts of *language* or *community* as ideologically constructed European inventions, the multilingual receptive practices observed in locations of extreme multilingualism such as Warruwi pose a challenge to it. On the one hand it appears to be another prime example of a translanguaging space, on the other hand people in the multilingual speech community are fully aware of their respective traditional languages and associated cultural values, which suggests that they have traditionally conceived of these as somewhat holistic entities and continue to do so.

4.4 Language policy making in contemporary Australia

Despite trends of reconciliation and acceptance of multiculturalism as part of a new post-colonial identity in recent decades (cf. Joppke 2004; Levey 2019) present day Australia still displays a great deal of contrast between the active accessing of fluid multilingual resources by a significant portion of its population and the use of monolithic language concepts. This becomes strikingly clear when looking at recent developments in language policy making. Heugh (2014: 335) points out that the notion of fluidity as a function of horizontal communicative practices has already been acknowledged in Australia by the *National Policy on Languages* first devised in the 1990s, thus seemingly adopting a linguistically informed contemporary view on multilingualism, but at the same time the policies maintain a hierarchical order of linguistic codes, each ranked according to perceived relevance for the benefit of a larger, multicultural society. This in effect represents a continuation of the colonial paradigm that places English on top, while community and indigenous languages are assigned second and third position, respectively. In doing so official policy making somewhat contradicts its own insights into fluidity, as this ranking in terms of relevance presupposes a conception of languages as clearly separable entities.

Mainstream discussions in Australia that ultimately result in educational policy making follow an agenda of monolingualism motivated by perceived socio-economic pressures that foster English as the most versatile and consequently more "valuable" language, while at the same time not enough attention is given to the reality of multilingualism apparent in society. This is evident, for instance, in the continuum of Australian Aboriginal English that is prevalent in school education, and which seems to directly reflect the traditional fluid approach to the use of language as a means to cross geographic, ethnic, and societal boundaries (cf. Heugh 2014). As we have seen in Section 4.3, however, this continuum and bounded language concepts are not mutually exclusive per se: speakers can take advantage of fluidity while simultaneously being aware of all their linguistic resources and where to place them. This is also evident in the observation that English-lexified Kriol is perceived in some communities as a substandard variety of English, even a "killer language" in competition with traditional languages that are held in higher esteem, while efforts on the part of field linguists result in valuing the code as a language in its own right and thereby gaining recognition (cf. Meakins 2014: 391; Vaughan and Loakes 2020: 721). Fixed language concepts serve a good purpose not only as a point of reference for identification, but also as descriptive labels that prove helpful whenever there is a need to reflect upon their multi-source repertoire or chart out its resources. Thus, the seeming contradiction between fixed language concepts and fluid practices is by no means unique to Europe.

Heugh (2014) views Australia as a highly polarized society in which the minority of ca. 500,000 indigenous people finds itself marginalized against ca. 24 million migrant settlers largely from a European background. These two subsets represent the extremities of what we understand by the *global south and north* (cf. Heugh 2014: 339). Accordingly, Australia is in stark contrast to numerous developing countries around the world that have not only accepted multilingualism as a reality permeating all social contexts but gone further by adopting "multilingual system-level policies and curriculum decisions that do not result in a monolingual point of educational exit" (Heugh 2014: 337), thus moving away from conceptual predominance of a singular colonial language. Heugh (2014: 338) attributes this to the overall degree of societal multilingualism, whether this is conceived of as linguistic continua of communicative practices or bounded written varieties of separate languages as means of instruction. In this respect Australia is different from India or Africa, where "the concept of a single language representative or constitutive of the nation state has never sat well with complex linguistic ecologies" (Heugh 2014: 337).

4.5 Fluid registers and fixed language concepts in present day Australia

Australia can be described as a postcolonial space characterized by a contradiction between the use of fluid registers, where speakers situationally gravitate to multiple codes and a lingering conception of English as the codified colonial language. Speakers take different perspectives on the colonial language, ranging from motivations of continuance of the colonial heritage to appropriation by those who highlight the colonial past still shimmering through in the English language in order to meet their own communicative ends.

In sum we can represent present day Australia linguistically as a multidimensional network of codes manifest in a continuum that spans local indigenous languages, pidgins and creoles, mixed languages and an overarching distinct postcolonial variety of English, where each code carries a specific ideology as well as indexicality within speaker groups of varying size, of which Australian English is the most wide-ranging and dominant, in all likelihood the only code readily available to all speakers.

In regards to the hypotheses formulated in Section 2 we can in fact corroborate at least two of the three: While there is indeed an increasing fluidity of registers especially in contact zones of the indigenous and non-indigenous, i.e. those sections of the postcolonial space where speakers have equally strong ties to both, traditional identities and ways of life as well as modern society largely grounded in the uniquely Australian brand of European heritage, it co-exists with metapragmatic knowledge of the respective usefulness of distinct codes for distinct purposes such as of course the awareness that English still carries the most prestige.

Given that English has no significant competitors for the status of colonial language in Australia – unlike other postcolonial spaces such as Mauritius, which will be discussed in some detail in Section 5, and also the south-western United States, where English has superseded Spanish in the course of the Americas' colonial history, but Spanish is still extremely dominant and even extending its influence to this day – we do not find separate or even competitive evaluation of colonial languages. What we do find, on the other hand, is stereotypical values of Australianness grounded in the distinct dialect of English that has emerged over the more than two hundred years of continuous European settlement.

With respect to the third hypothesis, we must acknowledge that unlike many other postcolonial spaces modern Australia represents a relatively stable society that has long ago joined the ranks of the first world. While codes are being evaluated by all speakers in terms of their usefulness in regards to social upward mobility, it is for this reason that specifically Australian English represents the endpoint of any individual's projected upward movement. There is no need for speakers to evaluate other codes with the intent to seek their personal fortune, as long as they remain in Australia.

In the light of the given multilingualism, we could argue that the reality of English in Australia as a whole today can no longer be adequately described by *colonial language* in any narrow sense. Rather it has emerged as a new code with a repertoire of linguistic features fed by diverse sources out of what was once the exclusive language of oftentimes aggressive colonizers. As such it is continually enriched by the plurality of voices from a multitude of backgrounds through communicative practices such as translanguaging to various extents.

While it seems intuitive that European traditional conceptions of language in regards to English as a hermetic entity employed for all communicative purposes have been carried over into the postcolonial period and even prevail in modern Australia, it remains to be investigated further if and how fixed concepts of English, indigenous and immigrant languages, respectively, can be upheld as such.

5 Two colonial languages – or not? The example of Mauritius

A glance at another postcolonial space, the small insular Republic of Mauritius in the Indian Ocean, may also serve to visualize the problem of the tension between colonial language(s) and fluid registers, focusing on the multilingual society and surveying the metapragmatic reflections.

Mauritius is fundamentally shaped by colonialism, sociohistorically as well as linguistically, as the island was uninhabited prior to the arrival of French colonizers around 1721, except for a brief, failed Dutch settlement attempt. Consequently, there is no indigenous population group that could claim to be the true or native Mauritians. In fact, the population of 1.3 million Mauritians is composed of various diasporic groups that found their way to the island in the course of the last three centuries, mainly through forced (but later also voluntary) migration. Northern Frenchmen actually came first, but they immediately transferred enslaved people from Africa (mainly Mozambique and Madagascar), as well as to a much lesser extent from India to the colony they called *Isle de France*. In the 18th century, a French-based creole language was already established in the colonial-era slaveholding society – the island being mainly characterized by sugar cane plantations. In 1810, France lost the territories to Great Britain, which granted Mauritius independence in 1968.

During more than 150 years of British rule, Mauritian history was marked fundamentally by two main facts: 1) Great Britain did not plan to populate the island on its own and allowed the French living there to retain their customs, laws, and religion – consequently, French remained the most important language of the upper class and the Mauritian creole language remained the lingua franca and target language of the dominated strata; 2) After the abolition of slavery in 1835, the British established a forced labor system ("coolie labor") and brought over half a million people from India to Mauritius to replace the former slaves on the plantations. They still form the largest, albeit ethno-religiously diversified, group. During the 19th century, southern Chinese petty traders completed the plural society. Thus, issues of cultural hybridization and creolization, which are also reflected in the highly complex linguistic situation, are firmly rooted in Mauritian history (cf. e.g. Eriksen 1999, for a detailed overview).

5.1 A sociolinguistic situation shaped by historically grown colonial structures

As a result of the aforementioned historical developments, Mauritius has become multicultural and multilingual, featuring a variety of exogenous languages and one endogenous language, each of which having particular functions for (parts of) the society. Yet not only is the island's society multilingual, but almost all individuals have repertoires that could be assigned to what is socio-culturally constructed as different *languages* (cf. Tirvassen and Ramasawmy 2017; cf. also Section 5.2).

In the wake of independence in 1968, Mauritius, like many other African countries, continued to follow historically grown colonial structures and retained what is referred to as *nested diglossia* (cf. Baggioni and Robillard 1990: 54–55)[12] that had grown over centuries: The lower functions are served by Mauritian Creole and the vernacular Mauritian Bhojpuri, the latter being much less commonly used only among Indo-Mauritians. The higher functions, on the other hand, are dominated by English, used mainly for official and written contexts (in administration, parliament, laws, the legal system, and public education), and French, which is considered the oral language of prestige and the written language of the media, church, and civic elites. These two languages thus fulfil, in the Mauritian context, the first three criteria of *colonial languages* according to our definition in Section 2. The last criteria, however, the collective perception of the languages as colonially anchored, must be examined separately.

---

12 Despite significant developments in this domain, in particular regarding the standardization and thus prestige of the Mauritian Creole, Baggioni and Robillard (1990) remains a revealing study, highlighting the Mauritian Francophonie.

Although in public discourse French is often not explicitly associated with the colonial period, its status in Mauritius can be linked to the ethno-socioeconomic structures that grew as a result of colonialism. Thus, Eisenlohr (2018: 193) emphasizes that the relevance of French in Mauritius overshadows that of English in various respects and that it

> is largely due to the dominant role Franco-Mauritians settlers and their descendants have always played in the island's economy, and their very important role in the politics of the colony even after the end of French rule [...].

This observation aligns with the "ideal to be aspired to" established by French-speaking elites cited by Judge (2005: 32). Baggioni and Robillard (1990: 71) also argue regarding French that, as the first language of the socioeconomically dominant elite since settlement, it was almost inevitably bound to influence the language perception and language practice of the rest of the Mauritian society, which led, at one point, to a situation in which many previously traditionally creolophone and bhojpuriphone classes became "neo-Francophones" aiming for social upward mobility. Hence, the authors distinguish an endolingual (=L1) and several exolingual (=L2/L3 or new L1) regional varieties of French in Mauritius, differing phonetically, lexically but also syntactically from each other and from Standard French:

> [I]l faudrait être outrageusement dogmatique pour ne pas donner à ses enfants les armes linguistiques aptes à les faire sortir de la situation de diglottes ou de locuteurs d'« entre-langue » où ils sont autrement condamnés à demeurer, même si l'on a du mal soi-même à assumer la nouvelle identité que l'on s'est procurée en devenant francophone (Baggioni and Robillard 1990: 72).[13]

In the public eye, the few neo-Anglophones are also well-regarded, because active oral competence in the de facto official language English is normally extremely limited among most Mauritians (cf. Ludwig et al. 2009: 167).

The fact that Asian languages locally known as *ancestral languages* or *oriental languages* are present in Mauritius, where they are mainly considered points of reference for ethno-religious (self-)identification, is largely due to colonialism and the associated displacements of human labor (for a detailed ethnolinguistic analysis of the Indian diaspora in Mauritius, cf. Eisenlohr 2006). Paradoxically,

---

13 Translation MF: "One would need to be outrageously dogmatic not to give one's children the linguistic weapons to get them out of the situation of speakers of 'in-between-languages' where they are otherwise condemned to remain, even if one has difficulty in assuming the new identity that one has acquired by becoming a Francophone".

the Indian and Chinese migrants did not speak the standard languages postulated today as *ancestral languages* and taught in Mauritian schools, i.e. Arabic, Hindi, Urdu, Tamil, Telugu, Marathi, or Mandarin, but mainly their related varieties and other (partly unrelated) languages with a comparatively lower prestige, such as Bhojpuri (North India) or Hakka (South China). While religion certainly plays a major role in this, it should not be underestimated that Mauritius is shaped by a *standard language ideology* concerning French and English that has been imported in colonial times and consolidated since then (cf. Hüning and Krämer 2018), the presumed self-evidence of which is certainly transferred to other languages.

Finally, Mauritian Creole, the only born-and-raised language in Mauritius, occupies a particular position. Its emergence and role as a target language in the colonial context, its use by all Mauritian communities as a language of proximity (L1 of over 84% of the population, cf. Kriegel 2017: 687) even for communication across the different diasporic groups (as "langue supracommunautaire" ['intergroup language'], cf. Stein 1982) and its lexical proximity to French (and to a lesser extent English and Indian languages), make it in some ways the most obvious colonial offspring – at the same time, it is a persistent symptom of some sort of 'inferiority complex' that has been challenged by the mentioned intergenerational pursuit of francophonization with only moderate success. Once again, it is also the lack of standardization of Mauritian Creole (considerably successful only after 2004, cf. Carpooran 2014), that contributes to this to a particular extent.

Unlike Australia (cf. Section 4.4), Mauritius has mirrored its multilingualism into the educational system. In addition to the compulsory colonial languages, which are supplemented by Mauritian Creole as an instruction tool at least at the primary school level, various ancestral languages, Mauritian Creole, and international languages, such as German and Spanish, can be selected as optional subjects.

All these sociolinguistic particularities point to an integrative multilingualism and a pragmatics of fluid registers in Mauritius, which Baggioni and Robillard (1990: 61) still classified as a deficient "entre-langue". This is a representation that remains widespread in the population and is based on fixed concepts of language. However, scholars are beginning to take a new epistemological perspective and detach their research from rigid concepts that fail to grasp reality, such as *language* and *diglossia* (cf. Tirvassen and Ramasawmy 2017). Recent studies show that almost every Mauritian is able to use elements of the numerous existing *languages* for his or her communicative, rhetorical-pragmatic purposes and for negotiating social identities (cf. Ludwig et al. 2009: 197–198).

What would be described as tags from and code-switching into varieties not associated with the speaker (*Crossing*) are quite conceivable (cf. examples (8)–(10) in Section 5.2). Thus, *translanguaging spaces*, as defined by Li (2011) are to be found in Mauritius. As Eisenlohr (2018: 193–194) puts it:

> Mauritians often have large linguistic repertoires. They creatively draw on them in order to take stances, define situations, and to enact social, ethnic, and religious identifications in everyday life. [T]his is not just a matter of code-switching from one defined language to another, but also involves considerable register variation within the vernacular languages Mauritian Creole, Mauritian Bhojpuri, and French.

5.2 Fixed language concepts versus fluid registers shown in metapragmatic data

We conducted data collection at Faculty of Social Studies and Humanities of the University of Mauritius in 2017, which yielded interesting results in terms of perceptions of the Mauritian multilingual environment. We are therefore able to test the hypotheses H1–H3 stated in Section 2 at least for a specific young and educated group that presumably reflects critically on languages and society, as these are main topics of their study programs.

Namely, 52 students, aged 19 to 21, were approached by means of a sociolinguistic questionnaire. 100% of the respondents indicated that they had good to very good active and passive proficiency in Mauritian Creole and in the two colonial languages,[14] French and English. In addition, the indication of at least low competencies in Bhojpuri (15%[15] active, 35% passive), Hindi (56% active, 15% passive), and Urdu (17% active, 15% passive), as well as isolated mentions of passive competencies in Arabic, Telugu, Marathi, Gujarati, and Tamil, confirm Eisenlohr's assessment of broad linguistic repertoires, also for the sampled generation Z, i.e., born shortly before the turn of the millennium. When assessing the data collected from this group, it is important to keep in mind that this is a generation and social class largely "modeled for and by" French and English, meaning that many of them grew up in neo-Francophone contexts, as this 25-year-old teacher of French and Mauritian Creole confirms:

---

14 In the questionnaire, all languages were referred to neutrally, i.e., without mentions such as *colonial languages* or *ancestral languages*.
15 All percentages have been rounded.

Nou, nou zenerasion, nou finn depas anfet sa kestionnman kolonial-la, mo panse, parski nou finn modele par sa, nou finn modele pou sa, nou finn modele pou ena enn sertin elevasion sosial, me nou pa kone ofet, nou pa realize ki li koumsa.[16]

In the questionnaire, the students were asked, for instance, about their personal pragmatics, offering not only the *named languages* Mauritian Creole, French, and English for selection, but also *language mixtures* of any kind. Interestingly, 20 participants identified no language mixtures at all (38%; five respondents made no statement), 27 participants (52%) claimed that elements of different languages were mixed in the most diverse situations (circle of friends, family, but also at work). According to the students, this type of mixing would also be practiced in written contexts (SMS/chats, etc.). These data show the tension in metapragmatic reflection, in which the acceptance of the practice of fluid registers, which cannot be denied, competes with the notion of fixed language concepts (cf. H1). The proportion of those who imagine an additive multilingualism is considerable, although more than half of all participants recognize an integrative multilingualism, i.e., multilingualism characterized by *Translanguaging*. Since six of them claim to have recognized language mixing in only one surveyed context each (school or SMS), the figures even give a somewhat distorted impression in favor of the perception of translingual practices. After all, only two participants put their crosses exclusively in the segment of *language mixtures* and neglected the *named languages* available for selection. One person even answered the question about the preferred language stating "J'aime bien le mélange de langues" ['I really like the mix of languages'] and thus provides a remarkable outlier in terms of metapragmatic reflection and evaluation of linguistic practices.

The contradiction of translingual practices and metapragmatic notions of fixed language concepts is indeed repeatedly apparent in the questionnaires: for instance, several participants who do not cite language mixtures in their metapragmatic reflections provide excellent examples (8)–(10) of precisely those practices in which speakers use different linguistic features (in syntax, morphology, and lexicon) in the free writing section that they would probably assign to the *languages* English, French, and Mauritius Creole in their own perceptions. Yet the written survey certainly led to increased use of English elements here:

---

16 Translation MF: "We, our generation, we have gone beyond this colonial questioning, because we are shaped by it, we are shaped for it. We are shaped to have a certain social elevation, but, actually, we don't know, we don't realize that it is like that".

(8) *pu montre so statut social and niveau l'éducation*
Mauritian Creole: 'pou montre so stati sosial ek nivo ledikasion'
French: 'pour montrer son statut social et le niveau d'éducation'
English: 'to show his/her social status and level of education'

(9) *acoz li sound gross sometimes*
Mauritian Creole: 'akoz parfwa li sonn grosie'
French: 'car cela peut parfois paraître grossier'
English: 'because it sounds gross sometimes'

(10) *Zot ti capav servi sa l'argent la pu improve the existing transport system rather than introducing a new means of transport*
Mauritian Creole: 'Zot ti kapav servi sa larzan-la pou amelior sistem transpor ki deza ena olie introdwir enn nouvo mwayin transpor'
French: 'Ils auraient pu utiliser l'argent pour améliorer le système de transport existant au lieu d'introduire un nouveau moyen de transport'
English: 'They could have used the money to improve the existing transport system rather than introducing a new means of transport'

The consolidation of the metapragmatic notion seems to be even more pronounced for the colonial languages English and French than for the still consolidating Mauritian Creole – as in the explicit reflection on language mixture, a Mauritian Creole influenced by English or French is indicated significantly more often than the other way around. In the diasporic context of Canada, when Mauritians with their emerged Mauritian regional lects meet Canadian English or Quebec French speakers, for example, a recurring finding is that Canadians do not speak Standard English or Standard French, as Mauritians do in their imagination. Thus, Mauritian regional French is not perceived as such by certain groups, but is equated with the prestigious standard, most probably as a result of the aforementioned standard language ideology imported during the colonial period (cf. Hüning and Krämer 2018).

Tirvassen and Ramasawmy (2017: 53) argue that

> [t]he unsettling paradox multilinguals display, with on the one hand, their language ideologies grounded in monolingualism, a view of named languages as separate, static and bounded entities, and in neoliberal imperatives, and on the other, their hybrid language practices, is testimony to the epistemicide they have been subjected to.

5.3 "Colonial" languages: useful and almost uncontested legacy

The assumption H2, namely that there is not necessarily a generalizable rejection of colonial language(s) or even a connection between colonial languages and the horrors of the colonial era in the postcolonial space, can also be verified with the help of the data collected for Mauritius. The survey's section on language evaluation – once again without explicit reference to the term *colonial language* in the questionnaire – recalls the "purpose-driven idealization" mentioned for Togo (cf. Section 2): The colonial languages dominate both the question about the "preferred language" (21% French, 38% English) and the question about the "most beautiful language" (27% each).[17] There is absolutely no evidence, that these languages are largely registered by the surveyed generation Z as imposed or even "terrifying" because of the historical linkage with the atrocities committed by French and British colonial masters against slaves and forced laborers.

However, at this point it is necessary to repeat the peculiarities specific to Mauritius, namely that English and French did not challenge or replace any autochthonous languages here and have been part of Mauritius since its settlement, i.e., for more than 200 and 300 years, respectively. Recognized as being thus endogenous languages, a certain distance from their colonial past seems to have been established. This distance already appeared during the pre-independence, i.e. still British era, when two ethno-politically distinct elites emerged as protagonists, each supporting one of the two colonial languages in an almost ironic way: While Indo-Mauritians were largely in favor of independence and (!) the maintenance of English as administrative language, the White and Creole elites tended to support the British guardianship and (!) were avowed Francophiles (cf. Carpooran 2014: 115). Hence, it is even more questionable that French and English are still registered as "colonial" among younger Mauritians, whereas their status as legitimate languages of social advancement remains, with few exceptions, unchallenged. In lower social classes, for instance, the disrespectful Creole expression *bann ferblan* ['those who pretend to be white'] is established for neo-Francophones.

In fact, Mauritian Creole, the only competitor for status and prestige that could be considered because of its widespread use among the population, is struggling on various fronts, including standardization, the ethnic connection with the Creoles (i.e. Afro-Mauritians) that is attributed to it, and, last but not least, stigmatization due to its emergence in the 18th century as a "waste product"

---

[17] Multiple responses included. Ten participants gave no response (19%).

of the colonial languages (or as Eriksen (1999: 12) puts it: "the poor cousin of French"), which would unmistakably be reflected in its lexical proximity to French and its receptivity to English elements, among others. Thus, a single response in the questionnaires refers to the colonial period or *colonial languages*: "[Kreol] enn langaz ki sorti depi enn langaz kolonial ek ki bann esklav ek zot bann desandan servi".[18] There is a reason why pro-Creole activists keep emphasizing that they only want to see Mauritius Creole granted its rightful place, but that they do not want to endanger the position of either English or French: "A nouveau, introduire le créole au Parlement ne voudrait pas dire exclure l'anglais ou le français, mais donner au créole sa juste place" (Y. Bosquet-Ballah in an interview cited in Ladouceur 2020).[19]

However, languages with a colonial history – in Mauritius these are de facto all of them – are valued quite dynamically and differently according to groups, also depending on the opportunities associated with them and the interests of certain communities. While the Indian and Chinese languages, which qualify as truly *ancestral* only in a few rare cases, were initially promoted primarily for ethno-religious reasons, there is also increasingly an underlying political and economic interest to postulate Hindi, Arabic, and Mandarin as *ancestral languages*: it is useful in order to emphasize a historically rooted connection to potential Asian investors and thereby to profit from the expansion of mainly India and China in the Indian Ocean and in Africa. In terms of usefulness for social promotion (H3), these languages could now slowly be penetrating spheres where, for a very long time, the *colonial languages* French and English were unassailable. However, these remain the most prestigious and promising *languages* in Mauritius, enabling numerous ties with the former colonial powers, for example through membership in the Francophonie, the Commonwealth, or the Cambridge Assessment International Education, providing qualifications for international admission. A pragmatic insertion of elements of these languages into discourses is, spoken with answers from the questionnaires, less "pour copier les Européens" ['to copy the Europeans'], but rather remains a "try to be seen as belonging to upper class/more educated in society". English and French seem to be registered in the collective Mauritian memory of the sampled generation Z as "de langaz internasional" ['two international languages'], useful and therefore valu-

---

18 Translation MF: "Creole is a language that comes from a colonial language and that is used by slaves and their descendants".
19 Translation MF: "Again, introducing Creole into Parliament would not mean the exclusion of English or French, but giving Creole its rightful place".

able, rather than as imposed "colonial" languages possibly associated with suffering and oppression. Still, more in-depth studies with different groups and generations are desirable to verify these findings.

6 Conclusions and outlook

This paper has aimed at a critical, multi-causal reassessment of what is meant by *colonial language* in the light of contemporary social dynamics in postcolonial spaces.

We started off by some fundamental considerations on the concept of *colonial language*. These led to the awareness that a perspective on the colonial layers of European languages must be part of the appropriate assessment of their international status. We have come to argue that the current international status of European languages cannot be captured by monocausal explanations, but has to be analyzed considering their colonial history, their instrumental character in colonial expansion and, particularly, their ties to decolonization and postcolonial diffusion. In particular, we have elaborated on the assumption that *colonial language* is not a static concept, but that features, classifications, and functions of colonial languages are negotiated in a purpose-driven way.

As a result, we argue for the need to explore the significance of fixed language concepts and theories, as well as practices of fluid repertoires for the conceptualization of *colonial languages*. Fixed and historically shaped notions of colonial languages, as metapragmatic ideologies, are obviously at odds with the pragmatics of fluidity in postcolonial spaces: While the assumption of fluid registers has been broadly accepted in sociolinguistics and related disciplines for quite some time already, the use of fixed categories still seems to dominate on the metapragmatic level. Thus, we argue for the importance of empirical research on postcolonial spaces and their fluid registers in tension with one or more colonial languages.

The tension between colonial languages and fluid registers has then been empirically discussed by drawing on two exemplary case studies: on the one hand Australia, which continues to show lingering conceptions of English as the codified colonial language and, on the other hand, Mauritius, which is characterized by the existence of more than one colonial language. In both postcolonial spaces, however, former "European" languages have evolved into national/regional lects that are discursively realized through practices such as *Translanguaging*. Fluid practices, in turn, do not prevent speakers' metapragmatic attribution of certain fixed and assumed valorizing labels. These may mirror autonomy on one side, e.g., the label "Australian English", or follow the ideology of the perpetual European Standard on the other, whether it fits or not.

Acknowledgements: We would like to thank Thomas Stolz for important comments and expert suggestions, which we have gratefully received.

References

Agha, Asif. 2007. *Language and social relations*. Cambridge: Cambridge University Press.
Ammon, Ulrich. 2014. *Die Stellung der deutschen Sprache in der Welt*. Berlin, München & Boston: De Gruyter.
Baggioni, Daniel & Didier de Robillard. 1990. *Île Maurice: une francophonie paradoxale*. Paris: L'Harmattan.
Baker, Beverley & Gillian Wigglesworth. 2017. Language Assessment in indigenous contexts in Australia and Canada. In Elana Shohamy & Nancy Hornberger (eds.), *Language testing and assessment. Encyclopedia of language and education, volume 7*. Dordrecht: Springer. 287–301.
Bhabha, Homi. 1994. *The location of culture*. London: Routledge.
Blommaert, Jan. 2010. *The sociolinguistics of globalization*. Cambridge: Cambridge University Press.
Blommaert, Jan & Ad Backus. 2011. *Repertoires revisited: 'Knowing language' in superdiversity*. Working Papers in Urban Language and Literacies 67.
Blommaert, Jan & Ben Rampton. 2011. Language and superdiversity. *Diversities* 13(2). 1–21.
Blommaert, Jan & Ben Rampton. 2016. Language and superdiversity. In Karel Arnaut, Jan Blommaert, Ben Rampton & Massimiliano Spotti (eds.), *Language and superdiversity*, 21–48. London: Routledge.
Bürki, Yvette & Carolin Patzelt. 2020. Contacto y migración. *Iberoromania* 91. 3–11.
Bradley, David & Maya Bradley. 2001. Changing attitudes to Australian English. In Peter Collins & David Blair (eds.), *English in Australia*, 271–286. Amsterdam: John Benjamins.
Calvet, Louis Jean. 1974. *Linguistique et colonialisme. Petit traité de glottophagie*. Paris: Payot.
Carpooran, Arnaud. 2014. Le créole mauricien dans sa marche vers le monde de l'écriture formelle et celui de l'univers scolaire durant la période post-2000. In Arnaud Carpooran (ed.), *Langues créoles, mondialisation et éducation. Actes du XIIIe colloque du Comité International des Études Créoles. Maurice, novembre 2012*, 109–136. Réduit: CSU-ELP.
Cheshire, Jenny, Paul Kerswill, Sue Fox & Eivind Torgersen. 2011. Contact, the feature pool and the speech community: The emergence of Multicultural London English. *Journal of Sociolinguistics* 15(2). 151–196.
Collins, Peter. 2012. Australian English: its evolution and current state. *International Journal of Language, Translation and International Communication* 1(1). 75–86.
Collins, Peter & David Blair. 2001. Introduction. In Peter Collins & David Blair (eds.), *English in Australia*, 1–16. Amsterdam: John Benjamins.

Cox, Felicity & Sallyanne Palethorpe. 2007. Australian English. *Journal of the International Phonetic Association* 37(3). 341–350.
Creese, Angela & Adrian Blackledge (eds.). 2018. *The Routledge handbook of language and superdiversity*. London: Routledge.
Diagne, Souleymane Bachir. 2019. Afrikanische Philosophie und die Sprachen Afrikas. *Merkur* 843. 94–99.
Eades, Diana. 1992. *Aboriginal English and the law: communicating with Aboriginal English speaking clients: a handbook for legal practitioners*. Brisbane: Continuing Legal Education Dept. of the Queensland Law Society.
Edjabou, Aqtime Gnouleleng. 2016. "Nos amis les Allemands" Zum Diskurs der aktuellen Deutschland-Begeisterung in Togo. *Journal for Discourse Studies* 3(2016). 265–280.
Eichinger, Ludwig M. 2017. Deutsch als Wissenschaftssprache. In Sandro Moraldo (ed.), *Die deutsche Sprache in Italien. Zwischen Europäisierung und Globalisierung*, 43–69. Frankfurt a.M.: Peter Lang.
Eisenlohr, Patrick. 2006. *Little India. Diaspora, time, and ethnolinguistic belonging in Hindu Mauritius*. Berkeley & Los Angeles: University of California Press.
Eisenlohr, Patrick. 2018. From language to religion in Mauritian nation-building. In Ramola Ramtohul & Thomas Hylland Eriksen (eds.), *The Mauritian paradox. Fifty years of development, diversity and democracy*, 191–215. Réduit: University of Mauritius Press.
Eriksen, Thomas Hylland. 1999. *Tu dimunn pu vini kreol: The Mauritian Creole and the concept of creolization*. Working Papers of the Transnational Communities Programme, University of Oxford. Retrieved from https:/www.potomitan.info/ki_nov/moris/creolization.html (checked 05/11/23).
García, Ofelia & Wei Li. 2013. *Translanguaging: language, bilingualism and education*. Basingstoke: Palgrave Macmillan.
Heller, Monica. 2007. Bilingualism as ideology and practice. In Monica Heller (ed.), *Bilingualism: A social approach*, 1–22. London: Palgrave Macmillan.
Heugh, Kathleen A. 2014. Turbulence and dilemma: Implications of diversity and multilingualism in Australian education. *International Journal of Multilingualism* 11. 327–363.
Hinrichs, Lars. 2014. Diaspora and sociolinguistic space. In Judith Misrahi-Barak & Claudine Raynaud (eds.), *Diasporas, Cultures of Mobility, 'Race'*, 235–268. Paris: Presses Universitaires.
Hüning, Matthias & Philipp Krämer. 2018. Standardsprachenideologie als Exportprodukt. In Birte Kellermeier-Rehbein, Matthias Schulz & Doris Stolberg (eds.), *Sprache und (Post)Kolonialismus. Linguistische und interdisziplinäre Aspekte*, 1–24. Berlin: De Gruyter.
Jørgensen, Jens Normann, Martha Sif Karrebaek, Lian Malai Madsen & Janus Spindler Møller. 2011. Polylanguaging in Superdiversity. *Diversities* 2(13). 22–37.
Joppke, Christian. 2004. The retreat of multiculturalism in the liberal state: Theory and policy. *British Journal of Sociology* 55. 237–257.
Judge, Anne. 2005. *French as a Tool for colonialism: aims and consequences*. UC Berkeley, Institute of European Studies. Retrieved from https://escholarship.org/uc/item/6t22342r (checked 05/11/23).
Kriegel, Sibylle. 2017. La Réunion, Maurice et Seychelles. In Ursula Reutner (ed.), *Manuel des francophonies*, 686–703. Berlin: De Gruyter.
Labov, William. 1966. *The social stratification of English in New York City*. Washington D.C.: Center for Applied Linguistics.

Ladouceur, Audrey. 2020. Langue maternelle: "Le 'kreol ghetto' a ce besoin constant de se ré-inventer", *Zordi* (21.02.2020). http://www.zordi.mu/culture/langue-maternelle-le-kreol-ghetto-a-ce-besoin-constant-de-se-reinventer (checked 05/11/23).

Lenz, Katja. 2017. *Lexical appropriation in Australian Aboriginal literature*. Baden-Baden: Tectum. https://doi.org/10.5771/9783828867437 (checked 05/11/23).

Léglise, Isabelle. 2018. Pratiques langagières plurilingues et frontières de langues. In Michelle Auzanneau & Luca Greco (eds.), *Dessiner les frontières*, 143–169. Paris: ENS Editions.

Levey, Geoffrey Brahm. 2019. Australia's "Liberal Nationalist" Multiculturalism. In Richard T. Ashcroft & Marc Bevir (eds.), *Multiculturalism in the British Commonwealth – comparative perspectives on theory and practice*, 83–103. http://dx.doi.org/10.1525/9780520971103-006 (checked 05/11/23).

Li, Wei. 2011. Moment analysis and translanguaging space: Discursive construction of identities by multilingual Chinese youth in Britain. *Journal of Pragmatics* 43. 1222–1235.

Lowe, Kevin. 2011. Aboriginal languages reclamation: countering the neo-colonial onslaught. In Carolyn Glascodine & Kerry-Anne Hoad (eds.), *Indigenous education: pathways to success*, 21–28. Darwin: Australian Council for Educational Research.

Ludwig, Ralph, Fabiola Henri & Florence Bruneau-Ludwig. 2009. Hybridation linguistique et fonctions sociales: Aspects des contacts entre créole, français et anglais à Maurice. In Vinesh Hookoomsing, Ralph Ludwig & Burkhart Schnepel (eds.), *Multiple identities in action: Mauritius and some Antillean parallelisms*, 165–202. Frankfurt a.M.: Peter Lang.

Lüdi, Georges & Bernard Py. ³2003. *Être bilingue*. Frankfurt a.M.: Peter Lang.

Makoni, Sinfree & Alastair Pennycook. 2005. Disinventing and (re)constituting languages. *Critical Inquiry in Language Studies* 2(3). 137–156. https://doi.org/10.1207/s15427595cils0203_1 (checked 05/11/23).

Matras, Yaron. ²2020. *Language contact*. Cambridge: Cambridge University Press.

McConvell, Patrick & Felicity Meakins. 2005. Gurindji Kriol: a mixed language emerges from code-switching. *Australian Journal of Linguistics* 25(1). 9–30.

Meakins, Felicity. 2014. Language contact varieties. In Harold Koch & Rachel Nordlinger (eds.), *The Languages and Linguistics of Australia: A comprehensive guide*, 365–416. Berlin & New York: De Gruyter.

Meakins, Felicity & Rob Pensalfini. 2021. Holding the mirror up to converted languages: two grammars, one lexicon. *International Journal of Bilingualism* (Special Issue). 1–33.

Meakins, Felicity, Rob Pensalfini, Caitlin Zipf & Amanda Hamilton-Hollaway. 2020. Lend me your verbs: Verb borrowing between Jingulu and Mudburra, *Australian Journal of Linguistics* 40(3). 296-318. https://doi.org/10.1080/07268602.2020.1804830 (checked 05/11/23).

Migge, Bettina & Isabelle Léglise. 2013. *Exploring language in a multilingual context. Vairation, interaction and ideology in language documentation*. Cambridge: Cambridge University Press.

Nugent, Maria L. 2008. 'To try to form some connections with the natives': Encounters between Captain Cook and indigenous people at Botany Bay in 1770. *History Compass* 6(2). 469–487.

O'Shannessy, Carmel & Felicity Meakins. 2016. Introduction: Australian language contact in historical and synchronic perspective. In Felicity Meakins & Carmel O'Shannessy (eds.), *Loss and renewal: Australian languages since colonisation*, 3–26. Boston & Berlin: De Gruyter.

Ostler, Nicholas. 2005. *Empires of the word. A Language history of the world*. New York: Harper Collins.

Otheguy, Ricardo, Ofelia García & Wallis Reid. 2015. Clarifying translanguaging and deconstructing named languages: A perspective from linguistics. *Applied Linguistics Review* 6(3). 281–307. https://doi.org/10.1515/applirev-2015-0014 (checked 05/11/23).
Pennycook, Alastair. 2007. ELT and Colonialism. In Jim Cummins & Chris Davison (eds.), *International handbook of English language teaching. Springer international handbooks of education*, 13–24. Boston: Springer.
Pennycook, Alastair. 2018. Repertoires, registers and linguistic diversity. In Angela Creese & Adrian Blackledge (eds.), *The Routledge handbook of language and superdiversity*, 3–15. London: Routledge.
Rampton, Ben. 1995. Language crossing and the problematisation of ethnicity and socialisation. *Pragmatics* 5(4). 485–513.
Rampton, Ben. 2011. From 'multiethnic adolescent heteroglossia' to 'contemporary urban vernaculars'. *Language and Communication* 31(4). 276–294.
Rampton, Ben. ³2018 [1995]. *Crossing: language and ethnicity among adolescents*. London: Routledge.
Rumsey, Alan. 2018. The sociocultural dynamics of indigenous multilingualism in northwestern Australia. *Language and Communication* 62(Part B). 91–101.
Russo, Katherine E. 2007. *Practices of proximity: appropriation in the Australian contact zone*. University of New South Wales dissertation.
Sánchez Moreano, Santiago. 2020. Análisis de la interacción social en contextos de movilidad transnacional y de superdiversidad. *Iberoromania* 91. 28–51.
Sarr, Felwine. 2016. *Afrotopia*. Paris: Philippe Rey.
Singer, Ruth. 2018. A small speech community with many small languages: The role of receptive multilingualism in supporting linguistic diversity at Warruwi Community (Australia). *Language and Communication* 62(Part B). 102–118.
Singer, Ruth & Salome Harris. 2016. What practices and ideologies support small-scale multilingualism? A case study of Warruwi community, Northern Australia. *International Journal of the sociology of language* 241. 163–208.
Schwörer, Emil. 1916. Kolonial-Deutsch. Vorschläge einer künftigen deutschen Kolonialsprache in systematisch-grammatikalischer Darstellung und Begründung. Diessen: Hubers.
Spitzmüller, Jürgen. 2013. Metapragmatik, Indexikalität, Soziale Registrierung. *Journal for Discourse Studies* 3(2013). 263–287.
Stein, Peter. 1982. Connaissance et emploi des langues à l'Ile Maurice. Hamburg: Buske.
Stolz, Christel (ed.). 2015. *Language empires in comparative perspective*. Berlin, München & Boston: De Gruyter
Tirvassen, Rada & Shalini Jagambal Ramasawmy. 2017. Deconstructing and reinventing the concept of multilingualism: A case study of the Mauritian sociolinguistic landscape. *Stellenbosch Papers in Linguistic Plus* 51. 41–59.
Turnbull, Paul, Chris Blackall, Alan van den Bosch & Christine Winter (eds.). 2004. *South seas: voyaging and cross-cultural encounters in the Pacific (1760-1800)*. Canberra: National Library of Australia.http://southseas.nla.gov.au/journals/cook/17700422.html (checked 05/11/23).
Vaughan, Jill. 2018. Translanguaging and hybrid spaces: boundaries and beyond in north central Arnhem Land. In Gerardo Mazzafero (ed.), *Translanguaging as everyday practice*, 125–148. Dordrecht: Springer.
Vaughan, Jill & Debbie Loakes. 2020. Language contact and Australian languages. In Raymond Hickey (ed.), *The handbook of language contact*, 717–740. Hoboken: Wiley.

Wallace-Bruce, Nii Lante. 1989. Two hundred years on: a reexamination of the acquisition of Australia. *Georgia Journal of International and Comparative Law* 19. 87–118.

Walsh, Michael. 2012. *Re-awakening Languages: Theory and Practice in the Revitalisation of Indigenous Languages.* Sydney: Sydney University Press.

Willoughby, Louisa J. V., Donna Starks & Kerry Taylor-Leech. 2013. Is the cultural cringe alive and kicking? Adolescent mythscapes of Australian English in Queensland and Victoria. *Australian Journal of Linguistics* 33. 31–50.

Andreas Jäger and Jascha de Bloom
Prolegomena to a study of code-switching in Togo and its metapragmatic functions

Usage contexts as a means to assess prevailing language attitudes

Abstract: In order to provide a theoretical foundation for future fieldwork we survey multilingual practices of code-switching in present-day Togo in terms of associated metapragmatic functions and structural constraints. We explore different code-switching events and explore their potential as markers of social positioning for the purpose of showing how the study of code-switching may serve as a useful investigative tool to evaluate the asymmetry of prestige that obtains between the many languages spoken in Togo today. We suggest that an analysis of code-switching events and their social significance may help to assess the current role of the majority language Ewe, which we characterize as a secondary colonial language, as well as the current status of French and German as primary colonial languages.

Keywords: borrowing, code-switching, colonialism, language ideology, metapragmatics, multilingualism, stance taking

1 Introduction

This contribution explores the potential of code-switching (henceforth CS) phenomena for the investigation of language attitudes in contact situations as well as linguistic effects of successive colonial administrations in multilingual postcolonial societies with a particular focus on the situation in modern day Togo. Given the country's specific history of multilingualism on both the individual and the societal level we believe it is an ideal testing ground for hypotheses about practices of mixing linguistic material, with a particular focus on associated func-

---

Andreas Jäger, University of Bremen, FB 10, Universitäts-Boulevard 13, 28359 Bremen, Germany. E-Mail: anjaeger@uni-bremen.de
Jascha de Bloom, Bremen, Germany. E-Mail: de_bloom@web.de

https://doi.org/10.1515/9783111323756-011

tions. We see our study as a contribution to the research program of Colonial Linguistics, which has produced various insightful articles and monographs since its inception in Bremen.[1]

Grounded in colonial as well as recent history we discuss structural properties as well as social dimensions of CS in Togo, thereby identifying the respective roles of former colonial languages as well as those of the most widespread indigenous languages. The paper is conceived as a preliminary theoretical foundation for future fieldwork in the specific multilingual context of Togo. The theoretical reflections and research questions sketched out here may serve as a basis for more detailed case studies on the linguistic legacy of the German and French colonial occupation, respectively, in terms of how language attitudes, ideologies and policies associated with former colonial powers are reflected in linguistic behavior observable in postcolonial Togo.

The social dimension of the effects of language contact and thus most significantly CS as spontaneous, temporary alternation of linguistic codes in situations of direct interaction is particularly interesting wherever there is a strong prestige asymmetry in a multilingual setting, because it reveals asymmetry of power and how speakers position themselves in society. This is encountered most strikingly in post-colonial societies where multilingual competence and usage is the norm, but languages differ greatly with respect to the scope of social acceptability and dominance, largely correlating with the degree of officiality they enjoy.

The history of Togo is interesting for a number of reasons. Not only is it a melting pot of communities whose linguistic codes do not always converge in terms of status and wide-spread popularity, but also there has been a change in recent history from one European language as the dominant and most prestigious code to another: After the end of German colonial rule in 1918 French soon became the official language dominating written communication for most organizational purposes, but always in competition with indigenous languages, which are the codes passed on through the generations.

In our analysis we interpret CS phenomena as linguistic variables and thus as components of linguistic styles (cf. Eckert 2008). In this regard we follow up on a succession of variationist works with a common core question: "what kinds of meanings can variables have, and how do they combine to yield the larger meanings of styles" (Eckert 2008: 458). If we deal with the functions of CS phenomena involving the majority language Ewe as well as the colonial languages

---

[1] For an impression of the goals of early Colonial Linguistics, its basic terminology and the various research fields that constitute the paradigm, see Dewein et al. (2012).

French and German and possibly others in the specific context of Togolese speakers, we continue a long thematic tradition within the subfield of sociolinguistics. Nonetheless this should not happen uncritically, which is why we also feel obliged to reflect on our own roles as European linguists researching post-colonial issues in the course of the investigation. Criticism has been raised for instance by Woolard (2006: 75), who points out that research on CS is often motivated against the background of the Eurocentric image of a monolingual standard which runs contrary to the predominant scientific self-conception. We are fully aware of this bias and it is for this reason that the present contribution poses a challenge for the European concept of colonial language[2] itself. Whether this concept exists at all in the minds of Togolese speakers and how tightly French, German, and also Ewe are associated with the colonial past by the speakers themselves can only be discovered through on-site fieldwork. If it turns out that these languages are indeed being perceived as colonial languages in the sense of a legacy of external oppression, we must take into consideration their respective assessment by the speakers and underlying issues of language ideology (stance-taking, see Section 4.1).

How do speakers in Togo position themselves when they switch to Ewe or the languages of the former colonial powers of Europe that have left their imprint on Togo? How are the colonial languages being evaluated? What role can be assigned to already existing assessments of these and to what degree do these constitute the background for a given CS event or even trigger it? In order to answer these questions, we suggest analyses using metapragmatic methods as "soziolinguistische Sprachideologieforschung"[3] (Spitzmüller 2013: 263). Metapragmatics may offer some explanatory potential when it comes to addressing the question "wie soziale Positionen und Sprachideologien diskursiv ausgehandelt, sozialsemiotisch aufgeladen und transformiert werden"[4] (Spitzmüller 2013: 263).

---

2 To this day, there is no common definition of the term *colonial language*. Concerning English and Arabic as two such languages in parts of the Middle East and Northern Africa, Shakib (2011: 117) draws a rather ambivalent picture of colonial languages: Among their key features we find a systematic (and frequently violent) imposition by the colonizers, but also the colonial languages' usage as a "practical alternative [...] both to enhance inter-nation communication [...] and to counter a colonial past through de-forming a "standard" Arabic tongue and re-forming it in new literary forms." (for a more detailed discussion of the term *colonial language* and possible ramifications of its use see Fischer et al. this volume).
3 'sociolinguistic research on language ideology' [translation JdB].
4 'how social position and language ideologies are discursively negotiated, charged with social semiotics and transformed' [translation JdB].

Given the colonial and post-colonial history of Togo, we are particularly interested in finding out whether speakers switch to either Ewe as a secondary colonial language[5], French or German as the current and former official language, and if so, with which intention in mind. Which social indexicality can be ascribed to the selective usage of Ewe, French or German expressions? Do we encounter the construction of we-groups on the part of Ewe, French, or German speakers or learners through CS? How could we characterize those types of person or behavior that a we-group dissociates itself from by way of CS in this case? A further step would then be to uncover possible correlations between the extent and structural makeup of a CS event and the degree of determination behind the associated stance-taking.

The metapragmatic approach serves as a means to find reasons for their occurrence in specific situations and constellations of discourse participants. To this end we have to first revisit definitions of the notion of language ideology. This can be achieved by conceiving of the language-ideological domain exclusively as the entirety of "Werthaltungen und Einstellungen, die diskursiv geäußert und verhandelt werden"[6] (Spitzmüller 2013: 265, following the widely accepted notion developed in Silverstein 1979). On this condition concrete instances of CS cannot be the object of metapragmatic analysis. However, instances of CS provide a window into usage patterns in situations of language contact, where languages themselves have an intrinsic social indexical value. For future fieldwork on the current status and sociofunctional spectrum of CS in Togo this means that speaker stance and attitudes need to be documented on grounds of attested instances of CS, which can then be analyzed in metapragmatic terms.

Exploring the ways in which members of the multicultural and multilingual society of Togo approach and employ linguistic structures from various sources will serve as a testing ground for traditional conceptions of languages and speech communities as distinct entities with clear boundaries, which of course also includes the concept of *colonial language*. In the light of communicative practices grounded in fluid registers we will also re-assess CS in the light of newer trends in sociolinguistics such as translanguaging (see Rampton 2011; García and Li 2013). This somewhat radical view expands traditional notions of languages as bounded linguistic entities in such a way that communicative practices in multilingual societies are characterized by accessing an intrinsically fluid repertoire including expressive features, elements, or structures also from multi-modal

---

5 Our usage of the term will be discussed in Section 5.1.
6 'values and attitudes that are uttered and negotiated in discourse' [translation JdB]

modes of expression. The relation between CS and translanguaging will be outlined in Section 3.

We will discuss how CS not only depends on the situation, its participants or the internal makeup of the social group a given speech event takes place in, but also on structural restrictions brought about by grammatical constraints characteristic of different source languages.

The paper is organized as follows: After a brief overview of the colonial history of Togo as well as its current situation in the light of considerable linguistic diversity in Section 2 we review relevant conceptions of CS from a structural and a sociolinguistic perspective in Section 3. In Section 4 we explore the potential of CS to convey speaker attitudes based on the theory of social indexicality and its relation to metapragmatic positioning. Section 5 outlines the envisaged application of metapragmatic tools of analysis in future field work in post-colonial Togo including a short excursus on the effects of multilingualism on the national educational system in the light of language politics.

The phenomenon of CS has been studied from multiple perspectives. Pioneering studies on bilingual behavior can, for instance, be found in Haugen (1953) and Weinreich (1968). For thorough overviews embedded in the larger context of language contact research the reader is referred to Thomason (2001) and Matras (2020). Auer (1999) thematizes conversational aspects of CS, i.e. its role in regulating discourse, while Clyne (2003) highlights the multifaceted nature of the matter when he argues for a multidimensional and multidisciplinary approach.[7]

In this paper the concept of CS can and will be interpreted as a convenient label for the employment of purely linguistic forms in multilingual speaker groups. These expressions stem from a variety of sources that are nonetheless subject to certain structural restrictions when used in a syntagmatic order (see Section 3.1 for a discussion of possible grammatical constraints). Any one of these sources may in turn be conceptualized as representing a subsection within an overall repertoire of expressions in which a linguistic form is significantly more common than in any other subsections, in much the same way as a word may be classified as part of the native lexicon of language X and at the same time as a loanword in language Y, notwithstanding the circumstance that it fulfills identical communicative purposes across X and Y. For the purpose of this paper such subsections then lend themselves to labelling in terms of traditional glossonyms despite the fuzzy boundaries, thereby focusing on purely linguistic expressions.

---

[7] For the import of the sociolinguistic history of the speakers in the outcome of linguistic change see Thomason and Kaufman (1988).

Consequently, we will continue using traditional glossonyms while at the same time acknowledging the fluid nature of the repertoires they represent.[8]

If we take into account the aforementioned structural restrictions governing the assembly of cohesive strings of linguistic signs in the practice of translanguaging, concepts that are traditionally defined as discrete entities, descriptive expressions such as *language* and *speech community* retain a descriptive value on some level of granularity, while their fluidity is acknowledged. In this regard CS means systematic construction of expressions drawing on resources of diverse origin. The meta-descriptive expression *to switch from L_B into L_A* may be re-interpreted as to combine features or expressions from L_A and L_B, where L_A is the dominant subsection of a repertoire that comprises forms as well as combinatorial restrictions from $\{L_A, L_B, ... L_n\}$ accordingly. For the purpose of this paper, we take the descriptive label CS to imply just that, on the condition of there being a strong asymmetry between these subsections in the sense that the majority of structures is drawn from one subsection. This is akin to the Matrix Language Frame Model (Myers-Scotton 1993a, see Section 3.2 for a brief discussion) in that it allows the analysis in a variety of language pairs or sets of languages regardless of their structural characterization.

Given the multi-faceted and interactive relation between structural and social factors to be investigated we suggest that data collection should be chiefly based on participant observation as "the systematic description of events, behaviors, and artifacts in the social setting chosen for study" (Marshall and Rossman 1989: 79). We also like to include an evaluation of metalinguistic knowledge as well as language attitudes and metapragmatic judgements of the informants that is to be gained from interviews.[9]

2 Multilingualism in Togo – its history and today's situation

Currently there are 49 languages in Togo actively spoken by ethnic groups of different sizes (Eberhard et al. 2019). Today Ewe and Gen of the Gbe family are the most widely spoken languages in the south of Togo as well as across the border in Ghana, while Kabiye and Tem claim this status for the north of the country.

---

8 For a detailed discussion of problems arising from diverging conceptualisations of traditional glossonyms see Good and Cysouw (2013).
9 For an overview of participant observation as a method see Kawulich (2005).

These belong to different branches of the Niger-Congo macro-family.[10] As a majority language in Togo it is mainly Ewe that enjoys a comparably high status, according to Amuzu and Singler (2014: 330). Ewe L1 and L2 speakers combined comprise 75 % of the population. While French has been the national language since 1960, in 1975 both Ewe and Kabiye were given this status.

German is by no means the first European language that has come into contact with indigenous languages on the territory of present-day Togo: From as early as the late seventeenth century Portuguese and English were used at the slave trading post of Aného on the south coast (Stickrodt 2001). Hamburg merchants began building further trading posts along the coast in the middle of the nineteenth century. From 1847 the *Norddeutsche Missionsgesellschaft* [‚North German Missionary Society'], known in West Africa as *Bremen mission*, systematically followed their agenda of christianizing the population of what is now southern Togo and Ghana and introducing school education. To this end they focused on Ewe as the majority language of the region, while other local languages were seen as a hindrance. In order to overcome the great degree of dialectal variation the missionaries aimed at establishing an Ewe standard variety, which was then promoted in churches and schools (Yayoh 2015: 132). While direct political involvement by German officials was avoided initially in the tension between competing economic interests in the region on the part of British and German traders, this practice still had the effect of singling out and promoting one language out of many, thereby presumably adding much prestige to its status as majority language. As will be argued for in the course of this paper, the effect of this is noticeable to this day: "In a way Ewe became a prestige language. This practice of standardising and promoting one variant [sic] of a language by missionaries was not peculiar to Ewedome. It was very much the tool for the construction of ‚African custom and identity'"[11] (Yayoh 2015: 132).

Under the auspices of the Bremen Mission a somewhat standardised written variety of Ewe emerged with the publication of books in Ewe (Yayoh 2015: 132). Grammatical descriptions of Ewe written in English (Schlegel 1856) and – more extensively – in German (Schlegel 1857; Westermann 1907) as well as an Ewe-German dictionary (Westermann 1906) arguably contributed significantly to the growing prestige of Ewe in Southern Togo.

The territory of today's Southern Togo around the capital city of Lomé was proclaimed an official protectorate of the Empire in 1884. German as the language of

---

10 While the former is classified as a Kwa language, the latter represents the Gur family of the Northern Volta-Congo branch (Eberhard et al. 2019).
11 The quote is taken from Berman (1998: 322).

the first colonial power was taught in schools in this area from the 1890s until 1910 with the primary objective of creating a well-educated local elite of administrative assistants for the purpose of providing efficient support to the imperial government. The governor's initiative in 1904 to promote German as the exclusive language of instruction in all school subjects with the perspective of establishing German as a colony-wide lingua franca was met with criticism (Sokolowsky 2004: 58).

German quickly attained the status of a prestigious educational language, a status that remained long after France succeeded Germany as the colonial power after the Empire ceased to exist in 1918. It was used exclusively even in primary schools for a few years after the governor issued a directive that banned all other languages from school instruction (Sokolowski 2004: 85), but remarkably in 1910 the colonial administration decided in favor of Ewe as the main language of instruction in elementary education. The reason for this was that the government became increasingly afraid that too extensive education through the medium of the colonial language may eventually lead to claims of equal rights on the part of the indigenous elite (Stolberg 2015: 327)[12].

Before colonial administration was taken up by France under a League of Nations mandate, a large part of Togo including the South with the capital Lomé was occupied by Britain for one year. The Western part of Togoland became incorporated into the British Gold Coast with English as the official language of administration. English also functioned as a lingua franca in Southern Togo (Lawrance 2001: 517), German only became banned and replaced by French with the declaration of independence in 1960, several decades after the beginning of the French mandate (Kangni 2007: 9).

The colonial successors did not at all follow in utilizing an indigenous language to meet their own ends, as Lawrance (2001: 530) shows: "[...] this Ewe unity, or at least the plausible image thereof [...] presented a threat to the French administration. Consequently among certain circles within the mandate government, the Ewe "tribu" and even the Ewe language were held in great suspicion."

The French administrators feared a potential threat through the perceived ethnic unity of the Ewe, an impression that in all likelihood was propelled further by the German codification efforts, as Lawrance (2001: 530, also cf. sources cited therein) concludes: "[...] the German authorities supported missionary activities in the field, and by implication such unifying policies. It follows that one of the most important legacies of this period was a united, mobilized and educated Ewe

---

[12] A similar ideologically charged discussion with respect to whether German or an indigenous language should be fostered as the colonial lingua franca took place simultaneously in German New Guinea (Lindenfelser 2021: 19–21).

ethno-linguistic group." Another quote by Lawrance (2001: 517) further highlights the legacy of German language policy with respect to the Ewe language: "In its written and published form, the Ewe language spread beyond its immediate ethno-linguistic barriers and later proto-nationalist activity in Togo between the two World wars drew on this linguistic strength." As a countermeasure to this perceived Ewe unity as well as to the rising popularity of English at the time the French administrators actively attempted to destabilize all indigenous languages (Roberts 2011: 470), but at the same time did not actively push for a wider application of French throughout the colony. Instead French became a very domain-specific code (Lawrance 2001: 519): "While the German regime launched a grand scheme for the Germanization of Togo in 1903–1904, one would be hard pressed to argue for a similar francophonic phenomenon during the French mandate. French language policy, and more generally French education policy was dispersed, contradictory, irregular and often non-existent."

French colonial policy against the Ewe and other indigenous groups thus contrasts sharply with the ideology of the German predecessors. We therefore believe that today's prestigious status of Ewe owes much to the fact that the German colonial administration is still perceived as one that recognized and even valued indigenous languages, even though it did so for doubtful political purposes. That the German language as a linguistic reminder of this time is still considerably prestigious amongst the educated class of present-day Togo (see Edjabou 2016) becomes clear if we look at how despite the dominance of French as the official language German has managed to even gain popularity as a language of instruction in school (cf. Kangni 2007: 9), even though it had only been the official colonial language for a few decades before WW1[13].

In the contemporary Togolese school education system German is taught as a foreign language from secondary school onwards alongside Spanish and English. Language education can then be continued on an advanced level at the university of Lomé following the French model of tertiary German studies courses. Most German teachers working in schools usually receive their language training exclusively in Togo, university staff on the other hand will commonly have spent several years in German speaking countries (Kangni 2007). However, it should be noted that outside the educational and academic domain the German language plays no longer a significant role, so that effects of the German colonial rule are rather indirect.

In contrast to Kabiye, which is spoken mainly in the less densely populated north, Ewe – spoken as an L1 chiefly in Southern Togo – has been widely used as

---

[13] Yigbe (2017: 97) even speaks of a "pronounced positive attitude to its former colonial power".

a language of market transaction and negotiation for a long time, even in precolonial times. Large-scale CS can therefore be expected to occur between Kabiye or other local languages on the one hand and Ewe as a code available to most people on the other hand.

3 CS – structural and sociolinguistic aspects

Our contribution attempts to shed light on the phenomenon of CS in a twofold manner: we assess sociolinguistic functions and ramifications attributable to CS events, but at the same time take a systemic linguistic look at their inner workings. It is hoped that by converging these two perspectives we lay the groundwork for more detailed future investigations of CS in the post-colonial society of modern Togo with the aim of determining which roles can be assigned to the colonial languages German and French as well as to the majority languages.

The first perspective focuses on patterns of usage and the circumstances of their occurrence as well as associated sociopsychological effects. The second perspective pinpoints the morphosyntactic make-up of a given expression in terms of their source language and the possibilities of integration into a grammatical context (cf. Kelechukwu 2016). To analyze a linguistic event as a CS phenomenon in the sense outlined above it is necessary to point out on which linguistic scale we can assume CS phenomena to happen. Woolard (2006: 74) for instance includes languages, dialects, registers, and levels as possible codes that allow multilingual speakers to switch to.

3.1 Differences between CS and borrowing

In language contact the concepts of CS and (particularly lexical or material) borrowing are akin, but differ in terms of ascribable function as well as the degree of establishment in the repertoire. CS refers to spontaneous change from using one code to another in a conversation or, more precisely the usage of material from L_B in L_A structured according to grammatical requirements of L_B. Haspelmath (2009: 38–39) differentiates between material and structural borrowing (also cf. Matras and Sakel 2007), where the former refers to the interlinguistic transfer of form-meaning-pairs and the latter to the copying of grammatical or semantic patterns. For Grosjean (1982) as well as for Poplack and Meechan (1995) in order to qualify as a loan (or borrowed expression) an element is necessarily integrated into the matrix language not only morphosyntactically, but also phonologically, so that no cues as to its linguistic provenance are available to the speakers.[14] Language users may, however, switch from one morphosyntactic and phonological system within one and the same turn, where insertions of material range from single-word expressions to large syntagms. The chunks that occur during switches are temporary and do not usually become part of L_A. There is some dissent about where to draw the line between a single-word switch and a loan. Gumperz (1982), for instance, bases the distinction on the brevity of an insertion: short insertions – mainly single words – are interpreted as part of the lexicon of L_A, longer phrasal insertions are subject to grammatical rules of L_B and do not enter the lexicon of L_A.

As pointed out in Section 1, in regards to the problem of transgressing blurred boundaries we think that an investigation of the informant's metalinguistic knowledge might prove helpful, i.e. taking into account whether speakers identify the switched material as belonging to A, B or to a repertoire describable in terms of both A and B.

The distinction between CS and borrowing is relevant for an investigation of the social functions associated with codes and CS in a multilingual setting for the reason that even though both can contribute to the indexicality of a linguistic event, they differ in terms of their suitability for the conscious usage for specific intended purposes. It is probably wrong to say that the speaker's intention alone triggers CS in every case. Beside a speaker's individual motivation even functional necessities of a given conversation play a part when speakers draw on resources from a different code (cf. Woolard 2006: 84). For any functional and metapragmatic investigation one has to make sure not to overstate the intentionality of singular CS events by making it a basic component of one's own understanding of CS.

Frequently occurring elements may be incorporated into the inventory of the target language to the point that speakers analyse their usage no longer as switches to expression fragments from a different code but as genuine elements of the target language. In contrast to the rather ethereal nature of CS, loans are persistent, they are the result of integration from a source lexicon into a target lexicon. A crucial difference is that whereas CS requires all speakers involved to be bilingual, for borrowing no source language competence is necessary, in the same way as the etymology of native elements is irrelevant to their understanding to the monolingual speaker.

In a diachronic perspective borrowing, more precisely the effect of a borrowing process, can be regarded as the result of a repetitive process that begins with

---

[14] For a taxonomy of loans as well as a discussion of reasons for borrowing see Haspelmath (2009).

an initial CS event. Matras (2020: 115) discusses a CS-borrowing-continuum involving "an increase in the usage frequency of new word-forms and their potential adoption by monolinguals".[15] The idea of the continuum seems particularly interesting for the situation in Togo given the overall high degree of multilingualism.

The non-native status of a linguistic expression only becomes relevant if speakers are indeed aware of its history so that pragmatic and metapragmatic effects may be directly attributed to it in a bilingual setting. This is generally more likely with recently borrowed material, where the freshness of expression can have an indexical value of its own. If on the other hand the integration is complete, then the etymology becomes obscured and erstwhile foreign elements can no longer be identified as such, so that no metapragmatic effect is associable.

For the colonial and post-colonial situation in Togo we assume that a higher degree of awareness in regards to the origin of a given linguistic expression can be expected, not only on grounds of the prevalent multilingualism in general, but also because any borrowing process from European languages must necessarily be rather recent due to the comparatively short colonial history. Consequently, loans may be analysed in terms of their pragmatic and metapragmatic expressiveness in much the same way as CS events, perhaps they are even better analysed as instances of CS altogether.

It should not be left unmentioned that so-called ad-hoc loans have been described as an intermediate level, structurally as well as in terms of metapragmatic awareness (cf. Poplack and Meechan 1995). These are partially integrated expressions that are being used more or less spontaneously and therefore do not form part of either monolingual lexicon. Again, however, the diachronic dimension brings to light the overall gradience of the matter. Ad-hoc loans in this sense can be re-analyzed as CS situations with a high potential for usualization and sedimentation in the matrix lexicon, thus representing a middle ground between true CS and fully integrated loans, which points to the direction of diachronic development towards full integration. Arguably this potential is proportional to the length and complexity of the expression, so that morphemes or single-word expressions are more likely to undergo this development than syntactic structures (cf. Matras 2011 also discussed below).

With respect to the situation in Togo an analysis of the CS-borrowing-continuum may illustrate the aforementioned role of Ewe and French. In his analysis of loanword integration in Akebu (Niger-Kongo, Kwa) Koffi (2020: 12) remarks the following, also quoting Heine (1981):

---

15 For a discussion of an integrated approach see also Backus (2015: 21).

> The expansion and integration of loanwords from African lingua franca, Twi and Ewe has been reinforced by the role these languages have played in the colonial and post-colonial era, and as commercial and educational languages in Togo and Ghana. Concerning the loanwords of African origin, Bernd Heine (1968:131) [sic], notes that the Southern and Eastern Kwa (Central Togo) languages, borrowed mostly from Ewe, and their Western counterparts from Twi.

While there are traces of English and other European colonial languages of the region, French has had a comparatively minor influence despite its prevalence and official status. However, it does in fact occur in sociolinguistically relevant CS:

> Akebu speakers, namely Akebu elite or Akebu speakers who have attended school, and who tend to use French words as a code-switching. Moreover, some French loanwords are only used by Akebu speakers who live in urban areas and who are in touch with modern life. Relatively few French loanwords are used by the rural Akebu populations. (Koffi 2020: 10)

3.2 Structural positions for CS events and the relation to other contact phenomena

There is a distinction between intra- and extrasentential CS (the former is sometimes also referred to as code-mixing (Appel and Muysken 2005: 121; Auer 1999)) depending on whether it occurs on the lexical or phrasal level or at the sentence boundary. CS events are more likely at certain points in the structure than at others, they are subject to structural constraints. Poplack (1980) states linearity as a universal constraint: A switch may only occur at a point where it does not interrupt the surface constituent structure of the languages involved or where their respective phrase structure is identical.[16] Other authors (e.g. Di Sciullo et al. 1986; Appel and Muysken 2005: 124) assume dependency as a constraining factor, such as exemplified by case assignment as well as verb subcategorisation. If X governs Y, both constituents have to be taken from the same code. If an element is ungoverned such as exclamations, interjections, tags and most adverbs it may be taken from a different code. According to Appel and Muysken (2005: 124) there is ample evidence to support this claim, but they concede that we also find governed elements that are switched. Similar observations have been made with respect to loans, where the syntactic autonomy of an entity is likewise proportional to its borrowability (Matras 2011: 224). Rather than clear-cut cut-off points for switches

---

16 This highlights the linear aspect of CS as integration into a structural frame in contrast to the multi-dimensional view of translanguaging and its transcendent approach (cf. Appel and Muysken 2005).

that are universally valid we find tendencies or degrees of acceptability for switches in a given position.

Informed heavily by psycholinguistic findings the Matrix Language Frame Model (Myers-Scotton 1993a) has gained wide acceptance in CS research since the 1990s, largely on grounds of its usability for analyzing different CS situations involving various pairs of contact codes. The gist of the idea is that in every CS event one (matrix) language provides the morphosyntactic frame into which material from another (embedded) language can be inserted at certain points.

In this paper we align with the widely established view that one section of the repertoire, i.e. one language, is usually dominant in a CS situation and that this language provides the morphosyntactic frame in which material from another language can be embedded at certain points in the structure, which leads to restrictions in the linear order. It is the matrix language that licenses the intersections particularly for intrasentential switches. Although this presupposes that one language is dominant in a multilingual setting it seems feasible that speakers are equally competent in all languages involved in a given situation, which would blur the boundaries. Muysken (1995: 182, also cf. Muysken 2000), for instance, states more refined criteria for the identification of the dominant code, which also may prove helpful as a guideline for future research as proposed in this paper: If one language provides the main verb as the central grammatical unit of a sentence (see dependency constraints in intrasentential switches) and the speaker turn begins with elements of the same language, this counts as the matrix language.

Let us now turn to examples of language contact and CS in a specific Togolese context. In a comparative study of post-colonial contact scenarios involving genetically and structurally divergent languages Amuzu (2014) discovers interesting parallels. For instance, the integration of French verbs into Ewe/Gengbe in CS situations in Togo follows a similar pattern to that of English verbs into various matrix languages in Ghana. Both Ewe and Gengbe are closely related Gbe languages[17], which makes them ideal candidates for a cross-linguistic comparison of CS and the structural mechanisms that constrain the construction of multilingual chains of linguistic expressions from various sources. Amuzu (2014: 276) observes that in bilingual verb phrases only those verbs from either English or French are licensed that correspond neatly to their matrix language counterparts

---

17 As part of a dialect continuum these are morphosyntactically similar. While Essizewa (2007: 30, see also references therein) classes Gengbe (Mina) as a dialect of Ewe, Amuzu (2014: 251) points out that Gengbe has evolved amongst non-native speakers of Ewe.

in terms of argument structure. For instance, in contrast to CS from Ewe to English there are no double object constructions in CS from Gengbe to French. The following is thus possible because Ewe likewise allows double objects (Amuzu 2014: 276) as shown in (1).

(1) Ewe [Amuzu 2014: 276]
ne e **grant** srɔ̃-wo so much **liberty** la ne
if 2SG **grant** spouse-2SG so much **liberty** TOPIC if
'If you grant your spouse so much liberty'

Amuzu (2014: 276) explains this by the fact that English allows such structures and French does not. This means that abstract grammatical information is transferred from another language. Dependency as a relevant factor should therefore not be underestimated. To illustrate this Amuzu (2014: 280) states that verbs with obligatory adverbial complements may occur in Ewe[18]-English CS, because Ewe requires similar structures for corresponding verbs, where the deletion of the adverbial would likewise result in ungrammaticality, see (2a–b).

(2) CS Ewe-English [Amuzu 2014: 280]
a. *Fifia ya la, Blackstar **place** mí **firmly***
now EMPHATIC TOPIC Blackstars **place** 1PL **firmly**
*(on the map of world soccer).
on the map of world soccer
'Now the Blackstars have placed us firmly on the map of world soccer.'
b. *Kofi da atukpa *(ɖe kplɔ-a dzi)*
Kofi put bottle on table-DEFINITE TOPIC
'Kofi put (the) bottle on the table.'

Myers-Scotton and Jake (2013: 9) cite examples of CS from Ewe into French (cf. (3a–b)) from Amuzu (2011) to illustrate the role of infinitive verb forms integrated into different matrix languages in lieu of finite forms otherwise expected in these positions.

(3) CS Ewe-French [Myers-Scotton and Jake 2013: 9]
a. *e la **promettre** na wò be ...*
3SG POT **promise** DAT 2SG COMP
'He will promise you that ...'

---

[18] Examples are taken from the Anlo variety of Ewe.

b.
wo	mu	**concevoir**	be	nuɖe
3PL	NEG.AOR	**imagine**	COMP	something
tsa	e	la	s'accompagner.	
too	3SG	POT	3SG.REFL.accompany	

'They don't imagine that something else can accompany it.'

As a reason for such switches the authors point out that these non-finite switched elements "do not project information about syntactic and argument structure" and thus "better serve the speaker's intentions regarding semantic and pragmatic meaning intentions" (Myers-Scotton and Jake 2013: 1).

3.3 Sociolinguistic prerequisites for CS situations

Hakibou (2017: 54) lists several factors for the occurrence of CS events. Accordingly, CS fulfills a broad array of pragmatic and metapragmatic functions, each calling for a sociolinguistic investigation. The Markedness Model of language choice, which assumes that "as speakers come to recognize the different RO (rights and obligations)-sets possible in their community, they develop a sense of indexicality of code choices for these RO-sets" (Myers-Scotton 1993b: 88), provides a useful framework for this kind of investigation. One possibility to do sociolinguistic research on the relation between CS situation types and social indexicality is to examine one and the same pair of contact languages under variable sociolinguistic circumstances (Alfonzetti 2005). In a pilot study Nartey (1982) compares CS situations in various West African languages in contact with English in a post-colonial setting on the one hand and in Great Britain on the other hand. Guided by the idea that English is associated with different degrees of prestige in these sociocultural environments Nartey (1982) concludes that purely linguistic factors are insufficient to explain either the different structural constraints observed in CS or the different patterns of usage.

As stated in Section 1, contrary to the assumption that multilingual speakers have clearly bounded and separable linguistic systems, newer approaches rather postulate a holistic repertoire of expressions that speakers can draw on, which has fuzzy boundaries and is fed by multilingual sources. Domain specification in multilingual speakers is presumed to be triggered by the need to use specific forms for specific social and situational purposes. This presupposes that while monolingual speakers have implicit knowledge of the appropriateness of a given linguistic expression in a given situation, multilingual speakers also know when to select which code. If comparably similar sociopragmatically identifiable situations recur frequently enough, expressions from distinct subsections of the overall repertoire will be selected repeatedly, which may help building up what can then be dubbed "demarcation lines" between languages but may be more appropriately described as "activation of selectional mechanisms" (cf. Paradis 2004; Matras 2011: 225). In terms of the aforementioned relation between translanguaging and CS this view in fact allows for diachronic development from the former to the latter in that separable codes "crystallize" out of a joint repertoire, where each one may subsequently be charged with different types of indexicality.

In addition to the sociocultural or sociopolitical context in which CS takes place, age or generation membership and possibly other demographic factors may play a role in predicting how and where CS is likely to occur in the syntactic structures of a conversation. Alfonzetti (2005) provides some evidence for the assumption that for a given pair of contact languages we cannot generalize across contact situations that one and the same structural CS pattern will be encountered. Rather, extralinguistic factors exert their effect on the structure of CS patterns in various ways.

4 Speaker attitudes to language selection and usage

4.1 CS as metapragmatic positioning and stance-taking

Linguistic variables such as the occurrence of CS have no fixed meanings. Instead their interpretation depends on multiple factors including the recipient's social identity (cf. Labov 1963 for a pioneering study), the situative context and/or the topic of the conversation at hand (cf. Woolard 2006). In the light of the aforementioned multitude of influencing factors, however, it makes sense – here likewise following Woolard (2006: 73) – to speak of indexical fields of possible meanings. Rather than having rigid structures, indexical fields can change continuously according to the possible meanings contained within. Linguistic variation such as that observable in CS events lends itself to an examination in terms of such "an indexical system that embeds ideology in language" (Eckert 2008: 454). The "indexical values" of such variations "are part and parcel of the ideological work of society and vice-versa" (Eckert 2008: 465). Furthermore, each embedding of ideology in language also entails an act of stance-taking – a speaker's self-positioning.

> Durch den Prozess der sozialen Positionierung werden Hinweise auf soziale Einordnungsstrategien der Diskursakteure beobachtbar und beschreibbar. Die soziale Positionierung ist

also nicht nur ein interaktiver, sondern auch ein sozialer Prozess, in dem Individuen sich als Subjekte konstituieren und durch den Prozess der Bewertung sozialer "Objekte" Einstellungen, Werthaltungen und Ideologien zum Ausdruck bringen. (Porstner 2017: 28)[19]

Whereas Woolard (2006: 76) explicitly targets the "social-indexical effect" of CS, Spitzmüller (2013) highlights the social indexicality of signs used in language and other forms of communication in general without limiting himself to variation of expression or other specific linguistic phenomena. This notion refers to the "Fähigkeit sprachlicher Zeichen, soziale Werte, Akteurstypen und Lebensformen zu evozieren bzw. zu kontextualisieren"[20] (Spitzmüller 2013: 265).

It becomes clear that the indexicality of CS events can only be examined by way of a multi-layered model that transcends the pairwise mapping of a given CS event to a specific meaning. Amuzu (2015), for instance, assesses Ewe-English CS by means of combining the Matrix Language Frame Model and the Markedness Model. This way he integrates structural and sociolinguistic findings.

For the intent of the present paper we have to assume that if a Togolese speaker switches into either Ewe, French or German it always and inevitably carries ideological implications. An example of Kabiye-Ewe CS is given in (4) (Ewe in bold print).

(4) CS Kabiye-Ewe [Essizewa 2007: 34]
Lɛlɪyɔ́ **nýɔ́nu**-wáa nɛ **ɖekadze**-wáa po-wók-I
Now woman-PL and young.boy-PL they-go-PRESENT
kɔ́ŋsɛtɪ-náa yém.
concert-PL free
'Nowadays, teenagers go to concerts without problem (from their parents).'

Example (5) illustrates CS by a Kabiye speaker going to be interviewed in Lomé by Essizewa (2010: 32), who conducts the interview mainly in Kabiye. The speaker inquires about the time of the interview.

---

19 'Through the process of social positioning hints towards social indexing strategies on the part of discourse participants become observable and describable. Consequently, social positioning is not only an interactive, but also a social process, in which individuals set themselves up as subjects expressing attitudes, sets of values and ideologies by means of a process of assessing and evaluating social "objects".' [translation AJ]
20 'capacity of linguistic signs to evoke and contextualise social values, types of participants and ways of life' [translation JdB].

(5) CS Kabiye-French [Essizewa 2010: 32]
Kabiye speaker:
Dimanche   quelle   heure   *ŋ-goŋ*   ***yé?***
Sunday   which   hour   you-come INTERROGATIVE
'What time are you coming in Sunday?'
Interviewer:
***Dix-sept   heure**-waa   taa   mbiyo.*
seventeen   hour-PL   in   around
'Around five pm.'

However, interpreting the meaning of any CS event is all but simple. Spitzmüller (2013: 264) at least ascribes to the domain of language ideology the "Summe aller Werthaltungen, mit denen die sprachliche Wirklichkeit von sozialen Akteuren diskursiv konstruiert wird".[21] Taking this into account, it is difficult to imagine how the indexicality of a CS event could possibly be grasped completely without explicit knowledge of or even participation in this "linguistic reality". Furthermore, as we have already stated, only metalinguistic exchange about language variation can be classified metapragmatically.

For the purpose of data collection on site in Togo we therefore believe that interviews are the most appropriate method when it comes to unveiling language ideological ideas and conceptions prevalent among Togolese speakers with respect to metapragmatics. We seek to investigate whether CS constitutes or even enhances *enregisterment* and also to what extent speakers are aware of the usage of different codes. *Enregisterment* refers to "processes and practices whereby performable signs become recognized (and regrouped) as belonging to distinct, differentially valorized semiotic registers by a population" (Agha 2007: 81; also cf. Johnstone 2016).

The complexity of the procedures involved in stance taking in regards to a particular language usage is ideally represented by means of Spitzmüller's (2013) model of metapragmatic positioning (see Figure 1). At the same time this model provides a road map for the analysis of the social indexicality of specific instances of language usage.

---

21 'entirety of sets of values according to which linguistic reality is construed discursively by social participants' [translation AJ].

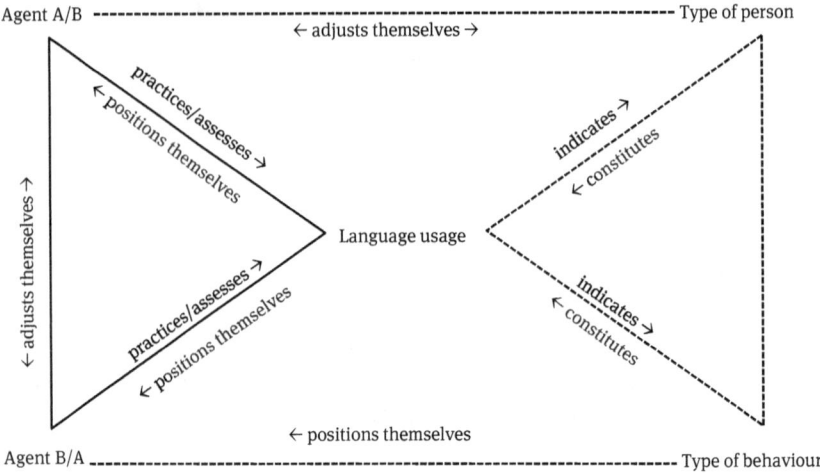

Figure 1: Spitzmüller's (2013) model of metapragmatic positioning.[22]

If we insert CS as language usage into the center of the model, several analytical pathways with respect to stance-taking spring to mind. Firstly, an interview may prove to be useful in eliciting metapragmatic statements about CS from Togolese conversation partners. The dashed lines in Figure 1 represent those meaning components associated with CS that are coded indexically, i.e. that are only interpretable with reference to knowledge of "linguistic reality" as stated above. More precisely it requires a more or less extralinguistic, social knowledge about the register that a particular instance of language usage refers to, or, as Romaine (2000: 21) puts it: "The concept of register is typically concerned with variation in language conditioned by uses rather than users and involves consideration of the situation or context of use, the purpose, subject matter, and content of the message, and the relationship between participants."

The various functions of a CS event can therefore not be fully grasped by merely describing its structural conditions. We intend to focus on metapragmatic statements in interviews in order to find out exactly how an "agent" (i.e. a discourse participant) indexes a type of person or behavior by means of a specific CS event, thereby taking a stance towards this type of person.

Assuming that switches are only licensed at certain points in the structure of a given matrix language and frequent CS events involving the same linguistic material result in the integration and sedimentation of forms similar to borrowing,

---

22 Translation JdB.

we can expect the emergence of distinct colonial varieties of those matrix languages. This concerns the accumulated effects of colonialism on the indigenous linguistic systems. By the same token, of course, one may ask how continuous CS has shaped and still shapes the varieties of European languages prevalent in the region (cf. Müller 2004).

4.2 Motivation for CS

While being subject to structural constraints, the motivation for CS stems from a multitude of social factors that manifest themselves inf discourse pragmatics (see Gumperz 1982; Malik 1994; Auer 1999). According to Gumperz (1982) CS is basically multifunctional, it operates on the level of social positioning as demonstrated in the categories "we-code" and "they-code" that he introduces, as well as on the level of situative discourse organization. Moreover, these are broad functional categories that call for a more fine-grained subdivision – for instance, social positioning with respect to the aforementioned type of person or behavior always entails further positioning toward any social group that is associated with this type in one way or another (cf. Spitzmüller's (2013) model of metapragmatic positioning in Section 4.1).

In order to illustrate this apparent multi-dimensionality of stance-taking, Agha (2005: 52) refers to a study undertaken by Alrabaa (1985) in Egypt. The study shows that young Egyptians both from the upper and the lower classes each demonstrate their linguistic affinity towards the respective other class by using different sets of second person personal pronouns, *inta/inti* (male/female informal) and *ḥadtritak/ḥadritik* (male/female formal) (Alrabaa 1985: 648). While members of the lower class are imagined by those of the upper class as being linguistically more informal, it is here that the formal forms of address are used more extensively. Conversely upper-class members, younger speakers in particular, tend to use the informal pronoun set in more settings regardless of age or class difference. In doing so, younger members of the upper class simultaneously set themselves apart from older members of the same class, which exemplifies the intricate social indexicality of this pronoun usage. Agha (2005: 56) concludes that this "multiplicity of role alignments simply reflects the multiplicity of engagements with real or imagined others that is characteristic of social life." In regards to CS such complex indexicality is more norm than exception.

Begum et al. (2016: 1644) list several pragmatic functions specifically attributable to CS: On the one hand there are social functions such as adaptation to a conversational partner, expression of formality, attitudes towards the hearer and change of social context. On the other hand, we find functions of discourse organizing such as marking of topic switches or expression of speaker identity. All these functions correlate with multiple structural means of expression.[23] It is paramount that any investigation of pragmatic functions associated with CS in a Togolese context must take into account all these and perhaps even identify further factors due to the specific historical and sociopolitical situation at hand.

Likewise medial differences may turn out to be insightful in this respect: We cannot neglect the possibility that CS presents itself in different ways – structurally as well as functionally – depending on whether it occurs in a real-time oral conversation, in formal contexts or in written electronic communication (cf. Begum et al. 2016).

5 Functions of CS in post-colonial Togo

5.1 Identity marking: the contrast between urban and rural

The following observation leaves no doubt that contact phenomena play a crucial role in everyday life in contemporary Togo with respect to social positioning: Essizewa (2010) notes a recent increase in CS and borrowing specifically from Ewe. He concludes that the reason for this is the growing consciousness of Kabiye speakers regarding the socioeconomic status of Ewe and consequently a heightened attractivity. We believe that this in fact constitutes a clear example of systematic stance-taking as outlined in the previous section. Essizewa (2010) provides evidence for the fact that among younger speakers of Kabiye in Togo there is a trend towards substituting traditional forms of address with those from Ewe [24], which is the dominant language in the south of the country, mainly in the capital region. This way French forms of address that have already been borrowed earlier indirectly find their way into Kabiye as well. Whereas the appropriate selection of forms of address has traditionally been highly relevant in Kabiye society, there is an ongoing shift in the direction of employing indirect forms from contact languages. These are mainly of French or Ewe origin. The former is exemplified by *frère* ('brother'), *soeur* ('sister'), or *mamani* ('mother'), while *fovi, fofovi, atavi* ('elder male cousin, paternal uncle') or *dadavi* ('elder sister/elder female cousin/paternal aunt') are taken from Ewe. In addition, a number of forms taken

---

23 We acknowledge that CS may not carry indexicality across the board. In some cases, lexical access difficulties may likewise trigger switches.
24 Essizewa (2010) includes Gengbe (Mina) here, which he classes as a variety of Ewe.

from Ewe can be traced back to either French (*tanti* ('aunt')) or English (*sista* ('sister') (Essizewa 2010: 38).

In addressing others, Kabiye traditionally differentiates between age brackets, particularly in early stages of a person's life, all based on a culturally specific series of initiations. Each of these initiations, which take place over a period of ten years, corresponds to an appropriate form of address for each stage reached by a speaker and also for the age group beyond. The passing of initiations has traditionally been marked by a change of name, of which the first is given and the second and third are chosen by an individual at ages 17 and 20, respectively (Essizewa 2010: 30–31).

This resembles the function of honorific person and number shifting in German or French pronouns of address, but in contrast to Kabiye rather than being associated with specific age brackets the category values in German are selected on grounds of showing respect towards a conversational partner. This in turn depends on a variety of factors, of which relative age is but one. Calques[25] such as given in (6) below, which show the use of plural prefixes by younger speakers on the model of French use of the 2.PL personal pronoun *vous* when addressing a single person of higher status, exemplify the change in Kabiye.

(6) Kabiye   [Essizewa 2010: 36]
    a.   *ḍadja/ḍoḍo*   *ŋ-liwaale*   *léé*   *ŋ-woki?*
         older.brother/older.sister   2SG-wake.up   where   2SG-go
         'How are you, where are you going?'
         is the older expression being replaced by:
    b.   *ḍadja/ḍoḍo*   *í-liwaale*   *léé*   *í-woki?*
         older.brother/older.sister   2PL-wake.up   where   2PL-go
         'How are you, where are you going?'

The shift that Essizewa (2010) describes has the effect that younger speakers of Kabiye in the south of Togo become increasingly dissociated from traditional customs when employing borrowed terms of address. Taking into account that outside of contact situations with Ewe the traditional terms of address are being used continually in Kabiye alongside the recently introduced ones, this indicates the highly charged interdependency between linguistic and cultural change in a multiethnic and multilingual population with a strong asymmetry of prestige.

---

25 See also Matras (2020: 254) for an overview of pattern replication.

As far as structure is concerned, it should be noted that a higher frequency of CS situations accelerates the usualization and sedimentation of borrowed expressions, particularly if these are short and morphosyntactically simple. Here we are obviously dealing with a borderline case on the diachronic path from ad-hoc loans as a subcategory of CS to expansion of the matrix language repertoire. This way frequent CS motivated by conscious social positioning within the same speaker group in similar contact situations leads to long-term linguistic change. With respect to the post-colonial situation of Togolese society in general the evidently recurrent CS scenario observed by Essizewa (2010) also shows an influence of French as the erstwhile colonial and now official national language. Presumably relevant expressions originating in French and reflecting the French categorization of forms of address had already been incorporated into Ewe when the Kabiye switches first occurred, but these also do not reflect the special honorific system grammaticalized in Kabiye. Consequently, when Kabiye speakers employ forms of address borrowed from French we may not speak of direct CS from Kabiye into French, but the former colonial language still exerts an indirect influence on the less prestigious Kabiye.

There is a noticeable orientation of Lomé-born descendants of Kabiye speakers (as well as of speakers of Kotokoli and other languages) toward Ewe, which signals their identification with an urban lifestyle. For Kabiye speakers Ewe becomes a means to affirm their urban identity and to distance themselves from their ethnic origins (Guyot 1997: 78, cited from Essizewa 2009: 62).

An opinion poll undertaken by Essizewa (2009) among native speakers of Kabiye attests an overall positive attitude towards both Ewe and their mother tongue, although for a variety of reasons: Whereas Kabiye is valued for the circumstance that it provides a sense of heritage and collective identity, Ewe is appreciated mainly for its association with modernity, connectedness with the outside world, progress and economic status. Command of Ewe is widely perceived as an additional social qualification that does not infringe on any established sense of identity.

Phenomena of this sort that manifest themselves in everyday language usage raise the question whether we are dealing with reverse cultural appropriation in the light of the mutual interferences between indigenous and European colonial languages. The current spread and increasing prestige of Ewe in modern, postcolonial Togo can be directly linked to the colonial history of the region, which harks back to political decisions of the late nineteenth century: Based on the discussion in Section 2 we assume that the attempts at codification and the actively fostered association of Ewe with the privileged class and last but not least the adoption of Ewe as the language of school instruction by the German colonial government have contributed largely to its present status despite the countermeasures of the French administration, which established French as the medium of instruction and disfavored the use of Ewe or other indigenous languages altogether, thereby provoking resentment (see Lawrance 2001: 531; also cf. Roberts 2011: 470). It should be noted in this context that amongst speakers of Kabiye there is a preference for the use of Ewe terms of address over those from French (Essizewa 2010: 42). We count this as a possible tendency for the use of Ewe as L2 as well as switches into Ewe to be valued higher than the use of French or switches into French. Further data on the CS behavior of speakers with different linguistic backgrounds will hopefully shed light on this issue.

As stated in Section 2, Ewe had attained the status of market language or lingua franca even in pre-colonial times mainly in southern Togo, where it enjoyed a wide distribution and with it a degree of dominance with respect to everyday conversation. Nevertheless, the lingering effect of the selection of Ewe as the chief medium of instruction in the school system by the German government should not be underestimated. Speakers were and still are conscious of the status associated with this social function and the enduring increase of prestige must be attributed to this at least partially, in the sense that said choice enhanced the increase.

We suggest that modern Ewe – more precisely the variety that has evolved under the circumstances described so far – can be characterized as a *secondary colonial language* understood as an indigenous language fostered by European administrations for the purpose of enforcing their own interests in a given colonial setting, which could and still can extend its reach and dominance in the region. The standardization and codification efforts with respect to Ewe helped to create an image of the language somewhat akin to that of the primary colonial languages in that its association with writing, education and upward mobility gained momentum and thus set it apart from other local languages. It is fueled by the lingering consequences of a colonial hegemony of a period long gone and it nowadays enjoys a status not unlike former European colonial languages in other post-colonial settings around the globe. This description is to be understood as a functional label for the dominant and most widely spoken language accessible to a majority of multilingual speakers[26] in Togo.

---

26 The term *multilingual* is understood here as having access to a complex repertoire paired with knowledge of which expression is appropriate in a given situation.

5.2 CS in the post-colonial classroom

As can be expected, CS plays an important role in school education in a post-colonial multilingual setting. In many post-colonial nations, the secondary and tertiary sector is still dominated by monolingual instruction, usually in English or another 'global language' (Milligan and Tikly 2016: 277)[27] such as French in Togo (Essizewa 2010: 30).

This can have far-reaching effects that go beyond the classroom. According to Gadet and Ludwig (2014: 21) normative French is taught in Togolese schools with 'severe discipline'. Example (7) underlines the complexities of language usage in modern Togo and the effect of focusing on normativity in language teaching. Here a middle-aged rural Ewe speaker uses French in a conversation with a fellow Ewe speaker while a German student well acquainted with both of them records the dialogue. Speaker A is a taxi driver, speaker B is a primary school teacher.

(7) [Gadet and Ludwig 2014: 21][28]
   A: *Ouais (…)* **docavitsotsodo émá** *eeehh.*
   'Yes (…) **intestinal.ulcer what.do.you.call.it** eeeh'
   B: *Ulcère*
   'ulcer'
   A: *Ulcère et … c'est n'est pas ulcère on l'appelle ẽẽ (…) Cette maladie qui coupe les-les …*
   'ulcer and … it's not ulcer what they call it (…) this illness that cuts the the …'
   B: *Les intestins*
   'the intestines'
   A: *Ouais ouais c'est pourquoi moi je crains de ça aussi (…) c'est pourquoi que je ne veux pas acheter le maïs **dans le marché** aussi c'est pourquoi que (…) cette année j'ai gagné un peu (…) **avec aide** de mon grand frère qui est en Europe aussi…*
   'Yes yes that's why I'm afraid of that, too (…) that's why I don't want to buy corn **on the market** that's why (…) this year I've earned a little money (…) **with the help** of my brother, who is also in Europe…'

---

[27] Quotation marks taken over from Milligan and Tikly (2016).
[28] Translation AJ.

CS (first line) in this example occurs alongside structural borrowings. The word *docavitsotsodo* is the name of an illness ('intestine ulcer', the topic of discussion here), for which the French expression is not known to the speaker. This circumstance is marked by *émá*, a demonstrative pronoun typically used in Ewe when a speaker searches for a word (Gadet and Ludwig 2014: 21). According to Gadet and Ludwig (2014: 21) the lack of (prenominal) articles in Ewe may explain the form *avec aide* instead of *avec l'aide* 'with the help', whereas the choice of preposition in the prepositional phrase *dans le marché* 'on the market' is a reflex of the corresponding locative postposition in Ewe shown in (8).

(8) [Gadet and Ludwig 2014: 21]
 Me   yi   asi-me
 1.SG go   market-in
 'I go to the market.'

Gadet and Ludwig (2014: 21) identify these and other features as cases of simplification as an avoidance strategy employed by speakers with limited secondary language teaching and access to a given normative prestige language when faced with norm uncertainty.

The education system of Togo prescribes French as the primary language of instruction on all levels from elementary to tertiary education. Ewe and Kabiye as majority languages are only used in primary schools (Kangni 2007: 91). We conjecture that the authorities disfavor multilingualism in the education system in general for the reason of adherence to older conceptions of the nation state as well as a sense of belonging to the francophone world. Hence the concept of monolingualism as a necessary unifying factor prevails in educational policy making, even though numerous studies show that, generally speaking, multilingualism is a resource rather than a hindrance in terms of learning outcome (cf. Kropp 2017 for an overview). It remains to be investigated, however, which attitudes students as well as teachers have towards the use of particular language codes in specific contexts.

In many post-colonial school classroom situations teachers find themselves challenged having to decide between adherence to prescriptions on the part of the education authorities on the one hand and matters of linguistic feasibility with respect to finding the right mixture of linguistic codes necessary to achieve the prescribed learning outcome on the other hand. In order to convey difficult subject matter most efficiently, they frequently revert to CS, thereby disregarding official requirements of monolingualism, the communicated rationale behind the latter being the envisaged provision of equal opportunities to all students regardless of their ethnic and linguistic heritage.

Taking into account differences in language competence among the students that form a cline of multilingualism, CS into a commonly understood code appears somewhat inevitable for the purpose of conveying the subject matter and making it equally understandable and also to warrant reliable organization of the curriculum (cf. Merrit et al. 1992; Moore 2002; Mokgwathi and Webb 2013). Ferguson (2003) also points out management of interpersonal relationships in the classroom as an important function brought about by CS into local languages. The result is a high degree of intrasituational language variation (Droste 2017).

While the conscious employment of CS has been in practice for a long time, it is in fact only recently that education authorities in post-colonial settings acknowledge the enormous advantage that is associated with the utilisation of CS to this end (see Ferguson 2003). Here another function of CS becomes apparent besides social positioning and stance-taking, namely the conscious and active overcoming of linguistic obstacles brought about by colonial rule in the first place. This type of CS, however, displays a reverse relation – rather than switching into high prestige languages, language teachers switch into numerous local languages with lower prestige. Because of CS from a single language into several we assume that in such situations utilitarian considerations outweigh functions of individual stance-taking.

Nevertheless, arguably a teacher's conscious decision in favor of a particular language itself carries social indexicality. As possible determining factors in this respect we may list the teacher's own native language, the respective majority language in the classroom and the location of the school. It can be assumed that all these factors are present simultaneously in a CS situation, but given different weight.

6 Concluding remarks: CS in Togo – outlook and research desiderata

In contemporary Togo CS mainly occurs in urban centres since they show the highest degree of linguistic diversity and likelihood of individual contact situations. One consequence of this is that people who return to their home regions after having spent long periods in a multilingual setting sometimes encounter difficulties due to the habituation process they have been exposed to brought about by frequent CS into mainly Ewe and French (cf. Essizewa 2010: 36). The difference becomes apparent particularly in interactions with older people that may have little experience with expressions from these languages.

If the array of languages or codes used in present day Togo is viewed in terms of a prestige hierarchy with European colonial languages mainly spoken in urban contexts at the upper end, widespread indigenous languages in the middle and local languages restricted in spread to rural areas at the bottom end, there is reason to believe that the languages on the low end of the hierarchy are in the dangerous process of becoming marginalised. Such a development is somewhat comparable to the interrelations between the German standard variety and the numerous dialects, where there is a noticeable decline in recent times of the traditional dialects and ongoing levelling towards the standard leading to the emergence of wider ranging regiolects. In the course of this process local features thus disappear due to increased mobility and multimedial communication (cf. Weiß 2005).

In the context of contemporary Togo CS can be expected not only into Ewe but also between local languages and the European languages German or French as representative codes of different colonial periods. German itself does not seem to have a significant function in post-colonial Togo outside of the specific academic context of language training and philology any longer. However, the observation that more than a hundred years after colonial authority has been ceded to France choosing career paths that involve German language training enjoys a high amount of popularity (see also Edjabou 2016 for a discussion of an enthusiasm for Germany in recent years) warrants an investigation of the indexical significance of German in and of itself including the possibility of CS into German in significant contexts, particularly in the light of far more common CS into Ewe or French. In this context a close investigation of Ewe CS and associated indexicality is furthermore highly relevant in terms of an on-going indirect legacy of the German occupation.

What we aim to find out is in which particular situations speakers are most likely to switch from less wide-spread local languages with low prestige into Ewe or else the primary colonial languages French and German.

We classify Ewe descriptively as a secondary colonial language on grounds of its sociolinguistic similarity to French and German in a post-colonial context in terms of associated functions and domains of usage. In addition to its pre-colonial status as a domain-specific lingua franca with a considerable range among the multiethnic and multilingual population of the region it could gain prestige through being established as the language of the colonial elite by the German administration[29]. Furthermore, we assume that the reason it maintains this status to this day lies in the comparatively lower popularity of French and consequently a lingering sense of glorification of the previous colonial rule, at least to some degree. However, a closer look is also necessary at the role of West African or even specifically Togolese varieties of French in terms of their sociolinguistic status and metapragmatic functions in contrast to that of the erstwhile colonial power itself.

All functions of CS must be listed and analyzed with respect to the specific context of Togo. Research on site should therefore be guided by questions such as the following: To what extent are speakers aware of CS? What is the respective indexicality of CS events? Do speakers perceive a switched expression as the "neutral" standard or as an indexical form? Does a frequently switched form necessarily become a borrowed expression and, if so, does it retain or alter its indexicality? In carrying out field work along these lines in order to avoid unwanted effects such as the observer paradox, we as researchers have to be prepared to also evaluate our own linguistic practices.

At the same time, we need to investigate how all these factors manifest themselves structurally and whether any predictions made by models of language contact are borne out in the peculiar and complex post-colonial situation encountered in Togo today. Once we have gained more insight, two further avenues of research present themselves immediately: Firstly, one may compare CS between specific language pairs, where one code is a local language and the other either a primary or a secondary colonial language and secondly it could be worthwhile to explore the degree of such differences depending on whether CS occurs in Togo itself or among Togolese expatriates elsewhere in the German speaking or francophone world, respectively.

Based on the assumption that CS between languages with a strong asymmetry in prestige is characterized by indexicality, identity-building and we-group constitution to a greater extent in a post-colonial context than elsewhere, a comparative study of CS between different sets of languages in Togo may help to evaluate prestige as a potentially measurable contributing factor. This possibly reveals more about the motivation for CS in specific situations and pragmatic effects brought about by it.

---

[29] In Togo, only 9 % of the children received school education during the colonial period and only a fraction was instructed in German (Speitkamp 2014: 101).

Abbreviations

AOR	aorist
CS	code-switching
COMP	complementizer
DAT	dative
NEG	negative
PL	plural
POT	potential
REFL	reflexive
SG	singular

References

Agha, Asif. 2005. Voice, footing, enregisterment. *Journal of Linguistic Anthropology* 15(1). 38–59.
Agha, Asif. 2007. *Language and social relations*. Cambridge: Cambridge University Press.
Alfonzetti, Giovanna. 2005. Intergenerational variation in code switching. Some remarks. *Rivista di Linguistica* 17. 93–112.
Alrabaa, Sami. 1985. The use of address pronouns by Egyptian adults. *Journal of Pragmatics* 9(5). 645–657.
Amuzu, Evershed Kwasi. 2011. *Ewe contact database (unpublished corpus)*. University of Ghana, Legon.
Amuzu, Evershed Kwasi. 2014. Comparative study of bilingual verb phrases in Ewe-English and Gengbe-French codeswitching. *Journal of language contact* 7. 250–287.
Amuzu, Evershed Kwasi. 2015. Combining the Markedness Model and the Matrix Language Frame Model in analysing bilingual speech. In Gerald Stell & Kofi Yakpo (eds.), *Codeswitching between structural and sociolinguistic perspectives*, 85–114. Berlin: de Gruyter.
Amuzu, Evershed Kwasi & John Victor Singler. 2014. Code-switching in West Africa. *International Journal of Bilingualism* 18. 329–345.
Appel, René & Pieter Muysken. 2005. *Language contact and bilingualism*. Amsterdam: Amsterdam University Press.
Auer, Peter (ed.). 1999. *Code-switching in conversation. Language, interaction and identity*. London: Routledge.
Backus, Ad. 2015. A usage-based approach to code-switching: The need for reconciling structure and function. In Gerald Stell & Kofi Yakpo (eds.), *Code-switching between structural and sociolinguistic perspectives*, 19–38. Berlin: de Gruyter.
Begum, Rafiya, Kalika Bali, Monojit Choudhury, Koustav Rudra & Niloy Ganguly. 2016. Functions of code-switching in tweets: An annotation scheme and some initial experiments. In Nicoletta Calzolari, Khalid Choukri, Thierry Declerck, Sara Goggi, Marko Grobelnik, Bente Maegaard, Joseph Mariani, Helene Mazo, Asuncion Moreno, Jan Odijk & Stelios Piperidis (eds.), *Proceedings of the tenth international conference on language resources and evaluation (LREC'16)*, 1644–1650. Paris: European Language Resources Association (ELRA).

Berman, Bruce J. 1998. Ethnicity, patronage and the African state: the politics of uncivil nationalism. *African Affairs* 97. 305–341.

Clyne, Michael. 2003. *Dynamics of language contact*. Cambridge: Cambridge University Press.

Dewein, Barbara, Stefan Engelberg, Susanne Hackmack, Wolfram Karg, Birte Kellermeier-Rehbein, Peter Muhlhäusler, Daniel Schmidt-Brücken, Christina Schneemann, Doris Stolberg, Thomas Stolz & Ingo H. Warnke. 2012. Forschungsgruppe Koloniallinguistik: Profil – Programmatik – Projekte. *Zeitschrift für germanistische Linguistik* 40(2). 242–249.

Di Sciullo, Anne-Marie, Pieter Muysken & Rajendra Singh. 1986. Government and code-mixing. *Journal of Linguistics* 22. 1–24.

Droste, Pepe. 2017. 'Enregisterment' aus praxisorientierter Perspektive: Der Fall narrativ inszenierter Kontrastierungen von Varietätengebrauch. *Arbeitspapierreihe Sprache und Interaktion (SpIn)* 78.

Eberhard, David M., Gary F. Simons & Charles D. Fennig (eds.). 2019. *Ethnologue: languages of the World*. 22nd edition. Dallas: SIL International.

Eckert, Penelope. 2008. Variation and the indexical field. *Journal of Sociolinguistics* 12(4). 453–47.

Edjabou, Aqtime Gnouleleng. 2016. "Nos amis les Allemands": Zum Diskurs der aktuellen Deutschland-Begeisterung in Togo. *Journal for Discourse Studies* 3. 265–280.

Essizewa, Komlan Essowe. 2007. Language contact phenomena in Togo: A case study of Kabiye-Ewe codeswitching. In Doris L. Payne & Jaime Peña (eds.), *Selected Proceedings of the 37th Annual Conference on African Linguistics*, 30–42. Somerville, MA: Cascadilla Proceedings Project.

Essizewa, Komlan Essowe. 2009. The vitality of Kabiye in Togo. *Africa Spectrum* 44. 53–76.

Essizewa, Komlan Essowe. 2010. Forms of address in Kabiye: A shift to borrowing terms of address among younger speakers in Togo. *Journal of Asian and African Studies* 80. 27–46.

Ferguson, Gibson. 2003. Classroom code-switching in post-colonial contexts, functions, attitudes and policies. In Sinfree Makoni & Ulrike H. Meinhof (eds.), *Africa and applied linguistics. AILA Volume Review 16*, 38–51. Amsterdam: John Benjamins.

Fischer, Magnus, Andreas Jäger, Carolin Patzelt & Ingo H. Warnke. this volume. Fluid registers and fixed language concepts in postcolonial spaces.

Gadet, Francoise & Ralph Ludwig. 2014. Introduction: French language(s) in contact worldwide – history, space, system, and other ecological parameters. *Journal of Language Contact* 7. 3–35.

García, Ofelia & Wei Li. 2013. *Translanguaging: Language, bilingualism and education*. Basingstoke: Palgrave Macmillan.

Good, Jeff & Michael Cysouw. 2013. Languoid, doculect, and glossonym: Formalizing the notion 'Language'. *Language Documentation and Conservation* 7. 331–359.

Grosjean, François. 1982. *Life with two languages: An introduction to bilingualism*. Cambridge: Harvard University Press.

Gumperz, John Joseph. 1982. *Discourse strategies*. Cambridge: Cambridge University Press.

Guyot, David. 1997. Plurilinguissme et métissage: Le cas des métis du Togo. *International Journal of the Sociology of Language* 128. 73–93.

Hakibou, Abdulaye. 2017. Borrowing and code-switching as linguistic phenomena in a multilingual community: The case study of Baatɔnum (Bariba), French and English in the northeastern border of Benin. *Journal of Humanities and Social Science* 22. 22–58.

Haspelmath, Martin. 2009. Lexical borrowing: concepts and issues. In Martin Haspelmath & Uri Tadmor (eds.), *Loanwords in the world's languages: A comparative handbook*, 35–54. Berlin: De Gruyter.

Haugen, Einar. 1953. *The Norwegian language in America: a study in bilingual behavior*. Philadelphia: University of Pennsylvania Press.

Heine, Bernd. 1981. Les langues résiduelles du Togo. In Perrot, Jean (ed.), *Les langues dans le monde ancien et moderne, Afrique Subsaharienne, Pidgins et Créoles texte*, 119–122. Edition du CNRS.

Johnstone, Barbara. 2016. Enregisterment: How linguistic items become linked with ways of speaking. *Language and Linguistics Compass* 10. 632–643.

Kangni, John Togbé. 2007. *Fremdsprache Deutsch in Togo und ihre Funktion im togolesischen Erziehungs- und Bildungssystem*. Universität Freiburg dissertation. https://phfr.bsz-bw.de/frontdoor/deliver/index/docId/23/file/Diss.06.04.07.pdf (checked 05/23/21).

Kawulich, Barbara B. 2005. Participant observation as a data collection method. *Forum Qualitative Sozialforschung / Forum: Qualitative Social Research* 6(2). https://www.qualitative-research.net/index.php/fqs/article/view/466/996 (checked 12/09/22).

Kelechukwu, Ihemere. 2016. Igbo-English intrasentential codeswitching and the Matrix Language Frame model. In Doris L. Payne, Sara Pacchiarotti & Mokaya Bosire (eds.), *Diversity in African languages: Selected papers from the 46th Annual Conference on African Linguistics*, 539–559. Berlin: Language Science Press.

Koffi, Yao. 2020. *Integration and morphology of loanwords in Akebu*. Dallas: SIL International.

Kropp, Amina. 2017. (Herkunftsbedingte) Mehrsprachigkeit als Ressource? Ressourcenorientierung und -management im schulischen FSU. In Tina Ambrosch-Baroua, Amina Kropp & Johannes Müller-Lancé (eds.), *Mehrsprachigkeit und Ökonomie*, 107–130. München: Open Publishing Ludwig-Maximilians-Universität.

Labov, William. 1963. The social motivation of a sound change. *Word* 18. 1–42.

Lawrance, Benjamin N. 2001. Language between powers, powers between languages – further discussion of education and policy in Togoland under the French mandate, 1919-1945. *Cahiers d'études africaines* 41(163-164). 517–539.

Lindenfelser, Siegwalt. 2021. *Kreolsprache Unserdeutsch. Genese und Geschichte einer kolonialen Kontaktvarietät*. Berlin & Boston: de Gruyter.

Malik, Lalita. 1994. *Sociolinguistics: A study of codeswitching*. New Delhi: Anmol.

Marshall, Catherine & Gretchen B. Rossman. 1989. *Designing qualitative research*. Newbury Park, CA: Sage.

Matras, Yaron. 2020. *Language contact*. Cambridge: Cambridge University Press.

Matras, Yaron. 2011. Universals of structural borrowing. In Peter Siemund (ed.), *Linguistic universals and language variation*, 200–229. Berlin: De Gruyter.

Matras, Yaron & Jeanette Sakel. 2007. *Grammatical borrowing in cross-linguistic perspective*. Berlin: De Gruyter.

Merrit, Marilyn, Ailie Cleghorn, Jared O. Abagi & Grace Bunyi. 1992. Socialising multilingualism: Determinants of codeswitching in Kenyan primary classrooms. In Carol M. Eastman (ed.), *Codeswitching*, 103–124. Clevedon: Multilingual Matters.

Milligan, Lizzy O. & Leon Tikly. 2016. English as a medium of instruction in postcolonial contexts: moving the debate forward. *Comparative Education* 52(3). 277–280.

Mokgwathi, Tsaona & Vic Webb. 2013. The educational effects of code-switching in the classroom – benefits and setbacks: A case of selected senior secondary schools in Botswana. *Language matters* 44. 108–125.

Moore, Danièle. 2002. Code-switching and learning in the classroom. *International Journal of Bilingual Education and Bilingualism* 5. 279–293.
Müller, Natascha. 2004. Afrikanisches Französisch oder Französisch in Afrika. Das Beispiel Togo. *Romanische Forschungen* 116. 155–182.
Muysken, Pieter. 1995. Code-switching and grammatical theory. In Lesley Milroy & Pieter Muysken (eds.), *One speaker, two languages: Crossdisciplinary perspectives on code-switching*, 177–198. Cambridge: Cambridge University Press.
Muysken, Pieter. 2000. *Bilingual speech: A typology of code-mixing*. Cambridge: Cambridge University Press.
Myers-Scotton, Carol. 1993a. *Duelling languages: Grammatical structure in codeswitching*. Oxford: At the Clarendon Press.
Myers-Scotton, Carol. 1993b. *Social motivations for code-switching: Evidence from Africa*. Oxford: At the Clarendon Press.
Myers-Scotton, Carol & Janice L. Jake. 2013. Nonfinite verbs and negotiating bilingualism in codeswitching: Implications for a language production model. *Bilingualism: Language and Cognition* 17(1). 511–525.
Nartey, Jonas. 1982. Code-switching, interference or faddism? Language use among educated Ghanians. *Anthropological Linguistics* 2. 183–192.
Paradis, Michel. 2004. *A neurolinguistic theory of bilingualism*. Amsterdam: Benjamins.
Poplack, Shana. 1980. Sometimes I'll start a sentence in Spanish y termino en español: Toward a typology of code-switching. *Linguistics* 18. 581–618.
Poplack, Shana & Marjory Meechan. 1995. Patterns of language mixture: Nominal structure in Wolof-French and Fongbe-French bilingual discourse. In Pieter Muysken, & Lesley Milroy (eds.), *One speaker, two languages: Crossdisciplinary perspectives on code-switching*, 199–232. Cambridge: Cambridge University Press.
Porstner, Ilse. 2017. Subjektpositionen in der postkolonialen Gesellschaft: Die diskursive Konstruktion von Selbstbildern junger Migrantinnen und Migranten. *Wiener Linguistische Gazette (WLG)* 81. 19–45.
Rampton, Ben. 2011. From 'multiethnic adolescent heteroglossia' to 'contemporary urban vernaculars'. *Language and Communication* 31(4). 276–294.
Romaine, Suzanne. 2000. *Language in society. An introduction to sociolinguistics*. New York: Oxford University Press.
Roberts, David. 2011. The development of written Kabiye and its status as one of the "national" languages of Togo. In Ochieng Orwenjo & Obiero Ogone (eds.), *Language and politics In Africa: Contemporary issues and critical perspectives*, 468–494. Newcastle-on-Tyne: Cambridge Scholars Publishing.
Schlegel, J.B. 1856. *Aongla-Primer*. Stuttgart: Steinkopf.
Schlegel, J. B. 1857. *Schlüssel zur Ewe-Sprache: dargeboten in den grammatischen Grundzügen des Aṅlo-Dialekts derselben, mit Wörtersammlung nebst einer Sammlung von Sprüchwörtern und einigen Fabeln der Eingebornen*. Bremen: Valett.
Shakib, Mohammad Khosravi. 2011. The position of language in development of colonization. *Journal of Languages and Culture* 2(7). 117–123.
Silverstein, Michael. 1979. Language structure and linguistic ideology. In Paul R. Cline, William Hanks & Carol Hofbauer (eds.), *The elements: A parasession on linguistic units and levels*, 193–247. Chicago: Chicago Linguistic Society.
Sokolowsky, Celia. 2004. *Sprachenpolitik des deutschen Kolonialismus: Deutschunterricht als Mittel imperialer Herrschaftssicherung in Togo (1884–1914)*. Hannover: Ibidem.

Speitkamp, Winfried. 2014. *Deutsche Kolonialgeschichte*. Stuttgart: Reclam.
Spitzmüller, Jürgen. 2013. Metapragmatik, Indexikalität, soziale Registrierung: Zur diskursiven Konstruktion sprachideologischer Positionen. *Beltz Juventa / Zeitschrift für Diskursforschung* 3. 263–287.
Stickrodt, Silke. 2001. A neglected source for the history of Little Popo: the Thomas Miles papers ca. 1789–1796. *History in Africa* 28. 293–330.
Stolberg, Doris. 2015. German in the Pacific: Language policy and language planning. In Daniel Schmidt-Brücken, Susanne Schuster, Thomas Stolz, Ingo H. Warnke & Marina Wienberg (eds.), *Koloniallinguistik. Sprache in kolonialen Kontexten*, 317–362. Berlin: de Gruyter.
Thomason, Sarah G. 2001. *Language contact: An introduction*. Washington: Georgetown University Press.
Thomason, Sarah G. & Terrence Kaufman. 1988. *Language contact, creolization, and genetic linguistics*. Berkeley: University of California Press.
Weinreich, Uriel. 1968 [1953]. *Languages in contact*. The Hague: Mouton.
Weiß, Helmut. 2005. Von den vier Lebensaltern einer Standardsprache: Zur Rolle von Spracherwerb und Medialität. *Deutsche Sprache* 4. 289–307.
Westermann, Diedrich. 1906. *Wörterbuch der Ewe-Sprache*. Berlin: Reimer.
Westermann, Diedrich. 1907. *Grammatik der Ewe-Sprache*. Berlin: Reimer.
Woolard, Kathryn Ann. 2006. Codeswitching. In Alessandro Duranti (ed.), *A Companion to Linguistic Anthropology (Blackwell Companions to Anthropology 1)*, 73–94. Malden, Oxford & Carlton: Blackwell Publishing Ltd.
Yayoh, Wilson K. .2015. German rule in colonial Ewedome (Ghana), 1890-1914. *African Notes* 39. 129–145.
Yigbe, Dotsé. 2017. Is Togo a permanent Model Colony? In Klaus Mühlhahn (ed.), *The cultural legacy of the German rule*, 97–111. Berlin: De Gruyter Oldenbourg.

Index of Authors

Aalberse, Suzanne. P. 137
Abd-el-Jawad, Hassan R. 112
Aboh, Enoch O. 206
Abu-Manga, Al-Amin 340
Achebe, Chinua 91
Agha, Asif 440, 495, 497
Ahearn, Laura. M. 394
Ahrens, Carolin 173
Akielewicz, Józef 5, 15ff., 21ff., 32, 34, 46, 55f., 58, 63, 66, 70, 76, 81
Al Sheshani, Ala 113, 115, 118f., 121ff., 128ff.
Alagozlu, Nuray 112
Alavi, Bozorg 334
Albalá Hernández, Paloma 328
Alfonzetti, Giovanna 492f.
Allières, Jacques 161
Alomoush, Omar Ibrahim 112, 114f.
Alrabaa, Sami 497
Al-Shawashreh, Ekab 132f.
Al-Wer, Enam 112ff., 125, 130, 132, 136
Ambrazas, Vytautas 33
Ammon, Ulrich 441f.
Amuzu, Evershed Kwasi 483, 490f., 494
Anchimbe, Eric A 92
Anderson, Benedict 378
Anderson, John M. 199
Andronov, M. S. 347f.
Angelo, Denise 206
Ansaldo, Umberto 206
Appadurai, Arjun 378
Appel, René 489
Aquilina, Joseph 167, 169, 171
Arkadiev, Peter 25
Arnaut, Karel 379
Ashton, E. O. 340
Atkinson, Louise 403, 406
Auer, Peter 481, 489, 497
Aurrekoetxea, Gotzon 159
Ayafor, Miriam 205
Aye, Daw Khin Khin 223f., 233
Azzopardi-Alexander, Marie 174

Backus, Ad 380, 394, 446, 450, 488
Baggioni, Daniel 463ff.

Bağrıaçık, Metin 112
Baker, Beverley 455
Baker, Philip 216f.
Bakker, Dik 69
Bakker, Peter 154
Bamgbose, Ayo 102
Baptista, Marlyse 213
Barbare, Dzidra 12f., 27f.
Bartens, Angela 94, 206ff.
Bashir, Elena 344
Bassiouney, Reem 116
Batac, Monica Anne 375
Bausani, Alessandro 330
Baxter, Alan N. 214
Beattie, Geoffrey 430
Begum, Rafiya 497f.
Berger, Hermann 349
Bergmane, Anna 11
Berman, Bruce J. 483
Bernaisch, Tobias 94
Berneker, Erich 36f., 45f.
Bhabha, Homi 428, 448
Bhambra, Guminder K. 374
Bhatia, Tej K. 345f.
Bhattacharya, Kakali 375
Bhattacharyya, Gargi 371
Biagui, Noël Bernard 214
Biber, Douglas 4
Biberauer, Theresa 209
Bickel, Balthasar 250
Bischoff, Alexander 390
Bittner, Maximilian 335
Blackledge, Adrian 380, 407, 411, 449
Blair, David 452
Blevins, Juliette 249, 281
Blinkena, Aina 11
Blinkena, Anna 69f., 74
Blokland, Tala 379, 428
Blommaert, Jan 379f., 394, 439, 446, 448, 450
Boas, Franz 203
Bollée, Annegret 216
Bonaparte, Louis-Lucien 146
Boretzky, Norbert 338

https://doi.org/10.1515/9783111323756-012

Borg, Albert 174
Boumans, Louis 129
Bovingdon, Roderick 168ff.
Bradley, David 453
Bradley, Jessica 403, 406
Bradley, Maya 453
Brato, Thorsten 98
Brear, Michelle R. 376
Brendemoen, Bernt 335
Brincat, Joseph M. 168ff., 172, 183
Broca, Paul 161
Brooks, Ethel 376
Brubaker, Rogers 373, 378, 427
Bruyn, Adrienne 206
Bugenhagen, Robert D. 132
Bührig, Kristin 390
Bukšs, M. 14, 16
Bürki, Yvette 446, 448
Burridge, Kate 92
Busch, Brigitte 380, 394, 403

Cadier, Linda 379, 394
Calabrese, Andrea 249
Callies, Marcus 92, 95, 97, 102, 104f.
Calvet, Louis Jean 443
Campbell, James 430
Cardona, George 346
Cardoso, Hugo C. 214
Carpooran, Arnaud 465, 469
Casamancese Creole 214
Casenave-Harigile, Junes 149
Čéplö, Slavomír 168ff., 176, 178
Chafe, Wallace 4
Chamoreau, Claudine 5
Chan, Thomas 96f.
Chechuro, Ilia Y. 112
Cheshire, Jenny 440
Chinuk Wawa 203f., 226
Chirikba, Viacheslav A. 112, 358
Chumakina, Marina 112
Cibuļs, Juris 63
Ciérbide Martirena, Ricardo 151
Clements, Clancy J. 214f.
Clements, G. N. 250
Clyne, Michael 481
Coghill, Eleanor 341
Cohen, Robin 378

Collins, Peter 452
Colot, Serge 216, 218, 222
Comrie, Bernard 112, 166, 169f.
Cowell, Mark W. 340
Cox, Felicity 452f.
Creese, Angela 380, 407, 411, 449
Creissels, Denis 196, 234
Croft, William 199
Crowley, Terry 198
Cysouw, Michael 482

Daija, Pauls 17
Dalli, Angelo 168ff.
Davies, Mark 98
de Sousa Santos, B. 389
Degani, Marta 92, 97
den Besten, Hans 209
Deuber, Dagmar 101
Deumert, Ana 395, 413
Devonish, Hubert 205, 208
Dewein, Barbara 478
Di Sciullo, Anne-Marie 489
Diagne, Souleymane Bachir 443
Dizdari, Tahir N. 332f.
Dodykhudoeva, Leila R. 344
Donakey, Andrea 384
Donaldson, Bruce C. 209f.
Douglass, Mike 379
Droste, Pepe 504
Durrleman, Stephanie 206
Dweik, Bader S. 112, 114

Eades, Diana 453
Eberhard, David M. 482f.
Eckert, Penelope 52, 478, 493
Eckert, Rainer 52
Edelman, D.I. 344
Edjabou, Aqtime Gnouleleng 444, 485, 505
Eichinger, Ludwig M 441
Eisen, Elad 281, 287
Eisenlohr, Patrick 464, 466
Elbert, Samuel H. 227
Elfenbein, Josef 347
El-Yasin, Mohammed Khalid 132
Emirbayer, Mustafa 394
Endzelin, J. 45, 50, 57, 62
Endzelīns, Janis 27

Engelberg, Stefan 5
Erhart, Sabine 216
Eriksen, Thomas Hylland 463, 470
Ersen-Rasch, Margarete I. 335
Escure, Geneviève 205
Essizewa, Komlan Essowe 490, 494f., 498ff., 504
Eyuboğlu, İsmet Zeki 337

Fa d'Ambô 214
Fabri, Ray 171f., 174
Fanselow, Gisbert 32f.
Faraclas, Nicolas 100, 206, 208
Farquharson, Joseph T. 206
Fattier, Dominique 216
Feinmann, Diego 196
Fenech, Edward 168, 170, 187
Ferguson, Gibson 504
Féry, Caroline 32f.
Fiedler, Astrid 102, 104
Field, Andy 185f.
Field, Fredric 166
Finney, Malcolm Awadajin 206
Finzel, Anna 96
Fischer, Magnus 479
Fischer, Wolfdietrich 333, 335, 340, 353
Florenciano, Lloret 211ff.
Flubacher, Mi-Cha 403
Forker, Diana 112, 139
Fragner, Bert G. 331

Gadet, Francoise 502f.
Gaibrois, Claudine 394
Gaiser, Leonie 383, 390
García, Ofelia 380, 446, 480
Gardner-Chloros, Penelope 112
Garibay, Cecilia 395
Gatt, Albert 172, 176
Gibbs, Raymond W. Jr. 102, 104
Gibson, Kean 205, 208
Gilroy, Paul 379, 430
Glick Schiller, Nina 379
Goilo, E. R. 211f.
Good, Jeff 135, 206, 482
Gordon, Matthew K. 254
Grant, Anthony 94, 203, 226, 338, 341, 357
Grawunder, Sven 286

Green, Lisa 205
Green, Melanie 205
Greene, Laurie A. 205
Grosjean, François 486
Grossman, Eitan 255
Guérin, Françoise 138
Güldemann, Tom 123
Gumperz, John Joseph 487, 497
Guyot, David 500

Haase, Martin 145f., 150, 154f., 158f., 161
Hackert, Stephanie 205, 233
Haddad, Mohanna 115
Hagège, Claude 181, 183
Hagemeijer, Tjerk 214
Haig, Geoffrey 118, 123, 136, 286, 341
Hakibou, Abdulaye 492
Hall, Stuart 374, 378, 428
Hall, Suzanne 379
Harder, Christoph 9f., 12f., 18f., 39, 43, 46f., 55, 62f.
Harris, Salome 458
Haspelmath, Martin 165f., 196, 201, 228, 232, 250, 252, 330, 486f.
Haugen, Einar 481
Heine, Bernd 332, 488f.
Hekking, Ewald 69, 166
Heller, Monica 379, 448
Hellwig, Birgit 341
Helmbrecht, Johannes 200
Herin, Bruno 113, 117f., 120, 125, 129f., 132, 136
Hesselberg, Heinrich 19, 43f., 46f., 55
Heugh, Kathleen A. 378, 459f., 460
Heynen, Nik 375
Hickey, Raymond 94
Hinrichs, Lars 445f.
Hober, Nicole 328
Hockett, Charles F. 282
Hofling, Charles Andrew 201
Höhlig, Monika 112
Holbrook, David Joseph 208
Holmes, Bernadette 407
Holmwood, John 374
Holvoet, Axel 53, 61f., 67
Honkanen, Mirka 100ff., 105
Horn, Paul 334, 336

Hornberger, Nancy H. 393
Huber, Magnus 206, 234
Hudelson, Patricia 390
Hudson, Joyce 207
Huerta Migus, Laura 395
Hüning, Matthias 465, 468
Hwa, Yen Siew 430
Hyman, Larry M. 249, 253f.

Intumbo, Incanha 214
Ivanova-Sullivan, Tanya 137

Jahani, Carina 343f.
Jaimoukha, Amjad 114, 117
Jake, Janice L. 491f.
Jansone, Ilga 14
Jean-Louis, Loïc 216, 218ff.
Jēgers, B. 12f., 68
Jennings, Marilee 395
Jeschull, Liane 135
Johanson, Lars 112, 335
Johnson, David Cassels 393
Johnson, Eric J. 393
Johnson, Mark 91, 97
Johnstone, Barbara 495
Jones, Russell 351ff.
Joppke, Christian 459
Jordan, Sabine 11
Jørgensen, J. Normann 380, 446, 449f.
Joseph, Cynthia 375
Jowitt, David 100, 104
Judge, Anne 443, 464

Kailani, Wasfi 112, 115
Kangni, John Togbé 484f., 503
Kantola, Ismo 422
Karasaev, A. T. 116
Karatsareas, Petros 411
Karulis, Konstantīns 11ff.
Kaufman, Terrence 481, 146
Kawulich, Barbara B. 482
Kelechukwu, Ihemere 486
Kelly, Michael 370, 407
Kelly-Holmes, Helen 395
Kerfoot, Caroline 378
Kerswill, Paul 380
Keshet, Yael 394

Khalidovna, Petimat Al'murzaeva 122, 138
Khalilov, Madžid Š. 112
Khubchandani, Lachman M. 346
Kieffer, Charles M. 344
Kiparsky, Paul 251
Kirkpatrick, Andy 94
Koffi, Yao 488f.
Kolbuszewski, Stanisław Franciszek 14
Komen, Erwin R. 113, 116, 120f., 124, 132
König, Ekkehard 252
Koptjevskaja-Tamm, Maria 341
Korn, Agnes 343f.
Kossowski, Tomasz 15, 54
Koul, Omkar N. 346
Kouwenberg, Silvia 209, 211
Kövecses, Zoltan 92, 97
Kperogi, Farooq A. 104
Krämer, Philipp 465, 468
Krause, Erich-Dieter 352
Kriegel, Sibylle 216f., 465
Kristiansen, Gitte 92
Kristovska, Ineta 15
Kutscher, Silvia 112

Labov, William 446, 493
Ladefoged, Peter 253
Ladouceur, Audrey 470
Lakoff, George 91, 97, 103
Lambert, James 96
Landmann, Angelika 332
Lang, Jürgen 213
Langlotz, Andreas 102
Lauffer, Pierre 212
Launitz, Christian Friedrich 5, 7, 12, 16ff., 23,
    29, 34, 40, 46, 59, 68, 70, 80f.
Lawrance, Benjamin N. 484, 501
Lee, Jamie Shinhee 105
Lefebvre, Henri 379
Léglise, Isabelle 5, 440, 446ff.
Leikuma, Lidija 18, 53, 63
Lenz, Katja 454
Lestrade, Sander 232, 234
Levey, Geoffrey Brahm 459
Levinson, Stephen C. 196
Levisen, Carsten 94
Levkovych, Nataliya 69, 135f., 158, 170, 196,
    249ff., 281, 328, 339, 357f.

Li, Michelle 205
Li, Wei 380, 411, 446, 448, 457, 466, 480
Liao, Min-Hsiu 395
Libert, Alan 166
Liddicoat, Anthony J 394
Lim, Lisa 206
Lindenfelser, Siegwalt 484
Lindström, Liina 58f.
Lo, Sandy 384
Loakes, Debbie 451, 454ff., 460
Löbner, Sebastian 220
Lorenz, Chris 375, 430
Lorenz, Manfred 334, 344
Lorenzio, Gerardo A. 213
Louisiana Creole 230
Lowe, Kevin 455
Lucas, Christopher 112, 168ff., 178
Lüdi, Georges 439
Ludwig, Ralph 216, 218, 222, 464f., 502f.
Luffin, Xavier 225
Luke, Nikki 375

Mac Giolla Chríost, Diarmait 379
Maciev, Axmed. G. 116, 126
Maddieson, Ian 251, 253, 282
Mahootian, Shahrzad 343
Makoni, Sinfree 448f.
Malik, Lalita 497
Manfredi, Stefano 112, 225
Manning, Frank E. 422
Mar-Molinero, Clare 379, 394
Marshall, Catherine 482
Martin, Jenni 395
Matras, Yaron 112, 118f., 129, 136, 165, 167, 181, 183f., 249, 327ff., 334, 340, 345, 355, 357f., 372f., 376, 379ff., 383ff., 388, 390, 393f., 407, 409, 411, 423, 425, 428, 439f., 481, 486, 488f., 493, 499
Matthews, Stephan 205
Maurer, Philippe 213f.
Mauri, Caterina 71
McConvell, Patrick 456f.
McGregor, R.S. 345f.
McLelland, Nicola 371, 400, 407, 412
McWhorter, John 206, 233
Meakins, Felicity 226, 228, 456f., 460
Meechan, Marjory 486, 488

Meeuwis, Michael 224
Mensah, Eyo O. 101, 103f.
Merrit, Marilyn 504
Mesthrie, Rajend 94, 200
Meyerhoff, Miriam 205
Michaelis, Susanne 196, 202, 216, 224, 234, 236
Michelena, Luis 148
Mieze, Silvija 28
Mifsud, Manwel 172
Migge, Bettina 5, 94, 206, 440, 446f.
Mignolo, Walter D. 374f., 431
Miller, Jim 4, 31, 69
Milligan, Lizzy O. 502
Mintz, Malcom W. 352
Mische, Ann 394
Mishra, Awadesh K. 348
Möhlig, Wilhelm J. G. 332
Mokgwathi, Tsaona 504
Molochieva, Zarina 113, 121, 125
Moore, Danièle 504
Mopan Maya 201
Mous, Maarten 227
Moutaouakil, Ahmed 125
Mufwene, Salikoko S. 224
Mühleisen, Susanne 94
Mukherjee, Joybrato 94
Muller, Enrique A. F. 212
Müller, Martin 413
Müller, Natascha 497
Muysken, Pieter 489f.
Myers-Scotton, Carol 129f., 482, 490ff.

Nartey, Jonas 492
Nau, Nicole 25, 27, 31, 33, 36, 47f., 52f., 57, 59, 63, 67f., 72ff., 76
Neary, Mike 375, 430f.
Neather, Robert 395
Neira Martínez, Jesús 151f., 160
Neumann-Holzschuh, Ingrid 216
Ngai, Ka Ming 390
Nichols, Johanna 113, 116, 121, 124, 126, 132
Nikolaev, Dmitry 255
Nintemann, Julia 196, 232, 234
Nītiṇa, Daina 12
Nordhoff, Sebastian 223
Nübling, Damaris 200

Nugent, Maria L. 452
Nwachukwu-Agbada, Joseph O. J. 100f., 104

O'Shannessy, Carmel 456f.
Offord, Baden 376
Ong, Aihwa 413
Onysko, Alexander 92, 97
Öpengin, Ergin 123
Osman, Mohamed Fathi 384
Ostler, Nicholas 441
Ostrowski, Norbert 70
Otheguy, Ricardo 448f.
Otsuji, Emi 380
Oyebola, Folajimi 105
Ozols, Arturs 6, 8, 12f.

Paauw, Scott H. 223
Palethorpe, Sallyanne 452f.
Palmer, Gary B. 92
Panayi, Panikos 378
Pantcheva, Marina 196, 234
Paradis, Michel 493
Patnaik, Manideepa 342
Patrick, Peter L. 372
Patzelt, Carolin 446, 448
Payne, John 343
Penny, Ralph J. 149
Pennycook, Alistair 380, 443, 446, 448f.
Pensalfini, Rob 457f.
Perez, Marilola 211
Peters, Pam 92
Peterson, John 197, 350f.
Petrollino, Sara 225
Pfänder, Stefan 216
Phillips, Judith Wingerd 216
Pidgeon, Michelle 376, 431
Pietikäinen, Sari 395
Plag, Ingo 206
Plakans, Andrejs 6f.
Plank, Frans 250f., 286f.
Platt, John 102
Pokrotniece, Kornēlija 12
Police-Michel, Daniella 216
Polzenhagen, Frank 92f., 96f.
Poplack, Shana 486, 488f.
Popper-Giveon, Ariela 394
Porīte, Tamara 70

Porstner, Ilse 494
Post, Marike 214
Powell, J. V. 203f., 226
Powell, Jonathan G. F. 33
Pratt, Mary Louise 413
Prescod, Paula 206
Procházka, Stephan 171, 341
Pukui, Mary Kawena 227
Purcell, Mark 379
Purkarthofer, Judith 403
Py, Bernard 439

Quint, Nicolas 214

Ramasawmy, Shalini Jagambal 463, 465, 468
Rampton, Ben 371, 379, 428, 446ff., 480
Rannut, Ulle 112
Rappaport, Roy A. 422
Redder, Angelika 379
Rehbein, Jochen 5, 426, 430
Revis, Melanie 216
Rialland, Annie 250
Roberts, David 485, 501
Roberts, Sarah J. 227
Robertson, Alex 379, 381, 384ff., 423, 428
Robillard, Didier 463ff.
Romaine, Suzanne 496
Rosalie, Marcel 216
Rosenberger, Otto Benj. Gottfr. 19, 43, 46, 55, 62
Roset, Caroline 225
Rossman, Gretchen B. 482
Rouchdy, Aleya 129
Rūķe-Draviņa, Velta 11
Rumsey, Alan 455, 457
Russo, Katherine E. 453ff.
Rusu, Mihai Stelian 422
Ryding, Karin C. 125, 225, 333, 335, 340, 350, 353
Rymes, Betsy 427

Saade, Benjamin 172
Saagpakk, Maris 5
Saari, Rami 165, 170, 174
Sadeghpour, Marzieh 92, 97
Said, Edward 374
Sakel, Jeanette 146, 330, 486

Salazar, Danica 96, 100
Salemann, C. 340
Samarin, William J. 227
Sánchez Moreano, Santiago 449
Sandefur, John 207
Sandefur, Joy 207
Sankowska, Julia 36
Sarasua Garmendia, Asier 145
Sarr, Felwine 444
Sassen, Saskia 413
Schiller, Maria 379, 389, 430
Schlaak, Claudia 147, 161
Schlegel, J.B 483
Schmidt, Emeli 17, 166, 170, 173
Schmied, Josef 103
Schneider, Edgar W. 93, 99ff.
Schröder, Anne 205
Schultze-Berndt, Eva 33, 206
Schuster, Michal 390
Schwegler, Armin 211
Schwörer, Emil 444
Scontras, Gregory 137
Sehwers, Johann 11
Senft, Gunter 198
Sepulveda, Leandro 379
Serracino-Inglott, Erin 171
Settegast, Daniel Gottlieb 16ff., 29, 34, 58, 60, 75
Shakib, Mohammad Khosravi 479
Sharifian, Farzad 92f., 97f.
Shaw, George C. 203
Shimelman, Aviva 198
Sian, Katy P. 430f.
Siegel, Jeff 206, 227
Silverman, Raymond Aaron 395
Silverstein, Michael 480
Simard, Candide 33
Singer, Ruth 458
Singler, John Victor 483
Sippola, Eeva 211
Skandera, Paul 103
Skujiņa, Valentīna 11
Slomanson, Peter 223
Smalley, William A. 4
Smith, Geoff. P. 206
Smith, Ian R. 214f.
Smith, Linda Tuhiwai 374f., 431

Sneddon, James Neil 222
Soares da Silva, Augusto 92
Sokolowsky, Celia 484
Soto Huerta, Mary Esther 395
Spagnol, Michael 169f.
Speitkamp, Winfried 506
Spevak, Olga 31, 33
Spitzmüller, Jürgen 444, 479f., 494ff.
Spivak, Gayatri 428
Sridar, Kamal K. 94
Stafecka, Anna 14f., 24
Steever, Sanford B. 348
Stein, Heidi 335
Stein, Peter 465
Steinkrüger, Patrick O. 211
Stender, Gotthard Friedrich 7f., 12, 18f., 28, 45, 49, 55, 62
Stevenson, Patrick 379
Stewart, Michael 376
Stickrodt, Silke 483
Stolberg, Doris 5, 484
Stolz, Christel 441
Stolz, Thomas 69f., 112, 135f., 158, 165, 167, 170, 173f., 182, 196f., 200f., 209, 211, 215, 225, 232, 234, 237, 249ff., 281, 328, 339, 357f.
Strods, P. 15, 68
Stroud, Christopher 378, 421, 423
Stubbs, Michael 95
Sturge, Kate 395
Suleiman, Yasir 112, 114
Suthar, Babu 346
Swift, Lloyd Balderston 224f.
Syrett, Stephen 379

Tadmor, Uri 126, 166, 169, 330, 351
Taiwo, Rotimi 99
Talmy, L. 196
Tannen, Deborah 4
Taylor-Leech, Kerry 394
Ternes, Elmar 286
Thomason, Sarah G. 146, 165, 481
Thompson, Dahlia 205, 208
Tikly, Leon 502
Tirvassen, Rada 463, 465, 468
Tomlinson, J. 378
Tosco, Mauro 331

Trimingham, J. Spencer 225
Tsotetsi, Cias T. 376
Turnbull, Paul 452
Turner, Mark 103

Udofot, Inyang 100

Valdman, Albert 216
Van den Berg, Margot 206
Van Langendonck, Willy 199
Van Putte, Florimon 212
Van Putte-de Windt, Igma 212
Van Sluijs, Robbert 209
Vanags, Pēteris 6, 8f., 11ff., 18, 63, 68, 76
Vaughan, Jill 451, 454ff., 458ff.
Veidemane, Ruta 13, 52, 54f., 62f.
Velupillai, Viveka 206
Veronelli, G. A. 377
Versteegh, Kees 123, 136
Vertovec, Stephen 379
Vorholt, Maike 181, 183

Wälchli, Bernhard 341
Wallace-Bruce, Nii Lante 452
Walsh, Catherine E. 375, 431
Walsh, Michael 455
Warnke, Ingo H. 5
Waters, Sophia 94
Webb, Vic 504
Weiers, Michael 349
Weil, Gotthold 335f.
Weinert, Regina 4, 31, 69
Weinreich, Uriel 481
Weiß, Helmut 505
Wellens, Werner 225f.
Werbner, Pnina 378
Westermann, Diedrich 483

Wetzels, W. Leo 249
White, Bob W. 469, 379
Wiemer, Björn 54
Wierzbicka, Anna 95
Wiese, Heike 200, 380
Wigglesworth, Gillian 455
Wilkins, Davin P. 196
Wilkinson, Erin 137
Williams, Raymond 95
Willis, David 154
Willoughby, Louisa J. V. 453
Winford, Donald 206
Winstedt, R. O. 352
Wohlgemuth, Jan 123
Woidich, Manfred 340
Woldeyes, Yirga Gelaw 376
Wolf, Eric R. 421f.
Wolf, Hans-Georg 92f., 96f.
Wolff, H. Ekkehard 341
Woolard, Kathryn Ann 479, 486f., 493f.

Yakpo, Kofi 206, 208
Yasugi, Yoshiho 201
Yayoh, Wilson K. 483
Yigbe, Dotsé 485
Young, David James 346
Yousef, Saaed 334f., 350

Zelkina, Anna 117
Zenner, Eline 96
Zimmermann, Klaus 5
Zola, Emile W.A. 224f.
Zribi-Hertz, Anne 216, 218ff.
Zwartjes, Otto 5

Index of Languages, Language Families, and Linguistic Areas

Abaza 275, 285
Abkhaz 275
Abkhaz-Adyghe languages 255ff., 262, 266, 268f., 271f., 274ff., 278ff., 285f.
Afghani 394
African languages 382, 394, 420, 443, 492
Afrikaans 208ff.
Afro-Asiatic languages 256f., 269, 271, 274, 278f., 281, 284f., 333, 341
Aghul 275
Aiki 123
Akan 382
Akebu 488f.
Albanian 332ff., 338f., 418
Amharic 407
Andi 278
Angolar 212f.
Anobonense 212
Arabic 111ff., 125ff., 139, 168ff., 178, 183, 225, 233, 235, 271, 274, 285, 327ff., 333ff., 343, 345, 349ff., 355, 357f., 371, 381ff., 388, 391, 400f., 405, 407, 410, 412, 418, 420, 465f., 470, 479
– Amman/Jordanian ~ 113f., 116ff., 120f., 125ff., 129, 131ff., 139
– Cairene ~ 340
– Classical/Quranic ~ 117, 125, 132, 330, 333, 335, 340, 353, 383, 407
– Çukurova ~ 271, 274, 341
– Cypriot/Kormakiti ~ 271, 274, 285
– Darfur ~ 225
– Iraqi ~ 341
– Juba ~ 225f.
– Modern Standard ~ 117, 125ff., 131, 134, 225, 330, 333, 335f., 338, 340, 350, 353, 410
– Neo-~ 225
– Palestinian ~ 116
– Sudanese ~ 225, 340
– Syrian 340
Aragonese 151ff., 160
Aramaic 271, 274, 278, 281, 284f.
– Neo-~ 341
Armenian 257, 268, 271, 274, 382f., 407, 410, 420
Aromanian 258f., 339
Asian languages 382, 394, 421, 464
Asturian 268
Australian languages 455
Austroasiatic languages 350f.
Austronesian languages 198, 332, 352

Badini 382, 394
Bahamian Creole 205, 233
Balkan languages 339
Balochi 343ff., 347, 354
Baltic languages 33, 52, 59, 62, 73, 79
Bangla 348
Bantu languages 224f., 236, 332
Bashkir 284f., 332ff.
Basque 145ff., 152ff., 156ff., 251, 256, 259, 261, 266, 268f.
Bavarian 411
Belarusian 71, 73, 80
Belizean Creole 205
Bengali 381ff., 391, 401, 405, 407
Berbice Dutch 208f., 237
Bhojpuri 463, 465f.
Bislama 205
Botlikh 278
Brahui 347ff., 354
Bravanese 391
Breton 285
Bulgarian 258f., 261, 278, 339
Burarra 459
Burushaski 348f., 354

Cameroon Pidgin 205, 207
Cape Verdean Creole 213
Caribbean Creoles 382
Caribbean languages 382
Casamancese Creole 214
Catalan 268
Caucasian languages 111f., 121, 136

Chabacano 211, 237
Chadic languages 341
Chechen 112ff.
– Jordanian ~ 113ff., 118f., 121f., 126f., 129, 132, 135, 137ff.
Chinese 371, 381ff., 391, 394, 400, 407, 409, 463, 470
– ~ Pidgin 205
Chinook 203, 226
Chinuk Wawa 203f., 226
Creolese 205, 207f.
Crimean Tatar 271, 274, 285
Czech 382, 407

Danish 449f.
Dari 382, 391
Dhivehi 359
Djinang 459
Domari 118, 129, 136
Dravidian languages 347f., 359
Dutch 202, 208ff., 229ff., 235, 285, 444, 462

English 29, 91ff., 98ff., 105, 115f., 127, 138, 154, 166, 168f., 197, 200, 205ff., 229ff., 235ff., 328f., 358, 370ff., 381ff., 386f., 389ff., 393f., 396ff., 401, 405, 414, 424, 441ff., 449ff., 479, 483ff., 489ff., 494, 499, 502
– African ~ 94, 103f.
– African American ~ 101, 205
– American ~ 100, 102f., 453
– Australian ~ 93, 452ff., 459, 461, 472
– British ~ 93f., 100, 102f., 453
– Canadian ~ 468
– Englishes 92ff., 96, 98, 104
– Ghanaian (Pidgin) ~ 98, 206f., 234
– Indian South African ~ 200
– Malaysian ~ 103
– New ~ 102, 104
– Nigerian ~ 92, 100, 104, 207
– Nigerian Pidgin ~ 92, 100f., 102ff., 206, 208, 382
– Postcolonial ~ 91, 93
– Singapore ~ / Singlish 102f., 206
– West African ~ 92f., 102
– West African Pidgin ~ 99
– World Englishes 91, 96f., 100, 102, 104f.

Estonian 67, 286
European languages 7, 31, 183, 251, 262, 268, 273, 287, 371, 382, 441f., 444, 471, 488, 497, 505
Ewe 478ff., 482ff., 488ff., 494, 498ff.

Farsi 123, 394, 407, 411
Finnish 67, 407
French 92, 145, 147ff., 152, 154f., 157ff., 202, 215f., 218ff., 229ff., 235f., 381f., 400f., 407, 409f., 414, 440ff., 449, 462ff., 478ff., 483ff., 488ff., 494f., 498ff.
– Mauritian ~ 468
– Quebec ~ 468
Fula 327
Fulani 418
Fulfulde 340
Fur 123

Gaelic 371
Galician 261, 268
Gascon 146, 149ff., 268
Gbe languages 482, 490
Gen 482
Gengbe 490, 498
German 3ff., 16, 18ff., 23f., 27, 29f., 33, 40, 43f., 46f., 49, 52ff., 56ff., 63, 69f., 72, 74f., 77ff., 154, 158, 199f., 334, 382, 400, 407, 411, 414, 418, 441ff., 445, 465, 478ff., 483ff., 494, 499ff., 505f.
– Swiss ~ 411
Goemai 341
Greek 10, 171, 261, 285, 338, 382f., 407, 421
– Italo-Greek (Sternatia) 261
Guadeloupean Creole 216, 222, 230
Guinea-Bissau Kriyol 214
Gujarati 345f., 353ff., 382f., 391, 466
Gur languages 483
Gurage 123
Gurindji 228, 456
– ~ Kriol 226ff., 456f
Guyanais 216
Haitian Creole 216, 221
Hakka 465
Harari 123
Hausa 99, 102, 327, 341, 382
Hawai'i Creole 206

Hawaiian 227
– Pidgin ~ 226f.
Hebrew 10, 383, 407
Hindi 123, 327, 345ff., 350, 353f., 356, 383, 391, 418, 465f., 470
– Fiji ~ 227
Hindustanic Pidgin 227
Hinukh 285
Hungarian 382

Igbo 99, 102ff.
Indian languages 470
Indo-Aryan languages 342, 345ff., 350, 359, 421
Indo-European languages 233, 235, 252, 256f., 259f., 266, 268, 271ff., 278, 283ff., 332, 334, 343ff.
Indonesian 222, 332ff., 351ff., 356
Iranian languages 112, 123, 252, 278, 334, 343ff., 347f., 411
Irish 278, 371, 418
Italian 154, 166ff., 174, 382, 401, 418

Japanese 407
Jingulu 457
Juang 342

Kabiye 482, 485, 494f., 498ff., 503
Kalmyk 251, 274
Karachay-Balkar 274
Karaim 274
Karata 278
Kartvelian languages 112, 256f., 269, 271, 274, 284, 286
Kashmiri 345f., 354
Kazakh 286
Kharia 197, 350f., 354
Khinalug 284
Kiezdeutsch 200
Kikongo-Kituba 224f.
Kinubi 225f.
Kipchak languages 332
Korean 383
Korlai 214f., 237
Kotokoli 500
Kreeol 209
Krio 206

Kriol 206f., 228, 453, 456, 460
Kumyk 274
Kunwinjku 458
Kurdish 118, 123, 136, 381ff., 388, 392, 394, 401, 407
Kurmanji 257, 271, 274, 341, 382, 394
Kurux 348, 354
Kwa languages 483, 488f.

Ladino 261
Latgalian 4, 14ff., 21f., 24, 31, 36, 38, 48, 52, 57, 63, 68, 71ff.
Latin 6ff., 10, 14ff., 19, 31, 33, 37, 43, 69, 78, 80, 117, 146, 148ff., 153f.
Latvian 3ff., 28, 34, 39ff., 45f., 48ff., 52ff., 57, 59, 61ff., 67ff., 73ff., 79ff., 382, 418
– (Modern) Standard ~ 4, 9, 21, 23, 27, 31, 36, 38f., 41, 47f., 50, 52, 57, 59, 63, 67f., 70, 74, 76, 78, 81
– High ~ 4ff., 10, 14ff., 21ff., 26, 28, 31ff., 37f., 40ff., 45, 49ff., 53ff., 63, 65ff., 70f., 73ff., 79ff.
– Low ~ 4ff., 8ff., 23ff., 27ff., 33ff., 39ff., 49ff., 65ff., 79ff.
Laz 257, 284
Lezgian 327
Lingala 224
Lithuanian 14ff., 33, 46, 50, 52, 57ff., 61, 63, 67f., 70ff., 79ff., 286, 382f., 407, 412
Livonian 3, 286
Luganda 397, 399

Macedonian 261, 339
Malay 103, 222ff., 230f., 233, 235, 237, 351ff., 356, 383
Malayalam 359, 382
Maltese 154, 165ff., 180ff., 186ff., 284
Malto 348, 354
Marathi 465f.
Martinican Creole 216, 218ff., 463
Mauritian Creole 216ff., 463, 465ff.
Mawng 458
Megleno-Romanian 339
Mirpuri 382, 391, 393, 401
Moghol 349, 351, 354, 356
Mongolic languages 251, 259, 269, 274, 349
Mopan Maya 201

Mudburra 457
Munda languages 342, 350f.

Nakh-Daghestanian languages 116, 126, 256f., 259f., 262, 266, 268f., 271ff., 278ff., 283ff., 339
Navarrese 145, 148, 151f., 160
Nengee 206
Ngbandi 227
Ngumpin-Yapa 456f.
Nicaraguan Creole 206ff., 229
Niger-Congo languages 332, 483
Nilo-Saharan languages 123
Noghay 257, 271, 274, 284f.
Nubian 129

Occitan 149, 268
Oghuz languages 335
Oriya 342, 348
Ossetic 274

Paamese 198
Pahari 382
Palenquero 211
Pama-Nyungan languages 456f.
Pāmir languages 343
Panjabi 381ff., 391, 393, 401, 407, 447
Papiamentu 211ff.
Papuan languages 198
Parachi 344, 353f.
Pashto 344ff., 354, 357, 381f., 401
Patwa 382
Persian 111, 118f., 121, 123, 135, 328ff., 334ff., 342ff., 355, 358, 382ff., 391, 394, 401, 411
Pichi 206, 208
Polish 4, 10, 14ff., 21f., 33, 36f., 42f., 50f., 54, 67f., 71, 73, 77ff., 381ff., 391, 400, 407, 410, 418
Portuguese 92, 105, 202, 212f., 215, 229ff., 235, 237, 381f., 418, 483
– Sri Lanka ~ 214f., 237
– Diu Indo-~ 214
Potwari 382, 401
Principense 212, 214
Prussian 16, 52
Punjabi 327, 345ff., 354, 418

Quechua 197f.

Reunion Creole 216, 230
Romance languages 145f., 148ff., 157ff., 161, 167ff., 183, 187, 261, 265, 268
Romani 261, 376, 382, 388, 393, 397, 420f.
– Kalderash ~ 261
– Romanes ~ 382, 397f.
Romanian 382ff., 393, 397f., 414
Russian 15, 17, 33, 51, 71, 80, 111f., 116, 121, 125, 127, 138ff., 261, 329, 383, 407, 411f.
Rutul 275

Saami 286
Sadri 348, 350
San Andres Creole 206, 237
Sango 227
Sanskrit 383
Santome 214
São-Tomense 212
Saramaccan 206
Sardinian 265, 284f.
Scots 371
Semitic languages 112, 116, 123, 168, 171f., 175, 177f., 180, 187, 333
Seychelles Creole 216
Shelta 382
Shona 382
Shugni 344, 353f.
Sicilian 154, 166, 168, 171
Sindhi 345f., 353ff.
Slavic languages 15, 33, 45f., 52, 62, 67, 71, 73, 75, 80, 261, 278
Slovak 382
Slovene 261
Somali 327, 381ff., 391, 397, 401, 407, 418
Sorani 382, 394
Sorbian Lower 284
Sorbian Upper 284
Spanish 92, 105, 145, 147ff., 156ff., 160f., 167, 202, 210f., 213, 229ff., 235, 261, 268, 328ff., 382, 400, 414, 420, 449f., 461, 465, 485
Sranan 206f.
Sundic languages 332, 352
Swahili 123, 224, 327, 332ff., 340, 382, 391, 418

Tajik/Tajiki/Tājikī 343
Tamazight 420
Tamil 382, 407, 465f.
Tatar 284ff.
Tayo 216, 230
Telugu 382, 465f.
Tem 482
Thai 383
Tigrinya 382
Tok Pisin 206
Turkic languages 111f., 118, 121, 123, 136, 256f., 269, 271, 274, 278, 283ff., 332, 335f., 339
Turkish 112, 140, 274, 327f., 334f., 337ff., 345, 353, 358, 382, 407, 450
– Ottoman ~ 335ff., 351
Turoyo 342
Twi 418, 489

Ubykh 275
Ukrainian 17, 382f., 407

Uralic languages 255f., 269, 276, 278, 283, 286
Urdu 123, 345f., 349, 354, 381ff., 391, 393, 401, 407, 418, 465f.
Uyghur 407
Uzbek 327

Vietnamese 383
Vincentian Creole 206
Volta-Congo languages 483

Wakhi 344, 354, 357
Welsh 284f., 371, 391
Wororran languages 457

Yanti 222
Yiddish 80, 382, 408, 418
Yoruba 99, 102ff., 381f.
Yucatec Maya 201

Zaza 257, 268, 271, 274

Index of Subjects

ablative 124, 197, 208, 210, 232
absolutive 116, 124, 158
acculturation/nativisation 91ff.
adjective(s) 16, 31ff., 35ff., 40, 42, 48, 78f., 114, 120f., 125, 129ff., 133, 138f., 166f.
adposition(s) 129, 166f., 196ff., 230, 232
adstrate(s) 146, 150, 152f., 236
adstratum/adstrara *See* adstrate(s)
adverb(s)/adverbial 29, 44, 46, 69, 71f., 74f., 119, 134f., 138, 156, 167, 218f., 336, 352, 489, 491
adversative(s) 71, 135, 159, 185, 328, 333ff., 344ff., 349f., 352, 355ff.
agreement 36, 116, 120ff., 130
allative 124, 128, 134, 156, 185, 197, 207, 212, 228, 232
areal/areality 249f., 258, 260f., 268, 274, 281, 286f.
article(s) 23, 28ff., 125, 131, 156, 173, 219ff., 503
– definite ~ 12, 23f., 27, 29f., 55, 68, 77, 81, 128, 130, 172f., 199f., 220f.
– indefinite ~ 12, 23f., 28, 30
auxiliary 13, 46ff., 52ff., 58f., 61, 66, 77f., 81, 122, 154, 157f.

bilingual/bilingualism 113, 115, 117f., 145, 150ff., 157, 160f., 249, 339, 341, 414, 481, 487f., 490
borrowability 166f., 328, 489
borrowing(s) 69, 75, 78, 93f., 103, 112, 119, 124, 131, 136, 139, 145f., 149f., 152, 154, 156, 159, 161, 166ff., 170, 172, 176, 187, 253, 282ff., 287, 328f., 338, 340f., 343f., 347, 349, 352, 355ff., 456f., 486f., 496, 498, 503
– grammatical ~ 146, 330
– lexical ~ 94, 96, 139, 154, 161, 166

calque/calquing 37, 67, 93, 103, 157
Caucasus/Caucasian 111ff., 116f., 125f., 136f., 252, 263, 269, 271, 274, 286, 327, 339, 358

causal 73f., 135, 159, 337f., 347, 353, 355, 357
code-switching 94, 96, 112, 115, 129f., 139, 336, 447, 457, 466, 477ff., 486ff., 500ff.
coding/encoding 196ff., 202, 204, 206, 208, 216, 226, 236
colonial language(s) 4f., 15, 79f., 378, 440, 443ff., 452ff., 460ff., 465f., 468ff., 478ff., 484ff., 489, 500f., 505f.
Colonial Linguistics 5, 478
colonialism 5, 377, 389, 399, 428, 441ff., 462, 464, 497
colonization 5, 11, 93, 99, 443, 445, 451
complementizer(s) 71f., 130, 135f., 140, 333, 336, 338, 346, 348
concessive 337, 347, 355ff.
conditional 28, 48, 55, 63, 72, 75, 77, 343ff., 348f., 352f., 355ff.
conjunction(s) 24, 70f., 136, 138, 159, 167, 169, 328, 330f., 333ff., 338, 340ff., 352f., 355ff.
– loan ~ 328ff.
conjunctive 135, 355f.
connective(s) 44, 69, 71ff.
consecutive 340, 347
contact
– ~ language(s) 5, 52, 79f., 98, 112, 116, 145, 152f., 160f., 170, 196, 224, 492f., 498
– ~ phenomenon/phenomena 96, 498
– ~ situation(s) 92ff., 112, 137ff., 152, 166, 249, 328, 457, 477, 493, 499f., 504
– ~-induced 96
coordination/coordinating 70f., 121, 135, 172f., 333, 336, 340ff., 355, 357f.
coordinator(s) 70f., 75, 78, 118
copula 32, 44, 48ff., 77, 79, 120, 122, 125, 133
corpus 8, 18f., 23f., 38, 47, 50, 54, 77, 95f., 98, 103, 113, 132, 168, 177, 352
correlative(s) 338, 340, 351, 357
creole(s) 94, 100, 195f., 198, 201f., 205f., 208f., 211ff., 215f., 218, 222ff., 229ff., 233ff., 447, 451, 456, 461f., 465, 469f.
creolisation/creolising 100, 378, 463

https://doi.org/10.1515/9783111323756-014

decoloniality/decolonial 372, 374f., 377, 380f., 389, 399, 406, 428, 430, 444
decolonising 374ff., 395
definiteness 120, 125, 130f., 199, 220
determiner(s) 24, 28, 32, 36, 39, 79, 130, 200
dialect(s)/dialectal 4, 9, 11, 14f., 24, 39, 50, 70f., 116f., 125, 145ff., 151f., 154, 158ff., 222, 333, 388, 396, 408, 410f., 420, 430, 451f., 461, 483, 486, 490, 505
differential marking/coding 158, 201f., 205ff., 213, 215, 222, 225f., 228f., 232, 234, 236
discourse marker(s) 118, 135, 167, 334
disjunction 70f., 135, 328
disjunctive 70, 135, 336, 340, 346, 355ff.
dominant language(s) 11, 112, 115, 137, 140, 358, 451, 498
donor(s) 15, 73, 124f., 168, 328ff., 334f., 338, 341, 347f., 351ff., 359
– distant ~ 328f., 340f., 343, 347, 357
– intermediate ~ 328f., 341, 352, 357
– near ~ 328f., 331, 333, 337, 339ff., 348, 350, 352, 357

encoding *See* coding/encoding
ergative 116, 123f., 134, 155, 158
Europe/European 5, 10, 69, 233ff., 250, 252f., 255, 258, 261, 266, 286f., 334, 339f., 357f., 370, 382, 391, 403, 414, 416, 419, 428, 442, 445, 449, 451f., 454, 459ff., 479, 489, 500f., 505

fluid
– ~ linguistic practices 450
– ~ registers 440, 445, 457, 460, 462, 465, 467, 471, 480
– ~ repertoires 445, 454, 456, 471
fluidity 380, 440, 445, 448, 455, 457, 459ff., 471, 482
frequency/frequencies 23f., 27, 48f., 54f., 63f., 77, 95f., 113, 132, 165ff., 170, 176ff., 183, 185ff., 224, 353, 488, 500
function word(s) 166, 168ff., 178, 183, 352

gender(s) 116f., 120ff., 139
– ~ assignment 125ff.
– ~ marker(s)/marking 124

genitive(s) 12f., 16, 38ff., 44, 57, 77ff., 124f., 130f., 139, 156, 160
grammaticalization 13, 23, 50, 74, 77

heritage language(s) 112, 114, 136f., 140, 396, 401, 409, 412, 414, 417, 420, 426
hierarchy/hierarchies 166f., 176, 184, 187, 237, 328, 355ff., 377, 392, 505
– markedness ~ 232f., 237

idiom(s) 92, 97, 102ff., 358
indigenous language(s) 93, 98f., 101, 103, 136ff., 328, 371, 451, 455f., 459, 461, 478, 483ff., 501, 505

language
– ~ change 3, 5, 77, 84, 94, 112, 380
– ~ contact 4, 69, 73, 77, 81, 92ff., 96, 103f., 111f., 118f., 136, 139f., 147, 158f., 161, 165ff., 170, 184, 188, 249f., 281, 283, 287, 328ff., 341f., 357ff., 446, 451, 457, 478, 480f., 486, 490, 506
– ~ ideology/ideologies 465, 468, 479f., 495
– ~ policy 94, 140, 371, 379, 392, 427, 429f., 441, 443, 459, 485
– ~ shift 115f., 137, 139, 149
language/linguistic empire(s) 331, 441
length 181ff., 185ff., 222, 231f., 237, 262, 488
– phonological ~ 177, 182f.
– vowel ~ 15, 20f.
lexifier(s) 204, 215, 226, 229ff.
linguistic ecologies 92, 104, 460
loan translation(s) 11, 69, 74, 103
loan(s) 112f., 118, 121, 124f., 127f., 135, 138f., 146, 154, 174, 281ff., 287, 334, 343, 348f., 486ff., 500
loanword(s) / loan word(s) 11, 15, 111, 117, 123f., 126f., 140, 146, 148f., 151ff., 156, 158, 166, 172, 249, 330, 352, 421, 481, 488f.
locative 12, 20, 26, 29, 57, 124, 128, 156, 207, 209, 215, 219f., 227f., 503

macro-area(s) 236, 250, 287
MAT-/material borrowing(s) 69f., 78, 146f., 249, 287, 333f., 347, 349
metaphor(s) 92, 96ff., 100f., 103

metapragmatic(s) 440, 444f., 450, 454f., 461f., 467f., 471f., 479ff., 487f., 492, 495ff., 506
monolingual/monolingualism 113, 411, 427, 439f., 446, 459f., 468, 479, 487f., 492, 502f.
multicultural/multiculturalism 9, 379, 395, 399, 405, 417, 440, 450, 452, 459, 463, 480
multilingual/multilingualism 6, 17, 96, 99, 200, 370ff., 379ff., 384ff., 392ff., 398ff., 406ff., 411, 413, 415ff., 423ff., 439f., 447ff., 454ff., 458ff., 462f., 465ff., 477f., 480f., 486ff., 490, 492, 499, 501ff.

named languages 396, 399, 449, 467f.
nativisation *See* acculturation/nativisation
noun(s) 24, 26ff., 46, 63, 70, 74, 78f., 114, 116ff., 120ff., 124ff., 131f., 138f., 156, 166f., 220ff., 228, 333
– common ~ 195, 201
– head ~ 13, 32, 34ff., 38ff., 42, 77, 120, 125, 130f.
number 29, 37, 120ff., 124f., 128f., 139, 499
numeral(s) 12, 24, 28, 30, 37, 79, 119f., 167

particle(s) 51f., 63, 66f., 70f., 79, 114, 118, 121, 135f., 138, 167, 220
– discourse ~ 118, 136
– focus ~ 118, 135
passive 5, 13, 47, 52ff., 61, 63f., 66ff., 77ff., 81
PAT-/pattern borrowing(s) 146f.
pidgin(s) 100f., 195f., 198, 201f., 205f., 208f., 211, 213, 215f., 223ff., 229ff., 233, 235ff., 382, 451, 461
place names 195, 201, 228
pluricentric languages 92, 97, 105
postcolonial 81, 94, 378f., 399, 428, 440, 442ff., 450ff., 455f., 459ff., 469, 471, 477ff., 486, 488ff., 492, 500ff.
postposition(s) 16, 132, 156, 165, 197, 209, 503
preposition(s) 11f., 29f., 57, 69, 73f., 132, 157, 165ff., 180ff., 197ff., 203ff., 215ff., 220, 222ff., 233, 237, 503

– loan/borrowed ~ 166, 168, 170ff., 175ff., 182ff.
pronoun(s) 12f., 23f., 27, 29f., 35, 37, 51, 59, 76, 131, 497
– demonstrative ~ 12, 23f., 27, 36, 51, 77, 503
– personal ~ 12f., 24, 497, 499
– possessive ~ 12, 16, 36f.
– reflexive ~ 12
proverb(s) 92, 97, 100ff.
purism 157, 159, 161
purposive 352, 355ff.

recipient language(s) 124, 136
repertoire(s) 61, 75, 80f., 101, 339, 372f., 380, 393f., 396, 399, 406f., 411, 420, 425, 430, 439f., 446, 448, 450f., 454, 456, 460, 462f., 466, 480ff., 486f., 490, 492, 500f.
replica(s) 154, 282, 286, 328ff., 333f., 336, 338ff., 343ff., 359

semantic(s) 11, 38, 69, 95, 98, 125f., 166, 177, 181, 183ff., 211f., 220, 224, 226, 233, 486, 492
sociolinguistic(s) 5, 80, 92, 97, 100, 104, 112, 114, 132, 136ff., 372, 378ff., 427f., 439f., 445f., 448, 450, 465f., 471, 479ff., 486, 492, 494, 505
source language(s) 102, 456f., 481, 486f.
spatial relation(s) 166, 195ff., 201, 203f., 233ff.
spoken language(s) 5, 9, 11, 15, 23, 27, 31, 33, 46, 52, 69, 73, 81, 171, 344, 396, 402, 482
subordination/subordinating 69, 71, 76, 121, 161, 336, 340, 343f., 347, 353, 355, 357
subordinator(s) 44, 74, 160, 357
substrate(s) 101, 146, 149f., 155, 212, 224, 236
substratum/substrata *See* substrate(s)
superdiversity 372, 379f., 385
syncretism 229, 234f.

translanguaging 372, 380, 399, 446ff., 457, 459, 462, 466f., 471, 480, 482, 489, 493
translingual practices 441, 467

typology/typologies 146, 170, 236, 250f., 253f., 258, 262, 286f., 395, 425

variation 4, 7, 10, 14, 21, 23, 31, 39, 41, 43, 80f., 94, 96f., 100, 128, 139, 183, 185ff., 202, 223, 235f., 256, 399, 407f., 410f., 413, 445ff., 452f., 466, 483, 493ff., 504
variety/varieties 8, 16, 18, 33, 41, 45, 48, 50, 52, 54, 57, 63, 67ff., 71f., 76f., 79ff., 92ff., 100, 102ff., 113, 116ff., 125, 137, 140, 147, 149, 152, 197, 200ff., 210, 213, 216, 222ff., 236, 251, 261, 330, 333, 340f., 359, 382, 391, 401, 410f., 426, 443, 446f., 449, 451ff., 456, 460f., 463ff., 481ff., 491, 497ff., 505f.
verb(s) 13, 32, 41, 44ff., 50, 52ff., 61ff., 67f., 75ff., 81, 98, 114, 117, 121ff., 125, 129, 132ff., 138f., 154, 157f., 160, 166f., 172, 197f., 207, 211f., 217, 219, 224, 226, 232, 234, 235, 489ff.
– motion ~ 197f., 208, 212, 217
– serial ~ 196, 198, 206, 209, 231f., 234
verbal 13, 21, 42, 57, 121, 125, 130, 132, 157, 347f.

word order 5, 9, 31, 33, 41, 43ff., 68f., 75, 81, 125, 131f., 134, 139, 157
written language(s) 4ff., 9, 31, 67, 71, 73, 77ff., 463

zero 24, 27, 78, 200f., 203, 207f., 230, 232, 235
– ~ -marked/coded 197, 201, 207ff., 211, 214ff., 216ff., 221ff., 227, 232f., 236f.
– ~ marking/coding 196, 200ff., 206, 211, 213ff., 220ff., 225, 227f., 230ff.